# The Templars in the
## *Corona de Aragón*

UNIVERSITY OF DURHAM
PUBLICATIONS

# The Templars in the
# *Corona de Aragón*

―――

A. J. FOREY

LONDON
OXFORD UNIVERSITY PRESS
1973

*Oxford University Press, Ely House, London W. 1*

GLASGOW   NEW YORK   TORONTO   MELBOURNE   WELLINGTON
CAPE TOWN   IBADAN   NAIROBI   DAR ES SALAAM   LUSAKA   ADDIS ABABA
DELHI   BOMBAY   CALCUTTA   MADRAS   KARACHI   LAHORE   DACCA
KUALA LUMPUR   SINGAPORE   HONG KONG   TOKYO

ISBN 0 19 713137 9

*Printed in Great Britain*
*at the University Press, Oxford*
*by Vivian Ridler*
*Printer to the University*

# PREFACE

I HAD not been long engaged in the study of the Templars in the *Corona de Aragón* before it became apparent that, because of the wealth of manuscript material available and because of the general lack of adequate catalogues and calendars, it would be impossible to examine all the relevant unpublished material thoroughly and that some limits would have to be imposed. The manuscript sources on which this book is based are therefore primarily those which are contained in the Archivo Histórico Nacional in Madrid and the Archivo de la Corona de Aragón in Barcelona, where the main collections of materials concerning the Templars are housed. Even so it has not been possible to examine fully all the relevant royal manuscripts in the Archivo de la Corona de Aragón, for to do this would in itself require years of sustained research. Nevertheless, the many thousands of documents which have been consulted should be sufficiently representative to provide a reliable guide to the history of the Templars in the *Corona de Aragón*.

During the preparation of the book I have received welcome assistance from a number of people and institutions. The early stages of my work on the Templars were supervised by Professor P. E. L. Russell and Dr. J. R. L. Highfield, whom I would like to thank for much help and good advice. I have also benefited from discussions with Professor D. W. Lomax and Dr. A. T. Luttrell, and a number of valuable comments and suggestions were made by Miss E. E. S. Procter and Mr. R. D. F. Pring-Mill, who examined an earlier version of the work when it was submitted as a thesis. I am further indebted for their help and courtesy to many archivists and librarians in Barcelona, Madrid, Oxford, and Durham. I would also like to acknowledge grants received from the University of Durham Travel Fund, and to thank the Durham University Publications Board for accepting the work for publication. During the course of publication I have become very

grateful to members of the staff of the Oxford University Press
for the care and patience they have shown. I would finally like to
express my gratitude to my wife, without whose encouragement
and assistance this book would probably never have been finished.

*Durham, October 1972*

# CONTENTS

# MAPS

# ABBREVIATIONS

## I. ABBREVIATED TITLES

*AHDE*  *Anuario de historia del derecho español.*

Albon, *Cartulaire*  Marquis d'Albon, *Cartulaire général de l'Ordre du Temple, 1119?–1150* (Paris, 1913).

*BEC*  *Bibliothèque de l'École des Chartes.*

*BRABLB*  *Boletín de la Real Academia de Buenas Letras de Barcelona.*

*BRAH*  *Boletín de la Real Academia de la Historia.*

*BSCC*  *Boletín de la Sociedad Castellonense de Cultura.*

*CDI*  *Colección de documentos inéditos del Archivo general de la Corona de Aragón*, ed. P. de Bofarull y Mascaró, etc. (Barcelona, 1847–1910).

*Cortes de Aragón, Valencia y Cataluña*: *Cortes de los antiguos reinos de Aragón y de Valencia y principado de Cataluña* (Madrid, 1896–1919).

Delaville, *Cartulaire*  J. Delaville Le Roulx, *Cartulaire général de l'Ordre des Hospitaliers de Saint-Jean de Jérusalem* (Paris, 1894–1906).

Delaville, *Hospitaliers*  J. Delaville Le Roulx, *Les Hospitaliers en Terre Sainte et à Chypre* (Paris, 1904).

*EEMCA*  *Estudios de edad media de la Corona de Aragón.*

*ES*  *España sagrada*, ed. H. Flórez, M. Risco, etc. (Madrid, 1747–1918).

Ferreira, *Memorias*  A. Ferreira, *Memorias e noticias historicas da celebre ordem militar dos Templarios* (Lisbon, 1735).

Finke, *AA*  H. Finke, *Acta Aragonensia* (Berlin, 1908–22).

Finke, *Papsttum*  H. Finke, *Papsttum und Untergang des Templerordens* (Münster, 1907).

Font Rius, *Cartas de población*  J. M. Font Rius, *Cartas de población y franquicia de Cataluña* (Madrid, Barcelona, 1969–   ).

García Larragueta, *Gran priorado*  S. A. García Larragueta, *El gran priorado de Navarra de la Orden de San Juan de Jerusalén* (Pamplona, 1957).

Huici, *Colección diplomática*  A. Huici, *Colección diplomática de Jaime I, el Conquistador* (Valencia, 1916–22).

Javierre, *Privilegios*  A. L. Javierre Mur, *Privilegios reales de la Orden de Montesa en la edad media* (Madrid, n.d.).

Lacarra, 'Documentos'  J. M. Lacarra, 'Documentos para el estudio de la reconquista y repoblación del Valle del Ebro', *EEMCA* ii (1946), iii (1947–8), v (1952). Figures given in brackets in references refer to volume and page.

Lees, *Records*      B. A. Lees, *The Records of the Templars in England in the Twelfth Century* (British Academy Records of the Social and Economic History of England and Wales, vol. ix, 1935).

Léonard,      E. G. Léonard, *Introduction au cartulaire manuscrit du*
*Introduction*      *Temple du Marquis d'Albon* (Paris, 1930).

*LFM*      *Liber Feudorum Maior*, ed. F. Miquel Rosell (Barcelona, 1945–7).

Michelet, *Procès*      J. Michelet, *Procès des Templiers* (Paris, 1841–51).

Migne, *PL*      J. P. Migne, *Patrologiae cursus completus. Series latina* (Paris, 1844–55).

Miret y Sans,      J. Miret y Sans, *Les Cases de Templers y Hospitalers en*
*Les Cases*      *Catalunya* (Barcelona, 1910).

Prutz, *Entwicklung*      H. Prutz, *Entwicklung und Untergang des Tempelherrenordens* (Berlin, 1888).

Prutz, *MU*      H. Prutz, *Malteser Urkunden und Regesten zur Geschichte der Tempelherren und der Johanniter* (Munich, 1883).

*Règle*      *La règle du Temple*, ed. H. de Curzon (Société de l'Histoire de France, 1886).

Régné, 'Catalogue'      J. Régné, 'Catalogue des actes de Jaime I, Pedro III et Alfonso III, rois d'Aragon, concernant les Juifs (1213–1291)', *Revue des études juives*, lx–lxx (1911–20); and 'Catalogue d'actes pour servir à l'histoire des Juifs de la couronne d'Aragon sous le règne de Jaime II', ibid., lxxiii–lxxviii (1921–4). The figures given in brackets in references refer to volume and page.

Riley-Smith, *Knights*      J. Riley-Smith, *The Knights of St. John in Jerusalem and*
*of St. John*      *Cyprus, c. 1050–1310* (London, 1967).

Villanueva, *Viage*      J. Villanueva, *Viage literario a las iglesias de España* (Madrid, 1803–52).

Zurita, *Anales*      J. Zurita, *Anales de la Corona de Aragón* (Zaragoza, 1610–21).

## II. OTHER ABBREVIATIONS

ACA      Archivo de la Corona de Aragón, Barcelona.

AGP      Archivo del Gran Priorado de Cataluña (in ACA).

AHN, cód.      Archivo Histórico Nacional, Madrid, Sección de códices, códice.

AHN, Montesa, P.      Archivo Histórico Nacional, Sección de órdenes militares, Montesa, documentos particulares.

AHN, Montesa, R.      Archivo Histórico Nacional, Sección de órdenes militares, Montesa, documentos reales.

AHN, San Juan      Archivo Histórico Nacional, Sección de órdenes

| | militares, San Juan de Jerusalén, Castellanía de Amposta and Gran Priorado de Navarra. |
| --- | --- |
| CRD | Cartas reales diplomáticas. |
| *l.* (B., J., V.) | *libras* (of Barcelona, Jaca, or Valencia currency). |
| leg. | legajo. |
| *m.* | *morabetinos.* |
| *maz.* | *mazmodinas.* |
| parch. | parchment. |
| RAH | Real Academia de la Historia, Madrid. |
| reg. | register. |
| *s.* (B., J., V.) | shillings (of Barcelona, Jaca, or Valencia currency). |
| sign. | signatura. |

## NOTE

The Aragonese numbering of kings is used throughout, both in text and in references, but it must be remembered that the Catalan numbering is employed in the ACA.

Personal names have been anglicized and place-names modernized where possible.

ninth year.[4] The establishment of a new community would
obviously necessitate a period of discussion and negotiation, but
these references—if accurate—imply that the Templars com-
memorated a date towards the end of 1119 or at the beginning of
1120 as marking the start of their new way of life.[5]

Hugh of Payns, the founder and first master, derived his name
from a village some eight miles north-west of Troyes, and he is
said to have been related to the ruling house of Champagne and
to St. Bernard,[6] but little is known of his early life or of when he
settled in the Holy Land.[7] Nor can the observances adopted by
Hugh and his followers in the period up to the Council of Troyes
be fully described. A few are referred to specifically in the Templar
Rule, for at the Council of Troyes Hugh gave an account of the
community's customs to the assembled prelates, and the Rule was
in part based on these early usages.[8] It is clear from the Rule, for
example, that the community had taken its meals together in a
refectory and that during meals there was no absolute rule of
silence,[9] while the custom of prolonged standing during offices is
also mentioned.[10] The Rule further suggests that women members
had not at first been excluded.[11] But it is usually difficult to determine whether in the Templar Rule an old usage was being preserved or a new one introduced.[12] Some recent writers have seen
the early community as a kind of Third Order attached to the
canons of the Holy Sepulchre, but as its members took the normal
monastic vows and lived a common life, this is not a very helpful
description.[13]

If little is known about their early observances, there is more
certainty about the original function of the Templars. William of
Tyre's statement that their first duty was to guard roads and
protect pilgrims finds support in several other twelfth-century
sources.[14] In undertaking this task they were answering an obvious
need: descriptions of the dangers of the journey along the roads to
Jerusalem are a common feature of early twelfth-century pilgrim
narratives.[15] The welfare of pilgrims was thus the first concern of
the Templars, as it was of the Hospitallers. By the time of the
Council of Troyes, however, the Templars had become involved
in the defence of the kingdom of Jerusalem and fighting against
the infidel had become their main function.

It has been asserted by some writers that the Christian military
order, which devoted itself to fighting the infidel, emerged in

imitation of the Islamic institution of the *ribat*, which was a fortified convent whose inmates combined a religious way of life with
fighting against the enemies of Islam.[16] This argument is based on
no direct evidence of borrowing. It rests on the similarities between the Christian and Islamic institutions and on the claim that
the combining of a religious and a military way of life was alien
to Christian traditions, which forbade clerics to bear arms or shed
blood: St. Bernard's hesitancy in writing in support of the
Templars when requested to do so by Hugh of Payns is taken
by Castro as giving 'a measure of the great distance that
separated the new military orders from the Christian conception
of life'.[17]

In order to assess the validity of this argument it would be
helpful in the first place to ascertain whether the Franks settled in
the East after the First Crusade had contact with, and knowledge
of, the Muslim institution; but because of the paucity of evidence
and because the word *ribat* could be used to describe buildings
which were not military strongholds but served other purposes,[18]
this cannot be stated with certainty.[19] But even if it were assumed
that the Franks were in a position to borrow from the Muslims,
it may be doubted whether they did so. Although little information survives about the organization of and life within the *ribats*,
it is obvious that the Temple and the other military orders were
*in form* based on Christian monasteries and monastic orders,
especially Cîteaux. It cannot be maintained that in this respect
there was a borrowing from the *ribat*, most of whose occupants
apparently served only temporarily, as a kind of retreat, particularly during Ramadan.[20] But if it can be accepted that the Christian
military orders derived their organization from Christian institutions there remains the question whether the idea of combining
the religious and the military way of life could have been taken
from Islam. Certainly the military order was looked upon in
Christendom as something quite new: St. Bernard wrote that
'a new kind of militia is reported to have arisen . . . a new kind of
militia, I say, and unknown to the world',[21] and Peter the Venerable admitted that he had been amazed on hearing of the Temple.[22]
But although the military order was considered quite new, it was
quickly accepted by the Church. Peter the Venerable stated that
he had rejoiced on learning of the Temple and had venerated it
from the time of its foundation.[23] St. Bernard, besides playing an

important role in the composition of the Templar Rule,[24] gave
his encouragement to the Order in his *De Laude Novae Militiae*;[25]
and although he delayed before writing this work, the reason that
he gave for the delay was not that he questioned the validity of
the Templars' activities but he feared

> lest a lightly-given and hasty assent should be criticized, if I though
> ignorant should presume to undertake a task which a better person
> could fulfil better, and something which is so necessary should be
> rendered less agreeable through me.[26]

The papal legate and the other prelates at the Council of Troyes
were similarly ready to accept the new institution. Had the Order
been as alien to the outlook of western Christendom at the time
as Castro suggests, the combining of the religious and military
way of life would not have been acceptable to the Church;[27] and
it can be argued not only that the concept of the military order
was not completely at variance with Christian ideas but that it
evolved out of the existing Christian background. New con-
fraternities and religious communities were frequently established
in the Middle Ages to meet the changing demands of medieval
society. The needs of pilgrims, for example, led to the establishment of institutions which provided hospitality for those visiting
shrines and holy places. But pilgrims needed protection as well as
care, and at a time when the Church was proclaiming the Peace
of God and stressing the social and moral obligations of knighthood, it is not surprising that the idea was evolved of forming
a knightly community to protect pilgrims on the road to Jerusalem. Already before the First Crusade a group of nobles in
south-western France had formed an association for the purpose
of protecting the monastery of La Sauve near Bordeaux and the
pilgrims who visited it.[28] At this early stage in its history the
Temple had little in common with the Muslim *ribat*, and could
scarcely have been influenced by it, but the Templars were already
combining a religious way of life with an activity which must
have involved the use of force and the shedding of blood. And
once the Templars had adopted this way of life for the protection
of pilgrims, the transition to becoming a military order was not
a difficult one, especially when in the kingdom of Jerusalem there
was a lack of soldiers and when the Church was promoting and
giving its support to the war against the infidel. In this way the

Temple as a military order can be considered a product of early twelfth-century Christian society.

Nevertheless in the years immediately following its foundation the Temple appears to have made little mark. It is not, for example, mentioned in Fulcher of Chartres's *Gesta Francorum Iherusalem Peregrinantium*, which covers the period up to 1127.[29] William of Tyre's remark that after nine years there were still only nine members can probably be taken as a play on numbers,[30] but it does suggest that in the beginning there was no marked increase in membership. In the West the community appears to have been little known.[31] Certainly there is little record of patronage in western Europe in the early and middle 1120s. Ordericus Vitalis reports that when Fulk of Anjou returned from the pilgrimage on which he had embarked in 1120 he promised to make an annual benefaction to the Templars,[32] but the only indication of Templar acquisitions in the West at this time among the documents published by Albon is a reference in a charter, drawn up in the year 1124, to Templar rights in a church near Marseilles.[33] But as Fulk had been to the East, and as Marseilles was an obvious point of contact between East and West, these donations should not be taken as evidence of any widespread knowledge of the Templars in the West. This lack of support appears in fact to have demoralized some Templars. In a letter written at about the time of the Council of Troyes Hugh of Payns represents Satan as tempting them by saying

Why do you labour in vain? Why do you expend so much effort to no purpose? Those men, whom you serve, acknowledge you as partners in labour but are unwilling to share in brotherhood. When do the benefactions of the faithful come to the knights of the Temple? When are prayers said for the knights of the Temple by the faithful throughout the whole world?[34]

When therefore Hugh of Payns and some of his companions crossed to western Europe, apparently in 1127, they were seeking not only the approval which was obtained at the Council of Troyes, but also material support. Their activities in this sphere apparently lay at first mainly in north-eastern France—in Champagne and Flanders. In the former, donations were received at Troyes and Barbonne,[35] while in Flanders the Order gained the patronage of count William.[36] His gifts were confirmed by his successor in September 1128, and at the same time a donation was received from William, the castellan of St. Omer.[37] The fact that William of St. Omer's son was one of the first Templars probably explains this early expansion in Flanders.[38] Hugh of Payns, who was in Flanders in September 1128, also visited Anjou and Poitou,[39] and according to the Anglo-Saxon Chronicle and other English sources he met the English king in Normandy and then crossed to England.[40] The acquisition of patronage was not, however, dependent entirely on the activities of Hugh himself, for other members of the Order were being sent out to seek support, and some of them had reached the Iberian peninsula by the early months of 1128, for in March of that year the Templar Raymond Bernard received from the Portuguese queen Teresa the castle of Soure, which lay on the Moorish frontier.[41]

If the Templars had reached Portugal by March 1128, they must presumably have arrived earlier in the north-east of the Peninsula, but it is not until 1131 that they are mentioned there in dated documents which are altogether reliable. Certainly all the supposed references to the Templars in the north-east of Spain before 1128 must be rejected or at least very seriously questioned. There are no grounds for assuming, as some historians have done, that the *fratres de palmis* mentioned in Ordericus Vitalis's account of the attack on Benicadell in 1124 were Templars;[42] as they are linked in the narrative with the bishop of Zaragoza and the lord of Belchite they may have been members of the military confraternity founded at Belchite two years earlier.[43] Further, the dating must be questioned of all Templar documents which Miret y Sans assigns to the years before 1128.[44] The first is a decree concerning those who had claims against the Order; it bears the date '1125' and was issued by the count of Barcelona from the Aragonese town of Ejea.[45] As the count at that time had no authority in Aragon, and as in the document he is given the title *Princeps Aragonensis*, which did not come into use until 1137, the date must be inaccurate.[46] Secondly, Miret y Sans assumes that a charter recording a grant by Peter of Malán in Vallespirans, dated '24 February in the eighteenth year of Louis', belongs to the reign of Louis VI; he assigns it to the year 1126.[47] Yet in another charter concerning property at Vallespirans, which is dated 'in the seventeenth year of Louis the Younger'—that is 1154—the scribe and witnesses mentioned are the same as those named in the other document.[48] Peter of Malán's grant was therefore almost certainly made in the reign of Louis VII and his charter is to be assigned to the year 1155. Thirdly, Miret y Sans gives '1127' as the date of a donation to the Temple made by Titborgs, the daughter of Berenguer of Sta. Coloma; this, however, is a misreading of the document, and Miret y Sans himself later gives the correct date, which is 1197.[49] Finally, like García Larragueta, he follows Zurita in placing in the year 1127 Alfonso I's gift of Mallén, made jointly to the Temple and Hospital.[50] Yet it was pointed out by Fernández that the date given in the *Anales* is a misprint,[51] as is clear from its place in the text: 'V' has been printed for 'X', and the date should read '1132', as is given in Zurita's *Indices*.[52] It is perhaps also significant that a royal grant of privileges to the Mozarabs of Mallén, issued in the middle of 1132, makes no reference to the military orders, who may therefore not have gained Mallén until the second half of that year.[53] García Larragueta further accepts the date of 1125 for a primitive *fuero* issued jointly by the Hospital and Temple to the inhabitants of Novillas, which lies on the Ebro near Mallén.[54] But this document exists only in a suspect transcript made in the year 1271,[55] and the Navarrese ruler García Ramírez in 1135 issued a charter granting Novillas jointly to the two Orders.[56] The grant made in 1135 could, of course, have been merely a confirmation of an earlier gift; the document issued by García Ramírez was called a charter of donation and confirmation. But this was a formula often used when new grants were being made, and in view of the lack of evidence about the Templars in Europe generally as early as 1125 it seems probable that—if the transcript of the *fuero* is authentic—the transcriber omitted an 'X' when copying the date; this would bring the date of the *fuero* into line with that of the royal grant.

If the dating of all documents referring to the Temple which have been assigned to the years before 1128 must be rejected, or at least seriously questioned, the dates of those which have been attributed to the years 1128–30 are not altogether free from doubt. Among the documents published in the *Cartulario de 'Sant Cugat' del Vallés* is the will of Raymond Hugh, who held the castle of Tona, south of Vich; this document, which includes a bequest of a mule to the Temple and the Holy Sepulchre, is assigned by its editor to the year 1128.[57] The date of the will is given merely as

28 March in the twentieth year of Louis and the date of its execution as 29 June in the twenty-first year.[58] But a transcript of the
instrument of execution was made on 6 February in the twenty-
first year of Louis the Younger. Therefore, provided that the
dating is accurate, the will must be attributed to the reign of
Louis VI and must be dated 28 March 1128. But this would mean
that the instrument of execution was drawn up in the twenty-
first year of Louis VI and the transcript in the twenty-first year of
Louis VII, and this coincidence suggests that in fact a mistake was
made about the beginning of the regnal year and that the will
itself as well as the transcript of the instrument of execution
should be assigned to the reign of Louis the Younger.

Doubts must also be voiced about Albon's attribution to the
year 1129 of a grant which was made to the Templars by Miro
Peter and which consisted of rights in the churches of Razazol
and Boquiñeni, villages on the Ebro above Zaragoza.[59] This donation was inserted in a charter recording the gift of these rights to
Miro Peter by the Aragonese king Alfonso I, and the date given
appears to refer to the royal grant.[60] It is not known when the
donation to the Temple was made.

Lastly the date must be discussed of the charter in which Raymond Berenguer III of Barcelona granted the castle of Grañena
to the Templars and also gave himself 'in obedience to them,
without property, a knight of God, wherever they wish, for the
rest of my life'.[61] The date of this document has usually been
accepted as 14 July 1130, and it is argued that the count did not
fulfil his promise.[62] He continued to govern his territories and
drew up his will on 8 July 1131 'lying in his palace in Barcelona,
stricken by the illness from which he died'.[63] The clause 'if
meanwhile I happen to die', which appears in the charter, might
therefore be taken to indicate that the count was expressing a
future intention, which he did not in fact fulfil. But it is possible
that the charter should be assigned to the year 1131. Miret y Sans
discovered in the Catalan Hospitaller archive, then housed in the
convent of San Gervasio, a transcript which gave this date,[64]
while Rodríguez Campomanes, writing in the middle of the
eighteenth century, stated that the date is given as 1131 in several
(*aliquot*) manuscripts.[65] Admittedly all the copies of the document
on which Albon bases his text give '1130', but none of these
versions can be dated earlier than the second half of the thirteenth

century, and most of them appear to be derived from the late thirteenth-century Templar cartulary now known as register 310 in the Crown archive in Barcelona. If the charter was issued in 1131, it was drawn up after the count had made his will and only very shortly before his death, which according to the *necrologium* of Ripoll occurred on 19 July.[66] It would follow that right at the end of his life the count probably did enter the Temple, and support for this contention is found not only in a claim made by Raymond Berenguer IV in 1143 that his father had been a brother of the Temple, 'in whose Rule and habit he gloriously ended his life',[67] but also in the comment in the *Gesta Comitum Barcinonensium* that

at the end, offering himself to God and to the militia of Jerusalem, he ended his life very religiously in the house of the poor at Barcelona without property.[68]

The clause 'if meanwhile I happen to die' could then refer to the count's final illness in 1131 and to the possibility that he might die before he could implement his promises.

It is not until 1131 that the Templars are mentioned in dated documents of a reliable character in north-eastern Spain. Nevertheless, there appears to be an earlier reference to them in Aragon in an undated letter written apparently not later than 1130 by William, archbishop of Auch.[69] The letter concerns the militia which Alfonso I of Aragon had established at Monreal del Campo and mentions that this militia had been freed by Alfonso from paying the royal tax of a fifth of booty captured from the Moors 'like the militia of Jerusalem'. The Temple therefore appears to have been receiving privileges from Alfonso I by 1130.

## NOTES

1. xii. 7, in *Recueil des historiens des croisades: historiens occidentaux*, i (Paris, 1844), 520. Other twelfth-century accounts of the foundation of the Temple are contained in the *Chronique de Michel le Syrien*, xv. 11, trans. J. B. Chabot, iii (Paris, 1905–10), 201–3, and Walter Map, *De nugis curialium*, i. 18, ed. T. Wright (Camden Society, 1850), pp. 29 ff.

2. Op. cit. xii. 7, in *Recueil*, i. 520. The date of the Council is discussed by G. Schnürer, *Die ursprüngliche Templerregel* (Freiburg, 1903), p. 113. The Rule of the Temple was not completed at the Council: certain points were left for the

decision of the pope and the patriarch of Jerusalem, and the latter appears to have made some additions about the year 1130: ibid., *passim*.

3. *Règle*, p. 14.

4. Albon, *Cartulaire*, pp. 10–11, doc. 16.

5. V. Carrière, 'Les Débuts de l'Ordre du Temple en France', *Le Moyen Âge*, xxvii (1914), 309, note 2, and *Histoire et cartulaire des Templiers de Provins, avec une introduction sur les débuts du Temple en France* (Paris, 1919), p. xvi, note 2, argues that a document, which is published ibid., p. 111, doc. 93, and by Albon, *Cartulaire*, p. 6, doc. 9, dated 31 October in the eighth year of the Temple, must belong to the year 1127 and that therefore the Order could not have been founded before the beginning of November 1119. Although 1127 is the most likely date for this document, it cannot be definitely assigned to that year.

6. *L'Art de vérifier les dates*, i (Paris, 1783 edn.), 513; J. Richard in *Saint Bernard de Clairvaux* (Paris, 1953), pp. 13–14.

7. Carrière, 'Les Débuts', p. 308, note 1, suggests that he may have accompanied count Hugh of Troyes to the Holy Land in 1104; but according to Michael the Syrian he did not arrive in the East until the beginning of Baldwin II's reign: *Chronique*, xv. 11, trans. Chabot, iii. 201; and he was in the West in 1113: M. Barber, 'The Origins of the Order of the Temple', *Studia monastica*, xii (1970), 222.

8. *Règle*, p. 14.

9. Ibid., pp. 33–4, art. 8.

10. Ibid., p. 26, art. 7.

11. Ibid., p. 69, art. 56.

12. It has been argued that the verbs *collaudamus* and *preoptamus* were used in the text of the Rule when an earlier usage was being confirmed, and that the use of *vetamus* and *contradicimus* signified the rejection of an earlier custom: G. de Valous, 'Quelques observations sur la toute primitive observance des Templiers et la *Regula pauperum commilitonum Christi*', *Mélanges Saint Bernard* (Dijon, 1954), p. 35; see also Schnürer, op. cit., pp. 95–9. But it may be doubted whether the compilers of the Rule were always as precise and careful as this in their choice of words.

13. J. Leclercq, 'Un document sur les débuts des Templiers', *Revue d'histoire ecclésiastique*, lii (1957), 85; C. Dereine in *Le Moyen Âge*, lix (1953), 197.

14. *Chronique de Michel le Syrien*, xv. 11, trans. Chabot, iii. 203; Walter Map, op. cit. i. 18, ed. Wright, p. 29.

15. *The Pilgrimage of the Russian Abbot Daniel in the Holy Land*, ed. C. W. Wilson (Palestine Pilgrims' Text Society, 1888), p. 9; *An Account of the Pilgrimage of Saewulf to Jerusalem and the Holy Land*, trans. W. Brownlow (Palestine Pilgrims' Text Society, 1892), pp. 8–9.

16. J. A. Conde, *Historia de la dominación de los árabes en España* (Madrid, 1820), i. 619, note 1; J. Oliver Asín, 'Origen árabe de "rebato", "arrobda" y sus

homónimos', *Boletín de la Real Academia Española*, xv (1928), 540–1; M. Asín Palacios, *El Islam cristianizado* (Madrid, 1931), p. 138, note 2; A. Castro, *The Structure of Spanish History* (Princeton, 1954), pp. 203–7. That the Spanish military orders were derived in part from Islamic institutions has also been argued by M. Cocheril, 'Essai sur l'origine des ordres militaires dans la péninsule ibérique', *Collectanea Ordinis Cisterciensium Reformatorum*, xxi (1959), 247–8, and E. Lourie, 'A Society Organised for War: Medieval Spain', *Past and Present*, xxxv (1966), 67–8, although I have not been able to follow the latter's argument that 'the influence of the *ribat* on these orders is apparent in the fact that except, and then only initially, for Santiago, the Orders of Spain . . . were never Hospitaller foundations, unlike either the Temple or Hospital'. Islamic influence on the Spanish military orders has been questioned by the most recent writers on these Orders: J. F. O'Callaghan, 'The Affiliation of the Order of Calatrava with the Order of Cîteaux', *Analecta Sacri Ordinis Cisterciensis*, xv (1959), 176–8; D. W. Lomax, *La Orden de Santiago* (Madrid, 1965), pp. 3–4.

17. Castro, op. cit., p. 207.

18. A. Noth, *Heiliger Krieg und Heiliger Kampf in Islam und Christentum* (Bonn, 1965), pp. 72–6.

19. G. Marçais, 'Ribat', *Encyclopedia of Islam*, iii (London, 1936), 1152, argues that by the twelfth century the *ribats* were losing their military character and were becoming purely monastic establishments, but that there was a general development of this kind has been doubted by Noth, op. cit., p. 83. In maintaining that the *ribat* did not exist in Syria as a fortified convent and that the word was used there to refer simply to watchtowers, Lomax, op. cit., p. 3, seems to be reading too much into a statement by Mukaddasi, *Description of Syria, including Palestine*, trans. G. Le Strange (Palestine Pilgrims' Text Society, 1886), p. 61.

20. Noth, op. cit., pp. 78–80, 86–7; G. Marçais, 'Note sur les ribâts en Berbérie', *Mélanges René Basset*, ii (Publications de l'Institut des Hautes-Études Marocaines, vol. xi, 1925), 418–21. Marçais also doubts whether there were any links between *ribats*.

21. Migne, *PL*, clxxxii. 921; St. Bernard, *Opera Omnia*, ed. J. Leclerq and H. M. Rochais, iii (Rome, 1963), 214.

22. Migne, *PL*, clxxxix. 434; *The Letters of Peter the Venerable*, ed. G. Constable (Cambridge, Mass., 1967), i. 407, no. 172.

23. Ibid.

24. This seems to be the implication of the clause 'cui creditum ac debitum hoc erat' in the Prologue of the Templar Rule: *Règle*, p. 16.

25. Migne, *PL*, clxxxii. 921–40; St. Bernard, *Opera Omnia*, iii. 213–39.

26. When suggesting that St. Bernard may not at first have given his full approval to the Temple, E. Vacandard, *Vie de Saint Bernard* (Paris, 1927), i. 236–7, refers to a letter which St. Bernard wrote to Hugh, count of Champagne, when the latter joined the Temple: Migne, *PL*, clxxxii. 135–6; Albon,

*Cartulaire*, p. 3, doc. 5. But in this letter St. Bernard is not obviously doing anything more than mourning the absence of a friend.

27. The *De Laude* can of course be looked upon partly as a justification or apology for the Temple, but what it sought to justify primarily was the use of force against the infidel rather than the combining of the military and religious ways of life. The justness of the use of force against the infidel was similarly the point at issue when Hugh of Payns wrote to members of the Order that 'certain of you have been confused by some less prudent people, as if your profession, by which you have dedicated your life to bearing arms against the enemies of the faith and of peace for the defence of Christians, as if, I say, that profession were illicit or wicked': Leclerq, loc. cit., p. 87. In so far as these writings reveal criticism of the Temple, therefore, it is criticism of the use of force rather than of the particular character of the Temple.

28. —. Cirot de la Ville, *Histoire de l'abbaye et congrégation de Notre-Dame de la Grande-Sauve*, i (Paris, 1844), 297–9, 497–8; C. Erdmann, *Die Entstehung des Kreuzzugsgedankens* (Stuttgart, 1935), p. 253.

29. Ed. H. Hagenmeyer (Heidelberg, 1913).

30. Op. cit. xii. 7, in *Recueil*, i. 521; cf. F. Lundgreen, *Wilhelm von Tyrus und der Templerorden* (Historische Studien, vol. xcvii, 1911), p. 59. According to Michael the Syrian there were originally thirty members: *Chronique*, xv. 11, trans. Chabot, iii. 201.

31. A letter in which Baldwin II informed St. Bernard that he was sending two Templars, Andrew and Gundemar, to gain papal approval for the Order, has been assigned by some writers to the period 1119–26: Albon, *Cartulaire*, p. 1, doc. 1; R. Röhricht, *Regesta Regni Hierosolymitani* (New York edn., n.d.), i. 28, no. 116. But its authenticity has been questioned: Carrière, *Histoire et cartulaire*, p. xxv; M. Melville, *La Vie des Templiers* (Paris, 1951), p. 272.

32. *Historia Ecclesiastica*, xii. 29, ed. A. le Prevost, iv (Société de l'Histoire de France, 1852), 423.

33. Albon, *Cartulaire*, pp. 1–2, doc. 2. On the date of this document, see *Cartulaire de la commanderie de Richerenches de l'Ordre du Temple (1136-1214)*, ed. Marquis de Ripert-Monclar (Avignon, 1907), p. xxxiii, note 4.

34. Leclerq, loc. cit., p. 89.

35. Albon, *Cartulaire*, p. 16, doc. 22; p. 6, doc. 9. On this early expansion in France, see Carrière, 'Les Débuts', pp. 311–21.

36. Albon, *Cartulaire*, p. 5, doc. 7.

37. Ibid., pp. 10–12, docs. 16, 17.

38. Cf. Melville, op. cit., p. 25.

39. Albon, *Cartulaire*, pp. 5–6, doc. 8; pp. 8–10, docs. 12–15.

40. *The Anglo-Saxon Chronicle*, sub anno 1128, ed. D. Whitelock (London, 1961), p. 194; Henry of Huntingdon, *Historia Anglorum*, vii. 39, ed. T. Arnold

# The Foundation of the Temple 13

(London, 1879), p. 250; *Annales de Waverleia*, in *Annales Monastici*, ed. H. R. Luard, ii (London, 1865), 221.

41. Albon, *Cartulaire*, p. 7, doc. 10. C. Erdmann, 'Der Kreuzzugsgedanke in Portugal', *Historische Zeitschrift*, cxli (1929), 38, rejects the claim that the Templars had possessions in Portugal by 1126.

42. Op. cit. xiii. 4, ed. le Prevost, v (1855), 5-7; cf. M. Gual Camarena, *Precedentes de la reconquista valenciana* (Valencia, 1952), p. 12.

43. On this confraternity, see P. Rassow, 'La cofradía de Belchite', *AHDE*, iii (1926), 200-26; A. Ubieto Arteta, 'La creación de la cofradía de Belchite', *EEMCA*, v (1952), 427-34. The nature of this confraternity, which is known only through a confirmation issued in 1136, is obscure. While it was possible to serve in it for a short period, it was also envisaged that there would be life-members; but in the surviving confirmation there is no reference to the taking of monastic vows, as members of military orders did, and the wording of the confirmation seems to imply that private property was allowed. It seems to have been essentially a lay institution, whose members, however, like crusaders received indulgences.

44. Miret y Sans, *Les Cases*, p. 16.

45. AHN, cód. 471, p. 155, doc. 157.

46. Miret y Sans, *Les Cases*, p. 16, note 2, does, however, rightly reject another document supposedly issued by the count of Barcelona at Ejea in 1125: AHN, cód. 467, p. 170, doc. 183. The date must also be rejected of another charter recording a grant supposedly made by Raymond Berenguer IV in 1126: AHN, San Juan, leg. 333, doc. 1. Miret y Sans, *Les Cases*, pp. 15-16, further questions the date of a grant apparently made by the count of Urgel in 1123. The Templar named in the charter of donation—Gerald of Nocura—is mentioned in other documents drawn up between 1134 and 1137: Albon, *Cartulaire*, p. 57, doc. 73; p. 101, doc. 144.

47. AGP, parch. Cervera, no. 325.

48. Ibid., no. 374.

49. Miret y Sans, *Les Cases*, pp. 222-3.

50. Zurita, *Anales*, i. 51; García Larragueta, *Gran priorado*, i. 38, note 17; 54, note 110.

51. AHN, cód. 502, pp. 4-5.

52. J. Zurita, *Indices rerum ab Aragoniae regibus gestarum ab initiis regni ad annum MCDX* (Zaragoza, 1587), p. 59.

53. T. Muñoz y Romero, *Colección de fueros municipales y cartas pueblas de los reinos de Castilla, León, Corona de Aragón y Navarra* (Madrid, 1847), pp. 503-4.

54. *Gran priorado*, i. 38, 54; cf. M. L. Ledesma Rubio, *La encomienda de Zaragoza de la Orden de San Juan de Jerusalén en los siglos XII y XIII* (Zaragoza, 1967), p. 27.

55. AHN, San Juan, leg. 340, doc. 1. The hand in which the transcript is written is not characteristic of the later thirteenth century; it seems rather to be an imitation of a twelfth-century script.

56. Albon, *Cartulaire*, p. 73, doc. 100.

57. *Cartulario de 'Sant Cugat' del Vallés*, ed. J. Rius Serra, iii (Barcelona, 1947), 84–5, doc. 892.

58. Ibid. iii. 87–8, doc. 896.

59. Albon, *Cartulaire*, p. 18, doc. 26.

60. The document, of which only a late twelfth-century copy is known, is published in full by Lacarra, 'Documentos', no. 150 (iii. 548–9). It appears to bear the date December, Era 1167; Lacarra, however, assigns it to the year 1128, not 1129, because it was confirmed by Peter, bishop of Zaragoza, whom Lacarra identifies with Peter of Librana, who was dead by December 1129. But as Peter's confirmation immediately precedes that of Raymond Berenguer IV, which must have been made between 1137 and 1162, it is possible that the bishop in question is in fact Peter of Torroja (1153–84).

61. Albon, *Cartulaire*, p. 25, doc. 33.

62. e.g. A. de Bofarull y Broca, *Historia de Cataluña*, ii (Barcelona, 1876), 425; Miret y Sans, *Les Cases*, pp. 23–4; S. Sobrequés Vidal, *Els grans comtes de Barcelona* (Barcelona, 1961), pp. 199–200; F. Soldevila, *Història de Catalunya* (Barcelona, 1963), p. 134.

63. Albon, *Cartulaire*, pp. 28–9, doc. 38; *LFM*, i. 527, doc. 493.

64. Miret y Sans, *Les Cases*, p. 16.

65. P. Rodríguez Campomanes, *Dissertaciones históricas del Orden y Cavallería de los Templarios* (Madrid, 1747), p. 220.

66. Bofarull y Broca, op. cit. ii. 425.

67. Albon, *Cartulaire*, p. 204, doc. 314; *CDI*, iv. 94, doc. 43.

68. Ed. L. Barrau Dihigo and J. Massó Torrents (Barcelona, 1925), p. 38.

69. Albon, *Cartulaire*, pp. 3–4, doc. 6; Lacarra, 'Documentos', no. 151 (iii. 549–50). On the relations of the archbishop of Auch with Aragon at this time, see J. M. Lacarra, 'La restauración eclesiástica en las tierras conquistadas por Alfonso el Batallador (1118–1134)', *Revista portuguesa de história*, iv (1949), 267.

## II

## *Expansion: (i) The Reconquest and the Growth of Property*

THE century following the Templars' arrival in the Iberian Peninsula witnessed a very marked expansion of the Order in north-eastern Spain. In that region the Templars acquired more wealth than the Hospitallers, while the Spanish military orders failed to attain in the *Corona de Aragón* the importance which they possessed in the centre of the Peninsula. This Templar expansion resulted to a considerable degree from the favour shown to the Order by the rulers of Aragon and Catalonia in return for its participation in the *reconquista*.

By the time that the Templars arrived in Spain the raiding between Christian and Moor which had characterized much of the eleventh century had been partly replaced on the Christian side by a policy of conquest, and in the north-east of the Peninsula the later decades of the eleventh and the early years of the twelfth centuries had been marked by notable Christian advances. Alfonso I, the king of Aragon and Navarre when the Templars reached the Peninsula, had conquered much of the middle valley of the Ebro, including the city of Zaragoza, and had made further gains to the south along the rivers Jalón and Jiloca. And to assist him in preserving and extending his gains, Alfonso had in 1122 founded the military confraternity at Belchite. In these circumstances it is not surprising that in Aragon and Catalonia, as in Portugal, the Templars were immediately expected to give military assistance against the Moors. This expectation is apparent from the count of Barcelona's grant of the castle of Grañena, for this lay in the march or frontier area, and was given 'for the defence of Christendom according to the purpose for which the Order was founded';[1] and this wording was repeated in 1132 when Armengol VI, count of Urgel, gave the Temple the frontier castle of Barbará, which his family had

held of the counts of Barcelona since 1067.[2] The task of
defending frontier castles, which the Templars were later to
perform in the Holy Land, was already being assigned to them
in Catalonia.

Yet the Templars were at first reluctant to become involved in
the struggle against Islam in the Peninsula. At that stage in their
expansion they were no doubt wary of committing themselves to
fighting on a second front against the infidel.[3] They did not therefore immediately establish themselves in Grañena and undertake
its defence. When the count of Urgel granted Barbará, he stated
that it should be held by the Templars 'who shall have come with
arms and stayed in Grañena or in our march': the use of the
future-perfect tense, coupled with the reference to two possible
places of Templar settlement, implies that the Order had not then
occupied the castle of Grañena. And when—possibly in the following year—Raymond Berenguer IV confirmed the count of
Urgel's grant, the clause 'when they shall have come with arms
and stayed in Grañena or in the aforesaid march' was included in
the charter of confirmation,[4] again indicating that Grañena had
still not been occupied by the Temple, and apparently implying
that the count's confirmation was a conditional one, which would
explain why Barbará was included in a list of newly granted strongholds contained in a charter issued to the Temple by Raymond
Berenguer in 1143.[5] A further attempt to involve the Temple in
the reconquest appears, however, to have been made in Catalonia
about the year 1134, when the count of Barcelona and at least
twenty-six Catalan nobles promised to serve with the Temple for
a year and when Raymond Berenguer further undertook to provide equipment and land to support ten Templar knights.[6] As
William and Odo of Moncada promised to give this service in the
*cavalleria* of Grañena, the promises clearly referred to service in
Spain and not in the Holy Land. The significance of the promises
is made further apparent by the wording of Raymond Berenguer's
undertaking—apparently made later than the others[7]—for this
stipulates that the count is to serve not just for one year, but for
the first year. This wording seems to indicate that when the promises were being made the manning of frontier castles by the
Templars was being discussed and that the count was proposing
to serve the Order for a year from the date when the Temple
entered the struggle against the Moors in Spain. The *cavalleria* of

Grañena was thus a proposed Templar establishment and not an existing one.[8]

Attempts were similarly being made in Aragon to bring the Templars into the *reconquista*. The exemption from the tax of a fifth on booty which Alfonso I granted to the Templars provides an indication of the military role assigned to the Order by the Aragonese king, while Alfonso's bequest of his kingdoms—in the absence of an obvious heir—to the Temple, the Hospital, and the canons of the Holy Sepulchre in 1131 should probably also be partly explained in the same context.[9] The inclusion of the Holy Sepulchre among the beneficiaries shows that Alfonso was motivated partly by veneration for the Holy Places and a concern for the Holy Land; the importance attached by Spaniards to Jerusalem at this time despite the presence of Islamic power in the Peninsula is clear from their participation in crusades to the East[10] and from the idea expressed on a number of occasions that the expulsion of the Moors from Spain would open the way to Jerusalem.[11] But Alfonso's bequest, if carried out, would inevitably have involved the Temple in the conflict with the Moors in the Peninsula, and in view of Alfonso's aggressive policies towards the Moors and his foundation of militias to assist in the struggle against the infidel it may be argued that the Aragonese king was also trying to ensure the continuation of the reconquest by the Temple, when his own militias of Monreal and Belchite, which are not mentioned in the will, had presumably collapsed.[12] But although Alfonso confirmed his will shortly before his death in September 1134[13] it was not carried into effect. For the Aragonese and Navarrese nobles the situation in 1134 was similar to that which faced the English barons on the death of Henry I in the following year, since a large number of nobles had witnessed Alfonso's will and had sworn to enforce it.[14] As in England, the king's wishes were ignored. Aragon fell to Alfonso's brother Ramiro, who was a monk and bishop-elect of Roda; the *regnum Cesaraugustanum* came under the control of Alfonso VII of Castile; and García Ramírez was established as ruler of Navarre.[15] The will had therefore no immediate effect on Templar activities in Aragon.

It was nevertheless as a result of later negotiations between Raymond Berenguer IV and the Orders about the latter's claims to Alfonso's kingdoms that the Temple was brought into the *reconquista*. The background to these negotiations is, however, by no means clear. It has been argued by Ubieto Arteta[16] that the first step was taken by Alfonso VII of Castile in 1136, after Innocent II had in June of that year ordered the Castilian king to enforce the will; after receiving the papal letter, Alfonso VII broke his alliance with García Ramírez, who until then was holding the *regnum Cesaraugustanum* of him, and made a treaty with Ramiro II of Aragon. The text of the treaty has not survived, but Ubieto—basing his argument partly on scattered references in other sources and partly on what happened later—claims that Alfonso VII granted the *regnum Cesaraugustanum* to Ramiro, although he was still to hold it for life of the Aragonese king, and that the two kings agreed to take joint action against García Ramírez. According to Ubieto, the grant to Ramiro and the attack on the Navarrese

would be nothing but the carrying out of the papal orders about the fulfilment of Alfonso's will, for which the unification of the old royal lands under one person was necessary.[17]

It was then decided that Alfonso's will was impracticable. Fresh terms were therefore arranged—presumably later, although this is not made clear by Ubieto—under the guidance of the papal legate Guy. It was agreed that Ramiro's daughter Petronilla should be betrothed to Raymond Berenguer IV, count of Barcelona; the latter was to receive Aragon from Ramiro and was then to obtain renunciations of claims from the Holy Sepulchre, the Hospital, and the Temple. The surrender of the kingdom to the count was made in 1137. In 1140 the Hospital and the Holy Sepulchre gave up their claims, as did the Temple three years later.

   This account may be criticized on a number of points. It is not beyond doubt that the dispatch of Innocent's bull, which does not bear the year of issue, immediately preceded the agreement made between Alfonso and Ramiro in 1136; it may have been issued in 1135.[18] Ubieto Arteta assigns it to the year 1136 by linking it with the legation to Spain in that year of the cardinal Guy. Yet, although the cardinal's presence in 1143 when compensation was given to the Temple for its claims suggests that he was involved in the question of the Aragonese succession,[19] his legation need not from the beginning have been closely linked with Innocent's bull, especially as it is stated in the *Historia Com-*

*postellana* and elsewhere that the legate had been invited to Spain in the first place by Alfonso VII to settle ecclesiastical disputes.[20] Even if it is accepted that the bull belongs to the year 1136, and that Guy's legation was occasioned by the question of the Aragonese succession, it is difficult to link the papal order with the grant of the *regnum Cesaraugustanum* to Ramiro. It may be asked why it should have been necessary to unite all the lands of Alfonso I before surrendering them to the rightful heirs, and it is not easy to understand how an agreement which gave to Alfonso VII a temporary, and to the Aragonese kings a permanent, right over the *regnum Cesaraugustanum* could have contributed towards the execution of the will.[21] A different interpretation of the events of 1136 is suggested by a reading of the *Chronica Adefonsi Imperatoris* and the *Historia Compostellana*, both of which imply that in the war between García Ramírez and Alfonso VII hostilities were started by the Navarrese.[22] The *Historia Compostellana* states that the king of Portugal attacked Alfonso 'after he had heard that the emperor was being troubled by the same king García', while the *Chronica Adefonsi Imperatoris* says that 'king García of Navarre and all his fighting men rebelled against the lord emperor', and that the kings of Navarre and Portugal 'opened hostilities against the emperor and prepared for battle'. It may be doubted whether a medieval chronicler, writing a 'song of praise' of Alfonso VII,[23] would have said merely this if the war had been sponsored by the pope and had had the purpose of restoring Alfonso I's lands to the rightful heirs. García Ramírez apparently rebelled against Alfonso VII in 1136, just as in the previous year he had abandoned the lordship of Ramiro. The alliance of Alfonso and Ramiro therefore may well have been occasioned by, and not caused, the outbreak of hostilities, since the Castilian king was also being attacked by Portugal and needed support. The most obvious ally was Ramiro, and Alfonso's grant of the *regnum Cesaraugustanum* to him may, as Traggia suggested,[24] be interpreted as a bribe to win him over to the Castilian side at a time when the Aragonese king might have tried to reassert his own overlordship over García Ramírez or gain outright control of the *regnum Cesaraugustanum*.[25]

If the war with Navarre and the cession of the *regnum Cesaraugustanum* to Ramiro are interpreted in this way, it may be doubted whether the agreement between Alfonso and Ramiro in 1136 was concerned at all with the question of the Aragonese succession in the ways that Ubieto suggests, especially as the betrothal of Petronilla and the grant of Aragon to the count of Barcelona did not take place until a year after the 1136 agreement,[26] and as it is not even certain that Petronilla had been born by the time of the agreement.[27] Ramiro's abdication from power in 1137 may have been linked with the question of Alfonso's will in that his rejection of its terms aroused the opposition of the pope who, as a result, may have refused to grant a dispensation for Ramiro's marriage;[28] but there is nothing to suggest that his course of action in 1137 arose out of the agreement of the previous year. Nor is papal hostility the only possible explanation of Ramiro's cession of his kingdom. It may have been occasioned by his difficult relations with his own nobles and with the Castilian and Navarrese rulers, for in one document Ramiro stated that he was giving away his kingdom

because of the many deceptions and frauds which I have suffered from many and so that I shall not suffer any more.[29]

While no link can be shown between the 1136 agreement and Ramiro's actions in the following year, there is further nothing to indicate that the grant of Aragon to the count of Barcelona formed part of any plan whose culmination was to be the renunciation of claims by the Temple, the Hospital, and the Holy Sepulchre. The documents recording the cession of Aragon to Raymond Berenguer are silent on this point;[30] it is further not clear that in 1137 the count of Barcelona was in any better position than Ramiro to obtain renunciations;[31] and it was not until three years later that the Hospital and the Holy Sepulchre renounced their claims. To maintain therefore that the negotiations conducted between Raymond Berenguer IV and the beneficiaries of Alfonso I's will arose out of measures adopted by Alfonso VII and Ramiro in 1136 and 1137 is merely to put forward a hypothesis, for which no evidence can be adduced and to which a number of objections can be raised. The negotiations may well have been undertaken on the initiative of the count of Barcelona himself. When he gained Aragon he needed a legitimate title to it in the eyes of the Church; he also wanted to secure the assistance of the Templars in the *reconquista*.

In the negotiations with the count of Barcelona the Hospital and the Holy Sepulchre acted together. After proposals had apparently been made by Raymond Berenguer, the patriarch of Jerusalem wrote to Raymond, the Grand Master of the Hospitallers, asking him to act on behalf of the Holy Sepulchre and to make similar agreements for both Orders.[32] Raymond therefore went to Spain, where he realized that it was essential for the proper government and defence of Aragon that the Hospital should surrender its claims. In a charter drawn up on 16 September 1140 he renounced, with certain reservations, the third left to the Hospital.[33] On the same day a similar surrender, in almost exactly —*mutatis mutandis*—the same words and with similar reservations was drawn up on behalf of the Holy Sepulchre.[34] This surrender was made in the name of the patriarch, with the Grand Master acting as his proxy. This explains the further renunciation made by the patriarch in August 1141 in terms similar to those of 1140;[35] it was merely a confirmation of the action taken by Raymond in the previous year.

Several historians have assumed that the Temple joined with the Hospital and the Holy Sepulchre in these negotiations. Zurita writes as though the Temple was involved in 1140;[36] but although the other two Orders refer to each other, neither mentions the Temple. Zapater asserts that all three Orders made surrenders of claims in 1141.[37] But as the patriarch's charter in 1141 was merely a confirmation of the renunciation made on his behalf by the Grand Master of the Hospital, there is no reason for the existence of similar documents for the other Orders. Zapater probably saw the surrender by the Holy Sepulchre in 1141 and Adrian IV's later confirmation of renunciations by all three Orders,[38] and assumed that the Hospital and the Temple had made similar cessions at the same time.

The Temple negotiated separately, for the issues were to some extent different. One stage in the negotiations is revealed in an undated letter from the count of Barcelona to the Grand Master of the Temple, written between 1137 and 1143.[39] This letter begins:

How king Alfonso shortly before his death left his kingdom in three parts, to the Sepulchre of the Lord, namely, to the Hospital and the militia of the Temple is well known to all. I therefore, his successor in the kingdom, want to serve that militia in all ways and to honour it and to magnify it honourably. Considering the nature of your profession, it seems to me that, just as in the beginning under the blessed

Peter the Church of God then founded rejoiced through the preaching
of the apostles, so now the same Church is defended by your action.
Therefore we and all the clergy and people of the land of Spain beg
your brotherhood that you provide for the Church of God and aid it
in its necessity in so far as you are able and give and send to us at least
ten of your brothers, whom you think suitable for this task, by whom
in our land knights and others of the faithful, who shall have given
themselves to this militia, may be governed and ruled.

Although the count makes no direct reference to the renunciation
of claims to Aragon by the Temple, it is clear from the opening
sentences that he was thinking in terms of compensating the Order
for its share of the kingdom. But he was also reviving the idea—
first put forward when he promised to serve for a year in the
Temple—that the Order should provide ten knights, who were
to be sent from the Holy Land to form the nucleus of a Templar
force in Spain. The wording of the letter suggests that part of the
count's concern was with the loss of manpower which would
result if Catalans and Aragonese who joined the Order were sent
to the East. Like the Spanish rulers and the popes at the turn of
the eleventh and twelfth centuries, who had tried to prevent
Spaniards from going on crusades in the Holy Land,[40] he wanted
his subjects to remain in Spain to fight against Islam there. To
obtain the agreement of the Order, the count offered not only
sufficient land to maintain ten knights, but also the town of
Daroca, the castles of Osso and Belchite, lordship over one man
of each religion in Zaragoza, a quarter share in Cuarte, near
Huesca, and a tenth of all that he acquired or won from the
Moors.

At the end of the letter the count warned the Grand Master of
the dangers of delay in replying to his request; but if the letter
was sent[41] it did not win over the Templars,[42] and when agreement was finally reached in 1143 following negotiations conducted 'frequently and diligently through letters and envoys',
the Order managed to obtain considerably greater concessions.
The Templars were then given the castles of Monzón, Mongay,
Barbará, Chalamera, Belchite, and Remolins and royal rights in
Corbins; a tenth of royal revenues and in addition 1,000s. annually
from royal dues both in Zaragoza and in Huesca; a fifth of all
lands conquered from the Moors; and exemption from certain
taxes.[43]

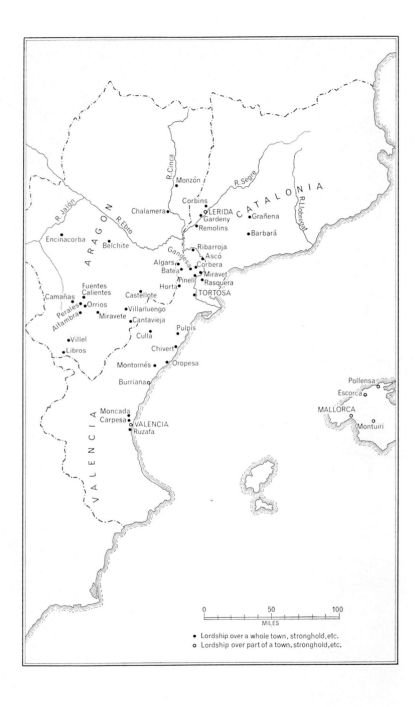

Lordship over a whole town, stronghold, etc.
Lordship over part of a town, stronghold, etc.

R.Cinca
R.Segre
R.Llobregat
R.Jalón
R.Ebro
Gandesa

Monzón
Corbins
LERIDA
Gardeny
Remolins
Grañena
Barbará
Chalamera
CATALONIA
Encinacorba
Belchite
ARAGON
Ribarroja
Ascó
Algars
Corbera
Batea
Miravet
Pinell
Rasquera
Horta
TORTOSA
Fuentes
Calientes
Camañas
Castellote
Orrios
Villarluengo
Perales
Miravete
Alfambra
Cantavieja
Villel
Culla
Pulpis
Libros
Chivert
Montornés
Oropesa
Burriana
Pollensa
Escorca
MALLORCA
Moncada
Carpesa
VALENCIA
Ruzafa
Montuiri
VALENCIA

0        50        100
MILES

In the charter recording the grant of these rights and privileges, as in the count's earlier letter, no reference is made to the renunciation of claims to the kingdom of Aragon by the Temple, but there can be no doubt that this was a condition of the grant. That the Temple made a formal renunciation is clear from the confirmation of it issued by Adrian IV in 1158,[44] and that it must have been made at this time is evident from the absence of any other grant to the Order by the count which could have comprised compensation for its claims to Aragon. The renunciation must have been made in a separate document drawn up at this time which has not survived.

But the count was not only gaining a renunciation of claims. In the charter he stated that

for the defence of the western Church which is in Spain, for the defeat, overcoming, and expulsion of the race of Moors and the exaltation of the holy Christian faith and religion, I have decreed that a militia shall be formed, on the model of the militia of the Temple of Solomon in Jerusalem, which defends the eastern Church, to be subject to the Temple and to follow that militia's rule and customs of holy obedience.

The Templars had agreed and 'sent their decree and counsel about the establishment of a militia of Christ in Spain against the Moors'. This agreement clearly meant not, as some writers have imagined,[45] that the Temple was first being introduced into Spain in 1143, but that it was then being brought into the struggle against the Moors in the Peninsula.[46] Up to 1143 the Order had been concerned only with obtaining property and recruits there. Now, with the consent of the Grand Master, the Temple was to serve the same purpose in Spain as it did in the Holy Land; and it was expected not only to provide troops but also to have a share in deciding policy, for Raymond Berenguer promised not to make peace with the Moors without the counsel of the Templars.

From 1143 onwards, therefore, the Templars fought in Spain and took part in the Aragonese reconquest up to its completion with the conquest of the kingdom of Valencia. In major campaigns the Templars formed part of the royal army, but they also undertook expeditions of their own, and the distinction made in some *fueros* between service owed to the provincial master and that due to the local Templar commander suggests that Templar activities included small-scale raids as well as larger expeditions.[47]

The Order was, in addition, often made responsible for the defence and protection of castles along the Moorish frontier. Although the evidence of their military activities and conduct in the field is sparse,[48] the Templars' participation in the struggle with the Moors during the period of the Aragonese reconquest cannot be called in question, as that of the Hospitallers has been.[49] In return for this military assistance the Temple received a share of the lands conquered from the Moors. But the attitude of the Aragonese rulers towards the 1143 agreement changed during the course of the reconquest. In the second half of the twelfth century they appear to have observed its provisions. In the early part of the next century, however, they came to consider that Raymond Berenguer's concessions to the Order had been excessive and tried to relate the Templars' rewards to the importance of the help they gave in the conquest of new territories.

The results of the 1143 agreement first became apparent during the expeditions which Raymond Berenguer undertook during the following ten years along the valleys of the lower Segre and Ebro, which then probably formed part of the kingdom of the Moorish ruler Lobo, who in the period following the collapse of Almoravide power controlled much of eastern Spain.[50] The participation of the Templars in the attack on Tortosa in 1148 is proved by an agreement which they made with the Hospitallers during the siege[51] and by a reference in the *Annali Genovesi*,[52] while their presence at the siege of Lérida in the following year is known from an agreement made there between the Order and the bishop of Roda.[53] There is also evidence to show that members of the Order were helping to besiege Miravet in the summer of 1152.[54] The size of Templar contingents on these expeditions is not known, but the Templars' role was important enough for the troubadour Marcabru to be able to comment that

> En Espaigna, sai, lo Marques
> E cill del temple Salamo
> Sofron lo pes
> E.l fais de l'orguoill paganor.[55]

By the middle of the twelfth century it had become a common practice among Christian rulers in Spain to anticipate conquests from the Moors and to make grants of territory which still lay in Moorish hands. This custom had been followed in the case of

Tortosa: Raymond Berenguer III had promised the city to Artal, count of Pallars;[56] Alfonso I stated in his will that if he captured it he would give it to the Hospitallers;[57] in 1136 Raymond Berenguer IV gave it in fee to William of Montpellier, who ten years later left it to his son;[58] in 1146 the count of Barcelona granted the lordship of the city, together with the castle called the Zuda and a third of the city's revenues, to the seneschal William Raymond of Moncada;[59] and at about the same time the Genoese were assigned a third of the city by the count.[60] After the capture of Tortosa only the last two of these grants were taken into consideration.[61] Nevertheless Miret y Sans has argued that because of these two donations the Temple gained only a fifteenth instead of a fifth of the city: Moncada and the Genoese were each assigned portions of the whole city, and the Templars were given a fifth only of the remaining third.[62] Yet shortly after the capture of the city William Raymond of Moncada complained that he had not been given a whole third. The count of Barcelona in reply maintained that he could grant William a third only of the part remaining to him and could give nothing from the third which the Genoese had won for themselves or from the Temple's fifth; and Raymond Berenguer's assertion was upheld in the count's court.[63] Priority was thus given to the claims of the Genoese and the Templars.[64] That the Templars in fact obtained the fifth promised in 1143 is further made clear in a confirmation of Templar rights in Tortosa issued by Alfonso II in 1175, for in this he not only referred to a fifth of the whole city, but also stated that all the revenues of Tortosa were to be collected by the bailiffs of the king and of others who had rights there, and that a fifth was to be assigned to the Temple before any other division was made.[65] The Temple's share of Tortosa consisted, however, merely in the right to receive a portion of the city's revenues. It was allowed no active part in the government and administration of Tortosa: in 1174 Alfonso II and Raymond of Moncada commuted the labour services of the Moors of Tortosa without reference to the Order[66] and in 1180 the king drew up constitutions for the city which were witnessed by Moncada but not by the Templars.[67]

The Temple also obtained a fifth of the city of Lérida after its capture in 1149. The Order's claim had been safeguarded in an agreement made in 1148 about the division of the city, whose territories were then defined as stretching from the boundaries of

Corbins in the north to those of Gebut in the south.[68] The lordship of the city, together with a third of the lands and revenues
there, was granted to the count of Urgel, but from the two-thirds
remaining to the count of Barcelona a fifth of the whole city was
to be given to the Temple and over this fifth the count of Urgel
was to exercise no rights of lordship; in compensation he was
given certain powers over the castellanry of Ascó. After the
conquest of Lérida the Order was apparently assigned specific
districts in the terms of the city,[69] and although it is nowhere
stated what lands were given to the Templars, later evidence
shows that they were granted Gardeny, situated on a hill to the
south of the city, where Alfonso I had built a castle in 1123 but
had failed to hold it;[70] they appear also to have been given rights
in Fontanet, on the opposite bank of the river from Gardeny, in
the district of Segriá to the north and west of the city and in the
parish of St. Lawrence within the city.[71]

In 1153, after the rest of the lower Segre and Ebro valleys had
been conquered, Raymond Berenguer further gave the Order
the equivalent of a fifth of the whole of the *ribera* of the Ebro
from Mequinenza to Benifallet.[72] His grant consisted of the castle
of Miravet, whose boundaries were delineated to include the
minor strongholds of Algars, Batea, Corbera, Gandesa, Pinell,
and Rasquera; estates at Mequinenza, Flix, Ascó, García, Mora
de Ebro, and Tivisa; and two *jovadas* at Marsá. In his charter the
count stressed the Temple's duty of defending these strongholds
by stating that he wanted Miravet to be entrusted to safe guardians.
By this time the Templars had probably also secured the castle of
Remolins, on the Segre, which had been promised in 1143, for in
1154 the arbiters in a dispute between the Order and the bishop
of Lérida confirmed possession of it to the Temple.[73] There is,
however, no record of the grant of a fifth of the lands along the
lower Segre below Lérida to the Order.

While the results of the 1143 agreement during the lifetime of
Raymond Berenguer IV are fairly clear, its importance in the
reign of Alfonso II is more obscure. Little information can be
found in either Christian or Arab chronicle sources about Alfonso's
expeditions in what became southern Aragon, and it is not known
what part the Templars played in these campaigns. Nor is it
altogether clear how far Alfonso II carried out the promises made
by Raymond Berenguer. The Order could expect a fifth of

Alfonso's conquests, but it was in fact excluded from the areas conquered by him. The military orders which enjoyed the patronage of the Aragonese king in these districts were those of Spanish origin. The stronghold of Alcañiz was given to Calatrava in 1179,[74] and a series of grants was made by Alfonso to the minor Order of Mountjoy, which had been founded about the year 1173 by the Leonese noble, Roderick count of Sarria.[75] Amongst the endowments of this Order were various frontier castles, including Alfambra, Villel, and Castellote. The special favour shown by the Aragonese king to this small Order, coupled with the absence of royal patronage of the Temple in these districts, suggests that Alfonso was becoming reluctant to entrust the defence of his Moorish frontiers mainly to a large international order, which might—as in the Holy Land[76]—pursue an independent policy, contrary to royal interests, and that he gave his support to Mountjoy because it could be more easily controlled than the Temple.

The exclusion of the Templars from southern Aragon apparently did not mean, however, that Alfonso was rejecting the 1143 agreement, for he made a number of important grants to the Temple, which were probably compensation for the Order's claim to a fifth of southern Aragon and some of which by their timing seem to be connected with his expeditions. The promises made in November 1169 of the Valencian castles of Oropesa and Chivert and of 1,000*m.* annually, to be paid whenever tribute was gained from the Moorish king Lobo, may thus have been linked with the expedition which Alfonso had undertaken in that year.[77] The promise of the Valencian stronghold of Montornés in 1181 may similarly have been made in compensation for a share in the conquests which Alfonso had made in the previous year.[78] Other important grants by Alfonso cannot be linked closely with his expeditions, and explanations of these grants are not provided in the charters of donation, but it may be suggested that these also comprised compensation for the Order's fifth of southern Aragon. These donations include the gift of the castle of Horta in ? 1174,[79] and that of Encinacorba in 1175,[80] and also the important grant made in March 1182 of royal rights of lordship, together with a half of royal revenues, in Tortosa, Ascó, and Ribarroja.[81] The king retained merely his demesne lands in Tortosa, his ecclesiastical rights, and half of the hunting and fishing when he or the queen was present; the Temple's fifth in Tortosa was, however, to be included in the revenues to be divided, together with the rents of any lands which either party acquired in future in the city.[82]

Although the Temple appears to have been given compensation for its fifth of Alfonso's conquests in this way, the necessities of frontier defence obliged the Aragonese king to make further donations to the Temple shortly before his death. The Order of Mountjoy, though expanding territorially, had become subject to difficulties. Already in 1186 a proposal had been made to incorporate it into the Temple. This plan had not been carried out presumably because of opposition from Alfonso II, who was still trying to exclude the Templars from southern Aragon. Mountjoy was instead in 1188 joined to the Hospital of the Holy Redeemer, which the Aragonese king had recently founded at Teruel for the ransoming of captives. But this did not bring an end to the Order's problems; and continuous rivalries and divisions within the Order finally led Alfonso to command that Mountjoy's possessions should be returned to the Crown or granted to an order which could defend them. It was decided, as Alfonso informed the pope in 1195,[83] that the Templars could protect them more effectively than anyone else; and in the following year Mountjoy was incorporated into the Temple by the Aragonese king and Fralmo of Lucca, the master of Mountjoy.[84]

By this amalgamation the Temple acquired a considerable amount of property in southern Aragon, most of which is listed in the instruments of union and in memoranda drawn up by the members of Mountjoy who opposed the amalgamation.[85] The most important gains mentioned in these documents consisted of the lordships of Alfambra—with which the neighbouring places of Camañas, Malvecino, Miravete, and Perales had been granted to Mountjoy in 1174[86]—Villel,[87] Libros, Fuentes Calientes, Orrios, Castellote,[88] and Villarluengo. These documents also mention a dozen churches of which Mountjoy had enjoyed the patronage through the gift of Peter, bishop of Zaragoza, besides other lands of minor importance in Aragon. Amongst the rights not mentioned in these lists, but which the Temple also gained in 1196, was the lordship of Cantavieja, of which the Templars were in possession by 1197,[89] and two further churches in southern Aragon.[90] By the end of Alfonso II's reign the Templars thus held many frontier castles and occupied an important role in frontier defence not only along the lower reaches of the Ebro but also in southern Aragon.[91]

Before the death of Alfonso II the Templars had further through their own military activities secured a temporary foothold in Valencia by capturing the castle of Pulpís, over which the Aragonese king then, in 1190, granted them lordship.[92] This was, however, lost again. According to the troubadour Gerald of Luc it was sold back to the Moors by Alfonso II:

> Gauch n'ant las gens d'outra.l Nil
> car lor fai tant gen socors
> c'us feus de lor ancessors
> c'avion conquist li fraire
> vendet, mas ges non pres gaire
> vas q'era grans la ricors.[93]

Riquer has pointed out that, in view of the troubadour's known hostility towards the Aragonese king, this assertion need not be accepted, but the poem does indicate that Pulpís had been lost again by the time of Alfonso's death in 1196.[94] Nevertheless, the episode had given the Templars a claim to the castle which could be put forward if the stronghold fell again to the Christians.

In Alfonso II's reign the Templars appear to have gained more than the fifth due to them according to the terms of Raymond Berenguer IV's charter. Royal generosity was not so marked in that of Peter II. His chief territorial acquisition from the Moors consisted of the Rincón de Ademuz, gained in 1210. In compensation for the Order's claim to a fifth of the lands conquered Peter granted the Temple his rights in Ascó,[95] and because they had taken part in the expedition 'with a praiseworthy band of brothers', he restored to the Templars the lordship of Tortosa,[96] which—since it formed part of the dowry which Peter's mother Sancha had been assigned by Alfonso II in 1174[97]—the Order had lost early in Peter's reign. The provincial master, Arnold of Torroja, had witnessed the grant in 1174 and reserved Templar rights, but at the time these consisted merely of a fifth of the city's revenues. After Alfonso's death, Peter II had become involved in disputes about his mother's rights, and although in 1200 she agreed to surrender certain claims, she retained Tortosa for life as Alfonso had held it before granting it to the Temple.[98] No compensation was given to the Temple, and though in 1202 the Templars were able to use the king's acute need of money to extract from him a charter granting the city back to the Order,[99] Sancha succeeded in retaining authority there until her death,[100] and the king's charter remained ineffective. Even when Sancha died in 1208, however, the city was not restored to the Temple. Peter granted it instead for life to William of Cervera, reserving only the military service and *questias* owed by the Christian inhabitants and jurisdiction over breaches of the peace.[101] This grant to William of Cervera lessened the value of the restoration of the city to the Templars in 1210. The king ordered William to do homage for the city to the Templars; he refused, but was overruled by arbiters appointed by the king;[102] and at the beginning of November 1210 a charter was drawn up stating that William of Cervera and his son were to hold Tortosa of the Temple for two lives, as William had previously held it of the king.[103] The Order had thus gained little beyond a claim to Tortosa, since William of Cervera still enjoyed most of the revenues of the city; the Temple had merely its fifth, its demesne lands, and the rights which Peter had reserved in 1208. The Order was therefore in 1210 obtaining only a partial restoration of what it could claim by right, and it did not recover all its former rights in Tortosa until William of Cervera in 1215 agreed to surrender the city to the Order, retaining for life only the king's share of the revenues and the royal demesnes as detailed in 1182.[104]

In receiving Ascó in 1210, the Order was gaining more than it did in the case of Tortosa, but at a price. This stronghold had also formed part of Sancha's dowry and was retained by her for life. Nevertheless Peter II did give the Temple compensation for its rights of lordship and share in the revenues of Ascó: in 1204 he assigned to the Order the castle and township of Serós, on the condition that when Ascó had been recovered from the queen-mother, it should be exchanged for Serós. To win this concession, however, the Temple was obliged to surrender temporarily certain rights, including the tenth from the royal demesne in Aragon.[105] This agreement was cancelled in 1206, when the king promised instead to pay the Temple 500*m.* annually from the revenues of Serós.[106] When Sancha died the Templars were therefore able to recover their rights in Ascó by surrendering the revenues in Serós. Peter's grant in 1210 thus comprised the half-share of the revenues which Alfonso II had kept in 1182. But Peter, besides retaining 200*m*. annually from the *lezda* and *peaje* of Ascó, also received in return for the grant the sum of 5,000*maz*. from the Templars. Since the annual value of a half-share of the revenues of Ascó was apparently 500*m*., the transaction in 1210 should therefore be viewed as a sale rather than a donation. The provincial master was nevertheless obliged to state that he would make no further claim about the fifth of the Rincón de Ademuz. It is true that Peter did make other grants to the Order for its military help: at the end of 1210 he rewarded the Templars for their services against the Moors by confirming two donations of rents in Lérida made by the count of Urgel,[107] and in June 1212 at the time of the battle of Las Navas de Tolosa he made further minor concessions to the Templars,[108] while the promises of the *alquería* and tower of Ruzafa and the castle of Culla in Valencia made in 1211 and 1213 respectively may have been occasioned by Templar participation in a Valencian expedition.[109] But although Peter might stress

how useful, how faithful, and how necessary they have been to our predecessors in everything which concerned the expansion of Christendom and how much they have sought to aid us ourselves in our necessities,[110]

the nature of the grants made to the Templars in 1210 following the conquest of the Rincón de Ademuz suggests that the Crown was becoming reluctant to make important new grants of territory to the Order.

The Crown's attitude towards the Temple finds a more precise expression in the reign of James I, especially at the time of the conquest of Mallorca from the Almohade ruler Abu-Yahya. At the meetings of the Cortes held in Barcelona at the end of 1228 and at Tarragona in September 1229 it was agreed that the land gained in the proposed expedition to Mallorca should be divided among the king, nobles, and clergy according to the size of contingents provided, and promises were made at these assemblies by various magnates and prelates to bring a certain number of troops.[111] After the conquest of Mallorca, these agreements were put into effect; as a result the Temple gained considerably less than a fifth of the island. All who had provided troops were assessed at a certain number of *caballerías*, according to the size of their contingents.[112] The term was here used merely to signify shares; it did not refer to actual pieces of land, as has often been thought.[113] The largest single assessment was that of the king, who was rated at 5,674½ *caballerías*, while of the rest the Templar assessment of 525½ *caballerías* was the fifth largest, coming after those of Nuño Sánchez, Gastoneto of Moncada, the bishop of Barcelona, and the count of Ampurias. As the total number of *caballerías* was nearly 13,450, the Templar assessment was just under a twenty-fifth of the whole. How large a contingent this figure represented is not clear. The chronicler Desclot states that in the Barcelona assembly the Order promised to contribute thirty horsemen and twenty crossbowmen;[114] but there is no reference to such a promise in the documents drawn up in the Cortes or in the Chronicle of James I, and Desclot's information about other contingents is inaccurate;[115] there seems therefore little reason for accepting his statement. And in the Cortes at Tarragona the lieutenant of the provincial master of the Temple merely promised to bring as many knights as possible. Nevertheless an indication of the number of troops which the Templar assessment represented is possibly provided by the evidence which survives about the share allotted to the Hospitallers. They had arrived too late to take part in the expedition but petitioned the king to give them some land in Mallorca. According to the Chronicle of James I the king agreed to give them the amount allotted for a contingent of thirty knights and also made them a further gift out of his own share;[116] and in the list of *caballerías* the Hospitallers are assigned first 148 *caballerías* and then 'by the donation of the king' another 152 *caballerías*. It may be suggested therefore that the 148 *caballerías* represented the share for thirty knights, and that each knight was assessed at five *caballerías*. The Templar contingent would therefore have consisted of just over a hundred knights or their equivalent.

Exactly what the Order gained as its twenty-fifth share is not known, since in the *repartimiento* the Temple's acquisitions are not given separately. The island was divided into eight parts, four of which were assigned jointly to the king, the Temple, William of Moncada, Raymond Alamán, and William of Claramunt, whose *caballerías* together comprised about half the total number.[117] Of these four parts the king gained approximately five-sixths and the others one-sixth. But details of the division of the sixth are not given, and it can only be stated what the Temple and these nobles were assigned together, although the proportions of each are known, for William of Moncada was assessed at 276 *caballerías* and Raymond Alamán and William of Claramunt jointly at 205. The Temple's share of the sixth was therefore a little over a half.

In the city of Mallorca the Temple and the three nobles were given 55 out of 320 *operatoria*, 4 ovens out of 24, 12 houses of the 89 in the Almudayna, and 393 elsewhere, besides 5 *alquerías* totalling 66½ *jovadas*.[118] Outside the city they were granted half of Pollensa, half of the Montaña, a quarter of Montuiri, and a twelfth of the Albufera.[119] The acquisitions in Pollensa consisted of 52 *alquerías* totalling 285 *jovadas*; in the Montaña they gained 26 *alquerías* of 129 *jovadas*; and in Montuiri their allocation comprised 36 *alquerías* of 193 *jovadas*.[120]

Thus in the division of Mallorca James I made no attempt to enforce Raymond Berenguer's charter, which he could have done by granting the Order part of his own share; the only donation he made to the Temple at this time other than those mentioned in the *repartimiento* was of a castle near the walls of the city of Mallorca given in April 1230 as a residence for the Templars.[121] And the precedent created following the acquisition of Mallorca was to be followed when further conquests were made: when James issued a confirmation of Templar privileges in 1233, during the siege of Burriana, he revoked the Order's right to a fifth of lands conquered from the Moors.[122] When therefore lands were distributed after the conquest of the kingdom of Valencia from the Moorish ruler Zaiyán, the Templars no longer enjoyed a privileged position. Their reward like that of others was to be determined by the extent of their help.[123]

No precise evidence survives about the significance of the Templar forces in the conquest of the Valencian kingdom, but entries in the Chronicle of James I suggest that the Order's troops were important not because of their numbers but because they could be quickly mobilized and could, with the men of the royal household, help to form the nucleus of an army. When early in 1238 the king set out towards the city of Valencia, his army—according to the Chronicle—included a commander of the Temple with about twenty knights. This was a small contingent compared with the royal retinue at that time of 130–40 knights, or Roderick of Linzana's following of thirty; but it was a force that was in the field earlier than many contingents coming from Aragon

and Catalonia.[124] That this was the importance of Templar troops
is also suggested by the Chronicle account of the Burriana campaign in 1233. Troops for the assault on Burriana should apparently
have been concentrated at Teruel. None appeared on the day
fixed, but messengers reported to the king that the provincial
masters of the Temple and Hospital, together with the Calatravan
commander of Alcañiz, had been waiting near Murviedro for two
days according to orders. These then joined James, and the attack
on Burriana appears, from the evidence of the Chronicle, to have
been undertaken by the king, the military orders, the men of
Teruel and of the bishop of Zaragoza, and a few nobles, who were
assisted only later by other lay contingents.[125]

In return for such aid the Templars received certain rewards.
In June 1233, during the siege of Burriana, James granted the
Templars the *alquerías* of Benhamet and Mantella, which lay
within the terms of Burriana, on the condition that they captured
them,[126] and the Templars' assistance was further rewarded after
the capture of Burriana by the grant on 25 July of part of the
town, including six towers.[127] Three days earlier, for the 'many
and gracious services' which the Temple had given in the siege
of Burriana, the king also confirmed the grant of Chivert to the
Temple.[128] At this time it still lay in Moorish hands, but—as in
many other Moorish strongholds—the inhabitants preferred to
capitulate on terms rather than withstand a long siege, and the
provincial master was able to negotiate for its surrender.[129] In
1237 the Templars were given the *alquería* of Seca in Burriana by
the king,[130] and in the next year, following the capture of the city
of Valencia, James

remembering the many and gracious services which you our beloved
and venerable brothers of the house of the Temple have given us and
give us daily and have given now in the conquest of the city and
kingdom of Valencia

granted to the Order in the city the *torre grande* at the gate called
Barbazachar for a residence, houses in the same part of the city,
land for a garden in La Xarea outside the gate, and twenty *jovadas*
of arable land.[131] In August 1244, following the siege of Játiva, at
which the provincial master had been present, the Order was
further given half of the shipyard at Denia[132] and later in the same
year, at the siege of Biar, James gave the Temple the right to

build houses on the walls of Burriana.[133] Two years later James also gave compensation for Ruzafa, which had been promised to the Temple by Peter II. The Order was assigned the *alquerías* of Moncada and Carpesa, which both lay near the city of Valencia and which James had bought from Peter of Moncada and the royal notary Bernard Vidal.[134] The Order lastly obtained Pulpís, although it was not until 1277 that the Templars gained possession of it from the Order of Calatrava, which claimed to have captured it.[135]

Yet the gains made by the Temple from the Crown following the conquest of Valencia were limited. New donations of property by the king were comparatively few and unimportant, and very little was granted to the Order in the more southerly parts of the kingdom; the Templars were not assigned a leading role in frontier defence there.[136] Nor were all the promises made by previous kings carried out, even though some of the places promised had apparently comprised compensation for the Order's fifth elsewhere. Culla was given by the king in 1235 to Blasco of Alagón, and Montornés in 1242 to a royal notary Peter Sánchez;[137] and although Oropesa had been promised with Chivert to the Temple in 1169, no reference was made to it when James confirmed the Temple's claim to Chivert in 1233, and after its capture it was assigned to the Hospital, which had been promised it in 1149 by Raymond Berenguer IV.[138] No compensation was received by the Temple for any of these places, even though the Order plainly had charters to support its claims.[139] Although the evidence about the conquest of, and allocation of lands in, Valencia is not so precise as that concerning Mallorca, the Templars clearly failed to gain either the fifth promised by Raymond Berenguer IV or all of the other rights to which they could lay claim in the kingdom of Valencia.

While in the first half of the thirteenth century the Temple's share in the Aragonese conquests was declining, this source of new wealth disappeared almost entirely after the acquisition of Valencia, which completed the conquest of the territories assigned to the Aragonese kings in the treaty of Cazorla in 1179. The only further property in reconquered districts that the Order gained from the Crown were houses and land in Murcia, granted by James I in 1266 after the Aragonese expedition there, in which the Templars had participated.[140] The Order's undertaking in 1143 to take part in the conflict with the Moors had therefore proved most profitable to the Temple in the twelfth century, when it received important lordships and rights from Raymond Berenguer IV and Alfonso II; through the grants received from these rulers it had become particularly powerful along the lower valleys of the Segre and Ebro and in southern Aragon. Its rewards in Mallorca and Valencia were of lesser importance.

While the Order was gaining important estates from the Aragonese rulers in return for its participation in the *reconquista*, it was increasing its wealth throughout the *Corona de Aragón* through other donations and purchases. These other acquisitions were in a variety of forms. Some gifts to the Temple were of cash and movables, especially horses and arms. A considerable number of grants of this kind were made by *confratres* of the Temple. Although some religious orders founded at the end of the eleventh century, such as Citeaux and Grandmont, prohibited the practice of confraternity, the Rule of the Temple permitted the custom, which soon received encouragement from the papacy.[141] The Order had *confratres* in Aragon as early as 1131,[142] and the rapid extension of such ties in north-eastern Spain is apparent not only from individual contracts of confraternity which have survived, but also from several lists of *confratres* which have been preserved. A parchment roll, covering the period up to 1225, thus lists some 450 Aragonese and Navarrese *confratres* of the Temple.[143] A similar list is found in a late twelfth-century Templar cartulary; in part it reproduces the parchment roll and contains the names of 230 *confratres*.[144] This cartulary also includes a further list of *confratres* living in Novillas; fifty-two agreements of confraternity are here detailed.[145] Most of these *confratres* made bequests of movables to the Order. Those who possessed a horse and arms usually bequeathed these; women commonly left their best garment; and other bequests by *confratres* were of money. It is difficult to judge, however, how frequently acquisitions of movables were made by the Temple. Although gifts of horses and arms and cash are frequently recorded in contracts of confraternity, information about other donations in these forms has often survived only because these gifts were noted in wills which were preserved because they also referred to rights over landed property. An isolated gift of cash is unlikely to have left any surviving record. As wills not infrequently refer to bequests of movables to the Temple, however, acquisitions in this form may have been of some importance.[146]

Nevertheless, the sources are inevitably concerned mainly with rights of a more permanent kind. They show that some of the Order's acquisitions consisted of dues of a personal character, not linked with any landed or territorial rights gained by the Temple. Among dues of this type were those commonly paid by *confratres* of the Order.[147] Most of the surviving documents, however, record acquisitions of rights over landed property. Comparatively little of this property lay in the most northerly parts of Aragon and Catalonia; much more was situated further south in recently reconquered areas, where there was still a threat of Moorish attack and where lands were often of little value until they had been resettled. The surviving evidence perhaps to some extent distorts the true picture of the distribution of Templar property, for several groups of documents concerning Templar rights in northern Catalonia are known to have been lost,[148] but it is clear from the small number of Templar convents established in the most northerly parts of the *Corona de Aragón* and from the limited incomes of these houses that only a small part of the Order's landed property was situated in these regions.[149]

The surviving sources reveal that the Templars gained lordship over a considerable number of castles and townships, especially in certain areas, such as the Ebro valley in Aragon. The castle and village of Novillas, situated on the Ebro near the frontiers of Aragon and Navarre, was granted jointly to the Temple and the Hospital in 1135 by García Ramírez of Navarre,[150] and the Templars gained full control of it by surrendering to the Hospital the rights which they had been given by Alfonso I in the neighbouring village of Mallén.[151] At about the same time the Order acquired lordship of the now deserted village of Razazol, further down the river, for this had been granted by Ramiro II to a certain Calvet towards the end of 1134 and the latter's grant of it to the Temple was confirmed by Raymond Berenguer IV four years later.[152] In 1151 the count of Barcelona further confirmed the Temple's rights of lordship over Boquiñeni, downstream from Razazol, but it is not known when the Templars acquired their rights there.[153] It is similarly not known when the Order gained Marlofa, on the right bank of the Ebro between the junction with

the Jalón and the city of Zaragoza; evidence of Templar rights
there is found only in thirteenth-century administrative documents.[154] It is clear, on the other hand, that the Temple's rights of
lordship at Alfocea—on the opposite bank of the river to Marlofa
—originated in 1143, when the Templars were given a fifth share
in the township,[155] while another fifth was acquired in 1194.[156]
On the Ebro below the city of Zaragoza the Templars gained La
Zaida. A three-quarter share in this township was given to the
Order in 1161 by Jordana, the daughter of Iñigo Fortunones, who
had been lord of Larraga;[157] in 1176 the Order acquired from
Peter López of Luna the rights which had belonged to Elvira, the
daughter of Gómez of Ruesta, formerly lord of Ayerbe and
Bolea;[158] and two years later the Templars purchased the share
belonging to Elvira's sister, Tota Gómez.[159] The Order in the
same way gradually acquired the lordship of the now deserted
place of Añesa, lying further north on the river Arba, which
flows into the Ebro at Gallur. The *almunia* of Añesa had been
given in 1117 by Alfonso I to Lope Garcés Peregrino,[160] who in
1133/4 left half of his possessions to his wife Mayor and the other
half to the Temple, the Hospital, and the church of St. Mary in
Zaragoza.[161] In 1144 Galindo Garcés of San Vicente gave the
Order the quarter share of Añesa which he had received from his
aunt, the widow of Lope Garcés,[162] and three years later Peter
Romeu gave the Templars another share, which was presumably
the other part of Mayor's portion.[163] Within a few years the
Order had also acquired the rights enjoyed there by the bishop
of Zaragoza in exchange for land elsewhere.[164] To the south of
the Ebro the Templars had early obtained the castles of Ambel
and Alberite from Peter Taresa, who according to some sources
was a candidate for the Aragonese throne in 1134,[165] and shortly
after the middle of the twelfth century the lordship of the castle
and village of Novallas, near Tarazona, was granted by Lazarus,
the son of Fortún Aznárez, lord of Tarazona.[166]

Groups of lordships were similarly built up in other districts.
One group, including Cofita, Castejón del Puente, Alfantega, and
Sta. Lecina, was concentrated in the neighbourhood of Monzón
in the valley of the river Cinca.[167] Further east, along the lower
reaches of the Segre, the Order gained the castles of Torres de
Segre and Gebut,[168] besides a number of lordships in the district
of Segriá to the north-west of Lérida and in the district to the

east of the city. Among these were Grallera, Barbens, Talladell, and a half of Pedrís.[169] In the region inland from Tarragona, slightly further east, the Order acquired another series of lordships, comprising rights over Selma, Ollers, Vallfogona, Albió, Espluga de Francolí, Montbrió, and Valldossera.[170] The last area where any considerable lordships were gained was the northern part of Valencia. In 1303 the Order purchased from William of Anglesola, who was lord of Bellpuig, the castle of Culla and the territory subject to it, which included Corbo (? Carbó), Buey, Vistabella, Benafigos, Adzaneta, and Molinell and the towers of Vina Rabina and Benasal.[171] Nine years earlier, however, the Templars had already considerably increased their possessions in northern Valencia through an exchange by which they surrendered to James II their rights in Tortosa. The king was anxious to recover lordship over this important coastal city, which could be of use to him in his Mediterranean policies, and the Temple was willing to give up its rights because of the difficulties it was encountering in exercising its authority there. In return James gave the Temple the castle and town of Peñíscola, with which were included Vinaroz and Benicarló; the castle and township of Ares; and the Tenencia de las Cuevas, which comprised Las Cuevas de Vinromán, Salsadella, Albocácer, Villanueva de Alcolea, Tirig, and Serratella.[172]

In other areas acquisitions of lordships were not so important. In the more northerly parts of Aragon only a few small villages— Arnasillo, Huerrios, Bien, and a share in Miquera—are known to have been gained.[173] In *Cataluña Vieja* apparently the only lordship of any significance that was obtained was that of Puigreig, on the upper Llobregat, which was bequeathed to the Temple in 1187 by the troubadour William of Bergadán.[174] Even this lordship the Order gained only after a long delay. Following William's death, which occurred between 1192 and 1196, the bequest was obviously disputed by the troubadour's brother, for Puigreig was included in the sale of the viscounty of Bergadán made to Peter II in 1199 by either the brother or the latter's widow.[175] Puigreig remained under royal authority until 1231, when James I, at last carrying out the conditions of William of Bergadán's will, assigned it to the Temple.[176]

A few of these lordships acquired in various parts of the *Corona de Aragón* were of considerable individual importance. Those

gained in northern Valencia at the turn of the thirteenth and fourteenth centuries were among the most valuable acquisitions made
by the Aragonese Templars.[177] But generally the most important
towns and castles under Templar authority were those obtained
from the Crown in return for aid in the *reconquista*; the lordships
gained in other ways tended usually to be of only moderate value
and consisted mainly of rights over minor castles and small townships and villages.

These lordships over castles and townships inevitably constituted only a small minority of the acquisitions made by the
Aragonese Templars. The majority consisted of lesser rights over
landed property. The type of acquisition most commonly made
by the Order comprised rights over pieces of land used for the
growing of corn or vines, or more rarely of olives. It is difficult,
however, to assess the importance of most acquisitions of this
kind, for measurements are only rarely given in charters. Terms
such as 'peca', 'campum', and 'vinea' are frequently employed,
without any indication of size, and although in Catalonia some
acquisitions consisted of manses, this word did not refer to properties of any uniform size.[178] Besides these very numerous rural
holdings the Temple also gained a certain amount of urban property. In Zaragoza, for example, the Order acquired rights over
houses and shops, especially in the neighbourhood of the Cineja
gate—the southern gate in the Roman wall—and near the western
gate, the Puerta de Toledo.[179] In Huesca houses and shops were
acquired particularly in the *barrio* of the Temple and in the suburb
outside the Alquibla gate, which stood at the end of the present
*calle de Ramiro el monje*;[180] by the early thirteenth century there
was similarly a Templar *barrio* in Tarazona.[181] Among other
acquisitions by the Order were rights over mills, including fulling
mills as well as those used for grinding corn; and in some places,
such as Jaca on the river Aragón and Cascajo on the river Gállego,
mills appear to have been the most important possessions which
the Order held.[182]

The Temple gained, lastly, considerable ecclesiastical properties. Unlike some monastic orders founded at about the same
time, the Temple was allowed to hold property of any kind. In
the Rule of the Temple the right to acquire tithes was conceded
and this right was confirmed by Innocent II in 1139 in the bull
*Omne datum optimum*.[183] It would have been possible to justify

this right by arguing that as the function of the Templars was fighting they could not maintain themselves by their own labour as some contemporary monastic orders sought to do, and that they therefore needed dues such as tithes, especially as the war against the infidel was a costly enterprise.[184] But the only reason given in the Rule was that, as the Templars had adopted a life of poverty, they should be allowed to possess tithes—a reference to the argument commonly expressed at the time that those who had given up their possessions should be counted among the *pauperes Christi* and should therefore be allowed to receive tithes.[185] The Rule of the Temple and the bull *Omne datum optimum* do not, on the other hand, make any reference to the patronage of churches; yet it is unlikely that the Templars would have been permitted to have tithes but not churches. If this had been the case a specific prohibition in the Rule would be expected.

Certainly within a very few years of the Council of Troyes the Templars were beginning to acquire rights over churches in the *Corona de Aragón*. In 1135 they gained the church of Novillas in the diocese of Zaragoza, and they may have obtained rights over the nearby churches of Razazol and Boquiñeni even earlier.[186] Besides these churches the Templars further gained in the same diocese, during the twelfth century, rights over the churches of Alberite, La Zaida, and Encinacorba,[187] and in 1204 the bishop gave the Order eight other churches in the districts which the Templars had taken over from Mountjoy.[188] The Order also possessed considerable ecclesiastical patronage in the diocese of Lérida, for from 1149 it held the church of St. John in Monzón, together with its subject churches, which in 1192 numbered twenty-three.[189] Along the lower valley of the Ebro, which formed part of the diocese of Tortosa, the Order acquired the patronage of the churches of Miravet, Algars, and Ribarroja; and further south in the same diocese it gained the churches of Seca and Chivert.[190] Elsewhere its importance as a patron was more limited. In the diocese of Urgel it had only the church of Puigreig,[191] and in the diocese of Barcelona only that of Selma.[192] Similarly in the Aragonese part of the diocese of Tarazona the Temple's only church was that of Ambel,[193] while in the diocese of Segorbe/Albarracín the Aragonese Templars enjoyed the patronage only of the church of Ademuz.[194] In the diocese of Valencia there appear to have been no churches under Templar patronage.[195] Throughout the kingdom of Valencia, however, which was divided between the dioceses of Tortosa, Segorbe, and Valencia, the Order received from its estates the share of the tithes which lords in that kingdom normally enjoyed from their lands.[196] It thus received from the bishop of Tortosa in 1244 a half of the tithes of Chivert and of all its lands in Burriana,[197] and in 1263 the bishop of Valencia gave the Templars a third of the tithes of Borbotó, which they had acquired from William of Portella.[198] A number of acquisitions of tithes were of course also made in other parts of the *Corona de Aragón* from both laity and clergy.[199]

This accumulation of property which was occurring throughout the *Corona de Aragón* while the Aragonese rulers were granting newly conquered lands to the Temple has parallels in the histories of other religious orders; but the motives of the donors of this property were, to some extent, different from those of patrons of monasteries. Whereas patrons of the regular clergy would often—if they had the means—found a monastery or convent and provide revenues for its support, none of the charters of donation recording gifts to the Temple is a foundation charter of a convent of the Order. The property which was granted to the Temple in various parts of the *Corona de Aragón* was given primarily in order to provide resources for the struggle against the infidel in Spain and the Holy Land or to further the work of resettlement in reconquered areas.[200]

Yet although these benefactors of the Temple did not found convents, they—like the Aragonese rulers when they granted frontier estates to the Order—expected the Temple to provide for their spiritual welfare in the same ways as monasteries did for their patrons. They hoped to gain spiritual reward through prayers said for them in the Order's houses and through good works performed by Templar convents, and sought by this means to avoid the agonies of hell and to share in the joys of paradise.[201] This aspect of patronage is revealed especially in contracts of confraternity, which sometimes give details of the spiritual benefits received by *confratres*. *Confratres* were included in the prayers said not only in their local Templar convents, but in all houses of the Order.[202] They were also considered to participate in the fasts and alms-giving undertaken by the Templars.[203] These benefits were usually extended to a *confrater*'s family and occasionally to a few friends as well.[204] The Temple in addition promised to bury *confratres* in its cemeteries and agreed to grant the habit, if it was demanded, even to female *confratres*.[205] In most cases, of course, a *confrater* would not seek the habit until he was dying and this promise by the Temple referred primarily to the custom known as *ad succurrendum*, which allowed individuals to die in the habit. The wording of the Templar Customs indicates, however, that as in some other orders those who took the habit when dying were not considered full members:

> If a man asks to be made a brother when he is dying, he who gives him the habit shall say nothing to him, but put it on him when he is on the point of death. The brother can take it off him again when he sees that he is dead; and if he dies in the habit there is no obligation to say the paternosters which must be said for a brother.[206]

The dying person merely had the habit placed upon him, without any proper profession; he was not buried in the habit nor was he treated as a brother after death.

Some patrons, considering further their spiritual welfare, provided through donations for the saying of masses or for the maintenance of lamps or candles which were to burn before the altars of Templar chapels. Those who had the means endowed chantries or lamps in perpetuity. In 1275, for example, G. of San Melione established two chantries in the Templar church at Valencia, ordering that

> the clerics who serve the said chantries in the said church are to celebrate daily a requiem mass for my soul and for those of all my benefactors, and are to be present by day and night at the offices which are said and celebrated in the said church every day and night, and are to go every day to my grave to absolve me and say prayers[207]

and when in 1282 Peter Cornel stated in his will that he would leave the castle of Fréscano to the Temple if he died without legitimate sons, he made the condition that the Order was to maintain ten priests to say masses for his soul and keep ten lamps burning day and night in the chapel in which he was to be buried.[208] Such provisions required a considerable endowment. The priests whom Peter Cornel provided for were to receive an annual salary of 150s. each, and in 1280 the bishop of Valencia considered that an income of 20*l*.V. was necessary to maintain a chantry priest and his boy and to provide for lamps and candles,[209] while an endowment of a lamp alone appears usually to have required a rent of from 10s. to 30s. a year.[210] Those who could not give enough to make perpetual endowments might merely provide for masses to be said on the anniversary of their death or state that masses should be said for a certain period or that a certain number of masses should be said. In 1295 Gayeta, the wife of Peter of Rueda, provided in her will for the celebrating of daily masses for a year, while by the terms of his wife's will, drawn up in 1208, Peter of Tena was obliged to see that 2,000 masses were said for her soul by a chaplain provided by the Templars in Zaragoza.[211] Alternatively a few shillings or a few pence might be left to the Temple and masses were to be said or candles and lamps kept burning until the money was used up.

While spiritual benefits were sought by all those who made gifts to the Order, at least a considerable minority of donors also sought a more worldly reward. In a world where *largesse* was extolled as a virtue, nobles could enhance their prestige by making generous benefactions. Some individuals, however, sought more precise material returns from the Order, although it cannot be stated what proportion of benefactors obtained benefits of this kind, for charters do not necessarily record all aspects of a transaction. It has been argued that during the civil war in England between Stephen and Matilda the Templars were given property in return for political support, and it has been maintained that the rival powers in the disputed borderlands between Poland and Pomerania sought to retain a hold over these districts by granting extensive properties there to the Templars.[212] There may similarly have been political motives behind some of the grants to the Temple in the disputed areas on the borders of Aragon and Navarre in the years following the death of Alfonso I. García Ramírez may have given Novillas to the Hospital and Temple in 1135 in the hope that they would defend it for the Navarrese, and a similar motive may explain in part the confirmation of Templar rights over Razazol issued in 1138 by Raymond Berenguer IV, for in the previous year García Ramírez had given it to Raymond of Cortes.[213] But the Order's reluctance to become involved in political disputes probably meant that gifts made for such reasons were few.[214]

There is clearer evidence of other material benefits obtained by donors. Those who entered into the confraternity of the Temple received a promise of protection from the Order, and this privilege was also sought by others. Many individuals, especially in *Cataluña Vieja*, bound themselves to make payments to the Order, which were considered partly as benefactions—in many of the surviving contracts the phrases 'for the salvation of our souls' or 'for the safety of our souls' occur[215]—and partly as payments for protection by the Temple. Requests for Templar protection are encountered not only in these formal contracts but also in a number of wills. The Temple was asked, in return for a donation, to give its protection to the testator's family after his death. In 1195, for example, a butcher called Arnold left a vineyard at Gardeny to the Templars and placed his wife and three children in their custody.[216] Some of those who sought the protection of the Temple were men who had no lords: thus in 1280 and 1281 several individuals who had redeemed themselves from the lordship of Galcerán of Pinós placed themselves under Templar protection.[217] Yet not all who sought the Order's protection lacked lords of their own.[218] In a society where violence was endemic many needed protection from any possible source and saw the advantage of having a Templar cross on their property, even though they already had a lord.[219] The frequency with which men turned to the military orders for protection is illustrated by a gloss on the Usage *In baiulia vel guardia*, which makes the comment

What of the Hospitallers and Templars, who daily receive custodies of this kind?[220]

and the need for protection was clearly important in bringing to the Temple a considerable number of small payments.

Besides seeking Templar protection for his dependants, a donor might also see to their interests by asking the Temple to pay off his debts after his death or to make payments to his family or other dependants. In 1255 Gonzalbo Gómez, an inhabitant of Teruel, gave a vineyard to the Templars on the condition that after his death they would pay off his debts and

make good all the injuries I have caused and also give to a certain woman named Mary by whom I have a child and who is now pregnant 100s.J. and to the son who has been born 200s.J. and to the one who is to be born, if he is then living, another 200s.;[221]

in 1219 after making several bequests Bernard of Savasona left the remainder of his possessions to the Templars on the condition that they would marry off his grand-daughter and provide her with a dower of 200*maz.*;[222] and in her will drawn up in 1298 Mary Rossa, an inhabitant of Valencia, asked the Temple to make an annual gift of a *cahíz* of corn to her servant for four years.[223]

Other donors sought to provide for themselves. It was common for benefactors of the Temple, especially *confratres*, to be granted regular corrodies during their lives. Sometimes a single payment in kind or money was made by the Order each year. When Bartholomew of Miracle and his wife became *confratres* of the Order in 1199 and gave it houses and land in Huesca, the Templars assigned them annually on All Saints' day three *cahíces* of wheat, two measures of wine, an *arroba* of cheese and 40*s*.J.,[224] and when Peter of Montañana gave the Temple some land at Torre de Bafes in 1169 the Temple agreed to give him a quarter of the produce during his life.[225] But most of those who received corrodies were promised a daily allowance of food and drink, and occasionally clothing or a payment for clothing as well: a *confrater* called Stephen of Monzón, for example, was given his food and drink and also 50*s*. a year, which were stated to be for his clothing.[226] But such promises did not necessarily mean that the recipient was in fact regularly maintained by the Temple. Benefactors were sometimes seeking merely the right to hospitality, which might be exercised only occasionally or when the donors were no longer able to maintain themselves. Thus although in 1176 the Templars promised Dominic of Batizo and his wife food and drink 'in our house of Huesca or of Monzón, wherever you want to receive it, all the days of your life', this couple lived in Pertusa and could scarcely have received regular maintenance at either Huesca or Monzón.[227] The desire on the part of benefactors to provide against future need is sometimes revealed very clearly in the sources. When Nina of Talladell gave the Templars a vineyard at Gardeny in 1196, they promised to give her assistance if she became poverty-stricken, and in the middle of the twelfth century a priest at Novillas named Gerald made a donation to the Temple on the condition that it would give him 10*s*. if he was ever in need of money because of illness and would provide him with a mount if he wanted to go on a pilgrimage.[228]

Most of the obligations entered into by the Temple in return for grants were of this temporary kind. Usually only ecclesiastical patrons obliged the Templars to pay rents in perpetuity for property given to the Order; but it was of course difficult for ecclesiastical institutions to make unconditional gifts. Thus when the abbot of Ripoll granted the lordship of Alfantega to the Order in 1217 he imposed an annual rent of 400s.B. on the Templars.[229] Grants to the Temple were not often looked upon by laymen as a means of exploiting property, although a few instances of this attitude are encountered in the sources. In 1176 Arnold of Murello gave a plot of land to the Templars on the condition that they built a mill there and that when the mill had been built Arnold would contribute half of the costs of running it and would receive half of the profits;[230] and in 1192 Alfonso II gave land at Lérida to the Temple on the same terms.[231] Nor was the rent of 1,000s. which James I demanded of the Templars for the Puente de Monzón and Castejón del Puente in 1219 merely a nominal sum; he admitted at the time that the grant was not then worth that amount and in 1224 the rent was reduced to 500s.[232] The imposition of permanent obligations on the Order by laymen occurred only occasionally, however, and in many charters the words 'per proprium alodium' or a similar phrase were included apparently to denote not that the property being transferred was necessarily free from all obligations but that the donor himself was not imposing any dues on the Order: such phrases were used to characterize the nature of the transaction, not the nature of the property.[233]

Some of those who made grants to the Temple did not seek any future material recompense from it, but did obtain a single payment from the Templars at the time of the transaction. Some charters recording the transfer of property to the Temple are worded as charters of donation but refer to payments made by the Order 'out of alms' or 'out of charity'. The earliest example of this practice occurs in ?1135 when Raymond Adalbert of Juiá received 20m. from the Temple for the gift of his rights over land at Collsabadell,[234] and numerous further instances are recorded, especially in Catalonia.[235] The amount paid by the Templars in such cases presumably did not represent the full value of the property, for in addition to the monetary return the donor was also gaining the spiritual benefits which resulted from a grant. Such transactions were therefore partly gifts and partly sales. The same may be said of conveyances by gift of land which was to be redeemed from pledge. An early example of this form of transaction is provided by Peter Taresa's grant of the castle of Alberite to the Templars, for the Order was obliged to pay 300m. to recover it from Simon Garcés of Bureta.[236] There was thus no clear-cut distinction between the gift and the sale of property; some transactions had the characteristics of both types of conveyance, and this is reflected in the wording of some charters. In a document drawn up in 1182, for example, it is stated that for the redemption of their souls and of those of their ancestors Berenguer Bafarul and his wife gave and sold to the Temple their rights in Torre de Bafes.[237]

Many benefactors of the Temple thus wished not only to further the work of the Order and gain spiritual reward; they also sought material benefits for themselves. But in any discussion of corrodies and the other payments made for gifts, it must be remembered that the desire to share in the life of a religious house was common amongst the laity in this period, and also that there were few ways of providing for one's old age or for the welfare of one's dependants except by making a gift to an ecclesiastical institution. It must also be remembered that the patronage of the Church which was expected of laymen must have placed a considerable burden on some individuals and families. Some individuals could scarcely afford to make an outright donation of any size during their lives. Gifts *post obitum* were therefore made in many instances;[238] but an alternative was to make a grant which was to be effective immediately and to seek maintenance in return. But many donors had to consider not only their own livelihood but also that of their descendants, and this may explain some of the money payments which were made in return for gifts. Donors had to ensure that their family estates were not eroded too much by the donations which were expected from each generation. They might therefore stipulate that the property they gave to a religious foundation should be held of it by their descendants;[239] or they might seek some monetary return for their gift.

Although some of the rights which the Templars paid for were said to have been given to the Order, straightforward sales of property to the Temple in the *Corona de Aragón* were very common. The Order began to purchase land there in the middle of the fourth decade of the twelfth century, and in many areas records of sales to the Order are more numerous than charters of donation. Sales of property in and around Huesca to the Temple occurred almost twice as frequently as gifts,[240] and while some twenty grants of landed property in the city of Zaragoza are recorded, nearly fifty sales of rights there to the Temple are known.[241] Sales of rights over landed property in and around Tortosa were similarly more than twice as numerous as donations there to the Templars.[242] This does not necessarily mean, however, that the Order acquired more property through sales than through donations. Most purchases by the Order were of only minor significance.

The purchase of landed property was one way in which the Templars could invest the wealth derived from the rights given to the Order, from grants of money and from the profits of war. By purchasing rights over land the Templars were also able to concentrate their possessions, and this end was also achieved through exchanges. Much of the property bought by the Templars bordered on land already held by the Order. Of seventeen purchases which they made in the parish of St. Mary in Zaragoza, twelve were of property adjoining lands belonging to the Order;[243] and a similar situation is encountered in many other places. The Temple also sought to concentrate its property by purchasing rights in lands where it already had certain claims. It often, for example, bought out the rights enjoyed by an overlord, as in 1150 when it purchased Raymond of Gurb's rights over land which had been left to the Temple at Parets, to the north of Barcelona.[244] At other times when it acquired the lordship of a town or village, it bought up fees held there: thus in the second half of the thirteenth century, after it had gained the lordship of Espluga de Francolí, the Order purchased a number of fees there, including those of Hugh of Cervellón, William of Jorba, and Arnold of Malgrat.[245] The Templars' acquisition of a mill at Cascajo, just to the north of Zaragoza, illustrates well the way in which through purchase they sometimes gradually built up their rights over a particular piece of property. In 1162 García of Albero and his wife Mary sold to the Temple the rent of 80s.J. per annum which they received for the mill from Duranda, the widow of a certain Folquer, and her children.[246] In the years following this initial sale, the Order gradually through a series of purchases acquired the rights of the tenants. In 1168 four of the children

sold a half share in the mill to the Templars for 400s.J., and three
years later a further eighth was purchased from one of Duranda's
sons for 12m.[247] In 1173 the Templars spent another 12m. in buying
from the bishop of Zaragoza the share of another son, who was
then a canon of Zaragoza,[248] and finally in 1178 the portion belonging to Arnold, a son of Duranda by her marriage to Alamán
of Atrosillo, was purchased for 13m.[249] Such purchases not only
led to a concentration of Templar property; they also served to
prevent the disputes which were almost inevitable when rights
over landed property were divided. After the Temple had gained
the lordship of Espluga de Francolí, for example, it recognized
Hugh of Cervellón's claim to a fee there;[250] but disputes arose
about particular revenues and it was necessary to resort to arbitration in 1257 and 1268.[251] When, therefore, the Templars bought
this fee in 1289 they were probably seeking not only to achieve
a concentration of property but also to avoid further dispute.
Besides purchasing land bordering on Templar possessions and
buying rights over property in which they already had an interest,
the Templars also through purchase concentrated their property
to some extent in the neighbourhood of Templar convents. This
tendency may be illustrated with reference to the convent of
Palau, to the north of Barcelona, which was one of the earliest
Templar foundations in Catalonia.[252] While grants of property to
that convent were scattered over a wide area, the lands purchased
by that house tended to be concentrated in Barcelona and in the
district of Vallés, just to the north—in Palau itself, in Parets del
Vallés, and in Sta. Perpetua de Mogudá.[253] Only occasional purchases are recorded at places further away from the convent, and
the only property of any importance that was bought outside
Barcelona and the district of Vallés was at Gurb, to the north-
west of Vich, where in 1200 the Order paid 800s. to Ferrer of
Andrea for a manse.[254] But although it is clear that the Templars
tried to concentrate their possessions in various ways, at times when
they were making a large number of purchases they were obliged
to buy whatever land was available, and they inevitably bought
a certain amount of property which neither adjoined the Order's
possessions nor was already partly under Templar control.

Opportunities for purchasing land were often, of course, provided by the financial difficulties of landholders, and this is sometimes made clear in the documents of sale. In 1163 the Order was

able to buy property at Montjuich in Barcelona because a certain Saurina needed money to redeem her son from captivity,[255] and difficulty in paying debts led the prior of St. Mary in Tarrasa to sell land there to the Templars in 1190;[256] and William of Anglesola in 1303 similarly stated that he was selling Culla to the Order because

we are liable for so many debts and injuries that we do not think that all the landed property we have in the kingdom of Valencia is sufficient for satisfying and emending them.[257]

But it would be wrong to assume that all those who sold property to the Order were in financial difficulties. Since marriage portions, for example, were often expressed in money terms, land was not infrequently sold in order to make payments to widows.[258] On other occasions the initiative in a transaction may have come from the Order, which wanted a particular piece of land and was prepared to pay a good price for it, so that the holder of the property would be persuaded to sell even if he had no need to do so for financial reasons. And in the reconquered districts, where land had often to be settled and brought under cultivation before it could be made profitable, landlords probably needed little persuasion before agreeing to sell. Some transactions which are recorded as sales, moreover, were really agreements following disputes over land. At a time when it was often difficult to establish clearly what rights different individuals enjoyed in a piece of property, it was a common practice for disputes to be settled by assigning the land in question to one claimant, who would then be obliged to compensate the other party by paying him a sum of money. And the documents recording such settlements are sometimes worded as instruments of sale: a charter drawn up in 1166 thus records that the Templars bought certain land in Razazol for 35s., but it also states that in return for this payment the sellers were abandoning the claims they had been making against the Temple about this property.[259]

The gradual growth of Templar property through gift and sale which was taking place throughout the *Corona de Aragón* while the Aragonese rulers were granting the Order large estates near the Moorish frontier in return for military aid inevitably owed little to the Crown; the Aragonese rulers appear to have made few other donations to the Temple.[260] Nor does the clergy appear usually to have been an enthusiastic patron of the Order. Admittedly most of the churches and many of the tithes gained by the Temple in the *Corona de Aragón* were given to the Order by bishops, but the great majority of these acquisitions lay in the reconquered areas, and the gifts appear to have been made in order to stimulate resettlement, which would in turn increase episcopal revenues. The bishops' point of view is made clear in a charter recording a grant of tithes at Horta to the Templars by the bishop of Tortosa in 1185, for this includes the clauses

you are to resettle the aforesaid castle of Horta and its territories and the settlers of that place are to give us and our churches established there the *primicias* of all produce and animals faithfully.[261]

It was therefore from the bishops of Zaragoza, Lérida, Tortosa, and Valencia that the Order received most of its ecclesiastical patronage. From the bishops in the more northerly parts of the *Corona de Aragón* it gained little. The only known grant by a bishop of Urgel was that of the church of Puigreig in 1278, and the only donations by bishops of Huesca were the gift of the church of Algás in 1176 and the bequest of the castle of Torres de Segre by James of Sarroca in December 1289.[262] No acquisitions at all are recorded from the bishops of Vich or Gerona. An examination of the surviving lists of *confratres* also reveals the limited clerical interest in the Order, for almost all of those listed were laymen. Very few individual clerics sought the confraternity of the Temple and there are no references in Templar records to any unions of confraternity with other religious houses. The clergy appear to have valued more highly the prayers said in monasteries, although unions between Spanish military orders and other religious institutions are not altogether unknown.[263] And many of the clergy may have felt that the Temple had acquired enough of their rights through papal concessions. The Order appears, on the other hand, to have been popular with all classes of the laity. While the *confratres* listed on the parchment roll of confraternity, for example, were almost all men of sufficient standing to possess a horse and arms and included some of the leading Aragonese and Navarrese nobles, the majority of the fifty-two agreements mentioned in the list of Novillas *confratres* concerned men of lesser rank.

Any attempt to discover with which families the Order had

particularly close links is hampered, however, especially in Aragon, by the difficulty of tracing family trees. Although it is clear, on the one hand, that the Order gained a certain amount of property in Boquiñeni and Pradilla from various members of the family of Rada[264] and, on the other, that the Templars had only tenuous links with some of the leading Aragonese families, such as the Romeu and the Cornel,[265] it is usually difficult to discover whether the Temple had ties with an Aragonese family for more than a generation or two. It is clear, however, that the Templars received a number of donations in Aragon from the French lords who had participated in Alfonso I's campaigns and from their families.[266] The French count Rotrou of Perche left land and houses in Zaragoza jointly to the Temple, the monastery of the Holy Cross at Tudela, and the sons of a certain Subiano, and by an agreement made in 1142 the Order was assigned the count's residence near the city wall and half of the land.[267] This residence presumably lay between the churches of St. Mary and St. Nicholas, where according to Zurita part of the count's property lay and where until recently the count's rights of lordship left a trace in the street named *conde de Alperche*.[268] Two years later Taresa, the widow of Gaston of Béarn, granted the Temple land at Sobradiel, on the Ebro above Zaragoza, and property in the city, presumably in the parish of St. Mary, where according to Zurita Gaston had been given rights in the former Mozarab quarter after the capture of Zaragoza.[269] In 1148 Peter, count of Bigorre, similarly granted the Order property in the city of Zaragoza.[270] In no case did the estates granted by Alfonso I to French lords remain intact long, and it has been suggested that one reason for their break-up was that these lords were not interested in settling permanently in Aragon.[271] Obviously efficient administration of distant properties was not easy and this may partly explain the donations to the Temple by these French lords.

In Catalonia genealogical problems are not so great, and the relationships between the Temple and some of the leading Catalan families can to some extent be traced. The Order appears to have gained comparatively little property from those families whose power was centred in the more northerly parts of Catalonia. The Templars had only occasional connections with the families of Pinós and Cardona and that of the counts of Ampurias.[272] The house from which the Templars acquired most property in northern Catalonia was probably that of the viscounts of Bergadán; the Order's acquisitions from this family included not only the castle of Puigreig, but also seven manses in Puigreig, Caserras, and El Funillet, given to the Temple by the troubadour's father in 1182.[273]

A more constant relationship can be traced between the Temple and some of the families which had considerable estates in the more southerly parts of Catalonia. These families in most cases both gave and sold property to the Order. The most important of them was that of the counts of Urgel, with whom the Temple had frequent contacts in the twelfth and early thirteenth centuries. Armengol VI not only gave the castle of Barbará to the Order, but also in his will drawn up in 1133 bequeathed his demesne at Calcina and his horse and arms to the Templars.[274] In 1147 he further granted land for the construction of mills near Balaguer, which had been gained in 1106 by Raymond Berenguer III and Peter Ansúrez, Armengol's grandfather.[275] Three years later the count gave the Templars permission to take water from Albesa to irrigate lands at Corbins, as had been done in the Moorish period.[276] Patronage of the Temple was continued by Armengol's son, Armengol VII, who succeeded to the county in 1154. The latter, with his wife Dulce, in 1161 founded a chantry at the Templar convent at Gardeny; until a proper endowment was made for it the count assigned to the Temple 100s.B. annually out of rents derived from Moorish shops, presumably in Lérida.[277] Armengol VII also gave the Order a half-share in the lordship of the castle of Pedrís, south-east of Balaguer. The charter of donation has not survived but the gift was confirmed by Armengol's widow and his son in 1185, the year after his death.[278] He also consented to the Temple's acquisition of lands in Fontanet and Lérida from two of his tenants[279]—his rights in these properties being clearly derived from the division of lands made after the conquest of Lérida—and finally in his will, drawn up in 1177, he bequeathed his horse and arms to the Order, together with further rights along the lower Segre.[280]

In 1201 Armengol VIII in turn promised the Temple dues in Lérida worth 100s.B. a year after his death; meanwhile the Order was to be given 10s.B. annually from these revenues.[281] In his will, drawn up seven years later, he also bequeathed to the

Temple his demesne at Albesa, with the right to build mills there,[282] while his wife Elvira, who later married William of Cervera, left 50*m.* to the Templars.[283] The relations of Armengol VIII with the Order were not, however, always friendly, but his quarrels with the Templars led to further transfers of property to them. Already before his father's death he had become involved in a dispute with the Order and seized some of its sheep. It was agreed in 1184 that compensation of 1,000*m.* should be given to the Templars, failing which the count's honour of Alchabez was to be surrendered. The money was clearly not paid, for in the next year Armengol VIII and his mother Dulce granted the Order their rights at Alchabez, although to gain this concession the Templars were obliged to give them 200*maz.* and a horse.[284] Further evidence of differences between the count and the Templars is found in an agreement made in 1201. In return for the confirmation of all Templar possessions in Lérida and a promise of protection by Armengol, the Order not only paid the count 250*m.*, but also agreed to surrender all claims which it had against him, and these were valued at the large sum of 15,000*s.*B.[285] Lastly, in 1205 Armengol gave the Order dues in Lérida worth 100*s.*B. annually in compensation for an attack on the Templar house at Barbens.[286] The last links with the house of Urgel occurred when Armengol VIII's nephew Gerald of Cabrera sold the castle of Mediona to the Templars and then entered the Order after he had been dispossessed of the county.[287]

There was thus a fairly constant, if at times uneasy, relationship between the Order and the counts of Urgel up to the early thirteenth century, although they had not especially favoured the Order and none had chosen burial in the Temple.[288] A similar link can be traced with the family of Torroja. The first member of that house to favour the Temple was Arnold, who in the middle years of the twelfth century made grants of vineyards in Lérida—received from the count of Barcelona after the city's capture—and of other land at Grallera, Aguilella, Barbens, and Tortosa.[289] Since the charters of donation have not survived, these gifts cannot be precisely dated. Nor is the identity of Arnold beyond dispute. Miret y Sans argues that he was related to the Templar of that name who became Grand Master of the Order.[290] Yet in a confirmation of his grant of rights at Aguilella it is stated that the gift had been made by the Arnold who later

became a Templar.[291] Unless there were two Templars of the
same name at the time, the patron of the Order must therefore
have been the man who afterwards became Grand Master.

Most of the gifts made by Arnold were confirmed in February
1164 by his kinsman Raymond of Torroja and the latter's wife
Gaia of Cervera; and Raymond at the same time made further
concessions to the Order.[292] These included land at Barbens, next
to that given by Arnold, and the tithe owed from Templar possessions there. Raymond also gave permission for the Order to
acquire rights in lands held of him at Barbens by Gerald of
Luzano and Raymond of Concabella, who in the following year
left half of his holding to the Temple.[293] For the confirmation
and concessions made in 1164 Raymond of Torroja received
400s.J. from the Temple, but three years later he did grant freely
that after his death the Order should have half of his land at
Barbens; if he left no legitimate sons or if his sons died without
legitimate offspring, the other half as well was to pass to the
Templars.[294] By the time that Raymond drew up his will in 1196
his son Raymond was already dead, but two other sons survived,
and one of these, called Hugh, inherited part of the family's lands
at Barbens, while the Templars received the rest.[295] In the meantime, the Order had purchased some houses from Raymond of
Torroja at Solsona, which he held of the count of Urgel.[296]
From Hugh the Templars in 1210 bought the lordship of the
castle and township of Grallera, after Arnold of Medalla had in
the previous year left the Templars 600*maz.* towards the cost of
its purchase.[297] Eight years later Hugh bequeathed a manse at
Espluga de Francolí to the Order.[298] Hugh had been left the
lordship of Espluga by his father, whose wife Gaia enjoyed certain rights there by inheritance and had in 1183 also purchased
those of her brother Pons, later viscount of Bas.[299] Hugh bequeathed Espluga to his sister Eldiardis, who in turn granted the
castle of Espluga de Francolí and that of Olmells to her son,
Simon of Palau, when he married Geralda of Anglesola in 1231;[300]
and Simon, who died in 1246/7, left Espluga de Francolí to the
Temple,[301] although the bequest was disputed by his widow and
it was only in 1255 that Geralda was receiving a payment of
1,000*m.* for surrendering the castle to the Templars, who also
undertook to pay her an annual pension of 2,000s.B.[302]

Amongst the other families in the more southerly parts of

Catalonia from which the Order made a considerable number of acquisitions were those of the Ribelles—from which the Temple gained rights in Lérida and at Barbens, Fuliola, and Guardiola[303]— and the Anglesola. Raymond Berenguer I had given the latter family a large stretch of uninhabited land between Tárrega and Lérida, which it had begun to settle by 1079, when Raymond Berenguer II confirmed his father's grant.[304] This family had further in 1118 been granted Corbins by Raymond Berenguer III,[305] and it was in these places that the Order gained a number of properties from the family, including the now-deserted places of Torre de Bafes and Escarabat, which both lay near Palau de Anglesola.[306] It was from members of this family too that the Order obtained the castles of Gebut and Culla.

One other Catalan family which may be mentioned in this context is that of the Moncadas. The Temple inevitably came into frequent contact with members of this family in Tortosa, where both the Order and the Moncadas enjoyed rights of lordship; but in addition a certain amount of the family's property, including important rights along the lower valley of the Ebro, passed into the Order's possession. In 1182 Raymond of Moncada granted the Templars his rights in the castle of Horta; for this and other minor concessions he received 1,000*m.* from them.[307] Twenty-five years later the Temple paid a further 1,000*m.* to Raymond's son, also called Raymond, for the lordship of the castle and town of Buriacenia, near Tortosa,[308] and in 1210 the Order spent 12,000*s.*J. in buying off the Moncadas' claims to Bene, which according to the Templars lay within the boundaries of Horta.[309] Finally, in 1216 the Temple gained from Raymond of Moncada the 200*m.* which the king in 1210 had retained in the *lezda* and *peaje* of Ascó. These dues had been given to Moncada in 1213, and the Templars bought them from him for 2,500*m.*[310]

Little was gained from these leading Catalan families after the early part of the thirteenth century, and acquisitions from other sources similarly became less frequent after the early decades of the century. Just as Templar expansion through grants by the Crown of newly conquered territories declined and stopped, so the growth of Templar property throughout the *Corona de Aragón* through other gifts and purchases slackened in the thirteenth century, although this did not happen simultaneously in all districts. Of sixty-five grants of landed property in Huesca,

Luna, Jaca, and elsewhere in the most northerly parts of Aragon, recorded mainly in a cartulary which covers the period from 1148 to 1273,[311] forty-four were made during the fifty years up to 1220 and only fourteen occurred in the following half-century. Of twenty-six donations of land to the Temple in Boquiñeni, Pradilla, and Tauste, most of which are recorded in volume five of the fourteenth-century Hospitaller *Cartulario Magno*,[312] only three dated grants occurred after the year 1200, compared with nineteen in the previous half-century. Apart from the royal grants of rights in Tortosa in 1148 and 1182, twenty-four gifts of landed property to the Temple in that city and the surrounding villages are known, mainly from a cartulary which was not completed before 1281,[313] and of these donations all except one took place between 1160 and 1220, while the remaining grant was made in 1226. Gifts in forms other than land appear to have undergone a similar decline. This can be illustrated by the declining numbers of *confratres*, for they did not usually give land to the Order. In the parchment roll of *confratres* of Aragon and Navarre, which covers the period up to 1225, the great majority of entries refer to contracts made before 1170; and although confraternity with the Temple became popular in Valencia during the years following the conquest of that kingdom, only two out of more than forty surviving contracts of confraternity with the Order there belong to the twenty years preceding the arrest of the Templars.[314]

Purchases by the Order underwent a similar decline. Of forty-six sales to the Temple of landed property in the city of Zaragoza—the records of these are found mainly in the *Cartulario Magno*[315]—twenty-four were made during the twenty years ending 1190 and thirty-six in the wider period from 1161 to 1220. Templar expenditure on property in the city was proportionate to the number of purchases. Almost half of the money spent by the Templars in Zaragoza was paid out in the twenty years up to 1190, and over three-quarters in the sixty years up to 1220.[316] Records of sales to the Temple in the towns and villages around Zaragoza, recorded mainly in the same fourteenth-century sources, reveal a similar pattern.[317] Four-fifths of the sales in these places occurred between 1161 and 1220, while of the money spent by the Temple more than four-fifths was expended between 1161 and 1220 and more than half in the last decade of the twelfth century. In the most northerly parts of Aragon the peak in the number of Templar purchases lay in the period between 1160 and 1190. The concentration of purchases in this period is well illustrated by what happened at Almudébar, for all the ten purchases made by the Order there occurred between 1176 and 1183.[318] After the end of the twelfth century the number of purchases made by the Temple in this area declined rapidly, although Templar expenditure did not markedly decrease until after 1250. In the more southerly parts of Aragon little property was bought by the Temple after the early decades of the thirteenth century. Of the purchases by the Order in the district of Castellote, which are recorded in a Templar cartulary compiled towards the end of the thirteenth century,[319] two-thirds had been made by 1220 and by that date an even larger proportion of the money expended there by the Temple had been spent; and although the first volume of the Hospitaller *Cartulario Magno* records a number of small purchases at Villel in the later part of the thirteenth century,[320] most of the money spent by the Templars in and around Villel had been expended by 1220. In the neighbourhood of Tortosa the decline in purchases is even more marked. No sales of land there to the Order are known after 1220, and in the quarter of a century up to that date they were made only occasionally. The period of greatest expenditure on land at Tortosa was during the years from 1165 to 1175, in which period the Order spent more than 3,000*m*.

In the later part of the thirteenth and at the beginning of the fourteenth centuries the Templars are known to have been making important purchases only in two districts in the *Corona de Aragón*. The first was the area inland from Tarragona, where the Temple bought the castle of Montbrió in 1269 and where it also acquired by purchase a number of fees held of the Order at Barbará, Albió, and Espluga de Francolí.[321] The other district was northern Valencia, where Culla was bought from William of Anglesola.[322] This was the most important single purchase ever made by the Order, but in assessing the significance of the transaction account should be taken of the arrangements which the Templars were obliged to make in order to pay for it. It was agreed that payment should be in instalments, and this meant that the Templars did not have to complete payment until a year and a half after the sale.[323] Nevertheless the Templars had difficulty in meeting their commitments, and in an attempt to obtain a longer period for payment they sought to take over some of William of Anglesola's debts.[324] But this did not solve the Temple's difficulties and it was therefore forced to sell rents to be paid out of the revenues it received elsewhere: in return for the sum of 16,000s.B., for example, a citizen of Lérida was assigned 1,000s.B. annually out of the income from the Temple's property in the district of Lérida.[325] The acquisition of Culla seems to have represented an attempt to create an extensive Templar lordship in northern Valencia, following the exchange of Tortosa for Peñíscola, and this was done partly at the expense of Templar possessions elsewhere. The Temple's landed wealth was probably only slightly increased by the purchase of Culla. The greatest increases had occurred in the twelfth and the early decades of the thirteenth centuries. It could, of course, be argued that this conclusion, like that concerning the geographical distribution of Templar property, is inevitably based on incomplete evidence. But the areas which have been discussed are those for which fairly full evidence is preserved in cartularies compiled in the late thirteenth or in the fourteenth centuries, and losses which had occurred by then would probably have been of early rather than late documents.

The slackening in the expansion of the Order's landed property during the thirteenth century can scarcely be accounted for by mortmain legislation. Mortmain decrees were admittedly included in the *Furs* of Valencia,[326] and these may at times have hindered the transference of property to the Order in that kingdom: when Bernard of Ganalor granted rights in a vineyard at Valencia to the Templars in 1259 he made the provision that if they could not obtain them 'through the impediment of the *fuero* of Valencia', they should—as stipulated in the *Furs*—have the price of the vineyard instead.[327] But legislation of this kind was not attempted throughout the *Corona de Aragón*.[328] It was, on the other hand, common for lords to impose restrictions on the alienation of individual holdings, but such restrictions were made in the twelfth as well as in the thirteenth century.

The decline in donations to the Order can, however, be fairly easily explained. The popularity of any religious institution tended to wane after an initial period of prosperity and growth. Most monasteries gained the majority of their endowments in the first century or so of their existence;[329] by the thirteenth century the great period of monastic endowment in Spain as elsewhere was over.[330] But there were also particular reasons why the Templars and the other military orders in north-eastern Spain no longer received extensive patronage.[331] The Aragonese reconquest had been completed before the middle of the thirteenth century and from that time onwards the function of the military orders in the *Corona de Aragón* was limited to frontier defence and raiding. In the Holy Land, of course, the Templars still had a more important task, which needed considerable resources. But although in the later thirteenth century much was written about the condition of the Holy Land and many crusading schemes were produced,[332] there was little enthusiasm for more practical measures of help. And in some countries it was being argued that the Templars were not making the best use of the property which they did possess in western Europe.[333] In this situation it is not surprising that patronage of the Order was declining.

The decline in acquisitions by purchase may have been occasioned in part by the diversion of Templar revenues into other types of investment. In the thirteenth century the Order occupied an important role as money-lender and some Templar funds were utilized in this way.[334] The Order may also have been investing money in commercial enterprises as an alternative to buying land: early in 1307 the Templars set up an attorney to recover from a certain inhabitant of Peñíscola not only the sum of 2,000*s*. which they had deposited with him but also the

share due to us of the profit which he made with the aforesaid money on the journeys which he made by sea and elsewhere with his ships.[335]

In this instance it is not clear, however, whether the money in question belonged to the Templars or consisted of cash that had originally been deposited with the Order. But whether or not revenues were being used in this way, probably the main reason for the decline in purchases was the deterioration in the financial position of the Temple. In the later part of the thirteenth century there was often little money available for investment. In many parts of the *Corona de Aragón* the Templars were experiencing difficulties in paying the annual dues which they owed to their superiors[336] and during the course of the century the evidence of borrowing by the Temple and of debts owed by it increases. Most of the money borrowed by the Order consisted, of course, of short-term advances, which were to be repaid when rents and dues were collected. This kind of loan was very common in the thirteenth century and does not in itself provide evidence of serious financial difficulties. But in practice the Templars sometimes had difficulty in repaying such loans: in 1254, for example, money owed to a Jewish money-lender in Barcelona was repaid by obtaining a further loan elsewhere.[337] And even if short-term loans were usually repaid when dues were collected, the Templars owed other debts which they had more difficulty in paying. This is apparent from an account drawn up in 1277, for this not only gives details of Templar obligations of various kinds amounting to over 100,000s.J., but also makes it clear that these were not all recent debts.[338] Although the Temple had very considerable estates in the *Corona de Aragón* the income derived from them was not always sufficient to meet such obligations; and in the thirteenth century the Order was at times obliged to alienate property and rights in order to obtain the money which it needed. It has been seen how rents were sold when money was required to pay the sums owed for the castle of Culla. Similarly when the Templars needed 1,000m. in 1255 to buy off the claims of Simon of Palau's widow to Espluga de Francolí, they sold their right of *questia* there for 1,200m.[339] These financial difficulties were apparently not the result of extravagance on the part of the Templars. Although, for example, they had to maintain expensive castles, they did not engage in extravagant building programmes. Templar buildings were neither elaborate nor unnecessarily large.[340] The explanation is to be sought rather in the increasing demands made of the Aragonese Templars both by the Order in the East and by the Aragonese kings. In the later part of the thirteenth century the Templars in the Levant were becoming increasingly dependent on aid from western Europe, and at the same time the Aragonese kings were not only developing new forms of taxation to which the Order was obliged to contribute, but also limiting some of the Temple's former immunities.[341] Nor was the situation improved by rising prices, which decreased the value of rents paid in money. In these circumstances the Order inevitably bought only a small amount of land in the later part of the thirteenth century, and by then the expansion of Templar property in the *Corona de Aragón* was coming to an end.

## NOTES

1. Albon, *Cartulaire*, p. 25, doc. 33.

2. Ibid., pp. 36–7, doc. 47 (the reference should be to ACA, parch. Raymond Berenguer IV, no. 14, not no. 7); *LFM*, i. 268–9, doc. 252.

3. On the Templar attitude to the reconquest in Portugal at this time, see C. Erdmann, 'Der Kreuzzugsgedanke in Portugal', *Historische Zeitschrift*, cxli (1929), 40.

4. *CDI*, iv. 18–19, doc. 6; Albon, *Cartulaire*, p. 53, doc. 70. The date is given as 3 January in the 25th year of Louis (1133) and in the year of the Incarnation 1134 (1135 N.S.).

5. *CDI*, iv. 93–9, doc. 43; Albon, *Cartulaire*, pp. 204–5, doc. 314.

6. *CDI*, iv. 32–3, doc. 11; Albon, *Cartulaire*, p. 55, doc. 72. In both of these versions one name is omitted. There are possibly two others which have now faded from the manuscript: ACA, parch. Raymond Berenguer IV, no. 28. M. Melville, *La Vie des Templiers* (Paris, 1951), p. 29, quotes Albon incorrectly in stating that the count and twenty-four others made promises. These promises, which are undated, are noted on the dorse of a charter which records a concession to the Templars made by the count of Barcelona and the archbishop of Tarragona during an assembly of prelates and nobles in April 1134 (this charter is published in *CDI*, iv. 29–32, doc. 11, and Albon, *Cartulaire*, pp. 53–5, doc. 71). As several of those who promised service appear as witnesses to the charter, the promises may well have been made during the assembly in April 1134.

7. The count's promise was inserted at the top of the memorandum after the other entries had been made.

8. It is possible that there was some kind of Templar establishment at Grañena by 1136, but the evidence is very tenuous: see below, p. 91; and there is nothing to suggest that the Templars themselves had taken over the defence of Grañena by that date.

9. *CDI*, iv. 9–12, doc. 2; Delaville, *Cartulaire*, i. 85–6, doc. 95; Albon, *Cartulaire*, pp. 30–1, doc. 40; *LFM*, i. 10–12, doc. 6; García Larragueta, *Gran priorado*, ii. 15–18, doc. 10.

10. At the turn of the eleventh and twelfth centuries some Spanish rulers had found it necessary to obtain papal bulls prohibiting Spaniards from going to the East; see, for example, Migne, *PL*, clxiii. 45, 64–5, docs. 26, 44; cf. J. Goñi Gaztambide, *Historia de la bula de la cruzada en España* (Vitoria, 1958), pp. 60–1, 64–5; see also A. Ubieto Arteta, 'La participación navarro-aragonesa en la primera cruzada', *Príncipe de Viana*, viii (1947), 357–83.

11. P. Rassow, 'La cofradía de Belchite', *AHDE*, iii (1926), 225; Albon, *Cartulaire*, pp. 3–4, doc. 6; Lacarra, 'Documentos', no. 151 (iii. 549).

12. Cf. J. M. Lacarra, *Semblanza de Alfonso I el Batallador* (Zaragoza, 1949),

p. 13. The significance of the inclusion of the Hospitallers among the beneficiaries is not clear because historians are not agreed about the character of the Hospitallers at this time. Delaville, *Hospitaliers*, p. 45, and E. J. King, *The Knights Hospitallers in the Holy Land* (London, 1931), pp. 32–3, argue that the Hospital had become a military order by 1126, when the office of constable is mentioned; this has been questioned by Riley-Smith, *Knights of St. John*, p. 53. As has been pointed out by the latter, ibid., p. 54, Alfonso in his will referred to the Hospital as 'Ospitale pauperum quod Jherosolimis est', and to the Temple as 'Templum Domini cum militibus qui ad defendendum Christianitatis nomen ibi vigilant', but it would be dangerous to attempt to base any conclusions merely on the wording of these descriptions.

13. Delaville, *Cartulaire*, i. 91, doc. 106; García Larragueta, *Gran priorado*, ii. 21, doc. 13.

14. Ibid., pp. 15–18, doc. 10; *CDI*, iv. 70–3, doc. 32; *LFM*, i. 17–19, doc. 12.

15. Contemporary accounts suggest that this occurred because of the need to maintain peace and to defend Alfonso's lands from the Moors. Ramiro at one time stated that he had become king 'not through ambition for office or desire for advancement but only because of the needs of the people and for the tranquillity of the Church': Villanueva, *Viage*, xv. 375, doc. 78; and when discussing the succession to Alfonso I the author of the *Chronica Adefonsi Imperatoris* stressed the need for defence and maintained that Alfonso VII intervened first to give aid to Ramiro and the Aragonese people, who were 'in great fear and trembling': ed. L. Sánchez Belda (Madrid, 1950), p. 51; cf. P. Kehr, 'El papado y los reinos de Navarra y Aragón hasta mediados del siglo XII', *EEMCA*, ii (1946), 160–1. But this may well have been written in an attempt to justify Alfonso VII's acquisition of the *regnum Cesaraugustanum*, and the acceptance of Ramiro as king suggests that military considerations were not of the greatest importance.

More recently it has been suggested that the provisions of Alfonso's will were rejected because they were contrary to the 'juridical tradition' of the country, which demanded that the ruler should be a member of the royal family: J. M. Ramos y Loscertales, *El reino de Aragón bajo la dinastía pamplonesa* (Acta Salmanticensia, vol. xv, 1961), pp. 99–100, 104; A. García-Gallo, 'La sucesión del trono en la Corona de Aragón', *AHDE*, xxxvi (1966), 46–7; cf. *Hispania*, x (1950), 417. It is not clear, however, to what extent a juridical tradition concerning the succession had been evolved by the early twelfth century. As it has been set out, the juridical tradition is merely a series of rules formulated by historians on the basis of what happened on a few particular occasions. Even if it is likely that a juridical tradition was being evolved, it may not have covered the circumstances existing in 1134, when the only close relation of the dead king was a monk. Certainly the fact that Alfonso's will was confirmed by the nobility suggests that its provisions were not considered illegal. Admittedly in 1134 the choice fell on Alfonso's brother and on García Ramírez, who was of royal descent, even if in an illegitimate line; but it does not necessarily follow from this that Alfonso's will was rejected because he had not designated a member of his family to succeed him. It is possible that it was rejected partly because the nobles preferred to have a king rather than ecclesiastical institutions in authority over them, while no doubt personal ambitions of claimants and their supporters were of some importance.

16. A. Ubieto Arteta, 'Navarra-Aragón y la idea imperial de Alfonso VII de Castilla', *EEMCA*, vi (1956), 49–53.

17. J. M. Lacarra, 'Alfonso II el Casto, rey de Aragón y conde de Barcelona', *VII Congreso de historia de la Corona de Aragón* (Barcelona, 1962), i. 101, similarly assumes that Alfonso's action was occasioned by Innocent's bull, but does not reach any conclusions about his motives.

18. The bull is published by Albon, *Cartulaire*, p. 373, Bullaire, doc. 2, and P. Kehr, *Papsturkunden in Spanien. I. Katalanien* (Abhandlungen der Gesellschaft der Wissenschaften zu Göttingen. Phil.-hist. Klasse, N.F., vol. xviii, 1926), p. 318, doc. 50. Kehr, 'El papado', p. 162, note 176, inclines to the date 1135, which is also accepted by P. E. Schramm, 'Ramon Berenguer IV', in *Els primers comtes-reis* (Barcelona, 1960), p. 14.

19. Albon, *Cartulaire*, pp. 204–5, doc. 314; *CDI*, iv. 93–9, doc. 43.

20. *Historia Compostellana*, iii. 46, in *ES*, xx. 570–1; Kehr, 'El papado', p. 163, note 178, refers to a document in the archive of Burgos which states that Alfonso invited the legate.

21. The sources are not consistent about the rights to be enjoyed by Alfonso and Ramiro over the *regnum Cesaraugustanum*. According to Ubieto, Alfonso was to hold it of Ramiro, but it has also been suggested that Ramiro held it as a vassal of Alfonso: cf. H. Grassoti, 'Homenaje de García Ramírez a Alfonso VII', *Príncipe de Viana*, xxv (1964), 60–1.

22. *Historia Compostellana*, iii. 51, in *ES*, xx. 585; *Chronica Adefonsi Imperatoris*, ed. Sánchez Belda, pp. 58–9.

23. Ibid., p. x.

24. J. Traggia, 'Ilustración del reynado de don Ramiro II de Aragón', *Memorias de la Real Academia de la Historia*, iii (1799), 493.

25. F. Balaguer, 'La vizcondesa del Bearn doña Talesa y la rebelión contra Ramiro II en 1136', *EEMCA*, v (1952), 102, suggests that the events of 1136 were occasioned by an appeal for help by Ramiro to Alfonso VII. This theory is based mainly on an entry in the *Chronica Adefonsi Imperatoris*, ed. Sánchez Belda, pp. 51–3, which has usually been taken to refer to Alfonso's seizure of the *regnum Cesaraugustanum* shortly after Alfonso I's death. Balaguer argues that as the entry follows an account of events which took place in the spring of 1135 it must belong to 1136. But it may be pointed out that the entry also immediately precedes accounts of other events which took place in 1135; and it may be noted that the same chronicler later gives a different explanation of the war with Navarre in 1136.

26. *CDI*, iv. 59–60, doc. 24; *LFM*, i. 12–13, doc. 7. Ubieto Arteta, loc. cit., pp. 49–50, argues that the *regnum Cesaraugustanum* was restored to Ramiro by 24 August 1136, but that the actual treaty between the kings took place later, at some time during the period up to 28 October 1136. He adopts this

argument because a document of 24 August was said to have been drawn up in the year in which Zaragoza was restored to Ramiro, while another document of 28 October was said to have been written in the year that Alfonso made an agreement with Ramiro: see Lacarra, 'Documentos', nos. 196, 197 (iii. 586–7); but it seems likely that both documents refer to the same event, and that the agreement was made by the later part of August.

27. Ubieto Arteta, loc. cit., p. 49, and 'La campana de Huesca', *Revista de filología española*, xxxv (1951), 50, suggests that Ramiro was married in January 1136. On the other hand, S. de Vajay, 'Ramire II le Moine, roi d'Aragon, et Agnès de Poitou dans l'histoire et dans la légende', *Mélanges offerts à René Crozet* (Poitiers, 1966), ii. 739–40, maintains that Ramiro married in the autumn of 1135 and that Petronilla was born not later than July 1136.

28. Cf. Kehr, 'El papado', pp. 162–3; Vajay, loc. cit., p. 737. On the question of the existence of a papal dispensation it may further be noted that after about a year of marriage Ramiro's wife returned to her own country: ibid., p. 742. Vajay also suggests that Innocent may have been influenced in his policy towards Ramiro by the fact that Ramiro's brother-in-law was one of the leading supporters of Anacletus, the other claimant to the papal throne: ibid., p. 741.

29. *LFM*, i. 13–14, doc. 8. The evidence about internal opposition has been subject to varied interpretations: see, for example, Ubieto Arteta, 'La campana de Huesca'; Balaguer, 'La vizcondesa del Bearn'.

30. *CDI*, iv. 59–60, doc. 24; *LFM*, i. 12–13, doc. 7.

31. According to F. Balaguer, 'La Chronica Adefonsi Imperatoris y la elevación de Ramiro II al trono aragonés', *EEMCA*, vi (1956), 14, 'only Raymond Berenguer could resolve the problem, since he was a Templar who safeguarded the rights of the Order in case the house of Barcelona died out'; and a similar statement is attributed to Lacarra in *Hispania*, x (1950), 418. The meaning of these remarks is, however, far from clear.

32. *CDI*, iv. 70–3, doc. 32. The main documents recording the negotiations of the Hospital and the Holy Sepulchre have also been published by C. Odriozola y Grimaud, *Ramón Berenguer IV, conde de Barcelona, caballero del Santo Sepulcro de Jerusalén. Memorias históricas referentes a la cesión en su favor de la Corona de Aragón, hecha por la Orden militar del Santo Sepulcro, la del Hospital y del Temple en el año 1140* (Barcelona, 1911). He does not, despite the title, offer any evidence about the Temple.

33. *CDI*, iv. 73–5, doc. 32; Delaville, *Cartulaire*, i. 111–12, doc. 136; *LFM*, i. 17–19, doc. 12.

34. *CDI*, iv. 70–3, doc. 32.

35. Ibid., pp. 78–81, doc. 36; *LFM*, i. 15–16, doc. 10; V. de la Fuente, *Historia de Calatayud*, i (Calatayud, 1880), 338–40, doc. 8.

36. *Anales*, ii. 4. The same assumption is made by M. Bruguera, *Historia general de la religiosa y militar Orden de los caballeros del Temple*, i (Barcelona, 1888), 186, and Riley-Smith, *Knights of St. John*, p. 44.

37. M. Zapater, *Cister militante* (Zaragoza, 1662), pp. 56–7.

38. *CDI*, iv. 317–18, doc. 130; Delaville, *Cartulaire*, i. 201, doc. 267; *LFM*, i. 19, doc. 13; Kehr, *Papsturkunden in Spanien. I. Katalanien*, pp. 364–5, doc. 81.

39. Albon, *Cartulaire*, pp. 102–3, doc. 145; *CDI*, iv. 368–70, doc. 153. The inclusion of 'princeps Aragonensis' among Raymond Berenguer's titles shows that the letter was written not earlier than 1137.

40. See above, p. 63, note 10.

41. The letter is now in the ACA in Barcelona: parch. Raymond Berenguer IV, undated no. 21.

42. R. Esteban Abad, *Estudio histórico-político sobre la ciudad y comunidad de Daroca* (Teruel, 1959), p. 49, suggests that opposition to the count's offer came from the inhabitants of Daroca because their privileges would have been affected; but their situation in fact would not have been changed.

43. This important document has been published most recently in Albon, *Cartulaire*, pp. 204–5, doc. 314, and *CDI*, iv. 93–9, doc. 43. It also appears in P. de Marca, *Marca Hispanica* (Paris, 1688), cols. 1291–4, doc. 402; P. Rodríguez Campomanes, *Dissertaciones históricas del Orden y Cavallería de los Templarios* (Madrid, 1747), pp. 221–4; P. Dupuy, *Histoire de l'Ordre militaire des Templiers* (Brussels, 1751), pp. 108–11, doc. 9; J. S. de Aguirre, *Collectio maxima conciliorum omnium Hispaniae et novi orbis*, v (Rome, 1755), 57–8; *ES*, xliii. 484–8, doc. 51. Albon identifies Mongay with the castle of that name to the east of Balaguer; but that place remained in royal hands. The castle granted to the Temple may have been the Mongay near Monzón. The Order failed to obtain Belchite, which remained in the possession of Lope Sánchez. On the lords of Belchite during the rest of the twelfth century, see M. Pallarés Gil, 'La frontera sarracena en tiempo de Berenguer IV', *Boletín de historia y geografía del Bajo-Aragón*, i (1907), 150–1.

44. *CDI*, iv. 317–18, doc. 130; Delaville, *Cartulaire*, i. 201, doc. 267; *LFM*, i. 19, doc. 13; Kehr, *Papsturkunden in Spanien. I. Katalanien*, pp. 364–5, doc. 81. This bull refers to the documents in which the renunciations made by the three Orders were recorded.

45. Zurita, *Anales*, ii. 4; in *CDI*, iv. 417, it is stated that Raymond Berenguer's grant marked the foundation of the Temple in the *Corona de Aragón*.

46. This interpretation has already been suggested briefly by Erdmann, loc. cit., p. 41, who also argues that after 1143 the Templars also participated in the reconquest in Portugal. M. Usón y Sesé, 'Aportaciones al estudio de la caída de los Templarios en Aragón', *Universidad*, iii (1926), 484, follows Miret y Sans, *Les Cases*, p. 29, in arguing that as a result of the count's grant the Order gained an 'official position' in Aragon and Catalonia, but neither explains what is meant by this phrase.

47. AHN, cód. 494, pp. 1–4, doc. 1; M. Albareda y Herrera, *El fuero de Alfambra* (Madrid, 1925), p. 25.

48. A few general rules about conduct in the field are found in the Templar

Customs: *Règle*, pp. 115–27, arts. 148–68; pp. 206–14, arts. 366–83; but no evidence survives from Spain on this subject.

49. S. García Larragueta, 'La Orden de San Juan en la crisis del imperio hispánico del siglo XII', *Hispania*, xii (1952), 483–524. The argument presented in this article relies heavily on the absence of evidence, and the interpretation given of some documents, especially a bull issued by Celestine III in 1193, may be questioned. In that bull the pope commanded the Hospitallers to continue fighting against the Moors when the Christian rulers made peace with them: P. Kehr, *Papsturkunden in Spanien. II. Navarra und Aragon* (Abhandlungen der Gesellschaft der Wissenschaften zu Göttingen. Phil.-hist. Klasse. N.F., vol. xxii, 1928), pp. 554–5, doc. 200. Whether the pope's orders were carried out is not known, but in 1205 the Aragonese king claimed that the Order of Calatrava did not dare to wage war on the Castilian frontier because the king of Castile had made a truce with the Moors: D. Mansilla, *La documentación pontificia hasta Inocencio III* (Rome, 1955), p. 351, doc. 321.

M. L. Ledesma, 'Notas sobre la actividad militar de los hospitalarios', *Príncipe de Viana*, xxv (1964), 51–6, emphasizes the difficulty of reaching any conclusion about the Hospital's military activity because of lack of evidence.

50. The exact extent of Lobo's kingdom is not known: cf. F. Codera, *Decadencia y desaparición de los Almoravides en España* (Zaragoza, 1899), pp. 123–5; I. de las Cagigas, *Los mudéjares*, i (Madrid, 1948), 266. Codera argues that in a treaty with the Genoese in 1149 Lobo sought to ensure the safety of the Moors in Tortosa; but the treaty refers to the Genoese in the city, not to the Moors there: S. de Sacy, 'Pièces diplomatiques tirées des archives de la république de Gènes', *Notices et extraits des manuscrits de la Bibliothèque du Roi*, xi (1827), 3–5.

51. Albon, *Cartulaire*, pp. 339–40, doc. 553; cf. pp. 349–50, doc. 564.

52. *Annali Genovesi di Caffaro*, ed. L. T. Belgrano, i (Fonti per la storia d'Italia, Rome, Genoa, 1890), 86.

53. Albon, *Cartulaire*, pp. 345–6, doc. 557.

54. AGP, Cartulary of Gardeny, fol. 53ᵛ, doc. 124.

55. *Poésies complètes du troubadour Marcabru*, ed. J. M. L. Dejeanne (Toulouse, 1909), p. 171. This poem has usually been assigned to the years 1137 or 1146–7, at the time of the Almería expedition: ibid., p. 235; P. Boissonnade, 'Les personnages et les événements de l'histoire d'Allemagne, de France et d'Espagne dans l'œuvre de Marcabru (1129–1150)', *Romania*, xlviii (1922), 219–20; C. Appel, 'Zu Marcabru', *Zeitschrift für romanische Philologie*, xliii (1923), 409. Yet in 1137 the Templars were not fighting in Spain; and as the count of Barcelona alone is mentioned, without any other Spanish ruler, it may be suggested that the poem was occasioned by Raymond Berenguer's expeditions rather than by the Almería campaign, in which several rulers participated. A date towards the end of the fifth decade of the twelfth century therefore seems more likely, as was suggested by C. Chabaneau, 'Sur la date du *Vers del Lavador* de Marcabrun', *Revue des langues romanes*, 3rd series, xiii (1885), 250–1.

56. *ES*, xlii. 102–3. The Hospitallers in 1242 put forward claims in Tortosa

based on the rights of the count of Pallars: ACA, parch. James I, no. 870; AGP, Cartulary of Tortosa, fols. 48ᵛ–49, doc. 148.

57. Albon, *Cartulaire*, pp. 30–1, doc. 40; *CDI*, iv. 9–12, doc. 2; Delaville, *Cartulaire*, i. 85–6, doc. 95; *LFM*, i. 10–12, doc. 6.

58. *CDI*, iv. 53–4, doc. 22; *ES*, xlii. 109.

59. *CDI*, iv. 113–14, doc. 51; *LFM*, i. 485, doc. 462.

60. *CDI*, iv. 332–4, doc. 141; 337–9, doc. 144.

61. The count of Barcelona obtained a surrender of the claims of the house of Montpellier: B. Oliver, *Historia del derecho en Cataluña, Mallorca y Valencia: Código de las costumbres de Tortosa*, i (Madrid, 1876), 68.

62. Miret y Sans, *Les Cases*, p. 61.

63. *CDI*, iv. 114–23, doc. 51; 347–55, doc. 147; *LFM*, i. 487–92, docs. 464, 465.

64. The Genoese sold their share back to the count in 1153: *CDI*, iv. 212–16, doc. 78; *LFM*, i. 485–7, doc. 463.

65. Oliver, op. cit. i. 393–4.

66. *CDI*, viii. 52–4, doc. 16.

67. ACA, parch. Alfonso II, no. 299. In February 1182 a charter was issued to the Jews of the city by the king and Raymond of Moncada, without reference to the Templars: AGP, Cartulary of Tortosa, fol. 86ᵛ, doc. 275.

68. *CDI*, iv. 126–9, doc. 54; *LFM*, i. 168–9, doc. 161.

69. Cf. J. M. Font y Rius, 'La reconquista de Lérida y su proyección en el orden jurídico', *Ilerda*, vii (1949), 15.

70. Lacarra, 'Documentos', nos. 29, 30, 31 (ii. 497–9), 117 (iii. 520).

71. This conclusion is based on the large number of Templar grants of property to tenants in these districts.

72. *CDI*, iv. 208–11, doc. 77. On the dates of Raymond Berenguer's conquests in these districts, see A. Giménez Soler, 'La frontera catalano-aragonesa', *II Congreso de historia de la Corona de Aragón*, i (Huesca, 1920), 487–8.

73. AHN, San Juan, leg. 324, doc. 1; leg. 333, doc. 1.

74. *Bullarium Ordinis Militiae de Calatrava*, ed. I. J. de Ortega y Cotes, J. F. Alvarez de Baquedano, and P. de Ortega Zuñiga y Aranda (Madrid, 1761), pp. 13–14.

75. On the history of the Order of Mountjoy, see J. Delaville Le Roulx, 'L'Ordre de Montjoye', *Revue de l'Orient latin*, i (1893), 42–57; A. Blásquez y Jiménez, 'Bosquejo histórico de la Orden de Montegaudio', *BRAH*, lxxi (1917), 138–72; F. D. Gazulla, 'La Orden del Santo Redentor', *BSCC*, ix (1928), 90–107, 157–60, 204–12, 370–5; x (1929), 38–41, 98–101, 124–6; A. J. Forey, 'The Order of Mountjoy', *Speculum*, xlvi (1971), 250–66.

76. R. C. Smail, *Crusading Warfare (1097–1193)* (Cambridge, 1956), pp. 102–4.

*Expansion*

77. *CDI*, viii. 45–7, doc. 13; *BSCC*, xiv (1933), 169–70; xxviii (1952), 298; AGP, Cartulary of Gardeny, fol. 14–14ᵛ, doc. 14; see below, p. 370. A peace was made with the Moors in the following year and Lobo apparently agreed to pay Aragon a tribute of 40,000*m.* annually. This treaty seems to have been observed until Lobo's death in 1172, but it is not known whether the Temple received the promised payment; cf. M. Gual Camarena, *Precedentes de la reconquista valenciana* (Valencia, 1952), pp. 26–7.

78. AGP, Cartulary of Gardeny, fol. 89–89ᵛ, doc. 221; cf. Javierre, *Privilegios*, p. 115, no. 7. On the 1180 expedition, see Gual Camarena, op. cit., p. 29.

79. AGP, Cartulary of Gardeny, fols. 16ᵛ–17, doc. 20; ACA, Varia 2, fol. 72–72ᵛ. Most versions of this grant give its date as 30 June 1177, and this is accepted by J. Miret y Sans, 'Itinerario del rey Alfonso I de Cataluña, II en Aragón', *BRABLB*, ii (1903–4), 403. J. Caruana, 'Itinerario de Alfonso II de Aragón', *EEMCA*, vii (1962), 149, 169, note 232, assigns the document to the year 1174 because Alfonso was unlikely to have been at Lérida, where the document was issued, at the end of June 1177; but the earlier date is given in only one late copy of the document: AHN, San Juan, leg. 354, doc. 6.

80. Ibid., leg. 285, doc. 2.

81. *LFM*, i. 492–5, doc. 466; Oliver, op. cit. i. 394–7. The date of this grant is discussed by Miret y Sans, 'Itinerario', p. 416. It would have been at this time that the Templar provincial master, Berenguer of Avinyó, confirmed certain privileges which Raymond Berenguer IV had granted to the Jews and Moors of Tortosa in 1148 and 1149: *CDI*, iv. 130–5, doc. 56; J. Miret y Sans, 'La carta de franquicias otorgada por el Conde de Barcelona a los judíos de Tortosa', *Homenaje a D. Francisco Codera* (Zaragoza, 1904), pp. 200–2.

82. Royal and Templar demesnes in Tortosa were defined in 1182 and 1184: ACA, parch. Alfonso II, no. 328; *LFM*, i. 495–7, doc. 467.

83. Kehr, *Papsturkunden in Spanien. I. Katalanien*, p. 560, doc. 254.

84. Gazulla, loc. cit. x. 99–101.

85. AHN, Ordenes Militares, Calatrava, sign. 1341–C, fols. 135–6.

86. Gazulla, loc. cit. ix. 370–1; Albareda y Herrera, op. cit., pp. 96–7.

87. The terms of Villel included Tramacastiel and Villastar.

88. The terms of Castellote included Las Cuevas de Cañart, Santolea, and Bordón.

89. There was a Templar commander of Cantavieja in that year. A document issued by Peter II in 1212 makes it clear that Alfonso had earlier granted it to Mountjoy: AHN, San Juan, leg. 231, doc. 2; published from two later versions by Gual Camarena, op. cit., pp. 72–3.

90. These are mentioned in a confirmation issued by the bishop of Zaragoza in 1204: AHN, San Juan, leg. 39, doc. 67.

91. Apart from the strongholds which it inherited from Mountjoy, the Temple

also obtained in southern Aragon from Alfonso II—apparently near the end of his reign—the frontier castle of Albentosa: cf. AHN, cód. 466, pp. 4–5, doc. 3.

92. AHN, Montesa, R. 8; cf. Javierre, *Privilegios*, p. 115, no. 8; see below, p. 373. For the date of this grant, see Miret y Sans, 'Itinerario', pp. 450–1.

93. M. de Riquer, 'El trovador Giraut del Luc y sus poesías contra Alfonso II de Aragón', *BRABLB*, xxiii (1950), 234. He also publishes a version of Alfonso's grant, taken from a fourteenth-century transcript in the ACA: ibid., pp. 247–8.

94. Ibid., p. 219.

95. AHN, San Juan, leg. 186, doc. 3; published from a later manuscript by Gual Camarena, op. cit., pp. 69–71.

96. Oliver, op. cit. i. 397–9.

97. ACA, parch. Alfonso II, no. 146.

98. ACA, parch. Peter II, no. 98; cf. Zurita, *Anales*, ii. 49, and J. Miret y Sans, 'Itinerario del rey Pedro I de Cataluña, II en Aragón', *BRABLB*, iii (1905–6), 240, 245–6.

99. ACA, parch. Peter II, no. 139. On the day when this charter was issued the Templars made a loan of 1,000m. to the king: Miret y Sans, 'Itinerario del rey Pedro', p. 266.

100. AGP, Cartulary of Tortosa, fols. 72ᵛ–73, doc. 235; ACA, parch. Peter II, no. 257.

101. Ibid., no. 308. In 1209 and 1210 William of Cervera and Raymond of Moncada acted together as lords of Tortosa: AGP, Cartulary of Tortosa, fol. 70, doc. 227; fol. 75–75ᵛ, doc. 246.

102. ACA, reg. 310, fol. 35ᵛ.

103. Ibid., fol. 35–35ᵛ.

104. ACA, parch. James I, no. 39. In a copy in reg. 310, fol. 35, the date is given wrongly as 1214.

105. ACA, parch. Peter II, no. 201. This compromise must have been preceded by another, for a reference survives to an agreement about Serós made by Raymond of Gurb, who was provincial master in 1200 and 1201; and in 1209 it was stated that the Templars had received revenues in Serós for more than eight years: reg. 310, fol. 31; parch. Peter II, no. 313.

106. ACA, reg. 310, fol. 31.

107. J. Miret y Sans, *Cartoral dels Templers de les comandes de Gardeny y Barbens* (Barcelona, 1899), pp. 22–3; see also ACA, reg. 310, fol. 37–37ᵛ.

108. AHN, San Juan, leg. 39, doc. 92; ACA, reg. 310, fol. 36.

109. ACA, parch. Peter II, no. 410; AHN, Montesa, R. 20; published from a different manuscript in *BSCC*, xi (1930), 355; cf. Javierre, *Privilegios*, p. 120, nos. 21, 22. Peter is known to have undertaken an expedition against the Moors in 1212: Gual Camarena, op. cit., p. 45.

110. AHN, San Juan, leg. 39, doc. 79; see below, p. 377.

111. *CDI*, vi. 95–101, docs. 16, 17; xi. 3–6; A. Lecoy de la Marche, *Relations politiques de la France avec le royaume de Majorque* (Paris, 1892), i. 403–5; Huici, *Colección diplomática*, i. 128–30, doc. 63; 138–40, doc. 70; *Chronicle of James I*, caps. 50–4, trans. J. Forster (London, 1883), i. 104–11.

112. *CDI*, xi. 37–9. The *repartimiento* of Mallorca has also been published, from a different manuscript, by J. M. Quadrado, *Historia de la conquista de Mallorca* (Palma, 1850).

113. e.g. M. Rotger, 'Los Templers a Mallorca', *Congreso de historia de la Corona de Aragón*, i (Barcelona, 1909), 143; Miret y Sans, *Les Cases*, p. 252; Lecoy de la Marche, op. cit. i. 79; S. Sobrequés Vidal in *Historia social y económica de España y América*, ii (Barcelona, 1957), 22–3. It is assumed by these writers that the *caballerías* were actual pieces of land, granted in addition to the *alquerías*, houses, etc., mentioned in the *repartimiento*. Yet since in the *repartimiento* it is frequently stated (*CDI*, xi. 75 ff.) that individuals were given *alquerías*, *operatoria*, etc., 'for their *caballerías*', it is clear that the *caballerías* were merely units of assessment. On the use of the term in this sense, see *Los fueros de Aragón*, ed. G. Tilander (Acta Reg. Societatis Humaniorum Litterarum Lundensis, vol. xxv, Lund, 1937), pp. 303–4. The word is also found in this sense in AHN, cód. 689, pp. 99–100, doc. 107.

114. B. Desclot, *Chronicle of the Reign of King Pedro III of Aragon*, trans. F. L. Critchlow, i (Princeton, 1934), 78.

115. His figures for Nuño Sánchez and the count of Ampurias are inaccurate. C. de Tourtoulon, *Jacme Ier le Conquérant*, i (Montpellier, 1863), 244, note 1, argues that Desclot confuses the Cortes held in 1228 at Barcelona with that held in 1229; but the promise which Desclot attributes to the Temple was not made in the later assembly either. Lecoy de la Marche, op. cit. i. 38, asserts that the promise mentioned by Desclot was made after the Cortes, but this claim is not based on any documentary evidence.

116. Cap. 97, trans. Forster, i. 186.

117. *CDI*, xi. 116, 131–3.

118. Ibid., pp. 74–5, 121, 125, 129–31.

119. Ibid., p. 132. Quadrado, op. cit., p. 434, identifies the Montaña with Escorca.

120. *CDI*, xi. 88–90, 107–8, 114–15. A further two *alquerías* of ten *jovadas* are also included in the list of Templar holdings at Montuiri, but these are said to be the king's, and were probably exchanged for the *alquería* of ten *jovadas* which the Temple was given in Petra: ibid., pp. 100–1.

121. ACA, reg. 310, fol. 45.

122. AHN, Montesa, R. 31; cf. Javierre, *Privilegios*, p. 124, no. 35.

123. The principle that rewards should be proportionate to the size of contingents was laid down after the conquest of the city of Valencia in 1238: *Chronicle of James I*, caps. 284–9, trans. Forster, i. 398–401; ii. 402–3.

124. Ibid., caps. 255–60, trans. Forster, i. 369–74.

125. Ibid., caps. 153–4, trans. Forster, i. 253–5.

126. AHN, Montesa, R. 25; cf. Javierre, *Privilegios*, pp. 122–3, no. 29; R. de María, *El 'Repartiment' de Burriana y Villarreal* (Valencia, 1935), pp. 12–14.

127. Huici, *Colección diplomática*, i. 202–3, doc. 114; *BSCC*, xv (1934), 68–9.

128. Huici, *Colección diplomática*, i. 200–1, doc. 112; *BSCC*, xiv (1933), 172–3.

129. *Chronicle of James I*, cap. 185, trans. Forster, i. 291. For the text of the agreement and discussion of it, see M. Ferrandis, 'Rendición del castillo de Chivert a los Templarios', *Homenaje a D. Francisco Codera* (Zaragoza, 1904), pp. 23–33. The date of the agreement is 28 April 1234. M. Gual Camarena, 'Reconquista de la zona castellonense', *BSCC*, xxv (1949), 436, argues that Chivert submitted to the Temple in September 1233 and that a draft of the later agreement was then drawn up. As the agreement which survives was written apparently at the time of the provincial chapter, it was probably a confirmation of terms which had been accepted earlier. G. de sa Vall, 'Rendición del castillo de Xivert', *BSCC*, xxiv (1948), 232, argues that the document was originally drawn up in Arabic.
   In 1225 James had promised Chivert to Roderick Jiménez of Luesia; he was given compensation for his claims in 1237: Javierre, *Privilegios*, pp. 131–2, no. 61.

130. ACA, reg. 310, fol. 47; cf. Javierre, *Privilegios*, p. 132, no. 62.

131. AHN, Montesa, R. 65; *CDI*, xi. 290; cf. Javierre, *Privilegios*, p. 134, no. 70. In a survey of houses in Valencia begun on 9 April 1239 fifty are attributed to the Temple in the quarter of the men of Lérida: *CDI*, xi. 589–90 (the total is given as fifty, but fifty-one are listed). These appear to be the same as the fifty noted in the Daroca and Teruel sector (ibid., p. 644), since there are several repetitions elsewhere in these groups. In the *repartimiento* of Valencia the area of land granted to the Temple is given wrongly as ten *jovadas*: ibid., p. 290.

132. AHN, cód. 471, pp. 107–8, doc. 103; Huici, *Colección diplomática*, i. 386, doc. 273.

133. AHN, Montesa, R. 78; cf. Javierre, *Privilegios*, p. 138, no. 83.

134. Huici, *Colección diplomática*, i. 412–15, docs. 298, 299; Javierre, *Privilegios*, pp. 66–7. Although the king gave securities, the Order had still not received full compensation twenty-five years later: AHN, Montesa, P. 321.

135. AHN, Montesa, P. 316, 372. James I stated in his Chronicle, on the other hand, that he had captured the castle: cap. 185, trans. Forster, i. 291. On Pulpís, see A. Sánchez Gozalbo, 'Notas para la historia del Maestrazgo de Montesa: el castillo de Polpís', *BSCC*, xiv (1933), 457–60.

136. Santiago seems to have been the military order with the most property in the southern part of Valencia: R. I. Burns, *The Crusader Kingdom of Valencia* (Harvard, 1967), i. 178.

137. Huici, *Colección diplomática*, i. 238, doc. 139; 356, doc. 246; *BSCC*, ix (1928), 86–7.

138. Delaville, *Cartulaire*, i. 141–3, doc. 181; *BSCC*, xxiii (1947), 279–80; xxviii (1952), 297. For the history of Oropesa up to 1270, see F. Sevillano Colom, 'Bosquejo histórico de Oropesa', *BSCC*, xxvii (1951), 77–82, although he confuses the Temple and Santiago when discussing the events of 1270. At the end of the thirteenth century, when Oropesa was held by Berenguer Dalmau, the Temple negotiated for its purchase, but the outcome of these negotiations is not recorded: ACA, CRD Templarios, no. 425. Although according to R. de María, 'Xivert y Oropesa', *BSCC*, xiv (1933), 180, the king in 1298 granted full jurisdiction to the Temple in both Chivert and Oropesa, there is in fact no reference to the latter in the charter of donation: AHN, Montesa, R. 169.

139. Burns, op. cit. i. 192, states that the king gave the Templars compensation for Oropesa in 1249; but, as he earlier points out correctly (ibid. i. 186), the grant in question was to the Hospitallers, not to the Templars; cf. *BSCC*, xxiii (1947), 280–2.

140. Huici, *Colección diplomática*, ii. 309, doc. 925; J. Torres Fontes, *La reconquista de Murcia en 1266 por Jaime I de Aragón* (Murcia, 1967), pp. 212–13, doc. 8; *Chronicle of James I*, cap. 446, trans. Forster, ii. 568.

141. *Règle*, p. 68, art. 55.

142. AHN, cód. 691, fol. 169ᵛ, doc. 422.

143. AHN, cód. 1311.

144. AHN, cód. 691, fols. 168–82, doc. 422.

145. Ibid., fols. 196–8, doc. 442; see below, p. 376.

146. A considerable number of bequests of cash are included in wills in AGP, parch. Testamentos.

147. See below, p. 110.

148. See below, pp. 99–100.

149. See below, cap. III.

150. Albon, *Cartulaire*, p. 73, doc. 100.

151. It is not known exactly when the exchange took place, although various dates have been suggested—not altogether consistently—by García Larragueta, *Gran priorado*, i. 52, note 98, and i. 55, and M. L. Ledesma Rubio, *La encomienda de Zaragoza de la Orden de San Juan de Jerusalén en los siglos XII y XIII* (Zaragoza, 1967), p. 25, note 9; p. 76, note 93. According to a document drawn up in 1173 Garner of the Temple and Peter Raymond of the Hospital made the exchange, which was later confirmed by the provincial masters of the two Orders at the siege of Tortosa: AHN, San Juan, leg. 290, doc. 2 (Albon, *Cartulaire*, pp. 339–40, doc. 553, and Lacarra, 'Documentos', no. 249 [iii. 624–5] publish this document from a copy in AHN, cód. 691, fols. 29ᵛ–30, which bears the date 1149). The exchange had therefore taken place by 1148,

and there are several reasons for suggesting that it occurred soon after García Ramírez made his grant. The Templar and Hospitaller who carried it out were those who received Novillas from the Navarrese ruler, and while Garner is mentioned in one other document drawn up in 1135 (*ES*, xlix. 336, doc. 13), there is no evidence of him after this—although a considerable number of documents concerning property at Novillas survive from the 1140s—except in a fourteenth-century transcript of a confirmation of the *fuero* of Novillas (AHN, San Juan, leg. 346, doc. 1), and this reference can be discounted. In two earlier versions of this document he is not mentioned: AHN, cód. 691, fols. 18ᵛ–19ᵛ, doc. 39; fols. 194ᵛ–195ᵛ, doc. 441; the names of Garner and other Templars and Hospitallers mentioned in the later version but not in the other two are exactly those found in the document already mentioned, drawn up in 1173, and it seems that they were taken from this document. The donation of the church of Novillas in 1135 to the Temple alone and not to the two Orders suggests that the Temple may even then have had complete control over Novillas: Albon, *Cartulaire*, pp. 70–1, doc. 94 (where the date is given wrongly). Further, although the records of Templar acquisitions in Novillas are numerous, there are none relating to Mallén. An early exchange would, moreover, have been convenient for both parties.

152. AHN, cód. 691, fol. 9–9ᵛ, doc. 26; Albon, *Cartulaire*, pp. 107–8, doc. 154. Calvet confirmed his grant in 1151: AHN, cód. 691, fol. 12–12ᵛ, doc. 32.

153. Ibid., fols. 11ᵛ–12, doc. 31.

154. e.g. AHN, San Juan, leg. 556, doc. 4; see below, p. 386.

155. Albon, *Cartulaire*, p. 191, doc. 292; Lacarra, 'Documentos', no. 230 (iii. 609–10).

156. AHN, San Juan, leg. 532, doc. 7.

157. Ibid., leg. 38, doc. 17.

158. Ibid., leg. 38, doc. 26.

159. Ibid., leg. 138, doc. 2. At the end of the thirteenth century La Zaida, together with some neighbouring properties, was given to Artal of Alagón in exchange for La Ginebrosa, Camarón, and Buñol, which were situated further south: AHN, cód. 467, p. 287, doc. 313; p. 453, doc. 441. According to I. de Asso, *Historia de la economía política de Aragón* (Zaragoza, 1947 edn.), p. 203, Buñol is a *despoblado* in the term of La Ginebrosa.

160. Lacarra, 'Documentos', no. 10 (ii. 482).

161. Ibid., no. 177 (iii. 570–1).

162. Albon, *Cartulaire*, p. 219, doc. 336.

163. Ibid., p. 283, doc. 455; Lacarra, 'Documentos', no. 245 (iii. 621).

164. AHN, cód. 691, fols. 1ᵛ–2, doc. 4.

165. Albon, *Cartulaire*, p. 122, doc. 177; p. 155, doc. 229; pp. 242–3, doc. 384 (the date of this document is given wrongly as 1146); Lacarra, 'Documentos',

nos. 342 (v. 564–5), 350 (v. 571–2). The dates of these acquisitions are discussed by Lacarra. In his will Peter Taresa also left the nearby castles of Borja and Magallón to the Temple and Hospital jointly, but presumably because of a rival claim by Peter's mother Taresa, Raymond Berenguer IV in 1151 forced the Orders to surrender Borja and Magallón to her inr eturn for a confirmation of the grant of Ambel and Alberite and a ratification of the exchange involving Novillas and Mallén: *LFM*, i. 20–2, docs. 14, 15; *CDI*, iv. 179–82, docs. 65, 66.

166. Lacarra, 'Documentos', no. 398 (v. 614–15). The document is undated, but there is a reference in it to the Templar Lope of Sada, who is mentioned in other documents drawn up between 1157 and 1175; cf. AHN, San Juan, leg. 340, doc. 10.

167. Lacarra, 'Documentos', no. 360 (v. 580–1); ACA, reg. 310, fol. 44–44ᵛ; AHN, San Juan, leg. 323, doc. 14; Delaville, *Cartulaire*, i. 452–3, doc. 677; 520–1, doc. 835; cf. A. Ubieto Arteta, *El real monasterio de Sigena (1188–1300)* (Valencia, 1966), pp. 20–1.

168. C. Rocafort, *Geografia general de Catalunya: Provincia de Lleyda* (Barcelona, n.d.), p. 190; ACA, Varia 1, fol. 53.

169. AGP, Cartulary of Gardeny, fol. 1, doc. 1; fols. 65ᵛ–66, doc. 160; fol. 103–103ᵛ, doc. 249; fol. 108–108ᵛ, doc. 259; parch. Casas Antiguas, no. 275; parch. Barbará, no. 71.

170. AGP, parch. Selma, no. 21; parch. Testamentos, no. 3; parch. Barbará, no. 78; parch. Espluga de Francolí, no. 394; ACA, parch. Alfonso II, nos. 150, 175; parch. James I, nos. 713, 1032; Miret y Sans, *Les Cases*, p. 346; cf. J. Miret y Sans, 'Lo castell de Montbrió', *Butlletí del Centre Excursionista de Catalunya*, ix (1899), 41–5.

171. AHN, Montesa, P. 582; published from a transcript in the municipal archive of Culla in *BSCC*, xii (1931), 134–8; cf. A. Sánchez Gozalbo, 'Notas para la historia del Maestrazgo de Montesa. Castillo de Culla', ibid., xxv (1949), 304–25.

172. AHN, Montesa, P. 523; cf. A. Sánchez Gozalbo, 'Notas para la historia del Maestrazgo de Montesa. Castillo de Cuevas de Avinromá', *BSCC*, xiv (1933), 289–99. In the same year the king gained William of Moncada's rights in Tortosa through another exchange: E. Bayerri, *Historia de Tortosa y su comarca*, vii (Tortosa, 1956), 625–6.

173. ACA, parch. Alfonso II, no. 293; Peter II, no. 128; AHN, cód. 499, pp. 37–8, docs. 89, 90. According to R. del Arco, 'Huesca en el siglo XII', *II Congreso de historia de la Corona de Aragón*, i (Huesca, 1920), 335, Miquera formed part of the city of Huesca, but when it was given to the Temple it was said to be near Huesca.

174. ACA, parch. Alfonso II, no. 451; published by M. de Riquer, 'El testamento del trovador Guilhem de Berguedán', *Mélanges de linguistique et de littérature romanes à la mémoire d'Istvan Frank* (Annales Universitatis Saraviensis, vol. vi, 1957), pp. 581–3. This confirmed an earlier bequest made in 1183: AGP, parch. Testamentos, no. 31. J. Miret y Sans, 'Los vescomtes de Cerdanya,

Conflent y Bergadà', *Memorias de la Real Academia de Buenas Letras de Barcelona,*
viii (1901), 160, wrongly attributes the earlier will to the troubadour's father.

175. Puigreig is not mentioned in two documents in the ACA concerned with
this sale: parch. Peter II, nos. 67, 82; but it is named in another charter dealing
with the sale in the episcopal archive of Barcelona; this is published by J.
Miret y Sans, 'Enquesta sobre el trovador Vilarnau, amb algunes noves de Guillem
de Bergadà, Ramon de Miraval i Guillem de Mur', *Revue hispanique,* xlvi
(1919), 261–2.

176. Huici, *Colección diplomática,* i. 166–7, doc. 86. In northern Catalonia the
Templars also made several acquisitions along the river Noguera. The castles
of Terrassa and Castellón de Encús were given to the Order: ACA, Varia 1,
fols. 56ᵛ, 58; AHN, San Juan, leg. 138, doc. 3. The castle of Palau which
Raymond of Castellvell gave to the Templars was said in a fourteenth-century
inventory to be in Pallars, and may have been Palau de Noguera: ACA,
reg. 310, fol. 43–43ᵛ; Varia 1, fol. 53ᵛ. Admittedly Miret y Sans, *Les Cases,* p. 84,
states that the church of Palau de Noguera was given to the Hospitallers in 1161
by the count of Pallars on the condition that they resettled the place; he maintains that from that time Palau was a dependency of the Hospitaller house at
Susterris. Yet he provides no further twelfth- or thirteenth-century evidence;
and according to A. Coy y Cotonat, *Sort y comarca Noguera-Pallaresa* (Barcelona,
1906), p. 339, the tithes of Palau de Noguera were granted to the Temple in
1180. It therefore seems possible that the Hospital did not resettle Palau and
that it later passed into the hands of the Temple; the Hospitallers may have
gained it only after the dissolution of the Temple.

177. Culla was easily the most expensive purchase made by the Aragonese
Templars. Its cost was 500,000s., not 50,000s., as is stated by Burns, op. cit. i.
192.

178. Cf. E. de Hinojosa, *El régimen señorial y la cuestión agraria en Cataluña*
(Madrid, 1905), p. 41.

179. AHN, cód. 468, p. 15, doc. 15; pp. 19–20, docs. 25, 26; pp. 154–5, docs.
137–9; pp. 158–62, docs. 144–51; pp. 164–5, doc. 155.

180. AHN, cód. 499, pp. 42–3, doc. 101; p. 44, doc. 104; p. 52, doc. 123;
pp. 60–1, doc. 150; p. 66, doc. 163; pp. 69–70, doc. 169; p. 76, doc. 185;
p. 86, doc. 203; pp. 93–4, doc. 216.

181. RAH, 12–6–1/M–83, doc. 95. It was not only in the cities and large towns,
however, that acquisitions of houses and shops were made. In some places
houses built within the walls of castles had no lands attached to them, and some
of the acquisitions made by the Templars at Novillas, for example, consisted
of properties of this type: e.g. AHN, cód. 691, fol. 31ᵛ, docs. 86, 87; fol. 36,
doc. 100.

182. AHN, cód. 499, pp. 26–7, docs. 53, 56, 57; cód. 469, pp. 354–6, docs.
299–301, 303; Albon, *Cartulaire,* pp. 216–17, doc. 331; Lacarra, 'Documentos',
nos. 352, 353 (v. 573–4).

183. *Règle,* pp. 59–60, art. 66; Albon, *Cartulaire,* p. 377, Bullaire, doc. 5.

184. Cf. G. Constable, *Monastic Tithes from their Origins to the Twelfth Century* (Cambridge, 1964), p. 142.

185. Ibid., p. 170, note 1; p. 231.

186. Albon, *Cartulaire*, pp. 70–1, doc. 94. On Razazol and Boquiñeni, see above, p. 8, and Albon, *Cartulaire*, p. 307, doc. 495.

187. AHN, cód. 691, fols. 1ᵛ–2, doc. 4; San Juan, leg. 138, doc. 4; leg. 285, doc. 3; see below, p. 371.

188. AHN, San Juan, leg. 39, doc. 67.

189. Albon, *Cartulaire*, pp. 345–6, doc. 557. The subject churches were listed in 1192 as those of Crespano, Cofita, Ariéstolas, Castejón del Puente, Pomar, Estiche, Sta. Lecina, Alcolea, Castelflorite, La Roya, Cascallo (?El Coscollar), Sena, Sigena, Ontiñena, Torre de Corneil, Chalamera, Ballobar, Filcena, Calavera, Casas Novas, Balcarca, Ripoll, Alfantega, San Esteban de Litera, and the Almunia de San Juan: AHN, San Juan, leg. 324, doc. 1. By that time the Order had in fact alienated the churches of Sena and Sigena. In 1192 the bishop of Lérida also granted the Order the churches of Binafut, Morilla, Monesma, and St. John in Selgua.

190. AHN, San Juan, leg. 308, docs. 1, 2, 6; Montesa, P. 78; AGP, Cartulary of Tortosa, fol. 95ᵛ, doc. 296.

191. ACA, parch. Peter III, no. 96.

192. Miret y Sans, *Les Cases*, p. 169.

193. Albon, *Cartulaire*, p. 236, doc. 369.

194. AHN, Montesa, P. 568.

195. At the end of the thirteenth century the Temple claimed the patronage of the church of Moncada, but it was not able to produce evidence to support its claim: AHN, Montesa, P. 507.

196. Cf. R. I. Burns, 'A Mediaeval Income Tax: The Tithe in the Thirteenth-Century Kingdom of Valencia', *Speculum*, xli (1966), 438–52; idem, *The Crusader Kingdom of Valencia*, i. 155–68.

197. AHN, Montesa, P. 78.

198. AHN, Montesa, P. 265.

199. e.g. AHN, San Juan, leg. 354, doc. 2; AGP, Cartulary of Gardeny, fol. 45, doc. 98; fol. 84, doc. 210.

200. Revenues were occasionally granted specifically for use in the Holy Land: e.g. AHN, Montesa, P. 438, 451; but usually no condition of this sort was made.

201. In a number of charters of donation it was stated that a gift was being made 'because I fear to see the agonies of hell and wish to arrive at the joys of paradise': e.g. AHN, cód. 499, p. 43, doc. 103; p. 81, doc. 195; see also below, p. 374.

202. AHN, cód. 466, pp. 47–9, doc. 47.

203. Ibid.; AGP, Cartulary of Tortosa, fol. 76, doc. 249.

204. AHN, Montesa, P. 410.

205. AHN, Montesa, P. 207, 223, 417.

206. *Règle*, p. 325, art. 632.

207. AHN, Montesa, R. 134.

208. ACA, reg. 55, fol. 2ᵛ.

209. AHN, Montesa, R. 134. In 1304 a chantry priest in Valencia was assigned 12*l*.V. a year: Montesa, P. 610.

210. AGP, Cartulary of Gardeny, fol. 2, doc. 2; parch. Gardeny, nos. 20, 455, 456.

211. AHN, Montesa, P. 535; cód. 469, pp. 184–6, doc. 145.

212. Lees, *Records*, p. xl; T. W. Parker, *The Knights Templars in England* (Tucson, 1963), p. 16; F. L. Carsten, *The Origins of Prussia* (Oxford, 1954), p. 13.

213. Albon, *Cartulaire*, p. 73, doc. 100; pp. 107–8, doc. 154; AHN, cód. 691, fol. 10, doc. 27. The Temple later obtained a renunciation of claims from Raymond of Cortes's widow: ibid., fol. 10–10ᵛ, doc. 28.

214. See below, p. 345.

215. e.g. ACA, parch. Alfonso II, nos. 266, 489; Peter II, nos. 31, 52, 68, 256, 380; see below, p. 375.

216. AGP, parch. Testamentos, no. 58.

217. ACA, parch. Peter III, nos. 221, 290.

218. Some individuals placed only part of their property under the Temple's protection; they presumably held the rest of another lord: e.g. ACA, parch. Peter II, nos. 46, 68. But at other times men holding of a lord put all their property under the protection of the Order, which promised assistance against all except the lord: e.g. parch. Alfonso II, no. 718; Peter II, no. 236. It was generally accepted that an individual could have both a lord and a protector, provided that the lord's permission was obtained: cf. Hinojosa, op. cit., p. 90.

219. Property under the Temple's protection was often stated to be 'under crosses': e.g. ACA, parch. Peter II, nos. 52, 68, 236, 286; see below, p. 375. P. Ourliac, 'Les villages de la région toulousaine au xııᵉ siècle', *Annales*, iv (1949), 268–77, shows how in some villages established by the Hospital in Toulouse Hospitaller protection by itself was not felt adequate.

220. Hinojosa, op. cit., p. 89, note 3.

221. AHN, cód. 466, pp. 47–9, doc. 47.

222. AGP, Cartulary of Tortosa, fol. 74–74ᵛ, doc. 242.

223. AHN, Montesa, P. 542.

224. AHN, cód. 499, p. 68, doc. 167.

225. AGP, Cartulary of Gardeny, fol. 48–48$^v$, doc. 107.

226. AHN, San Juan, leg. 575, doc. 112.

227. AHN, cód. 499, pp. 7–8, doc. 11.

228. AGP, parch. Gardeny, no. 280; AHN, cód. 691, fols. 19$^v$–20, doc. 41; fols. 100$^v$–101, doc. 276.

229. AHN, San Juan, leg. 323, doc. 14.

230. AHN, cód. 469, p. 523, doc. 534.

231. ACA, parch. Alfonso II, no. 698.

232. ACA, reg. 310, fol. 44–44$^v$; AGP, parch. Comuns, no. 142.

233. See, for example, Albon, *Cartulaire*, pp. 92–3, doc. 132; cf. R. Boutruche, *Une Société provinciale en lutte contre le régime féodal: l'alleu en Bordelais et en Bazadais du XI$^e$ au XVIII$^e$ siècle* (Rodez, 1947), p. 41.

234. Albon, *Cartulaire*, pp. 67–8, doc. 90. The date is given as November A.D. 1135, and in the 27th year of Louis; Albon assigns the document to the year 1134.

235. For similar transactions in the south of France, see M. Castaing-Sicard, 'Donations toulousaines du x$^e$ au xiii$^e$ siècle', *Annales du Midi*, lxx (1958), 57–64.

236. Albon, *Cartulaire*, p. 122, doc. 177; Lacarra, 'Documentos', no. 342 (v. 564–5).

237. AGP, Cartulary of Gardeny, fols. 98$^v$–99, doc. 239; parch. Casas Antiguas, no. 78.

238. Although such gifts were frequently made to the Temple, it cannot be stated what proportion of donations was of this type, for it was often not stated in charters when a donation was to take effect.

239. e.g. ACA, parch. Alfonso II, nos. 87, 382, 459, 463.

240. The documents concerning these transactions are found mainly in AHN, cód. 499.

241. Most of the evidence concerning Zaragoza is contained in AHN, cód. 468.

242. Most of the evidence concerning Tortosa is found in AGP, Cartulary of Tortosa.

243. AHN, cód. 468, pp. 14–24, docs. 12–15, 17–22, 25–31.

244. Albon, *Cartulaire*, p. 368, doc. 597.

245. ACA, parch. James I, nos. 1502, 1503; Appendix, no. 33; parch. Alfonso III, nos. 289, 290, 293, 294; Appendix, no. 4; AGP, parch. Espluga de Francolí, no. 474. Miret y Sans, *Les Cases*, p. 317, assigns the purchase of Arnold of Malgrat's fee to the year 1286, but at that time the seller merely stated that he had no documents concerning the fee: parch. Espluga de Francolí, no. 318; the sale had taken place twenty years earlier. The Temple acquired rights over Hugh of Cervellón's fee in the first instance only for seven years.

246. AHN, cód. 469, pp. 354–5, doc. 300; cf. p. 349, doc. 292.

247. Ibid., p. 354, doc. 299; p. 356, doc. 303.

248. Ibid., pp. 522–3, doc. 533.

249. Ibid., p. 355, doc. 301.

250. AGP, parch. Espluga de Francolí, no. 284. This claim was derived from an agreement between Pons and Raymond of Cervera in 1181, by which the latter was to hold a third of the revenues of Espluga in fee of the former: parch. Espluga de Francolí, no. 288. This right descended to Raymond's son William of Guardia: ACA, parch. James I, no. 441; and Hugh claimed the right through his aunt Marquesa, the wife of William of Guardia, and their daughter Geralda: parch. James I, no. 1550; parch. Espluga de Francolí, no. 284.

251. AGP, parch. Comuns, no. 258; ACA, parch. James I, nos. 1527, 1550, 1938, 1941.

252. On the convent of Palau, see below, p. 91.

253. Barcelona: ACA, parch. Raymond Berenguer IV, no. 312; parch. Alfonso II, nos. 53, 723; parch. James I, nos. 11, 977, 1644; Varia I, fols. 1–1ᵛ, 4–5. Palau: Albon, *Cartulaire*, pp. 140–1, doc. 202; ACA, parch. Alfonso II, no. 198; parch. James I, nos. 56, 88, 299, 454, 456; Varia I, fols. 9ᵛ–10, 14ᵛ–15. Parets: Albon, *Cartulaire*, p. 368, doc. 597; ACA, parch. Alfonso II, nos. 202, 280; parch. James I, nos. 47, 227, 314, 2193. Sta. Perpetua: ACA, parch. Alfonso II, nos. 282, 392, 720.

254. ACA, parch. Raymond Berenguer IV, no. 144; parch. Peter II, no. 78.

255. ACA, Varia I, fol. 1–1ᵛ; see below, p. 369.

256. Ibid., fol. 1.

257. AHN, Montesa, P. 582; published from a different manuscript in *BSCC*, xii (1931), 134–8.

258. e.g. AHN, Montesa, P. 463.

259. AHN, cód. 691, fol. 53, doc. 156.

260. e.g. AHN, San Juan, leg. 285, doc. 4; cód. 470, pp. 93–4, doc. 112.

261. AHN, San Juan, leg. 354, doc. 2; AGP, Cartulary of Tortosa, fol. 43, doc. 135.

262. A. Durán Gudiol, *Colección diplomática de la catedral de Huesca*, i (Zaragoza, 1965), 316, doc. 318; ACA, parch. Peter III, no. 96; C. Rocafort, *Geografía general de Catalunya: Provincia de Lleyda* (Barcelona, n.d.), p. 190. On James of Sarroca, see R. del Arco, 'El obispo Don Jaime Sarroca, consejero y gran privado del Rey Don Jaime el Conquistador', *BRABLB*, ix (1917–20), 65–91, 140–67; del Arco did not know, however, of the existence of the bishop's will and placed his death in December 1288 or January 1289.

263. T. Ruiz Jusué, 'Las cartas de hermandad en España', *AHDE*, xv (1944), 417–18; D. W. Lomax, *La Orden de Santiago* (Madrid, 1965), pp. 27–8.

264. AHN, cód. 470, pp. 5–6, doc. 4; pp. 65–8, docs. 75, 77, 78, 80; see below, p. 374.

265. In 1147 Peter Romeu, with his sons García, Peter, Blasco, and Simon, gave his rights at Añesa to the Temple: Albon, *Cartulaire*, p. 283, doc. 455; Lacarra, 'Documentos', no. 245 (iii. 621). These four sons became *confratres* of the Order: AHN, cód. 1311, sides K, R; and the Temple made exchanges of property at Pradilla with Blasco Romeu in 1173 and with García Romeu, who was lord of Pradilla, in 1271: AHN, cód. 470, pp. 81–2, doc. 99; pp. 85–6, doc. 103.

266. On these lords and their activities, see P. Boissonnade, *Du nouveau sur la Chanson de Roland* (Paris, 1923), pp. 38–69; M. Defourneaux, *Les Français en Espagne aux XIe et XIIe siècles* (Paris, 1949), caps. 3, 4; J. M. Lacarra, 'La conquista de Zaragoza por Alfonso I', *Al-Andalus*, xii (1947), 78–83; idem, 'Gastón de Bearn y Zaragoza', *Pirineos*, viii (1952), 127–34; L. H. Nelson, 'Rotrou of Perche and the Aragonese Reconquest', *Traditio*, xxvi (1970), 113–33.

267. Albon, *Cartulaire*, p. 183, doc. 280; Lacarra, 'Documentos', no. 229 (iii. 609).

268. Zurita, *Anales*, i. 44.

269. Albon, *Cartulaire*, p. 220, doc. 338; Lacarra, 'Documentos', no. 354 (v. 574–5); idem, 'Gastón de Bearn', pp. 133–4; Zurita, *Anales*, i. 44.

270. Albon, *Cartulaire*, p. 309, doc. 501; Lacarra, 'Documentos', no. 366 (v. 585–6); A. du Bourg, *Histoire du grand-prieuré de Toulouse* (Toulouse, 1883), Appendix, pp. xliii–xliv, doc. 62.

271. J. M. Lacarra, 'La repoblación de Zaragoza por Alfonso I el Batallador', *Estudios de historia social de España*, i (1949), 214–17.

272. In 1170 Galcerán of Pinós granted the Temple rights in the mountains of Encija and Palomera: AGP, parch. Cervera, no. 123; Cartulary of Gardeny, fols. 106–7, doc. 256. In 1211 Galcerán's son, Raymond Galcerán, gave the Order his rights over an inhabitant of Bergadán: parch. Cervera, no. 375. And in 1279 Galcerán of Pinós confirmed all the grants and sales made by his predecessors to the Temple, mentioning in particular two manses: parch. Cervera, no. 229.

In 1133 Bernard Amat, viscount of Cardona, made a grant of salt to the Temple: Albon, *Cartulaire*, p. 50, doc. 66. In 1221 the viscount William for 50s. surrendered to the Order mills in Puigreig which had been given to the Templars by the king and which William held in pledge: parch. Cervera, no. 227. In the next year William granted the Order a manse: parch. Cervera, no. 451; ACA, parch. James I, no. 193; and he also chose burial in the Temple, although the Order obtained the body only after a dispute with the abbot of Cardona: parch. Cervera, no. 517.

273. ACA, parch. Alfonso II, no. 333; AGP, parch. Cervera, nos. 232, 474.

274. J. Miret y Sans, *Investigación histórica sobre el vizcondado de Castellbó* (Barcelona, 1900), pp. 368–71; Delaville, *Cartulaire*, iv. 243–4, doc. 98*bis*.

Calcina was near Puigcercús: C. Rocafort, *Geografia general de Catalunya: Provincia de Lleyda* (Barcelona, n.d.), p. 809, note 288.

275. AGP, Cartulary of Gardeny, fol. 61–61ᵛ, doc. 150.

276. Ibid., fol. 56ᵛ, doc. 133. The date of this document could be read as 10 Kalends of October 1150 or the Kalends of October 1160. Miret y Sans, *Les Cases*, p. 73, accepts the latter; but as the Templar provincial master Peter of Rovira is mentioned in the document, it could not have been drawn up later than 1158.

277. AGP, Cartulary of Gardeny, fol. 15, doc. 15.

278. Ibid., fol. 103–103ᵛ, doc. 249; fol. 108–108ᵛ, doc. 259; AGP, parch. Casas Antiguas, nos. 263, 275. In 1194 the Hospitallers received a grant of Pedrís from the count of Urgel: Delaville, *Cartulaire*, i. 609, doc. 960. This must mean either that the donation to the Temple was not carried out or that the Hospitallers gained merely the other half of Pedrís.

279. AGP, Cartulary of Gardeny, fol. 21–21ᵛ, doc. 27; fol. 26, doc. 40.

280. D. Monfar y Sors, *Historia de los condes de Urgel*, in *CDI*, ix. 418–21; Delaville, *Cartulaire*, i. 351, doc. 515.

281. ACA, reg. 310, fol. 82–82ᵛ.

282. Monfar y Sors, op. cit., in *CDI*, ix. 433–7; Delaville, *Cartulaire*, ii. 91, doc. 1308; *El Cartulario de Tavernoles*, ed. J. Soler García (Castellón de la Plana, 1961), pp. 190–5, doc. 112.

283. Monfar y Sors, op. cit., in *CDI*, ix. 446.

284. AGP, Cartulary of Gardeny, fols. 103ᵛ–104, doc. 250; fols. 107ᵛ–108, doc. 258; fols. 108ᵛ–109, doc. 260. The Temple appears to have been slow in making this payment, for in 1190—in return for a confirmation of Alchabez— it agreed not only to pay the count 440s.B., but also gave him 200maz. and a horse: ACA, reg. 310, fol. 82. Alchabez should possibly be identified with Castellblanch de Litera: cf. Cartulary of Gardeny, fols. 109ᵛ–110, docs. 261, 262.

285. ACA, parch. Peter II, no. 119; AGP, parch. Gardeny, no. 451. Miret y Sans, *Investigación histórica*, pp. 171–2, refers to another dispute between the Order and the count in 1194.

286. ACA, reg. 310, fol. 83. The Order apparently gained altogether rents in Lérida worth 300s.J. annually from the count: ibid., fols. 82ᵛ–83.

287. J. Miret y Sans, 'Notes per la biografia del trovador Guerau de Cabrera', *Estudis universitaris catalans*, iv (1910), 323. The Order's rights over the castle of Mediona were later granted away in exchange for rights at San Iscle de Bages: Miret y Sans, *Investigación histórica*, p. 116, note 1.

288. Monfar y Sors, op. cit., in *CDI*, ix. 405–14, 421, 434, 445, 506.

289. AGP, Cartulary of Gardeny, fols. 62ᵛ–63, doc. 153; fols. 64ᵛ–65, docs. 157, 158; fol. 68, doc. 170.

290. *Les Cases*, p. 104.

291. AGP, Cartulary of Gardeny, fol. 64ᵛ, doc. 157.

292. Ibid., fols. 62ᵛ–63, doc. 153.

293. Ibid., fol. 64–64ᵛ, doc. 156.

294. Ibid., fol. 62–62ᵛ, doc. 152.

295. AGP, parch. Testamentos, no. 55; cf. ACA, parch. James I, no. 111.

296. AGP, Cartulary of Gardeny, fol. 99, doc. 240; cf. J. Serra y Vilaró, 'Relacions entre los senyors y la ciutat de Solsona al segle XIII', *Congreso de historia de la Corona de Aragón*, i (Barcelona, 1909), 70.

297. AGP, Cartulary of Gardeny, fol. 1, doc. 1; parch. Gardeny, no. 1540; parch. Testamentos, no. 104; cf. parch. Gardeny, no. 1494.

298. ACA, parch. James I, no. 111.

299. AGP, parch. Espluga de Francolí, no. 526. The district in which Espluga lay had been granted as waste land by the count of Barcelona to Pons Hugh of Cervera in 1079/80. On the early history of Espluga de Francolí, see A. Altisent, 'Un poble de la Catalunya Nova els segles XI i XII. L'Espluga de Francolí de 1079 a 1200', *Anuario de estudios medievales*, iii (1966), 131–213.

300. ACA, parch. James I, no. 432.

301. The will does not survive, but the bequest is mentioned in a document drawn up in 1278: AGP, parch. Espluga de Francolí, no. 394. On the date of Simon's death and the history of the family in general, see J. Miret y Sans, *Los vescomtes de Bas en la illa de Sardenya* (Barcelona, 1901).

302. AGP, parch. Espluga de Francolí, no. 390; Miret y Sans, *Les Cases*, pp. 313–14; cf. ACA, parch. James I, no. 1433. In 1260 the pension was reduced to 1,500s.B.: parch. Espluga de Francolí, no. 111; cf. no. 352. There was a further dispute about the pension in 1275: parch. James I, nos. 2221, 2232. In 1272 Sybilla, the daughter of Geralda and wife of the count of Ampurias, advanced a claim to Espluga: parch. James I, nos. 2109, 2111, 2112.

303. AGP, Cartulary of Gardeny, fol. 15ᵛ, doc. 17; fol. 50, doc. 113; fol. 66ᵛ, doc. 162; fols. 66ᵛ–67, doc. 164; fol. 68, doc. 169; fols. 76–7, doc. 193; fol. 90–90ᵛ, doc. 223; fols. 105ᵛ–106, doc. 255; parch. Gardeny, nos. 530, 589, 1743, 1744; parch. Testamentos, no. 330.

304. *LFM*, i. 174–5, doc. 165.

305. Ibid., pp. 175–6, doc. 166.

306. AGP, Cartulary of Gardeny, fol. 15–15ᵛ, doc. 16; fols. 20ᵛ–21, doc. 26; fol. 54–54ᵛ, doc. 127; fols. 72ᵛ–73, doc. 184; fols. 84–5, docs. 210, 211; fols. 93ᵛ–94ᵛ, docs. 229–31; fol. 97–97ᵛ, doc. 236; fol. 98–98ᵛ, doc. 238; parch. Gardeny, nos. 456, 525, 581, 1296; parch. Corbins, no. 95; parch. Casas Antiguas, nos. 2, 4, 38, 71, 83; parch. Espluga Calva, nos. 57, 60.

307. AHN, San Juan, leg. 354, doc. 6.

308. ACA, parch. Peter II, no. 277.

309. ACA, Varia 2, fols. 72ᵛ–74; AGP, Cartulary of Tortosa, fol. 94ᵛ, doc. 295.

310. ACA, reg. 310, fol. 36ᵛ; AGP, Cartulary of Gardeny, fols. 2–3, docs. 3, 4; Cartulary of Tortosa, fol. 90, doc. 284.

311. AHN, cód. 499.

312. AHN, cód. 470.

313. AGP, Cartulary of Tortosa.

314. AHN, Montesa, P. 533, 540.

315. AHN, cód. 468.

316. These calculations take into account the money spent in settling disputed claims to land and in redeeming from pledge land granted to the Order.

317. AHN, códs. 467–9.

318. AHN, cód. 499, pp. 29–31, docs. 64–72; pp. 89–90, doc. 209; published by M. D. Cabré, 'Noticias y documentos del Altoaragón. La Violada (Almudévar)', *Argensola*, x (1959), 149–55, docs. 2–11.

319. AHN, cód. 689. This cartulary originally covered the period up to 1272; a number of documents drawn up between 1274 and 1283 were inserted later.

320. AHN, cód. 466.

321. AGP, parch. Barbará, no. 78; parch. Espluga de Francolí, nos. 210, 474, 611; ACA, parch. James I, nos. 1502, 1938, 2179; Appendix, no. 33; parch. Alfonso III, Appendix, no. 4; parch. James II, nos. 623, 1028; reg. 291, fol. 262ᵛ.

322. AHN, Montesa, P. 582; published in *BSCC*, xii (1931), 134–8.

323. AHN, Montesa, P. 585.

324. ACA, CRD Templarios, no. 580; cf. AHN, Montesa, P. 611, 619.

325. ACA, reg. 291, fol. 226; cf. fols. 241–241ᵛ.

326. IV. xix. 5–8, and VI. iv. 37, 47, in *Volumen Fororum et Actuum Curiae* (Valencia, 1548), fols. 110, 150ᵛ, 151ᵛ; *Fori Antiqui Valentiae*, lxxii. 5–7, 14, and lxxxvi. 27, 31, ed. M. Dualde Serrano (Madrid, Valencia, 1967), pp. 114–15, 117, 165, 166.

327. AHN, Montesa, P. 224.

328. The right to alienate to the Church in Aragon and Catalonia was confirmed in 1235: *Cortes de Aragón, Valencia y Cataluña*, i (Madrid, 1896), 126. There is, however, a reference to a mortmain decree concerning Lérida in 1276: AGP, parch. Gardeny, no. 473.

329. Cf. G. de Valous, *Le Temporel et la situation financière des établissements de l'Ordre de Cluny du XIIᵉ au XIVᵉ siècle* (Vienne, 1935), p. 16.

330. J. Pérez de Urbel, *Los monjes españoles en la edad media*, ii (Madrid, 1934),

528; E. de Hinojosa, *El régimen señorial y la cuestión agraria en Cataluña* (Madrid, 1905), p. 57.

331. On a similar decline in donations to the Hospitallers, see M. L. Ledesma Rubio, *La encomienda de Zaragoza de la Orden de San Juan de Jerusalén en los siglos XII y XIII* (Zaragoza, 1967), p. 110, and A. Ubieto Arteta, *El real monasterio de Sigena (1188–1300)* (Valencia, 1966), pp. 69, 77.

332. A. S. Atiya, *The Crusade in the Later Middle Ages* (London, 1938), part 2; P. A. Throop, *Criticism of the Crusade* (Amsterdam, 1940), *passim*.

333. e.g. at a council at Norwich in 1291 it was argued that it should be ascertained how many knights could be maintained from the revenues of the Temple and the Hospital and that this number should be kept in the East: Bartholomew Cotton, *Historia Anglicana*, ed. H. R. Luard (London, 1859), pp. 208–9.

334. See below, cap. IX.

335. ACA, parch. James II, no. 2360.

336. See below, p. 319.

337. ACA, parch. James I, no. 1391.

338. ACA, parch. Peter III, no. 26.

339. Miret y Sans, *Les Cases*, pp. 314–15; cf. ACA, parch. James I, no. 1550. On the alienation of property by the Templars elsewhere in Europe to pay off debts, see E. Berger, *Les Registres d'Innocent IV*, iii (Paris, 1897), 159, doc. 6237.

340. This is apparent from the surviving buildings at Gardeny, one of the most important convents in the *Corona de Aragón*: see J. Puig i Cadafalch, *L'arquitectura romànica a Catalunya*, iii (Barcelona, 1918), 424–5, 578; E. Lambert, *L'Architecture des Templiers* (Paris, 1955), p. 93. Inventories of Templar goods show, on the other hand, that the Order's chapels were rich in ornaments, but it is not known how these came into the Templars' possession: see J. Rubió, R. d'Alós, and F. Martorell, 'Inventaris inèdits de l'Ordre del Temple a Catalunya', *Anuari de l'Institut d'Estudis Catalans*, i (1907), 391–407.

341. See below, caps. IV, VIII.

# III

## Expansion: (ii) The Creation of Provinces and the Foundation of Convents

THE development of Templar organization during the Order's early years in north-eastern Spain cannot be examined closely, for officials were not at first given precise titles; but it appears that in the beginning the Order merely appointed a number of Templars as bailiffs to collect revenues and administer the acquisitions made in a particular district. Those who are first mentioned in the sources had authority over fairly large areas, whose extent seems to have been determined by political divisions. Between 1128 and 1136 Hugh of Rigaud had charge of Templar possessions both in Catalonia and in the districts to the north of the Pyrenees, where the counts of Barcelona had political interests;[1] but neither he nor his immediate successor, Arnold of Bedocio, is mentioned in any Templar documents drawn up in Aragon or Navarre, both of which at the time of the Templars' arrival in Spain were ruled by the Aragonese house.[2] These first officials came in time to have under their command subordinate bailiffs, who were set in charge of smaller areas. Amongst such lesser officials was the Templar Raymond Gaucebert, who was frequently named in Templar documents concerning the districts of Barcelona and Vich between 1135 and 1142 and who was often given the title of 'bailiff'.[3]

As the Temple further expanded, however, a more elaborate and permanent form of organization was evolved. The early large administrative areas developed into provinces of the Order, ruled over by provincial masters, and at a more local level the basic unit of organization became the convent, a word which thirteenth- and early fourteenth-century evidence shows to have been used by the Templars to describe a community whose head was directly subject to the provincial master and was summoned to provincial chapters, and whose members usually included a chamberlain and chaplain.[4]

The institution of the province, the master of which acted as the intermediary between the headquarters of the Order and individual convents, was unknown in religious orders before the twelfth century. The Hospitallers began to evolve this form of organization in the early part of that century,[5] and it was developed both by them and by the Templars as presumably the best means by which men and resources scattered through most of western Christendom could be mobilized for use in the East, besides providing an effective instrument for regulating other relationships between the centre and individual houses, as is clear from its later adoption by a number of other religious orders.[6] The alternative system of the filiation of convents, which was being developed by some orders of monks and canons in the twelfth century, might have produced regional groupings, but it would have involved too many stages in the transmission of supplies to the East, while distance and slowness of communications made direct links between the headquarters and individual convents impracticable.

The convent became the accepted basis of local Templar organization everywhere. Convents were established not only where the Templars were engaged in fighting the infidel: in Spain they were set up in areas away from the Moorish frontier, just as they were founded throughout western Europe. To what extent this policy was the result of a conscious decision is not known, but it had advantages over the alternative of concentrating the members of the Order in the districts where the struggle against the infidel was being waged and entrusting the administration of estates to Templar or lay bailiffs. Although it was wasteful of Templar manpower—as was frequently pointed out towards the end of the thirteenth century[7]—the presence of Templar communities throughout western Christendom no doubt helped to stimulate recruitment and bring patronage to the Order;[8] and the dangers were avoided which would have resulted either from allowing Templar administrators to live permanently in isolation from other members of the Order or from committing the administration of distant estates entirely to laymen, who would have had personal and family interests.

The earliest reference to the province of 'Provence and certain

Mas-Deu

Castellón de
Ampurias

Huesca

Añesa

Aiguaviva

Novillas
Boquiñeni

Ambel

*R. Cinca*

Monzón

*R. Segre*

Puigreig

*R. Llobregat*

Ricla

Zaragoza

Corbins
Gardeny

Barbens

Grañena

Palau

Calatayud

Pina

Remolins?

Barbará

Selma

Barcelona

La Zaida

*R. Ebro*

Ribarroja

Juncosa

Ascó

Miravet

Castellote

Horta

Alfambra

Tortosa

Cantavieja

Villel

Chivert

Peñíscola

Burriana

Mallorca

Valencia

*R. Jalón*

0          50          100

MILES

parts of Spain', which evolved out of the early administrative unit straddling the Pyrenees, occurs in 1143, when Peter of Rovira was described as 'master of Provence and a certain part of Spain'.[9] The province as it existed in the years following that date was not, however, exactly the same in extent as the earlier division, for it also included the kingdoms of Aragon and Navarre. The linking of these districts with Catalonia and Provence was presumably occasioned by the political union of Aragon and Catalonia, just as later in the twelfth century the cession of certain parts of Navarre to Castile appears to have led to the transference of Templar rights in these districts to the Castilian province.[10]

The Spanish part of the province expanded as the Christian frontiers advanced. It came to include the more southerly parts of Aragon and Catalonia in the later twelfth century and Mallorca and Valencia in the first half of the thirteenth. It was by then so large that it was decided to divide it into two provinces, by separating the Spanish possessions from those in Provence. Stephen of Belmonte—last mentioned as provincial master in November 1239[11]—was still known as 'master of Provence and certain parts of Spain'; but his successor in the Spanish part of the old province, Raymond of Serra, who was in office by May 1240,[12] was given the title 'master in Aragon and Catalonia'. His authority was in fact more extensive and covered Roussillon, Navarre, Mallorca, and Valencia as well, but the change in title does mark the break-up of the former province. After 1240 the lands of the Temple in the *Corona de Aragón* and Navarre formed one province;[13] those in Provence constituted another. After the completion of the conquest of Valencia the only change in the extent of the Aragonese province was the temporary inclusion of certain possessions in Murcia, after the latter had been acquired by James II; but when agreement about boundaries had been reached between Aragon and Castile these reverted to the Castilian Templars.[14]

In the later part of the thirteenth century the Aragonese provincial master had over thirty convents subject to him in the *Corona de Aragón*, besides two in Navarre.[15] In *Cataluña Vieja* convents were founded at Palau, Aiguaviva, Castellón de Ampurias, and Puigreig, and further north, in Roussillon, one was established at Mas-Deu. To the west of the Llobregat, the castles of Barbará and Grañena, which had been among the Order's earliest acquisitions, became the sites of convents, as did the nearby

places of Juncosa and Selma. In the valley of the Segre there were
Templar convents at Gardeny, Corbins, and Barbens, and on the
Cinca—a tributary of the Segre—at Monzón. In Aragon along
the Ebro valley convents were founded at Novillas, Boquiñeni,
Ambel, Zaragoza, Pina, and La Zaida, and along tributaries of the
Ebro at Ricla, Añesa, and apparently briefly at Luna as well,
while another was set up at Huesca, to the east of Luna. In southern
Aragon there were four convents in the thirteenth century—at
Alfambra, Cantavieja, Castellote, and Villel—and five were
established along the lower reaches of the Ebro—at Miravet,
Tortosa, Horta, Ascó, and Ribarroja. In the kingdom of Valencia
further south, Chivert, Burriana, and the city of Valencia became
sites of convents, and lastly one was established on the island of
Mallorca.

It is not easy to trace the emergence of these convents. One
difficulty arises from the lack of precision in the use of terms. The
word most commonly employed to describe a Templar establishment was 'house' (*domus, casa*). In some cases a convent was being
referred to, but the term was also applied to minor Templar
establishments, which were dependent on a convent and not on
the provincial master. The word in itself therefore does not give
any indication of the nature of a Templar foundation. Similarly,
the heads of convents were usually called 'commanders' or 'preceptors', but these were titles which were given to almost any
Templars who were in positions of authority. Secondly, while
only convents were directly subject to the provincial master,[16]
the other characteristics of convents were not always peculiar to
them alone. Chaplains and chamberlains are very occasionally
encountered in places where convents were not established, and
the heads of convents were not the only Templars who were
present at provincial chapters.[17] And lastly, the early period of
Templar expansion is, of course, less well documented than later
periods. All that can be done therefore in tracing the development
of convents is to indicate when the term 'convent' came to be
used in different places, or when the sources suggest a development in organization in places where convents are known to have
been founded.

Neither the term 'convent' nor the features characteristic of
convents are mentioned in the sources referring to the period up
to 1143, but by that date Templar communities were apparently

being established at Palau and Novillas and possibly at Grañena, as well as at Mas-Deu in Roussillon, which was only later incorporated into the *Corona de Aragón*.[18] In 1140 a sale of land was made to 'Peter master of Rovira of the same place of Palau', to Raymond Gaucebert, Raymond Arnold, and to a chaplain Pons.[19] The wording is confused: Peter of Rovira appears to be called master of Palau, although at that time he probably had authority on both sides of the Pyrenees. But the apparent reference to a master of Palau, together with the list of other Templars, including a chaplain, suggests that the origins of the convent of Palau should be traced back as far as 1140, even though the first clear indication of a Templar community there does not occur until 1151.[20] The grant of Alberite in ?1139 was similarly made to Rigald 'master in Novillas', who seems by his title to have been not merely an official responsible for certain estates, but rather the head of a community;[21] in the confirmation of this grant in ?1141 Rigald was said to be acting 'with the will of our other brothers', and this wording again suggests the existence of a Templar community at Novillas;[22] and although the term 'convent' is not applied to Novillas until 1147,[23] there is a reference to the brothers of Novillas in a document drawn up in 1143/5,[24] while there was a chaplain there in 1146.[25] The evidence concerning Grañena is more tenuous. It is merely that according to the historian of the see of Vich, who quotes a document which no longer survives, the bishop of Vich in 1136 gave permission for a certain chapel in the castle of Grañena to be served by a Templar chaplain.[26] But no commander of Grañena is known before 1181; a Templar house there is not mentioned until 1190; and the first evidence indicating that a separate convent had been founded does not occur until the beginning of the thirteenth century.[27]

From 1143 onwards the process of establishing convents was inevitably influenced by the agreement made in that year between the Templars and the count of Barcelona. Most of the places granted by the Aragonese rulers to the Temple in return for its participation in the *reconquista* lay near the Moorish frontier when they came into the Order's possession, and as long as they remained in the frontier region they needed to be protected against Moorish attacks. The Templars therefore quickly began to establish communities in the most important of them in order not only to administer them but also to defend them against the infidel.

Although at Monzón there is no reference to a Templar community until 1153, ten years after the castle had been granted to the Order,[28] the house there was by then already sufficiently established to be looked upon as the centre of the Order in the *Corona de Aragón*: thus in 1153 it was said that the castle of Miravet had been granted to the 'brothers of Monzón'.[29] That this statement reflects Monzón's place in Templar organization at that time and was not merely occasioned by the circumstances of Raymond Berenguer's donation of the castle in 1143 is made clear by the wording of another document recording the grant of Alcanadre to the Order in 1155, for in this it is stated that the Templars who received the gift were acting on the advice of the brothers of Novillas, who were to administer the new acquisition, and of those of Monzón, implying that Monzón was considered to be the headquarters of the Aragonese Templars.[30]

Of the other castles granted in 1143, Corbins may quickly after its recapture have become the site of a convent, for in the dating clause of one document the year 1148 is referred to as the year in which 'García Ortiz served God in Corbins with those brothers',[31] and in the following year a bequest was made to the *caballeria* of Corbins.[32] But if there was then a convent there, it was apparently transferred to Gardeny after the conquest of Lérida, for in the second half of the twelfth century the commander of Gardeny conducted transactions involving property at Corbins, and at the end of the century some documents concerning rights at Corbins were being kept at Gardeny.[33] The word 'convent' is first used of Gardeny in the surviving sources in the year 1169;[34] but as early as 1151 Peter of Cartellá, who was later the head of the convent of Gardeny, was called 'master in those parts';[35] and in 1156 references occur to the master and brothers of the house of Gardeny and to a Templar chapel there.[36]

The convents founded along the lower Ebro at Tortosa and Miravet seem similarly to have been established soon after the conquest of this district by Raymond Berenguer IV in the mid twelfth century, although there is no specific mention of a convent at Tortosa until 1174 and at Miravet until almost the end of the century.[37] In 1156 there is a reference to Aymeric of Torreies as 'master of the brothers of the Temple in Tortosa';[38] and nine

years later there seems also to have been a Templar community
at Miravet, for in 1165 William Berard was master or commander
of Miravet and Tortosa, with Sancho of Vergea as his deputy in
Tortosa.³⁹ By then the centre of Templar authority along the
lower Ebro had apparently been transferred to Miravet, and it is
possible that this development had already taken place five years
earlier, for in 1160, when Aymeric of Torreies was still master
of Tortosa, Iñigo Sánchez was the official directly in charge of the
Templar house there.⁴⁰ Miravet is admittedly not included in
Aymeric's titles, but as all the surviving documents in which he
is named are concerned with lands in Tortosa, the omission is not
necessarily significant. The apparent transference of the seat of
Templar administration from Tortosa to Miravet, which could
have been occasioned by the strategic importance of the castle
and by the fact that the Templars enjoyed full lordship there and
not in Tortosa, suggests that the Templar community at Tortosa
may even have been established before Miravet was acquired in
1153, for otherwise Templar power along the lower Ebro would
probably from the beginning have been centred at Miravet. But
if in 1165 the master of Miravet and Tortosa based his authority
at Miravet, this situation may not have been maintained, for no
subordinate official at Tortosa is mentioned between 1165 and
1174, even though a considerable number of documents survives
from this period. The master of Miravet and Tortosa may for a
time have exercised direct control over both communities. From
1174 onwards, however, there was again an official at Tortosa,
and references soon begin to occur to a commander of Miravet
as well.⁴¹ Nevertheless the post of master or commander of
Miravet and Tortosa was retained, and the holder of the office
was apparently still considered as the head of the two convents:
most of the documents concerning Templar rights in Miravet
and Tortosa continued to be issued in his name, and his depu-
ties in the two convents were on occasion called merely 'sub-
preceptor'.⁴² And his authority was increased through the
acquisition of Horta, Ascó, and Ribarroja from Alfonso II. This
growth of power was reflected in a change of title: in 1192 he began
to be referred to as 'commander of Miravet, Tortosa and La Ribera', and later this title was contracted to just 'commander of La
Ribera'.⁴³ The actual administration of the newly acquired lordships at Horta and Ascó was soon delegated to subordinate

Templar officials. A commander had been set up at Ascó as
early as 1181, when the Order held it in pledge from the king,[44]
and this post was made permanent after Alfonso's grant in the
following year. At Horta, a commander was named in a document which must be dated before the end of July 1193;[45] the post
may, however, not have existed before 1192, for in the *carta de
población* granted to settlers at Horta at the beginning of that
year no commander is mentioned.[46] These subordinate commanders at Ascó and Horta in time became heads of convents,
although there is little evidence to suggest when this development occurred. The establishment of a convent at Ascó was no
doubt delayed by the temporary loss of lordship by the Templars
there in the reign of Peter II. But the convents at Horta and
Ascó had probably been established by 1236, after which date
the office of commander of La Ribera ceased to exist.[47] The
development of Templar administration at Ribarroja, the other
place granted to the Order by Alfonso II in 1182, appears to have
been much slower. In 1212 Templar rights there were farmed out
for life;[48] no commander of Ribarroja is known until the later
part of the thirteenth century; and for a time it formed part of
the commandery of Ascó.[49] But in 1277 and 1307 the Templar
community at Ribarroja was being assessed separately for payments to the provincial master:[50] a convent had thus by then
been established there.

Templar organization in the lands acquired from the Order of
Mountjoy in southern Aragon was fluid for several years after
1196. At first Templars—often commanders of convents further
north—were placed in charge of groups of castles and lordships.
In 1196 William of Peralta was commander of Novillas, Alfambra, Villel, and Teruel, and five years later he was commander
of Monzón, Castellote, Cantavieja, and Villarluengo. Yet the
Temple had been given these lands in order that they should be
properly defended and it was therefore under an obligation to
establish Templar communities as quickly as possible. It seems to
have been doing so by the turn of the century. The linking of
important castles in this region under the authority of one Templar
did not continue after 1201, except in the case of Alfambra and
Villel, which were both subject to the same official until 1207;
and already before 1201 subordinate commanders, set in charge of
one castle, were being appointed at Cantavieja, Castellote, Al-

fambra, and Villel. The disappearance at Cantavieja and Castellote of officials with authority in more than one place is probably an indication that convents were by then being established in these castles. A chamberlain and five other brothers at Castellote are mentioned in a document belonging to the year 1201,[51] and at least five brothers besides the commander were living there in 1205.[52] On the other hand, there is no definite information about Templar organization at Cantavieja as early as 1201.[53] A convent at Villel, however, is mentioned as early as 1198,[54] and the continued link with Alfambra presumably means that a convent was not founded at the latter place, which was further from the frontier, until about 1207. But this cannot be proved, since there are few sources for the history of Alfambra. The commander of Alfambra was present at a provincial chapter in 1212,[55] but no specific reference to a convent there occurs before about 1230.[56]

By October of the latter year, only a few months after the conquest of Mallorca, the Templars had set up a convent on that island,[57] and before the end of the decade they had begun to found convents in the kingdom of Valencia. At the time of the treaty with the Moors of Chivert in 1234 there was already a Templar commander of Burriana, and he was apparently the head of a convent by 1239, when a chamberlain of the house of Burriana is mentioned.[58] There is also a reference in the middle of that year to a convent at Valencia, only nine months after the city's capture.[59] The creation of this convent may have been achieved by transferring most of the Templar community recently established at Burriana, since for the next two decades there appears to have been no convent at the latter place. During that period the commander of Burriana was subordinate to, and holding office from, the head of the convent of Valencia; the latter is in some documents called the commander of the 'house' —in the singular—of Valencia and Burriana;[60] and no minor officials are mentioned at Burriana between 1239 and 1261. At least from the latter date, however, there appear to have been convents in both Valencia and Burriana.[61] It is not clear whether the Templars also established a convent at Chivert soon after its recapture. In 1234 it was made subject to the commander of La Ribera, who controlled Templar estates along the lower Ebro; no commander of Chivert is mentioned until 1243; and there is no clear evidence of a convent there until the last quarter of the century.[62] But as the office of commander of La Ribera ceased to exist after 1236, it is possible that a convent had by then been founded at Chivert.

The grants which the Aragonese rulers made to the Temple as a result of the 1143 agreement thus led to the foundation of sixteen convents—nearly half of the total number founded by the Templars in the *Corona de Aragón*. The establishment of these convents provides a further illustration of the importance of the royal grants in the expansion of the Temple in the Aragonese realms; and as most of these convents were, to begin with, in the frontier region, their foundation further serves to emphasize the military importance of the Templars, who not only gave assistance in conquering territories from the Moors, but also played a significant role in ensuring that lands were not lost again to the infidel.

While from 1143 onwards convents were being set up in the newly conquered areas at places given to the Temple by the Aragonese rulers, others were being established in the more northerly parts of Aragon as the Order acquired more land mainly from private individuals; since the accumulation of property was gradual, however, the process of founding new convents was often slow. It is clear from the activities of the members of the house of Novillas that until about 1160 that convent had control of all Templar properties in Aragon and Navarre, except those on the borders of Aragon and Catalonia which were subject to the convent of Monzón. Raymond Bernard, head of Novillas before the middle of the twelfth century, was concerned with rights and properties in an area stretching from Ribaforada in Navarre to Zaragoza, and from Añesa to Calatayud; Peter Martínez, who was placed in charge of the convent in 1159, was frequently involved in transactions in Navarre as well as in Aragon; and even members of the convent who did not hold office were often engaged in business over a similarly wide area. The convent of Palau likewise probably controlled for a considerable number of years Templar rights in most of the districts of Catalonia which were in Christian hands by 1143; certainly Templar lands in the more northerly parts of Catalonia were subject to the commander of Palau at least until the later part of the twelfth century, for in 1182 that official received a grant of lands in and around Puigreig[63] and he was also present when the will of the troubadour William of Bergadán—concerned mainly with rights in the same district—was drawn up in 1187.[64]

In these more northerly parts of the *Corona de Aragón* the establishment of a new convent was usually preceded by the delegation of a brother or several brothers to administer the Order's estates in a particular place. This was being done in Aragon and Navarre by the masters of Novillas before the middle of the twelfth century. As early as 1149 a brother Dominic was said to be in charge of the Order's rights at Boquiñeni,[65] and the Templar Raymond of Castellnou is mentioned consistently between 1146 and 1165 in documents concerning Templar lands in and around Huesca. Frequent references occur to a brother Ralph at Zaragoza between 1145 and 1157, and from the latter date Bernard of Salvi was in charge of Templar rights there. These officials were at first given no title—Raymond of Castellnou was never called anything other than 'brother' or 'servant'—but they soon came to be known as commanders. A brother Berenguer was commander of Boquiñeni in 1158,[66] and in 1162 Bernard of Salvi was called 'commander and obedientiary' of Zaragoza,[67] while from the end of 1155 references are also made to a commander of Novillas itself, in addition to the master, who was still in charge of the convent and who undertook the general supervision of properties in Aragon and Navarre. The title of commander in these instances merely denoted a Templar bailiff, subject to the master of Novillas: in 1165 the head of Novillas could still be given the title 'master of the militia of the Temple in the district of Zaragoza'.[68]

The establishment of new convents in northern Aragon, which gradually reduced the extent of Novillas's authority, appears to have taken place mainly in the second half of the twelfth century. One stage in this development is marked by the disappearance of the office of master of Novillas, which is not mentioned after 1169.[69] By then possibly three new convents had been set up in northern Aragon, for chamberlains besides commanders are mentioned at Huesca, Ambel, and Luna in 1160, 1162, and 1167 respectively.[70] The establishment of these officials may, however, mark only a stage in the development of communities independent of Novillas and not the completion of this process, for in 1162 the master of Novillas was involved with the commander and chamberlain of Ambel in buying land in the latter place.[71] And

if at this time Luna achieved independence of Novillas it soon
became subordinate to the head of the house of Huesca. From
1174 the commander of Huesca became known as *commendator
mayor* and participated in the administration of Templar property
in Luna; and in the early thirteenth century the establishment at
Luna was abandoned. The last reference to a commander there
occurs in 1217.[72] The proximity of Huesca and Luna and the
limited extent of Templar rights in that region clearly meant that
the maintenance of a convent in each place was not justified.
While these developments were taking place in *Alto Aragón* convents were apparently also being founded along the Ebro valley.
Although the Templar house at Zaragoza mentioned in 1170 may
still have been subordinate to Novillas, there is a reference to
a chamberlain there six years later.[73] And similarly although the
house at Boquiñeni referred to in 1170 may not have been an
independent convent, there was a chamberlain there in 1183.[74]
The convent which was founded at Añesa, on the river Arba,
appears to have been established rather later. No commander is
known there until 1185, and there is no indication of a Templar
community at Añesa until 1202.[75]

The creation of new convents on estates formerly subject to
Novillas was paralleled in Aragon by a similar development which
occurred slightly later and on a smaller scale on the lands subject
to the convent of Zaragoza. In this area new convents were
founded at Ricla, Pina, and La Zaida. In documents concerning
Templar rights at Ricla drawn up between 1173 and 1176 a
brother Nuño is mentioned, often together with Bernard of
Salvi, the commander of Zaragoza.[76] In 1184 Nuño was called
commander of Ricla and was accompanied by at least three other
Templars;[77] and there is a reference to a Templar house there
seven years later.[78] The convent at Ricla may therefore have been
established before the end of the twelfth century.

Bernard of Salvi also acted for the Temple in the 1170s in the
earliest transactions in the district of Pina and La Zaida;[79] but in
1182 García of Aragon—already mentioned in a document drawn
up in 1177[80]—was called commander in a charter concerned with
land in this area, though his title was given no territorial qualification.[81] He was probably, however, the predecessor of Michael of
Luna, who was commander of La Zaida and Pina from 1185 until
1188. These two places were still subject to a single commander

in 1200,[82] but the evidence is insufficient to show exactly how long this practice was maintained. There appear to have been convents at both Pina and La Zaida, however, by the 1230s, when there were commanders and subordinate officials at each of these places.[83] Yet in 1244 both Pina and La Zaida were again subject to a single official, and since no commander of Pina is known between then and 1263 and since in 1255 the commander of La Zaida made a grant of land in Pina,[84] it is possible that in this period there ceased to be a convent at Pina. But this could have been only a temporary development. In 1270 references were made to a chamberlain of the house of Pina,[85] and in 1277 Pina and La Zaida were assessed separately for payments to the provincial master.[86] And while the convent at Pina survived until the arrest of the Templars, it was the house at La Zaida that was abandoned after the Temple had alienated its rights of lordship there.

A gradual development of convents also occurred in the areas of Catalonia already in Christian hands before 1143, although little is known about the process of foundation. A commander of Barbará is mentioned in 1173 and there is a reference to the convent there a year later.[87] There was a commander of Selma in 1190, but the existence of a convent there is indicated only by much later sources.[88] Again, very few documents survive about the convent which was established at Juncosa, not far from Selma. According to Miret y Sans the house of Juncosa had originally been established at Gunyolas, where there was a commander in 1160.[89] When or why it was transferred to Juncosa is not known, but the transference must have occurred in the later part of the twelfth century, since the first known commander of Juncosa was a brother Dominic in 1199/1200;[90] but a convent there is not mentioned until 1243.[91]

The history of the foundation of convents in the more northerly parts of Catalonia is equally obscure. Very little can be discovered about the convent founded at Aiguaviva, south-west of Gerona. According to Miret y Sans it was in existence by 1192, but the only document now surviving in the Hospitaller archive is a transcript of three agreements dating from the year 1209, by which time a chapel had been built at the convent there.[92] Equally little is known of the convent which was established at Castellón de Ampurias, to the east of Figueras; its archives have completely disappeared. Again according to Miret y Sans a commandery had been set up there by 1168, when land in Castellón was sold to brother Berenguer of Mulnels, who was described as 'preceptor of that province'.[93] But this vague title suggests that there was in fact no convent at Castellón at that time and that Berenguer of Mulnels was merely a Templar bailiff, who administered the Order's possessions in that area. There is no reference to a Templar establishment at Castellón de Ampurias until 1217, when James I in an exchange granted his rights over a man in Besalú to the commander of the house at Castellón,[94] and the only clear indication that a convent was established there is the inclusion of Castellón among the places owing dues to the provincial master at the beginning of the fourteenth century.[95]

According to Monsalvatge y Fossas a further Templar convent was established in north-eastern Catalonia at San Lorenzo de las Arenas; he states that Pons Hugh II, count of Ampurias, was buried in the Templar chapel he had endowed there and that the Templars of the convent there later supported Hugh IV in a quarrel with the bishop of Gerona.[96] But a document drawn up in 1226, at the end of this dispute, makes it clear that the house in question at San Lorenzo belonged to the Hospitallers, not to the Templars.[97]

The only other convent established in northern Catalonia was at Puigreig. A Templar with the title of commander of Solsona was mentioned in 1169,[98] but from 1181 the official in charge of Templar estates along the upper Llobregat was usually called commander of Cerdaña or of Cerdaña and Bergadán.[99] The reference in these titles to a wide area and not to a single place indicates that at the end of the twelfth and in the early thirteenth century the commander was merely a bailiff in charge of the Order's possessions and that no convent had been established. When Puigreig was finally acquired it became the centre of administration in that area: the title of commander of Puigreig is found in 1239, although it did not at once completely supersede the older descriptions of the office. And in time a convent was created there. Yet it is not clear when the break from Palau occurred. There is a reference to a Templar house at Puigreig in 1248,[100] but for most of the thirteenth century the documents show the commander acting with only one or two other Templars, and no minor conventual officials are mentioned until 1285.[101]

Acquisitions from private individuals did not lead to a similar process of foundation in the more recently conquered areas. By the time that the most southerly districts were recovered from the Moors the Order was no longer increasing its property to any great extent through purchases or gifts from private individuals, and in the places conquered in the middle and later parts of the twelfth century the acquisitions which the Order made after the initial grants from the Crown did not usually compare in importance with these royal grants. The Templar convents in the more southerly parts of the *Corona de Aragón* were therefore almost exclusively those established in places granted by the Crown. Even when a convent was apparently founded late, as at Ribarroja, it was established in a place gained from the king. The only one that can be looked upon as an exception is that at Barbens, which was established on lands first subject to Gardeny and which was not founded as the result of royal patronage. The Order plainly had no establishment there in 1164, for in that year an individual promised that if a Templar house were built on any land at Barbens from which he received tithes he would surrender his right to them.[102] But there is a reference to a Templar house at Barbens three years later,[103] and a commander of Barbens is mentioned in a document drawn up in 1168. The authority of the head of Gardeny was not, however, then withdrawn from Barbens. He continued to conduct business there until at least the early part of the thirteenth century, and lack of evidence makes it impossible to say when Barbens became an independent convent; the first hint is provided by the presence of the commander of Barbens at what appears to have been a provincial chapter in 1244.[104]

Although, as in the case of Barbens, there is no evidence of some convents until almost the end of the Temple's history in the *Corona de Aragón*, it can be shown that most Templar convents had been set up by the middle of the thirteenth century, in the period when Templar property was expanding most rapidly; and there is no instance in which it can be definitely stated that a convent was established after the middle of the thirteenth century. The only changes that are known to have occurred after 1250 were in the siting of convents. Palau, to the north of Barcelona, was not a very convenient site for a convent, since the commander had frequent business with royal officials in Barcelona and with Barcelona merchants who transported Templar supplies

to the East.[105] These factors probably explain the transfer of the
convent to Barcelona, which—as changes in title indicate—
occurred in 1282. Romeo of Burguet was appointed as commander of Palau in 1280 or 1281, but from May 1282 his title was
changed to 'commander of Barcelona', although he continued to
administer all the possessions of the former commandery of
Palau.[106] The convent at Ricla had similarly by 1289 been transferred to Calatayud,[107] although the reason for the change is not
known, and after Peñíscola had been obtained from the king in
exchange for Tortosa it became the site of the convent previously
situated at Chivert.[108]

The way in which Templar convents were founded in order
to administer, and sometimes to defend, the possessions of the
Temple in a particular district meant that with a few exceptions—
such as the subjection of Torres de Segre to the convent at
Miravet[109]—the estates belonging to a convent were concentrated
in one area, and the possessions of different houses did not overlap
geographically. It did not mean, however, that any attempt was
made to ensure that all convents had possessions of approximately
the same value. It is clear from Hospitaller valuations which survive from the early fourteenth century, and from references to the
leasing of Templar estates by the Crown after the arrest of the
Templars, that the incomes of different convents varied considerably. While the revenues of Monzón were assessed by the
Hospitallers at 2,500*l*. and those of Miravet at 2,000*l*., Boquiñeni,
on the other hand, was valued at only 50*l*. and Añesa at even less.[110]
At times the income of the smaller convents was scarcely sufficient to maintain a community. In 1277 it was said that the convent of Boquiñeni had fallen into 'the greatest poverty', and it
was necessary to use revenues drawn from other convents to pay
off Boquiñeni's debts and to undertake essential expenditure
there.[111] Although some convents with small incomes were
situated in the more southerly regions of the *Corona de Aragón*—
Alfambra was valued at 100*l*. by the Hospitallers and Villel at
150*l*.[112]—most of the poorer convents lay in the more northerly
parts of Aragon and Catalonia. The convents of Selma, Castellón
de Ampurias, Aiguaviva, and Novillas, as well as Boquiñeni and
Añesa, were among the least wealthy Templar communities. The
reason for the creation of a number of small convents in these
areas is perhaps to be found in the fact that in the north Templar

possessions were more scattered than in the more southerly districts, where they tended to be concentrated in lordships granted by the Crown. It was probably more convenient to establish a number of convents than to try to administer these scattered possessions from just a few houses, which would have had lands at a considerable distance. There were therefore by the later part of the thirteenth century few places in the *Corona de Aragón* that were very remote from a Templar convent. It was only in parts of the extreme north and in the extreme south, in the southerly region of Valencia, that there was an absence of Templar foundations.

## NOTES

1. He is mentioned frequently between these dates in the documents published by Albon, *Cartulaire*; see also *Cartulaires des Templiers de Douzens*, ed. P. Gérard and E. Magnou (Collection de documents inédits sur l'histoire de France, série in-8°, vol. iii, Paris, 1965).

2. Arnold of Bedocio is last mentioned in 1139: Albon, *Cartulaire*, pp. 139–40, doc. 199. It is stated in the introduction to *Cartulaire de la commanderie de Richerenches de l'Ordre du Temple (1136–1214)*, ed. Marquis de Ripert-Monclar (Avignon, 1907), pp. cliv, clviii, that from 1136 to 1138 Arnold of Bedocio was in charge of the Templar establishment at Richerenches, north of Orange; but his authority was not limited to this area: see Albon, *Cartulaire*, p. 88, doc. 127; pp. 92–3, docs. 132, 133, etc. Léonard, *Introduction*, pp. 23, 40, states that Arnold at this time both held office at Richerenches and had authority over a wider area.

3. Albon, *Cartulaire*, p. 74, doc. 102; pp. 75–6, doc. 105; pp. 76–7, doc. 107; pp. 77–8, doc. 108, etc.

4. On the organization of convents, see cap. VII.

5. The earliest known Hospitaller province was in existence by about 1120: Riley-Smith, *Knights of St. John*, p. 353.

6. Cf. G. Le Bras, *Institutions ecclésiastiques de la chrétienté médiévale* (Histoire de l'Église depuis les origines jusqu'à nos jours, vol. xii, Paris, 1964), pp. 490–1.

7. In 1291, for example, in a letter to the pope, the French clergy argued that the Order should keep only a few Templars in the West and should concentrate its manpower in the East: Bartholomew Cotton, *Historia Anglicana*, ed. H. R. Luard (London, 1859), p. 213.

8. In some cases it can be shown that the most rapid growth of Templar property occurred in a district during the years following the establishment of a convent there.

9. Albon, *Cartulaire*, pp. 204–5, doc. 314; *CDI*, iv. 93–9, doc. 43. The word

'Provence' was not used in a precise sense; see J. A. Durbec, 'Les Templiers en Provence. Formation des commanderies et répartition géographique de leurs biens', *Provence historique*, ix (1959), 3.

10. See below, p. 107, note 75.

11. AHN, Montesa, P. 18.

12. AHN, cód. 689, pp. 96–7, doc. 103.

13. The Aragonese province of the Dominican Order created at the beginning of the fourteenth century covered the same territories: F. Diago, *Historia de la provincia de Aragón de la Orden de Predicadores* (Barcelona, 1599), fols. 2–3.

14. ACA, CRD Templarios, nos. 169, 278. The commander of Caravaca in Murcia is mentioned in a number of Catalan documents at the beginning of the fourteenth century: e.g. AGP, parch. Gardeny, nos. 231–6, 383–5, 2249, 2250.

15. Those in Navarre were at Ribaforada and Aberín. The most complete list of communities directly subject to the Aragonese provincial master is found in ACA, CRD Templarios, no. 81; see below, p. 415.

16. In 1250 reference was made to the 'convent' of the Holy Redeemer at Teruel, although this establishment was subject to Villel: AHN, cód. 466, pp. 361–2, doc. 438; but this is an isolated exception.

17. See below, p. 318.

18. There is a reference to a Templar house built at Mas-Deu as early as 1138: Albon, *Cartulaire*, p. 119, doc. 171.

19. Ibid., pp. 140–1, doc. 202.

20. ACA, parch. Raymond Berenguer IV, no. 132.

21. Albon, *Cartulaire*, p. 122, doc. 177; Lacarra, 'Documentos', no. 342 (v. 564–5).

22. Albon, *Cartulaire*, pp. 242–3, doc. 384; Lacarra, 'Documentos', no. 350 (v. 571–2).

23. Albon, *Cartulaire*, p. 279, doc. 447.

24. Ibid., p. 235, doc. 367.

25. Ibid., p. 248, doc. 395.

26. J. L. de Moncada, *Episcopologio de Vich*, i (Vich, 1891), 437–8. The document in question (Episcopal Archive of Vich, armario del derecho de diversas iglesias, no. 13) was destroyed during the Spanish Civil War. I am grateful to the Revd. M. S. Gros i Pujol for providing me with this information.

27. ACA, parch. Alfonso II, no. 578; parch. Peter II, no. 169.

28. AHN, cód. 499, p. 19, doc. 33. In 1146 the provincial master was said to be holding Monzón, but this refers merely to rights of lordship: Albon, *Cartulaire*, p. 246, doc. 390.

29. AHN, cód. 499, p. 19, doc. 33.

30. Lacarra, 'Documentos', no. 377 (v. 593–4).

31. Albon, *Cartulaire*, p. 308, doc. 499.

32. Miret y Sans, *Les Cases*, p. 66.

33. One section of the Cartulary of Gardeny in the AGP, beginning on fol. 54, consists of documents concerning Corbins. There was, however, a convent again at Corbins in the thirteenth century.

34. AGP, parch. Gardeny, no. 537.

35. AGP, parch. Corbins, no. 122.

36. AGP, Cartulary of Gardeny, fol. 24, doc. 35; fols. 33ᵛ–34, docs. 63, 65; fol. 41ᵛ, doc. 88; parch. Gardeny, no. 1. Albon, *Cartulaire*, p. 63, doc. 82, assigns to the year 1134 a will which includes the clause 'I leave my body to the militia of Gardeny'; but the French king by whose regnal year the document is dated must be Louis VII, not Louis VI. The will belongs to the year 1163.

A convent may also for a time have been established at the castle of Remolins, which had been given to the Order in 1143. In 1162 it appears still to have been under the authority of Gardeny since a record of a dispute in that year about rights there was made by the chaplain of Gardeny; and this document was later copied into the Cartulary of Gardeny (fol. 24ᵛ, doc. 37). The commander of Remolins mentioned in 1181 was probably therefore a subordinate of the commander of Gardeny. But in 1271 reference was made to land held of the commander and brothers of the house of Remolins, and six years later the commander and brothers there were involved in a dispute concerning land: AGP, parch. Gardeny, no. 1960; parch. Espluga de Francolí, no. 183. Yet if there was a convent at Remolins at this time, it was not maintained. At the beginning of the fourteenth century Remolins, together with Torres de Segre, was under the control of the commander of Miravet, who established a subordinate commander at Torres: AGP, parch. Torres de Segre, nos. 51, 58, 62.

37. AGP, Cartulary of Tortosa, fol. 26, doc. 77; S. A. García Larragueta, 'Fueros y cartas pueblas navarro-aragonesas otorgadas por Templarios y Hospitalarios', *AHDE*, xxiv (1954), 592–3; Font Rius, *Cartas de población*, i. 285–6, doc. 208.

38. AGP, Cartulary of Tortosa, fol. 30ᵛ, doc. 93. In the same year land was given in an exchange to Aymeric and the brothers 'who are with you in Tortosa': ibid., fol. 67ᵛ, doc. 217. Miret y Sans, *Les Cases*, p. 82, quotes a document from the Cartulary of Tortosa (fol. 50ᵛ, doc. 153) which records that William Berard, master and commander of Miravet and Tortosa, bought a vineyard in 1153 from Geralda, widow of Peter of Toulouse. But Peter of Toulouse was still alive in 1170 (ibid., fol. 34ᵛ, doc. 110), and William Berard held office from 1165 to 1174. Possibly the date of the document should be 1173.

39. Sancho of Vergea was called *procurator* of the house of Tortosa: ibid., fol. 60, doc. 185.

40. Iñigo Sánchez was called *gubernator*, *procurator*, and *ministrator*: AGP, Cartulary of Tortosa, fol. 33ᵛ, doc. 104; fol. 61–61ᵛ, docs. 191–3.

41. The first official who was clearly commander only of Miravet was R. Bernard in 1190. Dalmau of Godeto was given the title of commander of Miravet between 1178 and 1181: ibid., fol. 37ᵛ, doc. 118; fols. 67ᵛ–68, doc. 218; but he was probably commander of Miravet and Tortosa for he intervened in matters concerning Tortosa and no other commander of Miravet and Tortosa is known during this period.

42. Ibid., fol. 94ᵛ, doc. 295.

43. Dalmau of Godeto is called commander of La Ribera in a document bearing the date 1187: AHN, San Juan, leg. 529, doc. 1; but the titles of the other Templars mentioned show that the date is inaccurate, as does the reference in the document to another charter which was not drawn up until 1190: ACA, parch. Alfonso II, no. 561. In 1187 Bertrand of Conques was commander of Miravet and Tortosa.

44. AGP, parch. Comuns, no. 114.

45. AGP, Cartulary of Tortosa, fols. 41ᵛ–42, doc. 132. The document is undated, but it was issued by bishop Pons of Tortosa, who died in July 1193.

46. AHN, San Juan, leg. 351, doc. 1.

47. The last reference to it is in ACA, parch. James I, no. 422.

48. RAH, 12–6–1/M–83, doc. 14.

49. It was assessed with Ascó for the purposes of royal taxation: ACA, reg. 68, fol. 25ᵛ.

50. ACA, parch. Peter III, no. 26; CRD Templarios, no. 81; see below, p. 415.

51. AHN, cód. 689, p. 83, doc. 86.

52. Ibid., pp. 61–2, doc. 60. The commander and three brothers are named; 'others', in the plural, are not.

53. There is no reference to a convent there before 1244: ibid., p. 79, doc. 80.

54. AHN, cód. 466, p. 205, doc. 177.

55. RAH, 12–6–1/M–83, doc. 14.

56. M. Albareda y Herrera, *El fuero de Alfambra* (Madrid, 1925), pp. 39–41.

57. AGP, parch. Comuns, no. 197. Bertrand of Arlet was then head of the convent. He is also mentioned—without a title—in a slightly earlier document belonging to the same month: J. Miralles Sbert, *Catálogo del Archivo Capitular de Mallorca*, ii (Palma, 1942), 341, no. 7723.

58. AHN, Montesa, P. 18.

59. AHN, Montesa, P. 14.

60. AHN, Montesa, P. 73, 85.

61. For the convent at Burriana, see AHN, Montesa, P. 249, 251, etc.

62. ACA, parch. Peter III, no. 26.

63. AGP, parch. Cervera, no. 232; ACA, parch. Alfonso II, no. 333.

64. ACA, parch. Alfonso II, no. 451; published by M. de Riquer, 'El testa-mento del trovador Guilhem de Berguedán', *Mélanges de linguistique et de littérature romanes à la mémoire d'Istvan Frank* (Annales Universitatis Saraviensis, vol. vi, 1957), pp. 581–3. Riquer, ibid., p. 576, explains the presence of the commander of Palau by the fact that the troubadour held a few rights in villages near Palau; but these were of only minor importance. It seems more likely that he was present because the castle of Puigreig was to come under his authority.

65. Albon, *Cartulaire*, p. 333, doc. 543.

66. AHN, cód. 470, p. 10, doc. 11.

67. AHN, cód. 469, pp. 354–5, doc. 300.

68. AHN, cód. 468, p. 460, doc. 439.

69. In a document drawn up in 1172 William of Bais, who had been master, was placed at the head of a list of Templars at Novillas, but was assigned no title: AHN, cód. 691, fol. 121ᵛ.

70. AHN, cód. 499, p. 17, doc. 26; p. 54, doc. 130; A. Bonilla y San Martín, 'El derecho aragonés en el siglo XII', *II Congreso de historia de la Corona de Aragón*, i (Huesca, 1920), 236–7, doc. 3.

71. Ibid. The first occasion when there is a specific reference to a convent at any of these places is at Huesca in 1176: AHN, cód. 499, pp. 7–8, doc. 11.

72. AHN, cód. 468, p. 150, doc. 134.

73. AHN, San Juan, leg. 38, doc. 19; cód. 468, p. 154, doc. 137.

74. AHN, San Juan, leg. 38, doc. 19; cód. 470, p. 10, doc. 12. In 1184 the house of Boquiñeni was taken under royal protection: cód. 467, p. 129, doc. 146.

75. RAH, 12–6–1/M–83, doc. 52. The convents of Aberín and Ribaforada in Navarre were similarly established on lands formerly subject to Novillas. But the convent of Novillas seems to have lost rights in Navarre not only in this way but also as a result of the cession of the more southerly parts of Navarre to Castile in 1179—see the maps published by A. Ubieto Arteta as an appendix to his article 'Las fronteras de Navarra', *Príncipe de Viana*, xiv (1953)—for this apparently led to the transference of Templar rights in these districts, including Alcanadre, to the Castilian province. At the time of the arrest of the Templars Alcanadre was certainly in that province, and as in the thirteenth century the house at Alcanadre is never mentioned in the records of the Aragonese pro-vince, the transfer seems to have followed the political changes of 1179. By that date apparently no convents had been established in these southerly parts of Navarre. Although there is a reference to a Templar house at Alcanadre in 1175 (AHN, San Juan, leg. 718, doc. 6), the two Templars who held office as commander of Alcanadre in that year can both be traced at other times at Novillas and were probably merely bailiffs appointed by the head of Novillas.

The only other indication of Templar organization in these areas before 1179 occurs in a document in a cartulary of the monastery of Fitero, recording an agreement between the abbot and the Templar provincial master in 1173: M. Arigita, *Colección de documentos inéditos para la historia de Navarra* (Pamplona, 1909), p. 109. This charter makes reference to the 'brothers of the Temple of Solomon of Carbonera', but gives no indication of the character of the Templar establishment there.

76. Bonilla y San Martín, loc. cit., pp. 244–5, doc. 8; AHN, cód. 468, p. 516, doc. 502; San Juan, leg. 285, docs. 2, 3.

77. Bonilla y San Martín, loc. cit., pp. 255–6, doc. 19.

78. Ibid., p. 266, doc. 30.

79. AHN, San Juan, leg. 529, doc. 8; cód. 467, p. 472, docs. 566, 567.

80. AHN, San Juan, leg. 529, doc. 8.

81. AHN, cód. 467, p. 473, doc. 569.

82. Ibid., p. 432, doc. 405.

83. Ibid., p. 368, doc. 459; cód. 468, p. 521, doc. 530.

84. AHN, cód. 467, pp. 369–70, doc. 462.

85. Ibid., p. 378, docs. 474, 475.

86. ACA, parch. Peter III, no. 26.

87. ACA, parch. Alfonso II, no. 170 (the name of the commander mentioned in this document, which is dated 6 Kalends of March in the year of the Incarnation 1174, suggests that it was drawn up in 1174 and not 1175).

88. ACA, CRD Templarios, no. 81; see below, p. 415.

89. Miret y Sans, *Les Cases*, p. 174; cf. Font Rius, *Cartas de población*, i. 168–9, doc. 115.

90. The document in which he is mentioned is dated March 1199, and could thus belong to either 1199 or 1200: *Cartulari de Poblet* (Barcelona, 1938), p. 166, doc. 274.

91. AGP, parch. Vilafranca, no. 601. A. Alegret, 'Los Templarios en Tarragona', *Boletín arqueológico*, xvii (1905), 496–516, argues that the Templars built the church of St. Mary in Tarragona and had an establishment next to it. This argument is based on tradition and on the architectural style of the church. That there was no architectural style peculiar to the Templars has been shown by E. Lambert, *L'Architecture des Templiers* (Paris, 1955); and that the Templars had no establishment in Tarragona is apparent from the fact that they retained a right of hospitality in some houses there: ACA, parch. James I, no. 2273.

92. Miret y Sans, *Les Cases*, p. 172; AGP, parch. Aiguaviva, no. 3.

93. Miret y Sans, *Les Cases*, pp. 173–4. The document recording this sale has been published by F. Monsalvatge y Fossas, *Los condes de Ampurias vindicados* (Noticias históricas, vol. xxv, Olot, 1917), pp. 337–8.

94. Huici, *Colección diplomática*, i. 10–11, doc. 3.

95. ACA, CRD Templarios, no. 81; see below, p. 415.

96. Monsalvatge y Fossas, op. cit., pp. 102, 107.

97. *ES*, xliv. 265–6, Appendix 4. On the Hospitaller house at San Lorenzo de las Arenas, see Miret y Sans, *Les Cases*, p. 197.

98. AGP, Cartulary of Tortosa, fol. 38$^v$, doc. 122.

99. For the titles used, see Appendix II.

100. ACA, parch. James I, no. 1137.

101. ACA, parch. Peter III, nos. 460, 465.

102. AGP, Cartulary of Gardeny, fol. 63–63$^v$, doc. 154.

103. Ibid., fol. 66$^v$, doc. 162.

104. RAH, 12-6-1/M-83, doc. 110.

105. e.g. ACA, parch. Peter III, no. 292.

106. The change occurred between 2 April and 26 May: ACA, parch. Peter III, nos. 294, 301. Later in the same year Romeo of Burguet, as commander of Barcelona, granted out land at Sta. Perpetua: parch. Peter III, nos. 324–30.

107. J. Miret y Sans, 'Inventaris des les cases del Temple de la Corona d'Aragó en 1289', *BRABLB*, vi (1911), 65.

108. At the end of the thirteenth and beginning of the fourteenth century the commander of Chivert was merely a subordinate of the head of the house at Peñíscola: ACA, parch. James I, no. 2180; CRD James II, nos. 1737, 1747.

109. In the later thirteenth century Miravet appears to have been the chief house in the province (see below, p. 316), and presumably therefore incurred additional expenses, and this could explain why Torres de Segre was made subject to it.

110. Miret y Sans, *Les Cases*, pp. 399–400. In 1309 Templar revenues from Ascó and Ribarroja were farmed out for 10,000s.J. per annum, while those of Peñíscola were farmed for 13,000s. in one year and 10,000s. in another: ACA, reg. 291, fol. 187; Finke, *Papsttum*, ii. 228–9, doc. 124.

111. ACA, parch. Peter III, no. 26. Some of these revenues may have been used to buy property at Boquiñeni, for a series of small purchases of land was made there between 1260 and 1280; and these acquisitions may represent an attempt to put the convent on a sounder economic footing.

112. These houses had, however, recently been deprived of the patronage of certain churches: Miret y Sans, *Les Cases*, pp. 399–400.

# IV

## Rights and Privileges: (i) Secular

As a result of the acquisitions of property made by the Templars in the *Corona de Aragón* the Order's convents possessed a wide variety of rights, both secular and ecclesiastical, and to these were added privileges of exemption for the Templars and their vassals, obtained from both lay and ecclesiastical authorities.

Secular rights were gained over both persons and land. Rights of a purely personal character were acquired primarily through contracts of protection and confraternity. Those who sought the Order's protection or entered into the confraternity of the Temple usually agreed to pay a small annual rent to the Templars. Although it was very occasionally stated that this rent was to be taken from a particular piece of land,[1] the obligation was basically a personal one, resting upon the individual rather than upon his land. But while payments of this kind are mentioned in every contract of protection, not all *confratres* undertook to pay a fixed sum annually to the Temple. The amount which a *confrater* was to give was sometimes not specified—Peter Gómez of Zamora, for example, merely promised to give his 'charity' annually[2]—and in some agreements of confraternity there is no reference to an annual payment at all. Similarly although a contract of confraternity often gave the Templars a claim to a specific bequest from a *confrater*, this was not an essential characteristic of these agreements. When Mary, the daughter of Raymond of Centelles, was accepted into the confraternity of the Temple in 1259 she promised to leave merely 'something according to my desire and wish';[3] and some *confratres* made no bequest at all to the Order. *Confratres* were expected to give their patronage to the Temple, but the form of benefaction varied. Besides making payments or grants to the Order, *confratres* usually gave themselves to the Temple 'body and soul in life and death'. This phrase could be employed in a variety of contexts and does not of itself tell anything of the nature of confraternity ties.[4] But the obligations implied by this undertaking are made clear in a number of charters. The *confrater* was promising to be buried in a Templar cemetery; this would, of course, bring profit to the Order. He was also undertaking not to transfer his allegiance to or join another order without the permission of the Temple. To ensure that a *confrater* carried out this promise and fulfilled his obligations an oath of fealty, sworn on the Gospels, was exacted from him, and some *confratres* also did homage to the Temple 'with hands joined and on bended knees with hands and mouth'.[5] If a *confrater* wished to be released from his obligations he would normally have to give compensation to the Order. When Bernard of Odena in 1273 wanted to free himself from an undertaking to pay a pound of wax annually and one *morabetino* at death and to be buried in the Temple, he gave in perpetuity the rent of a pound of wax to the Order, and even then the condition was made by the Templars that if he died within a day's journey of Barcelona he was still to be buried in the Order's cemetery there;[6] and over a century earlier, in return for a surrender by the Temple of its right to bury his body, a *confrater* called Nicholas had abandoned his claim to three pieces of land.[7] It is not clear whether the Templars, like some other lords,[8] also usually obtained redemption payments from those who wished to free themselves from contracts of protection. Charters are usually brief and imprecise in wording, and in no document is it specifically stated that a redemption was to be paid. In one instance in 1279, on the other hand, the Templars promised not to demand any payment of this kind,[9] and in a number of charters it was stipulated that the Order was to seek nothing other than the annual rent,[10] while the reference in some documents to the protection of lands 'while they are between crosses' suggests that a merely temporary arrangement was being made.[11] But in many other cases it is clear that the agreement was intended to be of a permanent character, and as some of those under Templar protection promised not to seek another lord without Templar permission,[12] it is likely that on some occasions the Temple was able to exact redemption payments from those under its protection.

While contracts of confraternity and protection were concerned with personal ties, most of the acquisitions made by the Templars in the *Corona de Aragón* consisted of rights over landed property and over individuals as tenants of land or as inhabitants of places under Templar lordship. Exactly what the Order gained from such acquisitions is not always known, especially when small properties, such as manses, were acquired. Charters tend again to be short and vague in wording: an individual would merely state that he was giving or selling a particular piece of property, which apparently meant that he was surrendering whatever rights he had in it. But it was often not stated what these were; the defining of rights was often done orally, leaving ample scope for later dispute. But it is possible to some extent to distinguish two main kinds of secular lordship gained over landed property by the Order. In some instances the Temple was obtaining the rights of a landlord; this was commonly the case when small parcels of land were acquired and also when strongholds and townships in newly conquered areas were gained. Alternatively or in addition the Temple obtained what may be termed franchisal lordship, which included public rights and dues; this was gained whenever a castle or township was acquired and also in some instances when smaller properties were obtained. In practice of course these forms of lordship were not always clearly distinguished, but contemporaries did at times make reference to the two different kinds of authority: in 1280 Peter III contrasted the 'men' of the Temple with the 'tenants who hold lands and possessions of the Temple',[13] and in 1297 the queen similarly made a distinction between the 'men' of the Temple and the 'landholders and countrymen, who held lands and possessions of the said house of the militia of the Temple'.[14] While the Temple exercised franchisal rights over its 'men', the others merely held lands of the Order.

When the Temple acquired the rights of a landlord it gained either direct control of the land or—if the property was not held in demesne—dues such as land rents in money or kind, labour services, and in some parts of Catalonia the *malos usos*, besides the right to appoint a judge to settle disputes concerning the fulfilment of a tenant's obligations.[15] Thus when Beatrice of Castellón and her son confirmed the grant of a manse to the Order in 1238, the rights and dues listed in the charter of confirmation included rents, works, *intestias, exorquias, cugucias,* the redemption payments of the men and women on the manse, and judicial rights.[16] Most documents, however, are not so explicit, but it is clear that individuals who gave or sold rights of this kind to the Order normally transferred all the rights they possessed.

The rights which might be gained through the acquisition of franchisal lordship were partly of a financial character. They included the right to certain dues paid by the inhabitants of the land or district, such as *peita* or *questia, monedaje*,[17] *bovaje*,[18] and *cenas*. They also included—when lordship over a whole community was gained—the right to exact tolls and customs, such as *lezda* and *peaje*.

When the Temple gained this kind of lordship from private individuals, the latter appear usually to have surrendered all their financial rights, although these are often not defined in detail. The wording of early royal charters is often similarly imprecise and few financial rights are mentioned by name. The castles assigned to the Templars in 1143 were given merely with

all *usajes* and customs, with all *lezda* and *pasaje*, with all cultivated and uncultivated land, with plain and mountain, with meadow and pasture;[19]

and in 1169 Chivert and Oropesa were granted with *lezda, usajes*, and *pasaje* and with

all their terms and tenements, both by land and by sea, waste and settled, plain and mountain, pasture, woods and uncultivated land and with all water and *ademprivia*.[20]

Later royal charters are sometimes more explicit and give a fuller list of dues and financial rights granted to the Order: the places in Valencia given by James II in 1294 in exchange for Tortosa were granted with *lezda, peaje, usajes, herbaje, carnaje*, fishing and hunting rights, rights over treasure, control of the saltpans of Peñíscola, *monedaje*, control of weights and measures, ovens, mills, the office of public notary, *cena, peita, questia*, and *ademprivia*.[21] But even when few dues and rights were mentioned by name, a clause granting in general all other exactions and rights was often added, and it is clear that the king normally granted to the Temple all his financial rights: Peter II's retention of 200*m*. in the *lezda* of Ascó in 1210 was exceptional.[22] That the Order received all dues is also apparent from charters of exemption issued to the Temple by Peter II and James I, for in these the men of the Temple were exempted from the payment of *questia, peita, tolta, forcia, bovaje, monedaje*, or any other exaction to the Crown.[23] These dues were still paid by the Order's men, but the profits went to the Temple, not the king.

In practice these concessions were understood to mean that if men under the franchisal lordship of the Temple held lands elsewhere in *realengo*, the dues from these lands still belonged to the king. A decision to this effect was made by a royal justice in 1290 after a long dispute between the Temple and the *concejo* of Burriana about those living in the Order's *alquerías* of Mantella and Benhamet.[24] On the other hand, a royal writ issued in 1276 ordering officials in Valencia not to exact *questia* or other dues from lands held at rent from the Temple indicates that those who were not subject to the franchisal lordship of the Order, but merely held lands of it, were exempted from paying taxes to the king from these lands, and the dues from them fell to the Temple.[25] The same conclusion may be drawn from a Templar complaint in 1279 that officials in Burriana were compelling those who merely held land of the Temple to pay *questia* and other dues for the property which they held of the Order;[26] and the exemption of these men is clearly set out in a decree concerning the exaction of *bovaje* issued in 1297.[27] These rulings implied, of course, a blurring of the distinction between the different kinds of lordship, but not all those holding lands of the Temple would be affected, for presumably some would owe public dues to private individuals or institutions, not to the king.

The value of the financial rights acquired by the Temple was in several cases enhanced by the grant of special powers, such as the privilege of holding markets and fairs, which enabled the Temple to benefit from the commercial expansion of the period. James I allowed weekly markets to be held at Barbará, Castellote, and Gandesa,[28] and a similar privilege was granted in 1292 for Mirambel.[29] James I also permitted the holding of annual fairs at Monzón and Horta, which were to last for ten and eight days respectively.[30] Other concessions by the king included the permission given in 1263 to alter the course of the Zaragoza–Tortosa road so that it passed through Algars.[31] This increased the Temple's revenues from tolls, as did the right to have a ferry across the Ebro at Novillas, which was confirmed by James I in 1251.[32] The value of the financial rights gained by the Templars had, on the other hand, sometimes been reduced through concessions made by previous holders of these rights: in 1149, for example,

Raymond Berenguer IV had granted a number of exemptions to the inhabitants of Tortosa, including freedom from the payment of *lezda*, *portaje*, and *pasaje* in the city.[33]

Judicial as well as financial rights were normally gained through the acquisition of franchisal lordship, but the judicial rights which the Templars obtained either from nobles or from the rulers of Aragon and Catalonia are not usually defined in detail in charters. Thus in 1134 Raymond Berenguer IV issued a general statement to the effect that no one was to have the power to judge or distrain the Temple's men in secular matters and that the Order was to have the right to judge its men, provided that it was ready to do justice.[34] Later twelfth-century charters from the Crown seem similarly to grant wide powers, but these are not described in detail. In most instances the transfer of judicial rights is to be inferred only from general clauses and phrases, such as 'whatever right or reason I have or ought to have there', included in the charter recording the grant of Tortosa to the Temple in 1182.[35] Even when direct reference was made to judicial rights, no detailed account of them was given. In 1145, for example, it was stated merely that the places granted by Raymond Berenguer IV in 1143 had been given 'with all jurisdictions' and that the inhabitants were to have no recourse to the count or his court,[36] while a general privilege granted at the beginning of the thirteenth century by Peter II refers merely to the profits of justice, which were to go to the Order, without making it clear whether the Temple itself exercised jurisdiction.[37]

Later evidence helps, however, to clarify the situation. It is apparent in the first place that the Templars had their own courts over which their officials presided: in an agreement made in 1263 between the Temple and the inhabitants of Ambel it was stated that cases should be brought before the justiciar there appointed by the Order, and in the code of customs approved at Horta in 1296 it was decreed that the Templar commander and his officials should dispense justice.[38] It is further clear that despite the apparent comprehensiveness of the Order's privileges some offences were normally reserved for judgement by the Crown. Cases of default of justice were tried by royal officials. This reservation was made implicitly in the charter issued by Raymond Berenguer IV in 1134 and it was repeated in many later documents. It further quickly became accepted that royal officials might take action in

cases involving breaches of the *pax et treuga*.[39] At least in Catalonia, however, certain concessions were made on this point to
the Temple and other ecclesiastical lords. In the Cortes held at
Barcelona in 1200 it was decreed that if vassals of monasteries or
of other religious lords injured each other and a complaint was
made to the royal vicar, the latter was to return the accused to his
lord, who was to do justice within fifteen days.[40] A much greater
concession was apparently made in 1214, for the wording of the
decrees then issued implies that an ecclesiastical lord was to have
jurisdiction over his vassals in all cases involving a breach of the
peace;[41] but from 1218 onwards there was a return to the wording which had been used in 1200,[42] and this was also employed in
a decree for Roussillon issued in 1217.[43] At the Cortes of 1283
Peter III made the further concession that royal officials should
not intervene on account of breaches of the *pax et treuga* committed within the district subject to a castle held by a private
lord.[44] Entries in the royal registers show that these concessions
made in the Cortes were observed and enforced by the Aragonese
rulers: in 1294, following a complaint by the Temple, the royal
vicar of Vallés was reprimanded by James II for contravening the
peace decrees issued by Peter III,[45] and three years later, after a
further petition from the Order, the vicar of Cervera and Tárrega
was ordered to surrender to the Temple—in accordance with the
decrees of the *pax et treuga*—some inhabitants of Grañena who
had been involved in a dispute with the vassals of the monastery
of Stas. Creus.[46] One further concession had been made to the
Temple by James I in 1272 when he ordered royal officials not to
proceed against the Temple's men until it had been ascertained
for certain that the *pax et treuga* had been broken.[47] This necessitated
a preliminary investigation before action could be taken against
the Order's men. Thus in 1277 the royal bailiff and vicar of Lérida
commissioned Raymond of Vallés, a canon of Lérida, to discover
whether the peace had been broken at Corbins through the
seizure and detention of certain men there by the commander
and inhabitants of Corbins.[48]

While private individuals who gave or sold rights of franchisal
lordship to the Temple usually surrendered all their financial
and judicial powers, they sometimes retained certain claims to
military service, the right to which comprised the last main
characteristic of this kind of lordship. When Raymond Galcerán

of Pinós granted the Temple his rights over an inhabitant of Bergadán in 1211, he stipulated that the man was still to perform castle-guard for him and assist in local defence,[49] and when Bernard of Anglesola in 1176 gave the Order his rights over Torre de Bafes, he retained the military service of the knights there.[50] The Aragonese and Catalan rulers, on the other hand, usually granted to the Temple all their rights of military service. The earliest reference to this practice seems to be made in a charter issued by the count of Barcelona in 1145 concerning the castles given to the Order two years earlier, for in this document Raymond Berenguer states that

since we gave to God and the Temple the said castles and other places mentioned in the charter that the race of Moors might be confounded, we will that all men or the greater part of the men of the said castles and places participate with the said lords always and on every occasion in campaigns and expeditions wherever these take place.[51]

Templar rights were defined more precisely, however, in charters issued by the Aragonese kings later in the twelfth century and early in the thirteenth. In 1182, for example, Alfonso II promised not to seek *hueste* or *cabalgada* from the inhabitants of Tortosa or Ascó,[52] and when in 1174 the king granted the Temple his rights over an individual called Martin Moçarau, he freed him from the obligation of *hueste* and *cabalgada* to the Crown.[53] And in a confirmation of Templar privileges issued by Peter II at the beginning of the thirteenth century the exemption of all those under the franchisal lordship of the Temple was clearly set out: they were freed from *hueste, cabalgada, apellido,* or any payment in lieu of these obligations to the Crown.[54] Although these terms were not always clearly differentiated in meaning, the word *apellido* normally referred to a defensive action, and *cabalgada* signified an offensive expedition, while *hueste* could be used for either.[55] A complete exemption from military service to the Crown was thus being granted; all service was to be owed instead to the Temple. The Templars were of course from 1143 onwards expected to participate in Aragonese campaigns against the Moors and to bring their vassals with them; but no precise military obligation was ever imposed upon the Temple, except in Mallorca, where the Order was obliged to provide the service of four knights.[56]

Besides these rights over men and land, the Templars gained a number of other privileges and exemptions for both themselves and their men. Among these were exemptions from tolls and customs. In Raymond Berenguer IV's charter of 1143 it was conceded that no *lezda*, *costumbre*, or *pasaje* was to be taken from the Order's own property.[57] During the course of the twelfth century freedom from royal tolls and customs was extended to the Temple's men. In 1180 Alfonso II granted that the inhabitants of Miravet should be exempt from *lezda* and *pasaje* on both land and sea,[58] and by the time of Peter II's confirmations of Templar privileges in 1208 and 1209 it was accepted that all men of the Temple—Christian, Jew, or Moor—with all their possessions and merchandise were exempt from the payment of *herbaje*, *carnaje*, *lezda*, *portaje*, or any other custom to the Crown.[59] In the same way the count of Urgel in 1189 exempted the inhabitants of Tortosa from the payment of tolls in Mequinenza, and in 1248 Berenguer of Villafranca granted the Templars a similar exemption in Montblanch, but only a few privileges of this kind granted by nobles have survived.[60]

The Templars further obtained from the Crown certain judicial immunities for themselves. In 1134 Raymond Berenguer had stated that the Templars, like their men, should be free in secular matters from distraint and justice in the count's courts,[61] but more detailed information about the Templars' judicial immunity is not found until the thirteenth century. The Crown then accepted that the Templars should not normally be obliged to appear before lay courts. In 1221, during a dispute about tolls between the Temple and the inhabitants of Zaragoza, James I upheld the commander of Monzón's assertion that the Order was not obliged to answer the charge made against it

except under the examination and by the judgement of an ecclesiastical judge according to the practice and custom of the Temple;[62]

and in 1261 the same king commanded his bailiffs and vicars not to force the Temple to receive justice from them, provided that it was prepared to do justice 'in the power of its ordinary judge'.[63] In practice, however, since arbitration was the most common method of settling disputes, the Templars did often submit to the judgement of laymen, including the king. In 1273 a dispute with the Hospitallers of Mallén, involving charges of homicide, arson, and the devastation of property, was submitted for arbitration to Martin Pérez, *zalmedina* of Zaragoza, and John Giles Tarín, later *merino* of the same city;[64] and in 1284 the provincial master offered to appear before Peter III when the inhabitants of Zaragoza, Huesca, and Barbastro were complaining about the exaction of tolls by the Order at Monzón and Tortosa.[65] Similarly, when the Temple made a complaint to the king, a counter-claim by the other party appears sometimes to have been heard by him; this was possibly done with the agreement of the Order.[66] But there were some occasions when the king intervened more directly. He took action to bring the Templars to justice if they refused to satisfy their opponents, and when he himself had claims against the Order about land or other rights, he appointed judges to hear the dispute, just as the Templars did when they had claims against their own vassals: in 1284, for example, Peter III appointed William Aymeric, a Barcelona lawyer, to hear his claim to rights in the castle of Ollers.[67]

The Temple lastly gained promises of protection for itself and its men. In 1134, in the earliest grant of general privileges made to the Order in north-eastern Spain, the count of Barcelona joined with the archbishop of Tarragona in placing the Templars and their lands under the truce of God, and at the same time the count took the Order's possessions under his own protection.[68] The grant of protection was renewed in the peace proclamations issued by the Aragonese rulers in the Cortes. In Catalonia the Templars were first included in these decrees at the Cortes of Fontaldara in 1173,[69] and from 1192 onwards the Order's vassals were also mentioned in them.[70] At the Aragonese Cortes held at Huesca in 1188 the king's protection was extended to the clergy in general and their property,[71] while at the later meetings of the Aragonese Cortes at Almudébar in 1227 and at Zaragoza in 1235 the Templars with their possessions and vassals were specifically placed in the king's peace.[72] The Templars, their men, and their property were similarly included in the peace decree for Roussillon issued in James I's minority by Nuño Sánchez,[73] and in that for Valencia published by James I in 1271.[74] The Aragonese kings, in addition, issued charters of protection to individual Templar convents. Alfonso II in 1184 took the house of Boquiñeni under his protection,[75] and the convents for which charters were issued in

James I's reign included Palau, Gardeny, Zaragoza, Huesca, and Valencia.[76]

In 1173 Alfonso II left the enforcement of his decrees—in so far as they touched the Church—mainly in the hands of the bishops;[77] but in time royal officials took over the work of enforcement. In the thirteenth century writs were often issued ordering royal agents to proceed against those who molested or harmed the Templars or their possessions;[78] and these officials could if necessary summon the inhabitants of a district to assist them in carrying out the peace decrees.

Charters of protection were also granted to the Temple by members of the lay nobility. In the thirteenth century, for example, the convents of Barbará and Puigreig received charters of this kind from the viscounts of Cardona,[79] and at the beginning of the fourteenth century the house of Puigreig also enjoyed the protection of the Catalan family of Pinós and of the count of Pallars.[80] A promise to protect the Order was also included in some contracts of confraternity, although the amount of protection which a *confrater* could give inevitably varied according to his status. It was stated in some contracts that the *confrater* would inform the Temple of anything to its detriment which came to his knowledge, and this was probably the limit of the obligation of those of lesser rank.[81] To men of greater standing promises of protection brought an increase in judicial revenues and sometimes a small annual payment by the Order;[82] but probably the main purpose of promises of protection was in fact the protection of the Temple at a time when rights and legal processes were readily ignored and when the use of force was the rule rather than the exception. It was a layman's duty not only to endow but also to protect the Church. The grant of protection appears not, however, to have brought the Temple any more positive advantage, for there is no evidence to show that it led to the manipulation of justice in favour of the Order.

The Templars thus acquired in the *Corona de Aragón* very considerable secular rights and privileges, most of which were gained in the twelfth and early thirteenth centuries. During the course of the thirteenth century, however, the Aragonese rulers sought to recover many of the rights which they had earlier granted to the Temple. The Crown's lack of resources led the Aragonese kings in the first place to seek money from every possible source. The

Order, like the Church generally,[83] suffered a diminution of its rights. By the end of James I's reign the Temple's privileges concerning the payment of *monedaje* and tolls had been considerably reduced, as had its right to a tenth of royal revenues, and the Crown had further established a claim to exact *cena* from the Temple. But not all of James's attempts to limit the Order's financial rights were successful, nor were his successors able to add to his encroachments on Templar privileges. Royal policies provoked a reaction which found expression in the meetings of the Cortes in 1283, and after that date it was usually accepted by the Crown that it should be bound by the custom and practice of James I's reign.

For most of the thirteenth century the king took half of the *monedaje* owed by the Order's men. This was apparently done as early as 1219, and even then it seems not to have been an innovation;[84] and although there is no continuous evidence, the statements in royal writs that the division was made in 1284 'as is customary and ordained between the lord king and the Temple' and in 1289 'as has been customary until now' show that it became a regular practice, which the Order had sanctioned.[85] This division seems to represent a working compromise between the conflicting claims of the Temple and the Crown to the full enjoyment of the tax from the Order's men, and it was paralleled by similar arrangements on other ecclesiastical estates, where there were rival claims to the tax.[86] For most of the century the compromise was accepted by both sides. The only known occasion when the Temple failed to give the king his half was at Tortosa in 1279, when Peter III complained that the Order had retained a whole third of the *monedaje* from the city, instead of surrendering half of that amount to the Crown.[87] Similarly the king seems only rarely to have tried in practice to take all the *monedaje* from the Order's estates. In March 1264, when James I arranged to pay a debt of 4,000m. to the Temple from the *monedaje* exacted from the Order's men, the Templars were commanded to give the king all that remained.[88] But this demand obviously brought a protest from the Order, for later in the same month the king recognized the Temple's claim to half of the tax, although he commanded that it should produce documents in support of this claim.[89] This practice of dividing the *monedaje* left undecided the question of right, and this meant that both sides could still preserve their theoretical claims to full enjoyment of the tax. Thus when James I reached a settlement with the Temple on a number of disputed issues in 1247 he maintained his claims while not denying that the Order might have rights:

> We except *monedaje*, however, from this agreement and remission, and retain it for ourselves and our successors in towns and castles under Templar jurisdiction in our lands and kingdoms, to be paid in full to us and our successors, as it is customarily paid in cities and other places of our land. Through this retention or exception of *monedaje*, however, we do not wish any harm to be done to the Temple's right or privilege, if it has any, of not paying *monedaje*.[90]

At the same time the Temple similarly maintained its claim to exemption, while conceding that the king might have a right:

> We retain and keep for ourselves and our successors and for the brothers of the Temple, now and in the future, the right of not paying the said *monedaje*. . . . Through this protestation and retention, however, we do not wish any harm to be done to your right, if you have any, or privilege of demanding and taking the said *monedaje*.[91]

That the payment of half of the *monedaje* to the king should prejudice neither royal rights nor Templar privileges was further stated in royal writs issued in 1277, 1284, and 1289.[92] By this arrangement the Crown was able to gain a profit without disproving Templar claims. Yet despite these statements about safeguarding privileges, the custom of dividing the *monedaje* was in fact destructive of the Temple's immunity—even though this exemption was clearly set out in charters obtained from the Crown—for practice led in time to the abolition of privilege. The force of custom manifests itself in the agreements about *monedaje* made in 1283 between Peter III and the opponents of the Crown, for these had as their basis the practice of James I's reign; and although in the decrees issued in that year at Barcelona a clause was inserted safeguarding particular privileges, this was of little value to the Temple.[93] And finally in 1292 the force of established usage made it possible for James II formally to revoke the Temple's complete exemption from the payment of *monedaje* and to establish for the Crown the right to half of the *monedaje* paid by the Order's men.[94]

By the middle of the thirteenth century the Order's exemption from royal tolls and customs had also been reduced. During a dispute in 1245 about the exaction of *lezda* and *peaje* from the inhabitants of Ambel, the Infante Fernando was ordered by James I not to exact these dues from the Temple's men unless they were merchants.[95] Although only those who bought goods and then resold them were to pay *lezda* and *peaje*, such individuals must have comprised a considerable proportion of the Templar vassals who journeyed about the country carrying goods; the king's order therefore represented a marked encroachment on the Temple's immunities. It was repeated in a general decree issued at the beginning of the next year,[96] while in 1247 the ruling was also applied to the exaction of *herbaje* and *carnaje*.[97] This interpretation of the Order's privileges was maintained throughout the rest of the century: in 1268 James I commanded royal officials to exact *lezda*, *peaje*, and *pasaje* from merchandise carried by the Temple's men,[98] and in 1285 Peter III ordered that

if their [the Templars'] men were merchants and traded in merchandise from which *peaje* or *lezda* ought to be given, they should pay on these wares as other men pay.[99]

This restriction on the Order's privileges apparently resulted from a compromise made between the king and the Temple at Biar in 1244, at the time of the completion of the Aragonese reconquest,[100] but no text of the agreement has survived and the exact circumstances in which it was made are unknown. There was, however, no formal revocation of the Order's immunities, for total exemption from royal tolls was still included in a confirmation of the Order's privileges issued by James II in 1292.[101] The Crown was thus, as in the exaction of *monedaje*, giving verbal recognition to the Temple's immunity, while in practice disregarding it, and this is reflected in the wording of several royal writs. In a letter written in 1286 following a Templar complaint about the exaction of *lezda*, Alfonso III made reference to usage and custom as well as to the Temple's privileges,[102] and in 1291 the collectors of *lezda* and *peaje* in Daroca were commanded not to force payment in contravention of the Order's privileges 'except as has been accustomed until now'.[103]

A restriction on the Temple's right to a tenth of royal revenues was imposed at about the same time as the limitation of freedom from tolls and customs. Although in 1227 James I confirmed the charter issued in 1143 by Raymond Berenguer IV,[104] twenty years later the Order was obliged to accept that the promise of the tenth did not apply to the districts conquered or otherwise acquired by James himself.[105] There is no indication, however, that there was any attempt to stop payment of the tenth in the lands ruled by James when he first came to the throne, although the Order had temporarily lost the tenth from the royal demesne in Aragon early in Peter II's reign, when with Templar rights in Ascó it was given in exchange for the lordship of Serós,[106] and in James I's reign the tenth was on occasion withheld by the king as a loan from the Order; this was done between 1238 and 1244, in 1246, and apparently again in 1258, when the commander of Palau drew up an account of certain tenths in Barcelona which the king had retained for use on the fleet.[107]

Although only occasional references occur to the exaction of *cenas* from the Temple in James I's reign [108] and although most of the evidence about the payment of this tax by the Templars is found in the registers of James's successors, it is clear that by the time of his death the taking of *cenas* from the Order by the king and the royal *procurador* had become a firmly established practice.[109] Peter III's promise in 1283 not to exact *cenas* except in places where his predecessors had enjoyed them, and not even in these places if immunity through privilege could be established,[110] brought no general benefit to the Temple, for the Crown's claim was by then too well established; and although the Aragonese Templars later persuaded Clement V that *cenas* had been exacted 'almost by violence and with them always protesting and opposing',[111] in practice they had come to accept the obligation well before the end of the thirteenth century. Apparently the only occasion when the royal claim to *cena* was generally questioned was in 1296 following the publication of the bull *Clericis laicos*.[112] At other times the Templars were merely concerned to ensure that the limits established by custom in the exaction of *cenas* were not exceeded.

The obligation to pay *cenas* was not, however, imposed uniformly on all Templar convents. A few gained complete exemption through particular privileges. The immunity of Castellón de Ampurias was established as the result of an inquiry carried out in 1293; *cenas* had been taken from this convent in the time of Peter III and Alfonso III, but the registers of James I's reign showed that it was not liable for payment.[113] Further exemptions were gained in the following year. When James II recovered the lordship of Tortosa from the Templars he granted that the commanderies of Tortosa and Chivert and the districts given to the Order in exchange for Tortosa should enjoy exemption.[114] But when the majority of houses owed *cenas*, the exemption of a particular convent could easily be overlooked, and there was the further danger that a *cena* given voluntarily by an exempt house might be used as a precedent: when the queen was given hospitality for several days in 1303 by the convents which had gained exemption in 1294, the Templars felt it necessary to obtain from her a charter stating that this hospitality had been given freely and should not prejudice the Order's privileges.[115]

Some other convents enjoyed the privilege of giving *cenas* only when the king or *procurador* was present and took them in kind, which meant in practice that the *cena* would not be exacted every year. This right was established in 1298 for the commanderies of Castellote, Cantavieja, and Horta.[116] Although *cenas* in money had been taken in these places in the early years of James II's reign and in the reigns of his father and brother, an investigation of royal registers revealed that James I had not exacted *cenas* from these commanderies *in absentia*, and James II therefore accepted that they should not be obliged to pay *cenas* in money. In 1305 the house of Monzón also claimed the privilege of giving *cenas* only in kind, but although payment had usually been in this form, it is not known whether the convent managed to establish an exemption from the payment of *cenas* in money.[117]

From most commanderies *cenas* could be taken either in kind or in money. In practice they were usually taken in the latter form. In 1282 the convents of Miravet and Ascó were ordered to provide *cenas* in kind for the king, including twenty sheep, a cow, two sides of salted meat, thirty pairs of hens, bread and wine to the value of 50s., and ten *cahíces* of grain,[118] but on all other known occasions *cenas* were exacted from these houses in money. The king could obviously not exact *cenas* in kind everywhere in every year, and the right to commute the *cena* into a money payment provided him with a useful additional source of income.

While the convent or commandery was the normally accepted unit of assessment for *cenas*, the Aragonese kings attempted to gain further revenues by applying to Templar estates the policy followed elsewhere of exacting *cenas* separately from *aljamas* of

Jews and Moors.[119] And although in 1290 Alfonso III abandoned his claims to a separate *cena* from the Jews of Monzón,[120] demands were made of the Jews and Moors of Tortosa right up to the time when the lordship of the city reverted to the Crown.[121]

James I also asserted that the Jews under Templar lordship, like those subject to other private lords,[122] should pay *peita* to the Crown. But he did not succeed in establishing his claim. Admittedly for a time payments were apparently obtained from the *aljamas* of Tortosa and Monzón: in 1260 the tribute paid to the king by the Jews of Tortosa was increased by 800s. to make good a deficit elsewhere,[123] and in undated lists compiled towards the end of James's reign the *aljama* of that city was assessed at 2,000s. and 6,000s., while the Jews of Monzón were to pay 4,000s.;[124] and in 1283 the Infante Alfonso ordered all Jews assessed for *peita* with the *aljama* of Monzón to contribute to a payment then being made to the Crown 'just as you have been accustomed in the past to pay and contribute to royal exactions with that *aljama*'.[125] But an investigation into the royal right to exact *peita* and *questia* was made in 1289 after the provincial master had protested that the Jews of Monzón should be exempt. Alfonso III entrusted the inquiry to Raymond of Besalú, archdeacon of Ribagorza, but in the following year he ordered the judge delegate to take no further action because the matter had already been decided in the reign of James I, when a privilege had been drawn up.[126] This decision had obviously been in favour of the Temple, for Alfonso ordered that payments which were to have been made out of the *peita* of the Jews of Monzón should now be made from other revenues.[127]

James similarly failed to establish a right to a fifth of the booty taken by the Templars. He asserted a claim to this due in the 1240s and, when the Order opposed his demand, he even appealed to the pope, who in April 1247 appointed as judges delegate the prior of the Dominicans in Barcelona and the sacristan of Gerona;[128] but in July of the same year James gave up his demand.[129] The surrender of royal claims to the fifth formed part of a compromise settlement on a number of disputed issues, and the Temple in return made several concessions. But while it is possible to account for the abandoning of this royal claim, it is not known in what circumstances James gave up his demand for *peita* from the Jews under Templar lordship.

The failure of James's successors to establish a right to exact *bovaje* at the beginning of a reign in Catalonia and to take *quinta* from Templar estates in Aragon is easier to explain. In February 1277 Peter III ordered that *bovaje* should be collected without exception for his benefit in Catalonia since he had the right to exact it on succeeding to the throne.[130] Both the Templars and the Catalan prelates protested, but whereas on 13 April the latter were ordered not to impede the collection of the tax on their estates, the collectors of the *bovaje* were on that date commanded to delay collection from the Temple until a further order had been issued;[131] and a further order to delay was sent out a month later, even though the tax was then being collected from other ecclesiastical lordships.[132] At this time, however, the Templars appear to have been unable to maintain their immunity, for although in 1279 officials were still being ordered not to exact the tax from the Order's men,[133] in 1280 the inhabitants of Tortosa were being compelled to contribute and there is also evidence that at least some men subject to the commander of Puigreig made payments to the king.[134] Early in Peter III's reign the Temple's men in Aragon were similarly being obliged to pay the *quinta* to the king.[135] But in this, as in other matters, royal policy was attacked in 1283. At the Cortes of Zaragoza complaint was made about the *quinta* 'which has never been given in Aragon, except by request for the expedition to Valencia', and Peter was forced to concede that 'henceforth it is never to be given from any cattle or from any thing.'[136] In the Cortes at Barcelona the king further promised not to exact *bovaje* except in the places where his predecessors had taken it and in the accustomed form;[137] royal rights were to be established by Easter 1285, although in fact the matter was apparently still under examination at the end of 1286, when the lieutenant of the provincial master was summoned to an assembly to discuss the 'form of the payment of *bovaje*'.[138] After 1283 there is no evidence of further demands for *quinta* from Templar vassals, but the Order's immunity from the payment of *bovaje* was again questioned in the last years of the century. Although exemption from *bovaje* was included among Templar privileges confirmed by James II in 1292, the Order was in October 1296 again protesting about demands for *bovaje* from its men.[139] The Temple's complaint led to a further investigation of the Order's privileges, and its immunity was established early in 1297 by reference back to the practice of Peter III's reign;[140] and in the following years the Crown appears to have adhered to this ruling.[141]

James I's successors were, however, able to extract increasing sums from the Temple and its men in the form of extraordinary taxes, since these were given voluntarily, at least in theory. James I had already obtained by consent grants of *bovaje* for his expeditions, and to these the Temple had contributed;[142] he had also sought subsidies from particular places under Templar lordship.[143] But while in his time such taxes were exceptional, in the reigns of his successors they became common. They were usually levied under the names of aid (*auxilium*), subsidy (*subsidium*), or assize (*cisa*), and consisted either of general taxes consented to in the Cortes, such as those granted at Monzón in 1289 and Barcelona in 1292,[144] or of more local and particular levies. The Templars contributed to these taxes only reluctantly. In 1289, for example, when Alfonso III was demanding a subsidy of 20,000*s*.B. from the Temple towards the expenses of a royal embassy to Rome, the king was obliged to repeat his demand and to threaten seizure of Templar possessions if the tax was not paid;[145] and in 1292 James II complained that the provincial master had ignored a royal letter commanding him to ensure that the *cisa* decreed in the Cortes was imposed at Monzón.[146] The Templars showed reluctance partly because they feared that their privileges might be endangered by this form of taxation: thus in 1286 they sought to obtain from Alfonso III a promise that payment of the subsidy then being demanded should not prejudice their immunities or be used as a precedent.[147] Perhaps as important, however, was the weight of the burden which royal demands placed upon the Temple and its men. This is particularly apparent in 1292, when a separate subsidy was being demanded from the clergy in addition to the *cisa* granted in the Cortes. The Temple was asked to contribute 20,000*s*. towards this ecclesiastical subsidy.[148] On this occasion, however, it managed to persuade the king to abandon his demands;[149] but usually it could gain no more than a reduction in assessment, as in 1286 when its contribution was reduced from 12,000*s*.B. to 10,000*s*.B.[150]

The Jews under Templar lordship were expected to contribute separately to extraordinary taxes, which were either demanded directly from individual *aljamas* or negotiated at meetings attended by representatives of all the *aljamas* of Aragon or Catalonia. Thus in July 1282 the sum of 1,500s. was demanded as an aid from the *aljama* of Monzón,[151] and towards the end of the same year representatives from both Monzón and Tortosa were summoned by Peter III to an assembly at Barcelona in order to negotiate a further aid.[152] In the following year, however, the provincial master and Raymond of Moncada supported the *aljama* of Tortosa in its claim that it had never been accustomed to contribute to taxes jointly with the other *aljamas*.[153] It is clear that on this occasion the Jews of Tortosa managed to establish an immunity, for the Infante Alfonso ordered that their contribution should be paid by the other *aljamas*.[154] But if the Jews of Tortosa were able to establish a right not to be taxed jointly with other *aljamas*, the Aragonese kings could still make separate demands of them: in 1285 Peter III ordered them to send delegates with powers of attorney to answer certain questions put to them concerning a proposed subsidy,[155] and in 1287 Alfonso was seeking an aid of 10,000s. from them.[156] The collection of this subsidy was delayed,[157] but it is not known whether the *aljama* of Tortosa succeeded in excusing itself usually from such taxes. The position of the *aljama* of Monzón is clearer. It opposed the exaction of extraordinary taxes and gained certain concessions. Subsidies demanded in 1286 and 1289 were reduced from 15,000s.J. to 10,000s.J. and from 6,000s.J. to 4,000s.J. respectively,[158] while in 1294 the Jews of Monzón were freed from the obligation to contribute to a tax of 30,000s.J. originally demanded jointly from the *aljamas* of Monzón, Lérida, and Fraga;[159] and when in 1300 James II asked the Jews of Monzón to give 10,000s.J. to help meet war expenses he admitted that he had excused them from the payment of earlier subsidies.[160] But petitioning for concessions was not just a customary ritual whose outcome was known beforehand. All depended on the will of the king, whose favour could equally be withheld. In 1300 James forced payment by the removal of protection, the denial of justice, and the requisitioning of debts owed to the Jews of Monzón.[161] In this situation his promise that their contribution should not endanger their privileges could have provided little consolation.[162]

The demands for extraordinary taxes which were being made in the later part of the thirteenth century only indirectly affected Templar privileges, since such taxation was in theory obtained by consent. Nor did the more direct attacks on Templar financial privileges made by the Crown in the last quarter of the thirteenth century have any permanent consequences, for after 1283 the custom and practice of James I's reign became the criterion against which royal claims were judged: the Crown thus found itself obliged at the end of the century to abandon its demands for *bovaje* and some *cenas*. But most of the encroachments on the Order's financial rights appear to have occurred before the death of James I, and these were not affected by the concessions made in 1283. The Temple's privileges were therefore subject to considerable permanent reductions. Some of these, such as the restriction on freedom from tolls, were imposed at the time when the Aragonese reconquest was coming to an end and it is possible that royal policy towards Templar privileges was in some instances influenced by the completing of the *reconquista*; but it is clear that the Aragonese rulers were attempting to increase their revenues from all sources: the restricting of the Temple's financial rights formed only part of a wider policy pursued by the Crown in the thirteenth century.

In that century the Aragonese rulers also sought to extend their judicial powers. This was done partly by invoking the concepts of Roman law. In 1251 James I claimed the exclusive right of *merum imperium* in Valencia: no one else was to exercise justice of 'life and limb'.[163] And a similar claim was made in the *Fuero* of Aragon.[164] The king sought to apply this principle to places under Templar lordship; thus in 1254 he decreed that royal officials could enter the lands of the convent of Mas-Deu not only when there had been a default of justice or a breach of the *pax et treuga*, but also in order to punish and execute those guilty of homicide.[165] He claimed that the Crown customarily exercised these powers. But royal claims were not readily accepted by the Templars, who maintained that they should enjoy the right of *merum imperium* over their men. In a dispute which occurred apparently in 1271, for example, the Order claimed this right in Roussillon, Conflent, Vallespir, and Cerdaña. This claim was contested by the Infante James, who argued that the Temple's charters of privilege did not specifically mention the rights comprising *merum imperium* and that the Order should therefore not exercise this kind of jurisdiction. And the Infante's arguments were accepted by arbiters, who agreed that the Crown should have cognizance of all offences for which the punishment was death or mutilation.[166] The Templars nevertheless continued to question royal claims. They were clearly doing this in 1272, for in answer to a complaint by the Order about the way in which royal officials enforced the peace decrees James I maintained that the Temple could not exercise jurisdiction in cases involving capital punishment or mutilation.[167] A similar claim was asserted by the Crown in the next reign: in 1282 the royal sub-vicar in Tortosa was ordered to exercise rights of *merum imperium* in the city and the Templars and Raymond of Moncada were commanded not to impede him.[168] But royal policy, pursued generally, again aroused widespread opposition, which found expression in the meetings of the Cortes held in 1283. At Zaragoza the nobles objected to the introduction of the term *merum et mixtum imperium*, which they claimed 'had never been used before', and they demanded that the king should not 'set up justiciars or cause judgements to be made in any township or in any place which is not his own'.[169] Peter III was obliged to grant this demand, just as later in the same year at the Cortes of Barcelona, which was attended by the provincial master, the king was forced to restore the right of *merum imperium* to the nobles and clergy who had previously enjoyed it.[170] Although in the following years royal officials continued to challenge the Order's claim to exercise this kind of jurisdiction,[171] the Crown itself gave temporary recognition to the Temple's right; it was unable to establish a claim based on earlier custom. Yet at the end of the century James II made a further attempt to deprive the clergy of their rights of *merum imperium*. He adopted a method similar to that often employed in the thirteenth century to obtain taxes from the Church: in 1297, when he was at peace with the pope and when the latter was trying to persuade him to take action against his brother in Sicily, James instructed his envoys in Rome to ask Boniface VIII to grant him *merum imperium* in all places under ecclesiastical lordship, including those subject to the military orders.[172] An alliance of this kind between king and pope would—if achieved— no doubt have silenced any protests from the clergy, who would no longer have been able to appeal to the pope to act in defence of their privileges. But James's request was refused, as was a similar demand made three years later,[173] and the Templars were able to retain their rights of *merum imperium* until their arrest.[174]

The other judicial matter over which there was conflict between the Crown and the Temple was the right to hear appeals.
The Order both claimed and exercised this right in the thirteenth
century. In 1263, following a dispute about jurisdiction between
the Order and the inhabitants of Ambel, the provincial master
decreed that appeals against the judgements pronounced by the
justiciar of Ambel should be made to the commander there and
that appeals against the latter's judgements should be taken to the
provincial master; and a similar procedure was laid down for
Horta in 1296.[175] The actual exercise of the right is illustrated by
the hearing of appeals in 1277 and 1296 by Peter of Butzenit, a
lawyer set up as an appeal judge by the commander of Gardeny,[176]
although admittedly both of his judgements were concerned only
with dues and services owed to the Order and there are no surviving examples of appeals in cases of other kinds. This right to
hear appeals was called in question in the second half of the thirteenth century. The evidence remaining from James I's reign does
not provide any precise statement of royal claims, but shows that
at that time the king heard some appeals from the Temple's men,
who were obviously ready to take their cases to him. Thus in
1261 James promised Amato of Monzón that if by Christmas of
that year the latter had received no communication from the
Grand Master of the Temple, then those who had been exiled
from Monzón following disputes with the Order could return
to the town.[177] This promise clearly resulted from an appeal to
the king, after an earlier appeal to the Grand Master had apparently
had no effect. The provincial master's decree at Ambel two years
later suggests that the inhabitants of that place were similarly
making appeals to the king.[178] The royal claim to appeal jurisdiction is set out more clearly in the documents of James's successors. In 1282 Peter III decreed that appeals against decisions in
civil cases in Tortosa should be made to the royal vicar there and
then to the king; he claimed that the right to hear appeals was
part of royal jurisdiction.[179] Twenty years later James II argued
that appeals by men subject to the Temple in Aragon should be
brought before the justiciars of royal towns, the Justiciar of
Aragon, or the king.[180] He commanded the provincial master to
revoke the decree, made by the Temple, that appeals should be
made only to the Order's commanders or to the provincial
master, and he wrote to the inhabitants of Templar towns, telling

them to take their appeals to royal officials or to himself. James maintained that the hearing of appeals by the Templars was a recent innovation and that in the reigns of his predecessors appeals had been made to the king or royal officials; he claimed the right to hear appeals by reason of royal right and ancient custom. But although during a similar dispute with the bishop of Tortosa the king was advised that he could find support for his claims in the *Fuero* of Aragon and in the writings of the jurist Vidal of Canellas,[181] James did not produce any evidence to substantiate his claims against the Templars, and he was clearly unable to prove his case, for in 1318, after the Hospital had taken over the Temple's property, he was still trying to establish his right to hear appeals from those formerly under Templar lordship.[182]

Although from the middle of the thirteenth century onwards there was tension between the Crown and the Temple about rights of jurisdiction, it must nevertheless be remembered that the Templar attitude to royal interference was not one of complete hostility. The Order was ready to seek the aid of the king and royal officials against its members or its vassals when necessary. When in 1282 a Templar called G. of Monzón had discarded his habit and 'was going through the world rebellious and disobedient', the Infante at the request of the Temple commanded royal officials to assist in his capture;[183] and the Templars similarly sought the help of the Crown against vassals who failed to carry out their obligations to the Order.[184]

The military rights and exemptions of the Temple were, like its other privileges, called into question in the thirteenth century. It is possible that the Aragonese rulers put forward a claim to the *redenciones* of the Temple's men who did not serve against the Moors, although according to the Order's privileges these payments should have been received by the Temple. In 1305 royal officials attempted to collect *redenciones* from men of the Temple who had not participated in a recent expedition in Valencia. The Order protested and the king agreed that they should not pay. The reason that he gave, however, was not that they were exempt by privilege, but that as the provincial master had served with a large force of knights he had conceded *de gratia* that the men of the Temple should not be called out for the campaign and therefore should not be forced to pay a *redención*.[185]

More significant, however, were the demands which began to

be made for service against the Aragonese kings' Christian enemies. The Order's military privileges had been granted at a time when the conquest of Moorish territory occupied an important place in royal policy. But towards the end of the thirteenth century no further conquests to the south were possible and the Aragonese rulers needed service elsewhere, for they not only were trying to extend their power in the Mediterranean but at the same time also required military aid within the Peninsula against rebel nobles, against Castile, and against the French, who in alliance with Navarre and Mallorca attempted to put into effect the papal award of the kingdom of Aragon to Charles of Valois. It was inevitable that Templar houses sited along the Christian borders of Aragon should become involved in the defence of these frontiers: thus orders for the provisioning and fortifying of Templar convents near the Navarrese frontier were issued in 1283 and 1286.[186] But the Aragonese kings went further than this, as did some other rulers; they summoned the men of the Temple and even the Templars themselves for service in the royal army against the Crown's Christian enemies.[187] In 1275 James I summoned the men of the convent of Mas-Deu to serve against the count of Ampurias on the pretext that action was being taken against those who had attacked ecclesiastical persons and their property.[188] In the following reigns the Templars themselves were called out. The provincial master was summoned to serve with his men against the French in 1283 and 1285,[189] and against Castile in 1300 and 1301,[190] while the castellan of Monzón was called out in 1284 against the count of Foix. [191] In the last two decades of the thirteenth century the men of the Temple were also summoned frequently by themselves, as in 1280 for the siege of Balaguer,[192] in 1289 when the men of Monzón served in Cerdaña,[193] in 1293 against Artal of Alagón,[194] and in 1297 for a campaign in Pallars.[195]

When service was demanded only from the men of the Temple, the king issued summonses to them directly—although he sometimes also wrote to the Order telling it to send its men[196]—and this service was enforced by royal officials.[197] On these occasions military service was a matter between the Crown and the Order's men: when the inhabitants of Monzón served with Alfonso III in 1289 the king promised to support them if any objections to their serving in Cerdaña were raised by the provincial master or the castellan of Monzón.[198] It became the practice, however, to send summonses directly to the Temple's men even when members of the Order served.[199] This was probably done in an attempt to ensure that service was given; it does not imply that the Order's men did not then serve with the Temple. Although in August 1300 the inhabitants of Monzón were summoned directly by the king to fight against Castile, a letter was sent to the castellan of Monzón telling him to come for service with all the knights—both of the Temple and others—and the foot-soldiers of his commandery.[200] At such times the Order's men were still giving service to their lords, and on these occasions royal officials did not intervene. The royal sub-vicar of Urgel was reprimanded in 1283 for summoning the host in places under Templar lordship in that district 'especially because the host is being called out by the said brothers in these places in our aid'.[201]

Once the Crown had demanded military service directly from the Temple's men against Aragon's Christian enemies, it almost inevitably followed that it would also claim the *redenciones* of those who did not serve. Already in 1275 James I sought a payment of 1,000s. when the men of Mas-Deu failed to appear against the count of Ampurias;[202] and although *redenciones* were not generally sought at the time of the siege of Balaguer—the king ordered payment from Templar vassals only for lands which they held in *realengo*[203]—from the time of the French invasion in 1285 the Aragonese rulers claimed full payment from men of the Temple who had been summoned but did not fight. If none of the inhabitants of a township appeared, as happened in a number of cases in 1290 when service against Castile was demanded, the king imposed a joint *redención* of arbitrary amount on the township as a whole;[204] when only some failed to appear, a royal official was sent to inquire who they were, and the size of the *redenciones* was determined through negotiation and composition.[205]

When Peter III first sought the service of the Temple's men at the siege of Balaguer, he implied that such aid would be of a voluntary character, for at the end of letters issued on 23 June 1280 the clauses 'we will be grateful' and 'they will be thanked' were included, which are not encountered in other summonses sent out at the same time.[206] But this summons was accompanied by a request for a loan.[207] When a further summons was issued on the next day, the king asserted a more definite claim to service

by referring to the article *Princeps namque* in the Usages of Barcelona, which commanded all men to fight in defence of the
country;[208] and this became the basis of royal claims to service
from the Templars and their men against the Crown's Christian
enemies, and it was quoted in summonses which did not apply
merely to Catalonia.[209] The Usages did not, however, give the
king the right to service outside the frontiers of his dominions,
and in practice the Aragonese rulers did not try to assert any right
of this kind. In 1289 the inhabitants of Monzón did accompany
the king to Cerdaña, but Alfonso admitted that service had been
given 'not out of duty but as a special favour and at our prayers';
it was not to be used as a precedent.[210] The Aragonese kings
abided by this ruling. When the provincial master was summoned in 1301 to help repel a threatened Castilian invasion he
was told to join the king wherever the latter was 'within the
borders of our dominions';[211] and in 1306 before attempting to
use the Templars on a proposed expedition to Sardinia James II
considered it necessary to seek permission from the pope.[212] The
only obvious exception occurred in 1292, when the purpose of
the royal summons for troops to assemble at Tarazona was said
to be the invasion of Navarre. In fact the king intended merely
to exact *redenciones*; the circumstances were therefore exceptional.[213] It is not known whether on this occasion the men of
the military orders paid the sums demanded of them. Certainly
the collection of *redenciones* from those of the Hospital was delayed, which suggests that the Orders at least protested against
this imposition.[214]

Nevertheless the Usage *Princeps namque* could be used to justify
requests for service on a wide variety of occasions, when the king
was opposed by foreign invaders or by rebels. Yet the Aragonese
rulers did not try to exact service from the Templars and their
men at every possible opportunity. The Crown was clearly wary
of using the Templars themselves against its Christian enemies.
Members of the Order were admittedly called out when the
country was in danger of invasion from Castile or France and strong
measures were threatened to ensure that service was given; a summons to the master's lieutenant in 1300 thus contained the threat

if you do otherwise we will proceed against you and the possessions of
the said Order as is just against those who thus inhumanly refuse to
fight for their country.[215]

Yet the timing of summonses in 1285 indicates the king's hesitancy in demanding service from the Templars. On 22 April the Temple's vassals were ordered to join the king, who was at Figueras, and the master was commanded to send some men to the Navarrese frontier as well;[216] further summonses ordering the men of the Temple to join the royal army were issued at the beginning of May;[217] and it was only on 7 June that the military orders themselves were assigned the task of defending the coast, which was being threatened by the French fleet.[218] Nor was the aid of the Templars themselves usually demanded for suppressing risings of nobles. Similarly, although the men of the Temple were summoned more frequently than the members of the Order and were used against rebels, their services were not always sought. When Peter III, for example, called out the men of ecclesiastical lords in 1281, he commanded royal officials not to demand service from men subject to the Templars and Hospitallers, because he had excused them for the time being.[219] On such occasions royal officials who tried to exact service were rebuked by the king and ordered not to enforce service unless the men of the Temple were summoned by the king's command.[220] When the vassals of the military orders were summoned, it was often not until the middle of a campaign, when the king needed reinforcements. Thus although Peter III began to besiege Balaguer towards the end of May 1280, he did not seek the aid of Templar vassals until the later part of June.[221] Similarly, although the men of religious lords, including the Temple, were summoned for service in Pallars at the end of June 1297,[222] towards the end of May the royal vicar of Cervera had been ordered not to demand service from the Temple's men.[223] In the same way, the Aragonese kings did not always press their demands for *redenciones* from Templar vassals who did not serve. Although in order to enforce payment Alfonso III in 1289 commanded that all the possessions of the citizens of Tortosa on the island of Mallorca should be seized,[224] on some other occasions demands were abandoned, as in 1290 when the king *de gratia* gave up his claim to *redenciones* from the inhabitants of Monzón who had not served on a recent campaign in the north.[225]

The Crown's demands for service were being made at a time when royal encroachments on privilege were being denounced and when a return to earlier custom was being demanded. In this situation the Aragonese rulers were hesitant in making new claims to service, especially as there was in the 1280s the danger that the Temple might give its support to Aragon's French and papal enemies. The only solution for the king, as in the sphere of jurisdiction, was to persuade the papacy itself to agree to a diminution of the Order's privileges. James II therefore in 1297 sought not only the right of *merum imperium* but also that of *hueste* and *cabalgada* in places subject to the military orders and other ecclesiastical lords.[226] But the royal request was rejected, as was a demand made three years later that the king should lead the men of religious lords in expeditions undertaken in defence of the country;[227] and after the dissolution of the Temple the question of military service continued to be an issue in dispute between the Crown and the Hospitallers.[228]

The Aragonese kings' new demands for military service were probably more influenced by the completion of the reconquest than the claims they made in the fields of finance and justice, which formed part of a wider policy. But while royal demands for service against Christians are to be explained in part by the declining importance of the struggle against the Moors once the Aragonese reconquest was completed, it is possible that in seeking this kind of service the Aragonese kings were also influenced by the Templars' reluctance to fulfil the obligation which they still owed of fighting against the infidel. Although the Templars still participated in campaigns against the Moors,[229] they were often slow to respond to royal summonses and sought temporary exemptions for themselves.

The first clear indication of the Order's changing attitude is found in a papal bull issued in 1250, in which Innocent IV ordered the Temple and Hospital to assist in the struggle against the Moors in Spain.[230] This letter was sent in response to a petition from James I, who had obviously complained about the Orders' conduct. Fuller evidence of this reluctance is encountered towards the end of the century. It is revealed, for example, by the timing and wording of a series of royal summonses issued at the end of 1286 and early in 1287, after the treaty made with Granada in 1282 had been repudiated.[231] On 9 December 1286 the king wrote from Mallorca commanding the military orders to go without delay to Valencia to repel an invasion which the Moors were preparing.[232] This first summons was followed at the beginning of January 1287 by a further letter from Alfonso to Peter of Tous, the lieutenant of the provincial master, ordering him to prepare to repel the Moors and not to put forward any excuses; in this letter the king recalled that the Templars had been given lands on the understanding that they would always be ready to defend the kingdom against the Moors, and he threatened to seize some of their property if they did not serve.[233] On 11 April the military orders were further ordered to serve under Berenguer of Puigvert and Peter Fernández,[234] but it was necessary to write again ten days later to the Templars, Hospitallers, and the commander of Alcañiz to order them to go to Valencia immediately; on this occasion the king threatened to seize all their property in Valencia if they did not comply.[235] In the same way, when the Temple was commanded to serve on the frontier for the whole of January 1304, it was made known to the provincial master that

if, which is scarcely to be believed, he delays in carrying out this order, the king will take whatever action he thinks fit.[236]

The Templars did serve on the frontier in the early months of 1304, but after raiding into Granada in conjunction with troops from Murcia and with Alabes Abenraho, the leader of a Muslim force in the service of the Aragonese king,[237] the provincial master wrote from Lorca in May to James II, seeking to excuse the Templars from remaining on the frontier;[238] and the master was again loath to serve when the Templars were further summoned in September of the same year.[239]

This reluctance was apparently not the result of waning interest in the struggle against the Moors: in 1304 the provincial master was exhorting James II to attack and conquer Granada,[240] just as earlier the Templar Olivier in his poem 'Estat aurai lonc temps en pessamen' had urged James I to go on a crusade to the East.[241] It sprang primarily from a lack of adequate resources. In May 1304 the provincial master pointed out to the king that the Order had incurred heavy expenses on the frontier, to cover which it had been necessary to obtain loans;[242] and in September, when service was again being demanded, the master Berenguer of Cardona wrote to the commander of Alfambra, saying

Although we might make our excuses to him [the king] on the grounds that we have spent a large amount of money this year on frontier service and in the kingdom of Murcia, nevertheless, seeing that if we failed him great dishonour would fall on us and the Temple, especially as all the nobles and other ranks are going, and seeing that we want to serve God and uphold the honour of the Temple, we are preparing to go and help our lord the king.[243]

Yet in October he again complained to the king about costs. James therefore on 24 October asked him to bring merely twenty or thirty knights,[244] and on the next day the provincial master ordered the commanders of Alfambra, Villel, Calatayud, Añesa, and Aberín, who had been incurring expense while waiting at Murviedro, to return to their commanderies.[245]

Lack of resources not only made the Templars reluctant to serve; it apparently also meant that when they did serve they had difficulty in equipping an adequate force. Towards the end of the thirteenth century convents did not have enough horses for all fighting brothers: in 1289 the house of Monzón possessed only five hacks and two mules on which its members could ride.[246] Horses for those going to serve on the frontier were provided in part by the provincial master, who borrowed some from Templars who were not called out: on one occasion the master ordered a commander to give his horse to his companion and to borrow another from the commander of Miravet, who had been excused from service.[247] Even the horses which the Templars did possess were not always their own. In 1309 James II received a petition from an individual who was seeking to recover a horse which he had lent to the Order;[248] and in the following year requests were also made for arms and armour which had been loaned to the Templars.[249] Inventories compiled towards the end of the thirteenth century provide further evidence of the inadequacy of the equipment in some Templar houses. When the commander of Huesca drew up a list of his convent's possessions in 1289 he noted that three hauberks and three other coats of mail had been lent to Novillas on the order of the provincial master, and that all that remained at Huesca were four hauberks and seven and a half pairs of chausses.[250]

Such a situation easily explains James II's request to the pope that the Templars should devote all their resources to fighting the Moors of Granada and should send nothing for the support of the Order in the East.[251] But this request was refused. All that the Aragonese kings could do to ensure that the Templars provided an adequate number of troops—apart from threatening action against their lands—was to stipulate how many knights were needed for service on each occasion. In May 1287 the king ordered the Temple to maintain thirty knights on the frontier—the same number being demanded of the Hospital and twenty from Calatrava;[252] and in October 1303 the Temple was ordered to send a hundred knights to Valencia, while the Hospital, Calatrava, and Santiago were asked for contingents of sixty, thirty, and twenty respectively.[253] But since property on the mainland had not been granted to the Orders in return for a specific amount of service,[254] the king had difficulty in enforcing such demands. In the register containing the summons of October 1303 the figure '100' was crossed out and the words 'as large a force as you can manage' substituted, probably as the result of a Templar protest that the Order could not furnish the number required.

Even if it was occasioned by lack of money, this reluctance on the part of the Templars to fight against the Moors, and the Crown's difficulty in enforcing service, could well have helped to justify in the minds of the Aragonese kings a demand for military service against Aragon's Christian enemies: if the Templars did not fulfil the military obligations expected of them in one sphere, then an argument might be put forward for demanding service from them elsewhere.

The encroachments on Templar rights and exemptions which have been discussed apparently all resulted from attempts by the Crown to increase its wealth and power. Although on a number of issues the evidence is very incomplete, it is clear that charters of privilege issued by earlier rulers in themselves gave little protection against these royal demands, for kings did not feel necessarily obliged to accept concessions made by their predecessors: hence the practice of seeking frequent confirmations of privileges. Lip-service might admittedly be paid to the Order's rights and it might be stated that a particular demand was not to harm the Temple's immunities and was not to be used as a precedent, but the more often this was said the more meaningless it became. In some instances the Order was able to reach a compromise with the king, so that not all of the latter's demands were met, but royal encroachments could not be halted by individual action. The Crown could be effectively checked only when widespread hostility to royal policies was aroused, as happened in 1283. Thus, in contrast to the earlier policy of encroachment, there was from 1283 a reversion to past practice, if not an acceptance of all earlier privileges, and apparently the only new demand that was being enforced in the later thirteenth century was for military service against Aragon's Christian enemies; and although the Aragonese kings could put forward a claim based on the Usages of Barcelona, they were hesitant in demanding this service and turned to the papacy for assistance in establishing a right to *hueste* and *cabalgada* from the Temple's men.

The desire of the Aragonese kings to increase their power and wealth does not, however, account for all the Crown's contraventions of Templar rights and privileges. Some were occasioned merely by the inadequacies of royal administration, and in particular by a failure to maintain adequate records. A number of demands for *cena*, for example, were made of the Temple apparently because exemptions were not always properly noted. Thus although it was established in 1298 that the commandery of Horta was not obliged to give *cenas in absentia*, the convent was again assessed for money *cenas* in 1300 and in some later years, and in each case the Temple had to take action to ensure that Horta's privilege was observed.[255] During the reigns of Peter III and Alfonso III demands for *cena* from places subject to Monzón were similarly repeatedly made and then cancelled.[256] Charters of privilege did give some protection against abuses committed in these circumstances.

The Order's secular rights and immunities were contravened not only by the Crown. Rights might be called in question from any quarter. But the individuals against whom the Temple made the most frequent complaints were local royal officials and tax-farmers, who not only carried out royal orders but were also themselves responsible for many abuses. The activities of royal officials affected all the Temple's immunities and privileges, but it is in the financial sphere that the fullest information about their actions survives. The royal registers, for example, contain a very large number of writs to royal officials concerning the payment of the tenth of royal revenues to the Order, and numerous letters on the same subject are included in the *Liber super decimis*[257] and in the collections of royal parchments and paper documents. It is therefore primarily in this sphere that an explanation of the activities of royal officials is to be found and it was naturally with the Temple's financial privileges that tax-farmers were mainly concerned. In some cases, of course, encroachments on Templar immunities require little explanation. Farmers of revenues wanted to derive as much profit as possible from the dues which they farmed and officials similarly sought to gain by abusing privileges: in 1261 James I attacked those officials who proceeded against the Temple 'out of avarice rather than because of a zeal for justice'.[258] Yet such desires do not explain all the complaints made by the Temple. Abuses were again frequently caused by the difficulties which confronted medieval administrators and by the limitations of medieval administration. This was recognized by Peter II in 1205 when he blamed the Temple's difficulty in obtaining its tenth on frequent changes in personnel among royal officials.[259] The great variety of privileges enjoyed by different persons and institutions and the frequent lack of any adequate record of such immunities in the royal archives led to the issuing of general decrees on behalf of the Crown, which took no account of particular exemptions. Local officials and tax-farmers needed a detailed knowledge of the rights enjoyed by the inhabitants of their districts if friction was to be avoided. This was not always possible, especially when royal revenues were farmed out annually. Thus in 1293 the royal official in charge of the collection of *primicias* in the district of Teruel issued a general order, which his subordinate—ignorant of particular immunities—tried to enforce at Albentosa, where the Temple should have received the *primicias*.[260] An aggrieved person might be able to produce charters of privilege, but such documents were often vague in wording and the rights recorded in them had sometimes been modified by usage and custom. Charters did not therefore always provide a reliable guide, and a royal official might feel reluctant to accept them as evidence. He might also in these circumstances find himself confronted by a conflict of privilege, for rights were often granted by the king without reference to existing immunities, of which the Crown frequently had no record. In 1294 a dispute arose in Zaragoza because the Temple claimed to have privileges exempting certain Jews in the city from the payment of royal taxes, while the *aljama* of the Jews there asserted that they possessed a privilege which obliged all Jews in the city to contribute with them to these taxes;[261] and five years later, when the Temple complained that it was not receiving its share of royal revenues from Zaragoza, the *merino* of the city asserted that these revenues were not sufficient for paying out all the grants which had been made from them.[262]

Those collecting dues might be inadequately informed not merely about particular rights and privileges. Templar complaints that *cenas* were collected before a year had elapsed since the last exaction can probably be explained by ignorance of the proper date of collection on the part of the collectors. Orders for the exaction of *cenas* were not sent out at any particular time in the year, but were often issued well in advance of the proper date of collection. The first writs for the collection of *cena* from Templar commanderies for the year 1298 were sent out in September 1297,[263] while those for the year 1299 began to be issued in May 1298.[264] On these occasions the entries in the royal registers make clear which year's *cena* was being ordered, but in many instances this information is lacking in the registers and it may similarly have been omitted from the letters sent to officials. In this situation the latter probably sought to carry out their orders at once, thus provoking Templar complaints that two *cenas* were being demanded in one year.

At other times complaints might be occasioned by misunderstandings among royal officials and tax-farmers. When in 1295 the farmers of royal rents in the district of Prades were ordered by the king to pay the tenth due to the Temple, they claimed that the royal official who had farmed out the rents had promised to pay the tenth himself, and it was only after several months of dispute that it was agreed that the farmers should pay the tenth but should then deduct the amount involved from the sum which they owed to the Crown.[265] In these circumstances it is not surprising that when tax-farmers were appointed the Temple sought to extract charters from them, in which they guaranteed payment of the tenth to the Order.[266]

The limitations of medieval administration can also in part explain the slowness with which disputes were settled. The Aragonese kings certainly took action about complaints concerning the activities of royal officials and tax-farmers, but they could usually not give a definitive ruling without making an investigation of rights and privileges; and as complaints were frequent and administrative resources limited this could not always be done. Normally inquiries were instituted by the king only when the dispute was between the Templars and the Crown. When the issue lay between the Order and a royal official, the king often merely wrote to the individual concerned, ordering him not to go beyond right and custom, and to give up his demands if these exceeded established limits. Thus when the Templars complained in 1287 that the royal *procurador* in Valencia was unjustly demanding *cenas* from the Templar houses of Valencia, Burriana, and Chivert, the king merely ordered the *procurador* to abandon his demand if other *procuradores* had not received *cenas* in these places.[267] Similarly when in 1291 the Templars protested against the demand for *cenas* from both Torres de Segre and Remolins, the official concerned was merely ordered by the Infante Peter to give up his claim if he was satisfied that Remolins and Torres de Segre constituted one commandery.[268] The settlement of a dispute was thus often left in the hands of the official of whose conduct the Temple was complaining, and this could lead merely to the prolongation of a dispute. In 1291 after the Infante's letter had been read out to the collector of the *cena* and the Templars had asserted that Torres de Segre and Remolins formed one commandery, the collector merely said that he would deliberate on the matter; no quick solution was reached. This method of dealing with complaints was not therefore a very effective one, but in view of the administrative limitations of the time it was all that the king could do. He had difficulty in carrying out his duty of protecting right and privilege, and those enjoyed by the Temple were endangered not only by royal policy in the thirteenth century but also by the activities of many others, especially royal officials and tax-farmers. The defence of the Order's rights and privileges from outside interference was inevitably a matter of frequent concern to the Templars.

They did what they could to ensure that these rights and privileges were maintained, although they in turn were at times hampered by administrative limitations. Confirmations of rights were frequently sought and obtained; title deeds and charters of privileges were preserved and often copied: transcripts were made and cartularies were compiled both for individual convents and for the Order as a whole in Aragon.[269] Most of those that survive, however, were not compiled until the second half of the thirteenth century, by which time some documents had no doubt been lost;[270] and although—since most of the cartularies are now incomplete—it is usually difficult to assess how systematically the work of copying was done, there are several surviving parchments recording acquisitions by the convent of Tortosa which are not found in the cartulary of that house, even though this volume does appear to be complete.[271] Finally, the royal registers show that the Templars were quick to protest whenever they felt that their rights had been abused. By adopting such procedures and by taking such action, they were able to protect their rights and immunities from many attempts at encroachment, even if they were not able to prevent the Aragonese kings from restricting the Order's privileges.

## NOTES

1. ACA, parch. Alfonso II, no. 667; AHN, cód. 499, p. 80, doc. 193; cód. 691, fol. 173ᵛ, doc. 422.

2. AHN, cód. 1311, side A.

3. AHN, Montesa, P. 223.

4. J. Orlandis, ' "Traditio corporis et animae" (La "familiaritas" en las iglesias y monasterios españoles de la alta edad media)', *AHDE*, xxiv (1954), 136, seems to be reading more than is justified into the phrase when he says that it meant that the soul was given for prayers and the body for burial. It was used rather to signify the completeness of a gift.

5. AGP, parch. Tortosa, nos. 5, 64; AHN, San Juan, leg. 174, doc. 1.

6. ACA, parch. James I, no. 2151.

7. AHN, cód. 691, fol. 51–51ᵛ, doc. 149.

8. Cf. E. de Hinojosa, *El régimen señorial y la cuestión agraria en Cataluña* (Madrid, 1905), p. 87.

9. ACA, parch. Peter III, no. 164.

10. ACA, parch. Alfonso II, nos. 489, 718; Peter II, no. 52; see below, p. 375.

11. ACA, parch. Peter II, nos. 52, 68, 236, 286; see below, p. 375.

12. e.g. ACA, parch. Alfonso II, no. 266; Peter III, no. 175.

13. ACA, reg. 48, fol. 34.

14. ACA, parch. James II, no. 771; see below, p. 409.

15. Cf. Hinojosa, op. cit., pp. 93–4.

16. ACA, parch. James I, no. 730.

17. On this tax, see J. C. Russell, 'The Medieval Monedatge of Aragon and Valencia', *Proceedings of the American Philosophical Society*, cvi (1962), 483–504;

F. Mateu y Llopis, ' "Super Monetatico" o "Morabetino" ', *Mélanges offerts à René Crozet* (Poitiers, 1966), ii. 1115–20.

18. One view of the origins and nature of this tax is provided by F. Soldevila, 'A propòsit del servei del bovatge', *Anuario de estudios medievales*, i (1964), 573–84.

19. *CDI*, iv. 94, doc. 43; Albon, *Cartulaire*, p. 204, doc. 314.

20. *CDI*, viii. 45–7, doc. 13.

21. AHN, Montesa, P. 523.

22. AHN, San Juan, leg. 186, doc. 3.

23. ACA, parch. Peter II, no. 315; AHN, Montesa, R. 31. It may be noted that there is no specific reference to *cena* in this list. This is possibly because *cena* was not a tax that was assessed on individuals. The right of *cena* is, however, specifically granted to the Temple in some royal charters of the late twelfth and early thirteenth centuries concerning particular properties: AHN, cód. 470, pp. 93–4, doc. 112; AHN, Montesa, R. 20: published from a different manuscript in *BSCC*, xi (1930), 355.

24. AHN, Montesa, P. 491.

25. ACA, reg. 20, fol. 318$^v$.

26. ACA, reg. 41, fol. 92$^v$.

27. ACA, parch. James II, no. 771; see below, p. 409.

28. ACA, reg. 14, fol. 146$^v$; AHN, cód. 689, pp. 4–5, doc. 3; ACA, reg. 310, fol. 47; see below, p. 397. R. I. Burns, *The Crusader Kingdom of Valencia* (Harvard, 1967), i. 193, confuses Gandesa with Gandía on this point.

29. ACA, reg. 91, fol. 103$^v$.

30. ACA, reg. 16, fol. 162.

31. AHN, cód. 471, p. 112, doc. 108.

32. Huici, *Colección diplomática*, i. 536, doc. 397.

33. *CDI*, iv. 144–7, doc. 61.

34. Ibid., pp. 29–32, doc. 11; Albon, *Cartulaire*, pp. 53–5, doc. 71.

35. *LFM*, i. 493, doc. 466.

36. AHN, cód. 471, p. 210, doc. 212.

37. AGP, parch. Comuns, no. 136; see also below, p. 377.

38. AHN, San Juan, leg. 174, doc. 16; J. Cots i Gorchs, 'Les "Consuetuds" d'Horta (avui Horta de Sant Joan) a la ratlla del Baix Aragó', *Estudis universitaris catalans*, xv (1930), 312.

39. See *Cortes de Aragón, Valencia y Cataluña*, vol. i (Madrid, 1896), *passim*, for Catalonia; ACA, reg. 16, fol. 236, for Aragon; and B. Alart, *Privilèges et titres relatifs aux franchises, institutions et propriétés communales de Roussillon et de Cerdagne* (Perpignan, 1874), pp. 211–12, for Roussillon.

40. *Cortes de Aragón, Valencia y Cataluña*, i. 84.

41. Ibid., p. 94.

42. Ibid., pp. 100, 108, 118.

43. L. D'Achery, *Spicilegium sive collectio veterum aliquot scriptorum* (Paris, 1723), iii. 588.

44. *Cortes de Aragón, Valencia y Cataluña*, i. 149–50.

45. ACA, reg. 97, fol. 203ᵛ.

46. ACA, reg. 108, fol. 100ᵛ.

47. ACA, reg. 21, fol. 72ᵛ; reg. 310, fol. 59ᵛ.

48. ACA, reg. 40, fol. 27.

49. AGP, parch. Cervera, no. 375.

50. AGP, parch. Casas Antiguas, no. 71. In his will, however, Bernard bequeathed this service to the Church, and by paying his widow 250*m.* the Templars were able to ensure that it was assigned to them: AGP, Cartulary of Gardeny, fol. 98–98ᵛ, doc. 238.

51. AHN, cód. 471, p. 210, doc. 212.

52. *LFM*, i. 492–5, doc. 466.

53. AHN, cód. 470, pp. 93–4, doc. 112.

54. ACA, parch. Peter II, no. 315.

55. A. Palomeque Torres, 'Contribución al estudio del ejército en los estados de la reconquista', *AHDE*, xv (1944), 217–22.

56. *CDI*, xi. 38. As the result of the increase of Templar property on the island, the number was raised to seven, but then reduced to six in 1268: ACA, reg. 15, fol. 108.

57. *CDI*, iv. 93–9, doc. 43; Albon, *Cartulaire*, p. 205, doc. 314.

58. AHN, San Juan, leg. 306, doc. 5; ACA, reg. 310, fol. 22.

59. AGP, parch. Comuns, no. 136; AHN, San Juan, leg. 39, doc. 79; ACA, parch. Peter II, no. 315; see below, p. 377.

60. AGP, Cartulary of Tortosa, fol. 87ᵛ, doc. 277; ACA, parch. James I, no. 1128. In 1242 the Temple made an arrangement with the Hospital for a reciprocal exemption: parch. James I, no. 870; cf. E. Bayerri, *Llibre de privilegis de la vila de Ulldecona* (Tortosa, 1951), pp. 58–9, no. 57.

61. *CDI*, iv. 29–32, doc. 11; Albon, *Cartulaire*, pp. 53–5, doc. 71.

62. ACA, reg. 310, fols. 43ᵛ–44.

63. ACA, parch. James I, no. 1667.

64. AHN, San Juan, leg. 342, doc. 4.

65. AHN, San Juan, leg. 40, doc. 140.

66. AHN, cód. 471, p. 133, doc. 133.

67. ACA, reg. 43, fol. 83.

68. *CDI*, iv. 29–32, doc. 11; Albon, *Cartulaire*, pp. 53–5, doc. 71.

69. *Cortes de Aragón, Valencia y Cataluña*, i. 58.

70. Ibid., pp. 68, 73, 83, 91, 96, 103–4, 114.

71. J. M. Ramos y Loscertales, 'Textos para el estudio del derecho aragonés en la edad media', *AHDE*, i (1924), 398.

72. *Fueros y observancias del reyno de Aragón* (Zaragoza, 1667), fols. 182–183ᵛ.

73. D'Achery, op. cit. iii. 587–9.

74. *Aureum opus regalium privilegiorum civitatis et regni Valentie* (Valencia, 1515), fols. 27–8. A peace decree was issued for Mallorca shortly after the island was conquered, but it has apparently not survived: E. Wohlhaupter, *Studien zur Rechtsgeschichte der Gottes- und Landfrieden in Spanien* (Heidelberg, 1933), p. 149.

75. AHN, cód. 467, p. 129, doc. 146; see below, p. 373.

76. Huici, *Colección diplomática*, i. 263–4, doc. 161; AGP, parch. Gardeny, no. 471; ACA, reg. 12, fol. 133; AHN, cód. 471, pp. 116–17, doc. 114; Montesa, R. 96.

77. Wohlhaupter, op. cit., pp. 81–2.

78. e.g. ACA, reg. 21, fol. 72ᵛ; reg. 43, fol. 120ᵛ; reg. 44, fol. 235.

79. ACA, parch. James I, no. 1659; parch. James II, no. 688.

80. ACA, parch. James II, nos. 1490, 1668.

81. AHN, Montesa, P. 533, 540.

82. A penalty of 500m. was decreed in a number of charters of protection issued by the nobility. The viscount of Cardona received an annual payment of five pounds of wax from the Temple in return for his promise of protection: ACA, parch. James II, no. 688.

83. J. Vincke, *Staat und Kirche in Katalonien und Aragon während des Mittelalters* (Münster, 1931), *passim*.

84. In that year James I ordered the Templars to make a payment on his behalf 'from that half of the *monedaje* which pertains to us which you have collected from our [*sic*] honours': AHN, cód. 471, p. 107, doc. 102. The fourteenth-century scribe who copied this document into the *Cartulario Magno* appears to have confused 'vestris' with 'nostris'.

85. ACA, reg. 51, fol. 10ᵛ; reg. 80, fol. 25ᵛ. The *monedaje* was usually collected jointly by royal and Templar officials: AHN, cód. 471, p. 131, doc. 131; pp. 135–6, doc. 137.

86. Vincke, op. cit., pp. 28–9; L. Klüpfel, *Verwaltungsgeschichte des Königreichs Aragon zu Ende des 13. Jahrhunderts* (Berlin, 1915), p. 155; J. Delaville Le Roulx, 'Les archives de l'Ordre de l'Hôpital dans la péninsule ibérique', *Nouvelles archives des missions scientifiques*, iv (1893), 41–2, 199.

87. ACA, reg. 41, fol. 103ᵛ.

88. ACA, reg. 14, fol. 48ᵛ.

89. ACA, reg. 13, fol. 157–157ᵛ.

90. Huici, *Colección diplomática*, i. 452–7, doc. 330.

91. Ibid.

92. ACA, reg. 40, fol. 26ᵛ; reg. 46, fol. 174; reg. 80, fol. 25ᵛ.

93. *Cortes de Aragón, Valencia y Cataluña*, i. 143.

94. AHN, Montesa, R. 146. The royal right to half of the *monedaje* owed by the men of the Temple and the Hospital was confirmed in the Cortes of Alagón in 1307: *Fueros y observancias del reyno de Aragón*, fols. 172ᵛ–173.

95. Huici, *Colección diplomática*, i. 402–3, doc. 287.

96. Ibid., p. 407, doc. 292.

97. Ibid., pp. 452–7, doc. 330.

98. AHN, Montesa, R. 120.

99. ACA, reg. 43, fol. 117ᵛ.

100. ACA, parch. James I, no. 1011.

101. AHN, Montesa, R. 146.

102. ACA, reg. 63, fol. 89.

103. ACA, reg. 90, fol. 138ᵛ; see below, p. 405.

104. *CDI*, iv. 98, doc. 43.

105. Huici, *Colección diplomática*, i. 452–7, doc. 330.

106. ACA, parch. Peter II, no. 201; AHN, cód. 471, pp. 136–7, doc. 139.

107. Ibid., pp. 107–8, doc. 103; Huici, *Colección diplomática*, i. 450–2, doc. 329; ACA, parch. James I, Appendix no. 28.

108. e.g. ACA, reg. 23, fols. 18, 38; F. Fondevilla, 'La nobleza catalano-aragonesa capitaneada por Ferrán Sánchez de Castro en 1274', *Congreso de historia de la Corona de Aragón*, ii (Barcelona, 1913), 1151 (the reference should be to reg. 17, fol. 5ᵛ); F. Soldevila, *Pere el Gran: l'infant* (Barcelona, 1950–6), pp. 81, 446.

109. Most of the information about the payment of *cenas* by the Order in James I's reign comes from James's later years, and it cannot be stated when *cenas* were first exacted from the Temple. M. L. Ledesma Rubio, *La encomienda de Zaragoza de la Orden de San Juan de Jerusalén en los siglos XII y XIII* (Zaragoza, 1967), p. 154, note 19, states that the Hospitallers were paying *cena* in 1203; but the document to which she refers belongs to the year 1303: ibid., p. 268, doc. 90. J. Vincke, 'Das Gastungsrecht der aragonischen Krone im hohen Mittelalter', *Spanische Forschungen der Görresgesellschaft: Gesammelte Aufsätze zur Kulturgeschichte Spaniens*, xix (1962), 166, argues from the wording of the general exemption from taxation granted to the Hospital in 1221 that

Secular    151

the Hospitallers were then exempt from *cena*; but charters of this kind cannot always be accepted at their face value; some were already out of date at the time when they were issued.

Royal vicars in Catalonia had the right to exact *cenas* in Peter III's reign, but this was revoked by Alfonso III: ACA, reg. 66, fol. 55ᵛ.

110. *Cortes de Aragón, Valencia y Cataluña*, i. 144.

111. Finke, *Papsttum*, ii. 221, doc. 117.

112. Finke, *AA*, i. 34–5, doc. 27. Finke states that the tax mentioned in this document is the papal tenth; but he does not expand the word *cens*, although in the manuscript it has an abbreviation mark over it: ACA, CRD Templarios, no. 179. That the dispute involved the exaction of *cenas* is also apparent from the wording of ACA, parch. James II, no. 834.

113. ACA, reg. 100, fol. 350; reg. 333, fol. 74.

114. AHN, Montesa, P. 523.

115. ACA, parch. James II, no. 1714.

116. ACA, reg. 324, fols. 272, 281; AHN, San Juan, leg. 231, doc. 5.

117. ACA, reg. 55, fol. 66–66ᵛ; reg. 333, fol. 99. For assessments in kind, see reg. 59, fol. 11 (1282); reg. 68, fol. 5ᵛ (1286); reg. 68, fols. 31, 89 (1287); reg. 330, fol. 4 (1293); reg. 324, fol. 265 (1297); reg. 332, fol. 287 (1302); reg. 333, fol. 98ᵛ (1305). At the end of 1286, however, the king asked for 1,500s.J. instead of the *cena* in kind which he had earlier ordered: reg. 68, fol. 21ᵛ; and money *cenas* were demanded of the convent in 1290, 1292, and 1293: reg. 82, fol. 34; reg. 331, fol. 9; reg. 330, fol. 2.

118. ACA, reg. 59, fol. 8. For other examples of *cenas* in kind exacted from the Templars, see E. Ohlendorf, 'Zur "cena in presentia" des Königs von Aragon', *Spanische Forschungen der Görresgesellschaft: Gesammelte Aufsätze zur Kultur-geschichte Spaniens*, xxi (1963), 155–61.

119. Klüpfel, op. cit., p. 139; A. A. Neuman, *The Jews in Spain* (Philadelphia, 1944), i. 78–80.

120. ACA, reg. 81, fol. 93; cf. Régné, 'Catalogue', no. 2115 (lxix. 179).

121. ACA, reg. 330, fols. 14ᵛ, 176; reg. 331, fol. 21.

122. Cf. Klüpfel, op. cit., p. 145; F. Baer, *Studien zur Geschichte der Juden im Königreich Aragonien während des 13. und 14. Jahrhunderts* (Berlin, 1913), p. 50.

123. ACA, reg. 11, fol. 177ᵛ; cf. Régné, 'Catalogue', no. 127 (lx. 186).

124. ACA, reg. 17, fol. 20; F. Baer, *Die Juden im christlichen Spanien* (Berlin, 1929), p. 112, doc. 103; J. Jacobs, *An Inquiry into the Sources of the Jews in Spain* (London, 1894), pp. 133–4; cf. Régné, 'Catalogue', no. 484 (lxii. 40).

125. ACA, reg. 59, fol. 192; cf. Régné, 'Catalogue', no. 997 (lxiv. 230).

126. ACA, reg. 80, fol. 30ᵛ; reg. 81, fol. 213; cf. Régné, 'Catalogue', nos. 1980 (lxix. 157), 2241 (lxix. 199).

127. ACA, reg. 82, fol. 181; cf. Régné, 'Catalogue', no. 2339 (lxix. 216).

128. ACA, Bulas, leg. 9, doc. 30; cf. F. Miquel Rosell, *Regesta de letras pontificias del Archivo de la Corona de Aragón* (Madrid, 1948), p. 84, no. 141.

129. Huici, *Colección diplomática*, i. 452–7, doc. 330.

130. Villanueva, *Viage*, xvii. 360–1, doc. 64. Peter's claim is discussed by F. Soldevila, 'Alguns aspects de la política econòmica de Pere el Gran', *VI Congreso de historia de la Corona de Aragón* (Barcelona, 1959), pp. 186–7.

131. ACA, reg. 39, fol. 187; Vincke, *Staat und Kirche*, p. 121.

132. ACA, reg. 39, fol. 202.

133. ACA, reg. 42, fol. 122.

134. ACA, reg. 48, fols. 114, 184; reg. 49, fol. 1; reg. 59, fol. 120$^v$. It might of course be argued that in Tortosa the king was taking only the proportion of the *bovaje* that was due to him as his share of the city's revenues; but the evidence from Puigreig suggests that this was not so.

135. ACA, reg. 41, fol. 63; reg. 42, fol. 131, 131$^v$; reg. 48, fols. 3, 28$^v$.

136. *Fueros y observancias del reyno de Aragón*, fols. 7$^v$–8$^v$.

137. *Cortes de Aragón, Valencia y Cataluña*, i. 143.

138. ACA, reg. 70, fol. 18; published by F. Soldevila, 'A propòsit del servei del bovatge', *Anuario de estudios medievales*, i (1964), 586. Soldevila argues, ibid., pp. 581–3, that this assembly was concerned with the exaction of *bovaje* for Alfonso's Menorca expedition in 1287, but in the documents which he publishes there is no reference to the actual collection of *bovaje*.

139. ACA, reg. 105, fol. 130.

140. ACA, parch. James II, no. 771; see below, p. 409.

141. ACA, reg. 257 contains a number of orders for the collection of *bovaje* from the clergy in 1300, but none of these refers to the Temple; cf. Vincke, *Staat und Kirche*, p. 162.

142. ACA, reg. 310, fols. 44$^v$, 47–47$^v$; in this second document the tax is referred to as *monedaje*, but this must be an error in transcription. Cf. Soldevila, loc. cit., pp. 579–81.

143. F. Carreras y Candi, 'Rebelió de la noblesa catalana contra Jaume I en 1259', *BRABLB*, vi (1911), 536; Huici, *Colección diplomática*, ii. 281, doc. 882.

144. ACA, reg. 81, fols. 19$^v$, 212; reg. 306, fol. 2.

145. ACA, reg. 80, fol. 43$^v$.

146. ACA, reg. 306, fols. 8, 11–11$^v$; see below, p. 406.

147. ACA, reg. 64, fols. 133$^v$–134.

148. ACA, reg. 306, fols. 2, 8, 11, 39$^v$; reg. 331, fol. 50.

149. Ibid.

150. ACA, reg. 68, fols. 47–8.

151. ACA, reg. 59, fols. 50ᵛ–52; cf. Régné, 'Catalogue', nos. 935–7 (lxiv. 220–1).

152. ACA, reg. 59, fol. 147ᵛ; cf. Régné, 'Catalogue', nos. 982, 986 (lxiv. 228–9). On this aid, see D. Romano, 'El reparto del subsidio de 1282 entre las aljamas catalanas', *Sefarad*, xiii (1953), 73–86.

153. Ibid., pp. 80, 84–5.

154. Ibid., pp. 81–2, 85–6.

155. ACA, reg. 57, fols. 226ᵛ–227; cf. Régné, 'Catalogue', no. 1455 (lxvii. 68).

156. ACA, reg. 68, fol. 55ᵛ.

157. Ibid.

158. ACA, reg. 68, fol. 41ᵛ; reg. 80, fols. 16ᵛ, 31ᵛ; cf. Régné, 'Catalogue', nos. 1544 (lxvii. 198), 1969, 1974 (lxix. 156).

159. ACA, reg. 331, fol. 55ᵛ.

160. ACA, reg. 332, fol. 93.

161. Ibid., fol. 93ᵛ; see below, p. 412.

162. Ibid., fol. 93.

163. *Aureum opus regalium privilegiorum civitatis et regni Valentie* (Valencia, 1515), fol. 11ᵛ; cf. *Furs*, III. v. 72, in *Volumen Fororum et Actuum Curiae* (Valencia, 1548), fol. 74ᵛ.

164. *Fueros y observancias del reyno de Aragón*, fol. 166; cf. J. Guallart y López de Goicoecha, 'El derecho penal de la Compilación de Huesca, 1247', *Anuario de derecho aragonés*, iv (1947–8), 36, 66–7.

165. B. Alart, *Privilèges et titres relatifs aux franchises, institutions et propriétés communales de Roussillon et de Cerdagne* (Perpignan, 1874), pp. 211–12; Huici, *Colección diplomática*, ii. 30–1, doc. 487.

166. AHN, cód. 1032, pp. 158–62, doc. 98. This version of the document is undated. E. de Barthélemy, 'Étude sur les établissements monastiques du diocèse d'Elne', *Bulletin monumental*, xxiii (1857), 482, assigns the dispute to the year 1271, but gives no reference.

167. Prutz, *Entwicklung*, pp. 312–13, doc. 5. The date, which is given incorrectly by Prutz, should be 21 April 1272.

168. ACA, reg. 59, fol. 13ᵛ; see below, p. 400.

169. *Fueros y observancias del reyno de Aragón*, fol. 7ᵛ.

170. *Cortes de Aragón, Valencia y Cataluña*, i. 142.

171. e.g. AHN, Montesa, P. 434.

172. Finke, *AA*, i. 41, doc. 30.

173. Ibid. i. 83, doc. 59; cf. Vincke, *Staat und Kirche*, pp. 63–4.

174. The Hospital continued to exercise these rights in places taken over from

the Temple: A. T. Luttrell, 'The Aragonese Crown and the Knights Hospitallers of Rhodes: 1291–1350', *English Historical Review*, lxxvi (1961), 8.

175. AHN, San Juan, leg. 174, doc. 16; leg. 355, doc. 1.

176. AGP, parch. Gardeny, nos. 1291, 1532.

177. ACA, reg. 11, fol. 235.

178. A right of appeal to the king was also claimed by the inhabitants of Monzón in 1292: AHN, cód. 471, p. 238, doc. 221.

179. ACA, reg. 46, fol. 64ᵛ.

180. M. Albareda y Herrera, *El fuero de Alfambra* (Madrid, 1925), p. 47; cf. Delaville, *Cartulaire*, iv. 44, doc. 4579.

181. A. Giménez Soler, 'El poder judicial en la Corona de Aragón', *Memorias de la Real Academia de Buenas Letras de Barcelona*, viii (1901), 62, 103–4.

182. ACA, reg. 25, fols. 153–4. At the beginning of the fourteenth century a similar conflict was being waged over appeals in Mallorca, then ruled by a branch of the Aragonese house. In 1301 the king of Mallorca argued that only one appeal could be made to the Templar commander of the island; any further appeals were to be made to the king and his court: ACA, CRD Templarios, nos. 152, 153 extra saccos. In 1303 he made a similar claim with regard to the archbishop of Tarragona's estates in Ibiza: A. Pons, *Constitucions e ordinacions del regne de Mallorca*, ii (Mallorca, 1934), 8–10. But the outcome of this conflict is unknown.

183. ACA, reg. 59, fol. 43.

184. See below, p. 226.

185. ACA, reg. 307, fol. 136ᵛ.

186. ACA, reg. 61, fols. 115, 137, 171 (1283); reg. 63, fol. 74ᵛ (1286).

187. The English king Edward I had some Templars in his army at the battle of Falkirk in 1298: T. W. Parker, *The Knights Templars in England* (Tucson, 1963), p. 48.

188. F. Fondevilla, 'La noblesa catalano-aragonesa capitaneada por Ferrán Sánchez de Castro en 1274', *Congreso de historia de la Corona de Aragón*, ii (Barcelona, 1913), 1157–8. Service was demanded before this from the vassals of the Order of Calatrava: in 1254 James I conceded that the exaction of *hueste* and *cabalgada* against Castile from them should not injure Calatrava's privileges: J. Miret y Sans, *Itinerari de Jaume I 'el Conqueridor'* (Barcelona, 1918), p. 242; and four years later he claimed the right to service against Christians from the inhabitants of Alcañiz, who were under the lordship of Calatrava: *Bullarium ordinis militiae de Calatrava*, ed. I. J. de Ortega y Cotes, J. F. Alvarez de Baquedano, and P. de Ortega Zuñiga y Aranda (Madrid, 1761), pp. 731–2.

189. ACA, reg. 25, fol. 242; reg. 56, fol. 124; reg. 61, fols. 107ᵛ–108; cf. Delaville, *Cartulaire*, iii. 442, doc. 3826; 479–80, doc. 3903.

190. ACA, reg. 332, fols. 75, 77ᵛ, 152ᵛ; see below, p. 412.

191. ACA, reg. 62, fol. 58.

192. ACA, reg. 48, fols. 51ᵛ, 56; Delaville, *Cartulaire*, iii. 395, doc. 3727. On the siege of Balaguer, see F. Carreras y Candi, *Miscelanea histórica catalana*, ii (Barcelona, 1906), 33–56.

193. ACA, reg. 80, fols. 33ᵛ, 40.

194. ACA, reg. 98, fol. 229–229ᵛ; reg. 330, fol. 69.

195. ACA, reg. 253, fol. 14ᵛ.

196. ACA, reg. 48, fol. 51ᵛ; reg. 56, fol. 84ᵛ; reg. 62, fol. 144ᵛ.

197. ACA, reg. 62, fols. 57ᵛ, 144ᵛ–145.

198. ACA, reg. 80, fol. 40.

199. ACA, reg. 332, fol. 79–79ᵛ. Summonses for service against the Moors were apparently also sent directly to the Temple's men in some instances: AHN, San Juan, leg. 333, doc. 15.

200. ACA, reg. 332, fol. 79–79ᵛ.

201. ACA, reg. 61, fol. 188.

202. ACA, reg. 23, fol. 27ᵛ; Varia 38, fol. 4.

203. ACA, reg. 48, fol. 77ᵛ; reg. 50, fol. 160ᵛ.

204. ACA, reg. 82, fols. 75ᵛ–77ᵛ.

205. ACA, reg. 71, fol. 42ᵛ; parch. Alfonso III, no. 111.

206. ACA, reg. 48, fols. 51ᵛ–52ᵛ; cf. Carreras y Candi, op. cit. ii. 44–6.

207. ACA, reg. 48, fol. 55.

208. Ibid., fol. 56–56ᵛ. The Usage is published in *Cortes de Aragón, Valencia y Cataluña*, i. 26.

209. ACA, reg. 56, fol. 80ᵛ; reg. 61, fols. 107ᵛ–108; reg. 62, fol. 58. The first of these documents is published in J. Vincke, *Documenta selecta mutuas civitatis Arago-Cathalaunicae et ecclesiae relationes illustrantia* (Barcelona, 1936), pp. 21–2, doc. 41.

210. ACA, reg. 80, fols. 33ᵛ, 40.

211. ACA, reg. 332, fol. 152ᵛ.

212. V. Salavert y Roca, *Cerdeña y la expansión mediterránea de la Corona de Aragón* (Madrid, 1956), ii. 203–4, doc. 158.

213. ACA, reg. 331, fol. 60; cf. fols. 64ᵛ, 67ᵛ.

214. Ibid., fol. 66. When Templar vassals failed to answer a summons in 1290, Alfonso demanded payments from them towards the costs of his attack on Castile; but they had originally been summoned to defend the country against invasion: ACA, reg. 82, fols. 75ᵛ–77; reg. 84, fol. 41ᵛ.

215. ACA, reg. 332, fol. 75; see below, p. 412.

216. ACA, reg. 56, fols. 80ᵛ, 84ᵛ.

217. ACA, reg. 62, fols. 143$^v$, 144$^v$.

218. ACA, reg. 25, fol. 242; reg. 56, fol. 124; cf. Delaville, *Cartulaire*, iii. 479–80, doc. 3903.

219. ACA, reg. 49, fol. 87$^v$.

220. ACA, reg. 307, fol. 31.

221. ACA, reg. 48, fols. 51$^v$, 56; cf. Carreras y Candi, op. cit. ii. 37.

222. C. Baudon de Mony, *Les Relations politiques des comtes de Foix avec la Catalogne* (Paris, 1896), ii. 243–4, doc. 129.

223. ACA, reg. 108, fol. 67. The men of the Temple were furthermore not compelled to serve with the *juntas* established for keeping the peace; but if they did not serve, the *juntas* were then under no obligation to come to their aid: reg. 74, fol. 50.

224. ACA, reg. 80, fol. 124.

225. ACA, reg. 81, fol. 28.

226. Finke, *AA*, i. 41, doc. 30.

227. Ibid., p. 83, doc. 59.

228. Luttrell, loc. cit., pp. 8–9.

229. e.g. ACA, reg. 70, fol. 103; reg. 71, fol. 45$^v$; AHN, Montesa, P. 276; Finke, *AA*, iii. 122–4, doc. 54; J. Miret y Sans, 'Inventaris de les cases del Temple de la Corona d'Aragó en 1289', *BRABLB*, vi (1911), 68. In 1276 Peter of Moncada, who was then in charge of the Aragonese province, was captured by the Moors: *Chronicle of James I*, caps. 558–9, trans. J. Forster (London, 1883), ii. 668–70; *Gesta Comitum Barcinonensium*, ed. L. Barrau Dihigo and J. Massó Torrents (Barcelona, 1925), p. 63; F. Soldevila, *Pere el Gran*, II. i (Barcelona, 1962), 106, doc. 100.
R. I. Burns, *The Crusader Kingdom of Valencia* (Harvard, 1967), i. 184, states that for half of each year the masters of the Temple and Hospital took command of the Valencian frontier, each of them being in charge for a four-month period. The masters were in fact placed in charge of defence only temporarily when the king went to Montpellier shortly after the conquest of the city of Valencia: *Chronicle of James I*, cap. 295, trans. Forster, ii. 408.

230. Prutz, *Entwicklung*, p. 283, doc. 7; Delaville, *Cartulaire*, ii. 686, doc. 2517. D. Mansilla, *La documentación pontificia hasta Inocencio III (965–1216)* (Rome, 1955), pp. 116–17, doc. 98, publishes a letter written probably in 1155 by the papal legate Hyacinth, in which—according to the editor—he exhorted the Templars and Hospitallers to fight against the Moors. But in fact the legate was merely seeking pack animals and other necessary supplies from the Orders.

231. On the relations of Aragon and Granada in 1286–7, see F. D. Gazulla, 'Las compañías de zenetes en el reino de Aragón (1284–1291)', *BRAH*, xc (1927), 183–95.

232. ACA, reg. 70, fol. 25$^v$.

233. Ibid., fol. 63ᵛ; see below, p. 403.

234. ACA, reg. 70, fol. 92ᵛ.

235. Ibid., fol. 106.

236. ACA, reg. 307, fol. 96ᵛ. The relations between Aragon and Granada in 1303–4 are discussed by A. Giménez Soler, 'La Corona de Aragón y Granada', *BRABLB*, iii (1905–6), 301–24, 333–4.

237. ACA, CRD Templarios, no. 101; Finke, *AA*, iii. 122–4, doc. 54; A. Giménez Soler, 'Caballeros españoles en Africa y africanos en España', *Revue hispanique*, xii (1905), 365–9.

238. Finke, *AA*, i. 146–7, doc. 99.

239. ACA, CRD Templarios, no. 383; reg. 307, fol. 131ᵛ.

240. Finke, *AA*, i. 146–7, doc. 99.

241. M. Milá y Fontanals, *De los trovadores de España* (Barcelona, 1889), pp. 381–2.

242. Finke, *AA*, i. 146–7, doc. 99. Finke gives only a partial transcription of the document: ACA, CRD Templarios, no. 84.

243. ACA, CRD Templarios, no. 383.

244. ACA, reg. 307, fol. 131ᵛ.

245. ACA, CRD Templarios, no. 419. Neither in this letter nor in that to the commander of Alfambra is the year of issue given, but they can be linked with a series of royal letters issued in the autumn of 1304. On 1 September 1304 the king, who was at Stas. Creus, ordered the provincial master to prepare to join him in Valencia to repel a threatened invasion: ACA, reg. 307, fol. 107. The master's letter to the commander of Alfambra telling him to go to Murviedro was issued at Gardeny on the first Friday in September, which in 1304 was the 4th. On 12 September the king wrote from Tortosa saying that the Moors had retreated and therefore the Templars need not go to Valencia but should remain in readiness: reg. 307, fol. 116ᵛ. On 28 September, however, the king issued a new summons because of a renewed threat by the Moors, and this was followed by further royal letters sent on 8 and 9 October seeking immediate aid: ibid., fols. 120, 128, 128ᵛ. James's letter of 24 October was issued at Valencia, and the provincial master's order written on 25 October was sent from Peñíscola.

246. J. Miret y Sans, 'Inventaris de les cases del Temple de la Corona d'Aragó en 1289', *BRABLB*, vi (1911), 62.

247. ACA, CRD Templarios, no. 539.

248. ACA, reg. 291, fol. 235.

249. Ibid., fol. 285.

250. Miret y Sans, 'Inventaris', p. 63.

251. Finke, *AA*, i. 158, doc. 108; Salavert y Roca, op. cit. ii. 102, doc. 72.

252. ACA, reg. 70, fol. 101ᵛ; cf. Delaville, *Cartulaire*, iii. 500, doc. 3959.

253. ACA, reg. 307, fol. 96. The claim by James II's representatives at the papal court in 1309 that the Templars had provided 300 knights for service against the Moors was clearly much exaggerated: Finke, *AA*, iii. 195, doc. 90.

254. In 1303 James II claimed the service of seven knights for one castle belonging to Santiago, but this seems to have been exceptional: ACA, reg. 307, fol. 96–96ᵛ.

255. ACA, reg. 332, fol. 16; reg. 333, fols. 26ᵛ, 33ᵛ.

256. ACA, reg. 61, fol. 181; reg. 62, fol. 26; reg. 68, fols. 8ᵛ, 28; reg. 80, fol. 26ᵛ; reg. 82, fol. 109.

257. ACA, Varia 1, fols. 25–40; see below, p. 404.

258. ACA, parch. James I, no. 1667.

259. ACA, reg. 310, fol. 34–34ᵛ; AGP, parch. Cervera, no. 196; parch. Barbará, no. 124.

260. AHN, cód. 466, p. 64, doc. 63.

261. ACA, reg. 99, fol. 5–5ᵛ.

262. ACA, CRD James II, no. 641.

263. ACA, reg. 324, fol. 272.

264. ACA, reg. 332, fol. 1.

265. ACA, CRD James II, nos. 235, 236.

266. ACA, parch. Alfonso III, nos. 344–6.

267. ACA, reg. 74, fol. 42.

268. AGP, parch. Torres de Segre, no. 20; see below, p. 403.

269. The convents for which Templar cartularies survive are Castellote, Gardeny, Huesca, Novillas, and Tortosa. On these and other cartularies, see below, pp. 456–7.

270. Only those for Gardeny and Novillas were compiled earlier.

271. e.g. AGP, parch. Tortosa, nos. 8, 20, 56.

# V

## Rights and Privileges: (ii) Ecclesiastical

THE rights which the Temple enjoyed in the churches that it acquired in the *Corona de Aragón* normally comprised not only the right to present to livings but also control over the revenues deriving from them as appropriated benefices: apparently the only exception was at Selma, where in 1237 Bernard of Portella managed to establish before papal judges delegate a claim to hold the church there 'with full right as rector'.[1] But the Templar income from these churches was limited not merely by the need to provide for vicars, if these were not members of the Order, but also by the obligation to pay certain dues to the diocesan. Admittedly Alexander III conceded that in places which they gained from the infidel, where the Christian religion had not been established, the Templars could build churches which were to be subject only to Rome and in which the diocesan was to have no rights.[2] But the lands won from the Moors in Spain had earlier been in Christian hands, and as the *reconquista* proceeded the former ecclesiastical organization was restored; bishops in the re-conquered lands were able to claim rights inherited from distant predecessors. The churches which the Templars possessed in the *Corona de Aragón* were thus all subject to episcopal authority, and the majority were in fact granted to the Templars by the bishops themselves. And the latter not only retained powers of jurisdiction over Templar churches, including the right to institute vicars and the power to correct them,[3] but also in most cases reserved to themselves certain revenues.

When García, bishop of Zaragoza, granted the Templars the church of Novillas in 1135, he demanded a payment of only twelve pence annually,[4] but two years later his successor Bernard made a fresh agreement with the Order and reserved to himself a quarter of all tithes and of other revenues.[5] In the second half of the twelfth century, however, it became the custom in the diocese of Zaragoza for the bishop to take a quarter only of the tithes of

'bread and wine' from Templar churches. This was the amount
reserved by the bishop Peter when he confirmed Templar rights
in the churches of Novillas, Boquiñeni, and Razazol in 1157;[6]
and when he granted the church of Encinacorba to the Order
in 1176 he ordered the Templars to pay the quarter as it was
given from Novillas, Boquiñeni, and other Templar churches in
the diocese.[7] The Templars were similarly obliged to pay to the
bishop a portion of the tithe from the churches they held in the
dioceses of Pamplona, Urgel, and Tortosa, although in some cases
the obligation was commuted into a fixed payment: when the
bishop of Tortosa granted the church of Ribarroja to the Order in
1281 he reserved to himself 60s. per annum in lieu of the quarter,
and three years earlier the bishop of Urgel had similarly demanded 50s.B. annually from the tithes of Puigreig.[8] A few
bishops, however, surrendered their right to a portion of the
tithes. Although in 1145 Michael, bishop of Tarazona, retained
the quarter when he granted the church of Ambel to the Templars,
three years later he gave the Temple the quarter as well;[9] and when
in 1149 the bishop of Lérida granted the church of St. John in
Monzón to the Templars he made no reference to the quarter
among the rights which he retained.[10]

In the charter recording the gift of St. John at Monzón there is
similarly no reference to the episcopal right of hospitality, but
bishops usually retained the *cena* from Templar churches. The
only specific exemption was that granted by the bishop of Zaragoza in 1157 with regard to the church of Razazol.[11] This obligation did not, however, always fall on the Templars themselves.
In some instances vicars were made responsible for providing
hospitality. When a vicar was maintained in a Templar house,
as at Encinacorba or Añesa,[12] the bishop presumably received
hospitality there from the Order. When a church was not near
a Templar house or convent, the vicar might be obliged to provide hospitality for the bishop, as happened at Ademuz in the
diocese of Segorbe.[13] But there was no rigid rule. At Estiche in
1286 the obligation of *cena* was shared between the Temple and
the vicar who was then appointed.[14]

The financial rights which the Temple enjoyed in the churches
under its authority were determined primarily by local agreement. They were only rarely the subject of papal decrees. Innocent III stipulated in 1204 that the Templars could receive the

revenues of a church in their patronage for forty days during a vacancy, and this period was extended in 1255 to fifty days;[15] but the only statements made by the papacy about the division of revenues when a benefice was occupied—apart from decrees of a general nature[16]—were that the Templars 'should give a reasonable amount for temporal things' to a vicar,[17] and that after money had been set aside for him and for obligations to the diocesan the revenues should be used in aid of the Holy Land.[18]

The papacy did, however, confer a variety of other rights and privileges on the Order, and the Aragonese Templars were able to derive benefit not only from the ecclesiastical rights which they gained in the *Corona de Aragón* but also from these papal concessions. For most of the twelfth and thirteenth centuries the defence of the Holy Land occupied an important place in papal policies. The popes were therefore staunch supporters of the military orders, and sought in the first place to help to provide resources for the struggle against the infidel.[19] This they did partly by the grant of rights and privileges which helped to increase the military orders' income. These included first the right of burial in the Temple's cemeteries. In the bull *Omne datum optimum* Innocent II in 1139 allowed the Templars to have cemeteries attached to their houses, in which members of the Order and its *familiares* could be buried.[20] There is no specific statement until the beginning of Innocent III's pontificate that this privilege was extended to permit anyone to receive burial in the Temple's cemeteries;[21] the versions of *Omne datum optimum* issued later in the twelfth century add merely the right to bury travellers.[22] But the Order early established the practice of burying *confratres*, and the right to bury anyone is already implicit in Alexander III's bull *Dilecti filii nostri*, which refers to those who chose burial in the Temple.[23] When the papacy granted these privileges concerning burial to the Order, it sought to safeguard the interests of the secular clergy, and the latter's rights were defined in the bull *Dilecti filii nostri*. Of things granted to the Temple by persons in good health or by those who were ill but recovered or by those who were buried elsewhere, the secular clergy was to claim nothing; of bequests made by those who on their deathbed chose burial in the Temple, a quarter could be taken by the secular clergy. Urban III made it clear that nothing was to be taken from those who were not inhabitants of the diocese in which they were buried;[24] Innocent III further granted that horses and arms left to the Temple should be exempt from the regulation about the quarter; and he also allowed the Temple's priests to hear the confessions of those who had chosen burial in the Temple, and to bear their bodies 'with cross and procession' to the Order's cemeteries.[25]

Other papal privileges, like that concerning burial, provided further opportunities for the Temple to gain wealth. From the earliest period of the Order's history the popes offered a remission of penance to anyone who became a lay associate of the Temple and made an annual benefaction to it. The incentives were added that such people, provided they were not excommunicate, would not be denied a Christian burial, and that when the Templars came to collect these donations they could once a year open churches and hold services in places under interdict.[26] Further promises of indulgences were included in special appeals made in aid of the Temple when the situation in the East was causing alarm. After the Grand Master of the Temple had been killed and the Templar stronghold of Jacob's Ford destroyed in 1179, Alexander III sought aid for the Order from the rulers of Christendom in return for a remission of their sins,[27] and further remissions were offered by Innocent IV in 1253, after the Order had suffered heavy losses in the East during Louis IX's crusade and in Sicily at the hands of Frederick II.[28] Indulgences were also promised to those who patronized Templar churches: in 1249, for example, Innocent IV granted a relaxation of 40 days' penance to those who contributed towards the cost of building a church at the Templar house in Barcelona.[29] But it must be remembered that the granting of indulgences was becoming an increasingly frequent practice in this period and that the Templars were not securing an especially favoured position on this point. Also in order to increase its revenues, the Temple was in the thirteenth century allowed to receive the redemptions paid by any of its vassals who had taken the cross but were prevented by age or infirmity or other just cause from fulfilling their vows: this was a privilege which was normally enjoyed by secular lords who had taken the cross.[30] Urban IV further in 1262 permitted the Temple to receive property which members of the Order would have inherited, except that held in fee.[31]

In order to prevent financial loss on the part of the Temple, Urban in the same year granted the Aragonese Templars the privilege that if any of their vassals were convicted of heresy, the possessions which the latter held of the Temple should revert to it, instead of being confiscated by the lay authority.[32] A similar purpose lay behind the bull issued by Innocent III at the end of the twelfth century, which decreed that the vassals of the Temple should not be forced to fight against Christians, for the pope was here trying to prevent the expenditure of Templar resources on ransoms.[33] And Alexander III had earlier tried to ensure that the Temple's men were in a position to carry out their obligations to the Order by commanding prelates to impose penance and not monetary penalties on them.[34]

The papacy sought to provide resources for the Temple not only by granting these privileges, but also by exempting it from the payment of certain dues. Of the financial exemptions granted to the Order, the most important in the twelfth century was that concerning the payment of tithes. It is possible that a privilege in this matter had been obtained by 1130, for in article fifteen of the Latin version of the Templar Rule, which has been attributed to that year,[35] it is stated that

although the reward of poverty which is the kingdom of heaven is without doubt due to the poor, we nevertheless order you, whom the Christian faith counts among them, to give daily a tenth of all bread to your almoner.[36]

This may imply that the Order retained the tithes from its property and was itself to dispense alms from these dues, as did a number of monasteries which did not pay tithes to outsiders.[37] Certainly to have imposed the obligation of giving a tenth of bread to the poor in addition to the normal payment of tithes would have imposed a heavy burden on an institution which was only just establishing itself. The first direct reference to the Templar exemption is not found, however, until 1139, when in the bull *Omne datum optimum* Innocent II conceded that

since those who defend the Church should live and be supported by the goods of the Church, we entirely prohibit the exaction of tithes against your will from movables or animals or from anything which pertains to your venerable house.[38]

This was a vague privilege, and Anastacius IV stated more precisely that the Order should be exempt from the payment of
tithes on lands which it worked itself or at its own expense and on
the food of its animals.³⁹ Yet even if this was a new ruling for the
Temple, it was one which had been applied earlier to monks and
regular canons⁴⁰ and before the publication of Anastacius's bull
it was influencing the granting of local privileges to the Order.
When the bishop of Pamplona in 1149 granted the Templars
the right to build a church at Añesa, he conceded that 'as is your
custom' they should not pay tithes on lands which they cultivated
themselves,⁴¹ and in the same year in an agreement about the
church of St. John in Monzón the bishop of Lérida retained the
tithes of Tamarite, except those from the Order's animals and
from lands worked by the Templars.⁴²

The Templars were also exempted from the payment of certain
procurations. Alexander III decreed in 1160 that the Order should
give hospitality in kind to papal legates and nuncios, but should
not be liable for procurations in money, except to cardinals.⁴³

The papacy often justified the Templars' financial exemptions
on the grounds that the Order's resources were used in the Holy
Land. This argument had its most obvious application in the
sphere of extraordinary papal taxation, a considerable part of
which was destined for the East. It was put forward, for example,
in a papal letter to the archbishop of Tarragona in 1246 about the
twentieth for the Holy Land which had been imposed at the
Council of Lyons in the previous year.⁴⁴ The Temple's exemption
from this kind of taxation was defined in 1256 by Alexander IV
in the bull *Quanto devocius divino*. He granted that

> you are not to be held or in any way forced to contribute by reason
> of your churches, houses, or possessions in any *tallia, collecta*, sums of
> money, or other exactions, under whatever name they are taken, or
> to pay them for whosoever's benefit or for whatever reason they are
> imposed, on the authority of letters issued or to be issued by the Holy
> See or its legates, without a special order from that See, making full
> and express reference to this exemption.⁴⁵

This decree did not of course limit the pope's power of taxing
the Temple, but in practice the Templars were exempted from
papal taxes for the Holy Land and from those imposed by the
papacy for the benefit of secular rulers: the military orders were

thus exempted from payment not only of the twentieth for the Holy Land in 1245 but also of the tenth granted to James I by Clement IV in 1265.[46] But for much of the thirteenth century taxes were also being imposed by the papacy to further its own interests in Italy and Sicily, and contributions to these were sometimes demanded of the Order. At the end of Gregory IX's pontificate the churches under Templar patronage in the province of Tarragona paid a fifth to the pope to assist him in his struggle against Frederick II,[47] and in 1264 Urban IV sought a subsidy from the Temple during his conflict with Manfred,[48] while at the end of the thirteenth century Boniface VIII made several demands of the Templars. In 1298 he sought the sum of 12,000 florins from the Order for his war against the Colonna,[49] and the military orders were also asked to provide the pope with money for his Sicilian policies.[50]

Although the financial exemptions granted to the Temple by the papacy were primarily concerned with ecclesiastical taxes, the popes did also attempt to restrict the Order's liability for secular dues by exempting it from the payment of tolls and customs. Lucius III in 1182/3 commanded prelates to prohibit the exaction of *pedagium, vendum, passagium, lauragium,* or any other custom from Templar goods; and this order was frequently repeated by later popes.[51]

Besides concerning itself with the financial needs of the Templars, the papacy also sought to further the interests of the Order by placing it under papal protection. A promise of protection for the Temple and its possessions was included in the bull *Omne datum optimum* in 1139,[52] and the promise was renewed in later issues of this bull[53] and in others such as *Quociens a nobis petitur,*[54] besides being repeated, as in 1178 and 1179, with special reference to the Templars in Aragon.[55] In granting protection the papacy was of course merely extending to the Temple a privilege already enjoyed by many monasteries and churches, but in the case of the Temple in Aragon there is no evidence of any annual payment to the pope in return for protection.[56]

The value of this privilege is apparent from the frequency with which the Templars made use of it. The large number of appeals for protection which they made to the pope need not, however, be taken as a sign of widespread hostility to the Order, as Prutz would suggest;[57] it provides merely a further indication of the general lawlessness of medieval society, where force was commonly used and often took the place of legal action. Templar complaints against a particular individual or individuals were usually referred by the pope to members of the Aragonese clergy, who were either ordered to hear and judge the complaint or told merely to obtain satisfaction for the Temple by ecclesiastical censures. Thus in 1261 the archdeacon of Tarantona(?) and the cantor of Lérida were ordered to judge the grievances which the Temple had against Berenguer of Puigvert,[58] while the provost of Tarragona was ordered merely to compel Arnold of Belmonte to give satisfaction to the Templars, who claimed that he had attacked their property.[59] Orders of this latter kind were also contained in bulls of protection of a more general character which the Order obtained from the papacy.[60] The course of action which might be adopted when a bull of this type was issued is illustrated by a letter sent by the archbishop of Tarragona to his clergy in 1299; quoting a bull from Boniface VIII, in which he was commanded to obtain within a suitable period of time the restoration of rights and possessions seized from the Temple in his province, he ordered that

you are to publish and cause to be published the said privilege or letter in your churches in the presence of the people whenever and however many times the brothers of the Temple request it of you. A suitable period, namely ten days, is to be assigned to those harming the Order in the manner aforesaid, within which period they are to make satisfaction to the preceptor and brothers of the Temple or come to an agreement with them. If they fail to do this within a further suitable period, which you assign them for the purpose, you are then to promulgate a general sentence of excommunication on them.[61]

Papal orders to obtain satisfaction must frequently, however, have necessitated an examination of the Templar complaint before action could be taken. In the bull sent to the provost of Tarragona in 1261 the clause 'if it is so' was included, as in many royal writs concerning Templar complaints, and this implies that an investigation had to be conducted before sentence could be passed; and when the bishop of Sigüenza received a letter from Innocent IV in 1244, ordering him to take action against those who molested the Templars and their possessions, he ordered those accused by the Order to appear before his delegates so that Templar complaints could be investigated.[62]

The grant of protection in 1139 was not accompanied by the privilege of exemption from episcopal jurisdiction for the Order, but in the bull *Omne datum optimum* Innocent II restricted the rights of prelates over the Temple in several ways. He decreed that no ecclesiastical or secular person should alter the customs of the Temple, or exact oaths of fealty or homage from its members. If priests or clerks were admitted to the Order the permission of their bishop was to be sought but even if he refused they could still be received into the Temple. Once priests had become members of the Order, bishops were not to claim obedience from them. Finally, the Templars could have their clerks ordained by any bishop; they were not obliged to have recourse to the diocesan.

It is not known at exactly what date the Order's privileges were extended to include exemption from episcopal jurisdiction, but the Templars clearly enjoyed the immunity before the end of Alexander III's pontificate. When Honorius III in 1216 prohibited the passing of sentences of excommunication or interdict on the Templars or their servants, as long as they were in the Order's service, he referred back to a similar decree issued by Alexander III;[63] moreover, at the Third Lateran Council the prelates complained that the Templars tried to use their privileges to exempt *confratres* of the Order from episcopal sentences, and this implies that members of the Temple at least were exempt by 1179.[64] The Templars' immunity, like that of the Cistercians,[65] may in fact have been granted by Alexander III for, according to Giraldus Cambrensis, he is reported to have said that he especially favoured the Temple, the Hospital, and Citeaux.[66] These were apparently the Orders which gave him firmest support in his conflict with Frederick Barbarossa, and the privilege of exemption may have been granted to the Temple partly as a reward for its aid in the struggle against emperor and anti-pope.[67]

The papacy was not affected by the Order's ecclesiastical rights and privileges in the way that the Aragonese kings were by the Templars' secular immunities, and although there were differences between popes and the Temple in the thirteenth century[68] at no time did the papacy attempt a general reduction of the Order's ecclesiastical privileges. It did take action, however, over the payment of tithes. This was done in the interests of the secular clergy, who were directly affected by the exemptions enjoyed by the

Temple and other religious houses. In the middle of the twelfth century Adrian IV restricted the exemption of the regular clergy and decreed that it should apply only to *novales*.[69] Tithes were to be paid from all demesne lands except those newly brought under cultivation. His successor, Alexander III, later argued that Adrian's ruling had not applied to the Temple, the Hospital, or Citeaux;[70] but it has been shown that Citeaux's exemption was reduced in Adrian's pontificate;[71] the military orders were therefore probably subject to the restriction as well.[72] In arguing that Adrian's ruling had not applied to the Templars, Hospitallers, and Cistercians, Alexander was probably seeking to justify his own policy of allowing these Orders exemption from the payment of tithes on all lands which they cultivated.[73] But if Alexander reversed the policy of his predecessor in this respect for the benefit of the orders which he particularly favoured, these exceptional privileges were not maintained. Because of continued tension over tithes, the general chapter of Citeaux in 1180 imposed a restriction on its own privileges, and decreed that if Cistercians in future acquired lands from which tithes had been paid this payment should continue;[74] and at the Fourth Lateran Council in 1215 Innocent III extended this ruling to all regular clergy who enjoyed privileges similar to those of Citeaux: exemption was to be confined to demesne *labores* acquired before the Council and to demesne *novales*.[75] The only other Templar privilege which was not always respected by the papacy was that concerning the payment of procurations in money. Thus when Urban IV sent a papal clerk as tax-collector to the south of France and Spain in 1264 he ordered the clergy, including the military orders, to provide procurations both in kind and in money.[76]

But if the papacy normally respected the Order's ecclesiastical immunities, the rights and privileges of the Templars were frequently called in question, especially by the secular clergy, whose revenues and authority were reduced by these immunities. Yet, as was admitted by some Templars after their arrest,[77] the faults did not all lie on one side. The Aragonese evidence shows that the abuses which the prelates at the Third Lateran Council or writers like William of Tyre complained of bitterly were not uncommon.[78]

The churches and tithes which the Templars possessed were a subject of frequent controversy. Bishops sometimes tried to recover the churches which their predecessors had granted to the Temple. In 1193, for example, the bishop of Tarazona asserted a claim to the church of Ambel, which had been given to the Temple by the bishop Michael in 1145.[79] But on the other side there was the complaint that the Templars gained churches and tithes unjustly. At the Lateran Council in 1179 the prelates argued that the Order received gifts of churches and tithes without episcopal consent, even though in the bull *Omne datum optimum* the necessity of obtaining this consent had been stressed. At the Council it was decreed that churches and tithes which had been received 'in modern times' without consent should be surrendered.[80] This phrase was defined by Alexander to refer merely to the ten years preceding the Council, and this ruling was confirmed by Urban III in 1186.[81] The prelates' complaint was echoed in Catalonia in a dispute about tithes in 1181 between the Temple and the bishop of Urgel. The latter finally confirmed whatever the Order had gained in the past in certain places but decreed that in future it should not obtain tithes without episcopal consent.[82] But it is often difficult to determine whether episcopal consent was in fact sought; in the records of most grants of tithes by laymen in the *Corona de Aragón* there is no reference to the bishop, yet this does not necessarily mean that he was ignored. Possibly the abuse was less marked in Aragon than elsewhere, since the majority of acquisitions of churches and tithes by the Order there resulted from grants by the prelates themselves in the reconquered districts.

At other times there was abuse of the particular rights and powers which the bishops and the Order enjoyed over churches in Templar patronage. Disputes occasionally arose about the presentation and institution of clerics. It was stated in several papal bulls that some bishops sought to obtain Templar churches for members of their own households and therefore refused to accept candidates presented by the Temple;[83] and bishops also refused to institute secular priests living in Templar convents unless provision for them outside the Order's houses was made. A bull condemning this latter practice was addressed to the Templars in Spain in 1239,[84] but there is otherwise little evidence of a reluctance on the part of the Aragonese and Catalan bishops to accept priests put forward by the Order. The only known instance occurred in 1288 when the bishop of Urgel refused to

accept a candidate for the church of Puigreig on the ground that
he had celebrated divine offices while the country was under interdict. On this occasion the Temple easily found a supporter in
Alfonso III, who described the bishop's action as 'scandalous and
prejudicial to our country'.[85] But if the Templars had grievances
about the way in which some bishops exercised their powers, the
prelates at the Lateran Council in 1179 on their side complained
that the Templars failed to present candidates for benefices to the
diocesan and also removed priests from livings without episcopal
consent. It was therefore decreed that, unless a church was held
by the Temple 'in full right', presentation to the diocesan was to
be made; and the Order was at the same time forbidden to remove
priests without episcopal consent.[86] That these decrees were not
always observed is apparent from their repetition in 1215 at the
Fourth Lateran Council,[87] while in Spain the archbishop of Tarragona in 1193 ordered the Templars to observe them after the
bishop of Tarazona had complained that they were not being
respected,[88] and in 1221 a similar grievance was voiced by the
bishop of Zaragoza.[89]

Disputes arose more frequently, however, about the revenues of
Templar churches. Some bishops sought to recover dues which
had been granted away by their predecessors. Although in 1193
the bishop of Tarazona was not able to substantiate his claim to
the church of Ambel, he was awarded a quarter of the tithes of
'bread and wine' from that church, even though this quarter had
been assigned to the Temple in 1148.[90] A claim to a quarter of the
tithes of St. John at Monzón and its dependent churches was
similarly put forward by Berenguer, bishop of Lérida, in 1219;[91]
but the bishop failed to establish a right to these dues, and the
same happened in 1264, when a later bishop claimed a quarter of
these tithes.[92] It was, however, agreed in 1219 that the bishop
should have twelve *cenas* annually for himself and nineteen followers from these churches, although the right of hospitality had
not been specifically reserved when the church of St. John had
been granted in 1149; and the bishop's right of hospitality was
again accepted by arbiters in 1265, when it was amended to
consist of ten *cenas* for the bishop and twenty-five mounted
followers.[93] These arbiters nevertheless did uphold a Templar
protest against the exaction of *cenas* in money, contrary to papal
decrees. According to the Templars there was also abuse of the

decrees which limited the number of followers for whom bishops could claim hospitality: in 1226 Honorius III had occasion to write to the bishop of Zaragoza, saying that the Templars had complained that

not content with the number of persons and horses decreed in the Lateran Council, you bring with you such an unreasonable multitude of knights and horses that in your sole visit you consume what should suffice for many for a large part of the year.[94]

The Order could also argue that papal decrees were contravened when contributions to episcopal subsidies were demanded from Templar churches. When in 1301 the bishop of Lérida taxed Templar churches for the subsidy then being levied in aid of the newly established university of Lérida, the Order maintained that this demand was contrary to the privilege *Ante oculos mentis*, which stated that bishops should not demand more from Templar churches than their predecessors had done;[95] and when the bishop of Lérida sought a contribution from the vicar of Remolins towards a subsidy in aid of a royal expedition to Granada in 1273, the Templars maintained that this levy contravened the privilege which stated that, after provision had been made for vicars and episcopal dues, the revenues of Templar churches were to be used in the interests of the Holy Land.[96] Yet in 1229 an earlier bishop of Lérida had asserted that the Templars themselves abused this privilege by not assigning a sufficient amount for the maintenance of vicars and the fulfilment of obligations to the bishop.[97] In most cases it is not known what provision the Temple made for its vicars, and even when evidence does survive it sometimes consists merely of a list of dues, without any indication of their value.[98] But it may be noted that on some occasions the income of Templar vicars was determined by the diocesan;[99] that priests were sometimes given Templar churches as *beneficia personalia* and received most of the revenues attached to these churches;[100] and that at the beginning of the fourteenth century a number of Templar vicars in southern Aragon were being paid eightpence a day for food, together with 70s. a year for other expenses, and this compares not unfavourably with some of the provisions made for chantry priests at that time.[101]

The Templars' rights over churches and tithes were not the only causes of dispute between the Order and the secular clergy. The

Temple's right of burial reduced the income of the secular clergy and the latter's opposition to this privilege is referred to both in general decrees issued by the papacy and in local sources. A bull published by Alexander III shows that some prelates demanded a third instead of a quarter of bequests,[102] and Urban III in 1186/7 was obliged to remind bishops that nothing was to be taken if those buried in the Order's cemeteries left the equivalent of a quarter to the secular clergy,[103] while a further Templar complaint led Innocent III to decree that no one was to remove by force the bodies of those who had chosen burial in the Temple.[104] The Aragonese sources provide further evidence of particular abuses, committed by both sides: while the bishop of Zaragoza claimed in 1221 that he was not receiving the quarter due to him,[105] in 1296 the Templars were complaining that the bishop of Lérida was trying to prevent a certain priest from being buried at Gardeny.[106] These Aragonese sources also reveal that some bishops in the *Corona de Aragón* managed to impose permanent restrictions on the Templars' burial rights. In 1192, after a series of disputes between the Order and the bishop of Lérida, it was agreed that the Templars should exercise their right of burial in the diocese of Lérida only at Monzón, Chalamera, and Gardeny;[107] and elsewhere it seems to have become accepted that episcopal assent was necessary for the establishment of a new Templar cemetery. In 1204 the bishop of Zaragoza granted the Templars the right to have a cemetery at their house in Zaragoza, and a similar privilege was conceded for the Templar house in Barcelona in 1246 by the bishop of Barcelona.[108] Towards the end of the twelfth century the bishop of Tortosa had likewise allowed the Order to have a cemetery in the city of Tortosa, but he imposed the condition that the Templars

are to receive none of our parishioners for burial unless they can ascend to the Zuda on their own feet or on horseback without the aid of man or woman;[109]

this limitation was, however, removed in 1281.[110] But the bishop of Tortosa then imposed the restriction that if a horse other than the mount of the dead person was left to the Temple, or money in lieu of horse and arms, these should be included among the goods from which the secular clergy was to receive a quarter. In 1246 the bishop of Barcelona had similarly decreed that the

Templars should surrender a portion of any money left instead of horses and arms; and it was then further agreed that of movables and immovables left to the Order by inhabitants of the diocese of Barcelona, the bishop and chapter were to receive a half, which they were to divide equally with the parish priest.[111] Thus with regard to rights of burial it was common for the Aragonese bishops to restrict the privileges conceded to the Temple by the papacy. In the *Corona de Aragón* the Order's burial rights were often determined by agreements with the episcopate, and these modified papal privileges and restricted their application. The papal privileges were nevertheless important in that they forced the episcopate to allow the Templars to enjoy at least some rights of burial; they could not be completely ignored. If bishops sought to prevent the Order from exercising rights of burial altogether they were likely to incur papal displeasure, as happened at Huesca in 1200 when Innocent III threatened to call in the bishop of Lérida to bless the Temple's cemetery in the city if the bishop of Huesca continued to refuse to do so.[112]

The Temple's privileges concerning confraternity similarly led to conflict with the secular clergy. According to the Templars some ecclesiastics refused to allow members of the Order into their churches or demanded part of the money collected by the Temple.[113] But at the Lateran Council in 1179 the prelates on their side maintained that the Templars exceeded their rights by coming to places under interdict and opening churches there more than once a year.[114] There seem to have been faults on both sides, but the situation was made worse by the activities of those who pretended to be Templars or acting for the Temple and tried to collect for their own profit the alms intended for the Order.[115]

The secular clergy were further unwilling to accept the exceptional immunity from the payment of tithes enjoyed by the military orders and Citeaux in Alexander III's pontificate. Many prelates argued that these Orders were exempt only on demesne *novales*. Alexander was obliged to state in the bull *Audivimus et audientes* that if he had meant the privilege to apply only to *novales* he would have used that word.[116] Yet complaints by the Temple and the other Orders on this point continued and the bull *Audivimus et audientes* was frequently reissued.[117] The proceedings of the Lateran Council in 1179 apparently gave rise to a further abuse, for in the bull *Non absque dolore* Lucius III ordered the excommunication of those who exacted tithes from Templar *labores* held before the Council.[118] The origin of this abuse is not clear, but possibly Alexander at the Council confirmed his ruling that the Cistercians and the military orders should have the tithes from demesne *labores* as well as from demesne *novales*, and this was interpreted to apply only to *labores* acquired in future. The decrees of the Fourth Lateran Council were similarly quickly abused. Some prelates argued that in the Council the exemption had been cancelled on *labores* acquired before as well as after 1215, and it was to combat this claim that Honorius III issued the bull *Ex parte dilectorum filiorum*;[119] and in answer to others who claimed that all lands acquired before 1215 were liable to tithe Gregory IX in 1228 and 1229 defined the Order's exemption as consisting in freedom from the payment of tithes on demesne *labores* acquired before 1215, on demesne *novales* acquired before or after the Council, and on gardens, woods, fishing, hay, mills, and the food of its animals.[120]

Yet although dispute might turn on the interpretation of papal privileges concerning the payment of tithes, in Aragon these privileges, like those concerning burial rights, were usually of only limited importance. They often provided merely the starting-point for discussion about Templar obligations in individual dioceses, and in many parts of the *Corona de Aragón* the Order's exemption was reduced through local compromises and particular agreements. Some bishops sought to check their losses of tithes by placing a restriction on the amount of demesne land which was to be exempt from payment. At Horta, according to an agreement made with the bishop of Tortosa in 1185, the Templars were to enjoy exemption on twenty-five *parelladas*;[121] and when in 1263 the bishop of Valencia allowed exemption on a Templar garden at Borbotó, he stated that it was not to exceed six *fanegadas* in size.[122] Many other agreements obliged the Templars to pay a proportion of the tithes from lands which were exempted by papal privilege. When the archbishop of Tarragona arbitrated between the Temple and the bishop of Tarazona in 1193, he judged that—with certain exceptions—the Order should pay half of the tithes of 'bread and wine' from its demesne *labores* in the diocese of Tarazona.[123] This practice can be traced earlier in the neighbouring diocese of Zaragoza. The Templars agreed in 1147 to pay half of the tithes from the lands which they cultivated there, except those newly brought under cultivation;[124] and this concession was extended in 1204 when the provincial master agreed to pay half of the tithes from demesne *novales* as well as *labores*.[125] The custom of paying half of the tithe from demesne lands appears to have been most common in Aragon, but instances also occur in Catalonia: in 1192, for example, the bishop of Lérida retained half of the tithe from the Temple's demesne in Segriá.[126] Once such local agreements had been made, papal privileges were of little value. Although they might be quoted during the course of disputes by either side when it was convenient for them,[127] disagreements between the Order and the secular clergy were usually settled by reference to earlier local agreements rather than to papal privileges. Thus the arbiters in a dispute over tithes between the Temple and the bishop of Zaragoza in 1221 confirmed the agreement made in 1204, after the bishop had complained that the Templars were not paying the tithes owed from demesne lands;[128] and in 1265 the arbiters in a dispute between the Order and the bishop of Lérida referred back to a compromise made in 1154.[129]

The Templar exemption from the payment of tithes was affected not only by the claims of bishops and parish priests, but also by the rights which other individuals or institutions enjoyed over the tithes of Templar demesnes. In some instances the Temple was able to obtain a surrender of these rights, but it was usually obliged to give compensation. To gain the rights which the monastery of Poblet owned in the tithes from Templar *labores* at Barbens the Order was in 1182 obliged to give in exchange land elsewhere,[130] and among the rights which the Temple purchased from Bernard of Vallvert in 1216 was his share of the tithes from Templar *labores* at Palau.[131]

Lay interests were also at work in the sphere of extraordinary papal taxation. Although the papacy usually exempted the Templars from papal taxes imposed for the benefit of the Aragonese kings, James II made a number of attempts to obtain contributions from the military orders to the tenths which were granted to him by the papacy for his proposed expeditions to Sicily, Corsica, and Sardinia.[132] When Boniface VIII in February 1297 granted a tenth of ecclesiastical revenues to the Aragonese king for four years, he made no specific reference to the Temple, thus implying that it was exempt;[133] and this was explicitly stated early in September of that year, after collectors of the tax had tried to exact payment from the Order.[134] But in the same month James protested through his representative at the papal court that it had been agreed that the Temple should contribute. He asked Boniface to issue orders commanding payment and claimed that if the military orders were exempted the sum derived from the tenth would be reduced by at least a third, and the grant would have to be extended for a further two years.[135] In a reply sent in December Boniface postponed making a decision until he could meet James to discuss the matter.[136] But the king apparently gained nothing from the military orders, for in 1299 Boniface agreed to extend the grant of the tenth for a further two years.[137] Boniface again exempted the Temple in 1303 when he gave a tenth to James for three years for the conquest of Corsica and Sardinia,[138] but after Boniface's death James made fresh efforts to gain the tenth from the military orders. In June 1304 he was in negotiation with Benedict XI, but by the time of the pope's death in the next month James had been able to secure only a vague promise about contributions from the military orders.[139] The issue was raised again at the beginning of the next year, yet the military orders were again exempted when Clement V assigned the king a tenth for a further four years.[140]

When in 1297 and 1301 the collectors of these papal taxes demanded contributions from the Order, the Templars were able to quote to them the privilege *Quanto devocius divino*.[141] On these occasions the Order was making legitimate use of this bull, which concerned taxes levied on papal authority. But the Templars frequently sought to extend the application of this privilege and often used it to protect themselves when they were asked to contribute to episcopal subsidies. In 1290, when the bishop of Zaragoza demanded a subsidy from the clergy of his diocese, the Templars asserted that because of their papal privileges they were not obliged to contribute to any

> *collecta*, subsidies, sums of money or other exactions, under whatever name they are taken, or to pay them for whosoever's benefit or for whatever reason they are imposed, by reason of their churches, houses or possessions[142]

—a clear reference to the bull *Quanto devocius divino*; in answer to demands for money by the bishop of Lérida at the time of the

French invasion in 1285 and by the bishop of Gerona in the next year they similarly maintained that they were exempt from the payment of any *tallia* or *collecta*;[143] and requests from prelates in the following years received the same response.[144]

The Templars were, however, on firmer ground when they argued that the episcopate contravened the Order's clearly stated privilege that its members and servants could not be excommunicated except on papal authority. This right was abused especially during financial disputes with the Aragonese and Catalan bishops. In 1288 the bishop of Lérida pronounced a sentence of excommunication on the clerks in the convent of Gardeny when they refused to contribute towards an ecclesiastical subsidy for the king;[145] and at the turn of the century during a dispute about the tax for the university of Lérida the provincial master and his subordinates were excommunicated.[146] Prelates could, of course, pass sentence on the Order's vassals, but they appear at times to have used this power as a further weapon against the Templars themselves. A bull issued by Gregory IX, and renewed in 1246 and 1255, dealt with complaints by the Temple against certain bishops and their officials who, since they could not excommunicate members of the Order, imposed sentences on the Temple's men or on those using its mills and ovens or on those who traded with the Templars, thus preventing the latter from coming into contact with these people. Gregory pointed out that they were preserving the word but not the spirit of papal decrees.[147] The prelates on their side, on the other hand, asserted at the Lateran Council in 1179 that the Templars tried to exempt their *confratres* from episcopal jurisdiction and thus weakened the bishops' authority.[148]

Hostility between the Temple and the secular clergy was almost unavoidable, for the privileges which were granted to the Temple and an increasing number of other religious houses and orders constituted a growing threat to the jurisdiction and income of the secular clergy; and disputes were at times marked by bitterness and violence. In 1301 the Templars claimed that during the dispute about the tax for the university of Lérida the bishop had seized the Templar vicar of Ballobar and two other priests, burnt a bridge at Monzón and a number of Templar boats, carried off some of the Order's animals, and killed more than ten of its men, while others had been held to ransom; the bishop on his side maintained that the Templars were holding captive the vicar of Binaced and had threatened several other priests; he also asserted that they had destroyed a bridge at Conchel and damaged other property.[149] But it should not be supposed that there was continuous conflict. At times a more friendly relationship prevailed. As has been seen, the Aragonese clergy can be observed carrying out papal orders for the protection of the Templars,[150] and several promises of protection to the Temple by the Aragonese prelates themselves have also survived.[151] The clergy in the *Corona de Aragón* can similarly be seen giving their support to papal requests for aid to the Temple: one copy of the appeal sent out by Innocent IV in 1253, for example, is preserved in a letter which the bishop of Tarazona sent to the clergy of his diocese and in which he told them to exhort the faithful to make benefactions to the Order.[152] The surviving records also provide examples of the Templars' respecting episcopal rights. A number of documents record the presentation of candidates for benefices to the diocesan,[153] and in another charter drawn up in 1248 the bishop of Lérida's representative acknowledged that he had received full payment from the Order in respect of persons who had chosen burial at Gardeny.[154] Evidence of this kind is admittedly sparse, but it was obviously more important to keep records of the settlements of disputes than to preserve administrative documents of a routine nature.

It must further be remembered that not all the disputes between the Temple and the secular clergy were the result of deliberate abuse of right and privilege. In Church as in State the administrative methods in use were still rudimentary and conflict could easily be occasioned by administrative failings. Templar rights over parish churches were sometimes called in question apparently because of the inadequacies of episcopal archives. Bishops did not always know what rights had been granted away by their predecessors and therefore disputed Templar claims, as in 1221 when the bishop of Zaragoza demanded to know by what right the Templars held the church of Encinacorba and several others in his diocese.[155] He apparently did not have records of the grants made by earlier bishops.

Some other disputes seem to have been caused by uncertainty among the bishops about the extent of the Order's papal privileges. When in January 1292 the bishop of Lérida was demanding a contribution to an ecclesiastical subsidy, he stated that he was willing to examine the Order's privileges and would give up his demands if the Templars could prove their right to exemption,[156] and in May of the same year he promised to lift the sentence of excommunication which he had imposed if the Templars could show that this contravened their privileges.[157] But the Templars then faced the problem of producing evidence which a bishop would accept. During a dispute in 1288 the commander of Gardeny was able to place before the bishop of Lérida's official only a register containing transcripts of privileges; he said that the originals were at Miravet and could not be brought to Lérida because of the dangers of the journey.[158] But the excuses put forward by the Order on this point were not very consistent: while at times the Templars argued that the originals were at Miravet, on other occasions they maintained that they were in Cyprus and could be seen there or in the papal registers;[159] and while on occasion they claimed that documents could not be moved from Miravet because of the dangers of transporting them,[160] at another time they argued that the documents could not be examined except in the presence of the provincial master, who was away on the king's service.[161] The Templars appear at times to have had no desire to produce original documents for inspection. On the other hand, some bishops apparently sought to prevent the Order from showing originals by not allowing it enough time to produce them.[162] But even if privileges were produced, further dissensions might be occasioned by the differing interpretations to which they could be subject[163] or by a misunderstanding of their significance.[164]

Conflict might also arise out of a clash of rights. Thus Templar chaplains who became vicars of churches might claim as members of the Order to be exempt from episcopal jurisdiction but, on the other hand, the diocesan might claim obedience from them as vicars of churches subject to episcopal authority. Arbiters between the Order and the bishop of Lérida in 1264 tried to solve this problem by stating that such vicars should be subject to episcopal authority unless the Templars could produce privileges or agreements to the contrary.[165] A further clash of powers and privileges occurred in 1301. According to a decree passed in the provincial council of Tarragona in the year 1300, those who damaged ecclesiastical property were to be *ipso facto* excommunicate,

and it was argued by the bishop of Lérida in the following
year that the Templars were subject to this decree; the Templars,
on the other hand, asserted that they could not be excommunicated
except on papal authority. The evidence ends with the archbishop
of Tarragona hesitating between observance of the Order's
privileges and adherence to the decrees of the provincial council.[166]
Dispute might also be caused by conflicting papal decrees, for the
papal chancery, like that of the Aragonese kings, sometimes
issued general orders, which ignored particular privileges. Towards the end of the twelfth century Clement III sought to clarify
the situation and to protect Templar rights by stating that papal
letters which were contrary to the Order's immunities but which
did not mention the Temple by name could not be used against
it;[167] and in the middle of the thirteenth century it was decreed
that papal letters which generally set aside privileges of this last
kind but which did not mention the Temple by name could not
harm its immunities.[168] These decrees no doubt helped to protect
Templar rights, but they could not prevent disputes from occurring when papal letters were issued which clashed with Templar
privileges.[169]

The failure of bishops to enforce papal decrees for the protection
of the Order was again not necessarily the result of deliberate
negligence. In some instances the explanation is probably to be
sought in the weight of the administrative burdens placed on the
Aragonese prelates. The Templars clearly made full use of general
bulls of protection. That sent to the bishop of Sigüenza in 1244,
for example, was employed by the Order against the nobles
Berenguer of Puigvert and Peter of Queralt, the vicar of the
church of Alcolea, the rural dean of Monzón, the royal vicar of
Cervera, the abbot of Rocafort, and various others, including the
bishop of Lérida.[170] The custom of delegating the task of dealing
with petitions and appeals no doubt eased the work of the papal
curia, but it sometimes placed a heavy burden on the local clergy,
who may for this reason have sometimes failed to give satisfaction to the Temple. Their failure does not necessarily imply that
they were hostile to the Order.

The nature of medieval government and administration made
dispute inevitable, but probably the Templars—who took the
same measures to protect their ecclesiastical rights as they did to
safeguard their secular ones—did not usually have their rights and

privileges permanently reduced by conflicts arising out of administrative shortcomings. Their immunities were affected more by the activities of prelates who sought to maintain their jurisdiction and income by restricting Templar privileges, just as in the secular sphere the Crown's efforts to increase its power and wealth led to a diminution of the Order's secular rights.

## NOTES

1. AGP, parch. Selma, no. 22. The grant made to the Temple in 1171 had, however, included tithes and all other revenues: Miret y Sans, *Les Cases*, p. 169.

2. Ferreira, *Memorias*, ii. 823–5.

3. e.g. AHN, San Juan, leg. 308, doc. 1; ACA, parch. Peter III, no. 96.

4. Albon, *Cartulaire*, pp. 70–1, doc. 94.

5. Ibid., p. 100, doc. 143.

6. AHN, San Juan, leg. 340, doc. 4.

7. AHN, San Juan, leg. 285, doc. 3.

8. AGP, Cartulary of Tortosa, fol. 95$^v$, doc. 296; ACA, parch. Peter III, no. 96; Albon, *Cartulaire*, p. 334, doc. 545; AHN, San Juan, leg. 354, doc. 2; Montesa, P. 78.

9. Albon, *Cartulaire*, pp. 235–6, docs. 368, 369; p. 310, doc. 502. The bishop of Tarazona similarly gave up his claim to the quarter when he granted the church of Ribaforada in Navarre to the Templars.

10. Ibid., pp. 345–6, doc. 557.

11. AHN, San Juan, leg. 340, doc. 4.

12. AHN, San Juan, leg. 285, doc. 9; AHN, cód. 691, fols. 153$^v$–154, doc. 391.

13. AHN, Montesa, P. 568; cód. 466, pp. 56–7, doc. 56.

14. AHN, San Juan, leg. 277, doc. 30.

15. Prutz, *MU*, p. 49, no. 88; p. 64, no. 280.

16. e.g. J. D. Mansi, *Sacrorum conciliorum nova et amplissima collectio*, xxii (Venice, 1778), 219–20, 1019–22.

17. Ibid., cols. 223, 1047.

18. ACA, reg. 310, fol. 9.

19. Similar privileges were granted to all the leading military orders. Bulls for the Hospital are published or analysed in Delaville, *Cartulaire*; those for the Teutonic Order may be examined in E. Strehlke, *Tabulae Ordinis Theutonici* (Berlin, 1869). The papal privileges of the military orders have been discussed by H. Prutz in *Die geistlichen Ritterorden* (Berlin, 1908), caps. 5, 6, and in *Entwicklung*,

caps. 3, 4; but as Prutz did not know of any version of the bull *Omne datum optimum* before that issued in 1163 his interpretation of Templar privileges needs revision especially on this point.

20. Albon, *Cartulaire*, p. 378, Bullaire, doc. 5.

21. Prutz, *MU*, pp. 46–7, no. 57.

22. e.g. Ferreira, *Memorias*, ii. 811–21 (1186), 826–38 (1194); Migne, *PL*, cci. 1195–1200 (1183).

23. ACA, reg. 309, fol. 7–7ᵛ.

24. Ferreira, *Memorias*, ii. 821–3.

25. Prutz, *MU*, pp. 47–8, no. 64; cf. ACA, reg. 310, fol. 4.

26. This offer was made at least as early as 1144: Albon, *Cartulaire*, p. 381, Bullaire, doc. 8.

27. Marquis d'Albon, 'La mort d'Odon de Saint-Amand, grand-maître du Temple', *Revue de l'orient latin*, xii (1911), 281–2.

28. AHN, San Juan, leg. 713, doc. 19; see below, p. 391.

29. ACA, Bulas, leg. 11, doc. 49; cf. F. Miquel Rosell, *Regesta de letras pontificias del Archivo de la Corona de Aragón* (Madrid, 1948), p. 92, no. 160. See also AHN, cód. 471, p. 20, doc. 31.

30. ACA, reg. 310, fol. 11–11ᵛ.

31. ACA, reg. 309, fol. 22–22ᵛ.

32. Prutz, *Entwicklung*, p. 286, doc. 12.

33. Prutz, *MU*, p. 46, no. 51.

34. Ibid., p. 38, no. 3.

35. G. Schnürer, *Die ursprüngliche Templerregel* (Freiburg, 1903), p. 64.

36. *Règle*, p. 38.

37. G. Constable, *Monastic Tithes from their Origins to the Twelfth Century* (Cambridge, 1964), pp. 225–7.

38. Albon, *Cartulaire*, p. 377, Bullaire, doc. 5.

39. AHN, cód. 1312, p. 116, doc. 81. Constable, op. cit., p. 236, suggests that the word *sumptus* should be translated as 'use' or 'consumption' rather than as 'expense', on the grounds that it was occasionally replaced by the word *nutrimen*; but in one document quoted by Constable, op. cit., p. 260, note 2, *sumptus* is distinguished from *nutrimen*; and in thirteenth-century Catalan translations of papal bulls the word *sumptus* was rendered as *despeses* or *messions*: e.g. AHN, cód. 1032, pp. 4–5, doc. 4; pp. 18–19, doc. 19; pp. 22–4, doc. 23.

40. Constable, op. cit., pp. 240–4.

41. Albon, *Cartulaire*, p. 334, doc. 545.

42. Ibid., pp. 345–6, doc. 557. The phrase 'ganad ejusdem' is employed in this document and seems to refer to the animals themselves rather than their food.

43. Prutz, *MU*, p. 38, no. 5.

44. J. Delaville Le Roulx, 'Bulles pour l'ordre du Temple, tirées des archives de S. Gervasio de Cassolas', *Revue de l'orient latin*, xi (1905–8), 424–5, doc. 29.

45. C. Bourel de la Roncière, *Les Registres d'Alexandre IV*, i (Paris, 1902), 322, doc. 1075.

46. E. Jordan, *Les Registres de Clément IV* (Paris, 1893–1945), p. 32, doc. 134. The Templars were expected to contribute to the taxes for the Latin Empire imposed at the Council of Lyons in 1245: AHN, cód. 467, p. 49, doc. 71; cf. *Annales de Burton*, in *Annales Monastici*, ed. H. R. Luard, i (London, 1864), 277. But in 1246 Innocent IV stopped the collection of these from the Temple: AHN, cód. 466, p. 32, doc. 32; cf. cód. 471, p. 20, doc. 32; García Larragueta, *Gran priorado*, ii. 313–14, doc. 319.

47. AHN, cód. 467, p. 11, doc. 21.

48. J. Guiraud, *Les Registres d'Urbain IV*, i (Paris, 1901), 136–7, doc. 470; cf. Delaville, *Cartulaire*, iii. 88, doc. 3096.

49. G. Digard, M. Faucon, etc., *Les Registres de Boniface VIII*, ii (Paris, 1904), 29–31, doc. 2426.

50. Delaville, *Cartulaire*, iii. 709, doc. 4364. In 1295 Boniface also pledged the possessions of the Temple and Hospital in the *Corona de Aragón* for the payment of Blanche of Anjou's dower to James II: V. Salavert y Roca, 'El Tratado de Anagni y la expansión mediterránea de la Corona de Aragón', *EEMCA*, v (1952), 254, 358–60, doc. 46; Digard, Faucon, *Registres de Boniface VIII*, i (1907), 80–1, doc. 212; Delaville, *Cartulaire*, iii. 664–5, doc. 4281; cf. iii. 817, doc. 4520.

51. Prutz, *MU*, p. 42, no. 25, with the reissues mentioned there.

52. Albon, *Cartulaire*, p. 376, Bullaire, doc. 5.

53. Delaville Le Roulx, 'Bulles pour l'ordre du Temple', pp. 409–10, doc. 3 (1154); Ferreira, *Memorias*, ii. 774–84 (1163), etc.

54. AHN, cód. 471, pp. 9–10, doc. 14 (1217); ACA, reg. 309, fol. 19ᵛ (1236).

55. P. Kehr, *Papsturkunden in Spanien. I. Katalanien* (Abhandlungen der Gesellschaft der Wissenschaften zu Göttingen. Phil.-hist. Klasse. Neue Folge, vol. xviii, 1926), pp. 475–7, doc. 182; Delaville Le Roulx, 'Bulles pour l'ordre du Temple', pp. 413–17, doc. 11.

56. Only a few payments by the Temple for particular properties—mainly churches—are recorded in the *Liber Censuum*, ed. P. Fabre and L. Duchesne (Paris, 1889–1952).

57. Prutz, *Entwicklung*, pp. 32–3.

58. Delaville Le Roulx, 'Bulles pour l'ordre du Temple', pp. 430–1, doc. 40.

59. Ibid., p. 429, doc. 38.

60. e.g. in the bull *Non absque dolore*: ACA, reg. 309, fol. 9; reg. 310, fol. 7–7ᵛ; AHN, cód. 471, p. 73, doc. 69.

61. AHN, cód. 471, pp. 75–6, doc. 73.

62. RAH, 12-6-1/M–83, doc. 111; AGP, parch. Cervera, no. 472.

63. Prutz, *Entwicklung*, p. 268, no. 88; cf. Prutz, *MU*, pp. 51–2, no. 141; ACA, reg. 310, fol. 5ᵛ.

64. Mansi, op. cit. xxii. 223.

65. J. B. Mahn, *L'Ordre cistercien et son gouvernement* (Paris, 1951), pp. 138–9, 148.

66. Giraldus Cambrensis, *Opera*, ed. J. S. Brewer, iv (London, 1873), 205.

67. Cf. J. Rousset de Pina, in *Du premier Concile du Latran à l'avènement d'Innocent III* (Histoire de l'Église depuis les origines jusqu'à nos jours, vol. ix, Paris, 1953), ii. 62–4.

68. Finke, *Papsttum*, pp. 41–54.

69. Mansi, op. cit. xxii. 327–8, 330.

70. Ibid. xxii. 328. On the policies of Adrian IV and Alexander III, see P. Viard, *Histoire de la dîme ecclésiastique dans le royaume de France aux XIIᵉ et XIIIᵉ siècles* (Paris, 1912), pp. 42–4; Constable, op. cit., pp. 278 ff.

71. Mahn, op. cit., p. 107.

72. Constable, op. cit., p. 282, suggests that the Hospital was exempt from this ruling, but he provides no evidence on this point; and his remarks here seem inconsistent with what he later says about Alexander III's policy: ibid., p. 299.

73. Ibid.

74. Mahn, op. cit., p. 111; Constable, op. cit., p. 303.

75. Mansi, op. cit. xxii. 1042–3.

76. Guiraud, *Registres d'Urbain IV*, i. 128, no. 460.

77. Michelet, *Procès*, i. 199; ii. 9.

78. Mansi, op. cit. xxii. 222–3; William of Tyre, *Historia rerum in partibus transmarinis gestarum*, xii. 7, in *Recueil des historiens des croisades: historiens occidentaux*, i (Paris, 1844), 521.

79. AHN, San Juan, leg. 174, doc. 4.

80. Mansi, op. cit. xxii. 223.

81. Prutz, *MU*, p. 41, no. 17; p. 43, no. 29. Prutz assigns Alexander's decree to the years 1171–2, but the reference in it to the Council shows that it cannot have been issued before 1179.

82. AGP, Cartulary of Gardeny, fols. 86–7, doc. 214.

83. ACA, reg. 310, fols. 3, 9; Ferreira, *Memorias*, ii. 800–2.

84. L. Auvray, *Les Registres de Grégoire IX*, ii (Paris, 1907), 1217–18, no. 4721.

85. ACA, reg. 74, fol. 71.

86. Mansi, op. cit. xxii. 223.

87. Ibid. xxii. 1047–50.

88. AHN, San Juan, leg. 174, doc. 4.

89. AHN, San Juan, leg. 39, doc. 102; see below, p. 381.

90. AHN, San Juan, leg. 174, doc. 4.

91. AHN, San Juan, leg. 324, doc. 1.

92. AHN, San Juan, leg. 324, doc. 2.

93. AGP, parch. Gardeny, no. 2244–B.

94. AHN, cód. 471, p. 23, doc. 39.

95. AGP, parch. Gardeny, no. 2241–A.

96. AGP, parch. Gardeny, no. 2246–B.

97. AGP, parch. Gardeny, no. 2245–D.

98. e.g. AHN, San Juan, leg. 277, doc. 30; leg. 285, doc. 8.

99. AHN, San Juan, leg. 285, doc. 9; cód. 466, pp. 169–70, docs. 144, 145.

100. AHN, San Juan, leg. 277, doc. 30; leg. 333, doc. 5; see below, p. 410.

101. ACA, reg. 291, fol. 273–273$^v$.

102. ACA, reg. 309, fol. 7–7$^v$.

103. Ferreira, *Memorias*, ii. 821–3.

104. ACA, reg. 310, fol. 8.

105. AHN, San Juan, leg. 39, doc. 102; see below, p. 381.

106. AGP, parch. Gardeny, no. 2245–H.

107. AHN, San Juan, leg. 324, doc. 1.

108. AHN, San Juan, leg. 39, docs. 61, 67; ACA, parch. James I, no. 1029.

109. Villanueva, *Viage*, v. 277–80.

110. AGP, Cartulary of Tortosa, fol. 95$^v$, doc. 296.

111. ACA, parch. James I, no. 1029.

112. A. Durán Gudiol, *Colección diplomática de la catedral de Huesca*, ii (Zaragoza, 1969), 548, doc. 575.

113. ACA, reg. 310, fol. 4–4$^v$.

114. Mansi, op. cit. xxii. 223.

115. ACA, reg. 309, fols. 24$^v$–25.

116. Ferreira, *Memorias*, ii. 789–91; cf. Mahn, op. cit., p. 108.

117. e.g. Ferreira, *Memorias*, ii. 791–3 (1182/3), 793–5 (1186/7), 796–8 (1210).

118. Prutz, *MU*, pp. 42–3, no. 28.

119. AHN, cód. 471, pp. 19–20, doc. 30.

120. Prutz, *MU*, p. 53, no. 183; ACA, reg. 309, fol. 19.

121. AHN, San Juan, leg. 354, doc. 2. This agreement was confirmed in 1263: leg. 308, doc. 6.

122. AHN, Montesa, P. 265.

123. AHN, San Juan, leg. 174, doc. 4.

124. Albon, *Cartulaire*, pp. 285–6, doc. 460.

125. AHN, San Juan, leg. 39, docs. 61, 67.

126. AHN, San Juan, leg. 324, doc. 1.

127. AHN, San Juan, leg. 324, doc. 2.

128. AHN, San Juan, leg. 39, doc. 102; see below, p. 381.

129. AGP, parch. Gardeny, no. 2244–B.

130. AGP, Cartulary of Gardeny, fols. 97ᵛ–98, doc. 237; see below, p. 372.

131. ACA, parch. James I, no. 58.

132. According to A. T. Luttrell, 'The Aragonese Crown and the Knights Hospitallers of Rhodes: 1291–1350', *English Historical Review*, lxxvi (1961), 9, the Aragonese kings had sought contributions to papal taxes from the military orders as early as 1277; but in that year the king was concerned with the proceeds of papal taxes which had been deposited with the military orders, not paid by them: ACA, reg. 39, fol. 225–225ᵛ; Delaville, *Cartulaire*, iii. 350, doc. 3631.

133. G. Digard, M. Faucon, etc., *Les Registres de Boniface VIII*, i (Paris, 1907), 634–5, doc. 1679.

134. Ibid., col. 793, doc. 2059.

135. Finke, *AA*, i. 37–41, doc. 30.

136. Ibid. iii. 63–5, doc. 30.

137. Digard, Faucon, *Registres de Boniface VIII*, ii (Paris, 1904), 426, doc. 3088.

138. ACA, Bulas, leg. 23, doc. 4; cf. F. Miquel Rosell, *Regesta de letras pontificias del Archivo de la Corona de Aragón* (Madrid, 1948), p. 166, no. 312; A. Fábrega i Grau, 'La dècima per a la conquesta de Sardenya en els pontificats de Bonifaci VIII i Benet XI', *VI Congreso de historia de la Corona de Aragón* (Madrid, 1959), p. 466.

139. V. Salavert y Roca, *Cerdeña y la expansión mediterránea de la Corona de Aragón* (Madrid, 1956), ii. 122–3, docs. 90, 91; Fábrega i Grau, loc. cit., p. 473.

140. Finke, *AA*, iii. 134–8, doc. 60; Salavert y Roca, op. cit. ii. 151–4, doc. 116; 165–6, doc. 128.

141. ACA, CRD Templarios, no. 691; parch. James II, no. 1683.

142. Delaville Le Roulx, 'Bulles pour l'ordre du Temple', pp. 434–5, doc. 45.

143. ACA, reg. 57, fol. 192ᵛ; reg. 66, fol. 235–235ᵛ.

144. ACA, reg. 70, fol. 88; reg. 80, fol. 96ᵛ; reg. 92, fol. 161ᵛ; reg. 96, fol. 101ᵛ; AGP, parch. Gardeny, no. 2246–D.

145. AGP, parch. Gardeny, no. 2244–C.

146. AGP, parch. Gardeny, nos. 2241–B, 2244–D, –E, –F, –G, –H, 2246–G; parch. Comuns, no. 95; cf. Finke, *Papsttum*, ii. 6–7, doc. 5.

147. Prutz, *MU*, p. 57, no. 235; ACA, parch. James I, no. 2117; reg. 310, fol. 11. The version of this bull issued by Gregory IX to which Prutz, *MU*, p. 53, no.171, refers was apparently in favour of the Hospitallers and not the Templars: Delaville, *Cartulaire*, ii. 376, doc. 1894; but the later versions of the bull refer back to a similar privilege granted to the Templars by Gregory.

148. Mansi, op. cit. xxii. 223.

149. AGP, parch. Gardeny, nos. 2244–D, –G.

150. See above, p. 166.

151. In 1134 the archbishop of Tarragona and his bishops placed the Temple and its property under the Truce of God: Albon, *Cartulaire*, pp. 53–5, doc. 71; and in 1216 a later archbishop, Spartago, put the Order under his own special protection: AHN, cód. 471, p. 76, doc. 74.

152. AHN, San Juan, leg. 713, doc. 19; see below, p. 391.

153. AHN, cód. 466, pp. 169–70, docs. 144, 145; San Juan, leg. 285, doc. 9; leg. 324, doc. 4.

154. AGP, parch. Gardeny, no. 495; cf. AHN, Montesa, P. 278.

155. AHN, San Juan, leg. 39, doc. 102; see below, p. 381.

156. AGP, parch. Gardeny, no. 2245–F.

157. AGP, parch. Gardeny, no. 2246–C. Similar statements were made on a number of other occasions: e.g. parch. Gardeny, nos. 2244–C, 2245–H, 2246–G.

158. AGP, parch. Gardeny, no. 2244–C.

159. AGP, parch. Gardeny, nos. 2241–A, 2245–F, –H, 2246–D, –G.

160. AGP, parch. Gardeny, nos. 2244–C, 2246–D.

161. AGP, parch. Gardeny, no. 2245–F.

162. AHN, cód. 466, pp. 26–7, doc. 24; p. 58, doc. 58; pp. 67–8, doc. 67; see below, p. 399.

163. In 1301, for example, a different interpretation was placed on the bull *Ante oculos mentis* by the Templars and the bishop of Lérida: AGP, parch. Gardeny, no. 2241–A; and the Templars' exemption from extraordinary papal taxation appears to have been differently interpreted in different parts of the *Corona de Aragón*: see J. Rius Serra, *Rationes Decimarum Hispaniae (1279–1280)* (Barcelona, 1946–7), *passim*. For a disputation concerning the interpretation of Hospitaller privileges, see J. A. Brundage, 'A Twelfth-Century Oxford

Disputation Concerning the Privileges of the Knights Hospitallers', *Mediaeval Studies*, xxiv (1962), 153–60.

164. It is possible that the Templars misunderstood the significance of the bull *Quanto devocius divino*; certainly Delaville Le Roulx appears to have been misled by its wording, for he gives an inaccurate resumé of it: 'Bulles pour l'ordre du Temple', p. 431, doc. 42.

165. AHN, San Juan, leg. 324, doc. 2.

166. AGP, parch. Gardeny, nos. 2241–B, 2244–D, –G.

167. Kehr, *Papsturkunden in Spanien. I. Katalanien*, pp. 537–8, doc. 236; ACA, reg. 310, fols. 7, 7ᵛ.

168. AHN, cód. 1312, pp. 125–6, doc. 88; ACA, reg. 309, fol. 22. In these decrees, issued by Urban IV, there are references to similar bulls issued by Innocent IV and Alexander IV.

169. e.g. ACA, CRD Templarios, no. 691; CRD James II, no. 842.

170. RAH, 12–6–1/M–83, doc. 111.

# VI

## *The Exploitation of Property*

ANY attempt to examine the way in which the Temple exploited its varied rights and properties in the *Corona de Aragón* is hampered by a lack of vital evidence. No series of accounts and no court records have survived, and although a few rentals and custumals for particular estates have been preserved, there is for Templar lands in Aragon no survey comparable with that compiled by the English Templars in 1185.[1] The majority of the documents concerning the exploitation of property which have survived are charters recording grants of land to individual tenants, and from these only limited conclusions can be drawn.

It seems, however, that the Order usually pursued a policy of demesne exploitation, in the sense that it normally sought to retain direct control over its lordships and estates. There are only a few examples of the Temple's granting or farming out whole townships or all its rights in a certain district; and the concessions of this kind which were made were of a temporary nature and can in most instances be explained by particular circumstances. Lordships were occasionally assigned for a time to individuals as *beneficia* in return for concessions made to the Order: in 1244 the Templars granted the castle and township of Gandesa for life to Elvira, the widow of William of Cervellón, because she had given the Order the castle of Nonaspe together with rights in several neighbouring places;[2] and in the following year Bertrand of Naya was given the castle and township of Marlofa for life partly because he had granted irrigation rights to the Order.[3] But the concession of Marlofa was also made 'for the greater security of the Temple' and in return for an annual rent of thirty *cahíces* of barley and seventy of wheat. Temporary grants of lordships appear therefore to have been made not only as *beneficia* but also in order to ensure the defence and protection of castles which were not manned by the Templars themselves. On some other occasions Templar rights in a district were farmed out apparently because for reasons of distance it was more convenient for them to be administered in this way. Thus in the middle of the thirteenth century the Order's properties at Calatayud, on the river Jalón, were subject to the convent of Villel, some eighty miles further south, and it was probably their remoteness from the convent that accounts for their being farmed out in 1255 to two Jews, who were to pay an annual rent or farm of 120*m*.[4] But grants of this kind appear to have been few. In addition, of course, some places—such as Tortosa—were not directly subject to the Temple because enfeoffment had already taken place before the Templars acquired rights of lordship. But only a few earlier concessions of this kind are known and they did not necessarily mean that the Order was excluded altogether from a share in administration. Although the vicar who presided over the city court in Tortosa was appointed by the Moncadas, the latter had been assigned only a third of the revenues of the city, and the collection of dues was undertaken in part by the Order's officials.[5] And the records of conflicts between the Templars and the Moncadas show that in the thirteenth century the Order was trying to exert a direct influence in all matters of administration.[6] Most places under Templar lordship were, however, more immediately subject to the Order.

In Catalonia a town or village belonging to the Order was usually administered by a lay bailiff working under Templar supervision,[7] while in Aragon there was normally a lay justiciar as well as a bailiff in each township.[8] Besides these officers there were of course in each town or village a number of other subordinate officials, and similarly in places where the Temple possessed only scattered rights and properties the Order had a variety of officials, of whom many were laymen but some were members of the Order. Clearly this type of administration, provided that it was conducted efficiently, would bring greater profit to the Order than the system of farming out estates. But in the appointment of officials the Temple appears not to have been guided purely by considerations of efficiency, for at least towards the end of the thirteenth century bailiffs and justiciars of townships were commonly appointed for life[9] and offices were used by the Order as objects of patronage which it had at its disposal. Thus a bailiff was usually allowed a hundredth of some or all of the revenues of a bailiwick[10] and the office of bailiff was clearly

considered a desirable acquisition: individuals would seek to
obtain the promise of a Templar bailiwick already before the
existing holder of the office had died,[11] and in the years following
the arrest of the Templars the king received frequent petitions
from office-holders who saw their tenure endangered.[12] The
Templars therefore used offices as rewards to be given to those
who had served the Order well. In 1246 the bailiwick of Vallfogona was granted for life to Martin of Grañena, who had been
the personal servant of the master *deça mer*,[13] and at the beginning
of the fourteenth century Stephen of Castro, who had been servant to both the provincial master and the castellan of Monzón,
held several bailiwicks in the district of Monzón.[14] Offices could
alternatively be sold. In return for the grant of the bailiwick of
Puigreig Peter of Combes in 1269 gave the Temple his rights
over a manse there.[15] To men like Peter of Combes the acquisition of office not only brought the income normally assigned to
officials but also provided a means of access to other favours such
as the grant of a corrody or further financial rewards. In the years
preceding the arrest of the Templars Dominic Pérez of Ares, the
bailiff of Horta, was receiving *de speciali gratia* an annual payment
of 50s. and two *cahíces* of wheat,[16] and because of the services he
had rendered to the Temple Peter of Combes himself was in
1279 assigned part of the income of the church of St. Martin in
Puigreig in addition to his normal salary.[17]

The Temple did not always, however, have exclusive control
over the appointment of officials. The inhabitants of places under
Templar lordship were recognized as having a corporate existence
—signified by the term *concejo* in Aragon and *universidad* in
Catalonia—and they came to enjoy certain powers, which sometimes included the nomination of officials. In several places in the
more southerly parts of Aragon the *concejo* had either partial or
complete control over the appointment of the local justiciar. In
the *fuero* of La Cañada de Benatanduz, which was based on that
of Daroca, it was stated that the *judex* was to be set up 'by the
hand of the *concejo*'; presumably, as at Daroca, the *concejo* made
an annual appointment to the office.[18] A lesser degree of control
was gained by the inhabitants of Cantavieja in 1255. It was then
agreed that they should present ten men to the Templar commander
of Cantavieja and he was to select one of them to be justiciar.
The individual appointed was to hold office for a year and before

surrendering his post he—together with the other nine presented—was to nominate a further ten, from whom the commander was to name the next justiciar.[19] A similar procedure was
possibly followed also at Castellote and Las Cuevas de Cañart,
where at about the same time the *concejos* purchased from the
Temple the concession that the justiciar should be changed
annually.[20] As a consequence of this power of appointment, at
least some *concejos* obtained a share of judicial profits: at La
Cañada amercements were normally divided into three parts, of
which one was assigned to the Temple, another to the *concejo*, and
the third to the plaintiff.[21] But it was only in a limited number of
places in southern Aragon, where the influence of Castilian practice was felt,[22] that the inhabitants participated in the appointment
of the more important officials of a township. Elsewhere these
were nominated by the Order.[23]

It was, nevertheless, common both in southern Aragon and
elsewhere for the inhabitants of townships to appoint or share in
the appointment of *alcaldes* and *jurados* or similar officials, who
assisted in the exercise of jurisdiction. At La Cañada de Benatanduz the *alcaldes*, like the *judex*, were appointed 'by the hand
of the *concejo*', and at Cantavieja two of the ten men presented to
the commander were to be chosen by him to act as *jurados*.[24]
At Monzón, according to an agreement made in 1257, the *jurados*
or *adelantados* were to be nominated annually by the *concejo*,
although the candidates were to be presented to the commander,
who had the power to reject those of whom he disapproved;[25]
and in the code of customs compiled for Horta in 1296 the right
of the inhabitants to appoint *jurados* was confirmed, although
again the nominees were to be presented for approval to the
Templar commander.[26]

The inhabitants of some places under Templar lordship also
participated in the appointment of officials with more specialized
functions. According to the agreement made at Cantavieja in
1255 one of the ten men presented to the commander by the
*concejo* was to be appointed to the office of *almotazaf*, who had
charge of weights and measures,[27] while in the customs of Horta
the right of the inhabitants to nominate *corredores* was confirmed.[28]
And by the terms of a settlement made in 1275 the citizens of
Tortosa gained the right to assist in the selection of those who were
to carry out inquests: it was agreed that the citizens should choose

annually at Ascension sixteen *probi homines*—four from each parish—and from these the vicar was to select four who were to assist in the holding of inquests. Those appointed were to be known as *paciarii* or *paeres* and they were to receive a proportion of the fines which were imposed following the inquests.[29] It was not, however, common for special officials to be appointed to conduct inquests on Templar estates; the task was normally assigned to the *jurados* or other existing officials. At Horta in 1296 it was agreed that the *jurados* should assist the bailiff of Horta in undertaking inquests[30] and at Monzón in 1279, after the inhabitants had complained about the amount of crime being committed in the town, the Order had granted that for the next two years the *adelantados*, the counsellors of the justiciar and the heads of tithings could carry out inquests when certain offences were committed. They were, however, to present offenders to the justiciar of Monzón and fines were retained by the Temple.[31]

Participation in the appointment of officials formed merely one part of the activity of the *concejos* and *universidades* under Templar lordship. They often had an important role in administration even when they did not control appointments. In Tortosa the citizens were assisting in judicial administration long before 1275. Already in the twelfth century some of the *probi homines* were playing an important part in the judgements given in the city court. Thus in 1193 a dispute concerning some land which had been granted to the Templars was judged in the city court by four *probi homines*.[32] And the citizens of Tortosa were seeking to extend the competence of the city court and to increase their own importance in it. At the end of the twelfth century they put forward a claim that all cases should be decided there, but this was rejected by arbiters, who declared that disputes between inhabitants of Tortosa should be heard in the city court, but that suits between the Templars or the Moncadas and citizens should be brought before judges appointed by the lords of Tortosa.[33] In 1242, however, when the bishop of Lérida arbitrated between the citizens on the one side and the Templars and William of Moncada on the other, it was declared that certain civil cases between the lords of Tortosa and citizens should be heard in the city court.[34] The role of the citizens in the proceedings of the court was defined in 1272, following another prolonged dispute, during which the

Templars and Raymond of Moncada claimed that their authority was being weakened by the activities of the citizens. In the compromise that was finally reached the practice was confirmed whereby the vicar chose two citizens to decide with him civil cases and those involving monetary penalties; and, as in the past, appeals were to be heard by two or more citizens acting in conjunction with the vicar. It was also then agreed that inquests should be held in cases involving certain offences, such as homicide, rape, arson, and forgery, and that the vicar should choose citizens to assist him in conducting these.[35] The Customs of the city of Tortosa show that the citizens also had a number of other administrative functions. The checking of weights and measures, for example, was undertaken jointly by the vicar and the citizens, who received a third of the penalties imposed for infringements.[36] The inhabitants of Templar lordships also became involved in financial administration. At times they assisted in the assessment and collection of dues. Contributions towards the 400s. owed for *peita* by those living at Alfambra were clearly assessed by the inhabitants themselves, for in 1266 some of them complained that they had been forced to pay more than their share by the richer and more powerful members of the community;[37] and presumably the vassals of the Temple were similarly involved whenever dues were exacted by the Order in the form of a lump sum paid by the community as a whole.[38] Communities also not infrequently obtained the farms of Templar monopolies. In the middle of the thirteenth century, for example, the inhabitants of Grallera and Torre Farrera in the district of Segriá acquired the farms of the ovens of these places,[39] and in 1254 the *universidad* of Villalba similarly received the forge there at farm.[40]

In a few instances the *concejos* and *universidades* obtained complete control over certain aspects of administration, to the total exclusion of the Temple. In a sentence of arbitration given in 1242 the bishop of Lérida declared that the public baths in Tortosa pertained to the citizens and not to the lords of the city, and the citizens' rights in this matter were confirmed later in the century when the Customs of Tortosa were compiled.[41] In the first half of the thirteenth century the inhabitants of Monzón had control of the irrigation canals and also of weights in the town and presumably took the profits derived from these rights.[42] In 1173 the men of Monzón had also claimed a right to the profits of the ferry across the Cinca, and although when the matter was disputed before the bishop of Zaragoza they were obliged to accept the Order's claims, it was nevertheless agreed that the Temple and the inhabitants should each contribute half of the costs of maintaining the ferry and that the income from it should be divided between them.[43]

Finally, the communities subject to the Temple or the officials elected by them often had the power to issue their own decrees or by-laws and to receive a share of the amercements imposed for infringements. In the code of customs drawn up at Horta in 1296 the right of the *jurados* to issue by-laws was confirmed, and it was decreed that fines for breaches of them were to be divided between the *jurados* and the Temple as had been customary until then.[44] At Castellote, where the community enjoyed a similar right, the *jurados* and the Temple each received a third of the amercements imposed, as did the lords and citizens at Tortosa.[45] To safeguard its own interests the Order normally stipulated that enactments of this kind required the consent of the Temple, but clearly in practice this provision was not always observed. In 1263 the Templars complained that the *concejo* of Ambel had issued constitutions which were prejudicial to the Order,[46] and at about the same time the commander of Tortosa asserted that the citizens ignored Templar rulings when they wanted to issue decrees and accepted instead the decisions of the Moncadas.[47] It was therefore made clear in the Customs of Tortosa that all enactments were to be made in the city court in the presence of the bailiffs of both the Moncadas and the Templars.[48]

When the provincial master surrendered Templar rights of lordship in Tortosa to the Crown in 1294 he said that he was doing so

because the rights of the said militia of the Temple are being diminished and harmed in various ways.[49]

Clearly the exercise of power by the *concejos* and *universidades* subject to the Temple in some instances reflected a desire on the part of these communities to encroach on Templar authority and to appropriate some of the Order's revenues, and this desire was obviously particularly strong in the city of Tortosa, where the inhabitants had important commercial and trading interests.[50] But the activities of communities should not always be viewed in this light. The Templars, like other lords, had only a very limited administration at their disposal, and it was therefore often necessary for them to enlist the aid and seek the co-operation of their vassals in order that the Temple's rights of lordship might be exercised more effectively. This is apparent, for example, in the agreement made at Monzón concerning the holding of inquests. It might therefore be to the Temple's advantage to allow its vassals to perform certain functions, even if it was obliged to surrender part of the profits to them. It would thus be wrong to view the exercise of power by communities as always the result of an attack on Templar rights and as always prejudicial to the Order's authority. *Concejos* and *universidades* did not even always want to participate in the administration of Templar lordships. The problems and difficulties of administration sometimes led communities to surrender to the Temple the powers which they did possess and made them reluctant to accept any further duties. The inhabitants of Monzón in 1230 granted to the Temple the main irrigation canal there for a hundred years and agreed to pay *cequiaje* to the Order, and thirty years later they abandoned their control over weights there in return for 20,000s.;[51] and when in 1296 the Templars offered to reduce by 100s. the amount demanded for *questia* from the inhabitants of Barbará, provided that the community accepted responsibility for the collection of the tax, the favour was refused.[52]

The administration of the Order's estates was affected not only by the powers of the *concejos* and *universidades* but also by the rights of others who enjoyed authority within Templar lordships. In a number of places certain rights and revenues had been granted away by previous lords before the Temple gained possession, although not all of these earlier concessions had been in the same form or affected Templar administration to the same extent. In Espluga de Francolí, for example, the fee which Hugh of Cervellón held was essentially a money fief, consisting primarily of a third of the revenues of the lordship, and although according to a sentence of arbitration given in 1258 Hugh had the right to be present when justice was dispensed, the existence of this fee had little effect on Templar administration in Espluga, for most dues were collected by Templar officials, and Hugh received his third from these.[53] But some of the fees held by knights in Espluga when the Temple acquired it consisted of rights over particular properties and consequently those who lived on these lands were removed from the direct control of the Order.[54]

It is not altogether clear to what extent within their lordships and estates the Templars continued this practice of granting out rights and revenues. Certainly in the thirteenth century dues from Templar monopolies were commonly farmed out not only to communities but also to individuals either in perpetuity or for varying periods,[55] and the dues collected by public notaries were usually farmed by them for life: at the time of the arrest of the Templars the office of notary at Cantavieja was held for life at an annual rent of 60s.J., and that at Castellote for a rent of 80s.J. a year.[56] But the only other dues which are known to have been frequently granted out were those which were temporarily alienated when the Order was seeking to anticipate its revenues. When this happened the transaction usually assumed the form of either a sale or a loan. Thus in May 1275 rents worth 1,500s.B. which fell due during the course of the following twelve months were sold for 1,200s.B. to Isaac Adreti by the commander of Palau.[57] Several years earlier Isaac Adreti had also been involved in a transaction which took the form of a loan. He had lent the commander of Palau 2,000s.B. and had received in repayment the dues which had been assigned to the Order as its tenth of royal revenues in Barcelona.[58] The wording of several papal bulls issued in the second half of the thirteenth century and ordering the recovery of Templar rights which had been illicitly alienated would seem to imply, however, that it was a common Templar practice to grant out rights and revenues on a fairly extensive scale. In 1297 Boniface VIII was repeating the words of several of his predecessors when he wrote that

it has come to our hearing that not only the beloved sons the preceptor and brothers of the house of the Temple of Jerusalem in Aragon and Catalonia but also their predecessors have granted tithes, lands, houses, meadows, pastures, woods, mills, rights, jurisdictions and certain other goods of that house . . ., to the grave harm of the same house, to a number of clerics and laymen, to some of them for life, to some for a considerable period of time, and to others in perpetuity, at farm or for an annual rent.[59]

In the second half of the thirteenth century the papacy appears to have been seeking to check the continued Templar practice of granting out rights and dues. But a large number of papal bulls were issued on the subject of the alienation of rights by religious institutions,[60] and the form of wording employed by Boniface VIII in 1297 was also frequently used in bulls applying to other monasteries and orders.[61] He was adopting a common formula, which therefore does not necessarily provide very exact and precise information about Templar activities. Certainly another series of papal bulls issued on the same subject in the second half of the thirteenth century gives a rather different impression of Templar policies at that time. Boniface VIII was again repeating the words of several of his predecessors when in 1298 he wrote that *on the petition of the Templars* he was ordering the recovery of rights and lands previously alienated illicitly.[62] No doubt at all times some rights were likely to be granted out by the Templars to friends and relations, but that the second series of papal bulls gives a more accurate indication of Templar policies in the later part of the thirteenth century than the first set is suggested by the Temple's purchasing of fees in places such as Espluga de Francolí and Barbará, for these purchases appear to imply that the Order was itself seeking to recover rights rather than pursuing a policy of granting out more. That at this time it was trying to remove intermediate authorities and to maintain direct control of those who worked the land and paid dues is also indicated by its attitude to the question of the sub-letting of holdings by tenants in the later part of the thirteenth century. Sub-letting was a very common phenomenon on Templar estates. A tenant might let part of the land which he had received from the Temple; a prosperous tenant might alternatively buy land from his less fortunate neighbours and sub-let it; and the same might be done by an individual who had acquired wealth elsewhere through trade or business and wanted to invest it in land. In the middle decades of the thirteenth century, for example, Vincent of Viana, a Lérida apothecary whose wife came of a family established at Torre Farrera,[63] purchased a considerable amount of land in the latter place from tenants of the Temple,[64] and some of this was sub-let.[65] The sub-letting of lands held of the Temple was clearly a profitable activity for the Order's tenants: the rent paid by a sub-tenant was usually two or three times as large as that demanded by the Order from the tenant,[66] and in some instances the difference between the two payments was considerably greater.[67] But sub-letting brought little benefit to the Temple. If land was sub-let, it could not be so easily brought back into demesne, and as sub-tenants were often made responsible for fulfilling tenants' obligations to the Order[68] the Temple often had no direct authority over the individuals from whom it was meant to receive rents and services. Towards the end of the thirteenth century the Templars were attempting to remedy this situation, at least in the commandery of Gardeny, whose history can be traced more fully than that of others. On a number of occasions the Order acquired direct authority over the sub-tenant of a holding by purchasing the rights of the tenant of the property.[69] In the later thirteenth century the Templars of Gardeny also sought to check further sub-letting by forbidding new tenants to grant out their lands at rent.[70] In the 1260s they began to insert in charters issued to new tenants a clause stating that the property in question was not to be granted out at any larger rent than that paid to the Temple;[71] and for the rest of the Templar period at Gardeny charters recording grants of land to tenants included a clause of this kind, although from 1285 the form of wording was changed and new tenants were thenceforth forbidden to sub-let at any rent.[72]

Yet if towards the end of the thirteenth century the Temple was seeking to remove intermediate authorities and to recover rights earlier granted out, it is still not altogether clear how frequently concessions of revenues and rights of lordship had been made in earlier periods. Certainly the surviving evidence does not suggest that revenues were normally farmed out or that fiefs were commonly created by the Templars within their lordships. The great majority of the documents which are concerned with the exploitation of property record grants of small individual holdings to peasants and townsmen, and the work of Templar officials appears to have consisted primarily in the exaction of dues and services from these rather than in the supervision of fief-holders or farmers of revenues.

When the relations between the Temple and the peasants and townsmen on its estates are examined, it very soon becomes apparent that the Order was unable to exact all the dues and services to which it might claim a right. In many parts of the *Corona de Aragón* during the twelfth and thirteenth centuries concessions had to be granted in order to ensure that land was brought under cultivation and worked. This had to be done especially in the districts conquered from the infidel. In some parts of these regions concessions were made in the first place to the Moorish population. These were not only made in order to gain possession of territories during the reconquest but also had the purpose of checking widespread emigration to places further south still under Muslim rule, for although the Moors would not want to lose their lands, many would nevertheless be reluctant to live under alien domination, especially when they feared that the Christians would be hostile to them. The uneasiness which many felt when they were brought under Christian rule is illustrated by the agreement made in 1234 between the Templars and the Moors of Chivert, for this includes an undertaking by the Order to build a wall to protect the Moorish quarter and a promise on the part of the Templars that

if any Saracen within one whole year from the time when this agreement is made wishes to leave this stronghold and wants to go to pagan territories, he can do this without any impediment and can take with him his wife, children, slaves, cattle and anything else he has and can go to the land of the Saracens with the protection of the brothers of the Temple.[73]

And both on Templar estates and elsewhere Moorish fears were sometimes shown to be justified. In 1263, for example, the Christian inhabitants of Ambel admitted to attacking and plundering the Moorish quarter there and to killing five Moors.[74] But while in places such as Ambel and Chivert it is clear that there was a Moorish population living under Templar authority, it is difficult to judge exactly how successful the policy of granting concessions to Moors was. Although in some places along the lower Ebro, including Miravet, the Moors still comprised the greater part of the population at the end of the fifteenth century,[75] in most districts from which the Moorish population was not expelled the importance of the Moorish element living under Templar rule cannot be estimated. It is not known how many Moors decided to migrate to Muslim Spain. Emigration was, however, obviously common. The agreement made at Chivert in 1234 refers to those who had already moved to places under Moorish rule, and in other districts which came under Templar lordship references are frequently encountered to holdings which had previously been held by Moors but which had passed into Christian hands.[76] Of course, the population of reconquered places had not in the period of Muslim domination always consisted entirely of Moors. That there had been a Mozarab community living in some areas which became subject to the Templars is suggested by references in Templar documents to individuals whose names included the word 'Mozarab'.[77] It is also possible that some of the Jews to whom the Temple was granting land near Lérida just after the middle of the twelfth century had already been inhabitants of that district before it had been conquered from the Moors.[78] The numerical importance of such Mozarab and Jewish elements—which, unlike the Moors, would have had no reason for emigrating—is not known;[79] but clearly the existing population of reconquered places, whether it was Muslim, Christian, or Jewish, was usually inadequate. It was necessary to attract new settlers. Yet while newcomers might expect to be able to profit from raids into Moorish territory,[80] there were a number of drawbacks to settling in a reconquered district. Settlers often had to leave behind their families and friends; if they settled in a region which was still near the frontier they were likely to suffer from Muslim raiding; they often had to build their own dwellings before they even had anywhere to live;[81] and as the land had often lain waste for long periods hard work was essential before it could be made profitable. There were often more attractive lands being opened up in districts under Christian rule nearer their own homes, and the pressure of population was not sufficient to force large numbers to seek their livelihood in reconquered lands. In these areas concessions had therefore to be granted not only to prevent Moors from emigrating but also in order to attract new settlers.

The problem of manpower was not, however, peculiar to the districts reconquered from the Moors. In the more northerly parts of the *Corona de Aragón* the Templars, like other lords, were seeking to extend the area of land under cultivation. A supply of labour was obviously necessary for this purpose, and inducements might have to be offered in order to obtain it. Further, many of those who were attracted by offers of improved conditions of tenure in new settlements in the north or in the reconquered areas further south were tenants on old-established estates in the more northerly parts of the *Corona de Aragón*. As a result, these estates soon began to suffer from a shortage of manpower, which was made more acute by the fact that tenants were also migrating to the growing urban communities, where they could enjoy greater freedom.[82] The Templars sought to check desertion from their estates in *Cataluña Vieja* by adopting the practice of extracting charters from their men, in which the permanence of the Temple's rights of lordship were recognized and stressed. In 1229, for example, William of Sargantanes, an inhabitant of Voltregá near Vich, acknowledged that he and his children and possessions were under the lordship of the Temple

namely so that I or my descendants can never choose any other lord than the brothers of the Temple and no prescription of time or residence in village or city or town can benefit me or mine in any way or injure the said militia;[83]

and many similar charters survive from the rest of the thirteenth century.[84] But the exaction of charters was not in itself enough to prevent desertion. Concessions had again to be granted.

The concessions made by the Templars and other lords in order to ensure that land was worked covered a wide variety of issues. Moors who became subject to Christian lords in the reconquered areas were commonly allowed freedom of religion and law.[85] At Chivert the Moors were permitted to retain their mosque and cemeteries and were given the right to fast, to call worshippers to prayer, and to go on pilgrimage without hindrance. They were also to be judged by their own officials according to their own laws and were not to be compelled to swear any oath 'by any creature or thing except by Almighty God'.[86] Of course, to allow the Moors their own officials was probably a necessary concession in view of language differences, and to have rejected Muslim laws would have been out of keeping with the normal respect shown in the Middle Ages for local custom.[87] But these concessions probably helped to persuade some Moors to accept Christian domination. A concession sometimes made to attract new settlers to reconquered districts was to guarantee protection to those who had committed crimes elsewhere. The *fuero* of La Cañada de Benatanduz, for example, includes a clause stating that

if any murderer settles in La Cañada de Benatanduz and his enemies come after him to settle, they must either accept him in friendship or leave the township.[88]

Those who had fled from justice could thus seek a new home in the reconquered areas. The majority of concessions, however, were concerned with dues and services.

Temporary or partial exemptions from military service were granted by the Temple to Christian settlers in some reconquered areas. In the *carta de población* for La Cuba, in the commandery of Cantavieja, settlers were freed from the obligation of *hueste* and *cabalgada* for two years, while those at Villalba, which was subject to Miravet, were given exemption for fifteen years.[89] After that period the inhabitants of Villalba were to serve whenever requested against the Moors, as were those of Castellote,[90] but in the commandery of Cantavieja the obligation for *cabalgada* was limited to once a year with the provincial master and twice with the commander of Cantavieja.[91] Similarly, by the provisions of the *fuero* which had been granted to the inhabitants of Alfambra by the master of the Order of Mountjoy and which remained in force under the Templars, the commander of Alfambra could demand *hueste* and *cabalgada* only twice a year.[92] A fuller exemption was granted to the Moors of Chivert: they were obliged to give service only if Chivert itself were attacked, either by Christians or Moors.[93] When this privilege was granted Templar expeditions were directed primarily against Moorish Spain and the Order was obviously wary of using its Muslim subjects against men of their own religion. The only comparable exemption granted to Christian settlers seems to have been the freedom from *ejército* and *cabalgada* conceded in 1226 to those holding land at Fontanet near Lérida.[94] But by the early thirteenth century this district was no longer adjacent to Muslim territories. In areas which were still near the Moorish frontier at the time when they were settled the Temple could not afford to grant such full exemptions to their Christian vassals.

By contrast, it seems to have been in the more southerly areas that the fullest exemptions from labour services were granted to Christian settlers. On their estates in the district of Lérida, which was conquered in the mid twelfth century, the Templars usually demanded some labour services, though not as many as were owed by some of the Order's tenants in *Cataluña Vieja*. Each settler at Vencilló was obliged to perform annually one day's labour service on the Temple's demesne and to carry goods as far as Lérida once a year,[95] and a similar obligation was imposed by the Temple in the district of Segriá.[96] But further south Christian settlers on Templar estates seem often to have been completely exempt from labour services, for these are not mentioned in any document concerning Christian tenants living in the lower Ebro valley or in southern Aragon, while the only reference to such obligations in Valencia is that found in the *carta de población* for the *alquería* of Seca in Burriana, where one day's ploughing a year was demanded of settlers.[97] It is, of course, dangerous to assume that the absence of any reference to an obligation necessarily means that it was not owed: that dues and services owed were not always listed in full in *cartas de población* is apparent from the wording of the charter issued to settlers at Pinell in 1198, for in this the Temple reserved certain specified rights and 'other things which are seen to pertain to the lord of the land'.[98] Yet the almost complete absence of references to labour services in the more southerly parts of the *Corona de Aragón* strongly suggests that Christian settlers on the Order's estates in these districts were free from these obligations. In the more southerly areas, on the other hand, labour services were demanded from at least some of the Order's Moorish tenants. Those at Villastar in the commandery of Villel were obliged to provide one man from every household once a month,[99] and as in the charter granted to the Moors of Chivert in 1234 Moorish officials were specifically exempted from labour services, it seems that the other Moorish inhabitants there were expected to perform them.[100]

Tenants of the Order were sometimes not only exempted from performing labour services but also freed from the payment of rent for their lands. Thus in 1264 the commander of Villel conceded to the Christian inhabitants of Villastar that if the non-irrigated land there was worked, tithes and *primicias* should be paid from it, but no other rent.[101] But it is difficult to assess exactly how common this practice was. Certainly a considerable number of *cartas de población* refer to the payment of tithes and *primicias* but do not state that settlers were also to pay rent for their holdings. Those for Cantavieja, Villarluengo, and other places in the commandery of Cantavieja are of this type,[102] as are several issued in the northern part of Valencia, such as those for Pulpís and Castellnou de Chivert.[103] Yet in the absence of documents concerning individual tenements it cannot usually be ascertained whether in fact no rents were paid. Possibly the statement that no other *peita* was to be exacted—which is found in some of the charters concerning places in southern Aragon—should be taken to mean that the inhabitants of these districts did not pay rent for

their holdings; and it may be noted in this context that when
Alfonso II granted Villarluengo to the Order of Mountjoy in 1194,
he stated that it was to be settled at 'tithes and *primicias*'.[104] But
rents were clearly charged in some places whose *cartas de población*
might be taken to imply that they were not. In the charter granted
to Novillas it was stated that settlers were not to

pay any tribute to anyone except the tithes and *primicias* pertaining to
the Church of God.[105]

Yet other sources show that settlers there usually paid rents as well
as tithes and *primicias*.[106] The dues which were referred to in
*cartas de población* by the term *peita* may therefore not have included land rents, and it is possible that details of rents were
omitted from some *cartas de población* not because none were paid
but merely because they were not paid jointly by settlers or at a
standard rate. Certainly it was not the general policy of the Order
to grant lands free of rent, although when proportional rents were
charged it was not unusual for exemptions to be allowed on pro-
ducts of minor importance.[107] Rents were not, however, always
demanded immediately from settlers. The Christians who came
to Villalba, for example, were exempted from payment for two
years.[108] Concessions of this kind were obviously necessary when
land had been lying waste for a long time after being reconquered.
But not all the places where rents were not immediately demanded fell into this category. Thus an exemption for two years
was granted in 1234 to the Moors of Chivert.[109] In this case the
concession is perhaps to be explained by devastation which took
place at the time of the reconquest.

Because of variations in measures and quality of land, it is
difficult to ascertain whether the Templars sought to attract
settlers by charging low rents for land. Proportional rents demanded by the Order in reconquered areas were not noticeably
smaller than those exacted elsewhere, but it must be remembered
that in some reconquered districts rents might include a charge in
lieu of labour services. On at least one occasion, however, it was
asserted that land was not being worked because the Order was
demanding too high a rent for it, and the Templars appear in
several instances to have been obliged to reduce their demands to
ensure that land was brought under cultivation. Non-irrigated
land at Masarrochos near Valencia was still lying waste in 1286,

even though in the *carta de población* issued by the Temple in 1251 it had been decreed that this land was to be worked within four years.[110] The inhabitants maintained that it was not worth cultivating while the Temple demanded a third of the produce. The provincial master therefore reduced the rent to a fifth.[111] A similar reduction seems to have been made in the *alquería* of Seca in Burriana, for while in the *carta de población* issued in 1243 it was stated that a fifth of produce should be paid to the Temple,[112] in 1261 land there which was to be made into vineyards was granted to sixteen men at the rent of a ninth.[113] The need to attract settlers may also explain reductions in the rents charged at Fontanet near Lérida in the early thirteenth century, when the process of resettlement was apparently still incomplete. In 1225 rents were reduced from 15s. to 14s. per *fanegada* and in 1231 there was a further reduction to 12s.[114] Several references occur to arrears of rent at Fontanet at this time,[115] and it is possible that there as elsewhere the Temple had imposed too heavy a burden of rent and was finding difficulty in retaining settlers.

The concessions made by the Temple in order that land should be cultivated rarely included exemptions from the payment of tithes and *primicias*. In the *cartas de población* these are regularly mentioned among the rights retained and the only charters which include concessions are those of Alcalá and Castellnou de Chivert, where tithes and *primicias* were not taken from garden produce, fruit, wool, or cheese; but even in these cases it seems that the dues were merely being commuted, for it was stated that a chicken was to be exacted from every house for tithes and *primicias*.[116] But of course in the exaction of these dues the Temple did not have a completely free hand, for a proportion of them was usually owed to the diocesan. It appears to have been the Templar practice also to retain monopoly rights, for at least some of these are specifically reserved in every *carta de población*. The Templars possibly found that dues from monopolies were easier to collect and more profitable than others.[117] The few concessions which are mentioned in the *cartas de población* were made mainly in Valencia. At Seca settlers were allowed to bake up to five loaves in their own houses at Christmas, Easter, and Pentecost;[118] the Moors of Chivert were not obliged to make any payment for animals slaughtered in the *carnicería*;[119] and the settlers at Alcalá were allowed to have their own mills, provided that they were not powered by wind or water; hand-mills were thus permitted, and this would reduce Templar revenues, but presumably not to any great extent.[120]

Among the other concessions made by the Order were those concerning the exaction of tolls and the public due of *questia* or *peita*, and it is possible that the Order sometimes also abandoned its claim to a fifth of the spoils of war; but it is difficult to generalize about the incidence of these dues. They are usually referred to—if at all—only in *cartas de población*, and for some districts, such as that of Lérida, very few of these charters survive, while many of the *cartas de población* which have been preserved contain no reference to them. This omission is particularly common among the *cartas de población* drawn up by the Temple in Valencia; these do not usually mention any dues other than land rents, monopoly dues, tithes, and *primicias*. In a number of charters for places in the lower Ebro valley and in southern Aragon, the Temple reserved its right to *lezda*, including presumably that paid by the inhabitants of the districts in question, and the *cartas de población* for Cantavieja, Mirambel, and Iglesuela contain details about tolls to be exacted from inhabitants who took cattle or other animals into Moorish territory.[121] Yet, with the exception of that for Pulpís,[122] the charters which survive for Templar estates in Valencia contain no reference to tolls, and it cannot be ascertained whether the men living in these places paid them to the Order. But the absence of any reference to these dues in the *carta de población* which the Templars issued in 1192 for Horta, further north,[123] probably did imply that settlers were exempt from the payment of tolls there, for in 1165—when Horta was still under the lordship of the Crown—Alfonso II had conceded that those who settled there should not be obliged to pay *lezda* or *peaje* anywhere in the kingdom,[124] and in the customs confirmed in 1296 the inhabitants were exempted from the payment of *lezda* or *peaje* within the boundaries of Horta.[125] But the only exemptions from tolls which are known definitely to have been granted to settlers by the Templars themselves were those enjoyed by the inhabitants of the commandery of Miravet, who were freed from the payment of *lezda* and *peaje* in places subject to the convents of Monzón and Ascó, and by settlers at Villanueva de la Barca, who were allowed free passage across the Segre.[126] The incidence of *peita* and *questia* seems to have been very uneven.

While settlers at Villalba were exempted from *questia* in their *carta de población*, those at Gandesa paid it;[127] and while the inhabitants of Cantavieja and Mirambel were exempted from *peita*, those of Alfambra were subject to this due.[128] But no full information survives about the exaction of *peita* and *questia*, and the same is true of the right to a fifth of booty and prisoners taken in war. This right must have been of some importance, especially in the frontier districts, and it was retained by the Order in the *cartas de población* issued for Novillas, Pinell, Gandesa, and La Cañada de Benatanduz;[129] but there is no reference to it in any other settlement charter granted by the Temple,[130] and in none was a specific exemption conceded.

The situation is a little clearer with regard to the rights usually known in *Cataluña Vieja* as the *malos usos*. On some of its estates in the district of Lérida the Temple did not altogether abandon these rights. In the *carta de población* for Vencilló the right of *exorquia* was retained,[131] and in two charters recording grants of land to tenants near Lérida which were issued by the Order in 1234 the phrase 'with all evil custom ceasing' was included, which suggests that on these properties some of the *malos usos* had been retained up to that time.[132] There is no reference, however, to the exaction of *malos usos* on the Temple's lands along the lower valley of the Ebro, and in several *cartas de población* freedom from them was specifically granted. In the charter issued to the settlers of Horta the Templars promised to exact no *malos usos*,[133] and in 1198 the Order undertook not to demand *exorquia*, *intestia*, or *cugucia* from the inhabitants of Pinell, who were further freed from the *malos usos* when a new *carta de población* was issued in 1207.[134] A similar exemption was included in the charter issued for Batea, whose customs were later adopted at Algars.[135] It is clear that the Temple normally surrendered its rights to the *malos usos* on its estates along the lower Ebro valley. The Order similarly abandoned its claims to them in the *carta de población* issued for Moncada in Valencia,[136] but these rights are not mentioned in any other settlement charter granted by the Templars in that kingdom. Yet if the Order gave up these rights on its estates along the lower Ebro it is unlikely that it would have tried to reserve them in Valencia. Although the *malos usos* are usually associated with *Cataluña Vieja*, rights of a similar kind did exist in Aragon, and in the more southerly parts of that kingdom some were retained by the Templars. At Tronchón, in the commandery of Cantavieja, the Order claimed a right to a fifth of the goods of any inhabitant who died intestate, unless he had been killed by the Moors,[137] and at Cantavieja, Mirambel, and Iglesuela the Templars took a fifth of the possessions of those who died under sentence of excommunication or interdict.[138]

Yet although in some places several of the *malos usos* or similar rights were retained by the Order, there is no evidence in the reconquered lands settled by the Temple of the *remensa personal*. The only restrictions known to have been imposed on settlers were those which were considered necessary to guarantee that estates were worked. To ensure that land was brought under cultivation, alienation was often forbidden for a certain number of years. At Horta and Batea the period was five years, at Villastar three, and at Belloque and Cambor two.[139] A limitation of this kind was not, however, always imposed and the Templars sometimes merely decreed that the land should be worked or houses built within a certain period. Thus in the *carta de población* for Pulpís it was decreed that the Temple should have the right to seize any land that was not worked within two years,[140] and settlers who were given lands by the Order on the outskirts of Valencia were often obliged to build houses within three or four months.[141] To ensure that land was kept under cultivation, the Order frequently also decreed that a tenant must reside personally on his holding; failure to do so was punished by confiscation of the property. In the *carta de población* for Villalba it was stated that anyone who was absent from his holding for three years should forfeit it, unless he was being held captive,[142] and some lands at Carpesa were held on the condition that if the tenants did not reside personally within three months of being warned to do so, their lands would be confiscated by the Order.[143] The Templars sometimes also sought to enforce personal residence by decreeing that tenants could alienate their lands only to local inhabitants.[144] In imposing restrictions of this kind the Temple was, of course, merely doing the same as many other lords in the reconquered districts.[145]

Freedom from the *malos usos* was clearly one of the most important privileges which the Temple could offer to settlers, for it was commonly by granting this that lords in *Cataluña Vieja* sought to check emigration from their estates and to attract new tenants. The Templars were adopting the same policy as many other northern lords when in 1281, in an attempt to increase the population of Puigreig, they promised

> to all those settlers who wish to come to the said settlement and make continuous residence there and become *homines proprii* of the Temple that they are to be exempt in perpetuity and free from *cugucia* and *intestia* and *exorquia* and from the redemption of men and women; so that they can come freely to the said settlement without any redemption and that they can freely leave it whenever they wish without any redemption of their persons or their movables.[146]

This did not mean, however, that the *malos usos* disappeared altogether from Templar estates in *Cataluña Vieja*. At the end of the thirteenth and beginning of the fourteenth centuries many of those living on the Order's lands in this region were still subject to the *remensa personal*;[147] and elsewhere, if the Templars could not claim redemption payments, they might demand the due known as *laudimium*, which a lord could exact when he confirmed conveyances of property held of him.[148]

Some general trends can obviously be discerned among the concessions made by the Templars to ensure that land was worked. On the one hand, there was a tendency to abandon the *malos usos* and labour services and, on the other, monopoly rights and tithes and *primicias* were usually retained. But—except in the few cases when the customs of one township were adopted *en bloc* in another —the conditions of tenure varied to some extent from place to place. The picture of uniform concessions which has sometimes been presented in general discussions of exemptions clearly does not apply to Templar estates.[149] Of course, in some instances the Templars were probably merely confirming concessions made by previous lords, and some variations can be explained in this way. But there were also variations between places where the work of settlement was begun by the Templars. This was presumably because the conditions laid down in the *cartas de población* represented compromises between the wishes of the Order and those of settlers; just as the granting of the charter to the Moors of Chivert in 1234 was preceded by negotiations, so presumably the issuing of *cartas de población* to Christian settlements followed discussions between the Templars and the first settlers. And varying decisions could be reached as a result of such discussions.

It is not always easy to judge the success of this policy of concession. As has been seen, it is not known how many Moors left Templar estates and migrated to Muslim Spain. But it is clear that when lords wanted to attract new settlers it was not enough for them just to be ready to offer concessions: these needed to be publicized and the work of settlement organized. In some instances the Templars delegated part of this task to others. In 1151 land on a Templar estate at Castelldans was granted to two men on the condition that they undertook the work of resettling the whole estate.[150] The five individuals to whom the *carta de población* for Gandesa was issued were similarly assigned the task of finding further settlers, as was a certain Filiolo at Gorrapte,[151] while the charter for Castellnou de Chivert was granted to Bartholomew Amoros 'and to the settlers whom you send there'.[152] The men who undertook this work on Templar estates and elsewhere in Spain[153] can obviously be compared with the *locatores* who were employed to bring settlers to new lands in eastern Germany. Most of those who acted in this capacity on Templar estates in Aragon appear not, however, to have received as extensive privileges and rights as were usually conceded to the German *locatores*.[154] Although Filiolo was granted the office of bailiff and a quarter of judicial profits at Gorrapte, the two men who undertook the work of resettlement at Castelldans were merely exempted from the payment of rent and the performance of labour services, and in other instances there is no reference to any special privileges enjoyed by those who helped to resettle Templar estates. While some individuals resettled whole estates for the Order, others seem to have been given the task of finding tenants for particular holdings, for in some instances the Temple gave existing tenants additional lands, which they could then sub-let to newcomers at a profit. Thus in 1255 Arnold of the Ribera de Monzón was assigned land for building houses in Valencia next to the houses which he already held of the Temple, and in 1262 he granted away half of this land at more than twice the rent which he paid to the Order for it.[155] But it is not clear how frequently the Order delegated the task of finding settlers. It has been argued that the military orders resettled lands on the north-eastern borders of Germany by transferring some of their own tenants from estates further west.[156] In the *Corona de Aragón* the Templars adopted a policy of this kind when establishing Castellnou in Segriá,

and the evidence provided by names suggests that settlers on
Templar lands elsewhere in the Aragonese kingdoms were some-
times similarly drawn from the Order's own estates: Peter of
Horta, for example, was among the settlers to whom the *carta de
población* for Alcalá de Chivert was granted.[157] That settlers on
Templar estates in Aragon might be drawn from the Order's own
properties is also implied by the statement in the charter for
Puigreig that men could come there 'without any redemption'.
But presumably the Templars did not usually pursue a policy of
resettling lands by transferring tenants from other estates belonging to the Order, for if they had done so there would often soon
have been a lack of manpower on the old-established properties;
and in so far as can be ascertained from the evidence provided by
names, those who came to settle on Templar estates were drawn
from all parts of Aragon and Catalonia and possibly also from the
more southerly districts of France.[158]

Whether the task of resettling an estate was undertaken by the
Order itself or delegated to others, the Templars usually issued
a *carta de población*, and these charters are obviously an important
source for tracing the course of resettlement on the Order's lands.
Yet it must be remembered that they mark only a stage in the
process of settlement. Many were issued to just a handful of
individuals, and in many charters reference is made to future
settlers. And it is clear that in many settlements new land was
being brought under cultivation and houses built right up to the
end of the thirteenth century. But not all settlements prospered in
this way, and some *cartas de población* refer to merely abortive
attempts to bring land under cultivation. If *cartas de población* do
not therefore mark the completion of settlement, they do not
necessarily mark the beginning either. A second charter might be
issued not only after an earlier settlement had collapsed, but also
when conditions of tenure were being confirmed or changed. The
course of resettlement cannot therefore be traced just from the
evidence provided by the *cartas de población*. But even when all
the available material is examined, it is not always easy to follow
the progress of resettlement on Templar estates.

Some places in Aragon along the Ebro and its tributaries which
had been conquered in the early part of the twelfth century,
before the Temple entered into the *reconquista*, still needed resettling when they were acquired by the Order, although in some

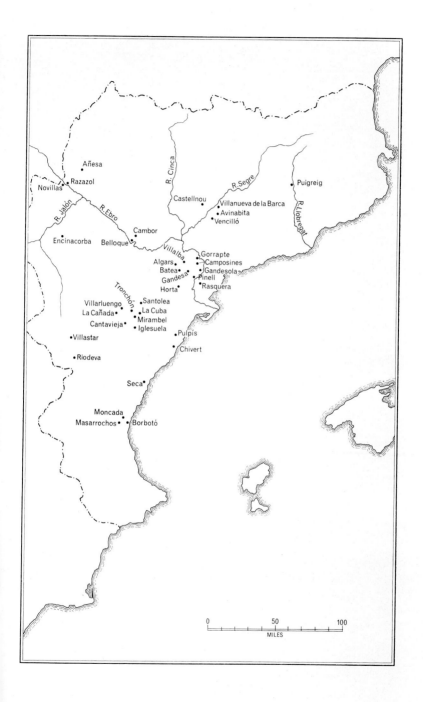

Añesa
Razazol
Novillas
R. Jalón
R. Ebro
R. Cinca
R. Segre
Puigreig
Castellnou
Villanueva de la Barca
Avinabita
Vencilló
R. Llobregat
Cambor
Encinacorba
Belloque
Villalba
Gorrapte
Algars
Camposines
Batea
Gandesola
Gandesa
Pinell
Horta
Rasquera
Tronchón
Villarluengo
Santolea
La Cuba
La Cañada
Mirambel
Cantavieja
Iglesuela
Villastar
Pulpis
Chivert
Riodeva
Seca
Moncada
Masarrochos
Borbotó

0        50        100
MILES

others a Christian community had been established before the Temple gained possession. Although the Templars issued a *carta de población* for Razazol in the later 1150s or early 1160s,[159] the work of resettlement was not then just beginning, for there were settlers at Razazol as early as 1129,[160] and the existence of charters recording conveyances of land there in the 1140s and early 1150s shows that this early settlement had not collapsed.[161] Boquiñeni had apparently also been resettled by 1129,[162] but it is not altogether clear whether or not Novillas was inhabited by Christians when it was given to the Order. In the middle of the twelfth century, when the *fuero* of Novillas was confirmed, it was stated that the work of resettlement had been carried out by the Temple: after the Order had gained the Hospital's rights there, the Templar Garner,

seeing that he could not defend the township of Novillas from the Saracens without the help of good men, settled it and allocated the lands of the said township of Novillas to settlers—holy men, knights and footmen—who wished to settle there.[163]

But it may be doubted whether the scribe who drew up this confirmation was well informed. The *carta de población* which survives—its authenticity is admittedly not beyond suspicion[164]— was drawn up in the name of the Temple and of the Hospital, not just in that of the Temple; and it is clear that even before 1135, when the *carta de población* was apparently issued, some allocation of lands had already taken place, for a bequest of a holding at Novillas was included in a will drawn up in 1133.[165] It may be suggested therefore that Novillas was already repopulated when it was given to the Orders and that the Templars —not alone but in conjunction with the Hospitallers—merely confirmed an existing settlement. At Añesa, La Zaida, and Encinacorba, on the other hand, resettlement was definitely the work of the Order. When the bishop of Pamplona granted the Templars the right to build a church at Añesa in 1149, he said that they were then establishing a settlement there;[166] and when the bishop of Zaragoza in 1177 gave the Order a similar right at La Zaida, he stated that

ever since it was ravaged by the Moors it has lain waste and uncultivated until the brothers began to work the land there with great labour and expense;[167]

while a year earlier the same bishop, quoting from Deuteronomy, had said of Encinacorba that it lay 'in a place of horror and waste solitude'.[168] Encinacorba was soon resettled by the Templars. They issued a *carta de población* for it in 1177[169] and late twelfth-century evidence shows that the settlement there did not collapse.[170] The work of repopulation may not have been carried out so effectively, however, at Añesa and La Zaida. Although a *carta de población* was issued for Añesa in 1157,[171] exactly a hundred years later a fresh charter was drawn up and lands were apparently then being allocated to settlers;[172] and in the fourteenth century Añesa was the least valuable of the former Templar commanderies. The Templars may similarly have enjoyed only limited success in attracting Christians to La Zaida. Although the Order had gained rights of lordship there in 1161, La Zaida was still without Christian inhabitants in 1177,[173] and when at the end of the thirteenth century the Grand Master gave permission for the alienation of La Zaida, he stated that he was doing this after being informed

of certain things in the bailiwick of Aragon which are in a poor state and unprofitable to the Temple,[174]

which suggests that the Order had not been altogether successful in resettling La Zaida. Certainly in 1275 the Templars were still trying to settle the nearby places of Belloque and Cambor, for in a *carta de población* issued in that year it was decreed that lands should be brought under cultivation there within two years.[175]

The Temple also participated in the resettlement of places in other areas which were already in Christian hands before the Order entered into the *reconquista*, but the process of repopulation is usually difficult to follow. In the thirteenth century, for example, there was clearly a Christian settlement at Selma, which had been lying waste in 1149,[176] but it is not known when this was established.

More information survives about resettlement in districts conquered after 1143. The Templars began to settle Christians on their estates around Lérida almost immediately after the city's capture. As has been seen, an agreement was made in 1151 about bringing settlers to the Order's lands at Castelldans,[177] and in 1158 the Templars, acting jointly with Gilbert of Anglesola, made grants of land for settlement at Avinabita, while in 1161/2 a *carta de población* was issued for Vencilló.[178] By this time land at Gardeny was also being brought under cultivation. In 1161 the commander of Gardeny granted gardens there to fourteen inhabitants of Lérida,[179] and in 1165 a further seven men were assigned as much land as they could irrigate there and another four were given land to make gardens,[180] while in the following year eight more individuals received plots at Gardeny for this purpose.[181] At this time the Order was similarly undertaking the resettlement of land at Fontanet, on the opposite bank of the Segre to Gardeny;[182] and by 1170 some Templar lands in Segriá were being worked by Christians, although it is not clear to what extent the Temple was responsible for resettling these lands.[183] But although the work of resettlement was begun early on Templar estates near Lérida, it was not quickly completed. That setbacks were not uncommon is suggested by a clause inserted in a charter recording the grant of three *fanegadas* of land by the Templars in Lérida in 1174; this stated that

if it happens that all the other settlers of that field leave it, we [the Templars] have the power to recover these three *fanegadas*.[184]

The extensive evidence which survives, however, about Templar estates in the region of Lérida shows that at least in many places there was continuous Christian settlement from the second half of the twelfth century. And in the early decades of the thirteenth century the Order could seek to draw upon the inhabitants of existing settlements in the area when it wanted to found completely new townships. This happened in 1231 when Castellnou in Segriá was being established. The land was assigned by the Order to the inhabitants of Riudovelles and of other nearby places under Templar lordship, and these were to undertake the building of the new township.[185]

The resettlement of Templar estates along the lower valley of the Ebro was not usually begun so early. Although Christian settlers soon established themselves in the city of Tortosa,[186] Christians did not come to live in many of the more rural parts of this region until the last years of the twelfth century or the early decades of the thirteenth, after Alfonso II's conquests had made the district less exposed to Muslim raids.[187] It was at this time that resettlement was undertaken on many of the Temple's estates in the region. *Cartas de población* were issued for Gandesa and Horta in 1192,[188] and Christian settlers at Pinell received charters in 1198 and 1207,[189] while a *carta de población* was drawn up in 1205 for Batea, in 1209 for Camposines, and in 1224 for

Villalba.[190] That these charters refer to an early stage in the work of repopulation and did not just confirm well-established settlements is apparent in the first place from the charters themselves. The *carta de población* for Gandesa was issued to only five settlers and the main work of resettlement clearly still lay ahead, while that for Pinell in 1207 was granted to only seven out of a proposed thirty settlers.[191] Other sources point to the same conclusion. In 1185 Horta was said by the bishop of Tortosa to need resettling, and although Miravet had some Christian inhabitants by then, these were not numerous enough to justify the building of a parish church.[192] A further indication of the lack of settlement on Templar lands in this region until towards the end of the twelfth century is provided by Alfonso II's grant of a *carta de población* for Algars and Batea in October 1181 and by his simultaneous gift of these places *ad populandum* to Bernard Granel; such action could obviously not have been taken if Algars and Batea had been settled by the Order and the Templars had been exercising their rights of lordship over tenants there.[193] The granting of *cartas de población* by the Temple is, moreover, paralleled at this time by similar activity on the part of other lords who had estates in this region.[194] But if the Templars were trying to establish communities of Christian settlers on their lands along the lower Ebro towards the end of the twelfth century, they were not always at once successful. As the seven settlers mentioned in the *carta de población* for Pinell in 1207 did not include the three named in the charter issued nine years earlier, it seems that the first attempt at resettlement had failed, as apparently had the king's essays at repopulating Batea and Horta, for which Alfonso II had issued a *carta de población* in 1165.[195] The resettlement of the lower Ebro seems in fact to have been a slow and laborious undertaking, which lasted throughout the thirteenth century: Gorrapte received a *carta de población* from the Order in 1237, as did Gandesola in 1248, while the Templars drew up a charter for Algars in 1281.[196] Admittedly at Algars there is evidence of some Christian settlement sixty years earlier,[197] and several references occur in the first half of the thirteenth century to a Templar official who supervised the administration of Algars.[198] But the wording of the charter issued in 1281, which shows that the customs of Batea were being adopted at Algars, does not suggest that the Order was then just modifying conditions of tenure for an existing settlement; and it may be noted that although the Temple had been granted rights of ecclesiastical patronage there in 1244,[199] Algars—like Miravet where there were very few Christian settlers[200]—is not mentioned in the accounts of papal taxes collected in 1279 and 1280.[201] It is probable therefore that in 1281 the Templars were seeking to re-establish a settlement at Algars, while in the case of Gorrapte it is made absolutely clear in the *carta de población* that the Templars were beginning the work of resettlement in 1237.[202]

Many places in southern Aragon were clearly already inhabited by Christians when the Temple acquired them from the Order of Mountjoy. Alfambra had received a *fuero* from Count Roderick, the founder of Mountjoy, and according to memoranda drawn up by members of that Order who opposed the amalgamation with the Temple, the possessions which the Templars gained there included churches with their ornaments, books, and vestments, and also mills and an oven.[203] The members of Mountjoy similarly asserted that the Templars had gained a church, mills, and an oven at Villarluengo. This place had been uninhabited when it was granted by Alfonso II to Mountjoy in February 1194,[204] but it had been repopulated almost immediately, for in the same year that Order rewarded an individual for his help in resettling it;[205] and when the Temple issued a *carta de población* for Villarluengo in 1197 there were at least twenty Christian settlers there.[206] At Villel, for which Alfonso II had drawn up a resettlement charter in 1180,[207] there were also Christian settlers in 1196, for in that year the Templars were said to have taken possession of a church there, and in the same year they began making purchases of land from some of the Christian inhabitants.[208] In 1196 the Order was similarly buying property from Christians at Castellote.[209] The places resettled by 1196 may also have included La Cañada de Benatanduz, for the Templars almost immediately issued a *fuero* for it.[210] But Cantavieja may have lacked settlers when it was gained by the Templars, for when Peter II confirmed possession of it to the Order in 1212, he stated that he was doing so

to settle our land and especially that which is situated on the Muslim frontier;[211]

and the only *carta de población* for Cantavieja that survives was drawn up in 1225.[212] And it seems to have been only after the conquest of Valencia had been undertaken, and this district had ceased to be a frontier region, that a number of places near Cantavieja were settled. *Cartas de población* for Iglesuela and La Cuba were issued in 1242 and for Mirambel in the following year, while Santolea, which was subject to Castellote, received a charter in 1261, and Tronchón was given one in 1272.[213] But the evidence concerning this part of southern Aragon is sparse and it is not clear whether these were all new settlements and whether they were maintained continuously. It may be noted, however, that the accounts of papal taxes collected in 1280 on the one hand mention La Cuba, Iglesuela, Tronchón, and Mirambel, and on the other indicate that some places in this area belonging to other lords had only recently been settled.[214] In the middle decades of the thirteenth century there was certainly some new settlement on Templar lands further south, again near the Valencian border, in the commandery of Villel. Although there were some Christian settlers at Riodeva before the middle of the century[215] a *carta de población* was not issued until 1260,[216] and that intensive settlement was only then being undertaken is shown by the wording of a charter drawn up in 1257, which refers to the possibility of re-settling Riodeva.[217] A few years later the settlement of Villastar, between Villel and Teruel, was also being undertaken. In 1264 a *carta de población* for this *alquería* was granted to twenty Christian settlers. That this was a new settlement is suggested by the absence of any earlier reference to Villastar in the first volume of the *Cartulario Magno*, which is devoted to the commandery of Villel, and also by two provisions included in the charter itself: it was decreed that settlers should not alienate their holdings for three years and that if the Order did not build a mill at Villastar they were to use the mill at Villel.[218] But this settlement did not immediately flourish, and in 1267 there were only four Christian *hereditates* there. In that year the Order granted all the rest of the land in the *alquería* to Moorish settlers. It was stated that

all the *hereditates* of the aforesaid *alquería* are to be divided equally and shared among thirty Saracen settlers of the same place except the four *hereditates* which the Christians have there.[219]

Yet in 1271 a further charter was issued to Christian settlers at Villastar, in which the terms of the 1264 charter were modified and in which it was said that all the land at Villastar was to be divided among seventeen settlers.[220] The resettlement of Villastar appears therefore to have suffered several setbacks, but it is clear from the evidence provided in the *Cartulario Magno* that the Christian settlement there was maintained during the rest of the thirteenth century.[221]

In the kingdom of Valencia resettlement appears to have been undertaken mainly in the middle decades of the thirteenth century. The Order was granting houses in the city of Valencia to tenants by June 1239, less than a year after the city's capture,[222] and there seems to have been no lack of settlers there, for in the middle of the century the Temple was creating a new suburb outside the walls of the city in La Xarea,[223] and was even able to charge small entry fines for land on which houses were to be built.[224] In the middle years of the thirteenth century the Order also granted *cartas de población* for several of the *alquerías* lying to the north of the city, but some of these may merely have confirmed settlements started by previous lords. This may have been the case at Masarrochos, for the charter granted to settlers there in October 1251 was issued apparently only a few months after the Temple had acquired the *alquería* through an exchange with Simon Pérez of Arenoso.[225] At Moncada as well in 1248 the Templars were probably issuing a charter to a settlement created before the Order gained possession. The wording of the documents recording the king's grant of Moncada and Carpesa in 1246 implies that these places were then already settled, and Moncada was clearly already populated in May 1248 when the Order issued the *carta de población*, for the charter was drawn up by the chaplain of Moncada and twenty settlers are mentioned in it by name.[226] The Templars may themselves, however, have resettled Borbotó, which they acquired from William of Portella in 1238.[227] The *carta de población* which they issued in 1265 clearly did not mark the very beginning of settlement,[228] for in January 1263 the Order had been prepared to agree to pay the bishop of Valencia 20 besants annually for the next twenty years for two-thirds of the tithes of Borbotó.[229] As the settlers paid the Order 800s. for the charter, its purpose was presumably to record a change in the conditions of tenure. But the settlement at Borbotó may not have been of long standing, for in 1265 there was no mill or forge there and it was decreed in the *carta de población* that certain land was to be brought under cultivation within three years.

In the middle decades of the century the Order was also under-taking the resettlement of lands further north. Settlers in the *alquería* of Seca in Burriana, which the Temple had been granted in 1237, received a *carta de población* in 1243,[230] as did those at Alcalá de Chivert in 1251—although lands had still to be allocated when their charter was issued[231]— and the work of resettlement at Castellnou de Chivert was being organized in 1262.[232] In the more northerly part of Valencia the Temple appears also later to have been obliged to undertake the main work of resettlement at Pulpís, for although the Order of Calatrava had issued a *carta de población* for it in 1244, the resettlement charter granted by the Templars was not issued until 1286, nine years after Pulpís had been awarded to the Order, and the terms of the Templar charter imply that a new settlement was being created: the *fuero* of Valencia was adopted instead of that of Zaragoza, which had been applied in 1244; settlers were to bring land under cultivation within two years; and they were also to build a church there.[233]

No further information about Pulpís in the Templar period survives, but it is clear that most of the settlements created or taken over by the Temple in the kingdom of Valencia were maintained throughout the rest of the thirteenth century. Never-theless, on Templar estates, as on those of other lords,[234] there was a problem of absenteeism, and because of the difficulty in obtain-ing new tenants the Order could not rigorously enforce regula-tions about personal residence. Although at Carpesa there was a rule that tenants would be deprived of their holdings if they did not take up residence within three months of being ordered to do so,[235] in May 1274 the Templars undertook not to deprive one individual of his land there provided that he came to live in Carpesa by the beginning of the following year;[236] and when in April 1275 he had still not taken up residence there, the Order allowed him a further two weeks' grace.[237]

A survey of the resettlement of conquered lands held by the Temple shows that its progress was uneven.[238] Settlers were attracted most easily and quickly to the large cities.[239] In the more rural areas, on the other hand, lands were often lying waste for long periods; and the evidence from the lower Ebro valley and southern Aragon suggests that it was particularly difficult to attract settlers to districts which were very close to the Moorish frontier and exposed to raiding. Along some parts of the frontier there was a belt of waste land between Christian and Moor. Admittedly the settlement of some rural districts, such as that around Lérida, began almost immediately after they had been reconquered. But in all regions there were likely to be setbacks[240] and the work of resettlement was only slowly completed. And in some places along the Ebro and its tributaries in Aragon the Templars may never have established satisfactory settlements. The Temple and other lords were competing for the available manpower, and the Order could only offer the same concessions as others. The Aragonese kings may further in the interests of their own estates have tried to check the flow of settlers on to private lands. This seems to be the implication of a charter issued in 1251 in which James I granted the Order the right to establish a further five settlers at Camañas, in the commandery of Alfambra.[241] Nevertheless, although it is impossible to gain a precise estimate of the size of settlements until the mid fourteenth century,[242] the success of the Templars generally in bringing reconquered lands into use, with either Christian or Moorish settlers, is apparent from the Hospitaller valuation of Templar commanderies drawn up in the earlier part of the fourteenth century, for this shows that many of the more wealthy Templar houses were situated in districts which had been gained from the Moors in the twelfth and thirteenth centuries.[243]

The Order was not always so successful, however, in preventing emigration from its more northerly estates. Although a *carta de población*, favourable to tenants, was issued by the Templars for Puigreig in 1281,[244] eleven years later permission to alienate the stronghold was given by the Grand Master because, like La Zaida, it was not profitable to the Order.[245]

The effects of the reconquest and resettlement were felt throughout the *Corona de Aragón* and influenced the Temple's policies towards its vassals not only in the reconquered districts. The need to bring land under cultivation and to keep it cultivated explains the majority of the concessions granted by the Order to its tenants. But a number of concessions were made for other reasons. Some were granted to individual tenants as special favours or in return for a payment. In 1154, for example, the Templars assigned land near Lérida free of rent to a scribe named Pons 'because of the service and love which you show to our house';[246] and in 1137, in return for a payment of 20m., the Order agreed to reduce the rent owed from some land at Collsabadell from a fifth to an eleventh.[247] It has been seen how the Order's lack of money in the thirteenth century similarly led it to free the inhabitants of Espluga de Francolí from the obligation to pay *questia* in return for a payment of 1,200m.[248] But not all the concessions made by the Order are fully explained in the sources. At Fontanet, near Lérida, the dues owed from some holdings were reduced in 1293 from 12s. to 10s. per *fanegada*,[249] and ten years later a further reduction of 2s. was made.[250] In 1303/4 the rent payable on some lands at Gardeny, on the opposite bank of the Segre, was similarly reduced from 12s. to 10s. per *fanegada*.[251] At Fontanet the rate of 12s. per *fanegada* had been in force since 1231,[252] and at Gardeny rents had remained unchanged in amount for at least forty years before the reduction made in 1303/4.[253] It cannot therefore be maintained that in these instances the Temple had imposed too heavy demands at the time of settlement and was forced to reduce them in order to bring land under cultivation, as had happened in some districts. The provincial master explained the reductions made in 1303/4 merely by saying that the land was so heavily burdened that the tenants were unable to pay their dues; he was therefore reducing Templar demands at the great insistence of the tenants and in order that the Temple should be more certain of receiving what was due. The difficulty which the commanders of Gardeny were experiencing at this time in collecting dues is apparent from the large number of references to non-payment and arrears of rent which occur in the documents of this convent at the end of the thirteenth century. Of fifteen references to non-payment or arrears at Fontanet, eight occur in the period between 1290 and 1304, and twenty-eight out of fifty-two references in the commandery as a whole come from the same period. In most cases from two to four years' rent was owed, but several instances of non-payment for ten years or more are recorded.[254] The seriousness of the situation is revealed in an inventory of Gardeny's possessions drawn up in 1289, for in this the commander made clear that he could not pay the dues he owed to the provincial master partly because of the difficulty the convent was encountering in the collection of rents.[255] But although it is apparent that rents were reduced in the commandery because of the tenants' inability to pay what was demanded of them, the sources do not explain why at this time the Order's vassals were in financial difficulties. The provincial master's statement in 1303/4 could be explained by declining productivity resulting from soil exhaustion. But an alternative explanation is suggested by the wording of a charter recording the sub-letting in 1284 of some land which was held of the Temple at Grallera in Segriá. In this document the recipient of the land undertook to pay all dues which were owed for it, including *bovaje* 'if, which God forbid, it is exacted'.[256] The Order's tenants may have had difficulty in paying their dues to the Temple because they were being impoverished by frequent royal demands for extraordinary taxes. If this was so, then all commanderies would of course have been affected. But much more evidence survives about Gardeny than about any other commandery, and it is not known whether other commanders were obliged to reduce rents at the end of the thirteenth century. Nevertheless, a considerable number of references to arrears and non-payment of dues occur at this time in other commanderies. Inventories drawn up in 1289 at Huesca and Calatayud include details of arrears owing in these commanderies,[257] and a list of debts owed to the convent of Corbins in 1300 similarly contains references to arrears of rent,[258] while a few years earlier the commander of Barcelona had nominated an attorney to recover debts and compel the men of the commandery to pay the dues which they owed.[259] In the commandery of Zaragoza at the end of the thirteenth century a number of tenants were deprived of their lands because rents had not been paid,[260] and the commanders of Zaragoza began to adopt the practice, when making grants of land, of stating that arrears would not be tolerated for more than a certain time.[261] Finally, the royal registers of the period refer not infrequently to Templar appeals to the Crown for assistance in the exaction of dues owed to the Order.[262]

Yet while some cases of arrears and non-payment of rent reflect the impoverishment of Templar vassals, others are to be explained by unwillingness rather than inability to pay. When demanding dues or services the Templars not infrequently encountered opposition from individuals or communities who asserted that the Order was exceeding its rights or who were trying to avoid the fulfilment of obligations and thus create an immunity through prolonged default. The Order's financial rights were those which were most commonly called in question, but dispute also arose on other issues. It has been seen how the inhabitants of Ambel questioned the Order's judicial powers, only to throw themselves on the mercy of the provincial master;[263] and at Monzón, where the Order claimed a right to military service whenever it needed it, the inhabitants on several occasions in the thirteenth century sought to restrict and limit their military obligations. In 1210 they admitted that they owed *hueste* and *ejército* but denied that they were liable for *cabalgada*. This claim was disallowed by Peter II who acted as arbiter in the dispute and who decreed that the men of Monzón should perform every kind of military service whenever the Temple demanded it.[264] Later in the century they asserted that according to the terms of a privilege issued by the Aragonese king Sancho Ramírez in 1076 they were not obliged to give *hueste* or *cabalgada*

if it was not done by their consent unless it was necessary for a battle in the field with bread for three days.

On these grounds they refused in 1287 to answer a summons to be at Játiva at Easter ready to serve for three months and in 1289 they neglected a further demand for service in Valencia.[265] Although Sancho Ramírez's privilege was confirmed by Peter III and Alfonso III,[266] the form in which it survives is suspect—in 1076, for example, Monzón was still in Moorish hands—and the fact that it had not been used in 1210 suggests that it could have been a thirteenth-century forgery.[267] The Templars did not go so far as to assert this, but they did point out that the privilege had never been used before and that at the time when it had been issued Monzón had not been resettled. By means of such arguments and by invoking the sentence given by Peter II the Order in 1292 finally compelled the inhabitants of Monzón to agree to pay 12,000s.J. as a penalty for default of service.[268] The inhabitants of Castellote, after refusing to serve, had similarly in 1265 accepted that military service was to be performed whenever the Order demanded it.[269]

Dispute between the Order and its men, as between the Temple and the Crown, was no doubt encouraged by the vague wording of documents, and this also hindered the settlement of differences. Although in the thirteenth century documents did tend to be more detailed, the charters which recorded grants to individual tenants, like the *cartas de población*, often failed to state fully what obligations were owed to the Order. A rather extreme example is provided by a charter drawn up in 1170 concerning two *cahizadas* of land in the district of Segriá: the only obligation placed on the tenants was that 'they are to pay rent as is the custom in Segriá.'[270] Throughout the Order's history in Aragon it was usual, however, for the Templars to seek to safeguard their rights by inserting in land charters a clause forbidding the alienation of property to knights or clerics.[271]

The ability of the Templars to enforce their rights depended, of course, not only on the manner in which documents were drawn up but also on the extent to which written records were kept. The Templars certainly tried to preserve a record of the obligations owed to them. Charters recording grants of land to tenants were usually drawn up in the form of chirographs, so that the Templars as well as the recipients of the land could have a copy. These documents were also copied into the Order's cartularies, although this was not a uniform practice. Whereas over half of the documents in the cartulary of Castellote are of this type, very few charters of this kind were included in that compiled for the convent of Huesca.[272] A further record of obligations was preserved in rentals and custumals: in 1214, for example, the commander of Gardeny drew up a list of the rents and labour services owed by tenants of lands in Segriá,[273] and Templar dues in Cerdaña were listed by the commander of Puigreig in 1275.[274] Although rentals and custumals were occasionally copied into cartularies,[275] very few now survive; but the compilation of such records was presumably a normal practice. Thus although no records of this kind have been preserved for the commandery of Monzón, it is known that, after the arrest of the Templars there, twenty-five books and *cuadernos* giving details of rents and dues owed to the convent were seized by the Crown.[276] The lists of *confratres* compiled by the Templars also served the purpose of recording what was due to the Order, for although these lists can be compared with the confraternity books which have survived from some monasteries and which were for use at the altar,[277] the Templar lists in all cases mention the obligation as well as the name of the *confrater*; and the copying of lists of *confratres* into the Novillas cartulary was no doubt done exclusively to provide a record of what was due to the Order.[278] But although the Templars adopted various common procedures for keeping records of the dues and services owed to them, the inadequacy of the written evidence at the Order's disposal was made apparent in 1275, when the commander of Puigreig drew up the list of dues owed in Cerdaña, for to do this he was obliged to rely not only on charters and earlier *capbreus* but also on 'the oaths of men'.[279] Much information was not recorded in writing, and as on other estates the inquest had to be employed as the only possible method of finding out what the lord's rights were;[280] and there must have been the danger that those who gave evidence would define existing practice, which might in fact contradict right and privilege.

The ability of the Temple to exact dues and services further depended on the efficiency of those who administered the Order's property. It has already been seen that considerations of efficiency did not always govern the choice of lay officials on the Temple's estates; and efficient administration was probably also hampered by the custom of appointing members of the Order to offices for only short periods of time, for this practice must have meant that Templar officials often had a very inadequate knowledge of the estates in their charge.[281] Nothing is known in detail of the workings of Templar administration, but its limited effectiveness is apparent from the fact that the Temple, like many other ecclesiastical lords,[282] was frequently obliged to seek the king's aid in enforcing its authority when—as often happened at least in the period for which royal registers survive—its officials encountered resistance. The Order clearly had difficulty in imposing its will when it was faced by united opposition from a whole community or from a considerable number of its men. In 1306, when a series of crimes was committed by a group of men at Puigreig, the commander there

could not by himself carry out inquiries against them, in view of the rebelliousness and power of the aforesaid, who were disobedient and rebelling against him, and he sought and invoked secular aid so that he could seek out and discover the truth in these matters. He therefore required and instructed the sub-vicar [of Berga] to assist him in executing justice.[283]

In such instances royal officials could obviously act more effectively than the Templars because they could, if necessary, summon armed assistance from neighbouring districts in order to coerce the Order's men. But many of the appeals made by the Temple were concerned with the activities of individuals rather than of groups or communities. In 1283, for example, the commander of Huesca complained that certain individuals in his commandery had not paid the dues they owed; he sent the king a list giving names and amounts and this was forwarded to the *sobrejuntero* of Jaca, who was ordered to enforce payment.[284] In 1291 a royal official in Mallorca was similarly commanded to compel individuals who alienated property held of the Temple to pay *laudimium* to the Order, and in the same year the justiciar of Calatayud was told to force a Jewess who had not paid rent for three years to surrender her house and land to the Templars.[285] The invoking of royal assistance in order merely to oust one Jewess from her property might, of course, appear to imply that the king's help was sought when it was not really needed and that by the end of the thirteenth century it had become customary for the Templars to seek royal aid whenever resistance, however slight, was encountered. But it must be remembered that there was always the danger that royal intervention in these circumstances might be used by the Crown as a precedent in order to create a right to interfere, to the detriment of the Temple's authority. The Templars were well aware of this possibility: when the commander of Puigreig invoked the assistance of the sub-vicar of Berga in 1306 he had it set down in writing that this was not to prejudice the Order's rights and immunities. The Templars were therefore unlikely to make unnecessary appeals to the king, for fear of the consequences. Other explanations of appeals against individual tenants must be sought. Possibly a tenant, whose lands were situated in a place which was far away from a convent and in which the Order had only a small amount of property, might through passive resistance be able by himself to withstand the Order's demands: this could explain why royal officials were frequently commanded to assist the Temple in the exercise of the rights which it inherited from the Order of Mountjoy, for Alfonso II had given the latter Order lordship over one man in every royal city or town of a hundred or more inhabitants and also over one man out of every hundred elsewhere on royal lands.[286] It was probably also difficult for the Order to coerce individuals who held land of the Temple but did not live on Templar estates: one complaint made to the king in 1299, for example, concerned certain inhabitants of Tárrega who held lands of the Order at Talladell and who were refusing to pay *questia*,

*cena,* and other dues for these lands.[287] On other occasions, however, the Order's difficulties may have arisen because individuals
were given support by neighbours and friends, who combined
to prevent the Temple's officials from taking action against a
defaulter.[288] Thus not only was the Order obliged to make concessions to its men and to surrender some rights in the *Corona de
Aragón*; it also encountered difficulty in enforcing the authority
and exacting the dues and services which it did retain.

The dues which the Order sought to collect from its lordships
and estates were demanded in one of three forms. In some
instances a proportional payment was exacted. When rents from
land were taken in this form the proportion varied from a half
of the produce—in which case the Order normally provided half
of the seed—down to an eleventh or *tasca.* At other times dues
were assessed as fixed payments in kind. When corn rents of this
kind were owed for arable lands, they were in most regions taken
either half in wheat and half in barley or in equal proportions of
wheat, barley, and oats.[289] Lastly, dues could be expressed as fixed
sums of money. Dues assessed in this last form appear not, however, to have always been paid in money. In many instances a
sum of money 'ad panem et vinum' or 'pani et vino' is referred
to,[290] apparently implying that the payment, although assessed in
money, was made in kind. But a clear distinction cannot be made
between dues described in this way and those which are simply
stated as amounts of money, for it is possible that in the latter
case payment may also in practice have been made in kind.

The form in which dues were demanded varied considerably
from one region to another and sometimes even within the same
region. In the more northerly parts of Catalonia rents from arable
land and vineyards subject to the Templars were for most of the
twelfth and thirteenth centuries predominantly of the proportional type,[291] and a similar situation is encountered in many
places in the northern half of Aragon, such as Novillas and
Boquiñeni,[292] although at Añesa fixed corn rents were demanded
from settlers in 1157.[293] In the more southerly parts of the *Corona
de Aragón* the variety is rather greater. In the district of Lérida,
land rents were expressed in money terms at Gardeny and Fontanet, while in Segári fixed rents in kind were usually exacted.[294]
Along the lower Ebro, Christian settlers in the commanderies of

Miravet and Horta and also those at Villalba paid fixed rents in kind for their lands,[295] but Moorish inhabitants of Miravet owed proportional rents,[296] while at Tortosa all forms of payment are encountered.[297] In the more southerly parts of Aragon, proportional rents were demanded of settlers at Villastar, fixed rents in kind were exacted from those settling at Riodeva, and money rents were asked of those coming to Santolea.[298] In the kingdom of Valencia, rents for lands in the city of Valencia were usually expressed in money terms, while proportional rents were demanded in the *alquerías* to the north of the city and also at Burriana.[299] Further north in the kingdom of Valencia, the Moors of Chivert paid proportional rents for their lands, but the Christian settlers at Alcalá de Chivert owed fixed corn rents.[300]

Other dues were similarly exacted in a variety of forms. Both hens and money were commonly demanded as rents for houses and gardens in all districts of the *Corona de Aragón*, while in some parts of Valencia and in the commandery of Castellote[301] payments of wax were also fairly common. Rents for mills and ovens granted out by the Order were taken in all forms, and even within a particular region there was no uniformity: although, for example, fixed rents in corn were usually demanded for mills in the district of Segriá, in some cases a money rent was exacted.[302] Not very much information survives about the payments made by tenants for using mills and ovens retained by the Order, but while in the kingdom of Valencia one loaf out of every twenty-seven baked was exacted for *fornaje* at Chivert and one out of every twenty-five at Burriana,[303] elsewhere there seems to have been more variety in the form of payment.[304] There is similarly little evidence about the form in which dues were exacted for the use of uncultivated land; in the charter granted to the Moors of Chivert in 1234, however, it was decreed that the Temple should receive a quarter of the *venatio grossa*, but that four rabbits should be paid to the Order annually by those who caught them.[305] Nevertheless, in the case of certain dues there does seem to have been greater uniformity. Payments for protection in *Cataluña Vieja* were usually in the form of a fixed rent in kind;[306] and *peita*, *questia*, and *cena* were normally expressed as money payments.[307]

Despite the diversity in forms of payment, some slight trends and developments can be discerned. There was in the first place a tendency in some districts for proportional rents to be replaced by fixed dues paid in kind or money.[308] This was clearly happening on some of the lands of the commandery of Barcelona at the end of the thirteenth and beginning of the fourteenth centuries. At Gurb, near Vich, for example, there are two cases in 1285 and another in 1288 of proportional dues for land being replaced by fixed rents,[309] and the same was happening at this time on lands subject to the convent of Barcelona in other villages.[310] A few examples of the replacement of proportional rents are also encountered in other districts: it was agreed in 1271 that the Christian settlers at Villastar should pay 200s.J. *pani et vino* instead of a seventh of the produce of their lands;[311] and in 1302 the rent for a mill at Peñíscola was changed from a proportional payment to twelve *cahíces* of wheat.[312] Proportional rents for lands appear also to have been replaced in some districts for which no records of change survive, for while early documents refer to proportional rents, later ones mention only fixed dues in money or kind; this is true of some districts in the commandery of Tortosa, such as Labar.[313] On some Templar estates there was a similar tendency to change the tithe from a proportional due into a fixed payment. At the end of the twelfth century the tithes from Templar lands in the district of Pardines near Lérida were commuted into fixed payments assessed in money,[314] and it was probably at about the same time that a similar change was made at Fontanet,[315] while in 1255 the tithes of wool and cheese were commuted at Alfambra and Orrios into a fixed annual payment of 100s.J.[316]

Besides this trend away from proportional dues there was in some places a replacement of fixed rents in kind by rents assessed in money. Again most of the clearest evidence comes from *Cataluña Vieja*, where some fixed rents in kind were being replaced by money payments at the same time as proportional rents were being commuted.[317] A few documents record similar changes in other districts,[318] and again comparison of early and late charters recording grants of lands to tenants indicates that changes were made in some places for which no specific evidence of commutation survives: at Villel up to the middle of the thirteenth century fixed rents in kind were in most cases exacted, but after that time rents were usually assessed in money.[319]

The significance of these changes should not, however, be exaggerated. They affected only a minority of the dues collected by the Order and there was no general trend towards the exaction of dues in any one particular form. There are even isolated cases where the change was in the opposite direction. Although it was agreed in 1157 that settlers at Añesa should pay a fixed rent in kind for their holdings, when the Templars issued a new *carta de población* a hundred years later they demanded proportional rents.[320] On other occasions in the second half of the thirteenth century when new lands were being granted out the Order sometimes similarly demanded a proportion of produce. The frequency of payments in this form in Valencia has been noted, and even in the commandery of Barcelona when some demesne land was granted out to tenants in 1295 a proportional rent was sought.[321]

As the rights which the Temple obtained in areas which were already settled were gained from a large number of different individuals and institutions, it might be expected that the dues it received in these districts would vary considerably in form; and the force of custom would make change slow. But if the variations in type of payment in some areas can be explained at least in part in this way, it is necessary to account for the variety of forms which the Templars themselves adopted in districts which they settled and to explain the changes which the Order did make.

The Templars were clearly influenced by a number of considerations. In making some changes in the forms of payment they may have been influenced by a desire for simplicity. If all the dues from a tenant were taken in the same form, it might be possible to exact just one payment instead of several, and the problems of administration would be eased. Certainly this was the effect of some of the changes which occurred in *Cataluña Vieja*. Thus in 1288 the various dues owed for a manse at Gurb, comprising money rents, fixed rents in kind, and a proportion of certain produce, were commuted into a single payment of 9s. 10d.B.[322] The commutation of some tithes in the commandery of Gardeny produced the same result. In the 1180s tenants on the Order's lands in the district of Pardines were paying a fixed rent of 8s. *ad panem et vinum* for each *fanegada* and in addition a proportion of produce for tithes and *primicias*.[323] In the following decade the proportional payments were commuted: tenants were now to pay for each *fanegada* 8s. for rent and a further 2s. *ad panem et vinum* for tithes and *primicias*;[324] and in the thirteenth century the obligation became expressed as a single charge of 10s. *ad panem et vinum*.[325]

More important, however, was the question of profitability. On this point there were advantages and disadvantages attaching to each form of payment. When prices were rising, as seems to have been happening generally in western Europe in the twelfth and thirteenth centuries, proportional rents and fixed rents in kind did not decline in value as did those paid in money. Proportional rents also had the advantage that they allowed the Order to share automatically in any rise in productivity which took place, and this might be an important consideration when lands were being newly brought under cultivation. But proportional dues also had their drawbacks. When the commander of Barcelona was commuting some proportional land rents in 1288 he said that these were unprofitable because of the sterility of the land.[326] Obviously in years of bad harvests the Templars might gain very little from proportional rents, whereas when fixed rents were charged the Order knew that it would receive a definite amount of produce or money every year. The commander of Barcelona's comment suggests that there had been a series of bad harvests in the years preceding 1288. Proportional rents would also be of only limited value if a tenant farmed his land badly: thus in 1260 the commander of Palau claimed that the Order had lost *agraria* worth fifty quarters of corn because for twenty years a tenant called Berenguer of Pradillo had failed to cultivate his manse properly.[327] When the commander of Barcelona was commuting proportional dues in 1288 he also referred to

the expenses which have to be incurred in the collection of the said proportional rents.

This was clearly an important disadvantage of rents paid in this form. When proportional dues were exacted close supervision was necessary to ensure that the proper amount was given. A representative of the Temple had to be present in the fields when produce like grapes or olives was gathered, and on the threshing-floor at the time of the grain harvest; and many documents recording grants of land to tenants included a clause forbidding the latter to gather their crops unless a Templar official was present.[328] In some places, moreover, it was the custom for the Temple to contribute to the cost of threshing when proportional rents were exacted;[329] and as rents of this kind were usually paid in the fields or on the threshing-floor the Temple often had the additional expense of transporting them to their houses—an expense which was not normally incurred when fixed rents in kind were charged: whereas the Order's tenants in the district of Segriá who paid proportional rents were usually obliged to make payment in the field or on the threshing-floor, those who paid fixed rents in kind were normally expected to bring these dues at their own expense to the convent of Gardeny.[330] The problems attached to the collection of proportional dues would be of particular significance when a convent had small parcels of property scattered over a wide area, and this may explain why the commutation of proportional rents is particularly evident on the lands of the commandery of Barcelona. In places where Templar properties were more concentrated geographically and were mostly situated near a convent these disadvantages lost some of their importance. In reconquered districts therefore, where the Temple had compact lordships and where also land was often being brought newly under cultivation, the Templars might be inclined to favour proportional rents, while in some other areas different forms of payment might be considered more profitable. The profitability of any type of payment varied according to the circumstances.

Decisions about the form in which dues were to be exacted were in some instances also influenced by the needs of the Temple. Rents were sometimes demanded in kind because the Order could then obtain produce needed in Templar convents for consumption purposes. Although the Temple usually charged money rents for houses in Zaragoza, in 1275 it demanded from one householder an annual rent of two *arrobas* of oil, in order to provide fuel for a lamp in the Templar chapel in the city.[331] The needs of the Templars may also explain why corn rents were paid for some lands at Gardeny which were described as vineyards.[332] But considerations of this kind were not usually of overriding importance. Templar convents were expected to pay in money the dues or responsion which they owed to the provincial master,[333] and it might therefore have been imagined that the Order would exact dues in kind for the needs of the members of a convent, and dues in money to meet obligations owed to the provincial master. But it is clear that this was not always done. Letters ordering the payment of responsions often included a clause stating that goods

might be sold so that payment could be made in money,[334] while
the inventory which survives for the house of Ambel from the
year 1289 shows that the commander of that convent set aside
wine and grain for his responsion;[335] and a list of responsions
drawn up in the year 1307 indicates that some were actually paid
in kind.[336] Some religious houses pursued a policy of demanding
dues in money from their more distant properties, while exacting
payments in kind from nearby estates in order to provide food
and other necessaries for the monastery;[337] but clearly the Templars
did not adopt this procedure. Such a policy, even if it had been
desirable, would perhaps have been hard to implement because
tenants would possibly have encountered difficulty in paying dues
in the form which the Order wanted. It is noticeable that the
predominance of rents expressed purely in money terms is most
marked in the larger cities: whereas in the *alquerías* to the north
of the city of Valencia proportional rents and fixed dues in kind
were usually exacted by the Order, all those holding land and
houses of the Temple within the city itself—with one exception—
paid a rent that was expressed purely in money terms. The rents
demanded from the Order's properties in Zaragoza and Barcelona
were again usually of this type. It cannot, of course, be ascertained
whether such rents were in fact always paid in money, but it is
possible that the inhabitants of cities could pay rents regularly in
money more easily than the Order's tenants in rural areas.

While the Templars were inevitably concerned with their own
needs and their own profits, they could not, when deciding the
form in which dues were to be exacted, altogether neglect the
wishes of their vassals, whose interests would obviously not always
coincide with those of the Order. Decisions about the form in
which dues were to be paid, like decisions about what dues were
to be owed, must in the newly settled areas have been reached
after negotiations between the Templars and early settlers; and
changes which were made elsewhere or at other times were presumably usually preceded by discussions between the Templars
and communities or individuals. On some occasions the Order's
vassals were apparently able to influence decisions by offering to
pay for the changes which they wanted.[338] At times even, presumably when the Templars felt that there was little to choose
between different forms of payment, tenants were offered a
choice: in 1285 the occupant of a manse from which the Order

had recently been demanding a rent of 17s. was given the choice of paying the proportional dues and other charges which had earlier been exacted or negotiating a new agreement with the Temple about the amount of rent to be paid.[339] Decisions about the forms in which dues were to be exacted were thus influenced by a variety of interests and considerations, and in this situation it is hardly surprising that different forms were adopted in different places and that the same changes did not occur everywhere.

Much less is known about the forms in which services were exacted by the Order. Although a number of references occur to both mounted and foot service, the only precise information found in the Templar sources about the different kinds of military service owed to the Order is that contained in a few *cartas de población* from southern Aragon which refer to *caballeros villanos*. A clause was included in the *fuero* of Cantavieja stating that any settler bringing a horse and arms was to receive a *caballería* and was always to give mounted service if the commander and *concejo* of Cantavieja considered that he was capable of doing so;[340] and in the *carta de población* for La Cañada de Benatanduz it was decreed somewhat obscurely that

an inhabitant who has a yoke of oxen and an ass and two beds and bread and wine from one year to the next, if he has more than this up to thirty shillings, he is to furnish a foal; if he has more he is to furnish a horse and maintain it.[341]

Nor is any full information available about the extent to which *redenciones* were demanded by the Order in lieu of military service. A few individuals are known to have had their service permanently commuted. It was noted in 1181 that the holders of two manses at Auzeda paid 4s. in lieu of *hueste* in those years when the host was called out,[342] and in 1263 the Temple agreed to commute permanently the military service owed against the Moors by the holder of part of a fee at Espluga de Francolí, although he was still to give service for purposes of local defence.[343] But these were concessions made to individuals in districts away from the frontier. There are no examples of the Temple's commuting permanently the military obligations of a whole community, and when in 1294 and 1295 the provincial master agreed that the inhabitants of places received in exchange for Tortosa should pay a lump sum in lieu of various obligations, the right to military service was retained by the Order.[344] Nevertheless at the end of the thirteenth and beginning of the fourteenth centuries, when the Order was in need of money and when the conflict with the Moors had tended to assume the character of raiding, the Temple on a number of occasions sought to obtain *redenciones* instead of personal service from communities. At the time when money was needed for the purchase of Culla from William of Anglesola, the provincial master received 12,000*s*.B. from Monzón in commutation of military service and sought a further 15,000*s*. from the Order's vassals in Valencia,[345] while a surviving fragment of a letter shows that one commander was ordered to seek at least 700*s*. in lieu of military service and to send this and any other money he had, since it was needed for paying William of Anglesola.[346] In these cases it is clear, however, that the question of commutation was a matter for agreement between the Order and its vassals, who could—if they wished—still insist on serving in person.

Similarly little is known about the extent of the commutation of labour services. Only an occasional reference survives to the permanent commutation of an individual's obligations.[347] But as *jova* and *tragina* are still specifically mentioned in a number of documents of the later thirteenth century,[348] it is apparent that at least in some districts labour services had not been permanently replaced by money payments which had become just part of the rent owed for a holding.

It was clearly still possible for the Templars to make use of all kinds of labour services, for in most places where they had considerable properties they continued to have a demesne in the sense of cultivated lands not granted out to tenants. Lands which were retained by the Order and used for corn growing or the cultivation of vines are mentioned in a number of documents: some *cartas de población* refer to land which the Temple did not grant out to settlers,[349] and agreements with the episcopate about tithes sometimes mention the demesne lands which were to be exempt from payment, [350] while all the inventories of Templar houses which have survived from the end of the thirteenth and the early years of the fourteenth centuries refer to oxen and mules used for ploughing.[351] From such sources it is clear that in most districts it was the custom for the Templars to keep some land in demesne; they did not abandon demesne farming in reconquered places, as happened in some newly settled parts of western Christendom.[352] And it is further shown by the inventories that the Order continued to keep land in demesne up to the time of the Templars' arrest.

In the absence of surveys, however, it is not easy to determine the proportion of land retained in demesne, although on a few occasions the size of the demesne is known. According to the *carta de población* issued for Vencilló in 1161/2 the Templars kept one *parellada* there in demesne, and the same amount of land was retained at Borbotó a century later.[353] Since in many places a *parellada* was the normal holding of an individual tenant,[354] the demesne was obviously of only minor importance in these places. Yet Vencilló and Borbotó were not places where Templar convents were established. It is probable that where Templar houses were built demesne lands were more extensive: at Horta, where the normal holding was a *parellada*, the bishop of Tortosa in 1185 allowed exemption from tithes on twenty-five *parelladas*, although it is not known whether all this land was in fact retained in demesne;[355] and in 1244 it was agreed that at Chivert the Templars should be exempted from the payment of tithes on six *parelladas*, as long as these were kept in demesne.[356]

It is similarly difficult to determine whether the amount of land in demesne tended to increase or decline. What evidence there is suggests movement in both directions. In 1295 the commander of Barcelona granted out a manse at Parets, which the Templars had previously kept in demesne,

seeing that it is better and more useful for us and the said house that the said manse with all its honours and possessions be given in emphyteusis at the rent and proportional payment mentioned below than be kept at the labour of the said house;[357]

and at various times in the twelfth and thirteenth centuries the Order made grants to tenants of *dominicature*, which were presumably portions of demesne land.[358] On the other hand, throughout the Templar period examples can be found of land being repurchased by the Order from tenants, and this was being frequently done in the commanderies of Valencia and Gardeny particularly at the end of the thirteenth century and at the beginning of the fourteenth.[359] Some of the land gained in this way was granted out again almost immediately,[360] and in some cases the

property had been sub-let by the Order's tenants[361] and the Temple
was therefore in these instances not bringing land back into
demesne. But on some occasions the demesne was apparently
being increased. The fullest evidence on this point is provided by
the documents concerning the holdings at Torre Farrera of the
Lérida apothecary, Vincent of Viana. When Vincent's son, also
an apothecary, died in 1293 the Order purchased his rights.[362]
Eleven years later some of this land was granted out again by the
Temple to various inhabitants of Torre Farrera.[363] Although some
of the Vianas' land had been sub-let,[364] it is difficult to believe
that in 1304 the Temple was granting out land already held by
tenants, since the Order would then have been obliged to accept
a lower rent than it had been receiving, and in any case the
Templars at Gardeny were at this time forbidding tenants to
grant out their lands at rent.[365] It seems therefore that in 1293
the Order was taking some land back into demesne. Thus at the
time when demesne land near Barcelona was being granted out to
tenants, elsewhere the Temple was recovering land from tenants.
The Templars' demesne policy appears to have been a flexible one,
and was presumably governed by such factors as the availability
of a labour force to work the demesne and the availability of
potential tenants. There is certainly no clear evidence of an over-
all decline of the demesne on Templar estates, such as has been
postulated for Catalonia as a whole during this period.[366]

Besides working some of their land, the Templars in Aragon
also engaged in pastoral husbandry as an adjunct to arable farming; it never completely replaced the latter. The inventories which
survive for the year 1289 show that some convents had considerable flocks of sheep and goats. Miravet had a total of 1,380
and Monzón possessed 1,061; at Cantavieja there were 400 ewes,
41 rams, 211 wethers, and 340 goats, while Horta possessed
1,060 goats.[367] An inventory of the possessions of the convent
of Peñíscola which was drawn up in 1301 similarly lists 700 ewes,
50 rams, 106 wethers, and over 200 goats,[368] and at the time of
the arrest of the Templars 1,025 sheep and goats were seized at
Miravet.[369] The keeping of large flocks of sheep and goats was
clearly not a thirteenth-century innovation on Templar estates,
for in 1184 the count of Urgel gave compensation to the commander of Gardeny for seizing 2,000 of the Order's sheep,[370] and
in 1201 part of the payment made by the Temple when buying

some land at Villel consisted of 400 sheep.[371] It seems, however—although inventories do not exist for all Templar houses and not all of the surviving inventories are complete—that the largest flocks were usually kept on the more southerly estates of the Order: at Huesca in 1289 there were only 30 ewes and 2 rams and at Ambel only 30 ewes.[372] Most houses, on the other hand, kept a number of pigs and some also had cows. The largest numbers of pigs recorded in 1289 were in the commanderies of Monzón and Gardeny, which had 182 and 71 respectively, while Tortosa had a herd of 42 cows besides 2 bulls.[373]

These animals were kept partly in order to provide food for Templar convents, where the diet was not so restricted as in monasteries: thus in 1289 it was noted that the 250 wethers in the commandery of Monzón were 'for the provisioning of the table of the castle'.[374] But animals were probably kept also to supply the needs of the Templars in the East[375] and much of the produce of the animals, especially wool, was no doubt sold, although little evidence survives on this point.

In some *cartas de población* and agreements with tenants the Order reserved certain lands exclusively for the use of its own animals. The Order's *dehesas* are, for example, mentioned in agreements between the Templars and the inhabitants of Castellote made in 1244 and 1260.[376] This was not, however, always done, for at Chivert both Moorish and Christian inhabitants were allowed to graze their animals anywhere in the term of the castle.[377] It was not only the use of pasture that was restricted by the Temple. Among other restrictions were those on fishing, as at Cantavieja, where a stretch of the river was reserved for the use of the Templars alone.[378] But as in the Rule members of the Order were forbidden to hunt animals, except the lion,[379] no lands were retained in Aragon for the purposes of hunting.

Even in those areas where labour services were retained, the tenants of the Order could have provided only a small part of the labour force needed for working demesne lands and tending the Temple's animals. For most of the year the Order was obliged to rely on other sources of manpower. One of these was the Order itself, for some Templars were employed on the land or put in charge of farm animals.[380] Another source was probably provided by the slaves and unpaid lay associates which most Templar convents contained.[381] Possibly as important, however, was hired

labour, although virtually nothing is known about it; the only
reference to this kind of labour is that found in a charter recording
the emancipation of a slave at Tortosa in 1226: the Temple
promised to pay him 2d. a day, as well as giving him his food,
whenever the Order needed his services for its 'works'.[382]

It is difficult to judge to what extent, either on the Order's
demesne lands or on those held by tenants, the Templars increased
the value of their rights during the twelfth and thirteenth centuries through developments in farming methods and techniques.
Only a few examples of Templar initiative in this sphere are
recorded. As elsewhere there was certainly a development of
viticulture: examples frequently occur of tenants being ordered
to plant vineyards on the lands assigned to them;[383] and that the
Order sought to increase pastoral farming on the part of its
tenants is implied by the statement made in 1255 that certain
tithes had been commuted at Alfambra so that the inhabitants
could acquire more animals.[384] But little else is known about
improvements in farming and farming techniques made by the
Templars. It would obviously have been in the Order's interests
to extend irrigation, for much higher rents could clearly be demanded from irrigated land: at Moncada near Valencia a proportional rent of a third was exacted from irrigated land compared
with a fifth from non-irrigated;[385] on lands held by Moors at
Villastar the proportions were a quarter and a seventh;[386] and in
the district of Segriá non-irrigated lands usually provided only
a quarter of the rent derived from irrigated land.[387] On a few
occasions the Order did certainly seek to extend irrigation. In
1238 the commander of Boquiñeni bought a strip of land in
order to construct a canal which would carry water to some of
the Temple's property,[388] and in 1245 Marlofa was granted to
Bertrand of Naya because he had given water from Pinseque to
the Order and agreed to open up a canal to bring it to Marlofa.[389]
But grants of water to the Temple did not necessarily mean that
irrigation was being extended—some donors may merely have
been confirming existing arrangements about the use of canals—
and some extensions of irrigation that did occur were undertaken
by the Order's tenants rather than by the Temple itself. A charter
drawn up in 1173 records that three of the Order's tenants had
converted some land in Segriá from *secanum* to *reganum*,[390] and

at Monzón the initiative in extending irrigation appears to have lain with the inhabitants: it was agreed in 1230 that the latter could, if they wished, increase the amount of land that was irrigated,[391] and the wording of an undertaking given twenty years later by the Order to construct a canal through Paúls and Sosils suggests that this was done as the result of a petition by the inhabitants of these places and not on Templar initiative.[392] It might, of course, be argued that the Templars did place an obligation on their vassals to increase the value of their holdings: charters recording grants of land to tenants often include a clause stipulating that the property was to be improved.[393] But it may be doubted whether very much significance was attached to this provision. Whenever precise details are given about the treatment of property, these reveal merely a concern on the part of the Templars to ensure that it was maintained in a proper state. The cutting down of trees without permission was often forbidden[394] and in some cases those who held houses of the Order were commanded to spend a certain amount of money on repairs, which were clearly frequently necessary if houses were to be maintained in a fit state.[395] Even if a tenant did increase the value of his property it was probably not easy for the Temple to derive any benefit from it. Unless a tenant paid a proportional rent the Order did not normally receive any automatic gain, and as grants to tenants were usually made in perpetuity it was probably difficult to increase rents.[396] In order to attract settlers and keep tenants, however, it was no doubt necessary to give them a hereditary interest in their holdings, and the Temple could not adopt a general policy of granting land for life or for a fixed term of years. Holdings were granted on these conditions only rarely and the grants of this kind that were made can sometimes be explained by particular circumstances.[397] Even if the Templars had been able to alter rents when they wanted to, they would have encountered difficulty in enforcing increases if, as has been suggested, the economic situation of the Order's tenants was deteriorating in the later part of the thirteenth century.

There can be little doubt therefore that the value of the Order's rights in the *Corona de Aragón* was increased much more through the resettlement of land than through any improvements in farming methods and techniques, whether they were undertaken on the initiative of the Templars or on that of their vassals.

Resettlement was the most important development which occurred on the Order's estates in the twelfth and thirteenth centuries. It was this that determined the prosperity of the majority of the Order's properties and it was this that most influenced the relations between the Temple and its vassals in the *Corona de Aragón*.

## NOTES

1. Lees, *Records*.

2. RAH, 12–6–1/M–83, doc. 110; cf. ACA, reg. 310, fol. 67–67$^v$.

3. AHN, cód. 469, pp. 177–8, doc. 136; San Juan, leg. 556, doc. 4; see below, p. 386.

4. F. Baer, *Die Juden im christlichen Spanien* (Berlin, 1929), pp. 98–100, doc. 95. The concession was made for fifteen years.

5. ACA, parch. James I, Appendix no. 31; AGP, parch. Tortosa, no. 81. That the vicar was one of the Moncadas' officials and not, as has sometimes been thought, a royal nominee, is apparent from ACA, parch. James I, no. 1746, and AGP, parch. Tortosa, no. 42.

6. ACA, parch. James I, no. 1746, Appendix no. 31; AGP, parch. Tortosa, no. 81.

7. See below, p. 271.

8. This was the normal pattern of administration throughout Aragon and Catalonia: cf. J. M. Font Rius, 'Orígenes del régimen municipal de Cataluña', *AHDE*, xvii (1946), 254–7.

9. ACA, reg. 291, fols. 135$^v$, 137, 149$^v$, 252–252$^v$, 256–257$^v$, etc.

10. ACA, CRD Templarios, nos. 36, 133; AGP, parch. Espluga de Francolí, no. 249.

11. ACA, reg. 291, fol. 326$^v$.

12. e.g. ibid., fols. 149$^v$, 171$^v$, 198$^v$–199.

13. ACA, parch. James I, no. 1031. On the master *deça mer*, see below, p. 328.

14. ACA, reg. 291, fols. 221$^v$, 259, 299–299$^v$.

15. ACA, parch. James I, no. 1978. In 1302 Peter Malet sold the bailiwick of Espluga de Francolí back to the Temple for 290s.B. when he was obliged to resign because of accusations made against him by the inhabitants of Espluga: AGP, parch. Espluga de Francolí, no. 249.

16. ACA, reg. 291, fol. 135$^v$.

17. ACA, parch. Peter III, no. 135.

18. AHN, cód. 494, pp. 67–72, doc. 12; cf. T. Muñoz y Romero, *Colección de fueros municipales y cartas pueblas de los reinos de Castilla, León, Corona de*

*Aragón y Navarra* (Madrid, 1847), p. 539; R. Esteban Abad, *Estudio histórico-político sobre la ciudad y comunidad de Daroca* (Teruel, 1959), p. 367.

19. AHN, cód. 494, pp. 17–19, doc. 4; see below, p. 390. The same procedure was still in use at the time of the arrest of the Templars: ACA, reg. 291, fol. 216.

20. AHN, cód. 689, pp. 76–8, doc. 78.

21. AHN, cód. 494, pp. 67–72, doc. 13.

22. Cf. J. M. Lacarra, 'Les villes-frontière dans l'Espagne des XIᵉ et XIIᵉ siècles', *Le Moyen Âge*, lxix (1963), 218. On the situation in Castile, see J. M. Font Rius, 'Les villes dans l'Espagne du moyen âge', *Recueils de la Société Jean Bodin*, vi (1954), 274–5; L. G. de Valdeavellano, *Historia de las instituciones españolas* (Madrid, 1968), p. 545.

23. The Order appears normally to have retained control over the appointment of the more important officials in the non-Christian communities under Templar jurisdiction. Although in the agreement made with the Moors of Chivert in 1234 nothing was stated about the method of appointing Moorish officials, the Templars presumably nominated them, for in 1359 the *aljama* was seeking the right to present three men, from whom the *alamín* was to be chosen: M. Gual Camarena, 'Mudéjares valencianos. Aportaciones para su estudio', *Saitabi*, vii (1949), 174–5. In the thirteenth century Moorish officials in Tortosa were appointed by the Order or the Moncadas: ACA, parch. Peter II, no. 258; parch. James I, nos. 43, 1746; cf. parch. Peter II, no. 257.

24. AHN, cód. 494, pp. 17–19, doc. 4; pp. 67–72, doc. 13; see below, p. 390.

25. AHN, cód. 471, pp. 258–9, doc. 233.

26. J. Cots i Gorchs, 'Les "Consuetuds" d'Horta (avui Horta de Sant Joan) a la ratlla del Baix Aragó', *Estudis universitaris catalans*, xv (1930), 313. The code of customs for Miravet which was confirmed shortly after the abolition of the Temple similarly included a clause stating that the inhabitants had the right to elect *jurados*: *Constituciones Baiulie Mirabeti*, ed. G. Sánchez (Madrid, 1915), p. 9; F. Valls Taberner, 'Les costums de la batllia de Miravet', *Revista jurídica de Cataluña*, xxxii (1926), 59.

27. AHN, cód. 494, pp. 17–19, doc. 4; see below, p. 390. On this office, see F. Sevillano Colom, 'De la institución del Mustaçaf de Barcelona, de Mallorca y de Valencia', *AHDE*, xxiii (1953), 525–38.

28. Cots i Gorchs, loc. cit., p. 315.

29. ACA, parch. James I, no. 2234; vernacular version in B. Oliver, *Historia del derecho en Cataluña, Mallorca y Valencia: Código de las costumbres de Tortosa*, iv (Madrid, 1881), 496–500, where the date is given wrongly.

30. AHN, San Juan, leg. 355, doc. 1. A similar procedure was followed at Miravet: *Constituciones Baiulie Mirabeti*, pp. 32–3; Valls Taberner, loc. cit., p. 74.

31. AHN, cód. 471, pp. 322–3, doc. 255.

32. AGP, Cartulary of Tortosa, fol. 77ᵛ, doc. 253.

33. Ibid., fols. 87ᵛ–88, doc. 278; published in Oliver, op. cit. ii. 55–6. This judgement was based on the charter granted to the inhabitants of Tortosa by Raymond Berenguer IV in 1149, in which it was stated that disputes between citizens should be settled by the judgement of the court and *probi homines* of Tortosa: *CDI*, iv. 144–7, doc. 61; Font Rius, *Cartas de población*, i. 121–6, doc. 75.

34. *CDI*, iv. 155–64, doc. 61. The bishop's decision was confirmed in the *Costums de Tortosa*, I. i. 9, in Oliver, op. cit. iv. 14.

35. ACA, parch. James I, no. 2136; a vernacular version of this document is published in Oliver, op. cit. iv. 487–91. Cf. *Costums de Tortosa*, III. i. 1; VII. vii. 1, 20, in Oliver, op. cit. iv. 104–5, 317–18, 323. A case tried by the vicar and two *coniudices* in 1242 is recorded in AGP, Cartulary of Tortosa, fol. 58, doc. 179.

36. *Costums de Tortosa*, IX. xiv. 3, in Oliver, op. cit. iv. 397–8.

37. M. Albareda y Herrera, *El fuero de Alfambra* (Madrid, 1925), pp. 44–5.

38. In 1294, for example, it was agreed that the Temple should receive 1,000s. annually from the men of Peñíscola for *cena* and certain other dues: ACA, parch. James II, no. 420; cf. nos. 408, 411–14.

39. AGP, parch. Gardeny, nos. 827, 1514.

40. AHN, San Juan, leg. 598, unnumbered document.

41. *CDI*, iv. 155–64, doc. 61; *Costums de Tortosa*, I. i. 15, and IX. xiii. 5, in Oliver, op. cit. iv. 16, 395–6; cf. A. Ruiz Moreno, 'Los baños públicos en los fueros municipales españoles', *Cuadernos de historia de España*, iii (1945), 153; L. Torres Balbás, 'Los baños públicos en los fueros municipales españoles', *Al-Andalus*, xi (1946), 444.

42. AHN, cód. 471, pp. 338–40, doc. 265; pp. 359–60, doc. 278.

43. Ibid., pp. 317–18, doc. 250.

44. Cots i Gorchs, loc. cit., p. 314.

45. AHN, cód. 689, p. 45, doc. 36 *bis*; *Costums de Tortosa*, I. v. 10, and IX. xx. 2, in Oliver, op. cit. iv. 44, 420.

46. AHN, San Juan, leg. 174, doc. 16.

47. *CDI*, iv. 154–5, doc. 61.

48. *Costums de Tortosa*, I. v. 9, and IX. xx. 1, in Oliver, op. cit. iv. 43–4, 420.

49. AHN, Montesa, P. 523.

50. It must be remembered, however, that at Tortosa the Templars were complaining of the activities of the Moncadas as well as of those of the citizens.

51. AHN, cód. 471, pp. 338–40, doc. 265; pp. 359–60, doc. 278. In the same year—1260—the *concejos* of Castellote and Las Cuevas de Cañart gave up the

concession which they had obtained concerning the appointment of the local justiciar: cód. 689, pp. 76-8, doc. 78.

52. ACA, parch. James II, no. 722.

53. ACA, parch. James I, no. 1550.

54. ACA, parch. James I, no. 1502; AGP, parch. Espluga de Francolí, nos. 210, 575.

55. ACA, CRD James II, no. 717; AHN, San Juan, leg. 306, doc. 16; AGP, parch. Gardeny, nos. 726, 941, 1473.

56. ACA, reg. 291, fols. 136ᵛ, 340ᵛ-341.

57. ACA, parch. James I, no. 2230.

58. ACA, parch. James I, no. 1332; see below, p. 388. The dues which are mentioned in the document were not in fact worth as much as 2,000s. annually.

59. J. Delaville Le Roulx, 'Bulles pour l'ordre du Temple, tirées des archives de S. Gervasio de Cassolas', *Revue de l'orient latin*, xi (1905-8), 436-7, doc. 47; cf. AHN, cód. 471, p. 71, doc. 65; ACA, Bulas, leg. 15, doc. 1; this last document is analysed by F. Miquel Rosell, *Regesta de letras pontificias del Archivo de la Corona de Aragón* (Madrid, 1948), p. 105, no. 187.

60. See, for example, F. R. H. Du Boulay, *The Lordship of Canterbury* (London, 1966), pp. 204-5; E. Miller, *The Abbey and Bishopric of Ely* (Cambridge, 1951), p. 167.

61. Cf. J. Guiraud and E. Cadier, *Les Registres de Grégoire X et de Jean XXI* (Paris, 1960), pp. 382-3, doc. 997; Delaville, *Cartulaire*, iii. 305-6, 378, 389, docs. 3534, 3683, 3712.

62. ACA, Bulas, leg. 22, doc. 2; cf. leg. 16, doc. 1; AHN, cód. 471, pp. 16-17, doc. 25. The first two of these documents are analysed by Miquel Rosell, op. cit., pp. 109, 160, nos. 195, 300.

63. AGP, parch. Gardeny, no. 794.

64. AGP, parch. Gardeny, nos. 701, 710, 729, 735, 813, 815, 818, 828.

65. AGP, parch. Gardeny, nos. 801, 806.

66. AGP, parch. Gardeny, nos. 284, 511, 1577, 2280, 2338.

67. AGP, parch. Gardeny, nos. 1641, 1648, 2425.

68. AGP, parch. Gardeny, nos. 865, 881, 916, 939, 944.

69. AGP, parch. Gardeny, nos. 503, 553, 595, 802, 1577, 1586.

70. This policy had been adopted by some lords in the south of France a century earlier: J. H. Mundy, *Liberty and Political Power in Toulouse, 1050-1230* (New York, 1954), p. 272. R. I. Burns, *The Crusader Kingdom of Valencia* (Harvard, 1967), i. 138, provides some evidence from Valencia on this point.

71. AGP, parch. Gardeny, nos. 326, 350, 484, 563, 750, etc.

72. AGP, parch. Gardeny, nos. 186, 583, 1621, 1857, etc. The change in wording was probably not very significant. No doubt in most instances land was

sub-let for profit and this practice was checked by the earlier form of wording. The later formula was more comprehensive, in that it also prohibited the sub-letting of land at a low rent, as might happen, for example, when an individual wanted to provide for one of his relations. But sub-letting at a low rent was probably comparatively rare.

73. M. Ferrandis, 'Rendición del castillo de Chivert a los Templarios', *Homenaje a D. Francisco Codera* (Zaragoza, 1904), pp. 30–1.

74. AHN, San Juan, leg. 174, doc. 16; cf. R. I. Burns, 'Social Riots on the Christian–Moslem Frontier (Thirteenth-Century Valencia)', *American Historical Review*, lxvi (1960–1), 378–400. A rather different picture of relations between Christian and Moor in Valencia is presented by F. Roca Traver, 'Un siglo de vida mudéjar en la Valencia medieval (1238–1338)', *EEMCA*, v (1952), 115–208, but this article is concerned primarily with the relations between the Moors and those in authority, especially the Aragonese kings.

75. J. Reglá, 'La expulsión de los moriscos y sus consecuencias. Contribución a su estudio', *Hispania*, xiii (1953), 263–4; J. E. Martínez Ferrando, 'Estado actual de los estudios sobre la repoblación en los territorios de la Corona de Aragón (siglos XII a XIV)', *VII Congreso de historia de la Corona de Aragón* (Barcelona, 1962), i. 160. For references to Moors at Miravet in the twelfth and thirteenth centuries, see AHN, San Juan, leg. 306, docs. 12, 14; leg. 308, doc. 2.

The Moorish population in the *Corona de Aragón* was probably in most cases static, but not all the Moorish settlements in Aragon at the end of the Middle Ages had had a continuous existence since the period of Muslim domination: there were said to be sixty-one Morisco households at the beginning of the seventeenth century at La Zaida, but in the mid twelfth century this place had apparently been lying waste: Reglá, loc. cit., pp. 247, 467; H. Lapeyre, *Géographie de l'Espagne morisque* (Paris, 1959), p. 110; see also above, p. 213.

76. e.g. AGP, Cartulary of Gardeny, fol. 15–15ᵛ, docs. 16, 17; fol. 16–16ᵛ, doc. 19; fols. 19–20, docs. 22, 23; Cartulary of Tortosa, fol. 37, doc. 116; cf. J. M. Font Rius, 'La reconquista de Lérida y su proyección en el orden jurídico', *Ilerda*, vii (1949), 11.

77. e.g. AGP, parch. Gardeny, no. 6.

78. AGP, Cartulary of Gardeny, fol. 16–16ᵛ, doc. 19; fol. 20–20ᵛ, doc. 24; fol. 42, doc. 90.

79. Cf. J. M. Lacarra, in *La reconquista española y la repoblación del país* (Zaragoza, 1951), pp. 72–4.

80. Regulations about raiding expeditions and the division of booty frequently occur in *fueros* issued to townships near the Moorish frontiers: see J. M. Lacarra, 'Les villes-frontière dans l'Espagne des xⁱᵉ et xııᵉ siècles', *Le Moyen Âge*, lxix (1963), 210–11.

81. Settlers were often required to build houses within a specified period of time: see above, p. 209.

82. Cf. E. de Hinojosa, *El régimen señorial y la cuestión agraria en Cataluña*

(Madrid, 1905), pp. 290-2; J. M. Font Rius, 'Franquicias locales en la comarca del alto Bergadá', *Pirineos*, x (1954), 459-88; id., 'Franquicias urbanas medievales de la Cataluña Vieja', *BRABLB*, xxix (1961-2), 17-46.

83. ACA, parch. James I, no. 380; see below, p. 385.

84. e.g. ACA, parch. James I, nos. 701, 1248; parch. Alfonso III, nos. 122, 124, 125.

85. Cf. M. Gual Camarena, 'Mudéjares valencianos. Aportaciones para su estudio', *Saitabi*, vii (1949), 168-70, 178-81.

86. Ferrandis, loc. cit., pp. 29-31.

87. Cf. C. Cahen, *La Syrie du nord à l'époque des croisades* (Paris, 1940), pp. 330-1.

88. AHN, cód. 494, pp. 67-72, doc. 13; cf. R. Esteban Abad, *Estudio histórico-político sobre la ciudad y comunidad de Daroca* (Teruel, 1959), p. 363; E. Sáez, R. Gibert, etc., *Los fueros de Sepúlveda* (Segovia, 1953), pp. 411-12. The *fuero* of La Cañada also contains the concession about the appointment of officials, but few concessions of this kind appear to have been made at the time of re-settlement on Templar estates.

89. AHN, cód. 494, pp. 104-6, doc. 20; San Juan, leg. 421, doc. 7 (in the relevant sentence of the version of this document published by Font Rius, *Cartas de población*, i. 344-6, doc. 244, there is a mistranscription, and 'hec' is given instead of 'nec'); cf. A. Palomeque Torres, 'Contribución al estudio del ejército en los estados de la reconquista', *AHDE*, xv (1944), 307-8.

90. AHN, cód. 689, p. 12, doc. 7.

91. AHN, cód. 494, pp. 1-4, doc. 1 (Cantavieja); pp. 19-22, doc. 5 (Mirambel); pp. 85-9, doc. 16 (Iglesuela); pp. 104-6, doc. 20 (La Cuba).

92. Albareda y Herrera, op. cit., p. 25. On similar limitations elsewhere, see Palomeque Torres, loc. cit., pp. 234-7.

93. Ferrandis, loc. cit., p. 31.

94. AGP, parch. Gardeny, no. 107. The settlement of this area had started much earlier, but it was apparently not complete by 1226. In the document recording this concession reference is made to the *populatores* who were already established there and to others who might receive land in the future. It may be argued therefore that the exemption from military service should be looked upon as a concession made in order to encourage resettlement.

95. Font Rius, *Cartas de población*, i. 169-70, doc. 116.

96. AGP, Cartulary of Gardeny, fols. 17-19, doc. 21. Tenants with a *parellada* of land were expected to provide a pair of oxen for ploughing and one animal for carting service; those who had larger holdings had to provide more. By comparison some tenants of the Temple in *Cataluña Vieja* at Auzeda were obliged to do two days' ploughing together with other services at the will of the lord, and the service owed from one manse at Palau consisted of three days'

ploughing, two days of other work, and also carting services: ACA, parch. Alfonso II, no. 327; parch. Peter III, no. 407.

97. AHN, Montesa, P. 73.

98. S. A. García Larragueta, 'Fueros y cartas pueblas navarro-aragonesas otorgadas por Templarios y Hospitalarios', *AHDE*, xxiv (1954), 592–3; Font Rius, *Cartas de población*, i. 285–6, doc. 208.

99. AHN, cód. 466, pp. 40–1, doc. 42; see below, p. 395.

100. Ferrandis, loc. cit., p. 29.

101. AHN, cód. 466, pp. 42–5, doc. 44.

102. AHN, cód. 494, pp. 1–4, doc. 1 (Cantavieja); pp. 19–22, doc. 5 (Mirambel); pp. 47–8, doc. 10 (Villarluengo); pp. 31–3, doc. 7 (Tronchón); pp. 67–72, doc. 13 (La Cañada); pp. 85–9, doc. 16 (Iglesuela); pp. 104–6, doc. 20 (La Cuba).

103. AHN, Montesa, sign. 542–C, fols. 30ᵛ–31, 44–45ᵛ; a version of the charter for Pulpís is published in *BSCC*, xxiv (1948), 65–6.

104. AHN, cód. 1032, pp. 79–80, doc. 50; published by F. D. Gazulla, 'La Orden del Santo Redentor', *BSCC*, x (1929), 98.

105. AHN, cód. 691, fols. 18ᵛ–19ᵛ, doc. 39; fols. 194ᵛ–195ᵛ, doc. 441. This wording is taken from a twelfth-century confirmation of the charter; in what purports to be a copy of the original charter, settlers are said to be freed from the payment of any rent (*censum*) except tithes and *primicias*: AHN, San Juan, leg. 340, doc. 1.

106. AHN, cód. 691, *passim*.

107. At Seca, for example, nothing was to be given from the produce of fruit trees: AHN, Montesa, P. 73.

108. AHN, San Juan, leg. 421, doc. 7. The version of this document published by Font Rius, *Cartas de población*, i. 344–6, doc. 244, changes the sense on this point by giving 'proximis' for 'pro eis'.

109. Ferrandis, loc. cit., p. 32.

110. AHN, Montesa, sign. 542–C, fol. 39–39ᵛ.

111. AHN, Montesa, P. 461. The Templars did, however, manage to extract a payment of 250s.V. in return for this concession.

112. AHN, Montesa, P. 73.

113. AHN, Montesa, P. 250.

114. For rents before 1225, see AGP, parch. Gardeny, nos. 85–9; in 1225 a payment of 14s. is mentioned: parch. Gardeny, no. 204; and early in 1226 the provincial master promised not to exact more than this amount: parch. Gardeny, no. 107. For the reduction to 12s., see parch. Gardeny, nos. 124–31.

115. e.g. AGP, parch. Gardeny, nos. 104, 117.

116. AHN, Montesa, sign. 542–C, fols. 26ᵛ–28, 44–45ᵛ. A version of the charter for Alcalá is published in *BSCC*, xxxiii (1957), 253–6.

117. Cf. G. Duby, *L'Économie rurale et la vie des campagnes dans l'Occident médiéval* (Paris, 1962), ii. 436–7, where the value of mills is stressed.

118. AHN, Montesa, P. 73.

119. Ferrandis, loc. cit., p. 31.

120. AHN, Montesa, sign. 542–C, fols. 26ᵛ–28.

121. AHN, cód. 494, pp. 1–4, doc. 1; pp. 19–22, doc. 5; pp. 85–9, doc. 16.

122. AHN, Montesa, sign. 542–C, fols. 30ᵛ–31.

123. AHN, San Juan, leg. 351, doc. 1.

124. Font Rius, *Cartas de población*, i. 184–5, doc. 126.

125. J. Cots i Gorchs, 'Les "Consuetuds" d'Horta (avui Horta de Sant Joan) a la ratlla del Baix Aragó', *Estudis universitaris catalans*, xv (1930), 312.

126. AHN, San Juan, leg. 310, doc. 18; Font Rius, *Cartas de población*, i. 329–30, doc. 236. The inhabitants of Tortosa had, of course, been exempted from *lezda* and other tolls by Raymond Berenguer IV: see above, pp. 114–15.

127. Font Rius, *Cartas de población*, i. 264–6, doc. 191; 270–1, doc. 196; 344–6, doc. 244. At Gandesa the due was referred to by the term *forcia*; cf. Hinojosa, op. cit., pp. 116–17.

128. AHN, cód. 494, pp. 1–4, doc. 1; pp. 19–22, doc. 5; Albareda y Herrera, op. cit., pp. 42, 44–5.

129. AHN, cód. 691, fols. 18ᵛ–19ᵛ, doc. 39; fols. 194ᵛ–195ᵛ, doc. 441; cód. 494, pp. 67–72, doc. 13; García Larragueta, 'Fueros y cartas pueblas', pp. 594–5; Font Rius, *Cartas de población*, i. 264–6, doc. 191; 270–1, doc. 196; 306–8, doc. 222.

130. The right was retained in the *fuero* issued for Alfambra by the master of the Order of Mountjoy: Albareda y Herrera, op. cit., p. 19.

131. Font Rius, *Cartas de población*, i. 169–70, doc. 116.

132. AGP, parch. Gardeny, nos. 654, 1757.

133. AHN, San Juan, leg. 351, doc. 1. In the code of customs drawn up in 1296 it was stated that *intestia*, *exorquia*, and *cugucia* 'have no place' in Horta: Cots i Gorchs, loc. cit., p. 321.

134. García Larragueta, 'Fueros y cartas pueblas', pp. 592–5; Font Rius, *Cartas de población*, i. 285–6, doc. 208; 306–8, doc. 222.

135. Ibid. i. 301–3, doc. 219; 505–7, doc. 344.

136. AHN, Montesa, sign. 542–C, fols. 15–16ᵛ.

137. AHN, cód. 494, pp. 31–3, doc. 7.

138. Ibid., pp. 1–4, doc. 1; pp. 19–22, doc. 5; pp. 85–9, doc. 16.

139. AHN, San Juan, leg. 351, doc. 1; cód. 466, pp. 42–5, doc. 44; cód. 467, p. 442, doc. 424; Font Rius, *Cartas de población*, i. 301–3, doc. 219.

140. AHN, Montesa, sign. 542–C, fols. 30ᵛ–31.

141. AHN, Montesa, P. 136, 174, 218, 220, 325.

142. Font Rius, *Cartas de población*, i. 344–6, doc. 244.

143. AHN, Montesa, P. 112 *bis*, 113, 214.

144. e.g. AHN, cód. 494, pp. 67–72, doc. 13.

145. Cf. S. Sobrequés Vidal in *Historia social y económica de España y América*, ii (Barcelona, 1957), 70.

146. Font Rius, *Cartas de población*, i. 507–8, doc. 345; cf. id., 'Franquicias locales en la comarca del alto Bergadá', *Pirineos*, x (1954), 459–88, especially pp. 482–3.

147. e.g. ACA, parch. James II, nos. 345, 356, 1088, 1443.

148. The Moors at Chivert were, however, exempted from this due: Ferrandis, loc. cit., pp. 29–30.

149. Cf. J. M. Font Rius, 'Orígenes del régimen municipal de Cataluña', *AHDE*, xvi (1945), 487–92.

150. AGP, Cartulary of Gardeny, fol. 49ᵛ, doc. 112; see below, p. 368; published from a later transcript by Font Rius, *Cartas de población*, i. 139–40, doc. 87.

151. Ibid. i. 264–6, doc. 191; 394–6, doc. 272.

152. AHN, Montesa, sign. 542–C, fols. 44–45ᵛ.

153. See, for example, *Los fueros de Sepúlveda*, pp. 175–8.

154. *Cambridge Economic History of Europe*, i. 471; F. L. Carsten, *The Origins of Prussia* (Oxford, 1954), pp. 28–32; cf. Duby, *L'Économie rurale*, i. 321–3, docs. 38, 39.

155. AHN, Montesa, P. 200, 263.

156. *Cambridge Economic History of Europe*, i. 462.

157. AHN, Montesa, sign. 542–C, fols. 26ᵛ–28; see above, p. 215. E. Lourie, 'Free Moslems in the Balearics under Christian Rule in the Thirteenth Century', *Speculum*, xlv (1970), 626, suggests that after the conquest of Mallorca the Temple transferred some Moors to the island from its estates on the mainland; but the evidence is by no means conclusive.

158. There was a considerable French element on some Templar lands along the Ebro near Zaragoza, but these immigrants may have settled before the Order acquired these estates: C. Higounet, 'Mouvements de populations dans le Midi de la France du xiᵉ au xvᵉ siècle', *Annales*, viii (1953), 6.

159. AHN, cód. 691, fols. 68ᵛ–69, doc. 209.

160. Lacarra, 'Documentos', no. 150 (iii. 548–9). On the date of this document, see above, p. 14, note 60.

161. e.g. Albon, *Cartulaire*, pp. 275–6, 295, 298, docs. 440, 473, 476; AHN, cód. 691, fol. 71, doc. 215.

162. Lacarra, 'Documentos', no. 150 (iii. 548–9).

163. This confirmation survives in two late twelfth-century versions (AHN, cód. 691, fols. 18ᵛ–19ᵛ, doc. 39, and fols. 194ᵛ–195ᵛ, doc. 441) and in a transcript which belongs probably to the later thirteenth century: AHN, San Juan, leg. 346, doc. 1. In the earlier versions the confirmation is undated, while in the later one the date is given as 1176 and as in the third year after the siege of Tortosa. The names of the witnesses suggest that the document was in fact drawn up about the middle of the twelfth century.

164. AHN, San Juan, leg. 340, doc. 1. See above, p. 7.

165. Lacarra, 'Documentos', no. 175 (iii. 568–9). In 1135 Novillas was granted to the Orders with all the land subject to it 'waste and settled': Albon, *Cartulaire*, p. 73, doc. 100; but this was a formula commonly employed in charters of donation, and no conclusions can be drawn from its use on a particular occasion.

166. Albon, *Cartulaire*, p. 334, doc. 545.

167. AHN, San Juan, leg. 138, doc. 4; see below, p. 371.

168. AHN, San Juan, leg. 285, doc. 3.

169. AHN, San Juan, leg. 286 *bis*, doc. 1.

170. AHN, San Juan, leg. 39, doc. 52.

171. AHN, cód. 691, fol. 145–145ᵛ, doc. 371. The date of this document is given wrongly in *Colección de fueros y cartas pueblas de España* (Madrid, 1852), p. 23, and I. de Asso, *Historia de la economía política de Aragón* (Zaragoza, 1947 edn.), pp. 7, 187.

172. AHN, San Juan, leg. 598, unnumbered document.

173. AHN, San Juan, leg. 138, doc. 4; see below, p. 371.

174. AGP, parch. Cervera, no. 484; see below, p. 405.

175. AHN, cód. 467, p. 442, doc. 424.

176. El '*Llibre Blanch' de Santas Creus*, ed. F. Udina Martorell (Barcelona, 1947), p. 51, doc. 43. The castle at Selma had been built towards the end of the tenth century: F. Bofarull y Sans, *El castillo y la baronía de Aramprunya* (Barcelona, 1911), p. 21.

177. AGP, Cartulary of Gardeny, fol. 49ᵛ, doc. 112; see below, p. 368.

178. Font Rius, *Cartas de población*, i. 160–1, doc. 108; 169–70, doc. 116.

179. AGP, parch. Gardeny, no. 5. Grants to a further four men are recorded on the dorse of this document.

180. AGP, parch. Gardeny, nos. 4, 6.

181. AGP, parch. Gardeny, no. 7.

182. AGP, Cartulary of Gardeny, fol. 32–32$^v$, doc. 59.

183. Ibid., fol. 35–35$^v$, doc. 69; fol. 45$^v$, doc. 100; parch. Gardeny, no. 1588.

184. AGP, parch. Gardeny, no. 1786.

185. Font Rius, *Cartas de población*, i. 365–7, doc. 256. The Order had similarly sought to attract men from Aguilar and Castellpagés when it was setting up Villanueva de la Barca in 1212: ibid., pp. 329–30, doc. 236. Aguilar and Castell-pagés were not, however, under Templar lordship. The township of Villa-nueva del Segriá, near Castellnou, had already been established by the early years of the thirteenth century, but no details of its foundation are known: cf. AGP, parch. Gardeny, no. 1292.

186. J. M. Font Rius, 'La comarca de Tortosa a raíz de la reconquista cristiana (1148)', *Cuadernos de historia de España*, xix (1953), 110; AGP, Cartulary of Tortosa, *passim*.

187. A considerable number of Moors, however, remained in this region after the reconquest: see above, p. 200.

188. AHN, San Juan, leg. 351, doc. 1; Font Rius, *Cartas de población*, i. 264–6, doc. 191.

189. García Larragueta, 'Fueros y cartas pueblas', pp. 592–5; Font Rius, *Cartas de población*, i. 285–6, doc. 208; 306–8, doc. 222.

190. Ibid. i. 301–3, doc. 219; 317–18, doc. 228; 344–6, doc. 244.

191. In the *carta de población* for Batea there is a reference to sixty settlers, but this is exceptional.

192. AGP, Cartulary of Tortosa, fol. 43, doc. 135; AHN, San Juan, leg. 306, doc. 35.

193. Font Rius, *Cartas de población*, i. 227–31, docs. 164, 165; *CDI*, viii. 68–9, doc. 23. There are several puzzling features about the *carta de población* issued by Alfonso II and his charter of donation to Bernard Granel: both are dated 30 October 1181, and while the *carta de población* refers to the *fuero* of Zaragoza, the charter to Bernard Granel mentions that of Barcelona. Font Rius, *Cartas de población*, i. 798, seeks to explain these peculiarities by arguing that the king at first attempted to resettle Algars and Batea and therefore issued the *carta de población*; when this attempt failed he granted these places to Bernard Granel, and 'in order to ensure the validity of this second concession' he ante-dated it so that it bore the same date as the *carta de población*. But in both documents the witnesses and scribe are the same, and there are reasons for suggesting that they were both issued at the same time. According to the charter issued to Bernard Granel, Alfonso was still to receive two-thirds of the revenues of Algars and Batea and he would therefore have been concerned about the way in which these places were resettled, even if Bernard Granel was to enjoy lordship over them. He might therefore have issued a *carta de población* at the time when he granted Algars and Batea to Bernard Granel. The fact that one document refers to the *fuero* of Zaragoza and the other to that of Barcelona does not

invalidate this argument, for the *carta de población* is concerned with settlers and the terms on which they were to settle, while the other charter gives details of the conditions on which Bernard Granel was to hold Algars and Batea of the king.

In 1182, when Alfonso II confirmed the Temple's right to the territories which had been granted with Miravet in 1153, he referred specifically to Algars and Batea, and this was probably done in response to a Templar protest against his action in the previous year: AHN, San Juan, leg. 306, doc. 6. Bernard Granel surrendered his claims to Algars and Batea in 1187: leg. 306, doc. 7.

The slowness of resettlement along the lower Ebro apparently also led Alfonso II to ignore Templar rights at Rasquera. Although Rasquera was among the places granted to the Order in 1153, in 1171 Alfonso granted it to the Hospital. But the Templars apparently recovered it, for they issued a *carta de población* for it, although the date of this charter is not known: Font Rius, *Cartas de población*, i. 797–8.

194. Font Rius, 'La comarca de Tortosa', pp. 110–11.

195. Font Rius, *Cartas de población*, i. 184–5, doc. 126. The fact that the surviving Templar charter for Batea was not issued until 1205 suggests that the settlement mentioned in Alfonso's charter of 1181 had collapsed.

196. Ibid. i. 394–6, doc. 272; 421–2, doc. 289; 505–7, doc. 344; García Larragueta, 'Fueros y cartas pueblas', pp. 598–9. The date of the charter for Gandesola is given wrongly as 1278 in *Colección de fueros y cartas pueblas de España*, p. 101.

197. AHN, San Juan, leg. 307, doc. 1.

198. Font Rius, *Cartas de población*, i. 411–12, doc. 283; AHN, San Juan, leg. 307, docs. 1, 2.

199. AHN, Montesa, P. 78.

200. It was said of Miravet at the beginning of the fourteenth century that 'not so many Christians come there as to other places': Finke, *Papsttum*, ii. 72, doc. 48; and at the end of the fifteenth century there were only three Christian households there: Reglá, loc. cit., pp. 263–4.

201. J. Rius Serra, *Rationes Decimarum Hispaniae (1279–1280)*, i (Barcelona, 1946), 165–78. These taxes were exacted in other places in the diocese of Tortosa where the Order enjoyed rights of ecclesiastical patronage.

202. In 1244 the Templars granted the valley of Batea to a group of men 'as the men of Nonaspe held and possessed it': Font Rius, *Cartas de población*, i. 411–12, doc. 283. This concession was presumably occasioned by the agreement by which Elvira of Cervellón ceded Nonaspe and several other places to the Order: see above, p. 189.

203. Albareda y Herrera, op. cit.; AHN, Ordenes militares, Calatrava, sign. 1341–C, fols. 135–6.

204. F. D. Gazulla, 'La Orden del Santo Redentor', *BSCC*, x (1929), 98.

205. AHN, cód. 689, p. 54, doc. 45. Admittedly the date of this document is given as 1184, but this must be an error in transcription. According to *Colección*

*de fueros y cartas pueblas de España*, p. 287, Villarluengo was resettled in 1184, but this is merely a repetition of a mistake made at one point by Asso, op. cit., p. 9, where it is stated that Villarluengo was granted to Mountjoy for settling in 1184; Asso later, however, ibid., p. 203, gives the date as 1194.

206. AHN, cód. 494, pp. 47–8, doc. 10.

207. A. López Polo, 'Documentos para la historia de Teruel', *Teruel*, i (1949), 187–8.

208. AHN, cód. 466, p. 204, doc. 173.

209. AHN, cód. 689, pp. 56–7, doc. 50. In 1197 the Templars came to an agreement with the inhabitants of Castellote on a number of issues: A. Bonilla y San Martín, 'El derecho aragonés en el siglo XII', *II Congreso de historia de la Corona de Aragón*, i (Huesca, 1920), 276–7, doc. 42. Bonilla gives the date as 1198, but see RAH, 12–6–1/M–83, doc. 48, and AHN, cód. 689, p. 11, doc. 6.

210. AHN, cód. 494, pp. 67–72, doc. 13. This document is not dated, but it is clear from the names of the Templars mentioned in it that it was issued before the end of the century. There is no justification for the date of 1142 which is given in *Colección de fueros y cartas pueblas de España*, p. 60, and repeated by R. Esteban Abad, *Estudio histórico-político sobre la ciudad y comunidad de Daroca* (Teruel, 1957), p. 185.

211. AHN, San Juan, leg. 231, doc. 2; published from later versions by M. Gual Camarena, *Precedentes de la reconquista valenciana* (Valencia, 1953), pp. 72–3. In 1204 the bishop of Zaragoza granted the Templars the church of Cantavieja, but this does not mean that a church had in fact been built by that time: AHN, San Juan, leg. 39, doc. 67.

212. AHN, cód. 494, pp. 1–4, doc. 1.

213. Ibid., pp. 19–22, doc. 5; pp. 31–3, doc. 7; pp. 85–9, doc. 16; pp. 104–6, doc. 20; cód. 689, p. 24, doc. 16.

214. Rius Serra, op. cit. ii (Barcelona, 1947), 103–4. Tronchón appears not to have been a completely new settlement in 1272, since a justiciar and *jurados* had already been established when the *carta de población* was issued.

215. AHN, cód. 466, p. 242, doc. 247.

216. Ibid., pp. 387–8, doc. 462.

217. Ibid., pp. 231–2, doc. 230.

218. Ibid., pp. 42–5, doc. 44.

219. Ibid., pp. 40–1, doc. 42; see below, p. 395.

220. AHN, cód. 466, pp. 41–2, doc. 43.

221. Ibid., p. 260, doc. 276; pp. 268–9, docs. 292, 293.

222. AHN, Montesa, P. 14.

223. AHN, Montesa, P. 123, 124, 136, 146, 157, 174, 177, 178, 180, 181.

224. AHN, Montesa, P. 123, 124. A larger entry fine was sometimes charged when the Temple was granting existing houses there: Montesa, P. 177.

225. AHN, Montesa, sign. 542–C, fol. 39–39$^v$; cf. Montesa, R. 99.

226. AHN, Montesa, sign. 542–C, fols. 15–16$^v$; Huici, *Colección diplomática*, i. 412–15, docs. 298, 299. In 1243 James I had issued a *carta de población* for Carpesa.

227. According to F. Diago, *Anales del reyno de Valencia* (Valencia, 1613), vii. 25, and Javierre, *Privilegios*, p. 67, the *alquería* of Borbotó was given to the Temple. This is also stated by J. Villarroya, *Real Maestrazgo de Montesa* (Valencia, 1787), i. 157, but in the same work (i. 62–3), he says that it was sold to the Temple. An incomplete copy of the instrument recording the transaction is contained in AHN, Montesa, sign. 543–C, fol. 38$^v$, and there it is worded as a gift. But in 1263 the bishop of Valencia said that the Templars had bought it: Montesa, P. 265. Possibly William of Portella received a payment *de caritate* for a grant.

228. AHN, Montesa, sign. 542–C, fols. 16$^v$–17.

229. AHN, Montesa, P. 266. There is another version of this document in the cathedral archive in Valencia: E. Olmos y Canalda, *Inventario de los pergaminos de la Catedral de Valencia* (Valencia, 1961), p. 43, no. 335.

230. AHN, Montesa, P. 73.

231. AHN, Montesa, sign. 542–C, fols. 26$^v$–28.

232. Ibid., fols. 44–45$^v$.

233. Ibid., fols. 30$^v$–31. The change from the *fuero* of Zaragoza to that of Valencia is perhaps not in itself very significant, as it was the usual practice of the Temple to adopt the latter: cf. M. Gual Camarena, 'Estudio de la territorialidad de los Fueros de Valencia', *EEMCA*, iii (1947–8), 271.

234. Cf. F. Soldevila, *Pere el Gran*, II. i (Barcelona, 1962), 16, 71–2.

235. AHN, Montesa, P. 112 *bis*, 113, 214.

236. AHN, Montesa, P. 348.

237. AHN, Montesa, P. 357.

238. The Aragonese sources provide little evidence about the resettlement of Mallorca. J. Lladó y Ferragut, *Catálogo de la sección histórica del archivo municipal de Pollensa y de las curias de los Templarios y Hospitalarios de San Juan de Jerusalén* (Palma, 1944), pp. 90–1, refers to a volume in the municipal archive of Pollensa which contains records of various Templar transactions, but these all belong to the last decade of the thirteenth and first years of the fourteenth centuries. On the existence of Muslim tenants on Templar estates in Mallorca, see E. Lourie, 'Free Moslems in the Balearics under Christian Rule in the Thirteenth Century', *Speculum*, xlv (1970), 625–9.

239. Cf. Sobrequés Vidal in *Historia social y económica de España y América*, ii. 47–8.

240. These were caused not only by the desertion of settlers dismayed by the hardness of the life or by Moorish raids; some settlements were destroyed as a result of feuds between the Templars and neighbouring lords: cf. F. Carreras y Candi, 'Entences y Templers en les montanyes de Prades', *BRABLB*, ii (1903–4), 217–57.

241. Huici, *Colección diplomática*, i. 536–7, doc. 398.

242. A hearth assessment for Catalonia survives for the year 1359: *CDI*, xii, *passim*. This, of course, refers to the period after the Black Death.

243. Miret y Sans, *Les Cases*, pp. 399–400.

244. Font Rius, *Cartas de población*, i. 507–8, doc. 345.

245. AGP, parch. Cervera, no. 484; see below, p. 405.

246. AGP, Cartulary of Gardeny, fol. 41ᵛ, doc. 87; cf. AHN, San Juan, leg. 437, doc. 2.

247. Albon, *Cartulaire*, p. 101, doc. 144; cf. ACA, parch. James I, no. 2001.

248. See above, p. 62.

249. AGP, parch. Gardeny, nos. 190, 191, 192, 193, 196, 197, etc.

250. AGP, parch. Gardeny, nos. 231-40, 243, 244, etc.

251. AGP, parch. Gardeny, nos. 383, 384, 385, 388, 389, 395, 567.

252. See above, p. 206.

253. AGP, parch. Gardeny, nos. 326–8, 330–2, 334, 337, etc.

254. e.g. AGP, parch. Gardeny, nos. 713, 967.

255. J. Miret y Sans, 'Inventaris de les cases del Temple de la Corona d'Aragó en 1289', *BRABLB*, vi (1911), 69; id., *Cartoral dels Templers de les comandes de Gardeny y Barbens* (Barcelona, 1899), p. 30.

256. AGP, parch. Gardeny, no. 1536.

257. Miret y Sans, 'Inventaris', pp. 63–5.

258. ACA, CRD James II, no. 1183.

259. ACA, parch. James II, no. 6; cf. AHN, cód. 466, pp. 366–7, doc. 444.

260. e.g. AHN, San Juan, leg. 559, docs. 39, 41, 61; cód. 469, pp. 415–16, doc. 354.

261. e.g. AHN, San Juan, leg. 551, doc. 7; leg. 552, docs. 18, 31.

262. e.g. ACA, reg. 48, fol. 71ᵛ; reg. 60, fol. 80ᵛ.

263. See above, p. 132.

264. AHN, San Juan, leg. 333, doc. 15; cód. 471, p. 135, doc. 136; p. 210, doc. 211.

265. AHN, San Juan, leg. 333, doc. 15; cód. 471, pp. 229–38, doc. 220. The privilege in question has been published by M. T. Oliveros de Castro, *Historia de Monzón* (Zaragoza, 1964), p. 588.

266. ACA, reg. 64, fol. 77–77ᵛ; AHN, cód. 471, pp. 129–30, doc. 128. When the privilege was confirmed its date was given as 1086.

267. Another suspect privilege supposedly granted to the inhabitants of Monzón by Alfonso I again in 1076 was also discussed during the course of this dispute: AHN, San Juan, leg. 333, doc. 15; the privilege has been published by Oliveros de Castro, op. cit., p. 589.

268. AHN, San Juan, leg. 333, doc. 15; cód. 471, pp. 218–19, doc. 215; pp. 229–38, doc. 220.

269. AHN, cód. 689, p. 12, doc. 7.

270. AGP, Cartulary of Gardeny, fol. 45ᵛ, doc. 100.

271. Usually *milites*, *sancti*, and *clerici* are mentioned, but some charters also forbid alienation to certain other individuals, such as lepers or the *donati* of another religious institution: AHN, cód. 467, p. 378, doc. 474; cód. 469, p. 171, doc. 132; cód. 499, p. 31, doc. 73; San Juan, leg. 553, doc. 141.

272. AHN, códs. 499, 689.

273. This is among the documents of Gardeny in the AGP, armario 11.

274. ACA, Varia 3.

275. e.g. AGP, Cartulary of Gardeny, fols. 17–19, doc. 21.

276. ACA, reg. 291, fol. 323ᵛ.

277. e.g. *Libri confraternitatum Sancti Galli, Augiensis, Fabrariensis*, ed. P. Piper, in *Monumenta Germaniae Historica* (1884); *Liber Vitae Ecclesiae Dunelmensis*, ed. A. H. Thompson (Surtees Society, vol. cxxxvi, 1923); *Liber Vitae: Register and Martyrology of New Minster and Hyde Abbey*, ed. W. de Gray Birch (Hampshire Record Society, 1892); cf. E. Bishop, *Liturgica Historica* (Oxford, 1918), pp. 349–69. A Templar list from the south of France similar to those compiled in Aragon has been published by A. du Bourg, *Histoire du grand-prieuré de Toulouse* (Toulouse, 1883), Appendix, p. xiv, doc. 21.

278. On Aragonese confraternity lists, see above, p. 36, and below, p. 376.

279. ACA, Varia 3.

280. The use of inquests for this purpose in England is discussed by R. V. Lennard, 'Early Manorial Juries', *English Historical Review*, lxxvii (1962), 511–18.

281. See below, pp. 266, 269.

282. Cf. J. Pérez de Urbel, *Los monjes españoles en la edad media*, ii (Madrid, 1934), 529.

283. ACA, parch. James II, no. 2325.

284. ACA, reg. 60, fol. 80ᵛ.

285. ACA, reg. 90, fols. 44ᵛ, 56ᵛ; see below, p. 405.

286. ACA, reg. 13, fol. 182ᵛ; reg. 48, fol. 71ᵛ; AGP, parch. Barbará, no. 127.

287. ACA, reg. 114, fol. 168ᵛ.

288. Cf. Duby, *L'Économie rurale*, ii. 529.

289. This does not, of course, imply that these crops were grown in these proportions.

290. Many examples of this kind of payment can be found among the parchments of Gardeny in the AGP.

291. Information about this district is contained in the collection of royal parchments in the ACA.

292. AHN, códs. 470, 691, *passim*.

293. AHN, cód. 691, fol. 145–145ᵛ, doc. 371.

294. Information about these districts is contained in AGP, Cartulary of Gardeny and parchments of Gardeny.

295. AHN, San Juan, leg. 351, doc. 1; García Larragueta, 'Fueros y cartas pueblas', pp. 592–5, 598–9; Font Rius, *Cartas de población*, i. 264–6, doc. 191; 270–1, doc. 196; 285–6, doc. 208; 301–3, doc. 219; 306–8, doc. 222; 344–6, doc. 244; 411–12, doc. 283; 421–2, doc. 289; 505–7, doc. 344.

296. AHN, San Juan, leg. 306, doc. 12; leg. 308, doc. 2.

297. Information about this district is contained in AGP, Cartulary of Tortosa and parchments of Tortosa.

298. AHN, cód. 466, pp. 40–1, doc. 42; pp. 42–5, doc. 44; pp. 387–8, doc. 462; cód. 689, p. 24, doc. 16; see below, p. 395.

299. On this area, see AHN, Montesa, documentos particulares, *passim*.

300. Ferrandis, loc. cit., p. 32; AHN, Montesa, sign. 542–C, fols. 26ᵛ–28.

301. AHN, cód. 689, *passim*.

302. See AGP, Cartulary of Gardeny and parchments of Gardeny, and also a *capbreu* drawn up in 1214 in AGP, armario 11.

303. AHN, Montesa, sign. 542–C, fols. 26ᵛ–28; Montesa, P. 73.

304. e.g. AHN, cód. 689, p. 24, doc. 16; pp. 75–6, doc. 77.

305. Ferrandis, loc. cit., p. 32.

306. e.g. ACA, parch. Alfonso II, nos. 266, 373, 489, 667, 718.

307. ACA, parch. James II, nos. 408, 411, 412, 413, 414, 420, 722; AHN, San Juan, leg. 598, unnumbered document; Albareda y Herrera, op. cit., p. 42.

308. Cf. E. de Hinojosa, *El régimen señorial y la cuestión agraria en Cataluña* (Madrid, 1905), pp. 200–1.

309. ACA, parch. Peter III, no. 474; parch. Alfonso III, nos. 80, 190; see below, p. 400.

310. ACA, parch. Peter III, nos. 1, 361; parch. Alfonso III, nos. 123, 201.

311. AHN, cód. 466, pp. 41–2, doc. 43.

312. ACA, parch. James II, no. 1688; cf. parch. Peter III, no. 277; AGP, parch. Selma, no. 29.

313. Proportional rents were exacted in the twelfth century at Labar, but when grants of land were made there to tenants in the thirteenth century a fixed money rent was demanded.

314. The change took place between 1185 and 1193: AGP, parch. Gardeny, nos. 1792, 1793, 1796, 1797, 1808.

315. Documents drawn up in the 1160s refer to tithe as a proportional due: AGP, Cartulary of Gardeny, fol. 32–32$^v$, doc. 59; fols. 37$^v$–38, doc. 77. From the early thirteenth century onwards rent and tithe were exacted in the form of a single payment assessed in money: parch. Gardeny, nos. 85–9, 91, 93–6, 203, 586.

316. Albareda y Herrera, op. cit., p. 46. At Castellote tithes were similarly exacted in the form of fixed money payments: AHN, cód. 689, pp. 1–4, doc. 2; A. Bonilla y San Martín, 'El derecho aragonés en el siglo XII', *II Congreso de historia de la Corona de Aragón*, i (Huesca, 1920), 276–7, doc. 42.

317. ACA, parch. James I, no. 1420; parch. Alfonso III, no. 190. Fixed payments in kind were possibly also being abandoned on some other occasions when it was stated that the *census* was being replaced by a fixed money payment: e.g. parch. Peter III, no. 474.

318. e.g. AGP, parch. Gardeny, no. 1579.

319. AHN, cód. 466, *passim*.

320. AHN, San Juan, leg. 598, unnumbered document.

321. ACA, parch. James II, no. 518; see below, p. 407.

322. ACA, parch. Alfonso III, no. 190.

323. AGP, parch. Gardeny, nos. 1787–90, 1792, 1793.

324. AGP, parch. Gardeny, nos. 1796, 1797, 1808.

325. AGP, parch. Gardeny, nos. 1807, 1829, 1834.

326. ACA, parch. Alfonso III, no. 201.

327. ACA, parch. James I, no. 1626.

328. e.g. AHN, San Juan, leg. 529, doc. 73; leg. 553, docs. 112, 144, 154.

329. AHN, Montesa, P. 113, 169, 214.

330. e.g. AGP, parch. Gardeny, nos. 594, 750, 785, 1596.

331. AHN, cód. 468, pp. 230–1, doc. 207.

332. AGP, parch. Gardeny, nos. 939, 985, 1570.

333. ACA, CRD Templarios, nos. 403, 457, 607; see below, p. 413.

334. ACA, CRD Templarios, nos. 403, 457, 507, 607; see below, p. 413.

335. Miret y Sans, 'Inventaris', p. 64.

336. ACA, CRD Templarios, no. 81; see below, p. 415.

337. e.g. E. Miller, *The Abbey and Bishopric of Ely* (Cambridge, 1951), p. 76; G. Duby, 'Économie domaniale et économie monétaire: le budget de l'abbaye de Cluny entre 1080 et 1155', *Annales*, vii (1952), 167.

338. Several documents recording changes refer to small payments made at the time by tenants to the Order: e.g. ACA, parch. James I, no. 1230.

339. ACA, parch. Alfonso III, no. 37; cf. AHN, San Juan, leg. 532, doc. 13.

340. AHN, cód. 494, pp. 1-4, doc. 1.

341. Ibid., pp. 67-72, doc. 13.

342. ACA, parch. Alfonso II, no. 327.

343. ACA, parch. James I, no. 2163.

344. ACA, parch. James II, nos. 408, 411, 412, 413, 414, 420.

345. ACA, CRD Templarios, nos. 616, 618.

346. ACA, CRD Templarios, no. 539.

347. ACA, parch. Peter III, no. 103.

348. AGP, parch. Gardeny, nos. 967, 969, 996, 1233; ACA, parch. James I, nos. 1938, 1941; parch. Peter III, no. 407; parch. Alfonso III, no. 120; parch. James II, no. 990.

349. e.g. Font Rius, *Cartas de población*, i. 169-70, doc. 116; 505-7, doc. 344.

350. AHN, San Juan, leg. 354, doc. 2; Montesa, P. 265.

351. Miret y Sans, 'Inventaris', pp. 62-72; ACA, CRD Templarios, nos. 116, 117, 118; CRD James II, nos. 1313, 1737, 1747.

352. *Cambridge Economic History of Europe*, i. 477.

353. Font Rius, *Cartas de población*, i. 169-70, doc. 116; AHN, Montesa, sign. 542-C, fols. 16ᵛ-17.

354. Holdings of this size are mentioned in a number of *cartas de población*, especially along the lower Ebro.

355. AHN, San Juan, leg. 354, doc. 2. In this document it is stated that this land was to be exempt from tithe whether the Templars kept it in demesne or not.

356. AHN, Montesa, P. 78. No attempt to estimate the size of the demesne from the numbers of ploughing animals is possible, even when no labour services were owed, because it is not known where in a commandery these animals were used.

357. ACA, parch. James II, no. 518; see below, p. 407; cf. parch. James II, no. 990.

358. e.g. AHN, San Juan, leg. 351, doc. 2; ACA, parch. Alfonso II, no. 575; parch. James I, no. 1446. In 1168 the Templars of Gardeny made two grants of land from their *condamina*, a term which could mean demesne land: AGP,

Cartulary of Gardeny, fols. 31, 34ᵛ-35, docs. 55, 68; but the exact significance of the word in this context is not clear: cf. parch. Gardeny, nos. 281-8, 297.

359. e.g. AHN, Montesa, P. 370, 453, 485, 554; AGP, parch. Gardeny, nos. 184, 438, 1501.

360. AHN, Montesa, P. 452, 453.

361. e.g. AGP, parch. Gardeny, no. 730.

362. AGP, parch. Gardeny, no. 719.

363. AGP, parch. Gardeny, nos. 686, 691, 703, 754, 776, 784, 804, 819.

364. AGP, parch. Gardeny, no. 748 *bis*.

365. See above, p. 199.

366. Hinojosa, op. cit., p. 203.

367. Miret y Sans, 'Inventaris', pp. 62-9. These Templar figures can be compared with some sixteenth-century sheep statistics provided by J. Klein, *The Mesta: A Study in Spanish Economic History, 1273-1836* (Harvard, 1920), p. 60.

368. ACA, CRD James II, no. 1313.

369. Finke, *Papsttum*, ii. 85-6, doc. 58.

370. AGP, Cartulary of Gardeny, fols. 107ᵛ-108, doc. 258; cf. fols. 103ᵛ-104, doc. 250. In 1201 the bishops of Zaragoza and Tarazona were ordered to investigate a Templar complaint that 1,000 of the Order's sheep and goats had been seized: AHN, San Juan, leg. 720, doc. 9.

371. AHN, cód. 466, p. 208, doc. 182. When the Temple took over the possessions of the Order of Mountjoy in 1196 it gained considerable flocks of sheep in southern Aragon, including 1,500 at Alfambra and 900 at Villel: AHN, Ordenes militares, Calatrava, sign. 1341-C, fols. 135-6.

372. Miret y Sans, 'Inventaris', pp. 63-4.

373. Ibid., pp. 62-3, 68-9.

374. Ibid., p. 62.

375. On the shipment of food supplies, see below, p. 324.

376. AHN, cód. 689, pp. 1-4, doc. 2; pp. 76-8, doc. 78.

377. Ferrandis, loc. cit., p. 31; AHN, Montesa, sign. 542-C, fols. 26ᵛ-28.

378. AHN, cód. 494, pp. 17-19, doc. 4; see below, p. 390.

379. *Règle*, p. 58, art. 48. Hunting the lion was justified by reference to Genesis 16: 12, and to 1 Peter 5: 8: 'your adversary, the devil, as a roaring lion, walketh about, seeking whom he may devour.'

380. See below, p. 281.

381. See below, pp. 285, 288.

382. AGP, Cartulary of Tortosa, fol. 7, doc. 22.

383. e.g. AHN, San Juan, leg. 529, doc. 73; leg. 546, docs. 4, 36; leg. 551, doc. 7; cód. 469, pp. 515–18, docs. 525, 526; pp. 521–2, doc. 531. These examples are taken from the district around Zaragoza. Cf. Duby, *L'Économie rurale*, i. 237 ff.; L. G. de Valdeavellano, *Historia de las instituciones españolas* (Madrid, 1968), p. 257.

384. Albareda y Herrera, op. cit., p. 46.

385. AHN, Montesa, sign. 542–C, fols. 15–16ᵛ.

386. AHN, cód. 466, pp. 40–1, doc. 42; see below, p. 395.

387. e.g. AGP, Cartulary of Gardeny, fol. 78, doc. 196.

388. AHN, cód. 470, p. 16, doc. 22.

389. AHN, San Juan, leg. 556, doc. 4; cód. 469, pp. 177–8, doc. 136; see below, p. 386.

390. AGP, Cartulary of Gardeny, fol. 51–51ᵛ, doc. 117; cf. parch. Gardeny, nos. 4, 7.

391. AHN, cód. 471, pp. 338–40, doc. 265.

392. Ibid., pp. 340–5, doc. 266.

393. e.g. AHN, cód. 466, p. 153, doc. 115; p. 157, doc. 123; AGP, Cartulary of Tortosa, fol. 11–11ᵛ, doc. 34; fols. 12ᵛ–13, doc. 39.

394. e.g. AGP, parch. Gardeny, nos. 196–9, 201, 427.

395. AHN, cód. 468, pp. 43–5, doc. 54; San Juan, leg. 587, docs. 34, 39; Montesa, P. 324.

396. In the document concerning the extension of irrigation in Segriá in 1173, however, the Order did stipulate that if irrigation was further extended then the rent should be increased; see also AGP, parch. Gardeny, nos. 524, 882. But provisions of this kind are rare.

397. In 1200, for example, when the Temple's right to a manse was being disputed, the commander of Palau settled the matter by granting the manse for life to the other party, who abandoned all other claims to it: ACA, parch. Peter II, nos. 94, 95; cf. parch. Alfonso II, nos. 423, 424.

# VII

## *Templar Organization and Life: (i) The Convent*

THE sites of Templar convents in the *Corona de Aragón* varied
considerably in character and reflected the different roles
which the Templars played in the Aragonese kingdoms.
Some convents were housed in large, strongly fortified castles,
which at the time of the arrest of the Templars were able to
withstand siege for months or even years. Amongst such convents
was that of Monzón, which was established in an impressive
castle dominating a hill by the river Cinca. Others were housed
in more modest strongholds, as at Gardeny, where the Templar
chapel and an adjoining two-storey building still survive.[1] Some
convents, on the other hand, whose situation was determined by
economic rather than military considerations, were set up in
cities and large towns. The convent of Zaragoza was established
apparently in the parish of St. Philip, where until the nineteenth
century the remains of the Templar chapel could be seen in the
*calle del Temple*.[2] The convent in the city of Huesca has similarly
left a trace in the names of the *calle de los Templarios* and the *plaza
del Temple*.[3] Despite these external differences, however, the
internal organization of Templar convents was essentially the
same throughout the *Corona de Aragón*.

As has been seen, the official in charge of a Templar convent
was usually known by the title of 'commander' or 'preceptor'.
The term 'master', which was sometimes given to the heads of
Miravet and Tortosa, Gardeny, Palau, and Novillas in the middle
years of the twelfth century, fell into disuse after the 1180s,[4] and
the only later change in terminology was the introduction of the
word 'castellan' from 1277 to describe the head of the convent of
Monzón. This title appears to have had no special significance,
and the position of the castellan can obviously not be compared
with that of the Hospitaller castellan of Amposta, who was the
head of a province. The title may have been introduced to distinguish the head of the convent from the subordinate commander

of the *villa* of Monzón, although this was not done in other places where a similar situation existed.[5]

Commanders of convents were drawn from members of both of the main ranks in the Order: from the knights and from the sergeants. As might be expected, however, it seems to have been the practice where possible to appoint knights. Of twenty-four commanders holding office between 1300 and 1307 whose ranks can be traced from documents concerning the dissolution of the Temple,[6] twenty were knights and only four were sergeants. The sergeants who did hold office, moreover, were usually placed in charge of minor convents, such as Selma and Añesa.[7]

The office of commander could be granted either for life or for a term.[8] The power to make a life appointment appears normally to have been reserved to the Grand Master and central Convent: when Berenguer of Cardona gave the commandery of Alfambra for life to Peter of San Justo in 1306 he did so not in his capacity as provincial master but by virtue of his office of visitor, to which were attached certain rights usually exercised by the Grand Master and Convent.[9] An examination of lists of commanders and their dates of office suggests, however, that few appointments of this kind were made. Appointments which were not for life were normally made by the provincial master and his advisers, although nominations could also be made by the Grand Master himself. The latter might intervene when he wished to promote the interests of a Templar whose services he valued, and he was no doubt also petitioned by members of the Order in the East who sought office as a means of returning to western Europe.[10] This situation could easily lead to conflict, and on such occasions the provincial master, who was on the spot, had the advantage. When Simon of Lenda was put in charge of the Aragonese province in 1307 the Grand Master James of Molay wrote to him, seeking an office for Peter of Castellón, after an earlier request to the previous provincial master had been refused. The Grand Master also complained that

when brother Bernard of Tamary left Cyprus we granted him the house of Ribaforada and when he arrived in Catalonia the provincial master had given it to another. It is a bad thing that orders are not obeyed when we give any bailiwick.[11]

During vacancies in the office of provincial master, the Grand Master was able to act more freely. After the death of Berenguer of Cardona, James of Molay made appointments to four commanderies in Aragon, granting at least three of these posts to Templars who were known to him personally.[12] It might have been expected that the provincial master would also be subject to pressure from the Aragonese king in the matter of appointments, but there is only one known instance of such interference. In March 1290 Alfonso III complained to the provincial master about the removal from office of Romeo of Burguet, the commander of Barcelona, whom the king had been employing in the collection of a royal aid;[13] and before the end of May the commander was restored to office.[14] But in this case the king was acting only because those involved in the collection of the tax were expecting the seal of the commander of Barcelona to be used as a sign of authentication. It does not suggest that royal interference in appointments at this level was common.

As the exact dates when commanders were appointed or removed from office are not known, the length of the terms of office of those who were not appointed for life cannot be determined precisely; but it is clear that there was no uniformity. The length of a term depended on the will of the provincial master. Nevertheless, with regard to a certain number of appointments a pattern is discernible. The Customs of the Temple refer to the appointing of commanders at the provincial chapter,[15] and that this was a common practice in the second half of the thirteenth century is suggested by the fact that a number of commanders were appointed to or removed from posts in April or May, which was the time when the annual provincial chapter was then usually held.[16] In 1286, for example, when the provincial chapter was in session on 17 April and had apparently begun on the 14th of that month,[17] Raymond Oliver is known to have been transferred from the charge of the convent of Villel to that of Tortosa between the 3rd and the 17th of April[18] and Peter of Tous was similarly moved from Gardeny to Miravet between the 6th and the 17th of April.[19] Some commanders thus held office for a whole year or for a number of complete years. But this was by no means a universal custom, for officials could clearly be appointed to and removed from posts at times other than during the chapter. William of Alcalá, who was commander of Gardeny in October 1254, was appointed to that post not earlier than August of that year,[20] and between the early part of June and the end of August

1269 Bernard of Pujalt was removed from office at Barbará in order to be given charge of the convent of Miravet.[21] Yet if it is clear that commanders could be appointed and dismissed outside the provincial chapter, it may nevertheless have been the custom to review all appointments annually during the chapter, as happened in the Teutonic Order, whose officials were obliged to surrender their offices each year at the chapter.[22] That this may have been a Templar practice as well is suggested by the obligation placed on commanders to present statements to the chapter each year giving details of the condition of their houses.[23]

Although a commander who was not appointed for life sometimes held the same post for more than twenty years,[24] offices were normally held—as in the Dominican Order[25]—for only two or three years. At Zaragoza in the thirteenth century thirty-six commanders are known, while for Castellote in the same period a list of thirty can be compiled. At both Villel and Gardeny there were forty. Almost inevitably this custom of short periods of office was accompanied by the practice of transferring Templars from the charge of one convent to that of another. William of Montgrí was in turn the head of Corbins (1243), Miravet (1244), Castellote (1246), Ambel (1246–9), Tortosa (1250–8), Ambel and Boquiñeni (1259), Monzón (1265–6), Alfambra (1267–71)—which he held jointly with Villel in 1271—Novillas (1272), and Huesca (1277). It was also common for Templars to have several periods of office at the same house. Raymond Oliver was commander of Tortosa from 1286 to 1287 and from 1290 until 1292, and head of Zaragoza from 1292 until 1294 and from 1297 until 1307. Raymond of Bastida in the same way was three times commander of Castellote between 1265 and 1278. Although these policies must have hampered efficient administration, they perhaps helped to prevent the growth of tensions which were liable to occur when a small community was subject to the same individual for a long period of years. But they were presumably adopted primarily in order to avoid the dangers which would exist if a Templar enjoyed too permanent a control over the possessions of a commandery and to emphasize that the holding of office in the Temple was regarded as a trust and responsibility rather than as a reward. This was also made clear by the not unusual practice of making commanders ordinary members of convents again instead of transferring them to the charge of other houses. John of

Corzano, for example, who was commander of Huesca from 1215 until 1221, remained in that house during the rest of 1221 without any office and later, in 1224–5, was holding a minor post there, before becoming commander of Zaragoza in 1226.[26]

Efficient administration was hindered not only by frequent changes in personnel but also by the practice of allowing a commander to rule over more than one convent at a time. There was apparently no regulation prohibiting the holding of commanderies in plurality, as there was at one time in the Hospital.[27] In most cases one of the houses held jointly was a minor convent: Boquiñeni was held by the commander of Ambel in 1256–7 and 1259, by the head of Añesa from 1271 until 1273, and by the commander of Novillas in 1282, while Juncosa was linked with Palau from 1246 to 1250 and from 1254 until 1258. It is possible—in view of the known financial difficulties of Boquiñeni in the second half of the thirteenth century—that appointments of this kind represented attempts to reduce the financial demands made on smaller convents which were in need of money. Although it is not clear whether a commander was assigned a fixed share of a convent's revenues,[28] such appointments would obviously save not only the expenses incurred by the commander himself, but also those of his attendants: according to the Customs of the Temple a knight commander was allowed an extra mount, which necessitated an additional arms-bearer,[29] and in practice during the second half of the thirteenth century Aragonese commanders sometimes had a companion as well as one or two arms-bearers.[30]

Some convents may at times have lacked commanders of their own for a different reason. In the Hospital several commanderies in each province were not assigned to commanders but were retained as *camere* by either the Grand Master or the head of the province, who drew revenues from them;[31] a similar practice is found in the Spanish military orders, in which a group of estates formed the *mesa maestral*.[32] There are hints that at the beginning of the fourteenth century the Temple was also following this custom. The post of commander of Gardeny was kept vacant from 1302 until 1307, and when the Grand Master James of Molay appointed Arnold of Banyuls to the commandery in the latter year he stated that the appointment was as commander, apparently stressing that he was not just installing a deputy to administer the commandery for his own benefit.[33] At the same time the Grand Master granted the commandery of Peñíscola 'as the provincial master of Aragon held it', apparently meaning that the latter had previously kept it in his own hands.[34] Clear evidence of the practice in the Temple is, however, lacking.

The commander of a convent occupied a dual role. He was in the first place the head of a community which followed a partly military, partly monastic, way of life. As such he had the duty of leading the members of his convent in the field and of seeing that both there and inside the convent the Rule and Customs of the Temple were observed. He had the right to punish those who contravened regulations, though if he was a sergeant commander he apparently could not deprive a knight of his habit.[35] In the same way a sergeant commander seems to have been unable to admit a knight into the Order, and apparently at the end of the thirteenth century permission had to be obtained from the provincial master before a commander could accept any new recruits to the Order.[36] A commander was secondly in charge of the rights and property attached to his convent and was responsible for their administration, although there is evidence which indicates that in the later thirteenth century and in the early years of the fourteenth, when the Temple was facing increasing financial demands, decisions about methods of exploiting property were taken by the provincial master: in a number of documents of this period it is stated that land was being granted to tenants by commanders on the order or with the licence of the provincial master;[37] and in 1305 the provincial master referred in a letter to a request by the commander of Mallorca for permission to 'give and establish certain lands and possessions'.[38] Out of the revenues of the property he administered a commander was obliged to make an annual payment or responsion to the head of the province.[39]

In carrying out these duties some commanders in the early thirteenth century had the aid of a sub-commander. This office is to be distinguished from that of lieutenant of a commander; the latter was merely a temporary replacement, appointed either when the post of commander was vacant or when a commander was absent from his house or wished to set up a delegate to act for him in a particular matter. In most cases the office of sub-commander is mentioned for the first time in the early years of the thirteenth century: at Barbará in 1200, at Grañena in 1203, and at Boquiñeni in 1211.[40] It came into being when the Templars were rapidly extending their property and possibly also increasing in numbers, and although it is nowhere stated what duties a sub-commander performed the office was clearly a sign of an organization expanding to meet growing needs. But in the more static conditions which characterized the middle and later decades of the thirteenth century the office must have been found superfluous, for it disappears from most convents in the fourth decade of the century, and the last reference to it is at Ambel in 1242.[41]

Whether there was a sub-commander or not, the head of a convent was assisted in the administration of the possessions of his house by an official who in Catalonia was always called a 'chamberlain' (*camerarius, cambrero*); this title was also used in Aragon from the middle of the thirteenth century, but until that time the term 'keeper of the keys' (*claviger, clavero*) was employed there. The nature of the surviving evidence does not permit a close examination of the work of these officials. The only traces of their activity are a few inventories which they drew up of the possessions of their convents and the stipulation contained in some charters that the chamberlain's permission was to be obtained before tenants could make alterations to property held of the Order.[42] It may be assumed, however, that their position corresponded to that of the cellarers in Cistercian houses, and the term 'cellarer' was itself used at Villel in the sixth decade of the thirteenth century as an alternative to 'chamberlain'.[43] The financial and administrative organization of a Templar convent, like that of a Cistercian monastery, was simple. With a partial exception in the case of property assigned by donors specifically to the Order's chapels,[44] there was no decentralization of control and no obedientiary system.

Chamberlains, like the heads of convents, usually held office for only a short period. The names of thirty-three are recorded at the house of Zaragoza in the thirteenth century, while twenty-five are known at Tortosa in that period and eighteen at Castellote, although the lists for the last two convents are by no means complete.[45] A few Templars moved as chamberlains from one house to another—Peter of Lena was chamberlain at Tortosa at the end of 1271 and at Castellote from 1272 to 1274—but the rapid change in personnel was usually effected by giving the office to various brothers within a convent and if necessary, in a small convent or presumably if Templars of administrative ability were lacking, by giving a brother several terms of office: at Zaragoza, Spañol was chamberlain from 1248 to 1249 and from 1255 to 1257; Bartholomew held the post in 1255 and from 1260 until 1263; and Dominic of Alcorisa was in office from 1264 to 1266 and from 1270 until 1274. The object of this policy was presumably to avoid placing a permanent burden of administration on one brother, but it must have provided a further obstacle to efficient administration, especially when a new chamberlain and a new commander took up their posts at about the same time.

Other Templars concerned with the administration of the property of a convent had more particular responsibilities. Within a commandery brothers were often placed in charge of dependent groups of estates and were responsible for the day-to-day administration of them: transactions such as the granting of land to new tenants were still conducted by the head of the convent. As has been seen, during the period of Templar expansion some of those placed in charge of groups of estates in time became the heads of new convents, but most remained as subordinate administrators. These minor officials were frequently called commanders or preceptors, but these titles were not universal; occasionally they were known as sub-commanders[46] and in a very few instances they were referred to as chamberlains,[47] while in the Templar Customs, in which they were assigned two mounts, they were called *freres casaliers*.[48] The number of these dependencies varied in different commanderies and at different times in the same commandery. The convent of Miravet had at times subordinate commanders of Nonaspe, Algars, Gandesa, and the *villa* of Miravet itself.[49] The Templars at Monzón similarly had a commander of the *villa*, besides commanders of La Ribera, La Litera,[50] Chalamera, Cofita, Estiche, and Zaidín, and a Templar —not called commander—at Armentera. By contrast, some convents had merely one or two dependencies. The only one subject to Boquiñeni was at Pradilla, and the commanders of Cabañas and Razazol were the only subordinate officials of Novillas in the thirteenth century. These officials spent part of their time on the estates which they administered, away from their convents. In some cases they were accompanied by several other Templars and a small subordinate community was formed. This appears to have happened at Cofita, for the priest who was given the living of Crespano in 1299 was promised food in the Templar house of

Cofita 'as is given to one of the brothers who live there';[51] and from the middle of the thirteenth century the house of Barcelona, which was then a dependency of Palau, had its own chapel and its own chaplain.[52] On the other hand, some of the Templars placed in charge of estates appear to have lived almost alone. This is implied by a complaint made in 1264 that the bishop of Lérida's men had expelled the brother and his servant who were staying at the Order's house at Armentera[53] and by a reference to the horse 'which the brother who is at Chivert rides', found in an inventory of the possessions of the convent at Peñíscola drawn up in 1302.[54] Yet it was not necessary for these Templars to be absent from their convents as continuously as Templar chaplains who were granted livings at a distance from their houses; and the rather scanty evidence which survives about these local administrative officials suggests that terms of office were short. Between 1294 and 1307, for example, William of Passenant, Peter of Montesquíu, and Bernard Belissén all had periods of office in Segriá and Urgel, which were dependencies of Gardeny.[55]

The relationship between these Templar officials and the lay administrators on Templar estates varied. On some occasions a subordinate commander's area of authority coincided with that of the lay justiciar or bailiff of a town. The commander of the *villa* of Monzón was concerned with Templar rights merely within the town, as were the lay justiciar and bailiff there. At the end of the thirteenth and beginning of the fourteenth centuries there were similarly both a Templar commander and a lay bailiff at Espluga de Francolí, which was subject to the convent of Barbará.[56] This situation appears to have existed, however, only in the more important townships under Templar lordship. Elsewhere a Templar official had a number of lay bailiffs and justiciars under his control. The commander of La Ribera, for example, had authority over the lay bailiffs of all the Templar lordships along the banks of the Cinca; and in a letter to James II Mascharos Garideyl in 1308 explained that the commander of Miravet used to establish lay bailiffs in all the places subject to Miravet, such as Gandesa, Corbera, and Nonaspe, and a brother of the Temple, who spent most of his time at Gandesa, was placed in charge of the bailiffs.[57] Alternatively the bailiff of a small town could be made directly responsible to the head of a convent, without the intervention of any subordinate commander.

Other members of a convent were sometimes assigned administrative duties of a more limited importance, such as the management of irrigation canals or mills. The title of commander was also occasionally given to these officials. A brother John was in charge of the canals at Pina from 1238 to 1255[58] and Peter of Montañana, a member of the convent of Monzón, was in 1269 the commander of the mills of Almerge,[59] while in the second half of the thirteenth century the house of Gardeny also had a Templar in charge of some of its mills.[60] But minor administrative tasks were not always performed by members of the Order. There was a flexibility in the employment of Templars and outsiders in the administration of the Order's property.

Besides these administrative officials, there was normally also a chaplain in each convent. In the Temple's early years there were apparently no clerical members of the Order, and the spiritual needs of the brothers were attended to by secular priests: the phrase 'chaplains or others staying for a period', found in article four of the Latin Rule, implies that priests and clerks were at first merely attached to the Order without becoming members.[61] In the documents of the later 1130s, however, references to clerical members begin to occur,[62] and the right to admit clerics was confirmed in 1139 by Innocent II in the bull *Omne datum optimum*.[63] In that privilege the pope stated that clerics could be received into the Temple after a probationary period of a year; they were to be subject to the Master and their share in the government and administration of the Order was to be determined by the Master and brothers;[64] and their food, dress, and bedding were to be the same as those of other brothers, except that they were to wear tight-fitting habits.[65]

Yet in practice the Temple may not have been able to attract a sufficient number of clerical recruits to enable every convent to have a chaplain who was a member of the Order. Although in some houses, such as Gardeny and Mas-Deu,[66] there were on occasion several Templar chaplains, for many convents no continuous list of Templar chaplains can be compiled, even where comparatively full evidence survives. And in some cases those referred to as chaplains of convents were secular priests: in 1280, for example, the cleric who was called 'chaplain of the castle' at Villel was not a Templar.[67] There may at times therefore have been a shortage of priestly brothers in the Order, as there was in the Hospital in the thirteenth century.[68] Nevertheless, the clerical members of the Order belong essentially at this level of Templar organization, for there is no evidence of an ecclesiastical hierarchy in the Temple, such as is encountered in the Hospital.[69] Although Honorius III granted special powers of absolution to the chaplain of the chief house in a province,[70] this does not imply the existence of several ecclesiastical ranks within the Order.

The powers of confession and absolution exercised by Templar chaplains in the Order's convents were considerable. They could hear the confessions of Templar servants as well as those of the brothers;[71] but the claims in the Templar Customs that 'they have from the pope greater powers than an archbishop to absolve brothers' and that they had power 'to absolve brothers always according to the quality and quantity of the offence' are not accurate.[72] The Customs elsewhere mention certain offences for which Templar chaplains could not give absolution,[73] and some of the limitations of their powers are further explained in papal bulls. They could not absolve a Templar who had killed a Christian; nor could they grant absolution when there had been fighting between brothers involving the shedding of blood. The right of giving absolution when there was no bloodshed was granted by Honorius III in 1223 to the chaplain of the chief house in a province,[74] and at least during Clement IV's pontificate this right was enjoyed by all Templar chaplains.[75] By these decrees the papacy was granting to Templar chaplains the same powers over members of the Order as abbots enjoyed over their monks. The third offence mentioned in the Customs for which they could not grant absolution was assault on a member of another religious order or on a clerk or priest. This may again refer to cases in which there was mutilation or bloodshed, for although Honorius III and Alexander IV reissued a decree of Innocent III which stated that offences of this kind which did not involve mutilation or bloodshed or the striking of a bishop or abbot could be dealt with by bishops,[76] the same two popes allowed Templar chaplains to absolve members of the Order for crimes of this nature committed by brothers before they had joined the Temple, unless the offences were of the more serious character mentioned above;[77] and it would be strange if the Order's chaplains could absolve Templars for certain offences only if they had been committed before the culprits had been received into the Order.

A Templar chaplain could lastly not absolve a brother who was found to have entered the Temple by simony or to have concealed that he was in orders.[78]

Despite the grant of these powers of absolution to Templar chaplains, it was not the papal intention that Templars should of necessity be absolved by them. The bull *Omne datum optimum* allowed brothers to be absolved by any 'honest' priest,[79] and in 1238 Gregory IX permitted those in captivity in the East to be absolved by Franciscans or by Jacobite priests.[80] The Temple itself, like many other religious orders,[81] placed some restrictions on freedom of confession, but the charge made against the Order that it compelled its members to confess only to their own chaplains was unfounded.[82] The Customs state merely that a Templar should confess to a Templar chaplain, if one was available, unless permission had been obtained to go to another priest.[83] The statements made by Templars at their trial show that—although some did not understand the regulation—the ruling in the Customs was normally followed. Bartholomew of Torre, a chaplain at Mas-Deu, said that if a Templar chaplain was not available, Templars should go to a Dominican or Franciscan, or if no friar was at hand to a secular priest.[84] The same opinion was voiced by many other Templars, while in the course of the inquiries conducted in Aragon after the arrest of the Templars, two Franciscans of Lérida testified that they had often heard confessions from Templars.[85]

The Templar chaplains' main work consisted in their religious duties in the Order's convents, but their time was not always exclusively devoted to these. They sometimes acted as scribes, particularly before the spread of the system of public notaries,[86] and in the thirteenth century some became vicars of churches under Templar patronage. This happened especially in and around Monzón, and also in other towns and villages where Templar convents were established, such as Novillas, Boquiñeni, and Miravet.[87] Most Templar vicars could thus live in one of the Order's convents; they usually avoided the life of isolation which the papacy saw as one of the dangers arising from the grant of parishes to members of religious orders.[88] Some became involved in administrative work. Towards the end of the thirteenth century the chaplain of the church of the Holy Redeemer at Teruel was placed in charge of the Order's lands there;[89] and although there was generally no obedientiary system, the Templar chaplains of Gardeny had charge of certain lands and revenues assigned to their chapel. The surviving sources show the Gardeny chaplains purchasing property with money bequeathed for the service of the altar or for the endowment of lamps, leasing out the land under their authority, and receiving rents from it.[90] But although the chaplains of Gardeny can thus be seen administering lands which provided revenues for their church, it was often stated that they were acting on the licence of the commander; they did not possess full authority over these properties, and the granting out of such land was sometimes done by the commander of Gardeny himself;[91] in a few documents concerning these properties the chaplain was not even mentioned at all.[92] Whether chaplains in other convents occupied a similar position with regard to such lands is not known.

Templar chaplains, like other officials in a convent, usually held office in the same house only for a short period. Although the Templar William of Albesa was a chaplain at Gardeny from 1208 until 1237,[93] the career of John of Monzón was more typical. In 1260 and 1261 he was chaplain at Villel;[94] in the next year he was transferred to Castellote;[95] in 1264 he was chaplain at Tortosa;[96] and in 1268 he returned to Castellote.[97]

The remaining brothers in a convent participated in the government and administration of their house only in the conventual chapter. This was held weekly: according to the Customs of the Order a chapter was to be convened on the eve of Christmas, Easter, and Pentecost and on every Sunday—except in the octaves of these three festivals—in any place where there were four or more Templars.[98] At such meetings a commander was meant to take the counsel of all present, asking first the advice of the most experienced individually and then that of the rest together.[99] These chapters were according to the Customs instituted in order that brothers might confess their faults there and amend them;[100] the chapter was considered primarily as a chapter of faults, such as was held in other religious communities,[101] and the section in the Customs on the holding of a chapter is mainly concerned with its judicial activities which are described in some detail.[102] Brothers were expected to confess their faults voluntarily, but if they failed to do so, accusations could be made against them, although a charge could not be sustained on the accusation of only one brother. When more than one Templar was prepared to bring a charge the commander could, if he suspected malice, question the accusers separately. To rebut a charge an accused was allowed to call upon brothers who could testify in his defence. The Customs do not elaborate all points of procedure, but it is made clear that the sentences imposed—which in the Temple ranged from a day's fasting and a beating to expulsion from the Order[103]—rested on a majority decision in the chapter. The Templar Customs give little information about the other work of a chapter, although they do state that the admission of new members had to take place there, and the evidence given by Templars after their arrest shows that this ruling was normally observed.[104] Presumably any matter that concerned the convent could be raised at the chapter. But conventual chapters in the Temple occupied a much more subordinate role than those in the Dominican Order, where the chapter elected the head of a convent and reported on his conduct.[105] In the Temple, authority in a convent rested to a large extent in the hands of the commander; and it is possible that in some convents his was the only seal, for although references occasionally occur to conventual seals,[106] some documents issued by commanders and their convents were sealed with the commander's seal and not that of the convent.[107] Nor is there any evidence of attempts to ensure that a commander did not have complete and undisputed control over his seal, as occurred in some other communities.[108] The nature of the Temple in fact made some centralization of authority inevitable. In the field the need for clear and decisive leadership made it necessary for members of a convent to be strictly subordinated to their commander and for the latter to carry out the commands of the provincial master. In the military sphere a commander was inevitably responsible to the master rather than to members of his convent, and the same was true in the economic sphere, where commanders were further responsible to the provincial master for the payment of dues owed by convents. Yet although the character of the Temple demanded that authority should be centralized in these respects, a commander usually consulted at least some members of his convent on matters concerning the administration of his commandery: documents were only very rarely issued on the authority of a commander alone.[109]

How many Templars there were in most Aragonese convents is

not known. In the Teutonic Order, whose customs were taken mainly from the Temple, a convent was expected to contain the common minimum of thirteen members,[110] and this may have been the rule in the Temple as well. But it is not clear whether Templar convents in fact usually housed as many brothers as this or how many Templars there were in the *Corona de Aragón* as a whole. In some countries the inquiries made before the dissolution of the Temple have been used to provide numerical evidence, and these have usually revealed small numbers.[111] Such sources can, of course, provide only minimum numbers, for it is not known how large a proportion of the Templars was arrested and interrogated. Certainly in Aragon some attempted to flee. Peter of San Justo, the commander of Peñíscola, was taken when trying to escape by sea[112] and three others who had tried to flee were handed over to the king by the bailiff of Tortosa.[113] Others may have been more successful for in the years following the arrest of the Templars there were rumours that some members of the Order had entered the service of the king of Granada.[114] In the Aragonese province a full record of those who were arrested survives only for the house of Mas-Deu, twenty-five of whose members were interrogated in 1310.[115] This figure suggests that Aragonese houses contained more Templars than those in other western countries, and this is possible in view of the Templars' participation in the struggle against the Moors; but Mas-Deu may not have been typical, since it was the only convent in Roussillon and possessed a considerable number of dependencies. The only other numerical evidence which exists for Aragon from the time of the dissolution of the Order is a list giving the names of 109 former Templars who were paid pensions; but as only fourteen of the twenty-five Templars interrogated in Roussillon received payments the list clearly cannot be used even to give an indication of the total number of Templars arrested.[116]

The references in documents to those who gave counsel to a commander have also been used for estimating numbers,[117] but this source is open to the criticism that it is often not clear whether all members of a convent are being mentioned by name. Three forms of wording are common. The first indicates that there are other brothers of the convent not mentioned individually: the commander acts with the advice of those named 'and of other brothers'. The second is ambiguous, merely listing names without

stating whether there are others. The third might seem to imply
that all members of a convent are being named: the commander
acts with the counsel 'of our brothers . . . namely . . .'; but it can
be shown that even this formula does not provide reliable evidence of the total numbers in a house.[118] This source, like the
inquiries, can therefore produce only minimum figures. They are
usually very low and bear no necessary relation to actual numbers,
although they do suggest that the latter varied in different convents. The greatest number of Templars at the convent of Mas-
Deu mentioned in any single document in the Aragonese archives
is seventeen, compared with ten at Castellote and five at Boquiñeni.[119] The greatest number of brothers without office who can
be traced in any one year at Gardeny is twenty-two, at Zaragoza
eight, and at Boquiñeni four.[120] It is further significant that in the
second half of the thirteenth century, when documents were
tending to become fuller and more detailed, the number of
brothers who can be traced in some convents, such as Boquiñeni,
decreases, for there is other evidence of declining numbers shortly
before the dissolution of the Temple. To a request made about
the year 1300 by the commander of Mallorca that some Templars
should be sent out to the island, the provincial master Berenguer
of Cardona replied

About the brothers which you ask us to send you, we must inform
you that we have none whom we can send.[121]

The same answer was given to a similar demand by Arnold of
Banyuls, the commander of Peñíscola.[122] The provincial master
was, however, ready to allow the commander of Mallorca to
create new brothers according to the needs of his convent and
this, together with the requests themselves, suggests that numbers
were not being limited for economic reasons, as happened in many
monasteries in the thirteenth century;[123] the decline in numbers
is to be explained rather by difficulties in recruiting at a time when
the Aragonese *reconquista* was complete and when enthusiasm for
crusades was waning.[124]

Although the records of the trial of the Templars are of only
limited value for calculating total numbers, they are of use for
estimating the proportions of knights, sergeants, and chaplains in
the Order's convents at the time of the Templars' arrest. At Mas-
Deu there were only three knights and four chaplains, compared

with eighteen sergeants, and of the thirty-two Templars mentioned
in a fragmentary record of an interrogation by the bishop of
Lérida in 1310 nine were knights, four were chaplains, and nineteen were sergeants.[125] Again, the majority of the Templars who
were being paid pensions in 1319 were sergeants.[126] The numerical
preponderance of sergeants in the Temple indicated by this
evidence is borne out by that drawn from other countries, with
the exception of Cyprus, where knights were in the majority.[127]
In the early fourteenth century the Temple was thus not predominantly a knightly order. Although most convents had a
knight as commander, most of those under his authority were
sergeants.

Yet while at the beginning of the fourteenth century most of
the Templars in a convent were sergeants, it is difficult to ascertain
whether this had earlier been the case. The only Templars whose
ranks were usually stated in documents were the chaplains; on a
few occasions brothers were described as *fratres milites*, but it can
be shown that Templars who are known to have been knights
were not always called *milites*.[128] It is further not even clear
whether in the Order's early years the distinction between knight
and sergeant was made. Bloch has argued that the Templar Rule
provides evidence of two ranks of fighting men in the Temple,
distinguished by clothing, equipment, and social status.[129] But it
may be questioned whether those whom he places in the second
rank—the *armigeri* of the Rule, who wore black or brown
clothing—were in fact Templars, for in article twenty-one it is
stated that some of those who should have worn dark clothing
had assumed white habits, and thus

have arisen . . . certain pseudo-brothers and married men and others
saying that they are of the Temple, when they are of the world.[130]

The term *miles*, moreover, is used in the Rule not to signify one
rank within the Order but as the equivalent of *frater*. On several
occasions the phrase *miles aut frater* is used,[131] and in the later
French translation, made when there were sergeants in the Order,
the word *miles* is translated as *frere chevalier* only in one clause
where the allowance of horses and servants mentioned is the same
as that later given to the knights;[132] elsewhere it is rendered as
*frere*, and in this way a distinction is made in the translation
between brothers of the Temple and the *armigeri*.[133] But if this was

the situation at the time when the Rule was compiled, the distinction of knight and sergeant was introduced soon afterwards, for in 1139 Innocent II could refer to 'brothers, both knights and sergeants'.[134]

The admission of sergeants implied really the establishment of two further ranks in the Order, for a distinction was made between sergeants-at-arms and *freres des mestiers*. The sergeants-at-arms were in some ways similar to the knights. They were fighting brothers and when they were living in a convent they were concerned with administration and the care of their horses and equipment; and in the Customs of the Order knights and sergeants-at-arms are sometimes grouped together under the title *freres du couvent*, as distinct from the *freres des mestiers*.[135] This distinction might seem to suggest that only the knights and sergeants-at-arms had a share in the government of a convent, but this was not so in the West: commanders are often said to be acting with the counsel of brothers who include *freres des mestiers*,[136] and there is occasional evidence of the presence of these brothers at chapter meetings.[137] Yet while there were similarities between the knights and sergeants-at-arms, the latter differed from the knights in dress, equipment, and social status. While knights, for example, wore white habits and were allowed three mounts and an arms-bearer, sergeants-at-arms were dressed in brown and were usually permitted only one mount;[138] and while in the thirteenth century knights had to be of knightly descent and legitimate birth, sergeants were merely required to be of free birth.[139] It may have been the growing stress on the hereditary character of knighthood in fact that led to the acceptance of sergeants-at-arms into the Order; and this step may in turn have made possible the admission of non-military sergeants.

The *freres des mestiers* fought only in an emergency and did not normally possess arms.[140] When they were living in a convent they were usually employed in household or agricultural work. The Templar Customs mention certain household duties performed by these brothers,[141] and further evidence of their activities is provided in the Aragonese sources. These show that those working inside a convent might perform the functions of cook, butler, or porter,[142] or be employed in a particular trade: some houses, such as Monzón, had Templar shoemakers,[143] while Miravet in 1241 had a brother Dominic as tailor,[144] and Monzón at times possessed a Templar smith and tanner.[145] Others were employed on the land. A brother Andico was a gardener at Castellote in 1237,[146] and G. of Albesa in 1212 worked in the vineyards at Gardeny.[147] Some had charge of the Order's farm animals: a brother Ferrer was a cowherd at Miravet in 1228;[148] Arnold of Corbins was 'preceptor of sheep' at Gardeny in 1182;[149] and Templar oxherds are mentioned at Zaragoza and Huesca.[150] Often no more specific title than 'labourer' (*operarius, obrero*) was given, presumably referring to manual workers with no special skill.[151] These *freres des mestiers* were the only members of the Order who normally performed manual labour; the Rule did not oblige all Templars to participate in this activity, and it was done by knights and sergeants-at-arms only as a penance.[152]

In the convent, as in the field, the Templars devoted themselves to practical occupations. The rarity with which Templar *signa* are found on documents suggests that throughout the history of the Order the majority of members were illiterate. Many could have described themselves, as a member of Mas-Deu did at his interrogation, as 'simple and ignorant', and many could have echoed the words of another Templar of the same house who said that his life had been 'given up to the land and the custody of animals'.[153] Meditative reading or literary and intellectual activity could therefore not be expected of them, and those Templars who were literate seem to have devoted little time to these pursuits. In the *Corona de Aragón* no Templar chronicle has survived or is known; and although Olivier—to whom the poem 'Estat aurai lonc temps en pessamen' is ascribed in an early fourteenth-century manuscript—may as Milá claims have been a Catalan Templar,[154] there is no evidence in the Templar archives to support Riquer's suggestion that, because of his knowledge of Pulpís, the troubadour Gerald of Luc may have been a member of the Order.[155] James of Garrigans knew how 'to write shaped letters well and to illuminate with gold' and wrote a book of hours for James II,[156] but he was probably exceptional, for he had been in minor orders before becoming a Templar.[157] The lack of intellectual and literary activity is further apparent from the small number and limited subject-matter of the books mentioned in Templar inventories. In a detailed list of the possessions of the convent of Corbins drawn up in 1299 only sixteen volumes are mentioned.[158] This list also demonstrates the limitations in subject-matter, for of the volumes listed three-quarters were service books, such as missals and psalters, and the rest consisted of two volumes of sermons and two of the lives of saints. Admittedly, the inventories of property seized by the Crown after the arrest of the Templars show that some houses had a wider range of books, although it is not known how they came into the Temple's possession or whether they were actually read.[159] Among eight volumes handed over to the king from Monzón in 1313 were the *Dialogues* of Gregory the Great, the *Exameron* of St. Ambrose, the *Historia Scholastica* of Peter Comestor, and the *Sentences* of Hugh of St. Victor.[160] These lists also refer to a vernacular version of the *Codex* of Justinian and of the *Secreta Secretorum*, then attributed to Aristotle:[161] and the royal officer Mascharos Garideyl reported that he had found a copy of 'lo Theoderich', which must be a version of the Dominican Theoderic's *Chirurgia*,[162] and also a book beginning 'De decayment de cabels', which was probably a translation of John XXI's *Thesaurus pauperum*.[163] Even a copy of part of the *Ars Poetica* was taken into royal hands.[164] But in most cases only one copy of each of these works is known and most convents, like Corbins, appear to have possessed few books other than those needed for the conduct of services: the books from the convent of Peñíscola which were listed in 1311, for example, consisted—apart from several copies of the Rule and Customs—almost entirely of service books.[165] The reference to translations among the books seized by the Crown is not the only evidence which suggests that literate Templars had often only an inadequate knowledge of Latin. The Aragonese Templars also had two translations made of a cartulary containing mainly royal and papal privileges to the Order,[166] and all the known versions of the Rule and Customs in the *Corona de Aragón* were written in the vernacular.[167] Moreover, when the Templars were interrogated after their arrest, it was necessary to explain the charges in the vernacular, even to the chaplains.[168]

Although the daily activities of the Templars were in marked contrast to those of others who followed the regular life, they were fitted when possible into the normal framework provided by the recital of divine office. Nor were services reduced to a minimum for, in addition to the canonical hours and mass, the offices of the Virgin and of the Dead and the gradual psalms before Matins were said.[169] But as most Templars were not in orders their participation in services was limited. They listened in silence to the recital of offices by their chaplains and were merely recommended to say a fixed number of paternosters for each office.[170] They were further excused from attending any additional masses that were said in their chapels, just as they were not obliged to take part in any processions other than the twelve stipulated in the Rule.[171]

Other aspects of the regular life were similarly adapted to suit the needs of the Templars and, apart from the vows of poverty, chastity, and obedience common to all regular clergy, Templar observances were often more like those of regular canons than those of monks. The Order's regulations about food were governed by a concern to ensure that Templars were strong enough to fight. They were allowed to eat meat three times a week, and fasting was limited mainly to Lent, to the period between the Monday before St. Martin in November and Christmas, and to Fridays between All Saints and Easter—very much less than that prescribed in the Benedictine Rule;[172] and Templars were forbidden both in the Rule and in a number of papal decrees to undertake any additional fasts without permission.[173] Silence was enjoined upon the Templars at meal times, but an exception was made for brothers who needed to speak 'through ignorance of signs', and similarly although silence was normally to be maintained after Compline a Templar was allowed to speak to his arms-bearer then, and brothers were also permitted to talk to each other if the military situation demanded it.[174] In matters of dress, the eastern climate was taken into consideration and brothers were allowed to wear linen from Easter to All Saints.[175]

Cistercian influence may, however, be seen in the Rule in the enforcement of a noviciate and possibly also in the prohibition on child oblation,[176] although opposition to this practice was growing throughout the monastic world,[177] and the prohibition in the Rule may be an addition made by the patriarch of Jerusalem.[178] Yet the first of these customs fell into disuse and the second was not fully observed. It was generally admitted by Templars who were interrogated at the beginning of the fourteenth century that individuals received into the Order were considered 'at once as professed brethren'.[179] It is not known how long this had been the custom. The provision for a probationary period was not, as

Curzon claims,[180] omitted when the Rule was translated into French—it was merely moved and attached to the clause concerned with the age of admission to the Order[181]—and at the beginning of the thirteenth century an individual in Aragon was ordered to spend a year as a *donatus* before becoming a full member of the Order: the condition was imposed on Bonsom of Villa in July 1204 at Castellote that

> you are to serve in this house like the other *donati* for one year from this July, and on the completion of that year you are to receive the habit and cross like other brothers.[182]

But no other evidence about the noviciate survives. Possibly, as in the Teutonic Order, it was abandoned because of the need to recruit new members rapidly after heavy losses in battle.[183] This is perhaps what was implied by the Templar William of Tamarite when he said in 1310 that individuals were accepted at once as professed brothers 'so that they can undertake and devote themselves to the exercise of arms against the Saracens'.[184] But clearly the period of noviciate had been discarded long before this and most Templars who were questioned at this time did not know why it had been abandoned; some even thought that it had never existed.[185]

In the prohibition on child oblation, it was stated that parents who wished their sons to enter the Temple should keep them at home until they were of an age when they could bear arms. Entrants were further expected to be old enough to make a final decision for themselves about entry, for the clause was added

> for it is better not to vow in boyhood than to retract violently after becoming a man.

But no definite age limit was fixed and it was left to the discretion of the Templars in a particular locality to determine whether a youth was old enough to be admitted. In practice some convents contained brothers who had been received when they were scarcely old enough either to bear arms or to make a final decision for themselves about entering the Order. Among the Templars interrogated by the bishop of Lérida in 1310 one had joined the Order at the age of twelve and another when only thirteen.[186] On the other hand, there are no clear examples in the *Corona de Aragón* of very young children being formally admitted as *oblati*, to be trained specifically for the profession of Templar, although the practice is found in other countries.[187] Some children did live in the Order's convents in Aragon, but they were apparently, like the young James I, merely being placed in the guardianship of the Temple and in some instances provided with a knightly education. When Peter Sánchez of Sporreto put his son in the wardship of the Templars of Huesca in 1217 for a period of ten years, he stated that the boy was to be free to leave the Huesca convent at the end of that period, and a similar condition was made by a widow, who in 1209 placed her three sons in the care of the commander of Zaragoza.[188] When on another occasion the Catalan noble Peter of Queralt asked the provincial master Berenguer of Cardona to accept the son of one of his knights, the master ordered the commander of Peñíscola to rear the boy 'in good customs . . . as you have been accustomed to do'.[189] It may not have been uncommon for the sons of nobles and knights to spend some time in a Templar convent in this way instead of being placed in a noble household; and as some no doubt later joined the Order, this could help to explain why knights tended to join the Temple at an earlier age than sergeants.[190]

These boys were by no means the only non-Templars who might be encountered in the Order's convents. In all houses there were a certain number of outsiders in the service of the Temple. Many of them took part in the everyday work of a house and some lived in the Templar community.

Templar convents in the first place often housed a considerable number of slaves. The thirteen commanderies for which inventories survive from the year 1289 had an average of twenty each, and Monzón, Miravet, and Gardeny had 49, 45, and 43 respectively; only in the inventory of the house of Calatayud is there no reference to the possession of slaves.[191] All were Moors, although some had been baptized,[192] and almost all were male: in 1289 the convent of Monzón was alone in possessing a female slave. In the inventories and elsewhere slaves were called captives, for in Spain they were usually prisoners either captured in the Peninsula or gained through piracy.[193] Some had no doubt been taken by the Templars themselves—when the provincial master wrote to James II in 1304 about a raid into Granada he mentioned that a number of prisoners had been taken[194]—but in the thirteenth century the Temple acquired many captives through purchase at prices which varied according to the number of Moors available, increasing during intervals between major campaigns and also generally towards the end of the thirteenth century.[195] The frequent purchase of slaves by the Templars illustrates one of the disadvantages of using this kind of labour force—namely, the constant diminution to which it was subject. Slaves were lost not only through death, but also by redemption[196] and through flight, which was perhaps not uncommon, especially when escaped slaves might hope for shelter and aid from the free Moorish population of the country;[197] on the other hand, since Templar slaves were usually male, few slave children could have been born on the Order's estates. But, despite the disadvantages of employing them, slaves were probably necessary in view of the difficulty in some parts of the *Corona de Aragón* of obtaining alternative forms of manpower. These slaves, who were placed in the charge of a Templar sometimes known as the 'keeper of the captives',[198] were probably in many instances not only maintained in Templar convents but also worked in them as household servants; convents like Monzón, however, which had large numbers of slaves—some of them living in Templar dependencies—could scarcely have used them all in this way and it may be argued that slaves were also employed as agricultural labourers.[199]

Templar convents also contained a number of free workers, for while household tasks might be performed by members of the Order, they were also carried out by non-Templars. There was no uniformity in the practice of household employment; the calling-in of outsiders apparently depended on the needs of a particular convent at a particular time. Huesca had a non-Templar cook in 1224, as did Gardeny in 1262.[200] Lay butlers can also be traced at the latter house, together with porters, a baker in 1238, and a water-carrier in 1225.[201] While some convents had a brother as tailor, at Palau in 1272 the monopoly of tailoring for the convent was granted to a *confrater*, Bernard of Gilida.[202] Similarly at the beginning of the fourteenth century Raymond of Sumerano was being paid two *cahíces* of wheat annually for acting as barber to the house of Gardeny.[203] It cannot be ascertained how often laymen were used for work of this kind, for these employees are encountered in the sources only as occasional witnesses to documents. The arms-bearers of the Templars, on the other hand, were always laymen. They similarly appear as witnesses and are never given the title of 'brother'. Some in fact were used by the king to guard the Templars after the latter's arrest.[204]

From lists of witnesses it is clear that there was also a considerable number of secular priests and clerks in the service of the Temple, who often lived in its convents. In the last decade of the thirteenth century more than a dozen such clerks and priests can be traced at Gardeny.[205] They were no doubt needed in part to assist the Templar chaplains in their duties or to replace them in convents which had no Templar chaplains of their own, but they were probably also increasingly required for the celebration of masses for the Order's benefactors. Although it would have been to the Temple's financial advantage to have these masses celebrated by members of the Order, rather than by secular priests, the numbers of Templar chaplains were clearly insufficient for this purpose, and only once was it stated that the chantry priest should be a Templar.[206] On other occasions—either when the founder of a chantry sought to provide for members of his family by decreeing that the chaplain should be a relation[207] or when no special qualifications were stipulated—secular priests were no doubt usually employed. Whether the latter lived and were maintained in Templar houses probably depended in part on the nature of the endowment. A chaplain who was assigned a fixed salary by the founder of a chantry or one who was himself assigned the lands given for his maintenance presumably did not usually reside in a Templar house.[208] On the other hand, when the Templars were asked to make general provision for a chaplain out of an endowment granted to the Order, they probably preferred for financial reasons to provide maintenance in a convent rather than pay a salary on which a priest could live; and in some cases it is clear that this was done.[209] This was possible when, as in most instances, the masses for which the Temple was responsible were celebrated in the Order's chapels; but it was sometimes stipulated that the masses should be said elsewhere and in some cases for reasons of distance chantry priests could not live in Templar houses. The chaplain who was to celebrate masses for the soul of Peter of Alcalá in a church at Pertusa could scarcely have been maintained in any of the Order's establishments.[210] In some other instances the Templars may have preferred to provide maintenance outside a convent because a chantry priest was married. Certainly some of the clerics in the Temple's service are known to have had families and were assigned houses in which to live; and the wording of documents suggests that this situation was not exceptional.[211]

As most of the Templars were illiterate and as their chaplains could not draw up all the Order's documents, scribes were employed by some convents in the twelfth and early thirteenth centuries. At Novillas in the middle of the twelfth century a scribe named Bernard agreed to draw up Templar documents for a period of five weeks each year after Michaelmas; during this time he received his food from the Order.[212] Zaragoza and Huesca are two other houses where notaries can be traced at the end of the twelfth and in the early decades of the thirteenth centuries.[213] But not all convents engaged scribes in this way. Templar documents were drawn up by a wide variety of people. Some were written by secular clerks living in the Order's convents: Peter of Zaidín wrote documents for Gardeny between 1247 and 1254, calling himself 'deacon and scribe of Gardeny';[214] others were drawn up by local parish priests and chaplains.[215] With the spread of the system of public notaries, the Temple began towards the middle of the thirteenth century to use these extensively, though not exclusively; and in places under Templar lordship the Order could stipulate that the notary should draw up documents for it free of charge.[216] The only house which had its own scribe in the second half of the thirteenth century was Gardeny, where at least from 1260 the Templars had their own public notary, even though Gardeny came within the boundaries of Lérida;[217] and it maintained this privilege until the time of the Templars' arrest, despite opposition in 1299 from the court and *paceres* of Lérida.[218]

While some of those who were employed in Templar convents were paid, others gave their services freely, as did some knights and some of those who worked on the Order's estates. Reference is made to these unpaid helpers in a papal bull which speaks of

your [the Templars'] priests and laymen, of whom some serve you freely and others for money,[219]

but it is not easy in practice to distinguish those who gave their services permanently without pay. They cannot be identified through terminology, for there was no attempt to achieve precision in the use of terms: although it has been argued that the word *donatus* or *donado* describes those who gave themselves to the Temple and participated in its life without actually taking vows,[220] the term was in fact often used of men who were merely entering into bonds of confraternity with the Order, and at least on some occasions nothing more was implied by the term *specialis donatus*.[221] A permanent unpaid servant can therefore be identified with certainty only if the sources provide a full description of his condition and activities. This is never done, but in a few cases sufficient information is given to make an identification probable, as in the case of Bartholomew of Tarba at Zaragoza in 1224.[222] He gave the Temple all his possessions, but retained for life a house and his movables. He received his food and drink in the Templar convent in the city and thus lived outside the convent but received his meals in it. This description at first sight resembles that of a *confrater* with a corrody, but the agreement between him and the Temple contains the clause

they [the Templars] are not to delegate me in town or outside it in any way without my consent nor transfer me from the aforesaid house,

and this suggests that he was in the service of the Order and was ensuring that he would not be obliged to do work which he did not like or be sent away from Zaragoza. The kind of work which the Temple might have asked of him outside the city included supervision of Templar lands; that unpaid servants were sometimes employed in this capacity is suggested, though not proved, by the wording of a document drawn up in 1222, in which the commander of Ambel's lieutenant in Tarazona is described as a *donado*.[223] A further example comes from Miravet, where in 1228 Peter of Luco gave himself to the Temple as a *conversus* and *donatus*.[224] He granted to the Order all his possessions, although the donation was not to be immediately effective. He also made the proviso that

if by chance, which God forbid, my wife complains to the aforesaid house and I am forced to leave your house, the aforesaid house is to have 500s.J. worth of goods . . . and if my wife dies before me, I will immediately enter the Order and receive the habit.

Peter of Luco seems to have had the desire to join the Temple, could not do so because he was married, and therefore entered its service as a layman.[225] The case of Iñigo Sánchez of Sporreto at Huesca appears to have been similar. In 1207 with his wife and son he made a donation to the Temple;[226] in 1214 he was a *donatus* and seems from the way in which he is mentioned to have been taking part in the life of the convent of Huesca;[227] and in the next year he became a brother, presumably after his wife had died.[228] These examples give little precise information about conditions of service and there could probably be variations in the terms agreed to, but they do suggest that the permanent unpaid servants of the Temple differed in character from the Cistercian *conversi*, who were subject to more rigorous regulations.[229]

Men giving temporary unpaid service are mentioned several times in the Rule of the Temple, and it seems to have been expected not only that the Order would satisfy its need of chaplains and servants in this way, but also that knights would give temporary service.[230] It was perhaps hoped that crusaders would stay in the East for a period and spend that time with the Order. Certainly in the early years of the Temple in Aragon it was not uncommon for nobles to promise service in the Peninsula against the Moors for a year. It has been seen how Raymond Berenguer IV and at least twenty-six nobles promised to serve for that length of time in ?1134,[231] and in 1148 García Ortiz, the lord of Zaragoza, spent a year with the Templars at Corbins.[232] At about the same time Peter of Piguera promised that if he recovered from wounds which he had received he would serve for the same period, and Iñigo of Rada when ill made a similar agreement.[233] Although this kind of service may especially have attracted young nobles and knights who were without responsibilities, clearly not all those who fought for a period with the Temple fell into this category. This form of knightly service may, however, have been characteristic only of the early years of the Order's history, since there are no further examples of it in Aragon after the middle years of the twelfth century and since the later Customs of the Order do not mention it. But there are indications that some kinds of temporary unpaid service were still being given in the thirteenth century. Innocent III in 1206 issued a bull directed against those who undertook to serve the Order for a period and then left before the term had expired;[234] and Gregory IX in 1227 ordered prelates not to hinder any of their clergy who wished to give unpaid service to the Temple for a year or two; he decreed that during such a period priests should not be deprived of their benefices and ecclesiastical revenues.[235] But priests may have been attracted particularly to such service by the hope of the Templar patronage which it could bring. The Order might give a priest one of its livings or petition the pope to provide him to a benefice.[236]

Besides those who gave their services to the Temple, probably many of the individuals who received corrodies from the Order either lived in Templar houses or at least received food and drink there, although the Templars were wary of allowing women into their convents. When Dominica of Sieste was promised food and drink by the commander of Zaragoza in 1248 he undertook to provide her with a house in which she could live, near to the Templar chapel.[237]

Maintenance was also given in Templar convents to the poor. The Rule and Customs provided for both regular and occasional almsgiving. In the Rule it was stipulated that all broken bread left after meals should be given to the poor or to servants and that altogether a tenth of the bread used in a house should be assigned to the poor.[238] The later Customs go further in stating that from the meat given to two brothers there should be enough left over to feed two paupers, while the house in which a provincial master was staying was obliged to feed three extra men.[239] Besides this regular almsgiving there were occasional charities. When a brother died one poor man was to be fed for forty days, and on the death of a person who was serving with the Order for a limited period a poor man was to receive food for seven days.[240] Old clothes were to be given to the poor, and on Maundy Thursday in each house thirteen paupers were to be washed and were to be given two loaves of bread, new shoes, and twopence each.[241] The office of almoner is frequently mentioned in the Rule and Customs and in some cases this official appears to have been assigned a separate building.[242] This and other references[243] show that alms were not just to be distributed at the door. The poor were to be fed inside Templar convents.

Although the office of almoner is referred to in Aragon only in three documents belonging to the convent of Boquiñeni,[244] it is clear that the Templars in the *Corona de Aragón* did not neglect the obligation of almsgiving. The inventories which survive from the year 1289 show that the convent of Gardeny allocated corn 'for alms, namely the tenth of bread', while the houses of Monzón and Huesca also set aside corn to be used for almsgiving.[245]

Further evidence of almsgiving comes from the time of the arrest of the Templars. In a letter to James II the commander of Mas-Deu in December 1307 asserted that alms were given daily by his own convent and three times a week by the Templars at Gardeny; he further maintained that 'at Miravet, as not so many Christians come there as to other places, alms are given to Christians and to Saracens'; and he also quoted the numbers of poor—undoubtedly exaggerated—who had been supported at Monzón and Gardeny.[246] If the validity of a claim made by the Templars at that time may be doubted, more certain evidence from the same period is provided by a royal writ issued in 1308, in which James II ordered that the alms formerly given by the Temple at Gardeny should still be distributed to the poor, the Dominicans, and the Franciscans.[247] There appears therefore to have been little substance in the charge made against the Templars at the beginning of the fourteenth century that alms were not given by the Order as they should have been.[248]

There was probably more truth, however, in the further charge that the Templars did not provide hospitality, for almsgiving appears usually not to have been accompanied by the care of the sick in Templar houses or by the dispensing of hospitality to travellers, although the Order was of course obliged at times to entertain the Aragonese king and some of his officials. The only provision in the Rule and Customs concerning hospitality to travellers is that the brothers who guided and protected pilgrims in the Holy Land should give food, transport, and shelter to those in need, but there is no evidence to indicate that this was a normal function of the Templars elsewhere.[249] In the Templar Rule and Customs there are no clauses concerned with the care of sick laymen, such as are found in the Rules of the Hospital and the Teutonic Order; the latter on this point imitated the Hospital and not the Temple.[250] The office of infirmarer is admittedly frequently referred to in the Templar Rule and Customs, but all the references concern the care of sick Templars.[251] It may therefore be presumed that the infirmarer mentioned in 1205, 1212, and 1231 at Gardeny—the only Aragonese house which is recorded as having this official—was concerned with sick members of the Order.[252] Certainly the infirmary of the Gardeny convent must be distinguished from the house of the sick which in a thirteenth-century document is stated to be

near Gardeny,[253] for the latter hospital is elsewhere referred to as
'the sick of St. Lazarus living close to the house of Gardeny'.[254]
In England, two Templar convents housed the sick and infirm
brethren from the whole country, and it is possible that the
infirmary at Gardeny was used for a similar purpose.[255] But while
Templar convents seem not to have provided for the sick, they
nevertheless contained a wide variety of men, and apart from the
Templars themselves were frequented by laymen employed there,
by those who received maintenance there, and by the poor who
sought alms at the Templar table. A Templar convent was by no
means an isolated community of warrior-monks, living away
from the world.

## NOTES

1. These were restored in the seventeenth century: F. Carreras y Candi,
'Excursions per la Catalunya aragonesa y provincia d'Osca', *Butlletí del Centre
Excursionista de Catalunya*, xviii (1908), 193–7; cf. J. Puig i Cadafalch, *L'arqui-
tectura romànica a Catalunya*, iii (Barcelona, 1918), 424–5, 578.

2. J. M. Quadrado, *Recuerdos y bellezas de España: Aragón* (Barcelona, 1844),
p. 290; M. de la Sala-Valdés, *Estudios históricos y artísticos de Zaragoza* (Zaragoza,
1933), p. 300. The Templar cemetery in Zaragoza, however, was in the parish
of St. Mary: AHN, cód. 468, pp. 21–2, doc. 29; see below, p. 380.

3. Cf. R. del Arco, *Catálogo monumental de España: Huesca* (Madrid, 1942),
i. 137.

4. It is last encountered in 1185: ACA, parch. Alfonso II, nos. 381, 382. The
term was used in the same way elsewhere by the Templars and also by the
Hospitallers: C. Erdmann, 'Der Kreuzzugsgedanke in Portugal', *Historische
Zeitschrift*, cxli (1929), 41, note 1; Lees, *Records*, pp. lxiii–lxiv; *Cartulaire de la
commanderie de Richerenches de l'Ordre du Temple (1136–1214)*, ed. Marquis de
Ripert-Monclar (Avignon, 1907), p. cxlviii; Delaville, *Hospitaliers*, p. 303.

5. e.g. Miravet.

6. Michelet, *Procès*; Villanueva, *Viage*, v. 226–32, doc. 9 (on the interpretation
of this document, see below, p. 299, note 126); Finke, *Papsttum*, ii. 364–78,
doc. 157; A. Mercati, 'Interrogatorio di Templari a Barcellona (1311)',
*Spanische Forschungen der Görresgesellschaft: Gesammelte Aufsätze zur Kultur-
geschichte Spaniens*, vi (1937), 246–51.

7. The sergeant P. of Lobera was commander of Selma in 1307, and Pascal of
Alfaro and Bernard Belissén, who were in charge of Añesa in 1301 and 1307
respectively, were similarly sergeant commanders. The other sergeant commander of this period, Berenguer Guamir, had a more important post as
commander of Barcelona.

8. Offices in the Hospital could similarly be granted either for life or for a term: see, for example, Delaville, *Cartulaire*, iii. 529, doc. 4022.

9. ACA, parch. James II, no. 2260; see below, p. 414.

10. When the provincial master Berenguer of Cardona was in Cyprus on one occasion, he received several petitions for the commanderies of Corbins and Gardeny: ACA, CRD Templarios, no. 247.

11. ACA, CRD Templarios, no. 86.

12. Ibid.

13. ACA, reg. 81, fol. 76–76$^v$.

14. ACA, reg. 82, fol. 47$^v$.

15. *Règle*, p. 103, art. 127; J. Delaville Le Roulx, 'Un nouveau manuscrit de la Règle du Temple', *Annuaire-bulletin de la Société de l'Histoire de France*, xxvi (1889), 200.

16. See below, p. 318.

17. AHN, Montesa, sign. 542–C, fols. 30$^v$–31; see below, p. 318.

18. AHN, cód. 466, p. 264, doc. 283; Montesa, sign. 542–C, fols. 30$^v$–31.

19. AGP, parch. Gardeny, no. 572; AHN, Montesa, sign. 542–C, fols. 30$^v$–31.

20. AGP, parch. Gardeny, no. 1296; at the beginning of August James of Timor was commander: parch. Gardeny, no. 1890.

21. AHN, cód. 471, pp. 326–7, doc. 259; San Juan, leg. 308, doc. 6.

22. M. Perlbach, *Die Statuten des Deutschen Ordens* (Halle, 1890), pp. 59–60.

23. See below, p. 320.

24. e.g. Arnold of Castellví was commander of Castellote for twenty-three years between 1283 and 1306 before being transferred to Mallorca.

25. G. R. Galbraith, *The Constitution of the Dominican Order* (Manchester, 1925), p. 123.

26. AHN, cód. 499, pp. 8–9, doc. 12; p. 23, doc. 46; pp. 61–2, doc. 151; pp. 73–4, doc. 179.

27. Delaville, *Hospitaliers*, p. 305; Riley-Smith, *Knights of St. John*, p. 349.

28. That he did is suggested by the wording of several documents: e.g. ACA, CRD Templarios, no. 133; AHN, cód. 469, pp. 505–6, doc. 512; but this evidence is not conclusive.

29. *Règle*, pp. 106–7, art. 132.

30. AHN, San Juan, leg. 169, doc. 10; leg. 277, doc. 1; leg. 333, doc. 5; cód. 689, p. 89, doc. 94; ACA, parch. James I, no. 1623.

31. Delaville, *Hospitaliers*, pp. 306, 308; Riley-Smith, *Knights of St. John*, pp. 351–2.

32. Javierre, *Privilegios*, pp. 65–9; M. Danvila, 'Origen, naturaleza y extensión de los derechos de la Mesa Maestral de la Orden de Calatrava', *BRAH*, xii (1888), 116–63; J. F. O'Callaghan, 'The Affiliation of the Order of Calatrava with the Order of Cîteaux', *Analecta Sacri Ordinis Cisterciensis*, xvi (1960), 7, 22–3; D. W. Lomax, *La Orden de Santiago* (Madrid, 1965), pp. 205–6.

33. ACA, CRD Templarios, no. 86.

34. Ibid. There was a commander of Peñíscola, however, until the early part of the year 1307.

35. *Règle*, p. 249, art. 466.

36. ACA, CRD Templarios, nos. 285, 400.

37. e.g. ACA, parch. Peter III, nos. 217, 324–30; parch. James II, no. 518; AGP, parch. Gardeny, nos. 165, 212, 329; AHN, Montesa, P. 249–51, 341, 342. Not all the documents recording grants of property to tenants at this time refer to the master's intervention, but this is not necessarily significant. Earlier documents of this type which mention the provincial master refer to his counsel rather than his command or licence.

38. ACA, CRD Templarios, no. 355.

39. See below, p. 319.

40. ACA, parch. Peter II, nos. 100, 169; AHN, cód. 470, p. 28, doc. 36.

41. RAH, 12–6–1/M–83, doc. 107.

42. e.g. ACA, CRD Templarios, nos. 116–18; AGP, parch. Gardeny, nos. 196–8.

43. e.g. AHN, cód. 466, p. 153, doc. 115; p. 157, doc. 123; p. 158, doc. 126.

44. See above, p. 275.

45. Lists of chamberlains are given in Appendix II.

46. RAH, 12–6–1/M–83, docs. 118, 119, 121; AHN, San Juan, leg. 174, doc. 15.

47. RAH, 12–6–1/M–83, doc. 120; ACA, CRD James II, nos. 1737, 1747.

48. *Règle*, p. 134, art. 181.

49. Lists of dependencies are given in Appendix III.

50. La Ribera referred to lands along the Cinca; La Litera lay to the east of Monzón.

51. AHN, San Juan, leg. 333, doc. 5; see below, p. 410.

52. On the building of the chapel, see ACA, parch. James I, no. 1162, and Bulas, leg. 11, doc. 49; cf. F. Miquel Rosell, *Regesta de letras pontificias del Archivo de la Corona de Aragón* (Madrid, 1948), p. 92, no. 160. In 1250 a brother William was chaplain there: parch. James I, no. 1189. In the second half of the thirteenth century there was similarly a chapel in the house of Vallfogona, which was subject to Barbará: parch. James I, no. 1410.

53. AHN, San Juan, leg. 324, doc. 2.

54. ACA, CRD James II, no. 1737.

55. Segriá: William of Passenant 1294–6
Peter of Montesquíu 1296–1302
William of Passenant 1303
Bernard Belissén 1303–4
Urgel: Peter of Montesquíu 1295–6
William of Passenant 1296–1302
Bernard Belissén 1306–7

56. AGP, parch. Espluga de Francolí, nos. 249, 319; ACA, parch. James II, no. 686.

57. ACA, CRD Templarios, no. 36.

58. AHN, cód. 467, p. 368, doc. 459; pp. 369–70, doc. 462.

59. AHN, cód. 471, pp. 326–7, doc. 259.

60. AGP, parch. Gardeny, no. 2435.

61. *Règle*, p. 64.

62. Albon, *Cartulaire*, pp. 112–13, doc. 161; J. L. de Moncada, *Episcopologio de Vich*, i (Vich, 1891), 437–8.

63. Albon, *Cartulaire*, p. 377, Bullaire, doc. 5.

64. Cf. *Règle*, pp. 165–6, arts. 270–1, where it is stated that the various chapters in the Order had the power to judge chaplains as well as other brothers. The Templar chaplains were not always ready to accept this subordination to the lay authorities in the Order. In 1255 the Aragonese provincial master complained to the pope that a number of Templar priests refused to obey him and had ignored a summons to appear before him: J. Delaville Le Roulx, 'Bulles pour l'ordre du Temple, tirées des archives de S. Gervasio de Cassolas', *Revue de l'orient latin*, xi (1905–8), 427, doc. 35; AHN, cód. 467, p. 21, doc. 30.

65. Cf. *Règle*, pp. 164–5, art. 268; pp. 235–6, art. 434. Their habits were normally of a dark colour; only those who became bishops were allowed white habits, such as the knights had. No Templars in Aragon are known to have become bishops but there are instances in the East: e.g. E. Langlois, *Les Registres de Nicolas IV* (Paris, 1886–93), p. 27, doc. 165.

66. A list of Templar chaplains at Gardeny is given in Appendix II. For Mas-Deu, see Michelet, *Procès*, ii. 428, 442, 454, 463.

67. AHN, cód. 466, p. 329, doc. 376.

68. Riley-Smith, *Knights of St. John*, p. 236.

69. Delaville, *Hospitaliers*, pp. 294–6; Riley-Smith, *Knights of St. John*, p. 235.

70. Prutz, *Entwicklung*, p. 282, doc. 4.

71. L. Auvray, *Les Registres de Grégoire IX*, ii (Paris, 1907), 567, doc. 3520; ACA, reg. 310, fol. 12.

72. *Règle*, p. 165, art. 269; p. 284, art. 542.

73. Ibid., p. 166, arts. 272, 273.

74. Prutz, *Entwicklung*, p. 282, doc. 4.

75. Ibid., pp. 288–9, doc. 16.

76. ACA, reg. 310, fol. 3ᵛ; AHN, cód. 471, pp. 65–6, doc. 56; Migne, *PL*, ccxvi. 643–4.

77. P. Pressutti, *Regesta Honorii Papae III*, i (Rome, 1888), 168, doc. 4530; ACA, reg. 309, fol. 35.

78. Recruits were questioned on these points when they were admitted to the Order: *Règle*, p. 234, art. 431; p. 343, arts. 673, 674; Finke, *Papsttum*, ii. 364, doc. 157. These abuses were attacked by Innocent III in the bull *Vitium pravitatis*: Migne, *PL*, ccxvi. 890–1.

79. Albon, *Cartulaire*, p. 378, Bullaire, doc. 5.

80. J. Sbaralea, *Bullarium Franciscanum*, i (Rome, 1759), 245.

81. J. B. Mahn, *L'Ordre cistercien et son gouvernement* (Paris, 1951), p. 82; M. Perlbach, *Die Statuten des Deutschen Ordens* (Halle, 1890), p. 63; J. F. O'Callaghan, 'The Affiliation of the Order of Calatrava with the Order of Cîteaux', *Analecta Sacri Ordinis Cisterciensis*, xvi (1960), 27; D. W. Lomax, *La Orden de Santiago* (Madrid, 1965), p. 97.

82. Michelet, *Procès*, i. 93.

83. *Règle*, p. 165, art. 269.

84. Michelet, *Procès*, ii. 432.

85. Finke, *Papsttum*, ii. 374–5, doc. 157.

86. e.g. ACA, reg. 310, fol. 72; AHN, cód. 689, p. 57, doc. 51; cód. 468, pp. 553–4, doc. 542.

87. e.g. Dominic of Monmagastre was vicar of St. John in Monzón in 1250, as was Raymond of Anis in 1278 and Peter of Torre from 1292 to 1304. William Vasco was vicar of Novillas in 1271, García of Rueda vicar of Boquiñeni in 1252, and Peter of Manresa vicar of Miravet from 1271 to 1288.

88. Cf. U. Berlière, 'L'exercice du ministère paroissial par les moines du xııᵉ au xvıııᵉ siècle', *Revue bénédictine*, xxxix (1927), 344–8. In 1255, however, the provincial master had occasion to complain of the dissolute life led by some Templar chaplains who had been granted parishes: AHN, cód. 467, p. 21, doc. 30.

89. AHN, cód. 466, p. 364, doc. 441.

90. AGP, parch. Gardeny, nos. 898, 995, 996, 998, 1000, 1411, 1535, etc.

91. AGP, parch. Gardeny, nos. 20, 21, 22, 892, 945, 1610, 1628.

92. AGP, parch. Gardeny, no. 951.

93. See Appendix II.

94. AHN, cód. 466, p. 322, docs. 359, 360; pp. 386–7, doc. 462.

95. AHN, cód. 689, p. 70, doc. 70.

96. AGP, Cartulary of Tortosa, fols. 34ᵛ–36, docs. 111, 112; fols. 56ᵛ–58, docs. 175, 178.

97. AHN, cód. 689, pp. 25–6, doc. 17; pp. 27–8, doc. 19.

98. *Règle*, p. 215, art. 385.

99. Ibid., p. 226, art. 412.

100. Ibid., p. 217, art. 389.

101. See, for example, G. de Valous, *Le Monachisme clunisien des origines au XVᵉ siècle*, i (Paris, 1935), 216–18.

102. *Règle*, pp. 216–84, arts. 386–543.

103. Ibid., pp. 227–76, arts. 416–523.

104. Ibid., p. 85, art. 97. That the procedure in the Customs was followed may be concluded from the fact that the admissions referred to in statements made by members of the convent of Mas-Deu in 1310 always took place on a Sunday: Michelet, *Procès*, ii. 423–515.

105. G. R. Galbraith, *The Constitution of the Dominican Order* (Manchester, 1925), pp. 45, 111 ff.

106. R. de Huesca, *Teatro histórico de las iglesias del reyno de Aragón*, vii (Pamplona, 1797), 121; *Costums de Tortosa*, I. iv. 9, in B. Oliver, *Historia del derecho en Cataluña, Mallorca y Valencia: Código de las costumbres de Tortosa*, iv (Madrid, 1881), 36. On Templar seals, see Appendix IV.

107. AHN, cód. 471, pp. 322–3, doc. 255.

108. Riley-Smith, *Knights of St. John*, p. 364.

109. e.g. AHN, San Juan, leg. 559, doc. 41; leg. 564, doc. 58; leg. 576, doc. 49.

110. Perlbach, op. cit., p. 41.

111. There were only 144 Templars in the British Isles, and even at the New Temple in London there were only five or six able-bodied Templars: C. Perkins, 'The Knights Templars in the British Isles', *English Historical Review*, xxv (1910), 222. In Cyprus only seventy-six Templars were arrested and interrogated: K. Schottmüller, *Der Untergang des Templer-Ordens* (Berlin, 1887), ii. 143–400.

112. Finke, *Papsttum*, ii. 229, doc. 124.

113. ACA, reg. 291, fol. 96ᵛ; cf. Finke, *Papsttum*, ii. 121–2, doc. 77.

114. Ibid. ii. 140, doc. 87; 145, doc. 88; 188, doc. 105. Certainly Bernard of Fuentes, who was arrested and interrogated at Lérida in 1310, later escaped and went to Tunis, where he became head of the Christian militia in the service of the sultan; in 1313 he returned to Aragon as the sultan's envoy: ibid. ii. 226–7, doc. 121; 372, doc. 157; A. Masiá de Ros, *La Corona de Aragón y los estados del norte de Africa* (Barcelona, 1951), pp. 171, 490–2, doc. 186; cf. C. E.

Dufourcq, *L'Espagne catalane et le Maghrib aux XIII^e et XIV^e siècles* (Paris, 1966), pp. 489–90.

115. Michelet, *Procès*, ii. 423–515.

116. Villanueva, *Viage*, v. 226–32, doc. 9.

117. This method is employed by García Larragueta, *Gran priorado*, i. 249.

118. This is apparent, for example, from a comparison of AHN, cód. 689, pp. 28–31, docs. 20, 22, 23.

119. Mas-Deu: ACA, parch. James I, no. 1773 (1264); Castellote: AHN, cód. 689, pp. 26–7, doc. 18 (1247); Boquiñeni: AHN, cód. 470, pp. 5–6, doc. 4 (1192), pp. 25–6, doc. 33 (1223), pp. 36–7, doc. 47 (1231), etc.

120. The figure for Gardeny refers to the year 1212; that for Zaragoza to 1213; and that for Boquiñeni to 1192–3, 1219, 1223, and 1230.

121. ACA, CRD Templarios, no. 285.

122. ACA, CRD Templarios, no. 371.

123. U. Berlière, 'Le nombre des moines dans les anciens monastères', *Revue bénédictine*, xli (1929), and xlii (1930); G. G. Coulton, *Five Centuries of Religion*, iii (Cambridge, 1936), 540–58.

124. A decline of this kind would mean of course that any conclusions about numbers derived from evidence concerning the dissolution of the Temple would not be valid for an earlier period.

125. Finke, *Papsttum*, ii. 364–78, doc. 157.

126. Villanueva, *Viage*, v. 226–32, doc. 9. The ranks of those receiving pensions are not given, but twenty-three can be traced from other sources as knights, and all of these received payments of 1,400s.B. or more. Similarly twenty-one can be traced as sergeants and these received payments of not more than 1,000s.B. John of Rosas who can be identified as a chaplain received 600s.B., as did another Templar described as Aznar Capella. It may therefore be concluded that the forty-five Templars who received payments of 1,400s.B. or more were knights, and that the sixty-three who received payments of 1,000s.B. or less were sergeants or chaplains, and of these the great majority would probably be sergeants. As none of the four chaplains interrogated in Roussillon received pensions, possibly most of the clerical members of the Order found employment elsewhere in the Church, and did not receive pensions.

127. In Britain only 15–20 of the 144 brothers were knights: Perkins, loc. cit., p. 224. In Cyprus more than half were knights: Schottmüller, op. cit. ii. 143–400. García Larragueta, *Gran priorado*, i. 237–8, shows that knights were probably in a minority in the Hospital in Navarre, and although Delaville, *Hospitaliers*, p. 290, argues that knights predominated in the Hospital, he does not substantiate this assertion.

128. A brother Cavler is mentioned in thirty-one documents in the Cartulary of Castellote (AHN, cód. 689), but is called *miles* on only three occasions.

129. M. Bloch, *La Société féodale*, ii (Paris, 1940), 58.

130. *Règle*, p. 67.

131. Ibid., p. 35, art. 11; p. 46, art. 35.

132. Ibid., p. 54, art. 51 of the French version.

133. Ibid., p. 46, art. 41 of the French version. A number of writers have suggested that the rank of sergeant did not exist at the beginning: e.g. Miret y Sans, *Les Cases*, p. 21; M. Bruguera, *Historia general de la religiosa y militar Orden de los caballeros del Temple*, i (Barcelona, 1888), 125; but they do not examine the question in detail.

134. Albon, *Cartulaire*, p. 377, Bullaire, doc. 5.

135. e.g. *Règle*, p. 269, art. 509.

136. e.g. AGP, Cartulary of Tortosa, fols. 12ᵛ–13, doc. 39; AHN, cód. 469, p. 372, doc. 322.

137. AGP, parch. Gardeny, no. 604; cf. Riley-Smith, *Knights of St. John*, pp. 123, 237, 348.

138. *Règle*, pp. 109–13, arts. 138–43.

139. Ibid., p. 194, art. 337; p. 234, art. 431; p. 240, art. 445.

140. Ibid., p. 129, art. 172; p. 229, art. 419.

141. Ibid., p. 113, art. 143; p. 115, art. 146; p. 161, art. 258; p. 178, art. 300; p. 189, art. 325, etc.

142. AGP, parch. Gardeny, no. 604; AHN, San Juan, leg. 308, doc. 5; cód. 466, p. 153, doc. 116; pp. 247–8, doc. 254.

143. AHN, cód. 471, pp. 340–5, doc. 266; AGP, parch. Comuns, no. 211.

144. RAH, 12–6–1/M–83, doc. 51.

145. AHN, San Juan, leg. 324, doc. 1; cód. 471, pp. 187–9, doc. 199; ACA, reg. 310, fol. 74.

146. AHN, cód. 689, p. 99, doc. 106.

147. AGP, parch. Gardeny, no. 604.

148. AHN, San Juan, leg. 309, doc. 5.

149. AGP, Cartulary of Gardeny, fol. 99, doc. 240.

150. AHN, cód. 469, p. 372, doc. 322; pp. 401–2, doc. 343; cód. 499, p. 45, doc. 107.

151. AHN, cód. 469, p. 363, doc. 310; AGP, Cartulary of Tortosa, fols. 12ᵛ–13, doc. 39; fol. 16–16ᵛ, doc. 50; parch. Tortosa, nos. 11, 20.

152. *Règle*, p. 163, art. 266; p. 251, art. 470; p. 263, art. 498.

153. Michelet, *Procès*, ii. 479, 493. In the thirteenth century it was decreed in the Teutonic Order that illiterate brothers should not learn to read and write without permission: Perlbach, op. cit., p. 64.

154. M. Milá y Fontanals, *De los trovadores de España* (Barcelona, 1861), p. 364; cf. J. Massó Torrents, *Repertori de l'antiga literatura catalana* (Barcelona, 1932), pp. 7–8; P. Meyer, 'Les derniers troubadours de la Provence', *BEC*, xxxi (1870), 436. Massó Torrents, op. cit., p. 241, suggests that the troubadour should be identified with the Templar Raymond Oliver, but as the latter was still alive in 1328 he is unlikely to have been writing sixty years earlier: AHN, San Juan, leg. 587, doc. 37. A further suggestion, made by G. Bertoni, 'Il serventese di Ricaut Bonomel', *Zeitschrift für Romanische Philologie*, xxxiv (1910), 701, note 4, is to identify him with the Oliver mentioned in the Catalan version of the Templar Customs: cf. J. Delaville Le Roulx, 'Un nouveau manuscrit de la Règle du Temple', *Annuaire-bulletin de la Société de l'Histoire de France*, xxvi (1889), 205.

155. M. de Riquer, 'El trovador Giraut del Luc y sus poesías contra Alfonso II de Aragón', *BRABLB*, xxiii (1950), 220.

156. ACA, CRD Templarios, no. 157; Finke, *AA*, ii. 924–5, doc. 596; cf. A. Rubió y Lluch, *Documents per l'història de la cultura catalana migeval*, ii (Barcelona, 1921), 16, note 1.

157. Finke, *Papsttum*, ii. 167, doc. 94.

158. J. Miret y Sans, 'Inventaris de les cases del Temple de la Corona d'Aragó en 1289', *BRABLB*, vi (1911), 70–2.

159. It was stated in the Rule that there should be a reading at meal times, but it is not known what was usually read: *Règle*, p. 34, art. 9.

160. J. Rubió, R. d'Alós, and F. Martorell, 'Inventaris inèdits de l'Ordre del Temple a Catalunya', *Anuari de l'Institut d'Estudis Catalans*, i (1907), 396–7, doc. 5.

161. Villanueva, *Viage*, v. 200; F. Martorell y Trabal, 'Inventari dels bens de la cambra reyal en temps de Jaume II (1323)', *Anuari de l'Institut d'Estudis Catalans*, iv (1911–12), 562, 565; Rubió, Alós, and Martorell, loc. cit., p. 406, doc. 17. There are two fourteenth-century Catalan versions of the *Secreta Secretorum* in the Biblioteca Nacional: J. Massó Torrents, *Manuscrits catalans de la Biblioteca Nacional de Madrid* (Barcelona, 1896), pp. 61, 69.

162. Villanueva, *Viage*, v. 200; Martorell y Trabal, loc. cit., p. 562. The earliest surviving copy of a Catalan translation of this work dates from 1310: L. Karl, 'Théodoric de l'Ordre de Prêcheurs et sa Chirurgie', *Bulletin de la Société Française d'Histoire de la Médecine*, xxiii (1929), 161–2.

163. Villanueva, *Viage*, v. 200; Martorell y Trabal, loc. cit., p. 562. In a Catalan version of this work contained in a fourteenth-century manuscript in the Episcopal Museum in Vich the heading of the first chapter is translated as 'De decayment de cabeyls': *Tresor de pobres* (Biblioteca de la revista catalana, 1892), p. 10; cf. J. Massó Torrents, 'Manuscrits catalans de Vich (Arxiu Municipal, Museu Episcopal, Biblioteca Episcopal)', *Revista de bibliografía catalana*, ii (1902), 238–9.

164. Rubió, Alós, and Martorell, loc. cit., pp. 403–4, doc. 14.

165. Ibid., pp. 393–6, doc. 4.

166. AHN, códs. 1032, 1312. It is not known who made these translations.

167. Rubió, Alós, and Martorell, loc. cit., pp. 393–6, doc. 4; Villanueva, *Viage*, v. 201; Martorell y Trabal, loc. cit., pp. 553, 562–6, where seven copies are mentioned; J. Massó Torrents, 'Inventari dels bens mobles del rey Martí d'Aragó', *Revue hispanique*, xii (1905), 415, 420, 422, 435, 453, nos. 6, 39, 53, 154, 285, where five are mentioned; Delaville Le Roulx, 'Un nouveau manuscrit'.

168. Michelet, *Procès*, ii. 423–515, *passim*.

169. *Règle*, pp. 202–4, arts. 355–8.

170. Ibid., p. 171, art. 282; p. 180, arts. 306–7; cf. Delaville, *Cartulaire*, ii. 558, doc. 2213.

171. *Règle*, pp. 171–2, art. 284; pp. 204–5, arts. 360–1.

172. Ibid., pp. 35–6, art. 10; p. 74, art. 76; pp. 200–1, arts. 350–1.

173. Ibid., pp. 41–2, art. 34; p. 202, art. 353; Ferreira, *Memorias*, ii. 893; ACA, reg. 310, fol. 4$^v$.

174. *Règle*, pp. 33–4, art. 8; pp. 39–40, art. 17.

175. Ibid., p. 31, art. 69.

176. Ibid., pp. 22–3, art. 58; pp. 25–6, art. 62.

177. M. P. Deroux, *Les Origines de l'oblature bénédictine* (Vienne, 1927), pp. 44 ff.

178. G. Schnürer, *Die ursprüngliche Templerregel* (Freiburg, 1903), pp. 54–6.

179. Michelet, *Procès*, ii. 423–515; Finke, *Papsttum*, ii. 366, doc. 157; A. Mercati, 'Interrogatorio di Templari a Barcellona (1311)', *Spanische Forschungen der Görresgesellschaft: Gesammelte Aufsätze zur Kulturgeschichte Spaniens*, vi (1937), 247.

180. *Règle*, p. iv.

181. Ibid., pp. 25–6, art. 14 of the French version.

182. AHN, cód. 689, p. 93, doc. 99.

183. E. Strehlke, *Tabulae Ordinis Theutonici* (Berlin, 1869), pp. 387–8, doc. 560; cf. K. Górski, 'The Teutonic Order in Prussia', *Medievalia et Humanistica*, xvii (1966), 28.

184. Michelet, *Procès*, ii. 451.

185. Ibid. ii. 429, 444, 481.

186. Finke, *Papsttum*, ii. 368–9, doc. 157; cf. A. Trudon des Ormes, 'Listes des maisons et de quelques dignitaires de l'Ordre du Temple en Syrie, en Chypre et en France', *Revue de l'Orient latin*, v (1897), 393, where an example of entry into the Temple at the age of eleven is quoted.

187. E. Magnou, 'Oblature, classe chevaleresque et servage dans les maisons méridionales du Temple au xiie siècle', *Annales du Midi*, lxxiii (1961), 389–90. Not all the cases referred to here were necessarily of formal oblation, but there is one very clear instance: cf. C. Brunel, *Les plus Anciennes Chartes en langue provençale*, ii (Paris, 1952), 18–19, doc. 372. Oblation appears not to have been unknown in the Hospital and in the Teutonic Order: Delaville, *Hospitaliers*, p. 290; *Cartulaire*, ii. 38–40, doc. 1193; Perlbach, op. cit., p. 51. In the Teutonic Order an individual was not supposed to make his profession before the end of his fourteenth year.

188. AHN, cód. 499, pp. 19–20, doc. 34; cód. 469, pp. 224–5, doc. 177; see below, p. 379.

189. ACA, CRD Templarios, no. 458.

190. Most of the Templars interrogated by the bishop of Lérida in 1310 gave their age on entering the Order: Finke, *Papsttum*, ii. 364–78, doc. 157. The average age of eighteen sergeants on entering was nearly twenty-seven, and only two had joined the Temple when below the age of twenty. The average for the nine knights was twenty and a half. One of them had joined at the age of fifty, but none of the others was over twenty when admitted, and the average age of the others on entering was seventeen.

191. J. Miret y Sans, 'Inventaris de les cases del Temple de la Corona d'Aragó en 1289', *BRABLB*, vi (1911), 62–9. Not all the slaves were housed in the convents; some were maintained in dependencies.

192. Miravet had two baptized slaves and there were also some at Alfambra. There was no obligation on Christian lords to free slaves who were baptized: see C. Verlinden, *L'Esclavage dans l'Europe médiévale*, i (Bruges, 1955), 300, 303–4.

193. Ibid. i. 252–61; cf. *Costums de Tortosa*, ix. vii, in B. Oliver, *Historia del derecho en Cataluña, Mallorca y Valencia: Código de las costumbres de Tortosa*, iv (Madrid, 1881), 376–80.

194. Finke, *AA*, iii. 122–4, doc. 54; A. Giménez Soler, 'Caballeros españoles en Africa y africanos en España', *Revue hispanique*, xii (1905), 366, note 1.

195. Verlinden, op. cit. i. 282–5; see below, p. 398.

196. AGP, Cartulary of Tortosa, fol. 7, doc. 22; Miret y Sans, 'Inventaris', p. 69.

197. Provisions concerning escaped slaves were included in a number of agreements made by the Temple: M. Ferrandis, 'Rendición del castillo de Chivert a los Templarios', *Homenaje a D. Francisco Codera* (Zaragoza, 1904), p. 30; AGP, Cartulary of Tortosa, fols. 48v–49, doc. 148; ACA, parch. James I, no. 870; cf. *Costums de Tortosa*, vi. i. 1–3, in Oliver, op. cit. iv. 265–6; Verlinden, op. cit. i. 299, 310–11. An instance where the Moorish population gave assistance to escaping Templar slaves is mentioned in ACA, reg. 48, fol. 117. On this problem in the following centuries, see Verlinden, op. cit. i. 481–509, and idem, 'Esclaves fugitifs et assurances en Catalogne (xive–xve siècles)', *Annales du Midi*, lxii (1950), 301–28.

198. AGP, parch. Gardeny, no. 144; Cartulary of Tortosa, fol. 17ᵛ, doc. 54.

199. Cf. Verlinden, *L'Esclavage*, i. 288; J. Miret y Sans, 'La esclavitud en Cataluña en los últimos tiempos de la edad media', *Revue hispanique*, xli (1917), 11.

200. AGP, parch. Testamentos, no. 134; parch. Gardeny, no. 2435.

201. AGP, parch. Gardeny, nos. 816, 907, 947.

202. ACA, parch. James I, no. 2127.

203. ACA, reg. 291, fol. 257ᵛ.

204. Ibid., fols. 302ᵛ, 306ᵛ.

205. References to these occur in the numerous parchments of Gardeny belonging to this period.

206. AHN, cód. 466, p. 36, doc. 36; pp. 354-5, doc. 423; see below, p. 384.

207. AHN, Montesa, R. 134; ACA, reg. 291, fol. 298.

208. These kinds of provision were made by some founders of chantries: AHN, Montesa, R. 134; P. 610; ACA, reg. 55, fol. 2ᵛ.

209. ACA, parch. James I, no. 1595.

210. AHN, cód. 499, p. 9, doc. 13; ACA, reg. 310, fol. 75-75ᵛ. That there was no Templar establishment of any kind near Pertusa at least towards the end of the twelfth century is apparent from the Templars' retention of the right of hospitality in certain houses there in 1176: cód. 499, pp. 7-8, doc. 11.

211. AHN, cód. 468, pp. 81-3, doc. 78; San Juan, leg. 531, doc. 9; cf. R. I. Burns, *The Crusader Kingdom of Valencia* (Harvard, 1967), i. 112-14; P. Linehan, *The Spanish Church and the Papacy in the Thirteenth Century* (Cambridge, 1971), caps. 1-5.

212. AHN, cód. 691, fols. 198ᵛ-199ᵛ, doc. 444.

213. At Zaragoza a certain Andrew was the scribe of the house from 1188 until 1207: AHN, San Juan, leg. 569, doc. 5; cód. 468, pp. 26-7, doc. 35, etc. In the Cartulary of Huesca (AHN, cód. 499), several scribes are mentioned between 1205 and 1247.

214. e.g. AGP, parch. Gardeny, nos. 50, 145, 209, 909, 1655.

215. e.g. AGP, parch. Gardeny, nos. 680, 683, 775, 777; parch. Casas Antiguas, no. 16.

216. ACA, reg. 291, fol. 361.

217. The name of the notary throughout the period was Bernard Menaguerra, but it is clear from references by one notary to the notebooks of his predecessor that there were at least two notaries of that name.

218. ACA, reg. 197, fols. 4ᵛ-5; AGP, parch. Comuns, no. 253.

219. D. Mansilla, *La documentación pontificia de Honorio III (1216-1227)* (Rome, 1965), pp. 199-200, doc. 256.

220. Trudon des Ormes, loc. cit., p. 420.

221. AGP, parch. Tortosa, no. 64, where the term is clearly used merely to denote a *confrater*. On the inconsistency in the use of the terms *confrater* and *donatus*, see J. Orlandis, ' "Traditio corporis et animae" (La "familiaritas" en las iglesias y monasterios españoles de la alta edad media)', *AHDE*, xxiv (1954), 125–30.

222. AHN, cód. 468, pp. 216–17, doc. 188; cód. 469, pp. 397–8, doc. 338.

223. A. Bonilla y San Martín, 'El derecho aragonés en el siglo XII', *II Congreso de historia de la Corona de Aragón*, i (Huesca, 1920), 289, doc. B.

224. AHN, San Juan, leg. 309, doc. 5.

225. Both Bartholomew of Tarba and Peter of Luco made promises of obedience to the Temple, and it is argued by Magnou, loc. cit., p. 386, that such a promise meant that an individual was becoming more than a *confrater*. In these cases it appears to have been so, but in the documents of the house of Tortosa promises of obedience are often mentioned in connection with those who were merely entering into the confraternity of the Temple.

226. AHN, cód. 499, pp. 18–19, doc. 32.

227. Ibid., p. 21, doc. 39.

228. Ibid., p. 81, doc. 195.

229. J. B. Mahn, *L'Ordre cistercien et son gouvernement* (Paris, 1951), pp. 51–3.

230. *Règle*, pp. 32–3, art. 29; pp. 64–5, art. 5; pp. 65–6, art. 32; p. 66, art. 61.

231. See above, p. 16.

232. Albon, *Cartulaire*, p. 308, doc. 499; p. 312, doc. 505.

233. AHN, cód. 691, fols. 137ᵛ–138, doc. 357; fol. 163, doc. 414; see below, p. 368. Iñigo of Rada was lord of Funes at least from 1155 to 1158: Lacarra, 'Documentos', nos. 259 (iii. 633), 262 (iii. 636), 264 (iii. 638).

234. ACA, reg. 309, fol. 11ᵛ.

235. Ibid., fol. 18–18ᵛ; repeated in 1245 and 1265: AHN, cód. 1312, pp. 90–4, doc. 57; ACA, reg. 309, fols. 25ᵛ–26.

236. AHN, San Juan, leg. 333, doc. 5; see below, p. 410. Papal registers contain several examples of the provision to benefices of secular priests patronized by the Temple: e.g. J. Guiraud, *Les Registres d'Urbain IV*, ii (Paris, 1901), 434–5, doc. 900; iii (Paris, 1904), 280, doc. 1786; 419, doc. 2487. None of these concerns Aragon, but there is no reason to suppose that the situation there was different from that in the rest of western Christendom.

237. AHN, cód. 469, p. 505, doc. 511. In the inventories which have survived from the year 1289 the food and drink of the brothers is sometimes listed separately from that of the *companyes*, and was no doubt of a different quality: Miret y Sans, 'Inventaris', pp. 63–4.

238. *Règle*, pp. 37–8, arts. 14, 15.

239. Ibid., pp. 104–5, art. 129; p. 119, art. 153; pp. 208–9, arts. 370, 371.

240. Ibid., pp. 62–3, art. 3; pp. 64–5, art. 5.

241. Ibid., p. 30, art. 24; pp. 198–9, arts. 346, 347.

242. Ibid., p. 142, art. 199; p. 163, art. 266; p. 198, art. 346, etc.

243. Ibid., pp. 83–4, art. 94; p. 137, art. 188.

244. AHN, cód. 470, pp. 5–6, doc. 4; pp. 66–7, doc. 78; pp. 73–4, doc. 88; see below, p. 374.

245. Miret y Sans, 'Inventaris', pp. 63, 69.

246. Finke, *Papsttum*, ii. 72, doc. 48.

247. ACA, reg. 291, fol. 114$^v$.

248. Michelet, *Procès*, i. 94. Trudon des Ormes, loc. cit., pp. 418–20, refers to statements made by Templars after their arrest in France, Cyprus, and Italy, showing that alms—especially the tenth of bread—were given in these countries; and a few years earlier James of Molay, when protesting against the proposed union of the military orders, stated that alms were given three times a week in Templar convents and also mentioned the giving of the tenth of bread: S. Baluzius, *Vitae Paparum Avenionensium*, ed. G. Mollat, iii (Paris, 1921), 151. About the year 1295 the Grand Master had, however, for financial reasons forbidden excessive almsgiving, and this could have given rise to the charge made against the Templars: Michelet, *Procès*, i. 629. But even in the twelfth century it had been noted that the Templars did not dispense alms on the same scale as the Hospitallers: John of Würzburg, *Descriptio Terrae Sanctae*, cap. 12, in Migne, *PL*, clv. 1087.

249. *Règle*, pp. 100–1, art. 121. It has been suggested that the Templars maintained hospitals in Navarre at Bargota, Sangüesa, Torres del Río, and Puente la Reina, along the pilgrim route to Compostela: M. Núñez de Cepeda, *La beneficencia en Navarra a través de los siglos* (Pamplona, 1940), pp. 38–9, 73, 218, 235; L. Vázquez de Parga, J. M. Lacarra, and J. Uría Ríu, *Las peregrinaciones a Santiago de Compostela*, ii (Madrid, 1949), 129. But the hospital at Bargota belonged to the Hospitallers, as probably did that at Sangüesa, where the Hospital had a commandery: García Larragueta, *Gran priorado*, i. 96, 155. The assertion that the Templars were established at Torres del Río seems to be based merely on the fact that the chapel there is in the octagonal form which has sometimes been considered characteristic of Templar architecture; but as has been seen (above, p. 108, note 91), there was no architectural style peculiar to the Templars. The Templars did enjoy the lordship of the old township of Puente la Reina, but there is no definite evidence to indicate that they established a hospital there for pilgrims. The only indication that they may have dispensed hospitality there is the wording of a charter issued by García Ramírez in 1146, which states that 'you [the Templars] may sell bread and wine, and give hospitality to any poor traveller for the love of God but not for money': J. M. Lacarra, 'Notas para la formación de las familias de fueros navarros', *AHDE*, x (1933), 260.

250. Delaville, *Cartulaire*, i. 67, doc. 70; Perlbach, op. cit., pp. 31–4; in a bull issued in 1199 Innocent III stated that 'with regard to the poor and the sick' the Teutonic Order adopted the customs of the Hospital: E. Strehlke, *Tabulae Ordinis Theutonici* (Berlin, 1869), p. 266, doc. 297.

251. See especially arts. 190–7, which form the *retrais* of the infirmarer: *Règle*, pp. 138–41.

252. AGP, parch. Testamentos, no. 103; parch. Gardeny, nos. 604, 1740, 1815.

253. AGP, parch. Testamentos, no. 165.

254. AGP, parch. Gardeny, no. 1753.

255. *Victoria County History of Cambridge and the Isle of Ely*, ii (London, n.d.), 260; Lees, *Records*, p. clxxx; T. W. Parker, *The Knights Templars in England* (Tucson, 1963), p. 41.

# VIII

## Templar Organization and Life: (ii) The Province and its Relations with the East

ACCORDING to article 87 of the Templar Customs, the head of the Aragonese province, like other provincial masters, was among the officials who were chosen by the Grand Master and chapter, as distinct from those whom the Grand Master could appoint merely with the counsel of some of the *prodomes* of the Temple.[1] The word 'chapter' is used in the Rule and Customs to signify any formal assembly, and in this context could therefore apply either to the meetings of the central Convent in the East or to the general chapter of the Order. In the next article, however, a distinction is made between unspecified officials appointed in the general chapter and those whom the Grand Master could appoint merely with counsel,[2] and in a Catalan version of the Customs of the Temple an article is included which specifically states that provincial masters could be appointed only in the general chapter.[3] At least in the second half of the thirteenth century, then, when article 88 and the Catalan version of the Customs were drawn up,[4] provincial masters were expected to be appointed in the general chapter. There is little evidence to show how far this ruling was observed in the appointment of the head of the Aragonese province. No records of elections exist and the only documents which survive about a particular appointment concern that of Simon of Lenda, the last provincial master, in September 1307. In the notifications of this appointment no reference is made to any assembly.[5] But at that time the Grand Master was in France; the pope had already decided to hold an inquiry into Templar conduct; and there were apparently dissensions among the Aragonese Templars.[6] The circumstances were therefore exceptional. But in the absence of precise information about dates of appointment and about the times when general chapters were held,[7] it is not clear whether on other occasions the procedure mentioned in the Customs was followed.

Whichever of the central authorities appointed provincial masters, it would be expected that the post would usually be given to a Templar who had served in the East and was known to the Grand Master and the leading officials of the Order; and it can be seen that this was certainly done in some instances. When notifying Simon of Lenda of his appointment in 1307, the Grand Master James of Molay referred to their long acquaintance with each other.[8] The new provincial master was an Aragonese Templar, and at the time of his promotion commander of Horta,[9] but he had been in Cyprus in 1292,[10] and his acquaintance with James of Molay probably dated from that time. His predecessor, the Catalan Berenguer of Cardona, is also known to have visited the East before his appointment, for in 1286 Alfonso III had given him permission to take horses from Aragon to the Holy Land.[11] With the disappearance of the central archives of the Order, however, it is impossible to determine whether the provincial master had always earlier been in the East. The only other known instances are of Gilbert Eral, who was Grand Commander in the Holy Land in 1183[12] and who became provincial master in 1185, and of Hugh of Jouy who was marshal of the Order in the East before being made provincial master in 1254.[13]

Yet the interests of the central authorities were not the only factor in deciding appointments to the post of provincial master. The wishes of the province itself were taken into account at least when a vacancy was caused by the death of a provincial master. In a letter to the Aragonese king, James of Molay in 1307 stated that

it is an established custom that when any preceptor of a province dies the brothers of his province, after informing the master of what has happened, advise according to their knowledge and opinion about the appointment of a new ruler for the province. And because our brothers have not yet done so, we have not been able without hearing their advice to establish a new preceptor.[14]

The other influence on appointments was likely to be that of secular rulers. Royal influence in the choice of provincial masters has been demonstrated in France,[15] and suggested in England,[16] and in Aragon in the fourteenth century Peter IV was able to secure the appointment of his nominee to a Hospitaller province.[17] Royal attempts to influence Templar appointments in Aragon are also recorded at the end of the thirteenth and beginning of the fourteenth centuries; they were never altogether successful and on some occasions they failed completely, but at times the choice of provincial masters may have been influenced by royal wishes. In an effort to win support for Charles of Valois's claim to the Aragonese throne, the French king Philip the Fair in 1286 wrote to Honorius IV, asking him to request the Grand Masters of the Hospital and Temple to appoint provincial masters in Aragon who would favour the French cause.[18] This petition, however, produced no result: the Templar provincial master Berenguer of San Justo remained in office. Four years later, apparently on the expiry of Berenguer of San Justo's period of office, the Aragonese king Alfonso III in turn tried to influence the choice of the provincial master. On 27 April 1290 he wrote to the Grand Master, William of Beaujeu, asking for the election of a Catalan as provincial master,

a person whom we can trust, and let him be experienced, prudent, and discreet, and suitable for the aforesaid position and a man who will be able to help us with counsel and aid.[19]

A further letter, written on the same day, requested the appointment of Peter of Tous, the commander of Miravet, who in the Cortes of Monzón had been placed on the king's council.[20] These letters, which sought to prevent the reappointment of a provincial master who apparently came of a Roussillon family[21] and to secure instead the election of a Catalan who could assist the king, were no doubt occasioned by political considerations, for Roussillon was subject to James of Mallorca, who was hostile to Aragon and in league with the latter's enemies. Already in February the king had decreed that all foreigners should leave the country[22] and he was obviously particularly anxious to ensure that positions of influence and importance were not occupied by men of divided loyalties. Alfonso did not gain all his demands: his nominee was not appointed. But Berenguer of San Justo was transferred to a post in Cyprus[23] and his successor, Berenguer of Cardona, was a Catalan. In April 1302 James II complained about Berenguer of Cardona, who had opposed him in the Cortes, and demanded that he should be removed from office.[24] No immediate reply was received and in September James reiterated his demand.[25] Two months later the Grand Master, James of Molay, wrote saying that he would willingly remove the provincial master if it were in his power to do so; but he was bound by the statutes of the Temple, which stated that offices granted *ad terminum* could not be revoked before the end of the term.[26] At the end of January 1303 James accepted this refusal on the grounds that the provincial master had apologized,[27] and Berenguer of Cardona remained in office until his death in 1307. In that year James put forward Dalmau of Timor, the commander of Barbará, as his candidate for the post of provincial master.[28] On this occasion, unlike those of 1290 and 1302, the king's intervention appears not to have been occasioned by any particular circumstances, and it might therefore be argued that the Crown was now beginning to assert a regular pressure on elections to the office of provincial master; but the Aragonese kings had long had reason to desire the appointment of amenable masters and they may well have acted earlier in this way: according to the Chronicle of James I the king had exerted influence on Hospitaller appointments as early as 1230.[29] In 1307 the royal candidate was again rejected, but the new provincial master, Simon of Lenda, was probably acceptable to the king, for he had been a royal envoy to Philip the Fair in 1301 and again in 1303.[30] As James of Molay reminded the new provincial master, the Temple needed not only to preserve its independence, but also to maintain good relations with the Aragonese king, on whose favour the well-being of the province depended;[31] and this double need may account for the choice of Simon of Lenda, just as it may explain the earlier appointment of Berenguer of Cardona.

That these local influences—whether of the Templars in the province or of the secular rulers—were of some significance in determining appointments is suggested by the predominance among the Aragonese provincial masters of men who were already known in the province before their appointment. Of thirty-two provincial masters in Aragon, twenty-two can be traced as Templars in the province before their promotion.[32] Of the rest, Peter of Moncada was the younger son of the Catalan noble Raymond of Moncada, killed during the conquest of Mallorca,[33] and Berenguer of San Justo probably came from Roussillon. Only one name—Hugh of Jouy—definitely suggests the appointment of a Templar who was not connected with the province, but his case was exceptional. According to Joinville, he was banished from the Holy Land for negotiating with the Muslims without Louis IX's consent, and it was therefore necessary to find him a post in the West.[34]

Several provincial masters, like Peter of Moncada, came from the leading noble families of the province. William of Cardona was the younger brother of the viscount Raymond Folz III[35] and Berenguer of Cardona belonged to the same family,[36] while Arnold of Castellnou was the brother of William, viscount of Castellnou.[37] Hugh Geoffrey came from the family of the viscounts of Marseilles[38] and Arnold of Torroja was a member of the house of that name, which richly endowed the Temple in Catalonia.[39] Such appointments, like the division between knights and sergeants, illustrate the influence which birth and secular rank inevitably exercised within the Order: St. Bernard's assertion that the Templars 'defer to the better, not to the more noble' was scarcely an accurate claim.[40] These appointments also show how the Temple provided a career for the younger sons of the nobility, who might find the Templar way of life more attractive than that of a monk. Yet the majority of provincial masters were of necessity drawn from lesser families. Peter of Rovira came of a knightly house settled in the district of Vallés to the north of Barcelona,[41] and Raymond of Gurb belonged to the family which held the castellanry of Gurb, to the north of Vich;[42] but in most cases their origins cannot be traced.

It is not known whether the office of provincial master was ever granted for life; it is apparent, on the other hand, that a number of Aragonese provincial masters were, like Berenguer of Cardona, appointed only for a certain period, for they later occupied other posts of similar or lesser importance. And as in the notification of the appointment of Berenguer of Cardona's successor it is not stated whether the office was to be held for life or not, it seems that such information was then not needed and that it was then the accepted practice to grant the office of provincial master for a period. The distance between the headquarters of the Order and many of the provinces meant that such appointments could not be reviewed annually, as may have happened in the case of posts within a province, for not all provincial masters could attend the general chapter each year: to have done so would have necessitated an absence from their provinces of many months every year. The Temple appears therefore to have adopted the practice of nominating for a term of four years those officials who were appointed by the central authorities and of summoning them to the East at the end of that time, just as the Hospitallers towards the end of the thirteenth century followed the custom of recalling the heads of western provinces every five years.[43] This is the implication of a letter sent by the Grand Master to the queen-mother Constance in 1290, in which, when refusing her request of an office for a protégé, he wrote

we cannot, while observing our statutes, because it is customary to recall our bailiffs at four-yearly intervals, otherwise our house would be ruined.[44]

A rule of this kind may have been in use throughout the second half of the thirteenth century, since although the length of the Aragonese provincial masters' terms of office is not known exactly, all those who are known not to have died in office appear to have occupied the post for approximately four years or for multiples of four years. William of Cardona, who was in the East in 1253,[45] was provincial master from 1244 to 1252. William of Montañana, commander of Sidon and Grand Commander of the Order in 1262,[46] held office in Aragon from early in 1258 until February 1262. His successor, William of Pontóns, was provincial master for slightly over four years before holding high office in the East.[47] Peter of Moncada, who was killed at the siege of Tripoli in 1289,[48] also held the post for about four years, as he was provincial master from April 1279 until late in 1282 or early in 1283.[49] The next provincial master, Berenguer of San Justo, appears to have held office for two terms: he went to the East in 1286,[50] when he had been master for some three and a half years, and surrendered his post in 1290, when a second term would have been completed.[51]

At the end of the twelfth century and in the early decades of the thirteenth, however, there was certainly no rule of this kind. The periods of office of those who were later transferred to other posts varied greatly and were not related to the term of four years. Pons of Rigaud, provincial master from 1189 to 1195, held office for some six years,[52] while Pons Marescalci was provincial master for two and a half years between 1196 and 1199.[53]

Before Provence was made into a separate province, a lieutenant ruled there as the delegate of the provincial master.[54] There was no similar office south of the Pyrenees. The Temple's participation in the *reconquista* inevitably meant that the provincial master spent most of his time in Aragon and Catalonia and a permanent delegate in these areas was not needed. In the Spanish districts, both before and after 1240, a lieutenant was appointed only on certain occasions. The provincial master might delegate his authority in the transaction of some particular business, and when he was away from the province he appointed someone to take his place during his absence. When Berenguer of Cardona went to Cyprus in 1300 he left Peter of Tous in charge of the province; and when the latter was transferred to Castile, the master delegated Raymond of Fals, the castellan of Monzón.[55] A temporary lieutenant was also appointed when the office of provincial master was vacant. The procedure laid down in the Customs of the Temple was similar to that followed during a vacancy in the office of Grand Master: a lieutenant—comparable with the Grand Commander in the Holy Land—was to be chosen by the heads of convents, to hold office until the naming of a new provincial master.[56] Those who were made lieutenants of the master in Aragon were usually Templars who were, or had been, commanders of Monzón, Miravet, or Gardeny, which were clearly regarded as the most important houses in the province.[57]

For most of the Temple's history in the *Corona de Aragón* the offices of provincial master and lieutenant were the only posts of importance in the central government of the province. At the headquarters of the Order in the Holy Land and Cyprus a seneschal, marshal, *drapier*, treasurer, and *turcoplier* are encountered,[58] and the Templar Customs suggest that the office of *drapier* existed in the provinces of Tripoli and Antioch and that there might be provincial marshals in the East.[59] This organization was not reproduced in the Aragonese province. The office of *drapier* is not mentioned in any document. A master's chamberlain appears only on one occasion,[60] while a marshal is referred to in only three charters in the middle decades of the thirteenth century;[61] and a letter written at the end of the century by the provincial master to one of his commanders, stating that 'at times of frontier service, the master gives horses and arms, both of wood and metal, to conventual brothers', indicates that the provincial master was then performing the duties which a marshal would normally fulfil.[62] Clearly these offices did not regularly form part of the provincial administration.

Those who surrounded the provincial master were more concerned with his personal needs than with the administration of the province. In the Templar Customs the attendants allowed to a provincial master are specified only with reference to the eastern provinces: the provincial masters of Tripoli and Antioch were assigned a knight as companion, a sergeant, a deacon, a Saracen scribe, and a boy,[63] while the commander of the kingdom of Jerusalem was permitted the *drapier* as companion, a sergeant, a deacon, a Saracen scribe, two boys, a *turcople*, and two arms-bearers.[64] The entourage of the Aragonese master was, however, obviously based on these regulations. He had a companion who first appears by name in the fourth decade of the thirteenth century.[65] This companion was drawn from among the young knights of the province and was usually later given the charge of a convent. Pons of Pontóns was the master's companion early in 1271[66] and later in the same year became commander of Novillas. Similarly Gaucebert Durbán, who was the master's companion in 1293,[67] was placed in charge of Villel in 1296. There is no reference to a sergeant in the master's entourage until the beginning of the fourteenth century,[68] but there is earlier evidence of a master's chaplain. William of Auvergne held this post in 1172;[69] even then it was probably the title rather than the office that was new. The early chaplains also acted as the master's scribes—William of Auvergne is known only because he drew up documents to which he added his *signum*—but in the thirteenth century a professional scribe joined the entourage of the provincial master and from 1239 a succession of master's scribes can be traced.[70] The other regular attendants of the provincial master were his arms-bearers, of whom there were usually two or three.[71] While the headquarters of the Temple in the East reproduced some of the great offices found in the household of a king or leading noble, the court of the Aragonese provincial master was thus much more primitive and simple in composition.

It was like the households of great lords, however, in being itinerant.[72] The master's duty of visitation[73] and the difficulty of conducting provincial business from one place meant that when he was not serving on the Moorish frontier he was constantly travelling with his court through the lands of the province. The records are too incomplete to allow the compilation of detailed itineraries, but for some years a certain amount of information survives, although this material reflects the necessity of journeying about the province on matters of special business rather than the duty of visitation. In 1292, when he was much concerned with the dispute at Monzón about military service, Berenguer of Cardona was in Barcelona in February[74] and in Monzón in June;[75] in October he was first at Huesca, then at Gardeny, and later at Barcelona;[76] and in December, after stopping at Algars, he returned to Monzón.[77] In 1294 he was at Lérida when the exchange of Tortosa was being discussed in August;[78] in September, when the exchange took place, he was in Tortosa itself;[79] and the next four months were spent largely either in Tortosa or in the places in Valencia which the Temple had received in the exchange.[80] On such journeys, hospitality for the master and his followers was provided by the Order's convents; and like kings, he seems to have claimed the right to commute his *cena* into a money payment when it was not convenient for him to take it in kind.[81]

This constant journeying about the province meant that the goods in the master's keeping were particularly liable to loss or damage. At least by the end of the thirteenth century the Aragonese provincial masters had therefore adopted the practice of establishing fixed places of deposit. By then a central archive and apparently a central treasury as well had been set up at Miravet. The indications of a central treasury are merely that a considerable sum of money was found at Miravet by royal officials in 1308, that part of it was found in the *torra del thesor*, and that no similar amounts are known to have been discovered in other convents.[82] The evidence is stronger, however, of a central archive. The claim made to the bishop of Lérida in 1288 and at other times[83] that original documents were kept at Miravet is shown to be genuine by an inventory of documents brought to Barcelona from Miravet after the arrest of the Templars. This lists not only sealed papal and royal privileges of a general character but also other documents of a more particular nature—some of them sealed—concerning eighteen convents other than Miravet.[84] The Temple, like the Order of Montesa later,[85] thus had a central archive in which were placed not only general privileges but also charters—including some original documents—relating to individual convents.[86] The administration of a central treasury and archive would have required at least a small staff, composed of Templars or secular clerks, but of this there is no trace in the surviving sources.

The government of the province did not rest entirely in the hands of this limited permanent administration, for a certain amount of business was conducted in the provincial chapter. In establishing this institution the Templars were probably influenced by the Hospitallers, who were holding provincial chapters by the year 1123,[87] and more indirectly by the Cistercians; but it is not known when it became a regular part of provincial administration. When the provincial master Peter of Rovira surrendered to the Hospital the Temple's claim to a fifth of Amposta in 1153 he stated that he was acting 'with the consent of the whole of our chapter',[88] and in 1176 a grant of land near Tortosa to the Temple was made 'in the presence of the whole chapter which was held at Gardeny'.[89] These references probably signify meetings of a general character in the province, but the first specific mention of a *capitulum generale* does not occur until 1212.[90] Even then the chapter may not have been an assembly which met at fixed intervals, for in that year there were *capitula generalia* in October and again in December. Towards the end of the thirteenth century, however, it was customary to hold provincial chapters annually. The place and date of the chapter were decided by the provincial master in consultation with his advisers, as was the practice among the Dominicans, although the decision was not made at the time of the preceding chapter, as happened in the other Order.[91] Up to the middle of the thirteenth century the provincial chapter was held most frequently at Monzón, which in that period was looked upon as the centre of the province;[92] but in the second half of the thirteenth century it often met at Miravet and Gardeny as well.[93] This change may have been introduced in order to relieve one house from the burden of providing for the chapter every year.[94] The selection of a meeting-place would be determined partly by geographical considerations, as the province was large and it would be convenient to choose a convent in a central position. But the choice of Miravet and Gardeny, in preference to other houses nearby, suggests that there was a further consideration—probably that not all convents were large enough to accommodate those attending the chapter. Towards the end of the thirteenth century it was customary to hold the provincial chapter at approximately the same time each year; when Berenguer of Cardona summoned a chapter to meet on the last Sunday in February, he mentioned that this was earlier than usual and referred to the 'time when the chapter is customarily held'.[95] From the surviving summonses it is clear that the normal time was in April or May and further that the chapter always began on a Sunday.[96] It was not always possible, however, to hold the chapter at the determined place and time, for on some occasions the master's arrangements were upset by royal needs, which took precedence over Templar convenience: in 1304 the chapter could not be held on the date fixed because James II was exacting frontier service from the Order[97] and in another year the date and meeting-place had to be changed because the master had been summoned to the royal *curia* to give counsel to the king.[98]

No regulation has survived limiting the duration of the provincial chapter; but it may be noted that documents drawn up during its sessions were always written on a Sunday, Monday, Tuesday, or Wednesday. This suggests that a provincial chapter normally lasted not more than four days, which was the maximum amount of time allowed for a Dominican provincial chapter in the mid thirteenth century.[99]

In the thirteenth century the provincial chapter was attended by all heads of convents, and a fairly complete list of commanders is given in some documents drawn up during its meetings.[100] But these documents also refer to brothers who were present in addition to the commanders; and a Templar interrogated in 1311 remembered a provincial chapter at Gardeny at which about a hundred members of the Order had been present.[101] It is not altogether clear who these brothers were. Some belonged to the convent in which the chapter was being held;[102] possibly commanders also brought their companions or other members of their houses with them, although the summonses refer to the attendance only of the commanders. There is certainly no evidence to suggest that there were elected representatives, such as are found at the chapters of the orders of friars.[103]

No full account of the procedure and work of a provincial chapter can be given. No *acta* have survived and the Templar Customs have nothing to say specifically about provincial chapters.

The surviving summonses reveal, however, that towards the end of the thirteenth century the payment of dues and stocktaking comprised an important part of the chapter's business. The head of each convent was ordered to bring his responsion, which was used partly for the province's contribution to expenses in the East and partly for expenditure within the province itself.[104] Only in exceptional circumstances were responsions from the whole province paid at times other than during the provincial chapter.[105] As no amount is mentioned in the summonses, it is clear that at the end of the thirteenth century the assessment of responsions was fixed. It is not known how the amount was determined, but a comparison of the only surviving list of responsions—for the year 1307[106]—with the Hospitaller evaluations of Templar commanderies[107] suggests that not all convents paid an equal proportion of their revenues. Of the twenty-two convents which both paid a responsion in 1307 and are mentioned in the Hospitaller evaluations, Monzón and Cantavieja paid the most (1,100*maz.*), but while Monzón was the second wealthiest house according to the Hospitaller evaluation, Cantavieja came only eleventh on the list; and while the average responsion in 1307 was about a tenth of the valuation given in the Hospitaller list, in some cases it amounted to about a half of the annual value and in others was as little as a twenty-fourth. It seems then that the size of a responsion was fixed by individual agreement between the provincial master and each convent, and that the size and needs of each community were taken into account.

It may be doubted, however, whether towards the end of the thirteenth century the provincial master ever received full payment of all responsions at the time of the chapter. In almost all documents which survive about payment there are references to defaulting by commanders. In 1277 six convents were unable to pay any of their responsions because of poverty,[108] and in 1289 the officials of Gardeny asserted that expenditure on mills and difficulty in collecting rents prevented them from making any payment in that year.[109] The 1307 list provides further evidence of arrears and default of payment. At least seven commanders appear to have been unable to pay in full the responsions which they should have brought to the chapter; and the wording of the document implies further that it was then the practice to excuse certain convents from payment either in a particular year or for longer periods. Juncosa was assessed at 40*maz.*, but the entry was made that 'it does not pay anything this year', suggesting a temporary immunity. The convent of Barbens, on the other hand, was exempt more permanently: no assessment was given for it; it was stated that 'it does not pay a responsion'; and the payment which it did make was in the form of a 'gift' to the master for that particular year. A similar exemption may have been enjoyed by Novillas, of which it was merely written that 'it does not pay anything', and by Añesa, against which the word 'nothing' was entered.

Yet if some convents were in financial difficulties and were unable to pay their responsions, others could afford to pay more than was demanded of them. As the fixed assessments did not take into account any extra revenues which might be available in a particular year, the provincial master in the summonses to the chapter asked commanders to bring any surplus which they had. In 1307 eight commanders made payments of this kind and in some cases the amounts were considerable: Monzón supplied 4,000*s.*J., and the surplus from Barbará amounted to over 3,600*s.*B. The discrepancy which there might be between the responsions and the revenues available is seen particularly in the case of Castellón de Ampurias, whose commander brought a surplus of 490*s.*B., but whose responsion was less than 30*s.*B.

In addition to responsions and surpluses, the houses in the lands subject to the Aragonese and Navarrese kings paid sums for the *legistres*, and those in the *Corona de Aragón* also gave money for the *taylla de la cort*, while a very few houses paid sums 'for the brothers overseas'. The payment for the *legistres* was probably for the pensions which the Temple gave to lawyers and justices at the king's court;[110] the second sum, sometimes said merely to be 'per la cort', may be related to the fixed annual sum which the Order paid for all documents drawn up for it in the Aragonese royal chancery.[111] The last of these payments probably consisted of donations made specifically for use in the East.

This part of the chapter's work was completed by the presentation of *albaras*, which described the state of the commanderies and which may have been linked with an annual review of offices. According to the summonses these statements were to include details of the corn and other goods left in the convents. Examples of *albaras* submitted to the chapter are probably pro-

vided by the inventories which have survived for a number of
convents from the year 1289,[112] for nine of the eleven which bear
a precise date were drawn up in the fortnight before the chapter
was held,[113] and several entries link them with the chapter: the
commanders describe *l'estament* of their houses, a word used in
the summonses to chapters; at Monzón dues had been paid 'up
to the day of the chapter'; the commanders of Ambel and Alfambra set aside amounts of corn and wine for the responsion and
other payments to the provincial master; and the head of Gardeny
stated that he was unable to pay the responsion. These inventories
contain lists of all movable property in the commanderies, including slaves, equipment, and stock as well as provisions. The commanders were thus merely stating what was in their houses. The
chapter appears not to have been concerned to ensure that the
property of a convent was being administered to the greatest
profit and apparently did not oblige commanders to present
accounts, although in view of the increasing financial demands
made of the Temple this might have been desirable. It merely
wanted to ensure that the property of convents was maintained
by commanders in the state in which they had received it.[114]

Apart from the payment of dues and stocktaking, and possibly
a review of appointments, the business of a chapter could cover
a wide range of subjects, including admissions to the Order,[115] the
dispensing of justice,[116] the granting out of land,[117] agreements
with tenants,[118] the issuing of *cartas de población*,[119] or even the
naming of an attorney in a dispute over tithes.[120] The chapter
could obviously transact any administrative or judicial business.
It was the formal meeting of the province, at which any matter
could be raised. Such affairs, however, unlike the payment of
responsions and stocktaking, were also dealt with at other times
outside the chapter; apart from these two items, and possibly a
general review of appointments, there appears to have been no
type of business which was specially reserved for transaction in
the provincial chapter.

The decision to bring a matter before the chapter was probably
largely based on convenience. Some commanders were unable to
try certain offences,[121] and on many questions heads of houses
might want advice from the master or other commanders. Such
matters would presumably be brought before the provincial
chapter if it was to be held soon; otherwise a commander might

seek the master's opinion or judgement when the latter was visiting his convent, or act with the counsel of neighbouring commanders.[122] The provincial master, for his part, was expected to
take advice on his actions,[123] but he could easily obtain it outside
the chapter. When he stayed at a convent he was often joined by
the commanders from near-by houses, and many documents
issued by the provincial master were drawn up on the advice of,
and attested by, a group of commanders from a particular
locality.[124] On other occasions he called a council of the most
important Templars in the province: an undated letter sent by the
lieutenant of the commander of Peñíscola shows that in one year
the provincial master took counsel at Gardeny on All Saints,[125]
and at another time Peter of San Justo, commander of Alfambra
and Peñíscola, was summoned to Miravet in October and told
that 'the council is being recalled to Miravet to discuss important
business.'[126] The wording of this summons, which belongs to the
early fourteenth century, indicates that the custom of taking
advice in this way had led by that time to the emergence of a
formal institution, which had become a recognized part of the
central administration of the province. Even in the exaction of
money the provincial master could act outside the chapter, for
although responsions and other dues were normally paid there he
could seek additional payments at other times of the year; and at
the end of the thirteenth century he did so frequently. This was
inevitable when the provincial master was responsible for much
of the financial business of the province, including the payment of
extraordinary taxes, which were being sought increasingly frequently by the Aragonese king and the Grand Master, and when
there was no attempt to relate the province's internal expenditure
in a year to the amount which had been collected at the provincial
chapter. The situation in which the provincial master must often
have found himself is illustrated by a letter in which Berenguer
of Cardona ordered the commander of Torres to

bring to the commander of Gardeny as soon as you have received this
letter all the money in your possession, whatever it is for, and any that
you can lay hands on, as we have great need of it for a payment which
we have to make.[127]

The provincial chapter thus played only a restricted part in the
government and administration of the province. Unlike the head

of a Dominican province, the provincial master was neither elected by his chapter nor answerable to it.[128] The chapter was, on the contrary, dependent on the master for its summoning, and documents drawn up during its sessions were issued in his name and sealed by him, for the provincial chapter had no seal of its own;[129] it could not act independently of the master. The chapter's lack of power meant that the government of the province rested mainly in the hands of the provincial master, as the delegate of the Grand Master. This centralization of authority in the province, like that in a convent, was to some extent inevitable. The masters of some provinces had to lead their men in the field, while the obligations owed by the western provinces inevitably meant that a provincial master's responsibility was to the Grand Master rather than to the brothers of his province.

The Templar Rule and Customs say little about the system of supplying the Order's needs in the East,[130] but it is clear from a bull issued by Nicholas IV in 1291 that the western provinces generally, like those of the Hospital, were obliged to send a third of their revenues to the East.[131] The Aragonese Templars, despite their participation in the *reconquista*, were not exempt from the duty of aiding the Order in the Holy Land. It seems probable, however, that in the thirteenth century they were expected to send only a tenth of their revenues, for during a dispute in 1221 about the tithes of certain parishes under Templar patronage the bishop of Zaragoza complained that the Templars

extracted a tenth from those tithes for the use of the master overseas before they gave the bishop his quarter.[132]

Further evidence of such an obligation is possibly provided by the existence in the mid thirteenth century of a *decimarius*, who was once referred to as the *decimarius magistri*,[133] and who on several occasions was also the commander of Corbins.[134] This official is clearly to be distinguished from the local *decimarii*, who are mentioned in the records of some convents and who collected tithes;[135] and it may be conjectured that he was concerned with the dispatch to the East of a tenth of provincial revenues.

By the beginning of the fourteenth century, however, the responsion owed by the province may have become expressed as a fixed sum of money instead of a proportional payment, for in 1304 the Templars negotiated with a Barcelona merchant about the transfer to Cyprus of a responsion of exactly 1,000 marks of silver.[136] The same conclusion is suggested by the assertion made in 1301 by the bishop of Lérida that the Aragonese Templars

do not pay a responsion to the Holy Land that reaches the sum of 1,000 marks and they convert all the rest of their income to their own uses,

for the 'not' seems to be out of place and may have been inserted by the scribe by mistake.[137]

At the end of the thirteenth century, when the Order's resources in the East had become severely depleted, the Grand Master was obliged to demand extra supplies in addition to the normal responsion. Such appeals explain some of the special levies exacted from convents by the provincial master. Houses were sometimes asked to provide a fixed sum determined by the provincial master,[138] but when the situation was desperate he resorted to more general appeals. After receiving a letter from the Grand Master in 1300 about the need for supplies, Berenguer of Cardona wrote anxiously to the commander of Corbins

we beg of your friendship as earnestly as we can that in so great a necessity and in so great a need as we now have you obtain for us from anywhere in the world as much money and salted meat as you can and anything else that is required, in such a way that you leave us in no doubt of your good will.[139]

Nothing is known of the response to such appeals.

In 1304 the responsion was paid in money, but this is the only example of help being sent to the East in this form. Normally payments were made at least partly in kind—a practice which was apparently followed by the Hospitallers as well.[140] Royal writs, granting freedom from dues or permission to export goods in times of scarcity or war, give an indication of the sort of supplies normally sent. In 1286 Alfonso III allowed the Templars to export thirty horses coming from Castile and ten from Aragon, together with mules, harness, salted meat, and other food;[141] four years later he gave permission for mules, arms, harness, oil, forty horses, 200 *cahíces* of wheat, and 100 of barley or oats to be sent to the Holy Land.[142] Letters written by the provincial master similarly contain references to the dispatch of corn and salted meat, and also mention the sending of animal fats and cheese.[143]

There were disadvantages in sending aid in this form. At a time when marine insurance was not common, the transport of goods by sea was subject to risk, while a transfer of money could be made without danger. In 1304 it was agreed that the responsion of 1,000 marks should be paid by the Barcelona merchant out of the money he obtained from selling his cargo in the East, and the Order was to reimburse him in Barcelona after he had certified that he had made payment in Cyprus. The responsion was thus paid without any transport of money. This form of transfer was probably also cheaper than sending certain goods. In 1304 the Templars undertook to pay the merchant up to 10,166s. 8d.B. to compensate him for the profit which he might have made if he had bought a new cargo in the East for sale in western Europe. This sum represented about 14½ per cent of the value of the responsion, but arrangements were made for calculating what the actual profit would have been on certain goods, and if it amounted to less than 10,166s. 8d.B., the Templars were to pay correspondingly less. The only precise evidence which exists for comparison about the cost of transporting goods is an agreement made in 1282, in which another Barcelona merchant undertook to ship horses and other animals from Barcelona to Acre at a cost of 2½ marks for each animal.[144] This sum may have amounted to only about 13 per cent of the value of a horse in Aragon at that time,[145] but it was more than the price of some mules.[146] Templar documents give no indication of the cost of transporting foodstuffs, but obviously the expense of carrying bulky non-luxury goods like corn—which sometimes made up a considerable part of a shipment—would be high in relation to their value.[147]

Although the dispatch of horses to the East might perhaps be explained by the quality of Spanish horses,[148] the transporting of other goods in these circumstances suggests that the economic situation of the Frankish states in the Levant towards the end of the thirteenth century was not very different from that found in the East a century later, when many essential goods were scarcer and more expensive than in the West.[149] The materials are lacking, however, for making a precise comparison between Aragon and the East at the end of the thirteenth century. Because of the paucity of evidence and the difficulty of relating accurately the currency and measures of one district to those of another, because no full examination of prices in Aragon has been made,[150] and because investigations of prices in the East have been based primarily on Muslim sources,[151] no adequate comparison of prices can be attempted.[152] Nor is it easy to discuss the comparative scarcity of goods, especially as permission to export to the East was given even when the goods were apparently needed in Aragon. The need to defend the Holy Land seems at times to have overruled other considerations: when Alfonso III allowed the export of horses and goods by the Aragonese Templars in 1290, he wrote to the Grand Master that

although these things are very necessary to us and our country because of the war in which we are involved, nevertheless for the honour of God, who protects and defends us and our people in our rights against our enemies in the said war, and because of our affection for you we have freely granted permission to the master.[153]

The transport of supplies necessitated fairly frequent voyages to the East. In an agreement made in 1233 between the citizens of Marseilles and the Grand Masters of the Temple and Hospital, it was stipulated that each Order should be allowed to load one ship with merchandise, pilgrims, or its own possessions free of charge in that port for the passage to the East in March and another for that in August.[154] This compromise suggests that the Orders made passages from Marseilles at both the normal sailing times each year, and the permission granted by James I to the Aragonese Hospitallers in 1262 to dispatch two ships a year free from any dues may mean that two journeys were made annually by the Hospital from Spain as well.[155] In the grant of a similar exemption to the Temple in 1272 James placed no restriction on the number of ships which the Templars might send;[156] Alfonso III in 1290 allowed only one ship to sail, but this was a limitation imposed in time of war.[157] It may be inferred, however, from the timing of preparations for voyages and from sailing dates, that at the end of the thirteenth century the Aragonese Templars did not normally undertake more than one passage to the Holy Land or Cyprus in the course of a year. Preparations were usually begun in April or May: orders for the purchase of supplies to be transported were then issued[158] and arrangements for transport made with Barcelona merchants, since the Aragonese Templars possessed no ships of their own;[159] special levies in kind were demanded from commanders[160] and, if necessary, permission was obtained to bring horses through the kingdom from Castile and to take supplies out of the country.[161] The work of preparation took several months[162] and the voyage was not made until August or September. A contract made in 1282 between the commander of Palau and a Barcelona merchant provided for a sailing in August;[163] similarly, several years later, Berenguer of Cardona stated that he was making a passage with supplies in that month.[164] Other letters contain references to his leaving Spain in the middle of August and arriving at Limassol on 8 October;[165] and at another time the provincial master ordered the Templars who were crossing to Cyprus with supplies to be at Barcelona on 8 September.[166] But though it is clear that the Aragonese Templars did not make more than one passage in any year, the surviving Templar records do not show whether the passage was made every year or whether supplies were sent only at intervals of several years.

The Aragonese province sent recruits as well as supplies to the East, and some indication of the importance of the Aragonese contingent at the beginning of the fourteenth century is provided by the records of the interrogations of the Templars in Cyprus carried out before the dissolution of the Order.[167] Of seventy-six Templars questioned there, just over half had entered the Order in France, and ten had joined it in the East, compared with seven who had made their profession in Aragon and Catalonia. The French element thus predominated, just as it did in the Hospital in Cyprus.[168] Yet while the French provinces provided the largest numbers of recruits, Aragon and Catalonia supplied more than any of the remaining western provinces at this time, although because of the Order's participation in the Spanish *reconquista* the Aragonese contribution at an earlier period may have been smaller. Even then, however, some of the central officials in the Holy Land had been drawn from the Aragonese province: the three provincial masters who became Grand Master all held the latter office before 1230.[169]

Not all Templars who travelled from Aragon to the East went to serve there: some merely made short visits for administrative reasons. According to the Templar Customs the provincial master was obliged to cross to the East for the election of the Grand Master, but otherwise he could go only on the summons of the Grand Master and Convent.[170] As has been seen, at the end of the thirteenth century provincial masters in the West appear to have been summoned to the general chapter every four years;[171] on these occasions they would report on their terms of office and participate in the business of the chapter. A provincial master might, however, be summoned at other times to give counsel on particular issues: Berenguer of Cardona was once ordered to go to Cyprus to discuss the recovery of the Holy Land, after Clement V had written to the Grand Master on the subject.[172] It is possible that some brothers from the province as well as the provincial master attended general chapters, for if the seventy-six Templars arrested in Cyprus represented the greater part of the Order's strength on the island,[173] the 400 Templars said to have been present in 1291 at a general chapter in Nicosia must—even if the number is somewhat exaggerated—have included brothers drawn from the provinces.[174] But although references survive about the summoning of Aragonese Templars to the East and their crossing to the Holy Land or Cyprus,[175] it is usually not clear whether they were attending the general chapter or whether they were going to serve in the East. The only documents which definitely suggest short visits are several letters in which the Grand Master granted individual Templars who had recently been in the East permission to return there again as many times as they wished; but these letters, of course, give evidence merely of particular favours.[176]

The summoning of provincial masters to the general chapter was one means by which the Grand Master and Convent maintained a check upon western provinces. Visitation was the other. Until the middle of the thirteenth century this was carried out by a master *deça mer*, whose authority embraced all the European provinces of the Order.[177] This office disappeared about the year 1250 and was replaced by that of visitor. Léonard has argued that the change was merely one of title and that the visitor, like the master *deça mer*, carried out his duties throughout western Europe.[178] But Léonard uses only French sources, and when in these a visitor is given a precise territorial qualification it never includes more than France, England, and Germany. A completely different list of visitors can be compiled from Spanish sources, and although the masters *deça mer* listed by Léonard can be traced in Spain, none of the visitors holding authority in France is mentioned in Spanish documents. The transition from master *deça mer* to visitor therefore implies not a change in title merely but the grouping of the European provinces into several districts for the purposes of visitation. One comprised France, England, and Germany; the Iberian peninsula formed another.

This new form of organization, which may have been copied from the Hospitallers,[179] was no doubt adopted in order to achieve a more effective visitation than could be undertaken by a single master *deça mer*. It tended, however, to weaken external control over the provinces, for while a master *deça mer* was only rarely also the master of the province which he was visiting, the visitor in Spain in the second half of the thirteenth century was nearly always the head of one of the two Spanish provinces. The first was Lope Sánchez, provincial master of Castile and Portugal;[180] three others—Arnold of Castellnou, Peter of Moncada, and Berenguer of Cardona—were masters of the Aragonese province;[181] and the only known visitor who was not a Spanish Templar was Simon of La Tour, who held office in 1277[182] and who can probably be identified with the Templar of that name who was commander of Safed in 1262 and Grand Commander of the Order in 1271.[183] This policy was perhaps dictated by considerations of expense. Its adoption shows that the danger of provincial independence was small, even though the Grand Master and other central officials rarely entered the Peninsula. William of Beaujeu in 1275 and James of Molay in 1294 are the only Grand Masters who are known to have visited Aragon,[184] while the only other central official encountered in Aragon in the second half of the thirteenth century is Peter of Castellón, the treasurer of the Order in Cyprus, who was sent by James of Molay on an embassy to James II.[185]

Almost the only surviving source of information about the office of visitor is a notification of the appointment of Berenguer of Cardona to that post in Spain, issued by the Grand Master in 1300.[186] As the provincial master had already held the post since 1297, the dating of the letter might seem to suggest that the office was granted for renewable periods of not more than three years; but since this letter was still being quoted as proof of authority in 1306, it appears that the office was held for an indefinite period and that the purpose of the letter was only to confirm Berenguer of Cardona's appointment. In the letter the Grand Master does not define the duties of a visitor very precisely; he merely states:

we have appointed brother Berenguer of Cardona as visitor general of our houses in all the five kingdoms of Spain, granting him in all the five kingdoms of Spain complete authority over all our houses, namely the power to visit our houses and brothers in all the five kingdoms of Spain, to sell, alienate and exchange our property, and to enter into and carry out obligations, placing the same brother Berenguer of Cardona, the aforementioned visitor, in our place in all and each of the aforesaid matters, and granting him the power to undertake each and all of the things which we, the Master and Convent, could undertake in all and each of the aforesaid matters.[187]

The only information found in other documents about the work of a visitor is a reference to a visit to Castile made by Berenguer of Cardona, during which he convened a chapter at Zamora.[188] It is therefore impossible to obtain any detailed impression of a visitor's activities, but it is clear from the Grand Master's letter in 1300 that a visitor not only undertook the visitation of provinces but also received certain powers normally reserved to the Grand Master and central Convent.

The Rule and Customs do not define the powers which the central authorities exercised in provincial affairs; these can only in part be discerned from particular examples. The Templars in the East, who depended on supplies from the European provinces, would obviously want to ensure that the Order's lands in the West were maintained; the right to alienate property was therefore reserved to the Grand Master and Convent. This is apparent not only from James of Molay's letter but also from a statement made by the castellan of Monzón in 1284 when he asserted that it was illegal to

subject or submit the men or possessions of the Temple to any person except by the special order of the Master overseas and the Convent;[189]

and in practice transactions involving the extensive alienation of Templar possessions and rights in the Aragonese province were normally made with the consent of the Grand Master and central Convent. This was obtained in 1246 for the exchange of Ruzafa for Moncada and Carpesa,[190] while James of Molay and the Convent in 1292 gave permission for the sale or exchange of La Zaida and Puigreig,[191] and the exchange of Tortosa was similarly carried out with their approval.[192] The Grand Master also, as has been seen, enjoyed the power of granting offices for life; that this

was included in a grant of authority to a visitor is shown by
Berenguer of Cardona's quotation of the letter of 1300 as his
authority when he gave the commandery of Alfambra for life
to Peter of San Justo in 1306.

Apparently the only other provincial affairs in which the Grand
Master and Convent took part were judicial decisions, although
no cases were specifically reserved for their judgement in the first
instance. They considered only appeals and those cases which a
provincial master wished to refer to them. Tenants of the Order
could appeal to the Grand Master against a decision brought by
a commander or provincial master; this is implied in a letter
written by James I in 1261 about persons exiled from Monzón,[193]
while James of Molay, obviously after an appeal from the inhabitants of Monzón, reduced from 12,000s.J. to 8,000s.J. the
penalty imposed on them by the provincial master in 1292 for
failing to fulfil their obligations of military service.[194] Although
there are no surviving examples, a member of the Order could
presumably likewise appeal against a sentence passed in the province. The Templar Customs give some indication of the other
kinds of cases which might be referred to the Grand Master and
Convent for decision. Templars of bad repute accused of minor
offences might be sent to the East for trial, and serious charges or
those which were new or difficult to judge could also be referred
to the Grand Master.[195] The case—mentioned in the Catalan version of the Order's Customs—in which several Catalan Templars
were sent to the Holy Land for trial on a charge of forging letters
from the papal *curia*,[196] was probably referred because of the
seriousness of the charge, while examples quoted in the Customs—
admittedly taken mostly from the eastern provinces—suggest that
cases involving offences for which the penalty was expulsion from
the Order were not infrequently referred to the Grand Master
and Convent.[197] Finally, though not mentioned in the Rule and
Customs, local disputes between the Temple and Hospital could
be settled in the East by the Grand Masters of the two Orders.
The procedure to be followed was defined in 1179 by the Grand
Masters Odo of Saint Amand and Roger of Moulins in an agreement similar to others made between religious orders in the
twelfth century: if any quarrel arose between the Temple and
Hospital, it was to be decided by the arbitration of three members
of each Order; if this failed, and counsel given by the supporters

of either side produced no settlement, the dispute was to be taken before the Grand Masters.[198]

Thus in practice, despite the centralized constitution of the Temple, the relations between the province and the headquarters of the Order were not very close. The distance between the province and the East and the slowness of communications meant that of necessity considerable freedom was allowed to the provincial master, and supervision by the Grand Master was therefore not strict. The most important link was economic, and provided that supplies were sent regularly to the East the provincial master could expect to rule his province with little intervention from his superiors.

## NOTES

1. *Règle*, p. 80.

2. Ibid., p. 81.

3. J. Delaville Le Roulx, 'Un nouveau manuscrit de la Règle du Temple', *Annuaire-bulletin de la Société de l'Histoire de France*, xxvi (1889), 201.

4. Although according to H. Prutz, 'Forschungen zur Geschichte des Tempel-herrenordens: I. Die Templerregel', *Königsberger Studien*, i (1887), 171, arts. 77–197 were drawn up before 1187, art. 88 is not found in the Dijon manuscript, which belongs to the early thirteenth century: *Règle*, pp. vi, 81; G. Schnürer, *Die ursprüngliche Templerregel* (Freiburg, 1903), p. 6; and it mentions the office of visitor, which did not come into existence until the middle of the thirteenth century: see above, p. 328.

5. ACA, CRD Templarios, nos. 46, 86 (to Simon of Lenda); parch. James II, no. 2470 (to members of the Order; see below, p. 419); Finke, *Papsttum*, ii. 43, doc. 28 (to James II; in this letter the Grand Master states merely that the appointment was made 'with the common counsel of our brothers').

6. These dissensions are mentioned in ACA, CRD Templarios, no. 86, but no details are given.

7. The timing of passages to the East by the Aragonese Templars suggests that general chapters may have usually been held in the autumn, as was the custom in the Hospital towards the end of the thirteenth century: Delaville, *Hospitaliers*, pp. 315–16; see also above, p. 326; but positive evidence is lacking.

8. ACA, CRD Templarios, no. 86. The part of this document in which the acquaintance is mentioned has been published by H. Finke, 'Nachträge und Ergänzungen zu den *Acta Aragonensia* (I–III)', *Spanische Forschungen der Görres-gesellschaft: Gesammelte Aufsätze zur Kulturgeschichte Spaniens*, iv (1933), 451–2, doc. 14.

9. He was a member of the convent of Zaragoza in 1276: AHN, San Juan, leg. 579, doc. 415; and in the next year he became commander of Cantavieja. He had been in charge of Horta since 1296.

10. AGP, parch. Cervera, no. 484; see below, p. 406.

11. ACA, reg. 66, fol. 62; see below, p. 402.

12. R. Röhricht, *Regesta Regni Hierosolymitani* (New York edn., n.d.), i. 167, no. 631.

13. Cf. Joinville, *Histoire de Saint Louis*, cap. 99, ed. N. de Wailly (Société de l'Histoire de France, 1868), pp. 182–4.

14. Finke, 'Nachträge und Ergänzungen', pp. 451–2, doc. 14.

15. Prutz, *Entwicklung*, pp. 286–8, docs. 13, 14. An attempt by Charles of Anjou and Clement IV in 1266 to have Amaury of Roche, master in northern France, transferred to Sicily appears, however, to have failed: E. Jordan, *Les Registres de Clément IV* (Paris, 1893–1945), p. 122, doc. 418; Léonard, *Introduction*, p. 114. In giving support to the Angevin request Clement was making an exception in favour of an ally; in the bull *Desiderio desiderantes vos* he attacked secular interference in Templar appointments: Ferreira, *Memorias*, ii. 915–16.

16. Lees, *Records*, pp. xlix–l.

17. A. T. Luttrell, 'The Aragonese Crown and the Knights Hospitallers of Rhodes: 1291–1350', *English Historical Review*, lxxvi (1961), 15.

18. G. Digard, *Philippe le Bel et le Saint-Siège* (Paris, 1936), ii. 219, doc. 2.

19. Finke, *AA*, iii. 8–9, doc. 5.

20. ACA, reg. 73, fol. 80.

21. B. Alart, 'Suppression de l'Ordre du Temple en Roussillon', *Bulletin de la Société agricole, scientifique et littéraire des Pyrénées-Orientales*, xv (1867), 102.

22. ACA, reg. 81, fol. 27ᵛ.

23. AGP, parch. Cervera, no. 484; see below, p. 406.

24. ACA, reg. 334, fol. 53ᵛ; published incompletely in Finke, *AA*, i. 115–16, doc. 78, where the reference is given inaccurately; cf. ibid. i. 127–8, doc. 88.

25. ACA, reg. 334, fol. 53ᵛ.

26. Finke, *AA*, i. 122–3, doc. 85.

27. Ibid. i. 127–8, doc. 88.

28. ACA, CRD James II, no. 2842. This document is misinterpreted in Finke, *Papsttum*, i. 35.

29. Cap. 95, trans. J. Forster (London, 1883), i. 183.

30. Zurita, *Anales*, v. 50, 58.

31. ACA, CRD Templarios, no. 86.

32. See Appendix II.

33. S. Sobrequés i Vidal, *Els barons de Catalunya* (Barcelona, 1957), p. 125.

34. Joinville, *Histoire de Saint Louis*, cap. 99, ed. de Wailly, pp. 182–4.

35. Sobrequés i Vidal, op. cit., p. 112; J. Ballaró y Casas, *Historia de Cardona* (Barcelona, 1905), p. 57.

36. ACA, parch. James II, no. 264.

37. C. Baudon de Mony, *Les Relations politiques des comtes de Foix avec la Catalogne* (Paris, 1896), ii. 147–9, docs. 62, 63.

38. C. Devic and J. Vaissete, *Histoire générale de Languedoc*, vii (Toulouse, 1897), 11.

39. According to S. Puig y Puig, *Episcopologio de la Sede Barcinonense* (Barcelona, 1929), p. 157, he was the brother of William of Torroja, bishop of Barcelona and later archbishop of Tarragona.

40. St. Bernard, *De Laude Novae Militiae*, cap. 4, in Migne, *PL*, clxxxii. 926.

41. ACA, parch. Raymond Berenguer IV, no. 120.

42. P. Bofill y Boix, 'Lo castell de Gurb y la família Gurb en lo segle XIII<sup>è</sup>', *Congreso de historia de la Corona de Aragón*, ii (Barcelona, 1913), 729.

43. Delaville, *Hospitaliers*, p. 305; Riley-Smith, *Knights of St. John*, p. 290.

44. Finke, *AA*, iii. 10, doc. 5.

45. E. González Hurtebise, 'Recull de documents inèdits del Rey en Jaume I', *Congreso de historia de la Corona de Aragón*, ii (Barcelona, 1913), 1203, doc. 24.

46. J. Delaville Le Roulx, *Documents concernant les Templiers extraits des Archives de Malte* (Paris, 1882), pp. 34, 36, docs. 21, 23; Delaville, *Cartulaire*, iii. 30–3, docs. 3028, 3029; 57–60, docs. 3044, 3045.

47. R. Röhricht, *Regesta Regni Hierosolymitani* (New York edn., n.d.), i. 366, note to no. 1413.

48. S. Runciman, *History of the Crusades*, iii (Cambridge, 1954), 407.

49. Peter of Moncada was called provincial master in 1276 and 1277 in several royal documents and in one private document: ACA, reg. 22, fol. 72ᵛ; reg. 38, fol. 11; AHN, cód. 470, pp. 20–2, doc. 27. But at the beginning of 1277 Arnold of Castellnou, who had become provincial master in 1267, was said still to be master although absent in Acre: ACA, parch. Peter III, no. 20; and he still held the post early in the following year: AGP, parch. Espluga de Francolí, no. 394. It seems therefore that in 1276 and 1277 Peter of Moncada was merely temporarily in charge of the province in the absence of the master.

50. ACA, reg. 66, fol. 61ᵛ.

51. He was 'comandor de la terre' in Cyprus in 1292: AGP, parch. Cervera, no. 484; see below, p. 406. By 1297 he had returned to Aragon, where he became commander of Miravet.

52. He was provincial master again from 1202 until 1206.

53. He was later commander of Monzón and of Miravet.

54. A list of lieutenants is given in Léonard, *Introduction*, pp. 25–6.

55. ACA, CRD Templarios, no. 181.

56. *Règle*, p. 81, art. 88; p. 302, art. 581; cf. pp. 143–4, arts. 201, 202.

57. See the list of lieutenants in Appendix II.

58. *Règle*, pp. 86–90, arts. 99–103; pp. 105–6, arts. 130–1; pp. 127–9, arts. 169–72; ACA, CRD Templarios, no. 99; AGP, parch. Cervera, no. 484.

59. *Règle*, p. 106, art. 131; pp. 90–1, art. 104. E. Rey, 'L'Ordre du Temple en Syrie et à Chypre', *Revue de Champagne et de Brie*, xxiv (1888), 255, stated that he had not found any examples of provincial marshals in the East.

60. AHN, cód. 499, pp. 12–13, doc. 20.

61. AGP, parch. Barbará, no. 131 (1235); AHN, San Juan, leg. 556, doc. 4 (1245; see below, p. 386); cód. 689, pp. 15–17, doc. 10 (1268). This office is also encountered at about the same time in the Castilian province: P. Rodríguez Campomanes, *Dissertaciones históricas del Orden y Cavallería de los Templarios* (Madrid, 1747), p. 31. An office of *decimarius* is similarly mentioned in a number of documents belonging to the middle decades of the thirteenth century: see above, p. 323.

62. ACA, CRD Templarios, no. 539. This document can be compared with article 127 of the Templar Customs which shows a provincial master in the East fulfilling the functions of a marshal: *Règle*, p. 103.

63. Ibid., p. 102, art. 125.

64. Ibid., p. 94, art. 110.

65. Hugh of Mirmanda was the first in 1239: AHN, Montesa, P. 14; but in 1227 there is a reference to García Royz 'who travelled with the lord master': cód. 466, pp. 235–6, doc. 237.

66. Ibid., pp. 61–2, doc. 61 *bis*.

67. AGP, parch. Gardeny, nos. 306, 370–5.

68. ACA, CRD Templarios, no. 537; parch. James II, nos. 2011 (1304), 2260 (1306); see below, p. 415.

69. AHN, cód. 467, p. 472, doc. 566.

70. The first was Peter of Cubells: AHN, Montesa, P. 14. They were not members of the Order.

71. Three are mentioned in 1281: AHN, San Juan, leg. 309, doc. 10; two are named in 1286 and 1290: AHN, Montesa, sign. 542–C, fol. 31; P. 487.

72. Cf. the remarks about the itinerant character of the English provincial masters in Lees, *Records*, p. lxv. According to García Larragueta, *Gran priorado*, i, caps. 2 and 4, the prior or provincial master of the Hospitallers in Navarre had a fixed residence.

73. This is referred to in *Règle*, p. 82, art. 91, and ACA, reg. 91, fol. 101.

74. AHN, cód. 471, p. 212, doc. 213.

75. Ibid., p. 238, doc. 221.

76. Ibid., pp. 239–40, doc. 222; pp. 241–4, doc. 224.

77. Ibid., pp. 213–18, doc. 214; pp. 247–8, doc. 226.

78. AHN, Montesa, P. 520.

79. AHN, Montesa, P. 523.

80. ACA, parch. James II, nos. 408 (Las Cuevas), 411–13 (Albocácer), 414 (Ares), 420 (Tortosa), 453 (Albocácer), 466 (Tortosa).

81. In a letter to Peter of San Justo, commander of Ambel, Berenguer of Cardona complained that the money for his *cena* had not been paid: ACA, CRD Templarios, no. 537. A further letter to the same Templar, when commander of Corbins, ordering him to prepare to receive the provincial master, can be compared with royal orders for *cenas* in kind: CRD Templarios, no. 643.

82. J. Rubió, R. d'Alós, and F. Martorell, 'Inventaris inèdits de l'Ordre del Temple a Catalunya', *Anuari de l'Institut d'Estudis Catalans*, i (1907), 391–2, doc. 2; ACA, CRD Templarios, no. 124.

83. AGP, parch. Gardeny, nos. 2244–C, 2245–F, 2246–D.

84. ACA, Varia 1, fols. 72–100ᵛ. The inventory was begun in February 1309. It is not a comprehensive one and it is probable that documents from other houses not mentioned were also kept at Miravet.

85. Javierre, *Privilegios*, pp. 86–8. The Hospitallers in Aragon did not create a central archive until 1428: A. L. Javierre Mur, 'El Archivo de San Juan de los Panetes de Zaragoza', *EEMCA*, iii (1947–8), 160; the scribes who copied Templar documents into the *Cartulario Magno* in the middle of the fourteenth century worked locally in the convents.

86. It is clear that not all original documents were kept at Miravet, for some were discovered in other Templar convents, such as Zaragoza and Cantavieja, after the arrest of the Templars: ACA, reg. 291, fols. 146–146ᵛ, 273ᵛ–274. The register of royal and papal privileges, which one of James II's officials found at Miravet at the end of 1308 (ACA, CRD Templarios, no. 147; reg. 291, fol. 184ᵛ) was probably one of the four inter-related cartularies of general privileges which have survived: ACA, regs. 309, 310 (in Latin); AHN, códs. 1032, 1312 (in Catalan).

87. Delaville, *Hospitaliers*, p. 364; Riley-Smith, *Knights of St. John*, p. 363.

88. Delaville, *Cartulaire*, i. 169, doc. 220.

89. AGP, Cartulary of Tortosa, fols. 63ᵛ–64, doc. 204.

90. AGP, parch. Gardeny, no. 604; RAH, 12–6–1/M–83, doc. 14. There is a reference to a provincial chapter in England as early as 1161: Lees, *Records*, p. li.

91. G. R. Galbraith, *The Constitution of the Dominican Order* (Manchester, 1925), pp. 54, 59. In the Temple the decision seems to have been made only a couple

of months before the holding of a chapter and commanders were given details in the summonses then sent out.

92. It is known to have been held at Monzón in:
    1212: RAH, 12-6-1/M-83, doc. 14.
    1225: AHN, cód. 494, pp. 1-4, doc. 1.
    *c.* 1230: M. Albareda y Herrera, *El fuero de Alfambra* (Madrid, 1925), pp. 39-41.
    1234: AHN, San Juan, leg. 673, doc. 2.
    1246: AHN, San Juan, leg. 663, doc. 3.
    1251: AHN, San Juan, leg. 663, doc. 5.
    1252: AHN, Montesa, sign. 543-C, fols. 39-42; Huici, *Colección diplomática,* i. 522-7, doc. 391; M. Gual Camarena, *Vocabulario del comercio medieval* (Tarragona, 1968), pp. 94-102, doc. 8; D. Sendra Cendra, *Aranceles aduaneros de la Corona de Aragón (siglo XIII)* (Valencia, 1966), pp. 63-4, doc. 7.
It was held at Gardeny in 1212: AGP, parch. Gardeny, no. 604.

93. Miravet: 1255: Albareda y Herrera, op. cit., p. 46.
            1275: AHN, cód. 467, p. 442, doc. 424.
            1296: ACA, parch. James II, no. 633.
            Undated summonses belonging to the late thirteenth or early fourteenth centuries: ACA, CRD Templarios, no. 507.
    Gardeny: 1281: ACA, parch. Peter III, no. 252.
            1286: AHN, Montesa, sign. 542-C, fols. 30$^v$-31.
            1294: ACA, reg. 97, fol. 294.
            ? 1303: AGP, parch. Gardeny, no. 231.
            Undated summonses: ACA, CRD Templarios, nos. 185, 403, 457 (these probably refer to the same year), 607; see below, p. 413.
    Monzón: 1271: AHN, cód. 466, pp. 41-2, doc. 43.
            Undated summonses: ACA, CRD Templarios, nos. 249, 278.
The chapter was held at Tortosa in 1263 and 1289: AHN, San Juan, leg. 529, doc. 2; ACA, parch. James I, no. 1796; P. Sanahuja, *Història de la ciutat de Balaguer* (Barcelona, 1965), p. 65. It met at Horta in 1307: ACA, CRD Templarios, no. 81; see below, p. 415.

94. Galbraith, op. cit., p. 60, suggests that this may have been the reason for the adoption of a similar practice by the Dominicans at this time.

95. ACA, CRD Templarios, nos. 185, 403, 457; see below, p. 413.

96. Chapters were summoned to begin on:
    The second Sunday in April: ACA, CRD Templarios, nos. 507, 607; cf. ACA, parch. James II, no. 633.
    The last Sunday in April:  CRD Templarios, no. 278.
    The second Sunday in May:  CRD Templarios, no. 249; cf. reg. 97, fol. 294; Finke, *AA,* i. 146-7, doc. 99.
    The last Sunday in May:    CRD Templarios, no. 81; see below, p. 415.

97. Finke, *AA,* i. 146-7, doc. 99.

98. ACA, CRD Templarios, no. 278.

99. Galbraith, op. cit., p. 72. The only apparent exception was in 1255. One document issued during the chapter of that year was drawn up on 4 May: Albareda y Herrera, op. cit., p. 46. But Miret y Sans, *Les Cases*, pp. 313–15, refers to two other charters issued by the chapter, one of which was similarly written on 4 May but the other of which was drawn up on 13 April. Both of these documents (AGP, parch. Espluga de Francolí, nos. 297, 423) have, however, disappeared and the accuracy of Miret y Sans's work at this point cannot be checked. But it seems very unlikely that the chapter would have lasted over three weeks.

100. Huici, *Colección diplomática*, i. 522–7, doc. 391; Sendra Cendra, op. cit., pp. 63–4, doc. 7; Gual Camarena, op. cit., pp. 94–102, doc. 8; AHN, San Juan, leg. 529, doc. 2. In these documents thirty and twenty-four commanders are named.

101. Michelet, *Procès*, ii. 16–17.

102. AGP, parch. Gardeny, no. 604.

103. Provincial chapters in the Hospital also consisted of commanders and other brothers: Delaville, *Hospitaliers*, p. 316, where it is assumed that the other brothers were members of the convent in which the chapter was held. The chapters of Calatrava were of similar composition: J. F. O'Callaghan, 'The Earliest "Difiniciones" of the Order of Calatrava, 1304–1383', *Traditio*, xvii (1961), 282.

104. Some payments made within the province were deducted from the responsions: ACA, CRD Templarios, no. 81; see below, p. 415.

105. In ? 1301, when the master was absent, his lieutenant did not summon a chapter but ordered that responsions should be brought to Gardeny on a certain date: ACA, CRD Templarios, no. 566.

106. ACA, CRD Templarios, no. 81; see below, p. 415.

107. Miret y Sans, *Les Cases*, pp. 399–400.

108. ACA, parch. Peter III, no. 26.

109. J. Miret y Sans, *Cartoral dels Templers de les comandes de Gardeny y Barbens* (Barcelona, 1899), pp. 29–30; idem, 'Inventaris de les cases del Temple de la Corona d'Aragó en 1289', *BRABLB*, vi (1911), 69.

110. Among those to whom pensions were paid at the beginning of the fourteenth century were Peter of Castro and G. of Jaffero: ACA, reg. 291, fol. 135. The former's perquisites at one time included falcons from Mallorca; the latter can probably be identified with En Jaffer, who was given a pension in 1305 when Raymond of Anglesola, precentor of Tarragona, was trying to secure his services as an advocate in a dispute with the Temple about the purchase of Culla: ACA, CRD Templarios, nos. 313, 560.

111. Cf. ACA, reg. 37, fol. 12; reg. 82, fol. 135.

112. Miret y Sans, *Cartoral dels Templers*, pp. 29–30; idem, 'Inventaris', pp. 62–9.

113. The chapter apparently met on 29 May, for it was in session on Tuesday, 31 May: Sanahuja, op. cit., p. 65. The other two inventories were compiled in April and June.

114. The importance attached to the maintenance of property in its existing state is illustrated by the evidence given at the time of the trial of the Templars by a cleric who said that when the provincial master had been requested to restore certain property unjustly held by the Temple he had replied that 'we ought not and cannot restore it; we ought rather to maintain it in the state in which we found it': Finke, *Papsttum*, ii. 376, doc. 157. In 1304 the commanders of the Order of Calatrava were ordered to bring similar statements to the chapter of that Order: O'Callaghan, loc. cit., p. 265.

115. Michelet, *Procès*, ii. 16–17.

116. J. Delaville Le Roulx, 'Un nouveau manuscrit de la Règle du Temple', *Annuaire-bulletin de la Société de l'Histoire de France*, xxvi (1889), 205–6.

117. RAH, 12–6–1/M–83, doc. 14.

118. Albareda y Herrera, op. cit., pp. 39–41; AHN, San Juan, leg. 673, doc. 2.

119. AHN, cód. 467, p. 442, doc. 424; Montesa, sign. 542–C, fols. 30ᵛ–31.

120. AHN, San Juan, leg. 663, doc. 3.

121. *Règle*, p. 249, art. 466.

122. e.g. AHN, cód. 468, pp. 77–8, doc. 73; cód. 689, pp. 73–4, doc. 74.

123. *Règle*, p. 86, art. 98; cf. AHN, cód. 466, pp. 61–2, doc. 61 *bis*, where the provincial master acts 'after common counsel and discussion had been held according to the statute and custom of our Order'.

124. e.g. AHN, San Juan, leg. 663, doc. 10; cód. 466, pp. 45–6, doc. 45.

125. ACA, CRD Templarios, no. 606.

126. ACA, CRD Templarios, no. 173.

127. ACA, CRD Templarios, no. 290.

128. Cf. Galbraith, op. cit., pp. 125, 132.

129. e.g. AHN, cód. 466, pp. 41–2, doc. 43. There is evidence, however, of a seal belonging to the provincial chapter in England in the mid twelfth century: Lees, *Records*, p. 245. On seals, see Appendix IV.

130. The only details given are that animals sent from the West should be given to the Marshal and that money should be paid into the treasury: *Règle*, p. 78, art. 84; p. 94, art. 111.

131. E. Langlois, *Les Registres de Nicolas IV* (Paris, 1886–93), p. 614, doc. 4204; Delaville, *Cartulaire*, i. 64, doc. 70. The Hospitaller regulation dates from before the middle of the twelfth century. The house of the Holy Sepulchre at

Calatayud sent a quarter of its revenues to the Holy Land: G. Tessier, 'Les débuts de l'Ordre du Saint-Sépulcre en Espagne', *BEC*, cxvi (1958), 21.

132. AHN, San Juan, leg. 39, doc. 102; see below, p. 382.

133. AHN, cód. 470, p. 47, doc. 62.

134. AHN, San Juan, leg. 306, doc. 12; ACA, parch. James I, nos. 1083, 1182.

135. AGP, parch. Barbará, no. 45; AHN, cód. 466, p. 145, doc. 108.

136. ACA, parch. James II, nos. 2071-3. In the first half of the fourteenth century the responsions of Hospitaller provinces were assessed as fixed sums of money: C. L. Tipton, 'The 1330 Chapter General of the Knights Hospitallers at Montpellier', *Traditio*, xxiv (1968), 303-4.

137. AGP, parch. Gardeny, no. 2241-A. The bishop assumed that 1,000 marks represented nearly a sixth of the province's income. This sum comprised about three-fifths of the total responsions owed in 1307, and the total responsions may have amounted to about a tenth of the income of Templar houses: see above, p. 319. The sum of 1,000 marks would thus be not only less than a sixth of the province's income but also less than the tenth which the Aragonese Templars earlier sent to the East.

138. ACA, CRD Templarios, no. 68.

139. Finke, *AA*, i. 79, doc. 55.

140. ACA, reg. 12, fol. 61ᵛ; R. Pernoud, *Histoire du commerce de Marseille*, i (Paris, 1949), 143, 247; S. García Larragueta, 'Relaciones comerciales entre Aragón y el Hospital de Acre', *VII Congreso de historia de la Corona de Aragón* (Barcelona, 1962), ii. 511-15.

141. ACA, reg. 63, fol. 89; reg. 66, fols. 57ᵛ, 58, 61ᵛ, 62, 127ᵛ; see below, p. 402.

142. ACA, reg. 81, fol. 81; reg. 83, fol. 13ᵛ; cf. reg. 73, fol. 81ᵛ; Finke, *AA*, iii. 8-9, doc. 5.

143. ACA, CRD Templarios, nos. 68, 310, 322, 357, 375, 376.

144. ACA, parch. Peter III, no. 292. This amount included the cost of transporting those who were to look after the animals during the voyage.

145. In 1279 the Templars sold a horse to the king for 1,500s.V., and the percentage is based on this figure: ACA, reg. 79, fol. 69. But some horses at this time were worth less: in 1289 the Order bought one for 800s.B.: ACA, parch. Alfonso III, no. 342; and horses were purchased in 1272 and 1298 for 1,000s.B. and 1,200s.B. respectively: C. E. Dufourcq, 'Prix et niveaux de vie dans les pays catalans et maghribins à la fin du xiiiᵉ et au début du xivᵉ siècles', *Le Moyen Âge*, lxxi (1965), 476-7. In these instances the percentage would be higher. A document drawn up in 1281 gives the value of a mark as 80s.: ACA, parch. Peter III, no. 250.

146. In a document belonging to the year 1288 mules are valued at 100-160s.: AHN, Montesa, P. 471. These may not, however, have been typical prices; in 1263 a mule was valued at 200s.: ACA, parch. James I, no. 1751; and at the

beginning of the fourteenth century prices of 703s.B. and 1,000s.B. have been found: Dufourcq, loc. cit., p. 477; while on one occasion at that time the provincial master was willing to pay 400s.B. for a mule: ACA, CRD Templarios, no. 346. Nevertheless 2½ marks would represent more than 14½ per cent of any of these prices.

147. Cf. C. M. Cipolla, *Money, Prices and Civilization in the Mediterranean World* (Princeton, 1956), p. 56. In 1302 the Templars sent 1,900 *cahíces* of wheat, worth nearly 700 marks: ACA, CRD Templarios, nos. 375, 376.

148. Cf. Y. Renouard, 'Un sujet de recherches: l'exportation de chevaux de la péninsule ibérique en France et en Angleterre au moyen âge', *Homenaje a Jaime Vicens Vives*, i (1965), 571–2.

149. J. Day, 'Prix agricoles en Méditerranée à la fin du XIVe siècle (1382)', *Annales*, xvi (1961), 629–56. There is some evidence to show that in the thirteenth century the cargoes carried by western merchants to the East included some essential goods like corn: e.g. Pernoud, op. cit. i. 155; cf. C. Cahen, *La Syrie du nord à l'époque des croisades* (Paris, 1940), p. 477; idem, 'Notes sur l'histoire des croisades et de l'orient latin. III. Orient latin et commerce du Levant', *Bulletin de la Faculté des Lettres de Strasbourg*, xxix (1950–1), 334.

150. Some information is provided by Dufourcq, loc. cit., pp. 475–520.

151. e.g. E. Ashtor, 'Le coût de la vie dans la Syrie médiévale', *Arabica*, viii (1961), 59–73; idem, 'La recherche des prix dans l'Orient médiéval', *Studia Islamica*, xxi (1964), 101–44; see also now the same writer's *Histoire des prix et des salaires dans l'Orient médiéval* (Paris, 1969).

152. An attempt at a comparison between Spain and the East has been made by E. Ashtor, 'Prix et salaires dans l'Espagne musulmane aux Xe et XIe siècles', *Annales*, xx (1965), 664–79, but this study does not go beyond the twelfth century and is concerned primarily with Muslim Spain.

153. Finke, *AA*, iii. 8–9, doc. 5.

154. Delaville, *Cartulaire*, ii. 462–4, doc. 2067; cf. Delaville, *Hospitaliers*, pp. 176–7. This agreement was the result of a dispute about an earlier concession by Hugh of Baux, which had been confirmed by Frederick II in 1216; this confirmation is contained in E. Winkelmann, *Acta imperii inedita seculi XIII* (Innsbruck, 1880), i. 117, doc. 139.

155. ACA, reg. 12, fol. 61v.

156. ACA, reg. 21, fol. 71.

157. ACA, reg. 81, fol. 81.

158. ACA, CRD Templarios, nos. 310, 322. Preparations would thus start at about the time of the provincial chapter.

159. ACA, parch. Peter III, no. 292.

160. Finke, *AA*, i. 79, doc. 55; ACA, CRD Templarios, no. 68.

161. ACA, reg. 66, fols. 57v, 58; reg. 81, fol. 81; Finke, *AA*, iii. 8–9, doc. 5.

162. In 1302 the commander of Peñíscola was ordered to buy corn on 9 May, but in the middle of August these supplies were still not ready for shipment: ACA, CRD Templarios, nos. 310, 322, 357, 375, 376.

163. ACA, parch. Peter III, no. 292.

164. ACA, CRD Templarios, no. 142.

165. ACA, CRD Templarios, nos. 377, 247.

166. ACA, CRD Templarios, no. 176.

167. K. Schottmüller, *Der Untergang des Templer-Ordens* (Berlin, 1887), ii. 143–400.

168. Riley-Smith, *Knights of St. John*, p. 284.

169. Arnold of Torroja (Grand Master 1181–4), Gilbert Eral (?1193–1201), and Peter of Monteagudo (1219–29).

170. *Règle*, pp. 80–1, arts, 87, 88; p. 144, art. 203.

171. See above, p. 313.

172. ACA, CRD Templarios, no. 142. The report which James of Molay sent to the pope on this subject probably followed this discussion: S. Baluzius, *Vitae Paparum Avenionensium*, ed. G. Mollat, iii (Paris, 1921), 145–9, doc. 32.

173. In the early fourteenth century the Hospitaller establishment of fighting brothers in Cyprus numbered eighty, but it is not known how many Hospitaller chaplains and *freres des mestiers* served there: Riley-Smith, *Knights of St. John*, p. 328.

174. Michelet, *Procès*, ii. 139.

175. e.g. ACA, CRD Templarios, no. 176.

176. ACA, parch. James II, nos. 31, 35, 2128.

177. A list of these officials, with variations in title, is given by Léonard, *Introduction*, pp. 15–17. The title *magister citra mare* was applied in 1146 to both Peter and Berenguer of Rovira: Albon, *Cartulaire*, pp. 256–7, docs. 408, 409; but at that time titles were used loosely and these Templars had no more than local authority.

178. Léonard, *Introduction*, pp. 17–18.

179. Cf. Delaville, *Hospitaliers*, pp. 355 ff.

180. J. Miret y Sans, *Itinerari de Jaume I 'el Conqueridor'* (Barcelona, 1918), p. 385. He held office in 1266. Thirty years earlier Fernando III made a grant to Stephen of Belmonte 'magistro ordinis milicie Templi in quinque regnis Hyspanie': AHN, San Juan, lengua de Castilla, donaciones reales, leg. 1, 1ª serie, doc. 13; but the royal notary was perhaps confusing offices in the Temple with those in the Hospital.

181. Arnold of Castellnou was visitor in 1278; Peter of Moncada held the post from 1279 until 1281; and Berenguer of Cardona was in office from 1297 until 1307.

182. ACA, reg. 40, fols. 26ᵛ, 38ᵛ; parch. Peter III, no. 46; AGP, parch. Barbará, no. 71.

183. J. Delaville Le Roulx, *Documents concernant les Templiers extraits des Archives de Malte* (Paris, 1882), p. 34, doc. 21; Delaville, *Cartulaire*, iii. 30–3, docs. 3028, 3029; S. Pauli, *Codice diplomatico del sacro militare ordine gerosolimitano*, i (Lucca, 1733), 194–5, doc. 152.

184. ACA, parch. James I, nos. 2233, 2234; AHN, cód. 467, p. 442, doc. 424; Montesa, P. 520. James of Molay apparently also intended to visit Spain in 1307: Finke, *Papsttum*, ii. 37, doc. 24.

185. ACA, CRD Templarios, no. 99.

186. ACA, parch. James II, no. 2260; see below, p. 414. A document recording the establishment of a proctor by the visitor of France and England in 1290 is published in Delaville Le Roulx, *Documents*, pp. 45–6, but the wording is imprecise and no indication of the powers and functions of a visitor is given.

187. On the use of the phrase 'five kingdoms of Spain', see L. G. de Valdeavellano, *Historia de las instituciones españolas* (Madrid, 1968), p. 232.

188. ACA, CRD Templarios, no. 322.

189. AHN, cód. 471, pp. 318–19, doc. 251. A promise not to sell or alienate property is also found in a copy of the oath to be sworn by a new provincial master in Portugal, which has been published from a manuscript belonging to the Cistercian monastery of Alcobaça by C. Henriquez, *Regula, Constitutiones et Privilegia Ordinis Cisterciensis* (Antwerp, 1630), pp. 478–9, and P. Dupuy, *Histoire de l'Ordre militaire des Templiers* (Brussels, 1751), pp. 103–4; but the wording of the document shows that it is one of the forgeries for which that monastery is well known.

190. Huici, *Colección diplomática*, i. 413–15, doc. 299.

191. AGP, parch. Cervera, no. 484; see below, p. 405.

192. AHN, Montesa, P. 520, 523.

193. ACA, reg. 11, fol. 235.

194. AHN, San Juan, leg. 333, doc. 15.

195. *Règle*, pp. 277–8, arts. 527–30.

196. J. Delaville Le Roulx, 'Un nouveau manuscrit de la Règle du Temple', *Annuaire-bulletin de la Société de l'Histoire de France*, xxvi (1889), 205–6.

197. *Règle*, pp. 289–90, art. 554; pp. 296–7, art. 569.

198. Delaville, *Cartulaire*, i. 378–9, doc. 558; cf. J. Sayers, 'The Judicial Activities of the General Chapters', *Journal of Ecclesiastical History*, xv (1964), 180–2. A similar agreement was made in 1262 by the Templars in Aragon with the Order of Calatrava: AHN, cód. 689, pp. 13–14, doc. 8. For other agreements among military orders in Spain, see D. W. Lomax, *La Orden de Santiago* (Madrid, 1965), p. 48; J. F. O'Callaghan, '*Hermandades* between the Military Orders of Calatrava and Santiago during the Castilian Reconquest, 1158-1252', *Speculum*, xliv (1969), 609–18.

# Secular Activities of the Templars

THE secular activities of the Templars included, as has been seen, participation in the reconquest and the administration of property, but they were not limited to these. The Order's temporal power in the *Corona de Aragón* made the provincial master an important political figure; and at a time when the Crown lacked an adequate body of professional administrators, the Temple—like other ecclesiastical institutions—was used as a recruiting ground for royal servants and officials; while the Templars were also commonly engaged in banking and money-lending activities.

The provincial master's standing gave him a natural place among the counsellors of the king. He was often in attendance at court and was regularly summoned to the Cortes.[1] But even among the leading men of the kingdom the master often appears to have enjoyed a particular prestige, for at times he was assigned tasks of special responsibility. William of Montrodón was thus made tutor to James I during the latter's minority,[2] and James in his first will drawn up in 1232 nominated the provincial master as a tutor for his own son Alfonso.[3] On several occasions the master acted as a mediator in major political disputes: in 1227, for example, the issues in dispute between James I and the Aragonese nobility were submitted for arbitration to the provincial master Fulk of Montpesat, the archbishop of Tarragona, and the bishop of Lérida.[4] On many other occasions the master was employed in the more normal activities of a king's servant, such as acting as a royal envoy. Among those who occupied this role were William of Pontóns, who was James I's representative at the papal court in 1262 when the marriage between the Infante Peter and Constance of Sicily was being negotiated,[5] and Arnold of Castellnou, who was one of James's ambassadors to the French king in 1272.[6]

Advisory and administrative functions were also performed by other members of the Order. At the Cortes of Monzón in 1289

Peter of Tous, the commander of Miravet, was appointed to the king's council.[7] The commander of Ascó was a royal representative at Rome in 1284,[8] and seven years later this position was occupied by the commander of the house of Ribaforada in Navarre.[9] In 1276 Peter Peronet, the commander of Burriana, was similarly ordered to negotiate on the king's behalf with the Moorish rebels of Eslida.[10] In the same year Peter Peronet also held the post of royal almoner and administered royal rights at Villarreal near Burriana.[11] Templars appear to have been employed most frequently, however, as financial officials, engaged in the reception of royal dues and taxes. In 1184 the Templar Pons of Azemar was one of those who received accounts from the royal bailiffs of Tarragona and Cervera.[12] In the same way, the commander of Palau, with a canon of Barcelona, received from the moneyers an account of the profits resulting from changes in the coinage made at the end of the year 1222,[13] while two years earlier a Templar had been appointed temporarily both in Aragon and in Catalonia to supervise the collection and administration of all royal revenues.[14] Similarly in 1289 the commander of Barcelona, Romeo of Burguet, was deputed to receive accounts from all royal officials,[15] and at the same time Templars were nominated to appoint collectors of an aid in the dioceses of Vich and Lérida.[16] The Order thus contributed a not inconsiderable number of those temporary officials on whom any royal administration of the period so much depended.[17] The Templars who carried out administrative tasks for the Crown would already have gained experience on the Order's own estates, where the administrative techniques would not have differed radically from those used by the Crown. By employing Templars the king was therefore obtaining the services of trained men, who could easily adapt themselves to the methods employed in the royal administration. There was, of course, the danger that in undertaking tasks imposed by the king the Templars would neglect their own duties; but these royal demands could not be refused if the Order wanted to remain in the king's favour.

Although individual Templars became involved in political affairs, the Order as a whole appears not to have played a major role in Aragonese politics.[18] The nomination of the provincial master as an arbiter in political disputes was made possible by the Temple's neutrality, and the Order's activities during the conflict between king and pope following the Sicilian Vespers suggest that its primary concern at that time was the preservation of its rights and property. In that struggle the Templars gave their support to the Crown, but they seem to have done so only reluctantly, and a number of protests against royal demands were made by the Order. This does not indicate, however, that the Templars sympathized strongly with the papacy, for their protests were not occasioned by Martin IV's sentence on Peter III. The protests were concerned merely with breaches of Templar privilege; such complaints were not new, nor did they cease when pope and king were reconciled. In giving support to the king, the Order appears merely to have been following the course which seemed to present the least immediate threat to its rights and privileges, although its siding with the Aragonese did create difficulties in Roussillon, where—at the instigation of the French king—James of Mallorca seized the house of Mas-Deu on the pretext that it was subject to the Aragonese Templars.[19] The Order's relations with the baronial opposition to the king at this time were similarly influenced by a concern for rights and privileges. Although its interests to some extent coincided with those of the nobles, the Temple was wary of entering into any commitment which might endanger its powers of jurisdiction: thus in 1284 the castellan of Monzón forbade his vassals to take any oath to the union of Aragonese nobles, because such an action would prejudice Templar authority.[20]

The Order was more important in the sphere of finance than in that of politics. The banking and moneylending activities of the Aragonese Templars were similar to those of their French and English colleagues, whose work in this sphere is well known,[21] but the surviving evidence suggests that in Aragon these activities were conducted on a rather smaller scale than in the other countries.

In Aragon as elsewhere Templar houses served as places of deposit, and they were frequently used for this purpose by all classes of men. At Gardeny there was even a special 'house of deposits'.[22] Anything could be deposited, including Moorish prisoners or a mule, left while its owner was abroad.[23] Early in the thirteenth century Gerald of Cabrera and his son had gold, silver, horses, and corn in safe-keeping at Gardeny.[24] Most deposits, however, fell into one of three classes: jewellery, documents, or money. In James I's reign royal jewels and ecclesiastical ornaments were at times kept at Gardeny and Monzón,[25] and among those of lesser rank who made deposits of this kind was a Valencian knight, Peter of Monteagudo, who in his will drawn up in 1256 stipulated that a ring deposited in the convent of Valencia should remain there until his son came of age.[26] The documents in Templar custody often included those placed temporarily in the Order's keeping while settlements and agreements were being put into effect. When Peter of Alcalá drew up his will in 1214 he handed over to the Temple all his title deeds, which were to be retained by the Order until the conditions of his will had been fulfilled,[27] and in 1241 Elvira, the widow of William of Cervellón, similarly entrusted to the commander of Palau several acknow-ledgements of debt, which were to be recovered by the debtors when they had fulfilled their obligations.[28]

Money was deposited in the Temple both by private individuals and by royal and papal officials. Gardeny in 1241 held cash belong-ing to the viscount of Cardona,[29] and seven years later the family of Moncada was using the Templar house at Tortosa for the same purpose,[30] while in 1275 the countess of Urgel received back money which she had deposited in the convent at Valencia.[31] Part of the crusading tenth exacted by Gregory X was deposited with the Aragonese Templars in 1277;[32] in 1270 the *peaje* exacted by royal officials at Alagón was for a time placed in the keeping of the commander of Zaragoza;[33] and five years later the houses of Zaragoza, Huesca, Tarazona, and Teruel for a while had custody of the *peita* paid to the Crown by the Jewish *aljamas* of those places.[34] In these last two instances royal officials were using Templar convents and houses merely as temporary local treasuries, and other depositors appear to have done the same. No one in Aragon is known to have used the Temple as his sole treasury and there is no evidence of the existence of current accounts, such as are encountered in France, into which money was regularly paid and from which disbursements were made by the Temple on behalf of its clients.[35] The Aragonese Templars did at times make payments on behalf of others, but in all the instances in which the circumstances are known they used money which either belonged to the Order or was derived from particular deposits.

Some individuals deposited money specifically in order that the Temple might make a payment on their behalf: when in

1256, for example, Lope of Fraga wanted to pay 200*maz.* to William of San Melione he used the commander of Tortosa as an intermediary.[36] Money might alternatively be deposited with the Temple for the purpose of having it transferred from one place to another: in 1270 a Catalan knight, William of Pujalt, received from the convent of Palau some money which he had deposited with the Order in the East.[37] Deposits might, on the other hand, be made merely for safe-keeping. The Temple's military and religious character made it particularly well suited for this task. Although Desclot reports that Peter III seized treasure which James of Mallorca had deposited with the Templars in Roussillon,[38] this was probably an exceptional occurrence; it was a seizure made by a king in time of war. There is no evidence to show that deposits might also be made with the Temple as a form of invest- ment, as they were with other bankers.[39] Most of the surviving documents are admittedly records of the withdrawal and not of the deposit of money and do not specify the terms on which deposits were made; but the few deposit agreements which have been preserved refer to 'demand' and not to 'time' deposits, such as are encountered in Genoese and other records of the twelfth and thirteenth centuries;[40] and in no document is there any refer- ence to the repayment of any sum other than the amount de- posited. It is not even clear whether the Templars made use of the money deposited with them. It has sometimes been assumed that the Order loaned it out,[41] but the scanty evidence which has been found on this subject does not support this assumption;[42] and there is with regard to Aragon the further point that as deposits were made on only a limited scale it would not have been easy for the Order to utilize them. The Temple might, however, derive benefit in other ways, even if immediately it was nothing more tangible than the goodwill of the depositor.

The moneylending activities of the Templars in Aragon can be traced back as far as the 1130s.[43] At that time it was not uncommon for ecclesiastical institutions to lend money, but whereas most other religious establishments soon lost importance in this sphere, moneylending became and remained a Templar activity of considerable significance. The surviving sources show that the Templars continued to make frequent loans up to the time of their arrest. These sources probably cover, however, only a fraction of the Temple's activity in this field, for there was no necessity to keep records of loans after the money had been repaid; records of advances made to the king have sometimes been preserved because the instruments of debt were copied into the royal registers, but documents concerning loans to private individuals have usually survived only by chance.

Money was borrowed from the Temple by men of all ranks and classes, including the Jews,[44] but the most important client was the king. In the early years of his reign Alfonso II obtained numerous loans from the Order, including 1,100*m*. in 1164, 1,200*m*. in 1167, 5,000*m*. in 1169, and 400*m*. in 1175,[45] while the royal registers show that in the second half of the thirteenth century the Crown was making constant recourse to the Temple for money. The demand for loans was such that, as in France,[46] the Templars had difficulty in satisfying it. When James I asked the Templars to lend him 4,000*m*. in 1264, he mentioned the possibility that they might have to borrow money themselves before they could make the loan, and in fact on a number of occasions the Temple was obliged to do this in order to satisfy royal demands.[47] The use of an ecclesiastical institution in the role of an intermediary—which was perhaps not uncommon[48]—probably facilitated the borrowing of money especially by rulers. Laymen would probably be more ready to make loans to an institution like the Temple than to advance money directly to the king, because a religious institution was less likely to repudiate a debt. The king, on the other hand, might be expected to honour obligations to ecclesiastical creditors more readily than those to laymen. Nevertheless the Templars in Aragon appear to have been reluctant to act in this role; they did so only 'at the great prayers' and 'the great insistence' of the king.[49] They no doubt feared lest, if the king defaulted, they would themselves be obliged to pay back not only the capital borrowed on his behalf but also the interest charged on that sum, thus incurring a double loss.

Most of the loans made by the Temple were short-term advances, which were sought by the Aragonese kings and others in order to overcome merely temporary financial difficulties and which could be repaid when clients' rents and dues were collected. A debtor normally repaid a loan of this kind by assigning some of his incoming revenues to the Order. If he usually received dues from the Temple, the Order was normally allowed to recoup itself from these. In the thirteenth and early fourteenth centuries royal debts to the Temple were frequently repaid out of the *monedaje* and *cena* which the Crown usually received from the Order's lands,[50] and in 1232 the bishop of Zaragoza in the same way made repayment out of dues owed to him by Templar churches in his diocese.[51] Occasionally debtors promised instead to pay back a debt on a certain date, but even then a clause was often inserted in the instrument of debt to the effect that if the debtor defaulted the Order was to recover its loan out of the income derived from certain properties.[52]

When revenues were assigned to the Templars in repayment of loans, it was often agreed that the Order could deduct part of the sum collected to cover its expenses, as was permitted in canon law:[53] when the Templars in 1169, for example, were assigned royal dues in Ascó in repayment of a debt owed by the king, they were allowed to retain a third of these revenues for this purpose.[54] But the Aragonese sources, like those of other countries,[55] do not reveal whether the Templars usually gained a direct monetary profit from lending. Only rarely can it be definitely stated that the Aragonese Templars did so. In a few instances they are known to have profited through the mortgaging of lands to them by debtors. Thus in 1189 a woman and her son pledged four vineyards and other lands to the commander of Boquiñeni and stated that the Order should retain this property and receive the produce from it 'for the souls of all our forebears' until they paid back a debt of 50*s.* which they owed to the Temple.[56] But even when references to mortgages do occur, it is not made clear whether the lands pledged were held of the Temple, and on this depended the legality of the transaction, for after the middle of the twelfth century a lender was allowed to retain the revenues of pledged land as profit only if he was the lord of the land and released the tenant from his tenurial obligations.[57] The mortgaging of lands to the Temple could not, however, have been a very common practice, because rents and dues were usually assigned to the Order for the repayment of the capital borrowed. When this was done the Temple sometimes charged interest at a fixed rate. When the bishop of Zaragoza in 1232 assigned the Order his revenues from Templar churches for a year, he stated that he was doing this in order to repay a debt of 550*m.*, 'namely 500 as capital and 50 as usury annually on the said 500*m*.'[58] This rate of 10 per cent *per annum*—2 per cent less than the maximum allowed to Christian moneylenders in Aragon and half of the Jewish rate[59]—appears to have been that normally charged by the Temple, for it was referred to several times by James I as the 'rate and custom of the Temple'.[60] In royal documents the exaction of interest by the Templars is mentioned only when the Order was acting as an intermediary, and in these cases the Templars were not deriving a profit but merely gaining compensation for the interest which they paid on sums borrowed on the king's behalf. But it cannot be proved that the Templars charged interest only in these circumstances. The 1232 charter of the bishop of Zaragoza makes no reference to the Templars' acting as intermediaries and it could well be referring to the exaction of usury by the Order for its own benefit.

While in a few instances the Templars definitely obtained a direct monetary gain from moneylending,[61] on some other occasions they appear not to have done so. Thus several loans made to Ramonedo of Moncada in 1302 were specifically stated to be free from usury.[62] But in the majority of documents there is no indication whether the Templars made a monetary profit or not. This silence does not necessarily mean that nothing was obtained, for interest could easily be concealed. The sums allowed to the Templars for expenses could easily hide an extra payment, especially when the Order was assigned a fixed proportion of revenues for this purpose. In some other cases it is possible that interest was deducted from a loan at the time when the money was lent, so that the amount mentioned in the instrument of debt would represent the sum loaned, but not the actual amount received by the borrower.[63] Interest might have been concealed in this way, for example, when the count of Urgel in 1186 granted the Temple revenues worth 175*s*.J. *per annum* for two years to repay a debt of 350*s*.J., without making any allowance for additional repayments.[64] But this could not have happened on every occasion when interest was not specifically mentioned, for it is made clear in some instances that the debtor received the whole sum that was to be repaid: when James I in 1227 assigned the Order revenues worth 500*s*.J. a year for eight years in repayment of a debt of 4,000*s*.J., he gave details of payments made by the Order on his behalf and these totalled exactly 4,000*s*.J.[65] But even if a document does not contain a concealed reference to interest it is of course possible that the Order still received some additional payment. Nevertheless, it would be dangerous to assume that a definite charge was made in all cases where there is no reference to interest. Peter II's restoration of Tortosa to the Templars in 1202 on the day that they lent him 1,000m.[66] suggests that in some cases the reward which the Temple gained consisted in the goodwill and favour of the borrower rather than in any precise monetary return. And the reference to usury in the bishop of Zaragoza's acknowledgement of debt in 1232 shows that not everyone tried to conceal the payment of usury to Christian moneylenders.[67] The absence of any reference to interest in a document might therefore sometimes mean that the Temple received no direct monetary return from a loan. But since moneylending was not just an occasional and peripheral activity for the Temple, it may be doubted whether many of the loans made by it were as completely gratuitous as the ecclesiastical authorities would have wished.

NOTES

1. *Cortes de Aragón, Valencia y Cataluña*, i (Madrid, 1896), 123, 140, 182–3, 197–8; J. Vincke, *Documenta selecta mutuas civitatis Arago-Cathalaunicae et ecclesiae relationes illustrantia* (Barcelona, 1936), p. 29, doc. 55; p. 52, doc. 94.

2. S. Sanpere y Miquel, 'Minoría de Jaime I', *Congreso de historia de la Corona de Aragón*, ii (Barcelona, 1913), 580–694, *passim*.

3. Huici, *Colección diplomática*, i. 187–9, doc. 101.

4. *CDI*, vi. 90–5, doc. 15.

5. D. Girona y Llagustera, 'Mullerament del Infant En Pere de Cathalunya ab Madona Constança de Sicília', *Congreso de historia de la Corona de Aragón*, i (Barcelona, 1909), 245, 268; J. Guiraud, *Les Registres d'Urbain IV*, ii (Paris, 1901), 29–31, doc. 94.

6. C. Baudon de Mony, *Relations politiques des comtes de Foix avec la Catalogne* (Paris, 1896), i. 221; ii. 147, doc. 62.

7. ACA, reg. 73, fol. 80.

8. ACA, reg. 47, fol. 131.

9. ACA, reg. 90, fol. 100v.

10. F. Soldevila, *Pere el Gran*, II. i (Barcelona, 1962), 23, 82, doc. 50.

11. AHN, Montesa, R. 132.

12. ACA, parch. Alfonso II, nos. 360, 361.

13. ACA, parch. James I, no. 207.

14. *CDI*, vi. 81–3, doc. 12; Huici, *Colección diplomática*, i. 33–4, doc. 16.

15. ACA, reg. 80, fol. 127ᵛ.

16. Ibid., fol. 136.

17. For examples of Templars in royal service in other countries, see M. L. Bulst-Thiele, 'Templer in königlichen und päpstlichen Diensten', *Festschrift Percy Ernst Schramm* (Wiesbaden, 1964), i. 289–308.

18. The Order of Santiago appears similarly to have avoided political entanglements: see D. W. Lomax, *La Orden de Santiago* (Madrid, 1965), pp. 30, 35.

19. The Templars in the East appealed to Nicholas IV to take action against James, but the pope's order for the surrender of the house was made conditional on its being administered by someone who was loyal to the pope and the king of Mallorca: S. Baluzius, *Vitae Paparum Avenionensium*, ed. G. Mollat, iii (Paris, 1921), 7–8, doc. 5.

20. AHN, cód. 471, pp. 318–19, doc. 251.

21. L. Delisle, *Mémoire sur les opérations financières des Templiers* (Mémoires de l'Institut National de France, Académie des Inscriptions et Belles-Lettres, xxxiii. 2, 1889); J. Piquet, *Des banquiers au moyen âge: les Templiers* (Paris, 1939); A. Sandys, 'The Financial and Administrative Importance of the London Temple in the Thirteenth Century', *Essays in Mediaeval History presented to Thomas Frederick Tout*, ed. A. G. Little and F. M. Powicke (Manchester, 1925), pp. 147–62; T. W. Parker, *The Knights Templars in England* (Tucson, 1963), pp. 58–80.

22. ACA, reg. 291, fol. 230.

23. AHN, cód. 466, pp. 53–4, doc. 52; ACA, parch. James I, no. 405.

24. AGP, parch. Gardeny, no. 461.

25. AHN, cód. 471, p. 124, doc. 119; p. 149, doc. 148; see below, p. 385.

26. AHN, Montesa, P. 204.

27. ACA, reg. 310, fol. 75–75ᵛ.

28. ACA, parch. James I, no. 864.

29. AGP, parch. Gardeny, no. 642.

30. AGP, parch. Tortosa, no. 38.

31. AHN, Montesa, P. 358.

32. ACA, reg. 39, fol. 225–225ᵛ; Delaville, *Cartulaire*, iii. 350, doc. 3631.

33. AHN, cód. 467, p. 396, doc. 333.

34. ACA, reg. 58, fol. 100ᵛ.

35. Piquet, op. cit., pp. 36 ff.; Delisle, op. cit., pp. 24 ff.

36. AGP, parch. Tortosa, no. 51.

37. ACA, parch. James I, no. 2034; published in part by M. Vilar Bonet, 'Actividades financieras de la Orden del Temple en la Corona de Aragón', *VII Congreso de historia de la Corona de Aragón* (Barcelona, 1962), ii. 584.

38. B. Desclot, *Chronicle of the Reign of King Pedro III of Aragon*, ed. F. L. Critchlow, ii (Princeton, 1928), 201–2.

39. A. E. Sayous, 'Les opérations des banquiers italiens en Italie et aux foires de Champagne pendant le xiiie siècle', *Revue historique*, clxx (1932), 10–11.

40. ACA, parch. James I, no. 379; AHN, Montesa, P. 212; cf. M. W. Hall, 'Early Bankers in the Genoese Notarial Records', *Economic History Review*, vi (1935–6), 77–8; R. de Roover, 'New Interpretations of the History of Banking', *Cahiers d'histoire mondiale*, ii (1954–5), 39. It seems, however, that not all demand deposits were returned on demand, and that deposits of this kind were in fact sometimes investments: A. E. Sayous, 'Les méthodes commerciales de Barcelone au xiiie siècle, d'après des documents inédits des archives de sa cathédrale', *Estudis universitaris catalans*, xvi (1931), 172, 192–3.

41. Delisle, op. cit., p. 15; Parker, op. cit., p. 66.

42. e.g. Joinville, *Histoire de Saint Louis*, cap. 75, ed. N. de Wailly (Société de l'Histoire de France, 1868), pp. 134–6, quoted by Delisle, op. cit., pp. 8–9. Parker, op. cit., pp. 60–1, mentions several occasions on which money deposits kept in chests and strong-boxes were seized from the English Templars.

43. Albon, *Cartulaire*, p. 64, doc. 84; p. 79, doc. 111; Lacarra, 'Documentos', nos. 183 (iii. 576), 188 (iii. 579–80).

44. AGP, parch. Tortosa, no. 22. Jews were of course forbidden to exact interest from or pay interest to fellow Jews.

45. ACA, parch. Alfonso II, nos. 13, 67, 179; AGP, parch. Gardeny, no. 648. Some of these loans are discussed by Vilar Bonet, loc. cit., pp. 579–81.

46. *Cambridge Economic History of Europe*, iii (Cambridge, 1963), 477.

47. ACA, reg. 13, fol. 157–157v; reg. 14, fols. 48v, 52v–53; reg. 28, fols. 37v–38; AHN, Montesa, R. 173; see below, p. 394.

48. *Cambridge Economic History of Europe*, iii. 444.

49. ACA, reg. 14, fols. 52v–53; reg. 28, fols. 37v–38; AHN, Montesa, R. 173; see below, p. 394.

50. ACA, reg. 13, fol. 157–157v; reg. 14, fols. 48v, 52v–53; reg. 332, fol. 280; reg. 333, fols. 33–4; parch. James II, nos. 1537, 2245; see below, p. 394.

51. AHN, cód. 467, pp. 258–9, doc. 265.

52. e.g. ACA, parch. Alfonso II, nos. 13, 239.

53. J. T. Noonan, *The Scholastic Analysis of Usury* (Cambridge, Mass., 1957), p. 112.

54. ACA, parch. Alfonso II, no. 67.

55. Cf. Delisle, op. cit., p. 87; Piquet, op. cit., pp. 52–6; Sandys, loc. cit., pp. 158–9; Parker, op. cit., pp. 69–72.

56. AHN, cód. 470, pp. 72–3, doc. 86.

57. Noonan, op. cit., pp. 102–3.

58. AHN, cód. 467, pp. 258–9, doc. 265.

59. *Cortes de Aragón, Valencia y Cataluña*, i. 126, 131; cf. F. de Bofarull y Sans, 'Jaime I y los judíos', *Congreso de historia de la Corona de Aragón*, ii (Barcelona, 1913), 852; A. A. Neuman, *The Jews in Spain* (Philadelphia, 1944), i. 200–1.

60. ACA, reg. 13, fol. 157–157$^v$; reg. 14, fol. 48$^v$.

61. M. Melville, *La Vie des Templiers* (Paris, 1951), pp. 75–6, maintains that in 1135 the Aragonese Templars profited from a loan which was made in the form of a purchase and later re-sale of land; their interest consisted of the revenues derived from the land while it was in the Order's possession. But it is by no means certain that they did receive the revenues in this instance, for they were to account for them when the land was repurchased by the original owners: Albon, *Cartulaire*, p. 79, doc. 111; Lacarra, 'Documentos', no. 188 (iii. 579–80).

62. AHN, cód. 467, pp. 263–5, docs. 273, 274.

63. Cf. G. Bigwood, *Le Régime juridique et économique du commerce de l'argent dans la Belgique du moyen âge* (Académie Royale de Belgique, Classe des Lettres, Mémoires, 2$^e$ série, xiv. 1, Brussels, 1921), pp. 453–4; Sayous, 'Les méthodes', p. 170.

64. AGP, parch. Gardeny, no. 1928.

65. AHN, cód. 471, p. 106, doc. 101.

66. See above, pp. 29–30.

67. Cf. J. Ibanès, *La Doctrine de l'Église et les réalités économiques au XIII$^e$ siècle* (Paris, 1967), p. 91.

# X

## *Conclusion: The Dissolution of the Temple*[1]

THE Templars maintained their banking and moneylending activities throughout the thirteenth century, but during the later part of that period their situation in the *Corona de Aragón* was becoming increasingly difficult. Although revenues in the reconquered areas were probably still rising to some extent as a result of continuing resettlement, the Order was gaining little new property through gift or purchase. On the other hand, increasing demands were being made on Templar resources through the exaction of extraordinary aids both by the Aragonese kings and by the Temple in the East, while the Order's income had been reduced through the restrictions imposed on its rights and privileges by the Aragonese rulers, who were seeking to increase their own wealth and authority.

Nevertheless, although James II like earlier rulers sought to reduce the Order's privileges, in 1307 he was reluctant to follow the example of the French king and arrest the Templars and seize their property. Philip IV wrote to the Aragonese king in the middle of October, informing him that he had ordered the seizure of the Templars and of their possessions in France on charges of heresy, idolatry, and immorality; and he invited James to do the same in Aragon.[2] News was also brought to James of the arrest of the Templars in Navarre, which was then ruled by Philip's son.[3] But instead of taking immediate action against the Templars the Aragonese king—like Edward II in England[4]—came out in their support. In the middle of November he wrote to Philip that

they have lived indeed in a praiseworthy manner as religious men up till now in these parts according to common opinion, nor has any accusation of error in belief yet arisen against them here; on the contrary, during our reign they have faithfully given us very great service, in whatever we have required of them, in repressing the enemies of the faith.[5]

Although James would have liked to reduce the Templars' power, he realized their value to him. He told Philip that he would take no measures against them until required to do so by the Church or until he was more certain that he ought to act. At this stage he merely wrote to the pope seeking advice.[6]

In the later part of November, however, further letters arrived from France, bearing the news that the Grand Master and other Templars had confessed to the crimes of which they had been accused.[7] Therefore at the beginning of December James commanded the bishops of Valencia and Zaragoza and the inquisitor John of Lotgers to undertake an investigation and ordered the seizure of the Templars and their possessions in the *Corona de Aragón*.[8] This was done before any instructions had been received from Clement V, and this earned the Aragonese king a rebuke from the pope, who obviously feared losing control of the proceedings against the Temple in Spain as well as in France.[9]

In some districts the seizure of the Templars and their possessions ordered by James II was carried out quickly and without difficulty. Peñíscola and other Templar strongholds in northern Valencia, for example, were taken into royal hands almost immediately.[10] But greater resistance was encountered in some other areas, especially Aragon. There the Templars fortified their castles and resisted royal forces, while at the same time protesting their innocence.[11] Villel and Castellote did not fall until the autumn of 1308 and Miravet held out until December of that year, while Monzón was not captured until May 1309.[12]

Clement V had in the meantime elaborated the procedure to be followed in investigating the conduct of the Templars. In the summer of 1308 he issued a series of bulls in which he appointed for each country a group of papal commissioners, who were to act in conjunction with the local bishops in carrying out the inquiries. The results of the investigations were to be presented to provincial councils, which were to pronounce sentence on individual Templars.[13] No complete record survives of the interrogations to which the Aragonese Templars were subjected. It is known that the questioning was completed by the summer of 1310,[14] but the only documentary evidence that has been preserved from the lands subject to James II is of the answers given by thirty-two Templars and several non-Templar witnesses when questioned at Lérida in February and March 1310 by the diocesan and some of the papal commissioners.[15] The only full record that exists for any part of the Aragonese province is that for Roussillon, which lay outside the territories ruled by James II.[16] The Templars who were questioned at Lérida, like those who were interrogated in Roussillon, admitted to a few of the minor charges, but denied all the more important and serious accusations. Thus while it was agreed that there was no noviciate, charges such as those concerning the denial of Christ, the worshipping of idols, and homosexual practices were vigorously contested. The non-Templar witnesses were not, however, so unanimous. Some spoke in support of the Order. The Franciscan William of Xesa, who claimed to have heard the confessions of many Templars, said that 'he found them good Christians and confessing faithfully and devotedly like true catholics.' The warden of the Franciscans in Lérida, who had also heard Templar confessions, similarly asserted that the Templars seemed to be good Christians. On the other hand, Raymond of Carcassonne, the rector of Aytona, was of the opinion that the accusations made against the Order were true. But none of the witnesses who appeared before the bishop of Lérida could do more than refer to rumours and suspicions, many of which had as their basis merely the secrecy in which Templar chapters were held. Reference was made by several of the witnesses to the placing of a guard on the door at the time of chapter meetings, while the Franciscan Peter Mir told how Raymond of Orchau had come 'pale and stupefied' out of the chapter which had received him into the Order. But none could produce any substantial evidence against the Templars.

The pope was not satisfied with reports sent to him by the Aragonese commissioners, and in March 1311 he ordered that the Aragonese Templars should be subjected to torture in order, as he said, 'that the truth might be elicited more clearly and more certainly from them'. Again the evidence which survives is limited, but eight Templars are known to have been subjected to torture and questioning again by the archbishop of Tarragona and the bishop of Valencia at Barcelona in August 1311. Some of these Templars feared that they might give way under torture and asserted beforehand that any confession of guilt they might make would not be true but only induced by the torture; but all in fact even under torture continued to maintain their innocence of all the main charges levelled against them.[17]

As the results of the inquiries conducted in many other countries were similarly favourable to the Temple, there was no justification for an outright condemnation of the Order. But on the grounds that the Order had been rendered suspect by the confessions of the Grand Master and others, and because it was alleged that no one would in future want to join it, in March 1312 at the Council of Vienne Clement V decreed the abolition of the Temple,[18] to the protests of the Aragonese prelates.[19] At the beginning of May he assigned the possessions of the Temple to the Hospitallers. From this ruling, however, were excepted Templar lands and rights in Portugal, Castile, Aragon, and Mallorca.[20] This reservation was made to a large extent as a result of the activities of James II and of his envoys.

Already before the end of 1307 James had begun to consider the possible fate of the Temple's Aragonese possessions,[21] and from that time onwards he was involved in negotiations about the Order's property, while retaining control of Templar possessions in Aragon until a decision was reached, despite orders to surrender them to the custodians named by the pope.[22] James's primary concern, whether the Temple was abolished or not, was the maintenance and extension of his own power and authority. If the Templars were exonerated, James wanted to use the trial as an opportunity to reduce their power. In 1308 he informed his envoys to the papal *curia* that if the Templars were found innocent he was not ready to allow them to recover their strongholds, especially those on the frontier or near the sea.[23] If, on the other hand, the Temple was abolished, James was anxious to ensure that his authority was at least safeguarded in any settlement made concerning the Temple's possessions and that another individual or institution did not secure complete control over them. In particular he wanted to make sure that if the Temple was dissolved the revenues from its Aragonese estates were devoted to uses within the Peninsula, for Clement V when ordering the arrest of the Templars and the seizure of their property had declared that if they were found guilty their wealth should be used to further the interests of the Holy Land.[24] James, who had earlier tried to prevent the Aragonese Templars from sending responsions to the East,[25] argued on a number of occasions that grants of property had been made to the Temple in Aragon for the purpose of defending the Church in the West and resisting the Moors in the

Peninsula, not in order to provide resources for the struggle against the infidel in the Holy Land.[26]

These considerations made James reluctant to accept any plan which would involve the transference of the Order's property to Rome, to the bishops, or to any secular prince, such as the king of Jerusalem, who would use the revenues in the interests of the Holy Land.[27] He was also opposed to any scheme whereby the Hospitallers would take possession of the Temple's property, just as earlier Spanish kings had resisted plans for the union of the military orders.[28] He feared the power which the Hospital would enjoy if it gained Templar property in his realms, especially as according to James the Templars had proportionately more possessions, especially castles, in the *Corona de Aragón* than elsewhere. He argued that

> if the Hospitallers or their master were unwilling to observe fealty to the king, which God forbid, they would be able to bring into the land of the said king whatever other power they might wish, nor could they be prevented in view of the very favourable opportunities they would have for doing this considering the said castles and strongholds which they would have on the frontiers and in other parts of the kingdoms of the said king, both by land and by sea.[29]

He was prepared to agree to the Hospital's acquisition of the Temple's Aragonese lands only on conditions which would ensure that the Hospital did not become over-powerful and that the Templar estates were not completely free from royal authority. He proposed that he should retain all Templar strongholds, that the Hospital as a result of the amalgamation should not have more than the Templars had previously held in Aragon, and that the inhabitants living on former Templar estates should do fealty to the king.[30] James was similarly unwilling to accept the establishment of a new military order, centred in the East and endowed with Templar property, except on certain conditions. He demanded that he should retain the rights which he had enjoyed over the Templars, that the members of the new Order in his kingdoms should be Aragonese and, notwithstanding the fact that the Templars had sent responsions to the East, that all the revenues which the new Order would have in the *Corona de Aragón* should be devoted to uses within the Peninsula.[31]

James's desires would have been fulfilled if he could have re-

tained the Temple's possessions for himself, and at an early stage
in the negotiations he appears to have considered this as a possibility. In 1308 his envoys were instructed to say that if Templar
lands in France passed to the French Crown, then he should
receive those in Aragon.[32] But when it became clear that this
solution was impossible he came increasingly to favour a plan
whereby Templar possessions in Aragon would be assigned to a
new Spanish military order. At one time it was suggested that the
Order of Mountjoy should be revived and given Montesa as its
headquarters,[33] but James's chief proposal was for the creation of
a new offshoot from the Order of Calatrava. Its members, who
would be Aragonese, would observe the rule of Calatrava but
would not be subject to its master: visitation and correction would
be carried out by the Cistercian monastery of Grandeselve or that
of Fontfroide. If necessary, James was willing to concede that the
new foundation should pay to the pope the responsion which the
Templars had sent to the East.[34] The creation of such an Order
would solve James's problems, for it would have only limited
power and James would be able to control it, especially if, as was
at one time suggested, one of the king's sons became its master.[35]
Most of its revenues would, moreover, be devoted to purposes
inside the Peninsula.

The solution that was finally reached in 1317 was inevitably
a compromise. It was agreed that a new military order should be
established, with its headquarters at Montesa in Valencia. The
members were to adopt Calatravan observances and were to be
subject to the master of Calatrava in that he was to have the
power of visitation and correction; this power was, however, to
be exercised in conjunction with the Cistercian abbot of Stas.
Creus. The new Order was to have all the possessions which the
Temple had held in the kingdom of Valencia and also—with
certain exceptions—those of the Hospital there. The lands in the
South were thus being assigned to a new Order, whose primary
concern would be the furtherance of the struggle against the
Moors in the Peninsula. Templar properties in the rest of James's
realms were to pass to the Hospital, which in this way gained
a considerable amount of property, for Templar possessions in
Aragon and Catalonia were far more extensive than those lost by
the Hospital in Valencia. But the interests of the Aragonese kings
were safeguarded by the provision that the Hospitaller Castellan

of Amposta was to do homage to the king before entering into office, and it was further decreed that the Aragonese king should continue to enjoy the rights which he had possessed in the past over Templar and Hospitaller properties.[36] The agreement was quickly put into effect, although James II certainly retained at least some of the movable possessions of the Templars.

The fate of the Aragonese Templars themselves was decided more quickly than that of their possessions. In May 1312 Clement V decreed that except in the cases of some leading members of the Order the power to judge individual Templars was still to rest with provincial councils. He also stated that all Templars except the impenitent and relapsed were to live in the Order's convents or in other religious houses, provided that there were no more than a few in any one house; and he ordered provincial councils to make provision for their maintenance out of the Temple's possessions.[37] In some countries provincial councils had already been held to determine the guilt of members of the Order, but it was not until November 1312 that the Aragonese Templars were absolved by a provincial council held at Tarragona. This council also decreed that they should be provided with accommodation and with a pension to be paid out of Templar revenues, and at the same time made it clear that they were subject to episcopal visitation and correction.[38] Although the payment of pensions meant that the Templars now possessed private property, the Church intended that in other respects they should continue to follow a monastic way of life: as John XXII later observed, the abolition of the Order did not mean that the Templars had been absolved from their vows.[39]

Yet although they were still bound by their vows, the task of contributing to the defence of Christendom was now denied to them. They had no function to fulfil and were merely unwanted survivals from the past. In this situation it is not surprising that some quickly rejected the manner of life which had been decreed for them. They left the convents and religious houses to which they had been assigned; they engaged in secular activities, including inevitably fighting; they dressed like laymen; and they ignored their vow of chastity. As early as 1313 one Aragonese Templar was charged with rape, and in the next year it was reported that Berenguer of Bellvís was openly keeping a mistress at Gardeny, while others took wives.[40] And much of the evidence which has been preserved about the Templars after the dissolution of the Order concerns the attempts made by the Church to ensure that they led strict lives. In 1317 John XXII wrote to the archbishop of Tarragona commanding him to force erring Templars to return to the convents to which they had been assigned, to correct their dress and way of life, and to obey the diocesan.[41] The archbishop in turn ordered that the Templars

were not to involve themselves in wars or secular business and were totally to abstain from wearing red, green, and striped clothes and all others dissonant and contrary to religion and were not to use any or various pelts other than sheepskin or any ornate silk for their clothing, so that their religious and honest way of life might be apparent in their habits and clothes.

They were to return to their convents and obey their bishops.[42] The problem was not, however, confined to Spain. At the end of the year 1318 the pope issued a general order, decreeing that prelates should summon the Templars and command them to transfer to a house of one of the approved religious orders, where they were to be received 'the clerics only as clerics, the laymen as *conversi*'. Care was to be taken to ensure that there were not more than two Templars in any one monastery, except in the convents of the Hospital. If any Templar refused to obey the papal decree he was to be deprived of his pension.[43] The size of the pensions paid to Templars was seen as one of the causes of trouble. In 1317 the Castellan of Amposta argued that the Templars led dissolute lives because of the amount of money they received,[44] and in the next year John XXII ordered that the scale of payments should be examined and pensions reduced if they were too large. He pointed out that the Templars needed only enough to provide themselves with food and clothing suitable for a member of a religious order and that they ought not to be in a position to hoard money.[45]

It is not altogether clear how far these decrees were enforced in Aragon. When an agreement was made by the Hospitallers about Templar pensions in November 1319, nearly a year after John XXII's decree, payments had apparently not been reduced in size, even though the amounts that were being paid were often very large. Dalmau of Rocaberti was receiving a pension of 8,000*s*. a year and Raymond of Guardia was paid 7,000*s*., while none received less than 500s.[46] In the agreement, however, the possibility of a reduction in pensions was mentioned. Nevertheless, in 1322 Gerald of Copóns was still receiving the same amount as in 1319, and of eleven Templars who are known to have been paid pensions in Roussillon in 1329 at least seven were receiving as much as in 1319.[47] And it was clearly possible for Aragonese Templars to accumulate wealth: in 1328 Raymond Oliver was leasing out property which he had acquired in Zaragoza.[48] Yet at least some pensions were reduced in size. In 1329 two Templars in Roussillon appear to have been receiving less than they had earlier been assigned, and in the following year William of Castellbisbal was paid only 1,000s. instead of the 2,000s. which he had been receiving in 1319.[49] The enforcement of other decrees seems to have been similarly slow but not altogether neglected. When the agreement was made in 1319 about pensions the Templars were still living in the Order's houses in fairly large groups.[50] But, on the other hand, James II was informed in 1325 that Berenguer of San Marcial had not been paid his pension for the last two years because he had refused to transfer to a religious house and accept the authority of the diocesan.[51]

It is difficult to gain an impression of the life of the Aragonese Templars as a whole after 1312. Not only is it uncertain how far the Church's decrees were enforced; it is also not clear what proportion of the Aragonese Templars required correction. But obviously the survivors were not usually beset by financial hardship, even if some were leading a frustrating existence; and as their numbers dwindled probably the Church's concern over them grew less and they were left to end their days with little interference.

The last of the Aragonese Templars died shortly after the middle of the century.[52] Their deaths marked the final disappearance in the *Corona de Aragón* of the Order which had first come to that country merely in search of resources, but which had later played an important role both in the Aragonese reconquest and in the resettlement of conquered lands, only then to be destroyed through the machinations of a French king. But although the Temple had ceased to exist, the concept of the military order had not seriously been questioned. New orders were still being founded in the fourteenth century and the institution of the military order still had centuries of life before it.

## NOTES

1. The dissolution of the Temple in Aragon has been studied in a number of works, especially Finke, *Papsttum*. See also Miret y Sans, *Les Cases*; Prutz, *Entwicklung* (Prutz like Finke publishes some documents on the subject); M. Usón y Sesé, 'Aportaciones al estudio de la caída de los Templarios en Aragón', *Universidad*, iii (1926), 479–523; B. Alart, 'Suppression de l'Ordre du Temple en Roussillon', *Bulletin de la Société agricole, scientifique et littéraire des Pyrénées-Orientales*, xv (1867), 25–115. I have not therefore sought to examine the subject at great length. There is room for a more detailed study, based primarily on ACA, reg. 291, and other sources in the Aragonese Crown archive, but this would require another book.

2. Finke, *Papsttum*, ii. 46–7, doc. 30.

3. Ibid. i. 283; ii. 50–1, doc. 33; Finke, *AA*, iii. 170–1, doc. 73.

4. T. W. Parker, *The Knights Templars in England* (Tucson, 1963), p. 91.

5. Finke, *Papsttum*, ii. 55–6, doc. 37; cf. 51–4, doc. 35; i. 286.

6. Ibid. ii. 62–3, doc. 41.

7. Ibid. ii. 47–9, docs. 31, 32.

8. Ibid. ii. 63–7, docs. 42–4.

9. A. Benavides, *Memorias de D. Fernando IV de Castilla* (Madrid, 1860), ii. 595, doc. 403. The bull *Pastoralis preminentie*, which ordered the arrest of the Templars and seizure of their possessions, was drawn up on 22 November 1307 but it was not received in Aragon until 18 January 1308: ibid. ii. 619–21, doc. 415; Villanueva, *Viage*, xix. 317–19, doc. 48; Finke, *Papsttum*, ii. 77, doc. 53.

10. Ibid. i. 287–8.

11. Ibid. ii. 70–3, doc. 48; 79–81, doc. 55.

12. The course of the action against the Temple can be followed in ACA, reg. 291. Extracts from this register have been published by Finke, *Papsttum*, ii. 85–7, doc. 58; 121, doc. 76; 131–2, doc. 84; see also Prutz, *Entwicklung*, pp. 349–52.

13. *Regestum Clementis papae V*, iii (Rome, 1886), 303–4, doc. 3484. At the same time Clement named the archbishop of Tarragona and the bishop of Valencia as custodians of Templar possessions in Aragon: ibid. iii. 312–15, doc. 3515.

14. Finke, *Papsttum*, ii. 202–5, docs. 108, 109.

15. Ibid. ii. 364–78, doc. 157.

16. Michelet, *Procès*, ii. 423–515.

17. A. Mercati, 'Interrogatorio di Templari a Barcellona (1311)', *Spanische Forschungen der Görresgesellschaft: Gesammelte Aufsätze zur Kulturgeschichte*

*Spaniens*, vi (1937), 246–51. Some other Templars were apparently later tortured at Lérida: Alart, loc. cit., p. 72.

18. Villanueva, *Viage*, v. 208–21, doc. 6; Benavides, op. cit. ii. 835–41, doc. 571.

19. Finke, *Papsttum*, ii. 286–8, doc. 140. In February 1308 the bishop of Gerona, together with the count of Ampurias and Dalmau of Rocaberti, had hindered action being taken in Aragon against the Templars: ibid. ii. 63–6, doc. 42. It is difficult, however, to generalize about attitudes in Aragon to the Templars at this time. Much would depend on circumstances. While some, for example, might welcome measures against the Templars because of old feuds, many others were vassals of the Order or had friends and relations in it and would be influenced by these ties: after the arrest of the Templars the king received a number of petitions on behalf of members of the Order from their friends and relations: ACA, reg. 291, fols. 232, 281, 286ᵛ.

20. *Regestum Clementis papae V*, vii (Rome, 1887), 65–8, doc. 7885.

21. Finke, *Papsttum*, ii. 73–4, doc. 49.

22. *Regestum Clementis papae V*, vi (Rome, 1887), 112–13, doc. 6740; Miret y Sans, *Les Cases*, p. 374; Alart, loc. cit., p. 67.

23. Finke, *Papsttum*, ii. 89–90, doc. 60.

24. Villanueva, *Viage*, xix. 317–19, doc. 48; Benavides, op. cit. ii. 619–21, doc. 415.

25. See above, p. 140.

26. Finke, *Papsttum*, ii. 230–8, doc. 125; 265–8, doc. 134; cf. 238–45, doc. 126.

27. Ibid. ii. 89–90, doc. 60; 246–8, doc. 127; cf. 258–61, doc. 132; 182–4, doc. 101; V. Salavert y Roca, *Cerdeña y la expansión mediterránea de la Corona de Aragón* (Madrid, 1956), ii. 553–4, doc. 433.

28. S. Baluzius, *Vitae Paparum Avenionensium*, ed. G. Mollat, iii (Paris, 1921), 150, doc. 32.

29. Finke, *Papsttum*, ii. 212–16, doc. 113.

30. Ibid. ii. 212–16, doc. 113; 217–19, doc. 115; 230–8, doc. 125.

31. Ibid. ii. 265–8, doc. 134.

32. Ibid. ii. 89–90, doc. 60.

33. Ibid. ii. 212–16, doc. 113.

34. Ibid. ii. 230–8, doc. 125; 265–8, doc. 134; 289–91, doc. 142.

35. Ibid. ii. 276–9, doc. 138.

36. Baluzius, op. cit. iii. 256–66, docs. 49, 50; P. Dupuy, *Histoire de l'Ordre militaire des Templiers* (Brussels, 1751), pp. 483–9, doc. 129.

37. *Regestum Clementis papae V*, vii. 303–4, doc. 8784; Benavides, op. cit. ii. 855–7, doc. 579.

38. J. D. Mansi, *Sacrorum conciliorum nova et amplissima collectio*, xxv (Venice, 1782), 515–18. There is evidence of the actual payment of pensions in 1313: Alart, loc. cit., pp. 81–3.

39. Dupuy, op. cit., pp. 511–14, doc. 137.

40. Finke, *Papsttum*, i. 383; Prutz, *Entwicklung*, p. 316, doc. 9.

41. *Jean XXII (1316–1334): Lettres communes*, ed. G. Mollat, i (Paris, 1904), 429–30, doc. 4670.

42. Finke, *Papsttum*, i. 384, note 1.

43. Dupuy, op. cit., pp. 511–14, doc. 137.

44. *Jean XXII: Lettres communes*, i. 429–30, doc. 4670.

45. *Bullarium Franciscanum*, v (Rome, 1898), 160–2, doc. 347.

46. Villanueva, *Viage*, v. 226–32, doc. 9; Miret y Sans, *Les Cases*, pp. 390–5; the payment mentioned for Raymond of Guardia was the same as that assigned to him in 1313: Alart, loc. cit., pp. 81–3.

47. Miret y Sans, *Les Cases*, p. 395; Alart, loc. cit., pp. 98–101.

48. AHN, San Juan, leg. 587, doc. 37.

49. Alart, loc. cit., pp. 98–101; Miret y Sans, *Les Cases*, p. 384, note 1. The two in Roussillon were the knights Bernard of Millas and Bernard of Furques. Both were paid 1,000s., whereas they had earlier been assigned 1,400s. It is possible, however, that the payments of 1,000s. did not in these cases amount to a full year's pension.

50. There were eleven Templars both at Barbará and at Gardeny.

51. Finke, *Papsttum*, i. 385–6.

52. Berenguer of Coll was still alive in 1350: Miret y Sans, *Les Cases*, p. 384.

# APPENDIX I

## *Illustrative Documents*

The following selection of hitherto unpublished documents is intended to illustrate the main themes discussed in this study of the Aragonese Templars, and to provide examples of the chief types of document which survive on the subject.

## I

AHN, cód. 691, fols. 137ᵛ–138, doc. 357          Mid twelfth century

*Peter of Piguera promises to serve with the Templars for a year if he recovers from his wounds; if he does not the Order is to receive his property in Oitura*

In dei omnipotentis nomine, ego Petrus de Piguera mortali vulnere sauciatus promitto domino deo et fratribus Templi Salomonis militie Iherosolimitani ut si deus me a morte substraxerit serviam deo in domo illorum fratrum ubi voluerint unum annum. Si vero ab hac plaga mortuus fuero, dimitto illis fratribus presentis et futuris pro remissione peccatorum meorum totam illam meam hereditatem qui est in Dotura. Totum videlicet quicquid habeo vel habere debeo, sive aliquis homo vel femina tenet ibi de me vel pro me. Similiter et manumitto fratribus illis predictis equum meum cum toto meo garnimento. Testes Fertunius de Bergua, Garcia Ortiç, Garinus de Mala, Arnald de Alagon, Fertunio Garceç de Oscha, qui omnes huic donationi et manumissioni interfuerunt et hanc cartam donationis post Petrum obitum firmaverunt.

## II

AGP, Cartulary of Gardeny, fol. 49ᵛ, doc. 112          25 August 1151

*Resettlement charter for Templar property at Castelldans*[1]

In nomine summi dei qui est trinus et unus amen. Ego Petrus de Cartila et ego Frevol et ego Aimericus et ego Guillelmus de Tavernos et simul omnes nostri fratres damus illam nostram hereditatem quam nos habemus in Castro de Asinos, excepto nostro domengue que nos retinemus, ad te Girbert et ad te Bernad Ferrer; que vos populetis illam ad honorem dei et Templi, et talis est convenientia inter nos et vos quod tu Girbert habeas et teneas duas pareladas de terra et una turre cum decima et primitia que reddas, et tu Bernad Ferrer similiter duas pareladas cum tua turre, decimam et primiciam reddendo. Hoc damus vobis atque concedimus et filiis vestris et vestre posteritati. Alii vero populatores quos vos feceritis populare ad honorem dei et Templi reddant nobis decimas et primicias et de unaqueque parelada reddant unoquoque anno una perna de XII.$^{cim}$ denariis et IIII. fogacas et uno iornal ad seminandum; ad unaquaque parelada que populaverit damus VI. modios de cervera in terra garachada. Facta carta VIII. kalendas septembris anno ab incarnatione domini M.° C.° L.° I.°, regnante Lodovico rege. Signum Petri de Cartila. Signum de don Frevol. Signum Willelmi de Tavernos. Petrus scripsit et hoc signum fecit.

## NOTE

1. This document has recently been published from a modern transcript by Font Rius, *Cartas de población*, i. 139-40, doc. 87.

## III

ACA, Varia 1, fol. 1-1$^v$                                    15 September 1163

*A certain Saurina sells property at Montjuich to the Temple in order to be able to redeem her son from captivity*

[S]it notum cunctis quod ego Saurina femina pro magna necessitate captivitatis cuiusdam filii mei Berengarii, quam redimere volo, vendo deo et milicie Templi alodium meum proprium quod per emptionem et per vocem genitorum meorum habeo in territorio Barchinonensi apud Monte iudaicum ad ipsam serram. Terminatur autem ab oriente in alodio quod fuit Mosse iudei, a meridie et ab hoccidente e a circio in alodio eiusdem milicie Templi. Sicut ab istis terminis concluditur et terminatur prefatum alodium cum introitibus et exitibus suis integriter vendo deo et milicie Templi ac, ut melius dici vel intelligi potest, ad utilitatem eiusdem milicie Templi de meo iure in ius et domin[i]um suum trado ad suum proprium, plenissimum et liberum alodium ad quod ibi vel ex inde magister et fratres ipsius milicie Templi facere voluerint sine vinculo ullius hominis vel femine et sine ullo retentu. Accipio pro hac venditione de bonis milicie Templi X. morabetinos bonos aiadinos in auro sine engan, et est manifestum. Siquis hoc fregerit supradicta in duplo componat et insuper hec venditio omni tempore maneat firma. Que est acta XVII. kalendas octobris anno

XVII. regis Ledoyci iunioris. Signum Saurine femine que hoc laudo et firmo, firmaria rogo. Signum Arnalli presbiteri Sancti Iusti. Signum Segunus. Signum Berengarii. Signum Bernardi de Cavallaria. Signum Iohannis Martini. Signum Petri medici. Signum Pīsane uxoris eius. Signum Berengarius Saurine. Signum Petri de Corron scriptoris qui hoc scripsit die et anno quo supra.


# IV


AGP, Cartulary of Gardeny, fol. 14-14ᵛ, doc. 14    11 November 1169
*Alfonso II grants the Temple 1,000m. annually out of tributes received from Moorish Spain*

In dei nomine et eius gratia ego Ildefonsus dei gratia rex Aragonensis, comes Barchinonensis et marchio Provincie bono animo et spontanea voluntate una cum consilio et voluntate baronum curie mee tam Aragonensium quam Catalanorum pro remedio anime mee et parentum meorum dono, laudo atque in perpetuum concedo domino deo et beate Marie et venerabili domui militie Templi Salomonis et omnibus fratribus eiusdem militie presentibus atque futuris quod ab ac hora in antea, quandocumque ego faciam pacem de Ispania cum rege Lupo vel cum successoribus suis, quod faciam dari ab eo vel ab eis iamdicte militie et fratribus eiusdem militie in unoquoque anno mille morabetinos. Et si ab illo rege Lupo vel a successoribus suis supradicta domus militie et fratres eiusdem iamdictos mille morabetinos habere non poterunt, ego laudo illis et dono atque concedo illis mille morabetinos singulis annis de illa palia quam ego et successores mei accipiemus de Yspania, undecumque ego accipiam paliam de Ispania et a quocumque habeam ipsam paliam. Supradictum autem donativum ego Ildefonsus rex facio iamdicte domui militie Templi Salomonis et omnibus fratribus presentibus atque futuris per secula cuncta amen. Hoc autem donum sive donativum ego rex facio in manu Arnalli de Turre Rubea tunc temporis in partibus Provincie et Ispanie rerum Christi pauperum procuratoris et fratris Begonis de Vireriis et in presentia fratris Geraldi de Castelpers et fratris Raimundi de Cubels et fratris Raimundi de Cervaria et fratris Berengarii de Zuiriana et fratris Petri de Balaug. Signum Ildefonsi regis Aragonensis, comitis Barchinonensis et marchionis Provincie. Signum Guillelmi Barchinonensis episcopi. Signum Raimundi de Montecatano. Facta carta in Iacha mense novembris, in die sancti Martini, era M.ᵃCC.ᵃVII.ᵃ, anno ab incarnatione domini M.ºC.ºLX.º VIIII.º Regnante me Ildefonso dei gratia rege in Aragonia et Barchinona et in Provincia. Episcopo Stefano in Oscha, episcopo Petro in Cesaraugusta, episcopo Martino in Tirassona. Comite Arnallo Mironis Palarensi in Ricla. Blascho Romeu maiordomo in Cesaraugusta. Ximino de Artusella stando alferiz domini regis. Petro de Castellazol in Calataiub. Sancio Necons in Darocha. Galindo Xemeniz in Belxit. Artallo in Alagon. Blascho Maza in Boria. Petro Ortiz in Aranda. Ximino de Orrea in Epila. Fortunio Aznariz in Tirassona. Petro de Arazuri in Oscha. Peregrino in Castelazol, in Barbastre et in Alchezer. Fortunio de Stada in Montclus. Arpa in Lodarre. Gomball de Benavent in Bel. Petro Lopiz in Lusia. Deusaiuda in Sos. Sunt testes, visores et auditores Petrus de Arazuri, Ximinus de Artusela alferiz domini regis, Ximinus Romeu, Petrus de Alcala, Doz de Alchala, Petrus de Sancto Vincentio. Ego Bernardus de Calidis scriba domini regis scripsi hanc cartam et feci hoc signum.

# V

AHN, San Juan, leg. 138, doc. 4                                    July 1177
*The bishop of Zaragoza grants the Templars the right to build a church at La Zaida and makes provision about ecclesiastical dues there*

Notum sit omnibus hominibus quod ego Petrus dei gratia Cesaraugustanus episcopus consilio et voluntate canonicorum Sancti Salvatoris Cesaraugustane sedis bono animo et spontanea voluntate damus et concedimus deo et fratribus milicie Templi in manu Arnaldi de Turre Rubea tunc temporis magistri ut faciant ecclesiam ad opus fratrum in loco qui dicitur Çeida ubi numquam fuit ecclesia, sed postquam a sarracenis fuit dissipatus semper fuit heremus et incultus usque modo quod fratres maximis laboribus et sumptibus excolunt eum. Et damus eis decimas et primicias illius loci cum suis terminis ut habeant et possideant ea in perpetuum; et donent nobis nostrisque successoribus pro recognicione episcopali unum kaficium frumenti et I. kaficium ordei et unam metrecam vini postquam fiunt ibi vinee per unumquemque annum in festivitate omnium sanctorum. Et si venerint ibi populatores christiani concedimus ut habeant fratres decimas et primicias eorum et de ipsis decimis parrochianorum habeat semper Cesaraugustanus episcopus suam quartam et postea fratres non donent supradictum censum. Sin autem teneatur sicut scriptum est. Huius rei sunt testes Bernardus archidiaconus, Petrus sacrista, Adam precentor, Guillelmus de Narbona, Petrus Ximini de Maria, Petrus minor sacrista, Garsias archidiaconus. De laicis Blascho Romeu, Petrus Ortiz, Blascho Maza. Berengarius dei gratia Terragonensis archiepiscopus. Petrus dei gratia Cesaraugustanus episcopus.

Factum est hoc in Cesaraugusta mense julii sub era M.ªCC.ªXV.ª

Johannes notarius jussione domini episcopi hanc cartam scripsit et hoc signum fecit.

Guillelmus de Albesa diachonus qui hoc translatavit et hoc signum fecit.

## VI

AGP, Cartulary of Gardeny, fols. 97ᵛ–98, doc. 237

18 September 1182

*Agreement between the Temple and the monastery of Poblet concerning lands, tithes, and* primicias

Sit notum cunctis tam presentibus quam futuris quoniam ego Berengarius de Avinione magister milicie Templi Salomonis in partibus Ispanie cum consilio fratrum nostrorum venimus ad finem et ad concordiam cum abbati de Poblet et eius conventu de ipso territorio Davibodi et de ipso termino et de ipsas domos de Tarrega quas fuerunt de Petro de Taladel. In tali modo quomodo ego Berengarius de Avinione cum nostris fratribus difinimus et reliquimus ad ipsos fratres de Poblet totum quantum nos habemus vel habere debemus in chastrum Davibodi et in suis terminis et ipsu censsum de ipsas casas de Tarrega difinimus et derelinquimus nunc et in perpetuum. Et ego Stephanus abbas de Poblet et nostris fratribus facimus emendam de ipsu honorem suprascriptum vobis fratribus XV. migeras de blad, VII. de forment et VIII. dordi, et istum blad accipiatis in ipsum decimum et in primicias de Barbenz quem nos debemus accipere a vobis et si aliquid superaverit nobis reddite et si forte minus evenerit convenimus vobis ipsas XV. migeras integrare. Et ipsu blad suprascriptum accipiatis in ipsas decimas et primicias qui debent exire nobis de vestra laboracione. Et hoc fuit factum in presentia B. de Avinione magistri in partibus Yspanie, fratris B. de Albespi preceptoris de Garden et fratris R. de Cubels preceptoris de Tortosa et fratris P. Dalmacii et fratris G. de Chaerzi et fratris B. de Cornela hac fratris P. Adalbert et aliorum plurium fratrum et domini abbatis Sthepani de Poblet et fratris P. prior et fratris R. de Sala et fratris B. de Borg et fratris A. Dartesa. Signum B. de Avinione magistri. Signum B. de Albespi. Signum R. de Cubels. Signum B. de Cornela. Sicnum P. prior. Sicnum R. de Sala. Sicnum B. de Borg. Signum A. Dartesa. Actum est hoc XIIII. kalendas octobris anno M.ºC.ºLXXX.ºII.º Sicnum R. Seger. Signum Guillelmi de Gardia. Sicnum Bernardi de Gardia. Nos sumus testes, visitores et auditores. Rimundus subdiachonus qui hoc scripsit et hoc signum fecit die et anno quo supra.

# VII

AHN, cód. 467, p. 129, doc. 146 September 1184

*Alfonso II takes the Templar house of Boquiñeni under his protection*

[I]n Christi nomine notum sit cunctis quod ego Ildeffonsus dei gratia rex Aragonensis, comes Barchinonensis et marchio Provincie recipio domum milicie Templi de Boquinyeneg et fratrem Simonem comendatorem et omnes fratres eiusdem domus sub mea proteccione et defenssione et omnes res eorum mobiles et inmobiles ubicumque sint in ullo loco terre mee vel in terra amicorum meorum. Ideoque volo et firmiter mando quod omnia vestra salva sint et secura et nemo audeat vos gravare nec pignorare pro ullo debito aliarum domorum vestrarum nisi pro vestro tantum modo debito faceret. Si quis autem contra hec precepta pervenerit vel ausu temerario corrumpere voluerit, mille morabetinos pectabit et insuper iram meam amittet.

Facta carta apud Pratellam mensse septembris era M.ªCC.ªXX.ªII.ª

# VIII

AHN, Montesa, R. 8 January 1190

*Alfonso II grants to the Templars lordship over Pulpís, which they have captured from the Moors*

Ne res gesta paulatim sub repente oblivione a memoria excidat debet literarum apicibus comendari. Igitur in nomine domini ego Ildefonsus dei gratia rex Aragonensis, comes Barchinonensis et marchio Provincie ob remedium anime mee predecessorumque meorum per me et per omnes meos dono, laudo atque concedo perpetuo deo et domui milicie Templi et universo conventui eiusdem loci presenti atque futuro castrum de Pulpiz et villam, quam superne virtutis subsidio ab inimicis crucis Christi adquisiverunt, absque retentu aliquo cum omnibus introitibus et exitibus suis, cum aquis, pascuis, cum silvis et nemoribus, cum omnibus honoribus et possessionibus suis cultis et incultis, et eciam cum cetero iure et omnibus pertinenciis suis, heremis scilicet et populatis, que pertinent vel pertinere debent prememorato castro et ville; hoc modo videlicet ut predictum castrum et villam et cetera omnia pertinentia eisdem libere, quiete et sine aliqua mei et meorum contradictione et contrarietate habeant, teneant atque possideant et ex eis plenam liberamque potestatem habeant faciendi omnem propriam voluntatem suam omni tempore ut ex suo proprio. Hoc autem donativum libenti animo et spontanea voluntate prout superius dictum est et declaratum dono, laudo atque concedo prememorate domui et universo conventui et per presentem conscriptionem corroboro atque confirmo, nulla aliquo tempore obstante causa firmiter duraturam. Datum apud Aquis in Provincia mense januarii anno ab incarnato domino millesimo C.°LXXX.°VIIII.° sub era M.ªCC.ªXX.ªVIIII.ª

Signum Ildefonsi regis Aragonensis, comitis Barchinonensis et marchionis Provincie, qui supradicta laudo et confirmo. Donacio ista facta est Poncio de Rigaldo adstante magistro in partibus Provincie et Ispanie. Frater Guillelmus de Sancto Paulo per manum ipsius commendator in partibus Provincie. Bernardus Catalani comendator in Sancto Egidio. Petrus de Sancto Gregorio in Montepesulano. Arnaldus de Claromonte tenens vicem predicti magistri in partibus Ispanie. Testes huius donacionis: Ennego Daveo; Bernardus de Benavent; Arnaldus de Alascun; Lupus de Darocha; Raimundus de Tirasona; Asalitus de Gudal; P. maior domus. Signum Barralli domini Marsilie. Signum Bertrandi de Baũc. Signum Ugonis de Baũc. Signum Guillelmi Raimundi Gantelin. Signum Berengarii de Sancta Eugenia.

Signum Johannis de Bãtx domini regis scriptoris qui mandato eiusdem hanc cartam scripsit mense et anno quo supra cum literis suprascriptis in prima pagina.

# IX

AHN, cód. 470, pp. 66–7, doc. 78                     December 1192

*García of Rada grants the Temple his hereditas in Pradilla*

[I]n Christi nomine et eius divina clemencia patris et filii et spiritus sancti, quatinus ego Garcia de Arrada timeo penas inferni et cupio delicias paradisi propter animam meam et per remissionem parentum meorum dono deo et ad domum militie Tenpli ex puro corde et obtima voluntate omnia mea hereditate quam habeo in Pratella, erma vel populata, casas et terras et vineas et ortos quanta que es nec habere debeo. Sic dono ego Garcia de Arrada ista jamdicta hereditate cum exiis et regressiis, cum aquis et pascuis, ad domum militie Tenpli Salomonis et a fratribus qui ibi sunt et postea venerint ut habeant et teneant atque possideant soluta et quieta, per dare et per vendere et per facere propriam voluntatem illi atque successoribus suis sine ingenio et absque contradiccio malo, sine clamo et sine ullo demando. Et accepit istum datum frater Garcia Centronico qui tunc erat preceptor Boquinyennic et alios fratres qui erant sub eo in bajulia sua, nomine frater Bernard de Terroç et frater Blasco et frater Petrus elemogin[arius?] et frater Arnaldus; in eodem tempore magister Poncius Rigaldus in Provincia, in partibus Yspanie. Et super hoc Garcia Arrada dedit fidança de salvetat ad usum terre scilicet Eximen de Arrada frater suus. Et quis voluerit disrrumpere hanc cartam disrrumptus sit, in inferno inferiori cum Judas traditori habeat porcionem. Amen. Sunt testes, visores et auditores Paschal de Florença et frater suus Johannes nomine. Facta carta in secunda emdopmada decenbris era M.ªCC.ªXXX.ª Dominicus scriba Petrole scripsit.

## X

ACA, parch. Peter II, no. 52                          1 August 1198

*Pereta of Argilager and her son put themselves and their dependants and property under the protection of the Temple*

Hoc est translatum cuiusdam instrumenti per alphabetum divisi quod subi istis continetur verbis. Notum sit cunctis quod ego Pereta de Argilager et filius meus Arnaldus et uxor sua Boneta insimul pro salute animarum nostrarum mittimus et ponimus in deffensione et proteccione sancte milicie Templi et fratrum eius totum ipsum nostrum mansum de Argilager et totum nostrum alodium quod ibi habemus et corpora nostra et omnes habitatores istius mansi cum omnibus rebus nostris. Et est ipse mansus et alodium in parrochia sancti Petri de Roda ad ipsas esplugas. Tali pacto ut fratres milicie deffendant et manuteant istum mansum et alodium et corpora nostra et habitatores istius mansi cum omnibus nostris rebus dum sint infra cruces sicuti res suas proprias, et accipiant in isto manso annuatim ipsi fratres unum par caponum in festo omnium sanctorum et nichil aliud ibi demandare possint sine nostra voluntate. Quod est factum kalendas augusti anno domini M.C.XC.VIII. Signum Perete de Argilager. Signum Arnaldi filii eius. Signum Bonete uxoris eius, qui hoc facimus et firmamus. Signum Guillelmi de Cerdaniola procuratoris milicie. Signum Raimundi Mironis bajuli. Signum Andree sacerdotis et publici ville Vici scriptoris. Raimundus levita qui hoc scripsit die et anno quo supra.

Ego Petrus de Pausa sacerdos Vicensis canonicus et decanus ac judex ordinarius qui predicta vidi in origonali non viciato legitime contineri firmo et meum signum pono. Signum Petri de Ayreis Vicensis canonici et publici ville Vici notarii. Signum Petri de Alibergo scriptoris jurati qui hoc translatum fecit fideliter translatari et scribi ac clausit mandato Petri de Ayreis publici Vicensis notarii cum dictione emendata in VI.ª linea ubi dicitur sint, V.° nonas octobris anno domini M.°CC.°LX.° quinto.

## XI

AHN, cód. 691, fols. 196–198, doc. 442          Later twelfth century

*List of Templar* confratres *at Novillas*

In dei nomine et eius divina clementia patris et filii et spiritus sancti. Hec est carta de ipsa confratria de Novellas. In primis Bernardus scriba XII. dnrs.[1] per unum quemque annum in festum sancti Michaelis, et ad obitum suum terciam partem de totum suum avere extra hereditate sua. Martin Pedriç VI. dnrs. et a sua fine meliorem unam bestiam quam habuerit. Arnal et uxor eius Matrona IIII. dnrs. et a sua fi II. sol. qualisque primus obierit. Michael et uxor eius III. dnrs. et a sua fi II. sol. Raimundus Gaschon et uxor eius III. dnrs. et a sua fi II. sol. Domingo de Madona et Johannes et eorum mater III. quartarios tri et a sua fi VI. sol. vel val'. Petrus Bernardus et uxor eius VI. dnrs. et et a sua fi V. sol. Arnal Ponç et uxor eius VI. dnrs. et a sua fi V. sol. Enecho cognato de Orti Oriç VI. dnrs. et a sua fi III. sol. Johannes de Ioan Taregeç et uxor eius VI. dnrs. et a sua fi V. sol. Sançio de Oblitcs et uxor eius III. dnrs. et a sua fi III. sol. Don Apparitio et uxor eius habent donato pro illa caritate I. peça de terra et melior bestia quam habeat a sua fine. Eneco Sanç et uxor eius et filius eius et sua germana VI. dnrs. et a sua fi V. sol. qualisque primus obierit. Rainallus et uxor eius arroa de trico et a sua fi V. sol. Sançio de Trist et uxor eius VI. dnrs. et a sua fi I. morabetin. Dominico del Espic XII. dnrs. et a sua fi III. morabetins. Petrus Albaro VI. dnrs. et a sua fi I. morabetin. Dominico Moçarau VI. dnrs. et a sua fi I. morabetin. Martin et uxor eius dona Goto VI. dnrs. et a sua fi I. morabetin. Petrus Carpenter et uxor eius et frater eius Guillelmus VIII. dnrs. et a sua fine I. morabetin qualisque primus obierit. Vales et uxor eius VI. dnrs. et a sua fi I. morabetin. Dominica de Feba IIII. dnrs. et a sua fi I. morabetin. Johannes lo pastor et uxor eius VI. dnrs. et a sua fi I. morabetin. Johannes IIII. dnrs. et a sua fi III. sol. Garcia Enecons et uxor eius VI. dnrs. et a sua fi I. morabetin. Martin Pastor et uxor eius VI. dnrs. et a sua fi I. morabetin. Johannes Ebral et uxor eius VI. dnrs. et a sua fi I. morabetin. Sançio Navarro et uxor eius IIIIII. dnrs. et a sua fi I. morabetin. Petro et uxor eius VI. dnrs. et a sua fine I. morabetin. Johannes de Oblitas et uxor eius VIII. dnrs. et a sua fi I. morabetin. Petrus Martini et uxor eius VI. dnrs. et a sua fi medio morabetin. Petro del Espic et filio suo Stephano I. arroa de trico et ad sua fi I. morabetin. Cecilia VI. dnrs. et a sua fine III. sol. Guillelmus Palarancho et uxor eius XII. dnrs. et a sua fine V. sol. Galino et uxor eius VI. dnrs. et a sua fi I. morabetin. Melendo et uxor eius III. dnrs. et a sua fi I. morabetin. Johannes Palarancho et uxor eius III. dnrs. et a sua fi I. morabetin. Steven Mozarau et et uxor eius VI.

dnrs. et a sua fine I. morabetin. Bona Fila, Guillelmus Alvernaç et uxor eius et filius de Bona Fila XII. dnrs. unusquisque IIII. dnrs. et unusquisque I. morabetin a sua fine. Martin nepoto de Steven VI. dnrs. et a sua fi I. morabetin. Dona Maior et filia eius IIII. dnrs. et a sua fine I. morabetin. Dona Endreça VI. dnrs. et ad obitum suum omnia que habebit. Johannes Egebal et uxor eius IIII. dnrs. et ad finem eorum omnia que habebunt. Petro Navarro VI. dnrs. et a sua fine I. morabetin. Sançio fil de Garçianecons IIII. dnrs. et a sua fine IIII. sol. Dominica uxor Guillelmus de Condom IIII. dnrs. et a sua fi III. sol. Vital et uxor eius VI. dnrs. et ad sua fi I. morabetin. Dona Gote VI. dnrs. et a sua fine quantum habet. Urti Oriç VI. dnrs. et a sua fine I. morabetin. Aimerig servus noster de Capanes unoque anno VI. d. et ad finem eius si non duxerit uxorem aut si non habuerit filium vel filiam quod habuerit totum sit de Templo, et si duxerit uxorem et cetera I. morabetin.

## NOTE

1. I have not expanded the abbreviations for pence and shillings.

## XII

AHN, San Juan, leg. 39, doc. 79         17 November 1208

*Peter II issues a confirmation of Templar privileges*

Pateat omnibus quod nos Petrus dei gratia rex Aragonum et comes Barchinonensis, attendentes quam fideliter, quam sollicite quamque devote fratres militie Templi ubicumque christiane fidei religio viget propagationi et defensioni eius intendunt, considerantes etiam quam utiles, quam fideles et quam necessarii fuerint predecessoribus nostris in omnibus que ad ampliationem christianitatis visa sunt expedire et quantum nos ipsos in nostris necessitatibus curaverint adiuvare, cum hoc presenti privilegio perpetuo valituro laudamus, concedimus et confirmamus ipsis fratribus presentibus et futuris omnes franchitates, libertates et immunitates et alia omnia que eis et eorum domibus ipsi predecessores nostri dederunt, concesserunt et alicubi assignaverunt et nos ipsi eis dedimus et concessimus sicut ea omnia hactenus melius tenuerunt, liberius habuerunt et plenius possiderunt. Volumus igitur et mandamus firmiter statuentes ut ipsi fratres de rebus suis propriis nullam lezdam, nullum pedaticum, nullum usaticum, nullum portaticum, nullam consuetudinem constitutam vel constituendam vel eorum proprii homines donent vel dare teneantur in aliquo loco terre nostre sicut usque modo minime consueverunt. Mandamus itaque et sub ea quam possumus pena et districtione iniungimus omnibus maioribusdomus, repositariis, merinis, justiciis, zahalmedinis, baiulis et vicariis et omnibus aliis, christianis scilicet, judeis et sarracenis, totius Aragonie presentibus et futuris ne contra hanc cartam in aliquo venire audeant, set eam plenarie observantes nichil de predictis a fratribus militie vel suis hominibus exigere vel eos ad horum aliquid dandum alicubi forciare presummant. Statuimus etiam ut nullus homo vel femina qui sit domus militie Templi vel ad eius iurisdictionem pertinere noscatur nullius rationis occasione libertatem aut franchitatem cum carta vel aliquo alio modo audeat impetrare vel infanzonem aut ingenuum sive immunem se facere, nisi hoc per cartam idoneam aut ingenuitatem aut testibus idoneis sufficienter poterit comprobare. Statuimus preterea ut nulla ecclesiastica secularisve persona infima vel sublimis predictos fratres militie aut homines suos vel res eorum possit vel audeat pignorare, nisi inventa fuerit prius fatiga directi in ipsis fratribus vel reppertus deffectus iuris sub sufficienti testimonio personarum. Precipimus etiam et statuimus ut nullum concilium alicuius civitatis, ville vel castri nec aliquod algemma iudeorum vel sarracenorum audeat pignorare, excomunicare aliquos christianos, iudeos vel sarracenos domus militie Templi alicuius ratione demande regalis vel vicinalis, vel eos a sua vicinitate eicere vel eis interdictum aliquod facere aut franchitates in aliquo violare. Constituimus preterea ut in omnibus que predicti fratres militie vel homines eorum possident vel possederint possint contra quamlibet personam per annum et diem secundum forum et consuetudinem Cesarauguste et libere valeant se tueri. Calonias vero, homicidia et iusticias predicti fratres semper ubique habeant et percipiant de suis propriis hominibus in toto Aragonie sicut hucusque habere eas soliti sunt et accipere. Quicumque autem contra hoc privilegium confirmationis, concessionis et constitutionis nostre venire presumpserit cuiuscumque dignitatis, professionis vel conditionis fuerit iram nostram et indignationem se noverit incursurum et insuper pro suo contemptu nostro a nobis mille aureorum pena sine aliquo remedio feriendum, hoc privilegio nichilominus in sue firmitatis robore permanente. Datum Barbastri XV. kalendas decembris era M.ªCC.ªXL.ª sexta per manum Ferrarii notarii nostri.

Signum Petri dei gratia regis Aragonum et comitis Barchinonensis. Testes huius rei sunt: comes Sanccius; Eximen Cornelii; Garssias Romei; Poncius Hugonis; A. de Alascuno; Eximen de Lusia; Assallitus de Gudal; Blasco Romei; Martinus de Caneto; G. de Alcalano; Poncius de Erillo; Albarus Guterriz maiordomus; Garssias Guterriz; Didacus Ferrandi; P. Lahyn.

Ego Ferrarius notarius domini regis hoc scribi feci mandato ipsius loco, die et era prefixis.

# XIII

AHN, cód. 499, pp. 19–20, doc. 34 May 1217

*Peter Sánchez of Sporreto enters into the confraternity of the Temple and makes various gifts to it; he also places his son in the guardianship of the Temple*

[S]ub Christi nomine et eius gratia. Hec est carta donationis et oblationis quam facio ego Petrus Sanz Desporret filius de Eneco Sanç Desporret domino deo et beate Marie domus milicie Templi Salomonis et omnibus fratribus dicte domus presentibus et futuris in manu de vobis fratre Johanne de Corzan preceptor domus milicie Templi Salomonis de Osca. Placuit mihi obtimo corde et voluntate et in presentia bonorum hominum non seductus non vi metuve inductus sed sincero corde dono et offero corpus et animam meam domino deo et beate Marie et fratribus dicte domus milicie Templi Salomonis ut dictum est in vita et in morte, ita quod de cetero non habeam potestatem me dare nec offerre nulle altere ordini aliqua racione vel causa, nisi erat cum voluntate et placimento magistri dicte domus milicie Templi Salomonis; et promitto de cetero sequi voluntates et mandata dicti magistri in omnibus et esse illi obediens, fidelis et legalis et dicte domui et fratribus ibi deo servientibus intus et foris bona fide; et de bonis mihi collatis dono et offero beate Marie dicte domus et fratribus omnibus ibi deo servientibus in perpetuum in manu de vobis dicto fratre Johanne de Corzan pro caritate et beneficio unas meas casas quas habeo in Luna in barrio porte de Lanava, et affrontant in una parte in casis Johannis de la Fiara et in secunda parte in casis Petri de Trasmut, et unam meam vineam in Luna in termino Vallis de Mazola et affrontat in una parte in vinea Bote Desporret soror mea et in secunda parte in vinea Martini Marce, et unum meum campum in termino de Ballellas et affrontat in una parte in vinea domus milicie et in secunda parte in campo filiorum Petri de Vall et in tercia parte in rivo de Larba et in quarta parte in çequia unde se rigat, et dono vobis similiter meam cortem quam habeo ad Fontes Saladas cum sua era et cum omni sua hereditate mihi pertinenti, et unum roncinnum ensellatum et emfrenatum ab integro et sine ullo retinimento. Dono vobis dictas casas de terra usque ad celum et vineam et campum et cort cum omni sua hereditate et roncin cum introitibus et exitibus eorum, ita ut totum mihi pertinet et pertinere debet et sicut melius ad donationem et caritatem dici et intelligi potest vestro salvamento; quod de cetero vos et successores vestri habeatis hoc totum franchum, liberum et quietum ad propriam vestram hereditatem per dare et vendere et impignorare et per omnes vestras voluntates facere in perpetuum sine mea meorum-que contradiccione vel impedimento. Tamen volo et mando quod si migravero ab hoc seculo antea quam abitum dicte domus acceptum habeam omne autem mobile quod ego et filius meus Enneco Sanz ad illum diem habebimus fratres domus milicie predicte per me et in mea voce dividant illud cum dicto filio meo, et dictus filius meus accipiat unam medietatem de toto mobile voce et racione matris sue et fratres domus milicie Templi medietatem de mea medietate. Tamen si vixero convenio dare et deliberare dare et deliberare in caritate et beneficio dictam medietatem mee medietatis de toto meo mobile dicte domui et fratribus ibi deo servientibus tunc quando abitum domus milicie Templi Salomonis accepero et magister mandaverit et voluerit. Et amore dei et mercedis rogo magistrum et dictum preceptorem domus milicie Templi de Osca et fratribus ibi deo servientibus quod dictus filius meus sit in eorum comanda cum omnibus suis bonis et nutriant illum amore dei et mei usque ad finem X. annorum et si filius meus interim obierit ab hoc seculo sepelliant illum in eorum fossario et medietatem suam de mobile habeant illam ad eorum proprias voluntates faciendas; et si ad finem termini vivus erit et voluerit stare in dicta domo milicie et remanere cum suo mobile bene; sin autem, vadat ubi voluerit cum omnibus rebus suis. Cartam et donum laudo et proprio signo corroboro. Et nos frater Johannes de Corzan dictus preceptor de Osca consilio et voluntate et auctoritate fratris Stephani cambrero et fratris Enneco Sanz de Sporret et fratris Petri Dalmudevar et fratris Dominici de Sporret et fratris Garcie preceptor Lune recipimus vos Petrum Sanz de Sporret in fratrem et socium nostrum in dicta domo et promittimus vobis de cetero habere panem et aquam sicuti unus ex nobis et ego fratres Johannes de Corzan predictus per me et omnes fratres dicte domus cartam et donum laudo et proprio signo corroboro. Sunt ex hoc testes Sancius de Osca filius Petri Frontini et Sancius de Cesaragusta. Fuit hoc mense madii in era M.ªCC.ªLV.ª Garcias scripsit et hoc signum fecit.

## XIV

AHN, cód. 468, pp. 21–2, doc. 29                    ?25 January 1218

*Raymond Longo sells some houses in Zaragoza to the Temple*

In Christi nomine sit notum cunctis quod nos Raymundus Longo et uxori mee Armesen et Dominica filie mee puro corde et animo volenti cum hac presenti scriptura perpetuo valitura vendimus vobis fratri Petro de Deo preceptor domus milicie Templi Cesarauguste et fratribus vestris, scilicet fratri Guillelmo vice-preceptoris et fratri Petro de Ricla clavigero et fratri Petro Carreter et omnibus aliis fratribus tam presentes quam posteri, unas casas quas habemus in collacione Sante Marie Maioris Cesarauguste; et habent afrontaciones ex tribus partibus casas et ciminterio domus milicie Templi et de quarta via. Sicut iste affrontaciones includunt vel dividunt per circuitum sic vendimus vobis predictas casas omnes ab integro de celo usque ad abissum cum introitibus et exitibus suis sine inganno et sine mala voce et absque ullo retentu pro C. solidis denariorum jaccensium monete curribilis. Unde sumus bene paccati tam de predictis denariis quam de alifala et stamus inde de manifesto omni tempore. Et vos et successores vestri habeatis et posideatis predictas casas salvas, liberas et quietas pro vestra propria voluntate jure hereditario dandi, vendendi, impignorandi et per facere inde omnes vestras proprias voluntates sicut melius et plenius dici et excogitari potest, vos [?] et successori vestri per secula cuncta. Et ut melius securi sitis nos Raymundus Longo et uxori mee Armesen et Dominica filie mee damus vobis fratri Petro de Deo preceptor et omnibus aliis predictis fratribus fidancias salvitatis per forum terre per salvare iam dictas casas, sicut superius scriptum est, Johan de Ongria et Johanes de Iacca filius Raymundo de Iacca. Testes sunt huius rey frater Pertegaz preceptor de Álfambra et frater Sancius de Avoro et de laycis Sancius de Lascarre et Bonmançip de la Cavalleria et Julianus de Xufof et Petrus Daniessa.

Facta carta ad exitum mensis januarii VI. dies, era M.ªCC.ªL.ªVI.ª Signum Petri qui hoc scripsit.


# XV

AHN, San Juan, leg. 39, doc. 102                                    4 July 1221

*Record of the settlement of a dispute about various issues between the Temple and the bishop of Zaragoza*

Notum sit cunctis presentem paginam inspecturis quod dompnus Sancius dei gratia Cesaraugustanus episcopus cum consensu et voluntate sui capituli ex una parte et frater Poncius Menes[calt te]nens locum magistri cum consensu et voluntate fratris Bernardi de Campanna comendatoris de Mirabeto et fratris Guillelmi de Soleças comendatoris de Alfambra et fratris Petri Murut comendatoris Cesarauguste et aliorum fratrum suorum ex altera parte compromiserunt in magistrum Petrum de Calathaiub et dompnum Petrum de Tolone super multis controversiis que inter eos vertebantur tunc; que controversie vel articuli denotantur inferius. Conquerebatur siquidem dominus episcopus quod non dabant ei quartas de hiis que dimitabantur in hora mortis a parrochianis episcopi qui eligebant sepulturas in ecclesias Templariorum. Et conquerebatur de quadam domo de Siest. Conquerebatur etiam de hereditatibus quas fratres ipsi adquisierunt post concilium. Conquerebatur etiam de primiciis quas nolebant ipsis dare ecclesiis quibus pertinebant. Conquerebatur similiter quod nolebant recipere suos homines in colligendis decimis secundum tenorem privilegii inter eos constituti. Conquerebatur etiam quod non presentebant ei clericum instituendum in ecclesiis suis. Conquerebatur etiam quod recipiebant decimas de ovibus parrochianorum suorum quas comendabant in capana Templariorum et similiter de decimis pastorum suorum. Conquerebatur etiam quod nolebant sibi dare iura episcopalia in Pena Roderici Dieç et in Libros et in Covas de Eva. Conquerebatur similiter quod non dabant ei decimam de Belestar; quod Belestar dicebat esse terminum de Villa Espessa. Conquerebatur similiter quod quando visitabat ecclesias Templariorum tam per se ipsum quam per vicarios suos in honeste ipsum vel eos recipiebant. Conquerebatur etiam quod nolebant dare sibi iura episcopalia in Laçaida. Conquerebatur similiter quod exrahebant decimam ab ipsis decimis ad opus magistri ultramarini antequam darent quartam suam ipsi episcopo. Conquerebatur etiam quod ecclesiam de Lizina Curva detinebant iniuste et volebat scire quomodo habebant eam. Conquerebatur similiter de ecclesiis de Villar Longo et de Lacannata et de Villatanduf. Conquerebatur siquidem de ecclesiis de Orrios et de Scalambrolosa. Conquerebatur etiam quod nolebant ponere medietatem decime hereditatum quam excolunt manibus propriis cum decimis parrochianorum, propter quod amittebat ipse quartam partem in ecclesiis illis ab eo concessis. Conquerebantur similiter Templarii de episcopo quod recipiebat decimas molendinorum iniuste. Super his inquam omnibus compromiserunt in predictos magistrum Petrum et Petrum de Tolone ut quicquid ipsi super premissis omnibus dicerent vel diffinirent sentenciando utraque pars ratum haberet et firmum et per omnia tempora inconcussum.

Magister vero Petrus de Calathaiub et Petrus de Tolone habita deliberatione per sentenciam diffinierunt sicut inferius est expressum. In primo siquidem capitulo convenerunt quod viderent fratrum compositione cum episcopo super ecclesiis de Novellas et aliis ecclesiis et tunc dicerent quod esset dicendum. Super domo de Siest convenerunt quod querimoniam episcopi iudicio dirimeretur. In capitulo hereditatum adquisitarum post concilium ienerale Rome tempore Innocentii habitum omnino dissenserunt. In capitulo vero primiciarum ita per sentenciam diffinierunt quod de hereditatibus infra quadraginta annos ab eis adquisitis dent medietatem primiciarum ecclesiis quibus pertinent. De hereditatibus vero quas adquisierunt ante XL.ª annos non darent primicias. In capitulo de decimis colligendis convenerunt similiter quod dominus episcopus poneret homines suos in unaquaque ecclesia cum fratre eorum qui similiter debet facere hominium domino episcopo quod fideliter colligat decimas cum homine episcopi, sicut continetur in instrumento inter episcopum et Templarios constricto. In capitulo instituendorum clericorum in ecclesiis sentenciando dixerunt quod fratres Templi nullum clericum in ecclesiis quas habent in Cesarauguste diocesi instituerent antequam dominum episcopum presentarent. In capitulo illorum qui habent oves comendatas cum ovibus Templariorum sentenciando diffinierunt quod ipsi darent decimas ecclesiis in quibus sunt parrochiani. In capitulo vero pastorum dubitarunt et de illo capitulo nichil diffinierunt. In capitulo vero de ecclesiis de Penna Roderici Dieç et de Libros et de Covas diffiniendo sentenciarunt quod in illis ecclesiis darent omnia iura sua domino episcopo. In capitulo de Belestar ita sentenciarunt quod probaret dominus episcopus Belestar esse terminum de Villa Espesa, et ita reciperet decimas de Belestar; et si probarent fratres quod esset in termino de Villel dimitteret episcopus Templariis et darent de eis quarta episcopo. In capitulo visitacionis ecclesiarum statuerunt quod cum dominus episcopus vel eius vicarii visitarunt ecclesias splendide et honorifice eum vel eos recipiant Templarii et habunde procurent et etiam nuntios eius bene recipiant. In capitulo de La Çaida ita dixerunt quod produceretur instrumentum vel compositio habita inter fratres et episcopum super La Çaida, et tunc habita deliberatione diffinirent. In capitulo quod dicebatur quia ipsi fratres extrahebant decima decimarum ad opus magistri ita sententiarunt quod fratres nunquam extraherent vel debuerunt extrahere decimam ad opus magistri antequam darent quartam domino episcopo de omni acervo. In capitulo de Licina Curva dixerunt quod fratres exiberent iusticiam domino episcopo qualiter detineant eam sub eis vel si noluerint sub domino archiepiscopo. In capitulo de ecclesiis de Vilarlongo et de Lacannata et de Villatanduf dixerunt quod exiberent iusticiam domino episcopo coram ipsis si voluerint vel coram domino archiepiscopo. In capitulo de Orrios et de Scalambrolosa in quarum possessione fratres fuerunt inducti per Bertrandum archidiaconum Cesaraugustanum dixerunt quod fratres essent in illa qualicumque possessione sive bona sive mala; postea responderent domino episcopo de proprietate illarum ecclesiarum. In capitulo quod dicebatur quod nolebant ponere medietatum decimarum suarum cum decimis parrochianorum sentenciando diffinierunt quod omnino mittant illam medietatem decimarum suarum cum decimis parrochianorum et ita darent quartam domino episcopo de omnibus. In capitulo quod dicebatur quod episcopus accipiebat decimam molendinorum omnino diffenserunt. Episcopus vero cum consensu capituli sui et dompnus Poncius Menescalt cum consilio fratrum suorum omnia in quibus supradicti dompnus magister Petrus et dompnus Petrus de Tolone concordarunt se in perpetuum servaturos promiserunt. In aliis vero in quibus supradicti duo non bene decesserunt sub arbitris iudicio stare compromiserunt. Testes huius rei sunt frater Bernardus de Campanna et frater Guillelmi de Soleças supradicti et magister Arnaldus Guillelmi canonicus Sancti Salvatoris et dompnus Ennechus Garsie de Azoara.

Actum est hoc in palatio domini episcopi Cesaraugustani sub era M.ªCC.ªLVIIII.ª, IIII.º nonas julii, sub anno incarnationis domini M.ºCC.ºXX.º primo. Ego Sancius qui iussu predictorum hoc scripsi et signum apposui.

## XVI

AHN, cód. 466, p. 36, doc. 36                    November 1221

*Mary, the widow of Peter Monzón, grants a vineyard to the Templars in order to endow a lamp and a chantry*

Pateat cunctis quod ego domina Maria que fuy coniux de Pero Moncon bono animo et voluntate bona stando in mea memoria do tradoque vobis fratri Stephano de Belmont comendatori de Villel et Sancto Redemptore et omnibus fratribus milicie Templi quomodo ibi sunt et in antea sunt venturi ipsam vineam quam habebam in loco qui dicitur Cegularia infra Vilianum Montisacuti et filios Arnaldi Fabri de Cedriellis et domina Oro et via pro anima mei mariti et filii et memetipse parentumque meorum atque omnium fidelium defunctorum ut eam plenarie et pacifice per omnia tempora hereditetis absque obstaculo et retentu sicut melius dici potest vel intelligi sine mala voce usque ad finem mundi. Hinc ego iamdictus Stephanus comendator de Villel et nos fratres Sancti Redemptoris qui sumus modo et in antea venturi concedimus vobis domine Marie predicte ut teneamus et faciamus tenere semper in ecclesia beati Redemptoris unam lampadem, que ardeat cotidie ante altare beate Marie, et cappellanum qui ibi decantet III. dies in ebdobmada missam pro animabus vestrum parentumque vestrorum et omnium defunctorum fidelium; set ex nostris fratribus debet esse cappellanus. Testes dompnus Paschasius Munyoz, J. Destrich, Andreas merinus, Andreas de Comdon, D. Pictor; de fratribus frater Raymundus cappellanus Sancti Redemptoris, frater Bernardus, frater Guillelmus; et R. de Gordan qui hoc scripsit signum, in era M.ªCC.ª L.ªIX.ª, actum est prima ebdobmada novembris.

# XVII

ACA, parch. James I, no. 380                    9 July 1229

*William of Sargantanes acknowledges that he and his descendants and possessions are all under the lordship of the Temple*

Notum sit cunctis quod ego Gillelmus de Sergentanis filius qui fui Bernardi de Sargantanis et Marie uxoris eius condam defuncte bona et libera voluntate recognosco et fateor in veritate corpus meum et omnes infantes meos quos habeo et habere debeo et omnes res meas habitas et habendas esse de milicia Templi suorumque fratrum. Ita scilicet quod unquam ego et mei non possimus alium dominum reclamare nisi fratres milicie Templi et nulla prescriptio tempororum sive habitacio villarum atque civitatum seu opidorum non possit mihi nec meis in aliquo prodesse nec dicte milicie suisque fratribus obesse; et pro possessione corporis mei infantumque meorum seu rerum dono vobis fratribus milicie ego et mei annuatim I. par caponum in festo omnium sanctorum. Ad maiorem etiam firmitatem juro ego dictus Gillelmus de Sargantanis manibus meis propriis per deum et super sancta IIII. evagelia ut hoc atendam et compleam omni tempore ut superius dictum est. Item recognoscho et fateor quod pater meus et mater fuerunt dicte milicie Templi. Quod est factum VII. idus julii anno domini M.CC.XX. nono. Signum Gillelmi de Sargantanis qui hoc laudo et firmo et iuro. Signum Gillelmi de Medala. Signum Ferrarii Bufil de Vila Seyna. Signum Arnaldi de Sargantanis. Signum Andree sacerdotis et publici ville Vici scriptoris. Signum Gillelmi sacerdotis qui hoc scripsit die et anno quo supra.

# XVIII

AHN, cód. 471, p. 124, doc. 119                    20 February 1240

*James I acknowledges receipt of jewels which had been deposited at Monzón*

[N]overint universsi quod nos Jacobus dei gratia rex Aragonum, Maioricarum et Valencie, comes Barchinone et Urgelli et dominus Montispessulani et nos Yoles eadem regina, comitissa et domina eorumdem locorum confitemur nos recepisse et habuisse omnes et singulas joyas quas in domo Templi Montissonis dimiseramus ac comendaveramus. Quare per nos et omnes nostros pro predictis joys omnibus domos Templi et omnes fratres clamamus quitios. Ita quod nunquam de cetero possimus aliquis nostrum vel nostrorum predictas joyas vel earum aliquas iterum demandare nec fratres aut domos aliquas nec bona aliqua Templi racione comande dictarum joyarum inculpare,

gravare aut etiam molestare. Datum apud Calataiubium X.° kalendas
marcii anno domini a nativitate M.°CC.°XL.° Signum Jacobi dei
gratia regis Aragonum, Maioricarum et Valencie, comitis Barchinone
et Urgelli et domini Montispessulani.

Huius rey testes sunt F. Infans Aragonum. Petrus Cornellii maiordomus Aragonum. P. Ferrer dominus de Albarrazin. G. Romei. A. de
Luna.

Signum Guillelmi scribe qui mandato domini regis et domine regine
pro domino Berenga Barchinonensi episcopo cancellario suo hanc
cartam scripssit loco, die et anno prefixis. Lecta fuit regi.

## XIX

AHN, San Juan, leg. 556, doc. 4                        9 October 1245

*The Templars grant Marlofa for life to Bertrand of Naya in return for certain
irrigation rights*

Noverint universi quod nos frater G. de Cardona domorum milicie
Templi in Catalonia et Aragonia minister humilis cum assensu et
voluntate B. deç Bosch comendatoris de Novelles, R. de Bera comendatoris de Boquinnenech, fratris P. de Sant Roman comendatoris
Cesarauguste, fratris P. de Mont Palau comendatoris de Villel, fratris
G. de Alcala, fratris S. deçmarii, fratris M. de Anessa, fratris P. de ça
Olivera camerarii Cesarauguste, fratris [?]Spaniolii et fratris Poncii de
conventu Cesarauguste, fratris G. de Tort socii nostri, fratris Poncii
menescalii nostri, fratris Johannis capellani nostri et aliorum fratrum
nobiscum existencium damus et concedimus vobis dompno Bertrando
de Naya et dompne Elbire Ximini filie dompni Alamandi de Luna
uxori vestre castrum et villam de Meçlofa cum ingressibus et egressibus
suis, cum vineis, campis, ortis et possessionibus universis, terminis
heremis et populatis, tributis, reditibus et cum omnibus juribus suis
que ad dictum castrum et villam pertinent vel pertinere debent aliquo
modo vel causa, quod habeatis, possideatis et explectetis omnibus
diebus vite vestre pacifice et quiete. Ita videlicet quod anno quolibet in
festo sancte Marie de augusto detis comendatori domus Cesarauguste
vel locum eius tenenti LXX. kaficia tritici et XXX. kaficia ordei boni
et pulcri intus in Cesaraugusta in domo Templi, non obstante aliqua
excusatione, casu fortuito, grandine, nebula, sterelitate temporis vel
aliqua alia tempestate vel causa, nisi forte solutio retardetur cum speciali
licencia comendatoris Cesarauguste; et procurabitis comendatorem
Cesarauguste cum tribus equitaturis bis in anno cum ipse illuc iverit
ad visitandum castrum et villam et hereditates de Meçlofa. Castrum
et domos reficiatis et in pede teneatis sine scalonibus, villam et hereditates melioretis sicut melius potueritis et meliorationes ibi factas nec

id quod hodie ibi est nullo modo deterioretis nec deteriorari faciatis nec permittatis. Illud açud teneatis in pede sicut Templarii facere tenentur hoc anno tantum usque ad mensem febroarii. Mundetis bene cequias dum castrum et villam tenueritis et faciatis omnia que Templarii facere debent, tenentur vel tenebantur ratione dicti castri, ville et hereditatum sive ratione vicinitatis sive qualibet alia ratione, ita quod Templarii dictum tributum liberum habeant et ad nichilum teneantur ratione dicti castri, ville et hereditatis. Et quod aperiatis in continenti cequiam unde fluat aqua de Pinsech ad Meçlofa et dabitis aquam ville de Meçlofa quanta transire poterit per unum foramen palmare ex utraque parte quadratum in qualibet septimana per unam diem et unam noctem ad rigandum dictas hereditates; quam aquam Templarii in perpetuum possideant ad suam propriam hereditatem. Sciendum tamen est quod qualibet septimana in die lune in occasu solis Templarii recipiant dictam aquam et in die martis in occasu solis dimitant eam, et si evenerit in aliqua septimana quod isti duo dies non sint de ador de Pinsech quod loco istorum habeant alios duos dies prout eis melius videbitur, ita quod in quocumque casu in qualibet septimana habeant dictam aquam per unam diem et unam noctem ut dictum est. Nec liceat vobis supradictis dompno Bertrando de Naya et dompne Elbire Ximini nec vestris nec alicui nomine vestro per dictam cequiam, dum castrum et villam tenueritis, aliquo tempore aquam passare ad vendendum aliis villis vicinis nec ad aliquid aliud faciendum nisi tantum ad rigandum hereditates de Meçlofa, nisi cum licencia comendatoris Cesarauguste expressa; et non possitis vendere, obligare vel alienare aliquo modo vel deteriorare aliquid de premissis. Et cum vos predictos B. de Naya et dompna Elbira Ximini mori contigerit vel religionem intrare, vel si mortuo vobis dompno B. de Naya dicta uxor vestra alium virum acceperit, vel si dictum tributum in dicto termino non solveritis, vel si dictas conveniencias omnes et singulas non adimpleveritis, vel si contra predicta in aliquo verbo vel facto vel machinatione aliqua veneritis, quod Templarii propria auctoritate et sine aliqua monitione vel denuntiatione dictum castrum et villam cum omnibus meliorationibus ibi factis, quocumque nomine censeantur, in continenti valeant emperare, salvo nichilominus quod magister et fratres Templi vel quilibet eorum mandato possit agere contra vos ambos supradictos vel alterum si forte contingat vos non servare omnia supradicta vel aliquod de predictis vel in aliquo contravenire et vos ipso facto, verbo vel machinatione ab omni jure vestro sine spe restitutionis penitus cadatis. Et nos dicti dompnus Bertrandus de Naya et dompna Elbira Ximini uxor eius dictam donationem castri et ville et hereditatum de vobis dominis Templariis gratanter recipimus sub conditionibus et pactis superius nominatis; et in presenti damus et offerimus deo et beate Marie et ordini Templi dictam aquam pro remedio peccatorum nostrorum et aliorum parentum nostrorum quod habeant eam ad propriam hereditatem in perpetuum pacifice et quiete sicut superius est premissum. Insuper ut omnia et singula bona fide et sine fraude attendamus et compleamus facimus vobis dicto magistro et fratribus Templi homagium manibus et hore, et insuper juramus corporaliter tactis sacrosanctis evangeliis. Preterea renuntiamus fori exceptioni ita quod si omnia predicta et singula non adimpleverimus vel si in aliquo contravenerimus ut dictum est, quod dominus papa vel delegati sui vel episcopi Tirasonensis, Cesaraugustanus, Oscensis nos excomunicent et totam familiam nostram in continenti et per suas dioceses denuntiari faciant excomunicatos cum a Templariis fuerint requisiti, nobis non citatis, non conventis, vocatis nec etiam expectatis nec aliqua excusatione nostra ex quacumque causa justa vel injusta audita, recepta vel etiam ascultata, vel alio modo prout eis videbitur per censuram ecclesiasticam compellant nos. Item concedimus quod tenemus in comanda de vobis in Meçlofa IIII. cupas que tenent XX. metros quas recuperetis quando castrum et villam recuperaveritis vel cupas alias bonas que teneant XX. metros. Et ad maiorem Templi securitatem damus vobis fidejussores quemlibet in solidum dompnum P. Martini de Luna dominum de Alcala, dompnum Guillelmum de Olivito et dompnum Gonisalvum de Libranas milites de Crisenet, qui renuntiant fori exceptioni eo modo et casu quo nos super obligavimus; et dompnum Johannem Petri de la Cabanna et dompnum Michaelem de Sancto Salvatore et dompnum Garsiam Lupi de Peralta habitantes in Alagona similiter quemlibet in solidum set non renuntiant fori exceptioni. Et nos dicti P. Martini de Luna, G. de Olivito, G. de Libranas, J. Petri, M. de Sancto Salvatore et G. Lupi constituimus nos fidejussores sicut superius continetur. Testes huius rey sunt dompnus Guillelmus Dasin miles, dompnus Egidius castellanus habitans in Crisenet, dompnus Sancius joglar et dompnus Michael çapatero cives Cesarauguste. Facta carta VIIII.º die introytu mensis octobris in era Mª.CC.ªLXXX.ª tertia. Ego Sancius de Valle publicus tabellio Cesarauguste hiis omnibus predictis interfui et hoc scripsi et hoc signum feci.

## XX

ACA, parch. James I, no. 1332            21 May 1253

*The commander of Palau acknowledges that Isaac Adreti has lent him 2,000s.B., and makes provisions for the repayment of this sum*

Sit omnibus notum quod ego frater Poncius de Hulugia comendator domus milicie Templi de Palacio concedo et recognosco tibi Yssacho

Adreti et tuis me a te de puro capitali numerando mutuo recepisse et habuisse duo millia solidorum Barchinonensium valente marcha argenti LXXX.VIII. solidos, quos in usibus propriis et necessariis dicte domus penitus convertimus, unde quia bene paccatus sum renuncio omni excepcioni non recepte peccunie. Quos assigno tibi et tuis habendos et plenarie recuperandos in solucionibus inferius scriptis, videlicet in quinquaginta solidis Barchinonensibus quos mihi solvere tenetur Bartolomeus Marchesius pro lezda vini, et in nonaginta solidis quos mihi solvere tenetur Guillelmus Pecuvinus de baiulia Sancti Petri de Auro, et in quinquaginta solidis quos Arnaldus Andreas mihi solvere tenetur de baiulia Minorise, et in centum quinquaginta solidis quinque solidis quos Guillelmus Ferre, Astrugus de Tolosa et Craschus Bonafusius mihi solvere tenentur de lezda molarum et catalli fusti, et in nongentis quadraginta solidis quos Petrus de Lissacho mihi solvere tenetur de lezdis domini regis Barchinone et quintario, et in ducentis triginta solidis quos Arnaldus Pelegrinus et Samuel Cap et Astrug de Tolosa et Abraham de Furno mihi solvere tenentur de baiulia Ville Mayoris, et in centum viginti quatuor solidis quos Bernardus Andreas mihi solvere tenetur de empcione macelli Barchinone, et in triginta solidis quos Bernardus de Furno mihi solvere tenetur de censu bocherie, et in quadraginta solidis quos Petrus de Rivo Primerio mihi solvere tenetur de empcione farnerie, et in sexaginta solidis quos Bernardus de Oltzina mihi solvere tenetur de censu Roudorii, et in triginta solidis quos Petrus de Sancta Cruce mihi solvere tenetur de mostalafia Barchinone, et in viginti quinque solidis quos Astrugus de Tolosa mihi solvere tenetur de albergis de Lupricato, et in triginta duobus solidis quos recipere debeo in censu Sancti Michaelis, et in nonaginta sex solidis quos recipere debeo in censu alfundici domini regis de mari cum macello, et in tribus solidis quos recipere debeo in barcha de Bagneolis, et in quatuor solidis quos recipere debeo in censu curie; quos omnes denarios assignavit mihi habendos et percipiendos Petrus de Castro Azol baiulus Barchinone racione decimi quod accipio in redditibus baiulie Barchinone; promitens tibi quod in predictis denariis aliquid non tangam nec accipiam nec tangi vel accipi ab aliquo promitant, et si forte dominus rex vel aliquis pro eo in predictis assignacionibus aliquid tetigerit, acceperit, emparaverit vel forciaverit in totum scilicet vel in partem aut aliquid fuerit ibi ab aliquo acceptum, forciatum vel diminutum racione mei et domus predicte de Palacio vel eciam racione guerre domini regis et Raymundi de Cardona tibi et tuis restituere promito statim cum a te fuero amonitus. Obligans super hiis tibi et tuis me et omnia bona dicte domus in quibus magis et melius accipere volueritis. Quantum autem ad hoc omni cuilibet juri et consuetudini et beneficio novissime constitucionis penitus renuncio. Actum est hoc XII. kalendas junii anno domini M.°CC.°L.° tercio. Signum fratris Poncii de Hulugia comendatoris predicti qui hoc laudo et firmo. Testes sunt fratris Guillelmus capellanus domus Barchinone et frater Berengarius eiusdem domus.

Signum Petri Carbonelli notarii Barchinonensis qui hoc scribi fecit cum literis appositis in linea I.ª et rasis et emendatis in linea XVII.ª, die et anno prefixis.

## XXI

AHN, cód. 494, pp. 17–19, doc. 4           11 September 1255

*The Templars make an agreement with the* concejo *of Cantavieja about the appointment of local officials and other matters*

Notum sit cunctis tam presentibus quam futuris quod nos frater Guillermus de Agero preceptor Cantavetulle cum consilio et voluntate tocius capituli generalis quod fuit celebratum apud Mirabetum, scilicet consilio et voluntate fratris Hugo de Joy domorum milicie Templi in Aragonia et Catalonia magistri et fratris Guillermi de Cardona comendatoris Miraveti et fratris Raymundi Berengarii Dager comendatoris Gardeni et fratris G. de Angularia comendatoris Orte et fratris Bernat de Altaripa comendatoris Montisoni et fratris G. de Mongri comendatoris Dartusse et omnium aliorum fratrum in dicto capitulo existentium, et eciam cum consilio et voluntate fratris Berengarii de Moncenis et fratris Johannis Ferrarii camerarii Cantavetule et fratris Petri Cosquella comendatoris Villarlongi et fratris Mercader et fratris Petri de la Cabana comendatoris de La Glesiolla et tocius conventus Cantavetule, per nos et omnes nostros successores damus et concedimus in perpetuum vobis universso consilio Cantavetule presenti pariter et futuro quod semper habeatis in Cantavetula justiciam vicinum Cantavetulle aut filium vicini Cantavetule. In tali modo quod presentetis comendatori et fratribus Cantavetule decem homines et ipse comendator eligat et possit eligere de illis decem hominibus unum quem ipse voluerit per justiciam; et de alis eligat duos juratos et unum almudacafium. Reliqui vero sex in simul cum ipsis juratis et cum almudatafio sint consiliarii per totum illum annum de justicia. Et quidquid illi decem homines fecerunt ad profectum sive utilitatem domini Templi et consilii Cantavetule ratum et firmum habeatur. Et transacto illo anno illi decem homines videlicet justicia et duo jurati et almudacafius cum illis sex consiliariis eligant alios decem homines antequam exeant de suo oficio; quos vos consilium universum Cantavetule presentetis comendatori et fratribus Cantavetule eodem modo sicut dictum est. Istud vero mutamentum fiat semper annuatim de festo in festam sancti Johannis Babtiste. Item volumus et concedimus quod habeatis in Cantavetule scribas sive tabelliones publicos ad forum Cesarauguste.

Item volumus et concedimus quod possitis manere in vestris mansiis donando fornaticum castro Cantavetule ad rationem de XXX.ª fogaciis unam sive de XXX.ª mensuris bladii unam. Non tamen diffaciatis vestras domos in Cantavetulla. Item volumus et concedimus quod omnes ministeriales sive omnes vicini Cantavetulle qui non potuerint dare unam fanecam bladii de decimo de suo labore sive unam saumandam racemorum aut duos agnos de suo bestiario dent II. solidos castro Cantavetule annuatim ad festum natalis domini de illis IIII.º solidis quos solebant dare. Item damus et concedimus vobis dicto consilio Cantavetule et vestris in perpetuum quod possitis piscare in omnibus rivis Cantavetule. Retinemus tamen pro nostra defesia in rivo de la Boxadella et de la Salçadella a molendino nostro totum superius cum illa nostra pesqueria que est circa ipsum nostrum molendinum. Item volumus et concedimus quod ponderetis sive pessetis in Cantavetulla ad forum Cesarauguste. Item volumus et constituimus quod donetis invicem introitum animalibus nostris et vestris ad covas nostras et vestras ubi animalia melius se potuerint recolligere vel recessare per totum terminum Cantavetulle. Omnia autem suprascripta promittimus per nos et omnes nostros successores tenere et observare incorrupta vobis dicto consilio Cantavetulle et vestris succesoribus in perpetum. Igitur nos Sancho de Sent Guillem justitia Cantavetulle et Dominicus Dalcanyzar et Petrus Martini Darman jurati eiusdem loci et Arnaldus Faber et Petrus Capater et Bernardus Ferrarius et Martinus Dalbalat et Lazaro Quarter et Garcia Pellizer et Dominicus Sancii Dixarch nos omnes insimul per nos et universum consilium Cantavetulle presens pariter et futurum recipimus a vobis dicto fratre Guillermo de Agero comendatore Cantavetulle et fratribus memoratis hanc graciam in omnibus supradictis a vobis liberaliter nobis factam, et promittimus per nos et omnes nostros successores esse semper fideles et legales vobis et vestris in supradictis et in omnibus aliis que vobis facere debeamus sicut boni vasalli debent esse suo domino naturali. Quod est actum III. idus septembris anno domini millesimo CC.LV.º Bernardus de Balagario scriba castri Cantavetule hec scripsit et hoc signum fecit.

## XXII

AHN, San Juan, leg. 713, doc. 19                      16 October 1260

*The bishop of Tarazona, quoting a letter from Innocent IV, orders his clergy to exhort the faithful to aid the Temple*

S.[?]dignatione divina Tirasonensis episcopus venerabilibus et karissimis in Christo dilectis filliis decanis, archidiachonis, prioribus, archipresbyteris, rectoribus, vicariis, capellanis et aliis ecclesiarum prelatis per nostram diocesim constitutis ad quos littere iste pervenerint, salutem et benedictionem. Litteras domini pape cum vera bulla et filis non cancellatas, non abolitas, non viciatas nec in aliqua parte sui suspectas nos recepisse noveritis sub hac forma:

Innocentius episcopus servus servorum dei venerabilibus fratribus archiepiscopis et episcopis et dilectis filiis abbatibus, prioribus, decanis, archidiachonis, archipresbyteris et aliis ecclesiarum prelatis presentes litteras inspecturis salutem et apostolicam benedictionem. Cadere debet super omnium corda fidelium frequens dilectorum filiorum . . magistri et fratrum domus milicie Templi Iherosolimitani contrictio si piis meditacionibus cogitetur et ad compaciendum eis ac pro viribus succurendum omnes qui aliqua humanitatis gestant viscera efficaciter invitare. Ipsi quidem pro universo christiano populo contra fidei catholice inimicos in partibus Iherosolimitanis, ubi redemptor noster in salutis humane precium sanguinem suum fudit, continuas excubias observantes, ne terra illa eodem sanguine consecrata infidelium dominio in tocius christianitatis obprobrium et christianorum periculum totaliter prophanetur, adversus continuos adversariorum insultus diei et estus pro certis comunis cause consortibus pondus portant et, vitam suam pro salute omnium exponere non verentes, temporibus preteritis quorum recens adhuc extat memoria multas personarum strages et immensa rerum dispendia pertulerunt. Non enim comunis fama subticuit eis qui presencialiter non viderunt quod a quindecim annis citra predicte domus fratres et homines fere usque ad internitionem novissimam hostilis impetus ter assumpsit eorumque facultates sic in equis et armis et bonis aliis fatigavit quod, nisi dominus qui lucernam eorum non permittit extingui semen modicum in paucis superstitibus reservasset, cecidisset omnino ibidem illa celebris columpna fidei orthodoxe; et quasi ad oppressionem eorum manus infidelium parum valida videretur, addidit crucis persecutoribus quondam Fr. olim imperator tyrampnidis sue robur ipsos magistrum et fratres possessionibus atque redditibus quos habent in regno Sicilie nequiter spoliando eosque detinendo per iniquitatis sue iniusticiam diucius occupatos, quibus adhuc incubant paterne malignitatis reprobi successores. Ut taceamus quot fratres ammiserint, quanta bona perdiderint in illa flebili strage quam karissimum in Christo filium nostrum . . regem Francorum illustrem cum christiano populo ex occulta dispensatione divini iudicii incurisse non absque dolore ac gemitu memoramur. Verum ad tot reparanda domus predicte dispendia et restauranda tam enormia divine substancie detrimenta ipsi magister et fratres tamquam viri constantes, tenaces, propositi et adversitatum congressibus viriliter reluctantes dura excogitavere remedia per que imminentibus facultatum suarum defectibus obvietur. Ut enim domus ipsorum pene succisa repullulet ipsiusque fore deiecta potencia vigore pristino reformetur, attenuant per indictam sibi censuram realis parsimonie vires suas, in archam corpora sua brevioris victus angustiam redigentes ac privatis detrahentes necessitatibus unde publice utilitatis negocium convalescat, ne per inflictam sibi sponte necessariorum indigenciam fratres ipsi circa terre predicte negocium remittuntur; quibus prefato regi et exercitui christiano assistant assidue ac continue collaborent vite non ociose miliciam in castrensibus occupationibus transigentes, pro zelo publici commodi quietis proprie comoditatibus abdicatis. Cum itaque domus ipsa sub hiis et gravium debitorum que propter hec subiit gravibus sarcinis nequeat diucius respirare nisi fidelium caritativis largicionibus adiuvetur, quin pocius timeatur quod graviter sit casura nisi supponat dominus manum suam, nos, ut tantum christiani nominis fulcimentum et tam validum propugnaculum quod contra hostes fidei divina erexit dispositio non vacillet, cupientes remedium adhibere universitatem vestram rogamus, monemus et hortamur attente per apostolica vobis scripta mandantes quatinus opus domini adiuvantes subditos vobis populos et christi fideles ut fratribus dicte domus ad exhonerationem debitorum huiusmodi manus porrigant adiutrices per vos et alios monere attencius ac sollicite inducere singuli procuretis, ita quod eadem domus ab imminenti sibi ruina valeat liberari ac hiidem fideles una vobiscum per hec et alia bona que domino inspirante feceritis ad eterne possitis felicitatis gaudia pervenire. Nos enim de omnipotentis dei misericordia et beatorum Petri et Pauli apostolorum eius auctoritate confisi ac illa quam nobis deus licet indignis ligandi atque solvendi contulit potestate, omnes qui eisdem fratribus de bonis sibi collatis a deo caritativum et competens ad hoc subsidium largientur volumus atque concedimus quod vos diligentius exponatis eisdem illius remissionis esse participes iuxta quantitatem subsidii et proprie devotionis affectum que transfretantibus in terre sancte subsidium a sede apostolica est concessa. Datum Perusii, III. kalendas februarii pontificatus nostri anno decimo.

Auctoritate igitur domini pape et nostra universitatem vestram rogamus et hortamur in domino in virtute obedientie vobis presentibus injungentes quatinus, dompnum Remirum fratrem et nuncium domus milicie Templi latorem presentium recipientes et tractantes benigne, subditos vobis populos et christi fideles ut fratribus dicte domus ad exhonerationem predictorum debitorum manus porrigant adiutrices per vos et alios monere attentius ac sollicite inducere singuli procuretis, necessitatem ipsius domus et dampna gravia que in personis, armaturis ac rebus aliis pro fide Christi in illis partibus pertulerunt et sustentamentum et auxilium quod fidei orthodoxe et populo christiano provenit ex ipsis qui pondus diei et estus portant pro ceteris comunis cause consortibus adversus continuos adversariorum insultus ne terra

sancta precioso Christi sanguine consecrata in tocius christianitatis obprobrium et christianorum periculum totaliter prophanetur et domini
pape et nostri ac aliorum prelatorum indulgencias eisdem subditis et
populis cum diligencia exponentes, et vos per hec et alia bona que
domino inspirante feceritis ad eterne possitis felicitatis gaudia pervenire.
Nos autem de omnipotentis dei misericordia confidentes omnibus vere
penitentibus et confessis qui dictis fratribus de bonis sibi collatis a
deo caritativum subsidium largientur quadraginta dies de injuncta sibi
penitencia singulis diebus quibus huiusmodi subsidium duxerint im-
pendendum misericorditer relaxamus, presentibus per annum tantum-
modo valituris. Datum Tirasone XVII. kalendas novembris anno
domini M.ºCC.º sexagesimo.

## XXIII

ACA, reg. 14, fols. 52ᵛ–53                                    10 April 1264
*James I acknowledges that the Templars have lent him 32,000s. J., and he
arranges to make repayment out of the* monedaje *due from Templar estates*

Confitemur et recognoscimus in veritate vobis venerabili fratri G.º de
Pontonibus magistro domus milicie Templi in Aragonia et Catalonia
et aliis fratribus eiusdem presentibus et futuris nos habuisse et mutuo
recepisse a vobis numerando triginta et duo millia solidos monete
jaccensis quos ad magnam instantiam nostram pro nobis a quibusdam
creditoribus sub usuris, videlicet ad rationem centum solidorum de
capitali pro decem solidis de usura in anno, mutuo recepistis, de quibus
bene paccati sumus. Et sic renunciamus excepcione non recepte
peccunie et doli. Quos triginta et duo millia solidos vobis et vestris
successoribus habendos et percipiendos assignamus in monetatico
omnium hominum villarum, castrorum et locorum vestrorum. Quod
monetaticum in festo sancti Michaelis septembris proximo venturo
debemus percipere et habere. Ita scilicet quod vos vel quos volueritis
loco vestri simul cum uno scriptore nostro et duobus probis hominibus
uniuscuiusque predictorum locorum colligant totum monetaticum
antedictum ab hominibus vestris predictis et inde vobis vel quibus
volueritis respondeant fideliter de eodem. Item assignamus vobis et
vestris successoribus habendos et percipiendos super monetatico antedicto omnes usuras quas predictis XXX.II. millibus solidis dictis
creditoribus solvere promisistis et omnia dampna et missiones que et
quas pro predicto mutuo vos forte facere oportebit. Item assignamus
vobis et vestris successoribus habendum et percipiendum in monetatico
supradicto totum illud quod G. de na Montagudo noster baiulus in

Ilerda de duobus annis proximo transactis retinuit de mandato nostro vel alia qualibet racione de juribus que vos et domus Gardenii annis singulis percipistis et percipere debetis in nostris redditibus Ilerde, facto tamen computo et albarano cum eodem bajulo de predictis. Promitentes vobis et vestris successoribus per firmam stipulationem quod nos in monetatico supradicto non tangamus vel tangi faciamus nec etiam permitamus nec assignacionem alicui vel aliquibus facimus famus super eodem. Immo faciemus ipsum vobis et vestris habere et libere percipere sine omni obstaculo et retentu. Mandantes universis hominibus dictorum locorum, castrorum et villarum vestrarum et collectori seu collectoribus et scriptori seu scriptoribus monetatici supradicti quod de dicto predicto monetatico vobis vel cui volueritis respondeant et non alicui alteri persone, et quod de ipso non donent nec solvant alicui vel aliquibus parum neque multum pro aliquibus nostris literis vel mandatis, quousque de supradictis XXX.II. millibus solidis, usuris, dampnis et missionibus et de omni eo etiam quod baiulus Ilerde de juribus vestris retinuit de duobus annis proximo transactis ut est dictum vobis et vestris successoribus et fratribus Templi fuerit plenario satisfactum. Datum apud Alagonem IIII. idus aprilis anno domini M.°CC.°LX.° quarto.

## XXIV

AHN, cód. 466, pp. 40–1, doc. 42                                 15 July 1267

*Carta de población granted by the Templars to Moorish settlers at Villastar*

In dei nomine amen. Noverint universsi quod nos frater A. de Castro Novo domorum milicie Templi in Aragonia et Catalonia magister humilis de consilio et voluntate fratris R. de Villalba comendatoris Orte et fratris G. de Montegrino comendatoris Alhanbre et fratris Dalmacii de Serone comendatoris Ambelli et fratris G. de Castro Veteri et fratris P. Dalbarels tenentis locum comendatoris Villeli et fratris Michaelis vicarii eiusdem et fratris P. de Timor et aliorum fratrum nostrorum per nos et succesores nostros damus, concedimus et stabilimus in perpetuum vobis Ferag de Pali et Abrahym Algebez et Jubamestar et Abdella Azir Abeyanet et aliis populatoribus sarracenis qui modo sunt vel in antea erunt ad populandum locum nostrum et alqueriam que notatur Bellestar que est in termino de Villelo cum domibus, ortis et ortalibus, agris et aliis hereditatibus heremis et populatis et terminis suis et pertinenciis universis; ita quod omnes hereditates predicte alquerie dividantur equaliter et quinyonentur inter XXX. sarracenos populatores eiusdem loci, exceptis quatuor hereditatibus quas christiani habent ibi prout eas tenent et fuerunt eisdem asignate, exceptis etiam domibus nostris turris sive statica superius posita, et excepta vinya et deffenssa quam ibidem habemus, que omnia retinemus ad opus nostri. Retinemus similiter nobis furnum et molendina et similia que ad dominum spectant ac plenam jurisdiccionem et senyoraticum nostrum tam etiam in zofris quam rebus aliis universsis. Predictas autem hereditates vobis damus et concedimus in hunc modum quod de omnibus bladis, vino, canamo, lino, ortaliciis et leguminibus et aliis omnibus fructibus et expletis et bonis que colligetis de eis detis vos et succesores vestri nobis et succesoribus nostris in perpetuum bene et fideliter quartam partem, et insuper dabitis nobis decimam et primiciam de omnibus que colligetis in hereditatibus antedictis. Preterea de unaquaque domorum predictorum triginta sarracenorum eiusdem populatorum habeamus semel in mense quolibet pro zofra unum pedonem et Templum det illa die qua eos habebit V. panes cuilibet prout est actenus consuetum. Insuper dabitis nobis annuatim in festo nativitatis domini pro unaquaque XXX. hereditatum unum par gallinarum. Item pro quolibet capite ovium et caprarum exivernatarum et pro qualibet arna apum detis nobis unum denarium annuatim in festo sancti Johannis babtiste; pro pollino vero equino et mulario dabitis XII. denarios, pro pollino asinino IIII. denarios et pro vezerro VI. denarios. De nutrimentis similiter animalium, videlicet de agnis, capritis sive edulis et pullis et anseribus et consimilibus decimam et primiciam nobis dabitis bene et fideliter et tam de predictis omnibus prout scriptum est quam de omnibus aliis que dici vel intelligi posint tanquam hic singulare posita dabitis nobis quartam partem et decimam et primiciam et omnia alia jura nostra bene et integre. Hec omnia faciendo et conplendo predictas hereditates habeatis, teneatis et posideatis et explectetis vos et succesores vestri. Set si quis hereditatem aliquam vendere aut alienare voluerit non posit hoc facere nisi suo consimili sarraceno qui ibi stet et maneat asidue et hoc de licentia fratrum Templi et de hiis que pro alla vendicione habuerit det Templo fideliter quartam partem. De vindemia autem quam in vineis quas in regano plantabitis colligetis quartam partem et predictam decimam et primiciam vestris expensis portabitis ad cellarium nostrum. De hiis autem quas in secano plantabitis dabitis septimam partem et decimam et primiciam de omnibus fructibus quos colligetis in vineis de secano. Nos autem predicti Ferath del Pali et Abrafim Algebez et Ajubamestar et Abdella Azir Abeyenet pro nobis et omnibus sarracenis presentibus et futuris ibidem habitantibus vel abitaturis hec omnia recepimus a vobis domino magistro et fratribus memoratis sub modis et condicionibus antedictis, promitentes esse fideles vassalli Templi et ibidem tenere hospicia nostra et predicta omnia et singula nec non et omnia alia jura vestra et servicia et ea que ad vestram jurisdiccionem vel senyoraticum pertineant dare et facere ac conplere bene et fideliter ut melius dici vel intelligi potest ad vestrum comodum et nostrorum. Et nos dictus magister ut presens instrumentum maiori vigeat firmitate ipsum sigilli nostri munimine duximus roborandum. Quod est actum idus julii anno domini M.°CC.°LX.° septimo. Signum fratris A. de Castro Novo magistri predicti. Signum fratris R. de Villalva comendatoris Orte. Signum fratris G. de Montegrino comendatoris Alhanbre. Signum fratris Dalmacii de Serone comendatoris Ambelli. Signum fratris G. de Castroveteri. Signum fratris P. de Albarels tenentis locum comendatoris Villeli. Signum fratris Michaelis vicarii Villeli. Signum fratris P. de Timor, qui hoc concedimus et firmamus.

Ego Raymundus de Montanyana notarius domini magistri auctoritate regis publicus hoc scripsi et hoc signum feci.

## XXV

AHN, cód. 689, pp. 4–5, doc. 3                    19 March 1268

*James I grants the Templars the right to hold a weekly market at Castellote*

Noverint universi quod nos Jacobus dei gratia rex Aragonum, Mayoricarum et Valencie, comes Barchinone et Urgelli et dominus Montispessulani per nos et per nostros damus et concedimus vobis venerabili et dilecto nostro fratri A. de Castro Novo magistro milicie Templi et fratribus eiusdem domus Templi et successoribus vestris in perpetuum mercatum in villa vestra que vocatur Castellotus. Ita scilicet quod de cetero in perpetuum in unaquaque die sabbati qualibet septimana teneatur et possit teneri et congregari mercatum in dicta villa libere et salve atque secure, et possint ibi vendi omnia que in mercato venduntur, et quilibet ad ipsum mercatum venientes possint vendere et ibidem res et merces eorum sicut ad mercatos allios terre nostre consueverunt et possunt vendere. Et recipiatis ibidem racione ipsius mercati ea iura que in aliis mercatis que nos dedimus in terra nostra recipiuntur. Nos autem recipimus et constituimus sub firma custodia nostra, proteccione, comenda et guidatico speciali omnes homines et mulieres qui et que ad dictum mercatum venient cum omnibus bestiariis seu bestiis grossis eorum et minutis et cum pane et vino ac quibuslibet aliis rebus et mercibus suisque quos ad dictum mercatum adducent vel inde extrahent seu portabunt, in eundo scilicet vel veniendo ad dictum mercatum et stando ibidem et redeundo. Ita videlicet quod nullus de nostri gratia confidens audeat ipsos homines vel mulieres ad dictum mercatum venientes seu inde redeuntes vel aliquas res vel merces suas quas ad dictum mercatum adducent vel inde extraent seu portabunt invadere, cape, detinere, impedire, marcare, offendere vel gravare culpa, crimine seu debito alieno, nisi homicide fuerint vel proditores manifesti vel debitores vel fidejussores pro aliis fuerint manifesti, nec in his etiam cassibus nisi prius in ipsis facta inventa fuerit de directo. Quicumque autem contra hoc presens guidaticum nostrum venire temtaverint iram et indignacionem nostram et penam quingentorum aureorum se noverint incursurum, dampno eis illato primitus et integre restituto. Mandantes firmiter vicariis, baiulis, civiis et universis aliis oficialibus et supditis nostris presentibus et futuris quod predicta firma habeant et observent ac faciant observari et non contra veniant nec aliquod contra venire permitant aliqua racione. Datum in Algizire XIIII.° kalendas aprilis anno domini M.°CC.°LX.° septimo.

Signum Jacobi dei gratia regis Aragonum, Maioricarum et Vallencie, comitis Barchinone et Urgelli et domini Montispessulani. Testes sunt Jacobus de Cervaria, Bernardus G. de Entenza, Jacebericus de Castro Novo, Gueraldonus de Capraria, G. de Angularia.

Signum Bartolomei de Pĩta qui de mandato domini regis hec scribi fecit et clausit loco, die et anno prefixis.


## XXVI

ACA, parch. Peter III, no. 33                                        3 May 1277

*William Sendre sells a Moorish slave to the commander of Barbará*

Sit notum cunctis quod ego Guillelmus Sendre junior civis Terrachonensis vendo vobis fratri Arnaldo Guarnerio comendatori de Barberano domus Templi et vestris pro undecim libris Barchinonensis monete de terno, de quibus sum a vobis bene paccatus et ideo renuntio exceptioni non numerate pecunie et doli, quendam sarracenum album nomine Mahometh ut eum habeatis ad omnes vestras voluntates. Teneor enim vobis et vestris quod non est furatus nec ablatus nec est de pace vel treuga nec habet morbum caducum. Et de hiis et aliis, pro quibus tenetur quis pro sarraceno vendito, teneor ego vobis et vestris pro isto ad consuetudinem Terrachone ubi eum vobis vendo. Et ipsum sarracenum faciam vobis et vestris habere et tenere in pace contra omnes personas. Et pro evictione et omnibus aliis predictis firmiter attendendis obligo vobis et vestris me et omnia bona mea habita et habenda. Insuper dono inde vobis ac vestris firmanciam Guillelmum Segarre de Vallibus qui mecum et sine me de predictis omnibus vobis teneatur et vestris. Et ego Guillelmus Sendre facio vobis fratri Arnaldo Guarnerio predicto et vestris hanc firmanciam sicut predictum est, obligando inde vobis et vestris me et omnes res meas habitas et habendas. Et ne possim super predictis per exceptionem principalis venditoris preconveniendi juvari in aliquo vel defendi renuncio nove constitutioni. Actum est hoc

quinto nonas madii anno domini M.ºCC.ºLXX.º septimo. Signum
mei Guillelmi Sendre. Signum Guillelmi Segarre, qui ambo hoc
firmamus et laudamus. Signum Guillelmi de Tever. Signum Arnaldi
Peladar. Signum Petri Simonis, testium.

Ego Petrus Vedelli publicus tabellio Terrachonensis sub Michaele
Boter hoc scribi feci et clausi vice ipsius. Ego Raimundus Vedelli hoc
scripsi mandato Michaelis Boter Terrachonensis notarii die et anno
prefixis.

# XXVII

AHN, cód. 466, pp. 26–7, doc. 24          22 September 1280

*Record of a dispute concerning the Temple's right to certain churches in the
diocese of Zaragoza*

Noverint universsi quod die dominica X.º kalendas octobris anno
domini millesimo ducentesimo octuagesimo frater Raymundus de
Pulcro Loco comendator de Villel conparuit coram reverendo patre
in Christo domino Petro dei gratia episcopo Cesaraugustano et eidem
ostendit duo translata duorum instrumentorum, in quibus videbatur
contineri jus quod Templum dicitur habere in quibusdam ecclesiis et
specialiter in ecclesiis de Serrion, de Alventosa, de Villestar, de Livres
et de Riodeva, super quibus dictus dominus episcopus mandaverat per
suas litteras dicto comendatori ut sibi inffra terminum in predictis
litteris contentum ostenderet quo modo tenebat vel posidebat Templum
ecclesias supradictas. Unum quoque eorumdem instrumentorum sicut
in suo translato facto per manum Johannis presbiteri manentis in castro
Mirabeti incipiebat: Quecumque pro religiosorum quiete statuta sunt
in sua debent stabilitate firmare, etc.; et finiebat: Ego Arnaldus notarius
mandato supradictorum hanc cartam scripsi et propria manu hoc
signum feci. Alter vero, sicut in suo translato facto per manum Garsie
de Laurencio notarii Turolii aparebat, incipiebat: Nunc et in eternum
sit cunctis hoc manifestum quod ego P. dei gratia Cesaraugustanus
episcopus, etc.; et finiebat: Petrus dei gratia Cesaraugustanus episcopus,
etc. Quibus translatis in presentia et audientia dicti domini episcopi
lectis, cum idem dominus episcopus noluerit credere eisdem translatis
et dixit velle videre originalia instrumenta, per dictum comendatorem
fuit dicto domino episcopo humiliter suplicatum ut terminum sibi in
predictis litteris asignatum, cum esset valde brevis nec infra ipsum poset
ipsa originalia instrumenta habere, prorogaret et sibi terminum
largiorem predicto conpetentem asignaret; quod dictus dominus
episcopus facere denegavit. Testibus ad hec dompnis Petro Eximini de
Ayerbe sacrista sedis Sancti Salvatoris Cesarauguste; Egidio Sancii et

Garsia de Vallibus canonicis eiusdem ecclesie; Guillelmo de Alcala domino de Quinto et Michaele Petri de Januis, militibus; Sancio precentore de Albarrazino et Garsia Guarini seniore, vicino Turolii, et Sancio Munyocii et magistro Bernaldo, vicario ecclesie de Villel; et me Raymundo de Laurencio publico Turolii notario qui predictis interfui et ad instantiam comendatoris predicti hoc scripsi et signum meum aposui et clausi die et anno prefixis scilicet in Cutanda.

## XXVIII

ACA, reg. 59, fol. 13ᵛ                                           24 June 1282

*The Infante Alfonso orders the royal sub-vicar of Tortosa to exercise rights of* merum imperium *in Tortosa*

Sabestiano de Manso. Vestras recepimus litteras et intellectis hiis omnibus que nobis significastis vobis respondemus quod volumus et vobis mandamus quod in omnibus et per omnia utamini in Dertusa et terminis suis vicaria et mero imperio juxta mandatum vobis factum per dictum dominum regem super eo. Nos enim scribimus magistro Templi vel eius locum tenenti et nobili R.º de Montecathano quod nullum impedimentum vel contrarium vobis faciant in predictis. Datum ut supra.

## XXIX

ACA, parch. Peter III, no. 474                                    9 May 1285

*The commander of Barcelona alters the rent to be paid for a manse at Gurb*

Sit notum cunctis quod nos frater Romeus Burgueti comendator domus milicie Templi Barchinone cum consilio et assensu fratris R.ⁱ de Trilano eiusdem ordinis gratis et ex certa scientia laudamus, approbamus, damus et stabilimus et ad certum censum redigimus per nos et successores nostros vobis Ferrario Paschalis et Berengarie uxori eius et vestris et progeniei atque posteritati vestre perpetuo ad bene colendum et meliorandum et ad habendum et tenendum omnique tempore in pace possidendum mansum nostrum de Serra cum omnibus honoribus, possessionibus cultis et heremis, in montibus et planis, per omnia loca, quem dicta domus milicie Templi per franchum alodium habet in parrochia Sancti Andree de Gurbo. Predictum itaque mansum cum honoribus, possessionibus, tenedonibus cultis et heremis, in montibus et planis, per omnia loca, introitibus, exitibus et pertinentiis suis et

arboribus diversi generis, prout melius et plenius tu et antecessores tui
hucusque habuistis et tenuistis ad certos census et agraria, deinde vos
et vestri et progenies atque posteritas vestra perpetuo habeatis, teneatis
et possideatis ad subscriptum censum pacifice et quiete. Sub tali tamen
conditione quod vos et vestri sitis in dicto manso homines nostri proprii
solidi et habitantes et affogati ad servicium et fidelitatem nostri et
successorum nostrorum, et quod pro censu dicti mansi et barquerie et
omnium honorum et pertinentiarum suarum et in compensationem
omnium agrariorum censuum exituum que dicta domus milicie Templi
ibi percipere consuevit tribuatis vos et vestri nobis et successoribus
nostris viginti et tres solidos monete Barchinonensis de terno tantum,
de quibus solvatis a primo festo omnium sanctorum ad unum annum
et deinde annuatim in eodem festo medietatem et a primo festo natalis
domini ad unum annum et deinde annuatim in eodem festo aliam
medietatem; et nullum alium censum vel agrarium vos vel vestri
teneamini nobis vel successoribus nostris dare nisi solum dictum
censum viginti trium solidorum per terminos supradictos. Constat
enim quod utilius et melius est dicte domui milicie Templi habere
et percipere annuatim predictum censum quam census vel agraria
consueta. In hiis autem non proclametis nec faciatis vos et vestri
alium dominum nisi tantum nos et successores nostros. Liceatque
vobis et vestris post dies XXX.ª, ex quo in nobis vel successoribus
nostris faticati fueritis, predictam adquisitionem cum omni melioramento quod ibi feceritis vendere vel impignorare sive alienare vestro
consimili et vestrorum; salvo tamen jure et dominio dicte domus
milicie Templi. Pro hac autem laudatione, approbatione, donatione
et stabilimento habuimus et recepimus a vobis unam libram
cere ad pondus Barchinone. Super quam quia bene paccati sumus
renunciamus exceptioni rei non recepte. Promitimus insuper vobis
quod faciemus vos et vestros dictum stabilimentum cum omnibus
melioramento quod ibi feceritis tenere, habere et possidere in pace
perpetuo contra omnes personas. Et pro hiis complendis obligamus
vobis et vestris omnia bona nostre domus, quecumque sint et ubicumque; sic etiam quod a nobis vel successoribus nostris nunquam
possitis demandari vel in causam trahi aut in aliquo conveniri in judicio
vel extra pretextu deceptionis cum in veritate nulla sit vel aliis modis
quibus posset dictum stabilimentum revocari. Immo imponimus nobis
et successoribus nostris in premissis silentium sempiternum. Volentes
et concedentes quod si aliquod instrumentum contra hoc decetero
apparuerit non possit vobis vel vestris in aliquo obesse. Ad hoc nos
dicti conjuges laudantes et acceptantes dictum stabilimentum sub
forma et conditionibus predictis promitimus vobis dicto comendatori
sub obligatione omnium bonorum nostrorum solvere dictum censum
annuatim per terminos supradictos. Actum est hoc VII. idus may anno

domini M.ºCC.ºLXXX.º quinto. Signum F. Paschalis. Signum Berengarie uxoris eius, qui hoc firmamus. Testes huius rei sunt Bernardus de Favario et Stephanus de Querchu presbiter. Signum fratris Romei Burgeti comendatoris domus Templi Barchinone qui hoc firmo salvo jure nostro. Signum fratris R. de Trilano predicti qui hoc firmo. Signum Arnaldi de Favario sacerdotis et rectoris ecclesie Sancte Cecilie de Voltregano in cuius manu et posse hanc cartam firmavit predicta Berengaria anno predicto et VI. kalendas julii, presentibus testibus Berengario de Podio, P. de Ecclesia et Jacobo de Rota.

Signum R.ⁱ de Prato Vicensis canonici tenentis loci Berengarii de Pulcro Visu publici Vicensis notarii. Signum Berengarii de Rimentol scriptoris jurati Vicensis scribanie sub Raymundo de Prato tenente locum Berengarii de Pulcro Visu publici Vicensis notarii in cuius posse hanc cartam sive hec omnia supradicta firmavit et laudavit dicta Berengaria XVII. kalendas decembris anno prefixo, presentibus testibus Andrea de Graello clerico Vicensi, P.º Simonis et Berengario de Bassil scriptoribus.

Signum Nicholai de Samares notarii publici Barchinonensis qui hoc scripsit et clausit cum litteris rasis et emendatis in linea VIII.ª ubi dicitur que et in X.ª ubi dicitur vos vel vestri, die et anno quo supra.

## XXX

ACA, reg. 66, fol. 62                                        25 April 1286

*Alfonso III informs officials and others that he has given the Templar Berenguer of Cardona permission to export six horses to the Holy Land*

Universis officialibus et aliis etc. Noveritis nos de speciali gratia concessisse venerabili et dilecto nostro fratri Berengario de Cardona ordinis milicie Templi quod possit extrahere de terra nostra et ducere ad partes transmarinas in defensionem terre sancte sex equos. Quare mandamus vobis quatenus super extrahendis equis predictis de terra nostra et ducendis ad dictas partes nullum eidem vel latori presentium eius loco impedimentum vel contrarium faciatis racione alicuius prohibitionis in contrarium facte; presentes vero in confinibus regni nostri volumus retineri. Datum Osce VII.º kalendas may.

# XXXI

ACA, reg. 70, fol. 63ᵛ                                     1 January 1287

*Alfonso III summons the Templars for service against the Moors*

Fratri Petro de Tous comendatori Miraveti locumque tenenti magistri
domorum Templi in Aragonia et Catalonia. Quia pro certo intelleximus quod janeti et alii sarraceni inimici fidei christiane se parant ad
veniendum et debellandum contra regnum nostrum Valencie, volentes
ipsorum sarracenorum multitudini resistere [ne] propter defectum
deffencionis regnum predictum valeat dissipari, dicimus et mandamus
vobis ac vos requirimus et monemus quatenus visis presentibus omni
excusatione posposita paretis vos et parari vestros fratres faciatis cum
equis et armis et aliis apparatibus ac necessariis ad veniendum apud
regnum Valencie et resistendum viriliter, cum ad hoc teneamini contra
inimicos fidei sarracenos, et ibidem regnum nostrum taliter deffendatis
quod adeo meritum[1] sciatis pro certo quod nos de bonis que Templum
habet in terra nostra tot et tanta occuparemus et acciperemus que large
poterunt sufficere ad tenendos in frontaria regni predicti milites et alios
cum armis paratos loco illorum quos vos tenemini ibi habere, quia
proprie predecessores nostri vobis illa que dederunt concesserunt ut
invenirent vos semper paratos ad defendendum terram christianorum
contra inimicos nostros perfidos sarracenos. Datum apud Maioricas
kalendas januarii anno domini M.ºCC.ºLXXX.º sexto.

## NOTE

1. Some words have obviously been missed out here.

# XXXII

AGP, parch. Torres de Segre, no. 20                        2 August 1291

*Record of a dispute about the exaction of cenas from Remolins and Torres*
*de Segre*

Noverint universi quod in presencia mei Petri Acerii notarii publici
Ilerdensis et testium infrascriptorum Bernardus Menaguerra presentavit
et legi fecit Romeo de Solerio portario Infantis P. quandam litteram
eiusdem domini Infantis P., tenor cuius talis est:

Infans P. illustris domini P. inclite recordacionis regis Aragonum
filius ac procurator regnorum Aragonie, Mayoricarum et Valencie ac

comitatus Barchinone fideli portario suo Romeo de Solerio, salutem et gratiam. Licet vobis mandaverimus quod petatis cenam in Villa Nova de Remolins et aliam cenam in Turribus milicie Templi, dicimus et mandamus vobis quatenus, si constiterit vobis dicta loca esse sub una bajulia seu comendatoria, non petatis nisi unam cenam et de altera penitus desistatis. Et si qua pignora inde fecistis ipsa comendatori dictorum locorum vel hominibus eorumdem restituatis et restitui faciatis. Datum Barchinone IIII.º kalendas augusti anno domini M.ºCC.ºXC.º primo.

Qua littera lecta et presentata, dictus Bernardus Menaguerra dixit dicto Romeo de Solerio quod cum loca de Turribus et de Villa Nova de Remolins sint sub una bajulia seu comendatoria quod ab altera duarum cenarum quas petebat locis predictis desisteret juxta mandatum domini Infantis predicti. Qui Romeus de Solerio predictus respondit quod deliberaret et compleret predictum mandatum predicti domini Infantis P. Presentata et lecta fuit hec littera prefato Romeo de Solerio quarto nonas augusti anno domini M.ºCC.ºXC.º primo, presentibus Ferrario dez Chaus curssore et Raymundo de Montaynnana mercatore Ilerdensi, testibus ad hoc specialiter rogatis ac convocatis.

Signum mei Petri Acerii notarii publici Ilerdensis qui hoc scripsi et predictis omnibus interfui et presens fui.

# XXXIII

ACA, Varia 1, fol. 28                                          27 August 1291

*James II orders the bailiff of Barcelona to ensure that the Temple receives its tenth of royal revenues*

Jacobus dei gratia rex Aragonum, Sicilie, Maioricarum et Valencie ac comes Barchinone fideli suo baiulo Barchinone vel eius locumtenenti salutem et gratiam. Dicimus et mandamus vobis quatinus visis presentibus compellatis et compelli faciatis omnes emptores et detentores nostrorum reddituum [et] proventuum ad solvendum sine diffugio comendatori domus milicie Templi Barchinone vel cui voluerit loco sui tam de anno preterito quam presenti decimum quod dicta domus habet et accipit et accipere debet et consuevit in nostris reddituus et proventibus supradictis, nisi alia justa causa in contrarium fuerit que obsistat. Datum Barchinone VI.º kalendas septenbris anno domini M.CC.XC. primo.

## XXXIV

ACA, reg. 90, fol. 56ᵛ                                          28 September 1291

*James II orders the justiciar of Calatayud to compel a certain Jewess to sur-*
*render her property to the Temple because she has failed to pay the rent owed for it*

Iusticie Calataiubii. Ex parte comendatoris domus milicie Templi
Calataiubii fuit coram nobis propositum et hostensum quod Jamilla
judea Calataiubii tenet quandam domum et ortum ad certum tributum
pro dicta domo Templi et cessavit ipsum tributum solvere per trien-
nium, propter quod secundum forum predicta domus et ortus dicuntur
fore comisse dicto comendatori. Quare mandamus vobis quatinus, si
est ita, compellatis dictam Jamillam ad tradendum dicto comendatori
dictam domum et ortum prout de foro fuerit faciendum, vel ad
faciendum inde fieri justicie complementum. Datum Cesarauguste
IIII. kalendas octobris.

## XXXV

ACA, reg. 90, fol. 138ᵛ                                          30 October 1291

*James II writes to the collectors of* lezda *and* peaje *at Daroca about the*
*exaction of these dues from the Temple's men*

Fidelibus suis leudariis et pedagariis Daroche, etc. Ex parte comendatoris domus milicie Calataiubii intelleximus quod vos cominamini
hominibus milicie Templi de Lina Curba ad compellendum eos dare
et solvere vobis lezdam sive pedagium de rebus suis, quodque ut ab
ipso comendatore asseritur esset contra privilegia ei indulta a nostris
predecessoribus et contra consuetudinem atque usum. Quare vobis
dicimus et mandamus quatinus non compellatis nec compelli faciatis
dictos homines ad dandum vel solvendum vobis pedagium sive lezdam
contra tenorem privilegiorum suorum nisi prout est actenus fieri consuetum. Datum ut supra.

## XXXVI

AGP, parch. Cervera, no. 484                                     20 April 1292

*The Grand Master, James of Molay, gives the Aragonese Templars per-*
*mission to alienate Puigreig and La Zaida; he also writes about the Templars'*
*privileges concerning* lezda *and* peaje

Frere Jaque de Molay per la grace deu humble mastre de la povre
chevalerie dou Temple et le c[ouv]ent de cele meissme chevalerie au
r[eli]gios et honeste frere Berenguer de Cardon . . . des maissons de

cele meissme chevalerie en Aragon et en Cateloingnie, salus en nostre seingnor. Cun vos nos ayes fait assaver d'aucunes chozes qui sont en la bailliee d'Aragon mal asizes des ques le Temple ne se peut ayder a nostre profit, nos reguardant vostre grant sen et vostre leaute et le grant sens qui est en les prodes homes de la baillyee d'Aragon et le bon portement qu'il ont en tos jors au profit dou Temple, dou chastel de Pui Rei et de la maisson de La Ssaide metons en vostre discrecio et en vostre conoissance et des prodes homes de la bailliee d'Airagoun et dou chapistre jeneral de la terre; que le devant dit chastel de Pui Rei et la maisson de La Ssayde puisses vendre ou changer por leuc coneu ou meismement le dit pris retorner en leuc coneu et d'autres piesses de terre; que vos puisses vendre et torner le pris en achat en leuc profitable ou changer por leuc profitable a la maisson o . . . cuns petis leus en les montaingnies mal assis et que ce faites per vostre grant consseill. Et de la leude et des payages de ques on ne vos laisse uzer ensi cun est droit et est acostume et cun vos aves les proveliges et vos contrasstent por le grant damage que nos entendons qu'en vient au Temple et en est avenu, laissons en vostre discrecion et en vostre conoissance se que vos en fer[es] per le conseil d'une grant partie des prodes homes de la baillyee d'Aragon et de vos sages que a nos plaist et tenons por ferme se que vos en feres, savut que vos n'ayes poer de vendre ni d'enguager ni de changer ni d'aliener le dit paiages et les leudes. Et nos prions a vos et as prodes homes de la baillyee d'Aragon que en cestes chozes menes a faire sagement et meurement en tal manere que il soient au profit dou Temple et al honor de vos et que vos puisses aver bon los dou monde et profit dou cors et de l'arme. Et en greingor fermete de ce nos avons fait faire ces pressentes lettres saclees de nostre seau de cire de la tube pendant o la guarentye de nos prodes homes des ques se sont les noms: frere Baudeuin de la Andrin mareschal; frere Berenguer de Saint Just comandor de la terre; frere Gaucher de Liencort tenant leuc de draper; frere Guillen de la Tor turcopler; frere Bertran l'Aleman; frere Semen de Lende; frere Ryenbaut de Caron; frere Raymon de Barberan sous-mareschal; frere Martin de Lou tressorer; frere Guillen d'Ourenc comandor de la vote. Ce fu fait a Nicosie en Chipre l'an de mil deus sens nonante et deu de Crist a XX. jors d'avrill.

## XXXVII

ACA, reg. 306, fol. 8                                                 5 July 1292

*James II orders the provincial master to allow the* cisa *to be imposed in places under Templar lordship*

Fratri Berengario de Cardona magistro milicie Templi in Aragonia et Catalonia. Cum, prout scitis, in generali curia quam nuper celebravimus

Barchinone ordinatum fuerit quod cisa imponatur, ordinetur et col-
ligatur per universa loca Catalonie tam nostra quam prelatorum,
nobilium, militum, civium et hominum villarum quam aliorum
scilicet a Cinqua usque ad Collum de Paniçars et a Portubus usque ad
mare et rivum de Uldichona, mandamus et dicimus vobis ac etiam vos
requirimus et monemus quatinus dictam cisam imponi et ordinari
faciatis et permitatis in Orta et in aliis locis Templi infra dictos terminos
constituta per ordinatores ad dictam cisam ordinandam deputatos
juxta ordinacionem curie supradicte. Etiam in hoc nullum impedimentum vel contrarium faciatis sive fieri permitatis, alias procederetur
contra vos prout secundum ordinacionem dicte curie fuerit proce-
dendum. Datum Ilerde III.° nonas julii.

<h1 style="text-align:center">XXXVIII</h1>

ACA, parch. James II, no. 518                    19 June 1295
*The commander of Barcelona grants out at rent a manse formerly held in*
*demesne*

Sit omnibus notum quod nos frater Romeus Burgueti comendator
domus milicie Templi Barchinone, attendentes quod melius et utilius
est nobis et dicte domui quod mansus subscriptus cum omnibus honoribus et possessionibus suis detur in emphiteosim ad censum et agrarium
inferius nominatum quam tenere eum ad laboracionem propriam dicte
domus, idcirco habita licencia et mandato a venerabili domino fratre
Berengario de Cardona magistro domorum milicie Templi in Aragonia
et Cathalonia qui predictis consenciit de consilio comendatorum et
fratrum in capitulo generali congregatorum, damus et stibilimus per
nos et successores nostros comendatores predicte domus vobis Petro
Guasqui et Dulcie uxori vestre de parrochia Sancti Stephani de
Parietibus et vestris et cui sive quibus volueritis perpetuo ad bene
laborandum, meliorandum, habendum et tenendum et perpetuo in
sana pace possidendum quendam mansum nostrum cum omnibus
honoribus et possessionibus suis, cultis et heremis, in montibus et planis,
per omnia loca et cum vinea et cum arboribus diversorum generum et
cum introitibus et exitibus et omnibus eius pertinenciis et tenedonibus
et cum columbario quod possitis facere quocumque volueritis infra
tenedones predicti mansi, quod tamen non excedat magnitudinem
aliorum columbariorum predicte parrochie. Quem mansum predicta
domus nostra per alodium franchum habet in predicta parrochia
Sancti Stephani de Parietibus et quem nos consuevimus tenere ad propriam culturam dicte domus; sicut terminatur predictus mansus cum

omnibus honoribus et possessionibus suis predictis ab oriente partim
in tenedone Raimundi de Plano alodio ecclesie Sancti Stephani et
partim in tenedone vestra alodio predicte domus et den Pedros et
partim in tenedonibus Berengarii Guasch et Luppeti alodio predicte
domus nostre et partim in alodio Sancti Christophori de Liçano; ab
occidente partim in flumine aque riarie de Parietibus et partim in via
publica; a meridie partim in tenedone Raimundi de Plano alodio
Sancti Michaelis et partim in tenedone vestra et predicti Luppeti alodio
predicte domus nostre; a circii in alodio Sancti Christophori de Lizano
et in tenedone mansi de Tereu alodio Poncii de Turri. Jam dictum
itaque mansum cum omnibus honoribus et possessionibus suis cultis et
heremis, in montibus et planis, per omnia loca et cum vinea et cum
arboribus diversorum generum et cum introitibus et exitibus et omnibus eius pertinenciis et tenedonibus et cum columbario quod possitis
facere quocumque volueritis infra tenedones predicti mansi, quod
tamen non excedat magnitudinem aliorum columbariorum predicte
parrochie, vos et vestri et progenies atque posteritas vestra habeatis,
teneatis et possideatis in perpetuum pacifice et quiete, sub tali tamen
condicione et pacto quod vos et vestri laboretis dictum mansum et
omnes suas possessiones tam vineas quam alias terras et quod faciatis
residenciam personalem in dicto manso et teneatis condirectum ipsum;
et quod sitis vos et vestri semper videlicet quicumque fuerit heres seu
possessor mansi predicti homines proprii solidi et affogati domus predicte; et quod detis vos et vestri sine omni missione dicte domus nobis
et successoribus nostris comendatoribus predicte domus de omni
expleto quod deus ibi dederit, exceptis paleis et arboribus et excepto
quodam cepo quod est ante januam dicti mansi, terciam partem fideliter
et decimum quod nos consuevimus recipere et retinere in possessionibus
supradictis. Detis etiam vos et vestri nobis et successoribus nostris
comendatoribus predicte domus pro censu domorum et orti sicut jam
fexuriatus est et columbarii, si quod ibi feceritis, unum par caponum
bonorum et receptibilium annuatim solvendorum in festo nathalis
domini. In hiis autem non proclametis neque faciatis vos vel vestri
alium dominum sive dominos nisi tantum nos et successores nostros
comendatores predicte domus. Liceatque vobis et vestris post dies
XXX.ᵃ, ex quo in nobis et successoribus nostris comendatoribus dicte
domus faticam inveneritis, presentem adquisitionem cum omnibus
melioramentis que ibi feceritis vendere et impignorare sive eciam
alienare vestro consimili et vestrorum, salvo tamen semper in omnibus
et per omnia jure, censu, agrario, senioratico et fatica XXXᵃ. dierum
predicte domus Templi et comendatoris eiusdem. Pro hoc autem
stabilimento confitemur nos habuisse et recepisse a vobis unam libram
cere, super qua renunciamus excepcioni cere non habite et non recepte.
Promitimus insuper vobis quod faciemus vos et vestros et quos

volueritis totam predictam adquisicionem cum omnibus melioramentis que ibi feceritis habere, tenere et possidere in pace perpetuo
contra omnes personas. Et pro hiis complendis obligamus vobis et
vestris omnia bona predicte domus mobilia et immobilia quecumque
sint et ubicumque. Actum est hoc terciodecimo kalendas julii anno
domini millesimo CC.° nonogesimo quinto.

Signum fratris Romei Burgueti comendatoris predicti qui hoc firmo
salvo jure et dominio Templi. Signum fratris Berengarii de Cardona
magistri domorum milicie Templi in Aragonia et Cathalonia, qui predictis consentimus et ea firmamus. Signum fratris Petri Comitis qui
predictis consencio. Testes huius rei sunt Petrus Saturnini clericus,
Raimundus Ferrarii, Guillelmus de Ladernosa, Berengarius Oliba et
Petrus Stagneolis.

Signum Arnaldi magistri notarii publici Barchinonensis qui hoc
scripsit et clausit die et anno quo supra.

## XXXIX

ACA, parch. James II, no. 771                    4 February 1297

*Queen Blanche gives instructions to the collectors of* bovaje *about the exaction
of the tax from those subject to the jurisdiction of the Temple and from those
who hold land of it*

Hoc est translatum sumptum fideliter a quadam littera papirea patenti
illustrissime domine Blanche dei gratia regine Aragonum, sigillo eiusdem cereo in dorso eiusdem littere impresso sigillata, cuius tenor talis
est: Blancha dei gratia regina Aragonum fidelibus suis Stephano de
Cardona et Berengario de Manso bovateriis ultra flumen Lupricati et
eorum substitutis salutem et dilectionem. Quamvis nos ordinaverimus
et vobis scripserimus quod ab hominibus milicie Templi non exigeretis
bovaticum tam de rebus mobilibus quam sedentibus quas tenerent pro
domo milicie Templi vel pro quibuscumque aliis dominis, et quod
terra tenentes seu campanerii qui terras et possessiones tenerent pro
dicta domo milicie Templi solverent pro eisdem, eo quia non sunt
homines eiusdem, postea deliberavimus cum nostro consilio diligenter
et aliter ordinavimus secundum quod usitatum et observatum esse
intelleximus super antedicto bovatico tempore illustrissimi domini
Petri inclite memorie regis Aragonum, videlicet quod homines predicte milicie Templi non solvant bovaticum de aliquibus suis bonis
mobilibus et semoventibus, in quibus specialiter intelligantur denarii,
ubique ipsos habeant vel eisdem debeantur, et cetera mobilia que predicti homines Templi habeant, et quod ipsi homines Templi non
solvant bovaticum de bonis sedentibus seu inmobilibus que teneant

pro domo milicie Templi nec pro alodiis propriis que habeant ipsi homines milicie Templi. Solvant tamen pro bonis sedentibus seu possessionibus que teneant pro aliis dominis. Et quicumque terra tenentes seu campanerii licet non sint homines dicte domus milicie Templi non teneantur solvere bovaticum supradictum pro hiis que tenent pro domo milicie Templi. Predicta declaramus ut superius continentur ita quod ex declaratione huiusmodi juri ipsius domini regis vel milicie Templi predicte vel hominum eiusdem in futurum aliquod prejudicium minime generetur. Quare auctoritate domini regis et nostra vobis dicimus et mandamus quatenus declarationem et ordinationem predictam observetis et observari faciatis prout superius continentur. Datum Barchinone II.ª nonas februarii anno domini M.ºCC.ºXC.º sexto. Signum Guillermi de Colle notarii Barchinonis. Signum Bernardi Payares notarii Barchinonis. Signum Nicholai de Samares notarii publici Barchinonis qui hoc translatum sumptum fideliter a dicto suo originali scripsit et clausit VII. idus februarii anno predicto cum litteris rasis et emendatis in linea IIII.ª ubi dicitur scripsimus et in V.ª ubi dicitur mi et in XI.ª ubi dicitur pro.

# XL

AHN, San Juan, leg. 333, doc. 5          21 February 1299

*The castellan of Monzón grants the church of Crespano for life to Bonanato Maçarech*

Noverint universi quod nos frater Raymundus de Falcibus Castellanus Montissoni, atendentes multa grata servicia que vos Bonanatus Maçarech clericus nobis et Templo fecistis et facietis prestante domino in futuro, de assensu, consilio et voluntate fratris Guillelmi de Castro Veteri, fratris Arnaldi de Baynuls, fratris Berengarii ça Rovira comendatoris Confite, fratris Guillelmi dez Bach, fratris Raymundi de Ontiynena, fratris Borracii de Cervaria camerarii, fratris Petri de Turre vicarii Sancti Johannis, fratris Bernardi de Rayols comendatoris ville et omnium aliorum fratrum conventus Monssoni, per nos et omnes successores nostros damus et concedimus vobis jamdicto Bonanato in beneficium personale ecclesiam nostram beati Petri de Crespano diebus omnibus vite vestre, cum omnibus decimis, oblacionibus, defunccionibus, lexiis et omnibus aliis iuribus pertinentibus seu pertinere debentibus quoquo modo ad dictam ecclesiam prout antecessores vestri eam melius et plenius habere actenus consueverunt. Damus etiam et concedimus vobis jamdicto Bonanato victum in domo nostra de Confita sicut datur uni ex fratribus ibi existentibus diebus omnibus vite vestre. Ita tamen et sub tali condicione predictam ecclesiam et alia vobis concedimus atque damus quod vos teneamini eam decantare et servire bene et honorifice ad honorem dei et beati Petri apostoli sicut decet et est actenus fieri consuetum. Et de omnibus redditibus, proventibus et exitibus que inde habueritis detis nobis et fratribus Templi successoribus nostris quartam partem fideliter atque bene. Que dicta quarta pars vel quartum nobis et Templo integre retinemus ad omnes nostras nostrorumque voluntates inde perpetuo faciendas. Teneamini insuper predictam ecclesiam pro posse vestro in libris, vestimentis et aliis necessariis ornamentis meliorare et augere taliter quod deus et nos debeamus inde esse paccati, et in ecclesia beate Marie de Confita tenere locum diachoni et esse omnibus horis diurnis pariter et nocturnis que in dicta ecclesia nostra de Confita celebrabuntur. Et si contingerit vicarium predicte ecclesie de Confita qui modo est vel qui pro tempore fuerit infirmari vel ire ad aliquam partem propter utilitatem et comodum predicte domus nostre de Confita quod vos teneamini esse ibi in locum vicarii et facere officium vicarii sicut decet. Preterea sitis ibi semper nobis et fratribus Templi bonus, legalis, fidelis, obediens et devotus, et non inducatis ibi alium dominum vel patronum nisi nos et successores nostros fratres Templi tantum; et nunquam per vos aut per alium aliquid petatis vel petere faciatis ultra hoc quod a nobis vobis datum est superius et concessum in omnibus hiis que nobis et nostris ibidem retinemus. Post obitum vero vestri predictam ecclesiam cum melioramentis omnibus ibi factis remaneat atque redeat nobis ac domui et fratribus Templi sine omni inquietacione, paciffice et in pace. Ego autem Bonanatus Maçarech clericus prenominatus recipiens humiliter et benigne hanc donacionem et gratiam dicte ecclesie a vobis venerabilibus dominis Castellano et fratribus memoratis mihi factam superius et concessam promito deo et vobis bona fide et legalitate omnia et singula que pro vobis notata sunt superius et expressa pro possibilitate mea facere, atendere et complere et non in aliquo violare.

Quod est actum IX.º kalendas marcii anno domini millesimo CC.º nonagesimo octavo.

Signum fratris Raymundi de Falcibus predicti Castellani Monssoni. Signum fratris Guillelmi de Castro Veteri. Signum fratris Arnaldi de Baynuls. Signum fratris Berengarii ça Rovira comendatoris Confite. Signum fratris Guillelmi dez Bach. Signum fratris Raymundi de Ontiynena. Signum fratris Borracii de Cervaria dicti camerarii. Signum fratris Petri de Turre. Signum fratris Bernardi de Rayols. Nos omnes fratres prenominati qui hoc per nos et successores nostros laudamus, concedimus et firmamus, testes rogamus et scribere mandamus. Signum mei Bonanati Maçarech predicti qui omnia supradicta laudo, approbo, concedo atque firmo. Signum Johannis Garssie de

412 *Appendix I*

Alfocea. Signum Guillelmi de Siscar, scutiferorum dicti domini Castellani testium huius rey.

Bernardi de Pulcropodio notarii publici castri Montissoni signum qui hoc scripsit.

## XLI

ACA, reg. 332, fol. 75            17 August 1300
*James II orders the lieutenant of the provincial master to prepare for military service against Castile*

Jacobus etc. Religioso viro gerenti vices in Aragonia magistri milicie Templi. Salutem etc. Cum ad notitiam nostram devenerit quod Ferdinandus natus quondam dompni Sancii de Castella cum gente sua equitum et peditum manu armata versus partes istas accedens ausu tam temerario proponat invadere regnum nostrum Aragonie, sic quod iam pervenit quasi ad confinia regni Castelle, et nos intendentes eidem resistere viriliter et potenter mandaverimus nobiles, mesnaderios, milites ac alios de dicto regno parari et vos in casu huiusmodi ad deffensionem regni nostri teneamini nos juvare, ideo vos requirimus ac vobis dicimus et mandamus firmiter et expresse quatenus statim receptis presentibus cum militibus et hominibus quos dictus ordo habet in regno Aragonie paretis vos equis, armis et aliis apparatibus vestris, sic quod statim cum per nos requisiti fueritis vel alias vobis innotuerit per appellitum vel aliis modis hostes nostros predictos accessisse adversus partes istas, ad nos personaliter ubicumque fuerimus preter alicuius more dispendium personaliter veniatis, nullo alio a nobis expectato mandato; scituri quod si secus feceritis contra vos et bona dicti ordinis tanquam contra illos qui sic inhumaniter pugnare pro patria negligunt prout juste fuerit procedemus. Datum Cesarauguste XVI.º kalendas septenbris anno domini M.ºCCCº.

## XLII

ACA, reg. 332 fol. 93ᵛ           5 September 1300
*James II orders officials to requisition debts owed to the Jews of Monzón; he also commands that they should be refused justice*

Vicario et curie Ilerde vel eius locum tenenti et universis aliis officialibus nostris ad quos presentes pervenerint. Cum nos judeos Montissoni manuteneri et deffendi hactenus mandaverimus ac debita sua eis solvi fecerimus per omnia loca dominationis nostre sicut judeis aliis terre nostre, et nunc ad requisitionem per nos eis factam de subveniendo nobis de quadam peccunie quantitate ratione presentis guerre quam habemus cum Castellanis contradixerint nobis auxilium facere vel succurssum, vobis dicimus et mandamus quatenus unusquisque vestrum in locis jurisdictionis sibi comisse faciatis publice preconizari quod quicumque debuerint aliqua debita predictis judeis Montissoni manifestent ea vobis loco nostri sub pena corporis et averi, et vos ipsa debita exigatis et recuperetis ab eisdem debitoribus pro parte nostra, in illis videlicet terminis in quibus ea prefatis judeis Montissoni solvere tenebantur. Mandamus etiam vobis quatenus predictis judeis Montissoni qui nobis in predicta necessitate inobedientes et rebelles se ut predicitur exibuerunt non faciatis fieri justicie complementum in suis petitionibus vel demandis, nec ipsos vel bona sua manuteneatis decetero seu etiam deffendatis. Datum Cesarauguste nonas septenbris anno predicto.

## XLIII

ACA, CRD Templarios, no. 457                                    *c.* 1301

*The provincial master, Berenguer of Cardona, summons the commander of Mallorca to a provincial chapter*

Frare Berengar de Cardona de les cases de la cavaleria del Temple en Arago et en Catalunya humil maestre et visitador general en Espanya al religios et honest frare P. de Sent Just comanador de la casa del Temple de Malorcha, saluts et bona amor. Fem vos saber que nos ab consel et ab voluntat dalguns dels promens del Temple avem ordenat de celebrar capitol a Gardeyn lo derer dicmenge de febrer qui ve. Per queus deym eus manam que al dit loc et dia personalment vengatz, et aportatz nos la responsio en or o en argent et tot ço de que ajudar nos podretz, et lexat en la batlia blat et vi et totes altres coses necessaries tro al novell be et bastantment et pagat vostres companyes de lurs soldades tro al temps que el capitol es acostumat de celebrar; et dam vos conger de vendre blat et totes altres coses per pagar la dita responsio, et si per ventura no podietz vendre per la brevea del temps asignasetz nos ho, et podetz pendre vostres rendes tro al temps que el capitol es acostumat de celebrar, no contrastant aqest abrevyament, et fet albara verdader del estament de la batlia et de les coses quy lexaretz et aportat lo al capitol. Datum en Tortosa XVI. dies anatz del mes de decembre. Fet en manera que per abrevyament del capitol les coses que remandran en casa non valen meyns.

## XLIV

ACA, parch. James II, no. 2260                    10 March 1306

*The provincial master, Berenguer of Cardona, announces that he has granted the commandery of Alfambra to Peter of San Justo for life, and quotes as his authority for doing this a letter confirming his own appointment as visitor in Spain*

Noverint universsi quod cum nos frater Berengarius de Cardona domorum milicie Templi in Aragonia et Catalonia preceptor humilis et visitator in Ispania generalis receperimus et habuerimus diu est ab excellentissimo domino fratre Jacobo de Molay sacre milicie Templi magistro ac venerabili conventu eiusdem milicie literas sagillo tumbe plumbee dicti conventus pendenti roboratas quarum tenor sequitur sub hac forma:

Universis presentes literas inspecturis frater Jacobus de Molay dei gracia pauperis milicie Templi magister humilis et conventus dicte milicie salutem in domino sempiternam. Noverit universitas vestra quod nos, attendentes racionabiliter et comffidentes ac etiam considerantes industriam et legalitatem ac laudabilia merita probitatis religiosi viri dillecti nobis in Christo fratris Berengarii de Cardona preceptoris domorum nostrarum in Aragonia et Catalonia et quod per eius industriam et sollicitudinem omnia bona que habemus in quinque regnis Ispanie poterunt erigi et in melius refformari, ipsum fratrem Berengarium de Cardona domorum nostrarum in omnibus quinque regnis Ispanie visitatorem constituimus generalem in omnibus quinque regnis Ispanie omnium domorum nostrarum sibi administracionem liberam concedentes, scilicet visitandi domos nostras et fratres per omnes quinque regnos Ispanie, vendendi de bonis nostris, alienandi, contrahendi et permutam trahendi et obbligaciones ffaciendi et tollendi; ponentes ipsum fratrem Berengarium visitatorem predictum loco nostri in premissis omnibus et quolibet premissorum, et generaliter omnia et singula faciendi et exercendi et procurandi que nos magister et conventus in premissis omnibus et quolibet premissorum facere possemus si personaliter presentes essemus. In cuius rei testimonium presentes literas nos prefatus magister et conventus fieri fecimus tumbe plumbee nostri conventus munimine roboratas. Cum testimonio fratrum nostrorum quorum nomina sunt hec: Frater Bartholomeus de Chinsi marescaldus. Frater Addam de Cronvalle draperius. Frater Valascus Ferrandi preceptor noster in Portugalia. Frater Riambaldus de Carona preceptor Nimocii. Frater Petrus de Bersi preceptor militum. Et frater Dalmatius de Timor torcuplerius. Datum Nimocii anno domini millesimo CCCº., dia decima mensis novembris.

Igitur nos frater Berengarius de Cardona preceptor et visitator predictus, attendentes et considerantes conversacionem in domino comendabilem, diligenciam et curam pervigilem ac alia laudabilia merita probitatis viri religiosi fratris Petri de Sent Just quod per vestri industriam et sollicitudinem bona castri et loci nostri de Alffambra et bajulie eiusdem poterunt de bono in melius refformari et meliori, auctoritate siquidem literarum predictarum et potestate nobis concessa in dictis literis a predicto domino magistro et conventu, damus et concedimus et confferimus vobis predicto fratri Petro de Sent Just iuxta potestatem predictam in omni vita vestra bajuliam castri nostri et ville de Alffambra cum omnibus proprietatibus, locis ac juribus et suis pertinenciis universis habendam, tenendam, regendam, possidendam et administrandam in fratris ac bonis et negociis suis in judiciis et extra quamdiu vobis fuerit vita comes; ita quod vos dictum castrum et bajuliam regatis utiliter ac vivere estudeatis honeste et quod solvatis responsiones et tallias et omnia alia consueta vel consuevenda et subvenciones inpositas vel inponendas pro subsidio terre sancte. Et teneamini superiores vestros venerari procurare ac recipere alios fratres Templi secundum consuetudinem domus Templi. Et in omnibus sitis in vita vestra obediens preceptori Aragonie qui pro tempore fuerit vel eius locum tenenti. Et vobis complendo omnia suppradicta non possitis relexari a predicta bajulia sine licencia domini magistri et conventus ultramaris vel eorum posse habentis. In cuius rei testimonium nos predictus et visitator presentem paginam sigilli nostri pendentis duximus munimine roborandam. Quod est actum in castro predicto de Alffambra VI.º idus marcii anno domini millesimo CCC.º quinto, presentibus et testibus: Fratre Bartholomeo de Villafranca comendatoris de Vilello. Fratre Gaucerando de Biure socio nostro. Fratre Dominico Martini capellano nostro. Fratre Raymundo de Sendaniol. Fratre Geraldo de Copons. Fratre Jacobo de Garrigans fratre serviente nostro.

Ego Jacobus Astruch scriptor predicti domini preceptoris qui de mandato eiusdem hoc scripsi et signum meum posui.

# XLV

ACA, CRD Templarios, no. 81                                    May 1307

*Account of responsions paid by convents*

Anno domini millesimo CCC.ºVII.º lonrat frare Berengar de Cardona de les casses de la cavaleria del Temple en Arago et en Catalonia honorable maestre tench et celebra capitol ab los promens del Temple en Orta lo dicmenge derer de mag del an damunt dit.

Lo Mas Deu: DCCC. matz.[1] qui . . . IIII. millia sol. jaqs. Los quals IIII. millia ss. de iaqs. fan a rao de XXX. mayla X. millia et C.LXX.II. sol. barchs. Per los quals paga VI. millia tornes. dargent, que valen a rao de XVI. drs. per tors. VIII. millia sol. de barchs. Item paga an R. Savina et an G. som frare II. millia DC.L.III. ssol. barchs. Et axi fan en suma X. millia DC.L.III. ssol. barchs. Et pagada la responsio ay de do CCCC.LXXX.I. sol.

Casteylo Dampuries paga la responsio et los taylles et als frares doltramer XX. tors. Dona de do CCCC.XC. sol. barchs. al seynor maestre zo es asaber CCC. sol. a Barchinona et al capitol C. sol.

Aygua Viva fa de responsio C. matz.; per legistres VI. matz.; item per la tayla de la cort XXX. sol. barchs. Paga an R. de Tovila CCCC. sol.

Pug Reg fa de responsio XXX.V. matz.; per legistres ;[2] per la taylla de la cort XX. sol. Et axi fa la responsio et la taylla de la cort CC.XX. sol. jaqs., los quals fan a rao de XXX. mayla D.L.IX. sol. et II. drs. barchs. Paga la responsio et els legistres et la tayla de la cort en asignacons. Encara de do part azo asigna CCC.XL.I. sol. meyns II. drs. barchs. Et axi es entre la responsio et les taylles et do mill sol. los quals el deu dar al seynor maestre.

Barchinona fa de responsio C.XL. maz.; per legistres XVIII. maz.; per la taylla de la cort XL. sol. Paga la responsio, els legistres et la tailla de la cort. Item paga per los frares doltramar XXX. tors. dargent. Los quals pres lo seynor maestre.

La Juncossa fa de responsio XL. maz.; per legistres XII. maz.; per la taylla de la cort XXX. sol. No paga res daquest an.

Celma fa de responsio XL. maz.; per legistres XII. maz.; per la taylla de la cort XX. sol. Pagao tot.

Barbera fa de responsio CCCC. maz.; per legistres XXX. maz.; per la taylla de la cort XC. sol. Munta per tot II. millia CC.XL. sol. jaqs. Pagao tot. Qui fan de barcs. a rao de XXX. maylia V. millia DC.XC.IIII. sol. et IIII. drs. barcs. Dona de do al seynor maestre III. millia DC.VI. sol. VIII. drs. barcs. Paga tot ab mil DCCCC. sol. que paga a la cavalria que compra. Item dona daltra part per LXXX. tors. dargent dels frares doltramar C. sol. barcs.

Graynena fa de responsio C.L. matz.; per legistres XV. matz.; per la taylla de la cort XL. sol. Munta per tot DCCC.XX.V. sol. jqs., que fan de barcs. II. millia XC.VII. sol. meyns III. males. Paga tot. Item paga per L. torn. dargent als frares doltramar LX.II. sol. VI. drs. bacs. Et part tot azo dona de do al seynor maestre DCCC.XL. sol. VIII. drs. et mala bacs. Et axi puxa per tot em fre la responsio et les talles de la cort et els legistres et los torn. dels frares doltramar et el do del seynor maestre III. millia sol. de barcs. Los quals son en la cambra del cambrer de Barbera.

La cassa de Barbenz no fa res de responsio ne taylla de registres ne de cort. Mas dona aqest an al seynor maestre DCCC. sol. barchs.

Corbins fa de responsio CC.XX. matz.; per legistres XX.V. matz.; per la cort XC. sol.

Gardeyn fa de responsio CCCC. matz.; per legistres XXX.VI. matz.; per la cort XC. sol. Paga tot.

Munso fa de responsio mill C. matz.; per legistres LX.V. matz.; per la cort XC. sol. Paga tot. Et dona de do IIII. millia sol. jaqs. al seynor maestre.

La cassa Doscha fa de responsio CCC.L. matz.; per legistres XX.V. matz.; per la cort LXX. sol. jaqs. Et axi munta per tot M.DCCCC. XL.V. sol. Dels quals paga an Michael Periz [?]Romeu C. sol. per son salari. Item an A. Garcia de Lozano official Doscha XXX. sol. Item paga al seynor maestre en CCC.L. kafices de forment a rao de V. ssol. mill DCCC.XV. sol. Et diu que pagara a compliment de la responsio LX.V. sol.

La casa de Pina fa de responsio LXXX. matz.; per legistres V. matz.; per la cort XXX. sol. Et axi munta entre tot CCCC.L.V. sol. Paga en drs. C. sol. Et asigna LXX. metros de vi a rao de II. sol. VIII. lo metro, fan C.LXXX.VI. sol. VIII. drs. Et axi fal de la responsio C.LX.VIII. sol. IIII. ds.

La cassa de Saragoza fa de responsio C.L. matz.; per legistres XX.V. matz.; per la cort LXX. sol. Munte la responsio et les taylles e la cort DCCCC.XL.V. sol. Paga a la justicia Darago CC.L. sol. Item an Johan de la Badia CC. sol. Item an Bertolomeu des Lava CC.L. sol. Item an D.º Marti C.L. sol. Item dona en drs. XC.V. sol. Et axi . . . a la responsio et ales tayles et a la cort.

Boquinenich fa de responsio XX. matz.; per legistres X. matz.; per la cort X. sol. Munta per tot C.LX. sol. Paga los quals asigna XXX. [?]kaffices de ce. . . na al compliment a la dita responsio.

Noveles. No paga res.

Anessa. No res.

Ribaforada fa de responsio C.L. matz.; per legistres XX.V. matz. Munta per tot DCCC.LXX.V. sol. Paga en DCCC. torn. dargent a rao de VI. drs. jaqs. CCCC. sol. jaqs. Et axi fal que roman a pagar de la responsio CCCC.LXX.V. sol.

Averi fa de responsio C.L. matz.; per legistres XX.V. matz. Munta la responsio DCCC.LXX.V. sol. Paga mill DCCC.XL. torn. dargent, que valen a VI. dr. DCCC.LXX.V. ssol. jaqs. Et axi a pagat la responsio els legistres.

Ambel fa de responsio D. matz.; per legistres XL. matz.; per la cort XC. sol. Munta per tot II. millia DCC.XC. sol. de jaqs. Los quals lo comanador Dambel los deu donar al seynor maestre.

Ricla fa de respo C.LX.V. matz.; per legistres XX.V. matz.; per la
cort L. sol. Munta per tot M. sol. de jaqs. Paga la responsio, els legistres
et tayla de la cort. Item paga per C.XIIII. mora. . . que deu fer al
maestre DCC.XC.VIII. sol.

Alfambra fa de responsio CC.XX. matz.; per legistres XX.V.
matz.; per la cort LX. sol. jaqs. Munta per tot mill CC.LXXX.V.
sol. jaqs. A pagat tota la responsio et taylles et legistres.

Vilel fa de responsio L. matz.; per legistres V. matz.; per la cort L.
sol. Munta per tot CCC.L. sol. jaqs. Paga la responsio, els legistres et
tailla de la cort.

Cantaveyla fa de responsio mill C. sol.;[3] per legistres XL. matz.;
per la cort XC. sol. Munta per tot V. millia DCC.XC. sol. Paga la
responsio, els legistres et les tayles.

Castelot fa de responsio C.X. matz.; per legistres X. matz.; per la
cort XXX. sol. Munta per tot DC.XXX. sol. Paga tota la responsio et
legistres et tayla.

Orta fa de responsio CC.L. matz.; per legistres XX.VIII. matz.; per
la cort LXX. sol. Munta per tot M.CCCC.LX. sol. Paga los quals
asigna en D. canters doli a rao de III. sol. lo canter, que fan M.D.
sol. Et axi a pagada la responsio et les taylles et los registres de la
cort.

Riba Roya fa de responsio CCC. matz.; per legistres V. matz.; per
la cort XXX. sol. Munta per tot mill D.L.V. sol. Paga en drs. CCC.
sol. jaqs. Et asigna al seynor maestre daltra part D. sol. Et axi fal de la
responsio DCC.L.V. sol.

Azcho fa de responsio DC. matz.; per legistres X. matz.; per la cort
LXX. sol. Munta per tot III. millia C.XX. sol. Paga la responsio, els
legistres et taylla de la cort.

Miravt fa de responsio D. matz.; per legistres XXX.VI. matz.; per
la cort XC. sol. Munta per tot II. millia DCC.LXX. sol. Dels quals
deu hom levar per La Zayda CCCC. sol. Et axi fa de responsio et
registres et tayla de la cort abacats los CCCC. sol. damunt dits II.
millia CCC.LXX. sol. Los quals a pagats.

Tortossa fa de responsio C.LXX. matz.; per legistres XIIII. matz.;
per la cort XXX. sol. Munta per tot DCCCC.L. sol. Paga M.DC. sol.
barchs. en drs. Item paga X. matz. an G. de Ceret. Fal lo [?]remanent
de la responsio.

Paniscola fa de responsio CCC. matz.; per legistres XX. matz.; per
la cort LX. sol. Munta per tot M.DC.LX. sol. Paga tot.

Buriana fa de responsio C.XL. matz.; per legistres V. matz.; per la
cort XX. sol. Munta per tot DCC.XL.V. sol. jaqs. Paga en drs. DC.
sol. de barchs. Fal lo [?]remanent.

La cassa de Valencia fa de responsio C. matz.; per legistres X. matz.;
per la cort XXX. sol. Munta per tot D.LXXX. sol. jaqs. Dels quals

paga an P. de la Costa L.V. matz. Item paga an Jafer daqesta pasca CC.X. sol. bacs. Et axi a a tornar de la responsio et tayles D.L. sol. barcs. Los quals diu que li pagara tan tost com sia a Valencia.

Maylorqes fa de responsio DCCCC.XX. matz.; no a pagat en cara res mas devo pagar.

## NOTES

1. Mazmodinas. I have similarly not expanded the abbreviations for shillings, pence, Jaca, Barcelona, or Tournois.

2. Left blank in the manuscript.

3. The manuscript should obviously read 'matz.' instead of 'sol.' here.


## XLVI

ACA, parch. James II, no. 2470                           8 September 1307

*The Grand Master, James of Molay, informs the Aragonese Templars of the appointment of Simon of Lenda as provincial master*

Frater Jacobus de Molayo dei gracia pauperis milicie Templi magister humilis universis eiusdem milicie fratribus in baillivia Aragonie et Cathalonie constitutis salutem in domino sempiternam. Noveritis quod nos, attendentes industriam et probitatem viri religiosi et providi fratris Eximini de Lenda preceptoris domus nostre de Orta, pensantes eciam utilitatem domus nostre et specialiter baillivie nostre de Aragonia et Cathalonia, ipsum fratrem Eximinum dicte baillivie de Aragonia et Cathalonia fecimus preceptorem. Quare vobis universis et singulis districte percipiendo mandamus quod dicto preceptori vestro obediatis ut decet, exhibentes eidem tanquam nobis in omnibus debitam reverenciam et honorem. Nos enim eidem fratri commisimus quod si quis vestrum in aliquo, quod absit, deliquerit ipsum puniat, corrigat et castiget secundum nostre religionis statuta. Rogamus vos insuper quod si hucusque ad regimen huius baillivie fuistis solliciti et attenti decetero ad reformationem ipsius de bono in melius efficacius procedatis. Ita quod devotionem vestram proinde possimus dignis in domino laudibus commendare. In cuius rei testimonium sigillum nostrum duximus presentibus apponendum. Datum Pictavis in domo nostra anno domini millesimo CCC. septimo, VIII.$^{va}$ die mensis septembris.

# APPENDIX II

# *Lists of Officials*

PROVINCIAL MASTERS[1]

| | |
|---|---|
| *Peter of Rovira | Nov. 1143–Jan. 1158 |
| *Hugh of Barcelona | 1159–April 1162 |
| *Hugh Geoffrey | May 1163–1166 |
| *Arnold of Torroja | Oct. 1166–March 1181 |
| *Berenguer of Avinyó | April 1181–March 1183 |
| Guy of Sellón | April–June 1183 |
| *Raymond of Canet | Nov. 1183–July 1185 |
| Gilbert Eral | Oct. 1185–Aug. 1189 |
| *Pons of Rigaud | Sept. 1189–Feb. 1195 |
| *Gerald of Caercino | Feb. 1196 |
| *Arnold of Claramunt | April–Nov. 1196 |
| *Pons Marescalci | Dec. 1196–June 1199 |
| *Arnold of Claramunt | Aug. 1199–April 1200 |
| *Raymond of Gurb | April 1200–Nov. 1201 |
| *Pons of Rigaud | April 1202–July 1206 |
| Peter of Monteagudo | July 1207–June 1212 |
| *William Cadell | Oct. 1212–May 1213 |
| *William of Montrodón | Jan. 1214–Sept. 1218 |
| *William of Azylach | Feb. 1221–July 1223 |
| Riperto of Puig Guigone | Jan. 1224 |
| *Fulk of Montpesat | 1224–Dec. 1227 |
| *William Cadell | March 1229–June 1232 |
| Raymond Patot | May 1233–April 1234 |
| Hugh of Montlaur | May 1234–April 1238 |
| *Stephen of Belmonte | June–Nov. 1239 |
| *Raymond of Serra | May 1240–June 1243 |
| *William of Cardona | Jan. 1244–May 1252 |
| Hugh of Jouy | Sept. 1254–June 1257/March 1258[2] |
| William of Montañana | May 1258–Feb. 1262 |
| *William of Pontóns | March 1262–Aug. 1266 |
| *Arnold of Castellnou | March 1267–Feb. 1278 |

Peter of Moncada          April 1279–Oct. 1282
Berenguer of San Justo    April 1283–May 1290
*Berenguer of Cardona     June 1291–Jan. 1307
*Simon of Lenda           Sept. 1307

## NOTES

1. Those marked * can be traced in the province before their appointment as provincial master. The dates given show when officials are known to have been in office; dates of appointment are usually not known.

2. Hugh of Jouy is mentioned in a document drawn up in March 1258 but the wording does not indicate clearly whether he was still master at that time.

## LIEUTENANTS OF THE PROVINCIAL MASTER IN ARAGON AND CATALONIA

| | | |
|---|---|---|
| Peter of Cartellá | July 1151 | |
| ?William of Albaix | July 1158 | |
| Arnold of Claramunt | Jan. 1190; April 1201 | Commander of Monzón |
| Pons Marescalci | June 1202; April 1204; Aug. 1207; March 1211; Sept. 1218; Aug. 1220; April, July 1221; June 1227; April, May, Aug. 1228 | Commander of Monzón Miravet, La Ribera |
| Raymond Berenguer | Oct., Dec. 1213; May 1214; Feb. 1215 | Commander of Gardeny |
| Bernard of Claret | Sept. 1216 | Commander of Gardeny |
| William of Sartol | Jan., May, Aug., Sept. 1219 | |
| Archibald of Sana | June 1226; Feb. 1227 | Commander of Monzón |
| Bernard of Campanes | April, Aug., Sept. 1229; April 1230; March 1231 | Commander of Miravet, La Ribera |
| Raymond of Serra | Dec. 1232 | Commander of Monzón |
| Peter Adalbert | Sept. 1234 | Commander of Novillas |
| Raymond Berenguer | July 1238 | |
| William of Cardona | Oct. 1238; July 1241 | Commander of Gardeny |
| Bernard of Portella | Sept. 1243 | Commander of Miravet |
| Bernard of Altarriba | Sept. 1249; Sept., Oct., Nov. 1257 | Commander of Gardeny, Monzón |
| James of Timor | Jan., April, May, Aug., Oct. 1253 | Commander of Gardeny |
| Peter of Queralt | Sept., Oct. 1261; March 1262; Oct. 1266 | Commander of Monzón, Gardeny |
| Bernard of Pujalt | Dec. 1269; Jan. 1270; Nov. 1272; Aug., Sept., Oct., Nov. 1274; March, May, Sept., Nov. 1275; July 1276 | Commander of Miravet |
| Peter of Moncada[1] | July, Aug., Nov. 1276; March 1277 | |

| Peter of Tous | July, Aug., Nov. 1277; July, Sept., Oct. 1278; Feb. 1279; Sept., Oct., Nov. 1286; Jan., March, April, May 1287; Oct. 1300; March, April, May, June 1301 | Commander of Miravet, Huesca |
| Arnold of Timor | July, Oct. 1290 | Commander of Monzón |
| Simon of Lenda | Dec. 1296 | Commander of Horta |
| Berenguer of San Justo | June 1300 | Commander of Miravet |
| Raymond of Fals | ?1301 | Commander of Monzón |
| Dalmau of Timor | Oct. 1306 | Commander of Barbará |

## NOTE

1. See above p. 334, note 49.

## HEADS OF CONVENTS[1]

*Aiguaviva*

| Berenguer of Arbores | 1192–March 1213 (with Palau in 1213) |
| John of Agde | June 1237 |
| Dominic | April 1239 |
| Cabot | May 1246 |
| Bernard of Montlaur | 1252 |
| Berenguer of Calaca | 1265 |
| Peter of Cánoves | 1272–*c.* 1288 |
| William of Abellars | 1293 |
| Berenguer of Vallvert | March 1303/4 |

*Alfambra*

| William of Peralta | Oct. 1196 (with Novillas, Villel) |
| Bernard of Claret | April–Aug. 1197 |
| Bernard of Cegunyoles | 1197–Oct. 1200 (with Castellote, Villel) |
| Gaucebert of Casales | Aug. 1201 (with Villel) |
| Peter of Castellnou | Sept. 1204–July 1206 (with Villel) |
| William of Senone | July 1207 (with Villel) |
| Peter of Barillas | July 1207 (subordinate commander) |
| Bernard Amil | Dec. 1212 |
| Pertegas | Jan. 1218 |
| William of Solesas | July 1221 |
| Peter of Campfet | June 1227 |
| Peter Adalbert | Jan. 1232 |
| Pons Maltos | Feb.–June 1242 |
| Gasco of Barrio | Jan. 1244–Jan. 1245 |

| | |
|---|---|
| Bernard of Palomar | April 1246 |
| Bernard of Montlaur | July 1249 |
| Raymond of Ledano | May 1251–March 1252 |
| William Mascarón | May 1255 |
| William Arnold | April 1259–Dec. 1260 |
| William Mascarón | May 1263–Dec. 1266 |
| William of Montgrí | July 1267–Oct. 1271 (with Villel) |
| Pons of Pontóns | June 1273; Dec. 1295 |
| Peter of San Justo | March 1306 |
| Berenguer of Olmos | 1307 |

*Ambel*

| | |
|---|---|
| Nuño | 1162 |
| Peter López | 1175–8 |
| Peter of Fraella | 1186 |
| Arnold Médico | June 1192–1206 (with Villel) |
| Fortún Aragonés | July 1207–1209 |
| Peter of Castellnou | Sept. 1210 |
| Raymond of Serra | Dec. 1214–May 1218 |
| William of Benasque | April 1222 |
| Peter Raymond | Jan. 1224–Sept. 1231 |
| Pons of Cervera | May 1236 |
| Peter Jiménez | Sept. 1239 |
| Andrew | Nov. 1241–March 1242 |
| Bernard of Palomar | May 1244 |
| William of Montgrí | May 1246–March 1249 |
| Berenguer of Monteagudo | Oct. 1249–Oct. 1252 |
| Sancho of Tena | March 1255–Feb. 1258 (with Boquiñeni) |
| William of Montgrí | Dec. 1259 (with Boquiñeni) |
| William Mascarón | July 1260–Nov. 1261 |
| Dalmau of Serón | May 1263–April 1264; July 1267[2] |
| Dominic of Jaca | May 1271 |
| Michael of Lison | Aug. 1272–May 1273 |
| Dalmau of Serón | Dec. 1278 |
| Arnold of Torroella | April 1289 |
| Lope Sánchez of Berga | Jan. 1296–Sept. 1301 |
| Gaucebert Durbán | Nov. 1302 |
| Peter of San Justo | April 1303 |

*Añesa*[3]

| | |
|---|---|
| Bernard of Serón | Nov. 1185–Jan. 1186 |
| Peter of Grañena | March 1189 |

| | |
|---|---|
| Bernard of Serón | June 1194 |
| Peter Cognado | June 1196 |
| William of Serón | *c.* 1200 |
| Peter of Luna | March–April 1202[4] |
| Michael of Luna | Before 1207 |
| Fortún of Arroniz | June 1207 |
| P. Arcez of Fillera | May 1218 |
| Sancho | Sept. 1239–Feb. 1242 |
| John of Ciresa | July 1244–May 1246 |
| Peter Jiménez | March 1249 |
| Peter of Molina | March 1252–Feb. 1257 |
| Martin Pérez | May–Sept. 1263 |
| García Jiménez | Dec. 1263 |
| Dominic John | Aug. 1271–April 1274 (with Boquiñeni) |
| Bernard Savit | Sept. 1282 |
| John of Sieste | Oct. 1287–July 1289 |
| Pascal of Alfaro | Sept. 1301 |
| Bernard Belissén | 1307 |

*Ascó*

| | |
|---|---|
| Bezo | Dec. 1181 |
| Fulk | May 1190–1197 |
| William of Torre | Aug. 1197 |
| Boniface | March 1209 |
| Jordan of Mesón | April 1224–Dec. 1225 |
| Raymond Seguer | April 1234 |
| Raymond Berenguer | Sept. 1237 |
| Dominic of Fraga | March 1242–Feb. ?1243 |
| Raymond of Serra | Jan.–March 1244 |
| Dominic of Fraga | Aug. 1250–May 1275 |
| Francis of Tallada | May 1279–May 1289 |
| William of Puignaucler | Aug. 1289; 1292[5] |
| Arnold of Torroella | July 1293–Sept. 1294 |
| Raymond of Belloch | April 1296 |
| Berenguer of San Marcial | 1302–7 |

*Barbens*

| | |
|---|---|
| Raymond Barufel | Nov. 1168–Feb. 1173 |
| Miro of Trilla | June 1176 |
| Bernard of Talladell | 1177 |
| Raymond of Monte | 1180 |
| Peter Adalbert | May 1181–Dec. 1190 |

# Lists of Officials

425

| William Amil | April 1204 |
| Raymond | Nov. 1208 |
| Peter Adalbert | Feb. 1210 |
| Geoffrey Badat | 1214 |
| Pons Galcerán | May 1244 |
| Peter of Gissona | March 1249 |
| Peter of Cervera | March 1252 |
| William of Palomar | 1255 |
| Raymond of Bastida | April 1263–Feb. 1264 |
| John of Balcarca | May 1271 |
| Arnold Guarner | Oct. 1282 |
| Bernard of Rocamora | 1292 |
| Peter of Redorta | Aug. 1294 |
| Peter Cestret | March 1303 |

## Barbará

| Bernard of Albespino | Feb. 1173–Feb. 1174 |
| Berenguer of Monte | Dec. 1174–Jan. 1181 |
| Gaucebert of Serra | May 1181–Dec. 1190 |
| Peter of Aguda | Dec. 1196–March 1198 |
| William Amil | Oct. 1198 |
| Peter of Aguda | Oct. 1199 |
| Raymond of Lorenzo | Sept. 1200 |
| Bernard of Claret | April 1202–Feb. 1203 |
| Gaucebert of Serra | April 1204 |
| William of Azylach | Feb. 1207–Aug. 1208 |
| Bernard of Claret | Feb. 1210–May 1214 |
| Bernard of Grañena | April 1215 |
| Riperto | May 1219 |
| Peter of Pertegas | June 1220–June 1233 |
| William of Trapos | May 1236 |
| William Acharia | Nov. 1236 |
| Pons of Oltrera | Sept. 1237–April 1240 |
| Bernard of Monfalcó | Dec. 1240 |
| Berenguer of Torá | March ?1242 |
| Raymond of Villalba | Sept. 1242–Oct. 1244 |
| William of Anglesola | Jan. 1246 |
| William of Tordo | April–June 1246 |
| Bernard of Palomar | Oct. 1247–Jan. 1249 |
| Dalmau of Busol | Sept. 1249 |
| William of Ager | April–Oct. 1250 |
| William of Prades | Feb. ?1251 |
| William Mascarón | Oct. 1253 |

Raymond of Baco                April 1256–June 1257
Berenguer of Torrefeta         June 1257
Berenguer of Villafranca       Sept. 1257–May 1258
William of Anglesola           Nov. 1258–Nov. 1260
Peter of Montpalau             Aug.–Oct. 1261
Arnold of Timor                Nov. 1262–Aug. 1266
Bernard of Pujalt              Oct. 1267–June 1269
Gallart of Josa                Dec. 1269–July 1270/April 1271[6]
Arnold of Timor                Feb./May 1271–Aug. 1276
Arnold Guarner                 May 1277
William of Abellars            June 1277–April 1279
Bernard of Rocamora            Oct. 1280
William of Abellars            May 1283–Dec. 1290
Bernard of Montolíu            June 1291–March 1302
Dalmau of Timor                Jan. 1305–July 1307

*Boquiñeni*

Giles                          ?
Berenguer                      Nov. 1158–Dec. 1173
Simon                          March 1182–Sept. 1184
Peter of Luna                  July 1188–Nov. 1189
Bernard of Serón               April 1190–March 1192
García of Cintruénigo          Nov. 1192–April 1196
Berenguer of Monte             June 1197–Aug. ?1197
García of Pradilla             May 1202
Arnold of Galliner             June 1211
Hugh                           April 1214
John of Corzano                Dec. 1214–March 1215
Raymond Grande                 March–Aug. 1219
García of Oliveto              Aug. 1220–April 1223
Diego                          Jan. 1224–May 1230
García of Oliveto              Aug. 1230–May 1233
Peruz                          Oct. 1233
Peter Martínez of Bera         Nov. 1238–Jan. 1242
Martin of Longares             Feb.–April 1243
R. of Bera                     June–Oct. 1245
Peter Martínez of Bera         March–July 1246
John of Ciresa                 Nov. 1248–March 1249
Peter of Olivella              Feb. 1251–April 1252
Sancho of Tena                 July 1256–Sept. 1257 (with Ambel)
Lope of Ribaforada             Sept. 1257 (subordinate commander)
William of Montgrí             Dec. 1259 (with Ambel)
Ramiro of Estella              Dec. 1259–Sept. 1260

| | |
|---|---|
| William of Castellnou | May 1263–March 1264 |
| Dominic John | June 1264–May 1273 (with Añesa) |
| Dominic of Vecino | April 1274 |
| Berenguer of Rovira | Oct. 1277–June 1280 |
| Sancho of Berga | March 1282 (with Novillas) |
| John Croyn | Sept. 1282 |
| Michael of Lison | June 1293–Jan. 1294 |
| John of Sieste | Jan.–July 1296 |
| Pascal of Alfaro | May 1306–1307 |

*Burriana*

| | |
|---|---|
| Buxardo | April 1234 |
| Sancho | Nov. 1239 |
| Bertrand of Guardia | May 1242 (with Valencia) |
| Walter | Sept. 1243–Oct. 1244 (with Valencia)[7] |
| Sancho | May–Oct. 1244 (subordinate commander) |
| G. Gonsa | Feb. 1250/1–March 1252 |
| García Sánchez | April 1260 |
| John of Cipriano | April 1261–Feb. 1262 |
| Peter of Castellbó | Nov. 1263–Oct. 1265 |
| Peter of Cellés | Nov. 1270 |
| Peter Peronet | Jan. 1276–July 1277 |
| William Sánchez | March 1282 |
| James of Vallfogona | Jan. 1286 |
| Berenguer of Aguaviva | Feb. 1287 |
| Michael of Lison | Aug. 1288–Nov. 1290 |
| John of Morella | Feb. 1295 |
| Raymond of Belloch | April 1295 |
| John of Morella | April 1296 |
| Peter of Redorta | March 1298 |
| Pascal of Alfaro | July–Dec. 1298 |
| Raymond of San Daniel | May–June 1300 |

*Cantavieja*

| | |
|---|---|
| Michael of Luna | 1197 |
| William of Peralta | May 1201 (with Monzón, Castellote) |
| Bernard of Madrona | July 1223–Jan. 1224 |
| Stephen of Belmonte | July 1224 |
| Raymond of Serra | April 1225; *c.* 1230; April 1234 |
| William of Monte | May 1240 |
| William of Ager | Jan. 1242–May 1244 |
| Bernard of Altarriba | April 1246–July 1247 |

| | |
|---|---|
| Walter of Alez | May 1250–Oct. 1253 |
| William of Ager | May 1255–April 1259 |
| Raymond of Villalba | Sept. 1261–May 1264 |
| Peter of Montpalau | Aug. 1268–March 1271 |
| Gallart of Josa | May–Aug. 1271 |
| Peter of Tous | June 1272–June 1273 |
| Raymond of Bastida | May 1275 |
| Simon of Lenda | July 1277–Feb. 1295[8] |
| Arnold of Torroella | April 1296 |
| Peter of Villalba | April 1300–Aug. 1306 |
| R. of Galliner | 1307 |

*Castellón de Ampurias*

| | |
|---|---|
| Geoffrey Badat | Sept. 1217 |
| Bernard of Montlaur | March 1252–May 1253 |
| William of Tamarite | May 1263–May 1264 |
| Raymond of Tallada | 1272 |
| Peter of Redorta | c. 1288 |
| Simon of Blanes | ? |
| Romeo of Burguet | ? |

*Castellote*

| | |
|---|---|
| Michael of Luna | Oct. 1196–Aug. 1197 |
| Bernard of Cegunyoles | 1197 (with Alfambra, Villel) |
| William of Badels | 1197–Sept. 1199 (subordinate commander) |
| William of Peralta | May 1201 (with Monzón, Cantavieja) |
| Bertrand of Ciresa | April 1203–Feb. 1209 |
| Raymond of Cervera | Oct. 1210–May 1211 |
| Peter Adalbert | Sept. 1211–Dec. 1213 |
| Stephen of Belmonte | Sept. 1217–Feb. 1220 |
| Bernard of Madrona | 1221 |
| Peter of Castellnou | July 1223 |
| Rubardo | July 1224 |
| Pons of Magallón | April 1225 |
| Vidal of Orles | Sept. 1231 |
| Bernard of Altarriba | March–May 1237 |
| Hugh Bremond | Sept. 1238 |
| Raymond of Bescarán | May 1240–May 1242 |
| Fulk | May 1243–Dec. 1244 |
| William of Montgrí | March 1246 |
| García Arnold | Aug. 1246–May 1247 |

Argol                          Sept. 1249–Sept. 1252
Berenguer of Tallada           Jan.–April 1253
Berenguer of Villafranca       Feb.–May 1255
Bernard of Pujalt              Dec. 1255–Sept. 1256
Berenguer of Tallada           Dec. 1257
Bernard of Montlaur            Feb.–April 1260
Berenguer of Villafranca       June 1261–April 1264
Raymond of Bastida             April 1265
Raymond of Montpaon            May 1267–April 1268
Raymond of Bastida             Aug. 1268–March 1269
James of Miravet               May 1271–May 1274
Raymond of Bastida             May 1277–Aug. 1278
Pons of Pontóns                July 1280–Oct. 1281
Arnold of Castellví            March 1283–May 1306
G. of Villalba                 1307

*Chivert*

William Almoravid              Sept. 1243
Bertrand of Lunel              Feb.–May 1244
Argol                          Nov. 1245
William of Prades              March 1251–May 1267
Arnold of Castellví            Nov. 1272
Bernard of Pineda              April 1286–April 1287
Lope Sánchez of Berga          *c.* 1289
Raymond of San Daniel          Aug. 1289–Aug. 1294

*Corbins*

Bernard of Griva               April 1167
Bernard of Ternera             March 1174
Miro of Trilla                 Jan. 1177
Arnold of Cerdaña              April 1181–March 1192
Raymond of Ferradella          April 1196
Raymond Oller                  April 1212; Aug. 1231
Arnold                         June 1239–March 1242
William of Montgrí             Sept. 1243
Sancho of Tena                 July 1247–March 1252
R. of Lledó                    Oct. 1256
Raymond Berenguer of Ager      May 1258 (with Gardeny)
Raymond of Baco                Dec. 1260
William of Anglesola           Sept. 1261
Gerald of Alentorn             Aug. 1262–April 1263
Sancho                         Feb. 1264
Raymond of Montpaon            May 1271–1273

| | |
|---|---|
| James of Miravet | July 1274 |
| Raymond of Montpaon | March–Nov. 1277 |
| Gerald of Corbella | 1282 |
| Francis of Tallada | Oct. 1289 |
| William of Puignaucler | 1290 |
| Bernard of Fuentes | Aug. 1294 |
| Peter of San Justo | April 1299–May 1300 |
| Bernard of Fuentes | Sept. 1301–Feb. 1303 |
| Bartholomew of Villafranca | March 1303–Feb. 1305 |

*Gardeny*

| | |
|---|---|
| Peter of Cartellá | Feb. 1156–Nov. 1161 |
| Aymeric | Feb. 1164–Sept. 1175 |
| Bernard of Cornellá | Nov. 1175 |
| Raymond of Concabella | June 1176–Jan. 1177 |
| Miro of Trilla | Feb. 1177 |
| Peter Uchor | Feb.–March 1178 |
| Peter of Colonges | May 1178–March 1180 |
| Bernard of Albespino | May 1180–Nov. 1185 |
| Bezo | May 1186–1189 |
| Bernard of Claret | Feb. 1190–Feb. 1195 |
| Peter of Aguda | Feb. 1196 |
| Bernard of Serón | April 1196–April 1197 |
| Peter of Aguda | May–Oct. 1198 |
| Bernard of Claret | Aug. 1199–June 1200 |
| Peter of Aguda | Aug. 1200 |
| William Amil | April 1201–May 1203 |
| Bernard of Claret | Sept. 1203–March 1206 |
| William of Montrodón | Aug. 1206–Feb. 1212 |
| Raymond Berenguer of Ager | March 1212–Feb. 1215 (with Monzón) |
| Bernard of Claret | May 1215–Nov. 1216[9] |
| Geoffrey of Castellnou | Dec. 1216–Sept. 1221 |
| Raymond of Cervera | Dec. 1222–June 1223 |
| Raymond of Serra | Oct. 1223–Feb. 1228 |
| Jordan of Peralta | March 1228–Jan. 1230 |
| Rigald of Roca | March–April 1230 |
| William of Monte | July 1231–Dec. 1233 |
| Peter of Campfet | Dec. 1233–Jan. 1239 |
| William of Cardona | June 1239–March 1243 |
| Peter Jiménez | May–Aug. 1243 |
| Pons of Oltrera | Jan.–May 1244 |
| Bernard of Altarriba | May–Nov. 1245 |

| | |
|---|---|
| William of Anglesola | Feb. 1246–Jan. 1247 |
| William of Tordo | Oct. 1247–April 1249 |
| Bernard of Altarriba | Sept. 1249–March 1251 |
| William of Alcalá | Sept. 1251–Feb. 1252 |
| James of Timor | March 1252–Aug. 1254 |
| William of Alcalá | Oct. 1254 |
| Raymond Berenguer of Ager | May 1255–March 1260 (with Corbins) |
| Bernard of Altarriba | July 1260–Feb. 1261 |
| Raymond Berenguer of Ager | Sept. 1261–March 1262 |
| Peter of Queralt | April 1265–Feb. 1267; Sept. 1267 |
| Vacant | Aug.–Sept. 1267; Jan. 1268 |
| Bernard of Altarriba | May 1268–Sept. 1269 |
| Arnold of Timor | Nov. 1269–Feb. 1271 |
| Vacant | July 1271 |
| Raymond of Baco | Aug. 1271 |
| Vacant | Feb. 1272; April 1272 |
| Raymond of Baco | May 1272–April 1274 |
| William of Miravet | July 1274–April 1284 |
| Peter of Tous | May 1284–April 1286 |
| Bernard of Montolíu | April 1286–March 1290[10] |
| Peter of Villalba | April 1290–March 1292 |
| Arnold of Timor | May–Nov. 1292 |
| Vacant | May 1293 |
| Raymond Oliver | Aug. 1294–March 1297 |
| Peter of Villalba | May 1297–Feb. 1298 |
| Arnold of Torroella | May 1298–Oct. 1301 |
| Vacant | 1302–7 |
| Arnold of Banyuls | 1307 |

*Grañena*

| | |
|---|---|
| Peter of Cuatrocasas | Dec. 1181 |
| Roig of Beviure | 1189–92 |
| Peter of Cardona | 1197–Oct. 1198 |
| William Amil | Oct. 1203 |
| Pons of Oluja | Nov. 1210–Dec. 1211 |
| P. Hugh | May 1228 |
| Raymond Pérez | Nov. 1233 |
| William of Lugols | Jan. 1234 |
| Albert | Oct. 1245 |
| Berenguer of Aguilella | April 1251–March 1252 |
| Bernard of Palomar | 1255 |
| Berenguer of Villafranca | Aug.–Nov. 1256 |
| Peter of Rocamora | May 1263 |

Pons of Pontóns                    1272
Berenguer of Vallvert              Dec. 1285–Feb. 1289
James of Oluja                     April 1293–Aug. 1294
Berenguer of Montornés             July 1297–March 1299
James of Oluja                     Aug. 1300–Nov. 1301
Peter of San Justo                 ?
James of Oluja                     1307

*Horta*

Bertrand Aymeric                   ?1193–April 1194
William of Nulger                  Aug. 1197
Peter of Deo                       June 1202
R. of Valdellobregat               Nov. 1205
Raymond of Cervera                 Aug. 1207
William of Monte                   June 1227
Arnold of Cursavell                March 1229
Bocardo                            May 1233
Bernard of Altarriba               April 1234
Rostagno of Coms                   April 1241–March 1244
Raymond of Serra                   Dec. 1251–March 1252
William of Anglesola               1255–June 1257
William of Pontóns                 Oct. 1259
Bernard of Altarriba               Sept. 1261–May 1263
Raymond of Villalba                April 1265–Dec. 1275
William of Benages                 Jan. 1281
William of Miravet                 April 1286–1296
Simon of Lenda                     April 1296–1307

*Huesca*

Raymond of Cervera                 Oct. 1171
Nuño                               Dec. 1174–Dec. 1176
William of Serón                   Oct. 1176–March 1178[11]
Nuño                               July 1178
García of Borja                    May 1179–June 1181
William of Serón                   Oct. 1181–March 1184
Peter Ralph                        Feb. 1185
Nuño                               April 1186–Feb. 1192
Bertrand of Vilafraser             Aug. 1192–June 1194
Bernard of Serón                   March 1195
William of Serón                   April 1196–Nov. 1197
Bernard of Serón                   May 1199–April 1200
Gaucebert of Serra                 Aug. 1200
Albert                             June–Sept. 1203

| | |
|---|---|
| William of Montrodón | Aug. 1204–Feb. 1206 |
| Aymeric of Estuga | Oct. 1206–Oct. 1207 |
| Stephen of Bot | Dec. 1208–Oct. 1209 |
| A. Salamón | Sept. 1210 |
| Guy | Oct.–Dec. 1210 |
| Orella | Oct. 1212–May 1215 |
| John of Corzano | Nov. 1215–Jan. 1221 |
| Aymeric of Estuga | May 1221 |
| William Folz | Nov. 1222 |
| Gaucelino | June 1224–Aug. 1227 |
| Peter of Torá | Aug. 1228 |
| Archibald of Sana | Feb.–July 1231 |
| William of Palau | June 1232–May 1233 |
| Pons of Magalas | April 1235–Feb. 1240 |
| Sancho of Hueso | Sept.–Dec. 1241 |
| Pons Maltos | March 1243–May 1244 |
| Sancho of Hueso | Nov. 1245–July 1248 |
| García Arnold | May 1251–April 1255 |
| William of Alcalá | July–Nov. 1255 |
| García Arnold | Nov. 1258–July 1262 |
| Bernard of Montlaur | May 1263–April 1264 |
| Dalmau of Serón | April 1265–April 1266 |
| William of Miravet | July 1266 |
| Arnold of Timor | June 1268–June 1269 |
| Peter of Tous | May 1271 |
| William of Miravet | Nov. 1273 |
| William of Benages | May 1275 |
| William of Montgrí | March–June 1277 |
| Peter of Villalba | June 1289 |
| Peter of Tous | July 1293–April 1301 |
| Bernard of Montolíu | Oct. 1306 |

*Juncosa*

| | |
|---|---|
| Dominic | March 1199/1200 |
| Peter Giles | April 1246–Aug. 1266 (with Palau) |
| Bernard of Barbará | April 1280 |
| Riambau of Montclús | ? |

*La Zaida*

| | |
|---|---|
| [García of Aragon | March 1182][12] |
| Michael of Luna | Jan. 1185–July 1188 (with Pina) |
| F. of Braza | June 1194 |
| Raymond of Lorenzo | Oct. 1199–April 1200 (with Pina) |

| | |
|---|---|
| William of San Pastor | July 1221 |
| Raymond of Salas | April 1223 |
| García of Navasa | April 1232 |
| Rostagno Walter | Jan.–Feb. 1244 (with Pina) |
| Sancho | Dec. 1245 |
| William Mascarón | March 1252 |
| Berenguer of Monteagudo | Aug.–Nov. 1255 |
| Peter Perenol | Oct. 1257 |
| Ramiro | May 1263 |
| Berenguer of Torá | ?Jan. 1264–Jan. 1266 |
| Sancho of Tena | Dec. 1269–Oct. 1270 |
| Miro | Oct. 1272 |

*Luna*

| | |
|---|---|
| Raymond of Cervera | 1167–March 1168 |
| Arnold of Sarroca | June 1174–Jan. 1177[13] |
| B. of Prades | 1184 |
| Sancho | Nov. 1197 |
| J. | May 1205 |
| R. | April 1214–May 1215 |
| García | May–Nov. 1217 |

*Mallorca*[14]

| | |
|---|---|
| Bertrand of Arlet | Oct. 1230 |
| Raymond of Serra | June 1231–Nov. 1232 |
| Arnold of Cursavell | 1234 |
| Raymond of Pelalaval | May 1236 |
| Dalmau of Fenollar | July 1240–June 1242 |
| Raymond of Montblanch | April 1244 |
| Bernard of Montlaur | April 1251 |
| Peter of Ager | 1252 |
| Peter of Agramunt | 1253 |
| Peter Sánchez | 1254 |
| Peter of Ager | 1255 |
| Arnold | 1257 |
| García Sánchez | 1258 |
| Peter of Montpalau | 1260 |
| Raymond of Baco | 1262–April 1263 |
| William of Castellví | May 1263 |
| Raymond of Bastida | 1270–May 1272 |
| Bernard of Rocamora | 1274 |
| Bernard of Montolíu | Dec. 1279 |
| Arnold of Torroella | 1284 |

| | |
|---|---|
| Raymond Oliver | Jan. 1290 |
| Raymond of Belloch | 1290 |
| William of Abellars | 1294 |
| Raymond of Miravalls | 1298 |
| Bernard of Fuentes | 1299 |
| Peter of San Justo | Oct. 1300–June 1301 |
| Lope Abri | 1301 |
| Bernard of Fuentes | 1304 |
| Arnold of Castellví | 1307 |

*Miravet, Tortosa, and La Ribera*

| | |
|---|---|
| Aymeric of Torreies | Jan. 1156–Jan. 1162 |
| William Berard | Jan. 1165–Feb. 1174 |
| Bernard of Albespino | June 1174–March 1178 |
| Dalmau of Godeto[15] | Dec. 1178–Aug. 1181 |
| Raymond of Cubells | Dec. 1181–Jan. 1183 |
| Bezo | May 1183–Aug. 1185 |
| Bertrand of Conques | July 1186–April 1189 |
| Lope | Jan. 1190 |
| Bartholomew | May–July 1190 |
| Bernard of España | April 1191 |
| Bezo | Jan. 1192–Nov. 1193 |
| William of San Pablo | April–June 1194 |
| Gerald of Caercino | Oct.–Nov. 1194 |
| Peter of Colonges | April 1196–April 1200 |
| William of Torre | March 1201–June 1202 |
| Bernard of Cegunyoles | Aug. 1204–Aug. 1207 |
| Peter of Castellnou | Dec. 1207–March 1210 |
| Pons Marescalci | July 1210–July 1211 |
| Raymond of Cervera | Oct.–Dec. 1212 |
| Bernard of Campanes | Jan. 1216–Jan. 1231 |
| Rigald of Roca | July 1231 |
| Peter Raymond | May 1233 |
| William Folz | April 1234–April 1236 |

*Miravet*

| | |
|---|---|
| R. Bernard | May 1190 |
| Gaucebert of Casales | Aug. 1197 |
| William of Torre | June 1198 |
| Fulk | Jan. 1202 |
| Peter of Deo | Nov. 1205 |
| Bernard of Campanes | March–Aug. 1207 |
| Raymond of Cervera | June 1209 |

| | |
|---|---|
| Geoffrey of Castellnou | July 1210–Dec. 1212 |
| Bernard of Rocafort | April 1224–June 1227 |
| Hugh | April 1234 |
| Raymond of Serra | July 1239–March 1241 |
| Pons of Oltrera | July 1241–June 1242 (with Tortosa) |
| Bernard of Portella | Sept. 1243 |
| William of Montgrí | May–Dec. 1244 |
| G. of Torre | Dec. 1245 |
| García Arnold | Sept. 1250 |
| Bernard of Altarriba | ?May 1251–Oct. 1253 |
| William of Cardona | March 1255–March 1258 |
| Raymond of Villalba | Aug.–Nov. 1258 (with Tortosa) |
| William of Ager | Sept. 1261 |
| Peter of Queralt | July 1262–May 1264 |
| Bernard of Altarriba | March 1267–March 1268 |
| Bernard of Pujalt | Aug. 1269–July 1276 |
| Peter of Tous | March 1277–Jan. 1282 |
| | April 1286–May 1290[16] |
| Peter of Villalba | May 1292–April 1296 |
| Berenguer of San Justo | Dec. 1297–1307 |

*Monzón*

| | |
|---|---|
| William of Albaix | Jan. 1163–May 1167 |
| Aymeric | 1167 |
| Raymond of Cubells | May 1173–Aug. 1181 |
| Jordan of Corbarieu | Feb. 1182–Jan. 1183 |
| Raymond of Cubells | June 1184–Jan. 1188 |
| Arnold of Claramunt | Jan. 1191–Nov. 1194 |
| Pons Marescalci | April–Oct. 1196 |
| William of Peralta | Jan. 1198–May 1201 (with Canta- vieja, Castellote) |
| Bernard of Claret | Oct. 1201 |
| Pons Marescalci | July 1202–March 1210 |
| William Cadell | April 1210–June 1212 |
| Bernard of Aguilella | Dec. 1212–Oct. 1213 |
| Raymond Berenguer of Ager | May–Oct. 1214 (with Gardeny) |
| Bernard of Aguilella | 1214 (subordinate commander) |
| Bernard of Claret | Sept. 1215[17] |
| Bernard of Aguilella | Nov. 1215–May 1217 |
| Pons Marescalci | Jan. 1218–Dec. 1221 |
| Archibald of Sana | April 1224–Feb. 1227 |
| Raymond of Mongay | May 1230 |
| G. of Rúa | *c.* 1230 |

| | |
|---|---|
| Raymond of Serra | Aug. 1231–April 1234 |
| Raymond Berenguer | Dec. 1237–July 1238 |
| Peter Jiménez | 1240 |
| Dalmau of Fenollar | April 1243–July 1244 |
| Dominic of Mallén | 1244 |
| Raymond of Serra | Feb. 1246–Nov. 1248 |
| Peter Jiménez | April 1250–March 1252 |
| Dalmau of Fenollar | May 1252 |
| William of Ager | Oct. 1253 |
| Bernard of Altarriba | May 1255–May 1258 |
| Peter of Queralt | Jan. 1260–March 1262 |
| William of Ager | May 1263–April 1264 |
| William of Montgrí | April 1265–Aug. 1266 |
| William of Miravet | May 1269–May 1271 |
| Dalmau of Serón | Nov. 1272–Nov. 1274 |
| Gallart of Josa | May 1275 |
| Arnold of Timor | March 1277–Jan. 1292 |
| Raymond of Fals | May 1294–Sept. 1301 |
| Berenguer of Bellvís | Sept. 1305–1307 |

*Novillas*

| | |
|---|---|
| Rigald Viger | ?1139–Nov. 1151 |
| Raymond Bernard | 1144–Sept. 1150[18] |
| Frevol | 1148–April 1158 |
| Raymond William | Dec. 1155–Aug. 1156 (subordinate commander) |
| William of Bais | Aug. 1156–April 1167 |
| William Bec | 1156–7 (subordinate commander) |
| García of Luna | June–Nov. 1158 |
| Lope of Sada | June 1158 (subordinate commander) |
| Peter Martínez | Feb.–Sept. 1159 |
| William of San Marcial | May 1159 (subordinate commander) |
| Lope of Sada | Jan. 1161–June 1162 (subordinate commander) |
| Peter Tizón | Oct. 1161–1169 |
| Sancho Iñiguez | July 1163 (subordinate commander) |
| Lope of Sada | March 1164 (subordinate commander) |
| Sancho of Berga | 1164 (subordinate commander) |
| Rothlan | 1164–April 1165 (subordinate commander) |

| | |
|---|---|
| Lope of Sada | May 1166 (subordinate commander) |
| Martin Sánchez | Oct. 1167 (subordinate commander) |
| Bernard of Griva | 1169 (subordinate commander) |
| Peter John | Dec. 1170–March 1175 |
| Raymond of Concabella | March 1180 |
| Orella | ?1182 |
| Bernard of España | 1186–9 |
| Raymond of Cubells | Oct. 1190 |
| William of San Pablo | July 1193 |
| P. of Barbastro | June 1194–May 1195 |
| William of Peralta | Dec. 1195–Oct. 1196 (with Alfambra, Villel) |
| Bernard of Claret | Jan. 1198–Feb. 1199 |
| Raymond of Torroja | April 1199–Oct. 1200 |
| Bernard of Cegunyoles | May 1202 |
| Aymeric of Estuga | Feb. 1203 |
| William Amil | 1206 |
| Peter of Barillas | 1209 |
| William of Azylach | Dec. 1212–1218 |
| Peter of Barillas | March 1218–1219 |
| Bertrand of Albero | 1225/9 |
| G. Arnold of Benasque | Dec. 1227 |
| Peter Adalbert | Sept. 1234 |
| Peter Arrieta | Sept. 1239 |
| Sancho of Hueso | Oct. 1240–April 1241 |
| Peter Jiménez | Nov. 1241–Jan. 1242 |
| Bertrand of Guardia | March 1243 |
| Sancho of Hueso | April 1243–May 1244 |
| Berenguer of Bosco | Oct. 1245 |
| William of Alcalá | Feb. 1246–March 1249 |
| Bernard of Palomar | 1250 |
| Dalmau of Busol | Dec. 1251–Sept. 1252 |
| Peter Martínez | March 1255 |
| Peter of Molina | Dec. 1259–April 1271 |
| Pons of Pontóns | May 1271 |
| William of Montgrí | May–June 1272 |
| Pons of Pontóns | Nov. 1272–June 1273 |
| Bernard of Montolíu | Dec. 1278 |
| Sancho of Berga | March 1282 (with Boquiñeni) |
| Arnold of Puig | July 1296 |
| William of Jumeda | Sept. 1301 |
| Bartholomew of Villafranca | April 1302 |
| Berenguer of Olmos | July 1304 |

### Palau/Barcelona

| | |
|---|---|
| Berenguer of San Vicente | Nov. 1151–Jan. 1172 |
| William of Solsona | Jan. 1175–Dec. 1176 |
| Gerald of Caercino | March 1179–Oct. 1180 |
| William of Cerdanyola | July 1181–Jan. 1199 |
| Raymond of Traveseras | July 1199–June 1202 |
| Raymond Bataia | 1202–Nov. 1211 |
| Guy | Nov. 1212 |
| Berenguer of Arbores | March 1213 (with Aiguaviva) |
| Raymond Arlet | July 1213–March 1216 |
| Gaucelino | 1217–Feb. 1223 |
| Gerald | Dec. 1224 |
| Ferrer | Dec. 1225–March 1230 |
| William | Aug. 1230–Feb. 1232 |
| Gerald | May 1232–May 1236 |
| William of Monzón | Jan. 1237 |
| Peter of San Félix | April 1237–Feb. 1238 |
| Peter Giles | Aug. 1238–Feb. 1250 (with Juncosa) |
| Pons of Oluja | May 1250–July 1254 |
| Peter Giles | Oct. 1254–May 1258 (with Juncosa) |
| Sancho of Tena | Oct. 1258–May 1259 |
| Peter Sutor | Jan. 1260–Jan. 1261 |
| Peter Peronet | March–Oct. 1262 |
| Arnold Guarner | Nov. 1263–April 1267 |
| Raymond of Barbará | May 1268–Dec. 1279 |
| Romeo of Burguet | April 1281–Jan. 1302 |
| Berenguer Guamir | Aug. 1302–June 1305 |

### Peñíscola

| | |
|---|---|
| Raymond of Guardia | July 1295–March 1298 |
| Bernard of Tous | June 1298 |
| Bernard of Fuentes | ? |
| Arnold of Banyuls | Dec. 1298–Feb. 1307 |
| Peter of San Justo | 1307 |

### Pina

| | |
|---|---|
| Michael of Luna | Jan. 1185–July 1188 (with La Zaida) |
| Raymond of Lorenzo | April 1200 (with La Zaida) |
| Martin López | April 1232 |
| Raymond Seguer | Sept. 1238 |
| Rostagno Walter | Feb. 1244 (with La Zaida) |
| Bernard of Cornellá | Nov. 1262–May 1263 |
| Simon | Jan. ?1264 |

| Bernard of Cornellá | May 1264–Feb. 1265 |
|---|---|
| Peter of Cocallo | March 1270–Feb. 1278 |
| Bernard of Barbará | March 1284 |
| John of Ambel | May 1295–March 1299 |

*Puigreig, Cerdaña, Bergadán*[19]

| [William | Feb. 1169][20] |
|---|---|
| Berenguer of Gaver (C) | April 1181 |
| Roig of Beviure (C, B) | Jan. 1186–1189 |
| William of Lugols (C, B) | May 1216–Jan. 1231 |
| B. of Pino (C, B) | 1231–Jan. 1234 |
| Raymond of Villanueva (C, B, P) | 1236–Jan. 1241 |
| Arnold of Prades (C, B) | Feb. 1243 |
| Raymond of Villanueva (C, B, P) | July 1244–May 1254 |
| Peter of Orpinell (P) | Jan. 1256 |
| Raymond of Villanueva (C, B, P) | April 1258–Jan. 1267 |
| Berenguer of Tallada (P) | Oct.–Nov. 1267 |
| Bernard of Cornellá (P) | May–Dec. 1269 |
| Berenguer of Portella (P) | June 1271 |
| Francis of Tallada (P) | Aug. 1274–Jan. 1276 |
| Peter of Zalona (P) | June 1277–Jan. 1278 |
| Francis of Tallada (P) | Sept. 1278–Feb. 1279 |
| William Scarich (P) | June 1279–May 1280 |
| William of Puignaucler (P) | Aug. 1280–June 1283 |
| Bernard of Torrellas (P) | July 1284 |
| Raymond Cazador (P) | Feb. 1285–April 1288 |
| Peter of Villanueva (P) | Jan.–Feb. 1289 |
| William of Passenant (P) | Aug. 1289–May 1292 |
| Peter of Villanueva (P) | Aug. 1293–Feb. 1299 |
| Arnold of Puig (P) | May 1300–March 1307 |
| Galcerán of Biure (P) | 1307 |

*Ribarroja*

| Robert | Oct. 1271–March 1277 |
|---|---|
| B. of Algars | May 1294 |

*Ricla/Calatayud*

| Nuño | April 1184 |
|---|---|
| Peter | Dec. 1191 |

| | |
|---|---|
| Giles of María | June 1194–April 1196 |
| Bernard of Cegunyoles | April 1197 |
| Diego | July 1221 |
| Bertrand of Rosseto | Nov. 1227–June 1239 |
| Sancho | Dec. 1240–March 1242 |
| García | May 1242 |
| Berenguer of Torá | March–July 1246 |
| Gómez of Puig | March 1252 |
| García Sánchez of Tena | July 1257 |
| Artuso | Sept. 1261–May 1263 |
| Michael of Lison | Nov. 1270–May 1271 |
| Dominic of Jaca | Aug. 1272 |
| Michael of Lison | June 1277 |
| Bernard of Pineda | Nov. 1284 |
| William of Puignaucler | Feb. ?1288 |
| Bernard of Barbará | May 1289 |
| Dominic Doron | April 1295 |
| Gaucebert Durbán | Feb. 1304–June 1306 |
| Berenguer of Monteagudo | ? |

## Selma

| | |
|---|---|
| Dominic | Dec. 1190 |
| R. of Soler | Dec. 1196 |
| William of Romano | 1225 |
| Raymond of Rossellón | June 1237 |
| Berenguer of Forcadela | March 1252 |
| P. of Lobera | *c.* 1290 |
| Arnold of Puig | Dec. 1292–Jan. 1293 |
| Riambau of Montclús | Aug. 1304 |
| P. of Lobera | 1307 |

## Tortosa

| | |
|---|---|
| Iñigo Sánchez | April 1160–June 1161 |
| Sancho of Vergea | Nov. 1165 |
| Peter Uchor | June 1174–July 1177; Aug. 1180– Aug. 1186[21] |
| Gerald of Caercino | April 1187 |
| Lope of Ciurana | Dec. 1188 |
| Gerald of Caercino | Jan. 1190–April 1191 |
| Raymond Bernard | Nov. 1193–Jan. 1195 |
| Bernard of Gaver | May 1197 |

| | |
|---|---|
| Peter of Calasanz | Aug. 1197–April 1198 |
| William of Torre | June 1198–April 1200 |
| Berenguer of Montblanch | March 1201–Jan. 1202 |
| Bernard of Campanes | Oct. 1205 |
| Armando | Aug. 1207–Oct. 1208 |
| Dalmau of Cervera | Aug. 1211 |
| Peter Adalbert | Jan. 1216 |
| Raymond of Avinyó | June 1216–Feb. 1219 |
| Rostagno | April 1219–June 1225 |
| William of San Pastor | May–Dec. 1226 |
| Pons of Cervera | June 1227–April 1228 |
| Dalmau of Fenollar | May–Sept. 1228 |
| Arnold of Cursavell | Sept. 1230–May 1233 |
| Raymond of Lunel | April 1234 |
| Peter of Molina | Nov. 1234 |
| Raymond of Serra | Nov. 1235–May 1236 |
| William of Aguilón | Aug. 1237 |
| Bernard of Lunel | March 1238–Feb. 1239 |
| Rostagno of Coms | Aug. 1239–April 1240 |
| Pons of Oltrera | Dec. 1240–March 1242 (with Miravet) |
| | |
| Gasco | April 1242 |
| Peter of Montpalau | Aug. 1243 |
| Bernard of Altarriba | Jan.–Nov. 1244[22] |
| Raymond of Serra | Nov.–Dec. 1245 |
| Pons of Oltrera | April–June 1246 |
| Peter of Montpalau | April 1248–Oct. 1249 |
| William of Montgrí | Aug. 1250–March 1258 |
| Raymond of Villalba | Aug.–Sept. 1258 (with Miravet) |
| Bernard of Altarriba | May 1259–April 1260 |
| Dalmau of Fenollar | May 1260–Dec. 1264 |
| Bernard of Altarriba | May 1265 |
| Dalmau of Serón | Aug. 1268–March 1272 |
| Gallart of Josa | Nov. 1272–Nov. 1274 |
| Dalmau of Serón | May–Dec. 1275 |
| William of Benages | Sept. 1276–Jan. 1277 |
| William of Abellars | Dec. 1280–Sept. 1281 |
| Bernard of Montolíu | Nov. 1285 |
| Raymond Oliver | April 1286–Aug. 1287 |
| Bernard of Rocamora | May–Sept. 1289 |
| Raymond Oliver | May 1290–May 1292 |
| Raymond of Belloch | May 1292–April 1295 |
| Berenguer Guamir | Oct. 1295–June 1298 |
| Giles Pérez | 1307 |

*Valencia*

| | |
|---|---|
| Everard | June 1239 |
| Bertrand of Guardia | May–June 1242 (with Burriana) |
| Walter | Sept. 1243–Feb. ?1250 (with Burriana, Villel) |
| Peter of Ager | Jan.–Nov. 1247 (subordinate commander) |
| Peter of Ager | Feb. 1251–June 1252 |
| William of Tordo | Aug. 1252–Oct. 1254 |
| Walter | Nov. 1254–March 1258[23] |
| Berenguer of Villafranca | Aug. 1258–Dec. 1259 |
| William of Castellví | June 1260–Jan. 1263 |
| Raymond of Baco | May 1263–Feb. 1265 |
| Raymond of Bastida | June 1266 |
| Peter of Albanell | Jan. 1269–April 1271 |
| Peter of Montpalau | May 1271–March 1276 |
| Gerald of Corbella | July 1277–Nov. 1280 |
| Raymond of Belloch | Dec. 1282–Feb. 1286 |
| Arnold of Torroella | May 1286–Jan. 1288 |
| Raymond of Miravalls | Jan.–May 1290 |
| William of Abellars | June 1291 |
| Raymond of Miravalls | Oct. 1292–April 1296 |
| Raymond of Belloch | Sept. 1297–March 1307 |

*Villel*

| | |
|---|---|
| William of Peralta | Oct. 1196 (with Novillas, Alfambra) |
| Bertrand Navarro | Oct. 1196 (subordinate commander) |
| Bernard of Cegunyoles | 1197 (with Alfambra, Castellote) |
| Peter Martínez | Jan. 1198–April 1199 (subordinate commander) |
| Arnold Médico | April 1199 (with Ambel) |
| Bernard of Cegunyoles | July 1199–Sept. 1200 (with Alfambra) |
| Bernard Amil | Sept. 1200 (subordinate commander) |
| Arnold Médico | ?Oct. 1200 (with Ambel) |
| Peter Martínez | ?Oct. 1200 (subordinate commander) |
| Gaucebert of Casales | Aug. 1201–Oct. 1203 (with Alfambra) |
| B. of Ciresa | Aug. 1201 (subordinate commander) |
| Peter of Castellnou | Jan.–July 1206 (with Alfambra) |
| Bertrand | Jan. 1206 (subordinate commander) |
| William of Senone | July–Sept. 1207 (with Alfambra) |
| Peter of Pertegas | July 1207 (subordinate commander) |
| Bernard of Campanes | Aug. 1210–Feb. 1213 |
| William Arnold of Benasque | Jan. 1214 |

| | |
|---|---|
| Bertrand Carbonell | July–Aug. 1214 |
| William Arnold of Benasque | Dec. 1214–Jan. 1220 |
| Stephen of Belmonte | June–Dec. 1221 |
| G. Folz | Jan. 1224–Nov. 1225 |
| William Arnold of Benasque | Aug. 1226–June 1227 |
| Raymond of Serra | May–July 1228; March 1228/9 |
| Peter of Campfet | Jan.–Dec. 1232 |
| William of Monte | May 1234–Sept. 1236 |
| Walter | July 1240–May 1243 |
| William of Monte | May 1243–Jan. 1245 |
| Peter of Montpalau | March–Oct. 1245 |
| Walter | April 1246–Jan. 1248 (with Valencia) |
| Peter of Ager | March 1248–Nov. 1249 |
| Berenguer of Palomar | April 1250–Jan. 1255 |
| Walter | Feb.–April 1255[24] |
| Berenguer of Villafranca | Oct. 1255–Jan. 1256 |
| García Arnold | Oct. 1256 |
| Berenguer of Torrefeta | Oct. 1257–March 1260 |
| Dalmau of Serón | Dec. 1260–Oct. 1261 |
| Gerald of Alentorn | May 1263–Aug. 1265 |
| Raymond of Montpaon | July 1270–March 1271 |
| William of Montgrí | Aug.–Oct. 1271 (with Alfambra) |
| Peter of Paen | May 1272–Aug. 1273 |
| Gerald of Puyades | April 1275 |
| Dalmau of Serón | April 1277 |
| Arnold of Torroella | Feb. 1279–May 1280 |
| Raymond of Belloch | Sept. 1280–March 1282 |
| Arnold of Torroella | Aug. 1282 |
| Raymond Oliver | Sept. 1283–April 1286 |
| James of Olvia | Aug. 1286–April 1289 |
| John Pérez | Sept. 1289–Feb. 1292 |
| Peter of San Justo | June 1292–Jan. 1294 |
| Gaucebert Durbán | Jan. 1296–Sept. 1299 |
| Berenguer of Montornés | July 1300–March 1302 |
| Berenguer of Olmos | March–June 1303 |
| Bartholomew of Villafranca | June 1305–1307 |

### Zaragoza

| | |
|---|---|
| Bernard of Salvi | April 1162–March 1182 |
| Peter of Grañena | April 1184 |
| Peter of San Gregorio | June 1186 |
| Gilbert of Costabella | July 1188–Feb. 1189 |
| Peter of Grañena | Sept. 1190–Dec. 1195 |

| | |
|---|---|
| Peter Galliner | April 1196 |
| Peter of Luna | Aug. 1196–April 1208[25] |
| Aymeric of Estuga | July 1208–April 1210 |
| Fortún Aragonés | May 1210–May 1211 |
| Bremond | Aug. 1213–May 1217 |
| Peter of Deo | Jan.–Nov. 1218 |
| Peter Murut | May 1220–July 1221 |
| Bertrand of Albero | Dec. 1223–May 1224 |
| John of Corzano | July–Dec. 1226 |
| Bertrand of Albero | Aug. 1228–Feb. 1229 |
| Peter of Deo | May 1229 |
| Peter Murut | Sept. 1231–March 1233 |
| William of Palau | Sept. 1234 |
| Pons of Montpesat | March 1235–Aug. 1236 |
| William of Monzón | Nov. 1237–May 1239 |
| Albert | Oct.–Dec. 1241 |
| Martin of Bera | April 1242 |
| Bernard of San Justo | May 1243 |
| Berenguer of Bosco | May–Aug. 1244 |
| Peter of San Román | April–Oct. 1245 |
| Arnold Ferrer | Dec. 1246–Oct. 1247 |
| Arto | July 1248–July 1255 |
| William of Alcalá | Aug. 1256–Feb. 1257 |
| Laurence of Olvia | Oct. 1257 |
| Borracio | May 1260–July 1262 |
| Dominic of Jaca | May 1263–Sept. 1267 |
| Arnold Guarner | May 1269–May 1275 |
| William Almoravid | Dec. 1275–Nov. 1279 |
| William of Monzón | June 1280–Feb. 1282 |
| Michael of Lison | July–Nov. 1284 |
| William of Puignaucler | Jan. 1289 |
| Gerald of Corbella | Aug. 1289 |
| Bernard of Barbará | May 1291 |
| Raymond Oliver | Aug. 1292–April 1294 |
| Berenguer of Montornés | Dec. 1294–Jan. 1296 |
| Peter of San Justo | July 1296 |
| Raymond Oliver | June 1297–1307 |

## NOTES

1. As it is not known exactly when convents were founded, all commanders of places where convents were established are listed. For the commanders of Mas-Deu, see Léonard, *Introduction*, pp. 89–90.

2. He was commander of Huesca in 1265–6.

3. Uncastillo was included in the title given to some of the early commanders of Añesa: RAH, 12–6–1/M–83, doc. 27; AHN, cód. 467, p. 404, docs. 505, 506.

4. He was apparently commander of Zaragoza at the same time.

5. He was commander of Corbins in 1290.

6. Gallart of Josa appears as commander in April 1271, although Arnold of Timor was named as commander in February. The latter is next mentioned as commander in May 1271, while the penultimate reference to Gallart of Josa as commander occurs in July 1270.

7. Although after 1244 the commanders of Valencia did not include Burriana in their title, they continued to exercise authority over Burriana for some years: see above, p. 95.

8. He was absent in the East in 1292: AGP, parch. Cervera, no. 484; see above, p. 406.

9. He was apparently commander of Monzón at the same time.

10. Peter of Tous is called commander in a document drawn up in 1288, but this must be a mistake, as he was commander of Miravet from 1286 to 1290: AGP, parch. Gardeny, no. 185.

11. There is obviously a mistake in the dating of the documents of the year 1176, but it is impossible now to determine where the error lies.

12. See above, p. 98.

13. From 1174 onwards the commanders of Huesca also had authority over the house of Luna, and some were called commanders of Huesca and of Luna; see, for example, AHN, cód. 499, p. 17, doc. 24; p. 18, doc. 31; p. 22, doc. 44.

14. In compiling this list I have made use of the list of commanders given by M. Rotger y Capllonch, *Historia de Pollensa*, i (Palma de Mallorca, 1897–8), 44.

15. See above, p. 106, note 41.

16. He was commander of Gardeny from 1284 until 1286.

17. He was apparently commander of Gardeny at the same time.

18. In the early years at Novillas there was more than one 'master' at the same time.

19. The titles given to the various commanders are indicated by the initials given after the names.

20. See above, p. 100.

21. He was commander of Gardeny in 1178.

22. He also appears as commander of Tortosa in September 1245, but there is apparently an error in dating, for he was commander of Gardeny in August and October 1245.

23. He was also commander of Villel in 1255.

24. He was at this time also commander of Valencia.

25. In March and April 1202 he was also commander of Añesa.

## CHAMBERLAINS[1]

### Castellote

| | |
|---|---|
| Bernard | May 1201 |
| Pons of Montpaon | July 1224 |
| Lope | March–May 1237 |
| Peter | Sept. 1238 |
| John | May 1240 |
| Lope | Jan. 1244 |
| Dominic of Huesca | March 1247 |
| García | May 1247 |
| D. of Tamarite | Sept. 1252 |
| Albert | Feb.–May 1255 |
| Ferrer | Dec. 1255 |
| Dominic of Huesca | Dec. 1257–April 1260 |
| S. López | June–Dec. 1261 |
| F. | Nov. 1262–May 1267 |
| P. of Olivella | Dec. 1268–March 1269 |
| Peter of Lena | Aug. 1272–May 1274 |
| Matthew of Balaguer | Aug. 1277–July 1280 |
| John Saguet | July 1283 |

### Tortosa

| | |
|---|---|
| Gerald of Caercino | Jan. 1184–Aug. 1186 |
| Pons of Borna | Aug. 1197 |
| D. of Stagno | Feb. 1200 |
| G. of Rocafort | June 1202 |
| Peter of Cardalac | July 1218–Feb. 1219 |
| Gilbert | Feb. 1221 |
| Arnold of Cursavell | May 1228 |
| Raymond of Lunel | Sept. 1228–Sept. 1231 |
| William | Oct. 1233 |
| Pelabous | April 1234 |
| William of Caercino | Nov. 1234–Sept. 1237 |
| Peter Zapater | March 1238 |
| William of Tornello | Dec. 1238–Aug. 1239 |
| Albert | Jan. 1240 |
| Dominic of Mallén | Dec. 1240–Aug. 1243 |

Lope                                Nov. 1244–Sept. 1245
Borracio of Oluja                   April 1246–March 1251
James                               Nov. 1255–March 1258
John of Alcover                     Sept. 1258–Feb. 1259
Bernard of Cornellá                 Jan.–May 1260
Peter Catalán                       March 1263–Aug. 1264
Bernard of Cornellá                 May 1265
Peter of Lena                       Dec. 1271
Peter of Guardiola                  Dec. 1275–Jan. 1277
Raymond of Otgers                   April–Sept. 1281
William Escarit                     Jan.–Nov. 1285
Bernard Roig                        May 1289


*Zaragoza*

Bernard                             Sept. 1176
John                                April 1203
Dominic of Rada                     Aug.–Oct. 1204
Arnold Raymond                      Dec. 1213
William                             Oct. 1214
Lope                                Oct. 1215
Peter of Ricla                      Jan. 1218
Giles                               May 1220
Gerald                              May 1224
Lope                                July–Dec. 1226
Peter of Sta. Lecina                Sept. 1234–April 1242
William of Palau                    July–Aug. 1244
Peter of Olivera                    April 1245
Dominic                             April–May 1245
Peter of Olivera                    Oct. 1245–Oct. 1247
Spañol                              July 1248–Nov. 1249
Bartholomew                         July 1255
Spañol                              July 1255–Jan. 1257
Bartholomew                         May 1260–Nov. 1263
Dominic of Alcorisa                 May 1264–Sept. 1266
John of Sieste                      May 1269
Dominic of Alcorisa                 Jan. 1270–Dec. 1274
John of Ambel                       Dec. 1275–Jan. 1278
William of Vallfogona                June 1278–Feb. 1279
John of Ambel                       April 1279–Feb. 1282
William of Vallfogona                July–Nov. 1284
Peter of Mora                       Jan. 1289
Sancho of Añesa                     Aug. 1289
Peter of Mora                       Dec. 1291–Sept. 1292

| | |
|---|---|
| Berenguer of Berga | April 1294 |
| John of Biscabella | Dec. 1294 |
| John of Torresecas | Aug. 1295–Jan. 1296 |
| Raymond of Vallebrera | July 1297–March 1299 |
| Peter of Tamarite | May 1299 |
| Bonanat of Vallebrera | Feb. 1300–May 1307 |

## NOTE

1. Only some of the more complete lists are given.

## CHAPLAINS[1]

*Gardeny*

| | |
|---|---|
| Richard | May 1165–Aug. 1167 |
| Berenguer | May 1176 |
| Peter | July 1180 |
| Arnold | Aug. 1181 |
| Peter of Pradillo | March 1191–Nov. 1203 |
| William of Albesa | Feb. 1208–March 1237 |
| Peter of Novillas | Sept. 1225 |
| Raymond | March 1237–Jan. 1238 |
| Berenguer | Oct. 1240–March 1243 |
| Sancho | Oct. 1247–April 1249 |
| John of Claramunt | Feb.–March 1248 |
| Martin | Feb. 1251–Oct. 1253 |
| John | Jan. 1257–May 1258 |
| Bartholomew | March–Sept. 1260 |
| James | Aug. 1260–July 1262 |
| Peter of Manresa | Aug. 1262–Nov. 1264 |
| Berenguer of Barbará | April–Oct. 1265 |
| Ferrer of Lletó | Aug. 1266–Sept. 1269 |
| Raymond Dans | Feb. 1271–Nov. 1275 |
| William of Roda | Feb. 1273–April 1274 |
| Dominic of Borja | Dec. 1275–Aug. 1276 |
| Michael of Boyl | Jan. 1277–Feb. 1278 |
| Ferrer Redón | April 1277–Oct. 1278 |
| Bernard of Graus | May–Sept. 1279 |
| Peter of Barbará | Dec. 1279–March 1281 |
| Peter Guamir | May 1280–Nov. 1282 |
| Peter of Torre | Feb. 1283–Feb. 1286 |
| Bernard of Benasque | Jan.–March 1288 |
| Giles Pérez of Tarazona | May–Sept. 1289 |

| | |
|---|---|
| John of Rosas | May 1292–Jan. 1305 |
| Peter of Terrats | Aug.–Oct. 1296 |
| John of Embrún | June 1299 |
| Aznar | July 1300 |
| Bernard of Monlleó | Feb. 1303 |
| Dominic Martínez | Oct. 1306–April 1307 |

## NOTE

1. Only the most complete list is given.

# APPENDIX III

## Dependencies of Convents[1]

*Aiguaviva*
  ?Libiano

*Ambel*
  Alberite
  Tarazona

*Barbará*
  Espluga de Francolí
  Vallfogona

*Boquiñeni*
  Pradilla

*Cantavieja*
  Iglesuela
  Villarluengo

*Gardeny*
  Escarabat
  Monlleó
  Segriá
  Torre de Bafes
  Urgel

*Huesca*
  Algás
  Arnillas
  Baibinum
  Loreto
  Pompién

*La Zaida*
  Belloque

*Miravet*
  Algars
  Gandesa
  Gebut
  Nonaspe
  Torres de Segre
  *villa* of Miravet

*Monzón*
  Armentera
  Chalamera
  Cofita
  Estiche
  Litera
  Ribera
  *villa* of Monzón
  Zaidín

*Novillas*
  Cabañas
  Razazol

*Palau*
  Barcelona

*Peñíscola*
  Ares
  Chivert

*Ricla*
  Encinacorba

*Tortosa*
  Prado

*Valencia*

   Moncada

*Villel*

   Libros

   Teruel

   Villastar

*Zaragoza*

   Alfocea

   Marlofa

   Sieste

## NOTE

1. Dependencies which became convents are not included. For the dependencies of Mas-Deu, see Léonard, *Introduction*, pp. 91–3.

APPENDIX IV

# Seals

## The seal of the provincial master

In 1224 the provincial master was using a round seal (25 mm. in diameter) of black or dark-green wax, depicting a lamb and bearing the legend: s. PVINCIE ET ARAGONIS.[1] According to a bull issued by Innocent IV in 1251 it was customary for successive provincial masters to use the same seal.[2] A change had been made, however, when the province of Provence and certain parts of Spain was divided into two. The master of Provence continued to use a seal depicting a lamb,[3] but the seal of the Aragonese master William of Cardona, although round (29 mm. in diameter) and of black or dark-green wax, depicted a knight on horseback, carrying a lance and shield, on which was a cross; it bore the legend: s. MINISTRI TEMPLI I ARAGON 7 CATALON.[4] This form of seal was also used by later Aragonese provincial masters.[5]

## Seals of convents and commanders

Alfambra    1248. Brown wax, round, 30 mm. in diameter, depicting a cross. Legend: ...... LUM CASTRI .... [6]

Barbará    Early fourteenth century. Yellow wax, round, 29 mm. in diameter, depicting a castle between two fishes. Legend: s. COMAND ..... BARBERA.[7]

Gardeny    Early fourteenth century. Yellow wax, round, 27 mm. in diameter, depicting a cross, with stars in two angles and shields with crosses in the other two. Legend: s. AR .......... GARDENNI. This is the seal of Arnold of Banyuls.[8]

Huesca    Round, depicting a castle. Legend: s. DOM. TEMPLI DE OSCA.[9]

Miravet    1278, 1287. Depicting a lion.[10]

Monzón    Early fourteenth century. Round, depicting a castle with three towers, with a griffin on each side. Legend: s. CASTELL ........ ONI.[11]

Tortosa    Late thirteenth century. Depicting a cross. Legend: SIGILLUM MILICIE TEMPLI IN DERTOSA.[12]

## NOTES

1. F. de Sagarra, *Sigillografía catalana*, iii (Barcelona, 1932), 473, no. 5667.

2. E. Berger, *Les Registres d'Innocent IV*, ii (Paris, 1887), 169, doc. 4970.

3. L. C. Douët d'Arcq, *Collection de sceaux*, iii (Paris, 1868), 242, no. 9870.

4. The seal is described in a document drawn up in 1245: RAH, 12–6–1/M–83, doc. 111; and examples survive from the years 1247 and 1251: Sagarra, op. cit. iii. 473, no. 5668; J. Menéndez Pidal, *Catálogo de sellos españoles de la edad media: Archivo Histórico Nacional: Sección de sigilografía* (Madrid, 1929), p. 182, no. 251, where the date of the second seal is given wrongly as 1241.

5. See the descriptions of the master's seal in AGP, parch. Gardeny, no. 2244–B (1264) and AHN, San Juan, leg. 342, doc. 6 (1273).

6. Sagarra, op. cit. iii. 473, no. 5669.

7. Ibid. iii. 473, no. 5670.

8. Ibid. iii. 474, no. 5671.

9. R. de Huesca, *Teatro histórico de las iglesias del reyno de Aragón*, vii (Pamplona, 1797), 121.

10. See the descriptions in ACA, parch. Peter III, no. 96, and AHN, San Juan, leg. 333, doc. 15.

11. Sagarra, op. cit. iii. 474, no. 5673.

12. *Costums de Tortosa*, 1. iv. 9, in B. Oliver, *Historia del derecho en Cataluña, Mallorca y Valencia: Código de las costumbres de Tortosa*, iv (Madrid, 1881), 36.

# BIBLIOGRAPHY

## (i) MANUSCRIPT SOURCES

*Archivo Histórico Nacional, Madrid*

Sección de órdenes militares: San Juan de Jerusalén: Castellanía de Amposta and Gran Priorado de Navarra.

| Legs. | | | | |
|---|---|---|---|---|
| 18–22 | papal bulls | 351–60 | Horta |
| 38–41 | miscellaneous docs. | 361–7 | Orrios |
| 135–41 | Alfambra | 385–93 | Huesca |
| 169–77 | Ambel | 419–25 | Villalba |
| 184–91 | Ascó | 426–32 | Villarluengo |
| 204–19 | Calatayud | 433–41 | Villel |
| 227–35 | Cantavieja | 442–58 | Zaragoza |
| 254–63 | Castellote | 528–99 | *treudos* |
| 274–80 | Chalamera | 626–72 | miscellaneous docs. |
| 281–6 | Encinacorba | 673–81 | Aberín |
| 287–99 | Mallén | 694–5 | Cogolludo and Melgar |
| 303–18 | Miravet | 701–6 | Villafranca |
| 319–37 | Monzón | 708–24 | miscellaneous docs. |
| 338–50 | Novillas | | |

Sign. 1439–C. *Fuero* of Alfambra and related documents.

On these sources, see A. L. Javierre Mur and C. G. del Arroyo, *Guía de la Sección de órdenes militares* (Madrid, n.d.), pp. 94–104; J. Delaville Le Roulx, 'Les archives de l'Ordre de l'Hôpital dans la péninsule ibérique', *Nouvelles archives des missions scientifiques*, iv (1893), 8–16; Delaville, *Cartulaire*, i, pp. cxl–cxlii, cliv–clv. The information provided by Delaville Le Roulx is not, however, always reliable.

Sección de órdenes militares: Montesa.

Documentos particulares. Over 600 survive for the period up to 1307 (the figures given in the *Guía*, p. 78, are inaccurate), and of these a large proportion concerns the Temple.

Documentos reales. These are analysed in Javierre, *Privilegios*.

Sign. 542–C and 543–C. These contain chiefly resettlement charters; see *Guía*, p. 232.

Sección de órdenes militares: Calatrava.

Sign. 1341–C. This register includes information about the property of Mountjoy.

Sección de códices.

Códs. 466–71    Cartulario Magno, 6 vols. These contain general privileges and documents for Villel (vol. i), Zaragoza (vols. ii, iii, iv), Boquiñeni (vol. v), and Monzón (vol. vi).

493    Resettlement charters.

494    Similar in content to cód. 493.

495    Cartulary of the Hospitaller convent of Ulldecona. A catalogue of some of the documents in this volume is provided by M. Magallón, 'Templarios y Hospitalarios. Primer cartulario en el Archivo Histórico Nacional', *BRAH*, xxxiii (1898), 257–66.

499    Cartulary of the convent of Huesca.

502    Writings by the archivist Fernández on the history of the Temple and Hospital.

689    Cartulary of the convent of Castellote.

691    Cartulary of Templar documents for Aragon and Navarre, compiled probably at Novillas.

1032    Catalan cartulary of papal, royal, and private privileges to the Temple.

1311    Lists of *confratres* of the Temple.

1312    Catalan cartulary, similar in content to cód. 1032. A catalogue of the documents in this volume is provided by M. Magallón, 'Los Templarios de la Corona de Aragón. Indice de su cartulario del siglo XIII', *BRAH*, xxxii (1898), 451–63, and xxxiii (1898), 90–105; he sometimes, however, confuses this volume with cód. 1032.

On these volumes in general, see *Guía*, pp. 252–5; A. L. Javierre Mur, 'El Archivo de San Juan de los Panetes de Zaragoza', *EEMCA*, iii (1947–8), 157–92; Delaville Le Roulx, 'Les archives', pp. 16–18; Delaville, *Cartulaire*, i, pp. cxlii–cxlv.

Sección de sellos.

This section, comprising documents of any kind which have seals attached, includes a few Templar documents.

### Real Academia de la Historia, Madrid

12–6–1/M–83. Among the parchments stitched into this volume are 63 documents concerning the Aragonese houses of the Temple.

### Archivo de la Corona de Aragón, Barcelona

Royal parchments. Raymond Berenguer III
                   Raymond Berenguer IV
                   Alfonso II
                   Peter II
                   James I
                   Peter III
                   Alfonso III
                   James II

The collection of royal parchments includes many Templar documents, especially for the convents of Barbará, Palau, and Puigreig. These documents were presumably retained by the Crown after the dissolution of the Temple.

Royal registers. James I
  Peter III
  Alfonso III
  James II

Over 350 registers survive for the period up to the death of James II, and as there are no adequate indexes or catalogues it has not been possible to do more than sample a number of the royal registers. A detailed list of registers is provided by L. Cadier, 'Les archives d'Aragon et de Navarre', *BEC*, xlix (1888), 80–4. Reg. 291, which deals exclusively with the arrest of the Templars and the administration of Templar property following the arrest, is particularly important for Templar history. The following Templar volumes are also included among the registers, although they do not form part of the series:

309   Cartulary of royal, papal, and private privileges to the Temple.
310   Similar in content to reg. 309, which is probably based on this volume.
Varia 1   This volume contains records of Templar transactions involving land in and around Barcelona; the *Liber super decimis*; and an inventory of Templar documents which were seized by the Crown after the arrest of the Templars.
Varia 2   Cartulary of miscellaneous Templar documents.
Varia 3   Fragment of a rental for the house of Puigreig, 1275.
Varia 5   Notebook of a Villel notary at the end of the thirteenth century.

Cartas reales diplomáticas. James II. Legs. 88–93 are devoted exclusively to Templar documents, of which there are nearly 700. Some Templar documents are also included elsewhere in this collection.

Real Patrimonio. 2349. This volume contains information about *cenas* exacted from the Temple.

Bulas pontificias. These are analysed by F. Miquel Rosell, *Regesta de letras pontificias del Archivo de la Corona de Aragón* (Madrid, 1948).

*Archivo del Gran Priorado de Cataluña* (now housed in the ACA)

Parchments.   Aiguaviva      Espluga de Francolí
  Barbará      Gardeny
  Bulas      Grañena
  Casas Antiguas      Selma
  Cervera      Testamentos
  Comuns      Torres de Segre
  Corbins      Tortosa
  Espluga Calva      Vilafranca

Cartulary of Gardeny. This is described by J. Miret y Sans, *Cartoral dels Templers de les comandes de Gardeny y Barbens* (Barcelona, 1899), pp. 5–6.

Cartulary of Tortosa.

Rental from the convent of Gardeny for the year 1214.

The contents of this Hospitaller archive are discussed—not always accurately—
by Delaville Le Roulx, 'Les archives', pp. 77–105, and *Cartulaire*, i, pp. cxlviii–
clii. See also J. Santachs y Costas, *Memoria sobre el archivo prioral de Cataluña
de la Orden de San Juan* (Barcelona, 1885).

## (ii) SELECT LIST OF PRINTED WORKS

ACHERY, L. D', *Spicilegium sive collectio veterum aliquot scriptorum* (Paris, 1723).
AGUIRRE, J. S. DE, *Collectio maxima conciliorum omnium Hispaniae et novi orbis* (Rome, 1753–5).
ALART, B., *Privilèges et titres relatifs aux franchises, institutions et propriétés communales de Roussillon et de Cerdagne* (Perpignan, 1874).
—— 'Suppression de l'Ordre du Temple en Roussillon', *Bulletin de la Société agricole, scientifique et littéraire des Pyrénées-Orientales*, xv (1867).
ALBAREDA Y HERRERA, M., *El fuero de Alfambra* (Madrid, 1925).
ALBON, MARQUIS D', *Cartulaire général de l'Ordre du Temple, 1119?–1150* (Paris, 1913).
—— 'La mort d'Odon de Saint-Amand, grand-maître du Temple', *Revue de l'orient latin*, xii (1911).
ALEGRET, A., 'Los Templarios en Tarragona', *Boletín arqueológico*, xvii (1905).
ALTISENT, A., 'Un poble de la Catalunya Nova els segles XI i XII. L'Espluga de Francolí de 1079 a 1200', *Anuario de estudios medievales*, iii (1966).
*Annali Genovesi di Caffaro*, ed. L. T. Belgrano (Fonti per la storia d'Italia, Rome, Genoa, 1890–1929).
ARCO, R. DEL, *Catálogo monumental de España: Huesca* (Madrid, 1942).
—— 'El obispo Don Jaime Sarroca, consejero y gran privado del Rey Don Jaime el Conquistador', *BRABLB*, ix (1917–20).
—— 'Huesca en el siglo XII', *II Congreso de historia de la Corona de Aragón*, i (Huesca, 1920).
ARIGITA, M., *Colección de documentos inéditos para la historia de Navarra* (Pamplona, 1909).
ASHTOR, E., *Histoire des prix et des salaires dans l'Orient médiéval* (Paris, 1969).
ASÍN PALACIOS, M., *El Islam cristianizado* (Madrid, 1931).
ASSO, I. DE, *Historia de la economía política de Aragón* (Zaragoza, 1947 edn.).
*Aureum opus regalium privilegiorum civitatis et regni Valentie* (Valencia, 1515).
AUVRAY, L., *Les Registres de Grégoire IX* (Paris, 1890–1955).

BAER, F., *Die Juden im christlichen Spanien* (Berlin, 1929).
—— *Studien zur Geschichte der Juden im Königreich Aragonien während des 13. und 14. Jahrhunderts* (Berlin, 1913).
BALAGUER, F., 'La Chronica Adefonsi Imperatoris y la elevación de Ramiro II al trono aragonés', *EEMCA*, vi (1956).
—— 'La vizcondesa del Bearn doña Talesa y la rebelión contra Ramiro II en 1136', *EEMCA*, v (1952).
BALLARÓ Y CASAS, J., *Historia de Cardona* (Barcelona, 1905).
BALUZIUS, S., *Vitae Paparum Avenionensium*, ed. G. Mollat (Paris, 1914–27).
BARTHÉLEMY, E. DE, 'Étude sur les établissements monastiques du diocèse d'Elne', *Bulletin monumental*, xxiii (1857).

BAUDON DE MONY, C., *Les Relations politiques des comtes de Foix avec la Catalogne* (Paris, 1896).

BAYERRI, E., *Historia de Tortosa y su comarca* (Tortosa, 1933– ).
—— *Llibre de privilegis de la vila de Ulldecona* (Tortosa, 1951).

BENAVIDES, A., *Memorias de D. Fernando IV de Castilla* (Madrid, 1860).

BERGER, E., *Les Registres d'Innocent IV* (Paris, 1881–1920).

BERLIÈRE, U., 'L'exercise du ministère paroissial par les moines du XIIᵉ au XVIIIᵉ siècle', *Revue bénédictine*, xxxix (1927).
—— 'Le nombre des moines dans les anciens monastères', *Revue bénédictine*, xli (1929) and xlii (1930).

BERNARD, ST., *De laude novae militiae*, in Migne, *PL*, clxxxii, and in *Opera Omnia*, ed. J. Leclerq and H. M. Rochais, iii (Rome, 1963).

BLÁSQUEZ Y JIMÉNEZ, A., 'Bosquejo histórico de la Orden de Montegaudio', *BRAH*, lxxi (1917).

BLOCH, M., *La Société féodale* (Paris, 1939–40).

BOFARULL Y BROCA, A. DE, *Historia de Cataluña* (Barcelona, 1876–8).

BOFARULL Y SANS, F., *El castillo y la baronía de Aramprunya* (Barcelona, 1911).

BOFILL Y BOIX, P., 'Lo castell de Gurb y la família Gurb en lo segle XIIIᵉ', *Congreso de historia de la Corona de Aragón*, ii (Barcelona, 1913).

BOISSONNADE, P., *Du nouveau sur la Chanson de Roland* (Paris, 1923).

BONILLA Y SAN MARTÍN, A., 'El derecho aragonés en el siglo XII', *II Congreso de historia de la Corona de Aragón*, i (Huesca, 1920).

BOUREL DE LA RONCIÈRE, C., *Les Registres d'Alexandre IV* (Paris, 1902–53).

BOURG, A. DU, *Histoire du grand-prieuré de Toulouse* (Toulouse, 1883).

BRUGUERA, M., *Historia general de la religiosa y militar Orden de los caballeros del Temple*, i (Barcelona, 1888).

BRUNEL, C., *Les Plus anciennes chartes en langue provençale* (Paris, 1926–52).

*Bullarium Franciscanum* (Rome, 1759–1904).

*Bullarium ordinis militiae de Calatrava*, ed. I. J. de Ortega y Cotes, J. F. Alvarez de Baquedano, and P. de Ortega Zuñiga y Aranda (Madrid, 1761).

BULST-THIELE, M. L., 'Templer in königlichen und päpstlichen Diensten', *Festschrift Percy Ernst Schramm* (Wiesbaden, 1964).

BURNS, R. I., *The Crusader Kingdom of Valencia* (Harvard, 1967).
—— 'A Mediaeval Income Tax: The Tithe in the Thirteenth-Century Kingdom of Valencia', *Speculum*, xli (1966).
—— 'Social Riots on the Christian–Moslem Frontier (Thirteenth-Century Valencia)', *American Historical Review*, lxvi (1960–1).

CABRÉ, M. D., 'Noticias y documentos del Altoaragón. La Violada (Almudévar)', *Argensola*, x (1959).

CADIER, L., 'Les archives d'Aragon et de Navarre', *BEC*, xlix (1888).

CAHEN, C., *La Syrie du nord à l'époque des croisades* (Paris, 1940).

*Cambridge Economic History of Europe*, i (2nd edn., Cambridge, 1966), iii (1963).

CARRERAS Y CANDI, F., 'Entences y Templers en les montanyes de Prades', *BRABLB*, ii (1903–4).
—— 'Excursions per la Catalunya aragonesa y provincia d'Osca', *Butlletí del Centre Excursionista de Catalunya*, xviii (1908).
—— *Miscelanea histórica catalana* (Barcelona, 1905–6).

CARRERAS Y CANDI, F., 'Rebelió de la noblesa catalana contra Jaume I en 1259', *BRABLB*, vi (1911).

CARRIÈRE, V., 'Les débuts de l'Ordre du Temple en France', *Le Moyen Âge*, xxvii (1914).

—— *Histoire et cartulaire des Templiers de Provins, avec une introduction sur les débuts du Temple en France* (Paris, 1919).

*Cartulaire de la commanderie de Richerenches de l'Ordre du Temple (1136–1214)*, ed. Marquis de Ripert-Monclar (Avignon, 1907).

*Cartulaires des Templiers de Douzens*, ed. P. Gérard and E. Magnou (Collection de documents inédits sur l'histoire de France, série in 8º, vol. iii, Paris, 1965).

*Cartulari de Poblet* (Barcelona, 1938).

*Cartulario de 'Sant Cugat' del Vallés*, ed. J. Rius Serra (Barcelona, 1945–7).

*Cartulario de Tavernoles*, ed. J. Soler García (Castellón de la Plana, 1961).

CARUANA, J., 'Itinerario de Alfonso II de Aragón', *EEMCA*, vii (1962).

CASTRO, A., *The Structure of Spanish History* (Princeton, 1954).

*Chronica Adefonsi Imperatoris*, ed. L. Sánchez Belda (Madrid, 1950).

*Chronicle of James I*, trans. J. Forster (London, 1883).

*Chronique de Michel le Syrien*, trans. J. B. Chabot (Paris, 1899–1910).

COCHERIL, M., 'Essai sur l'origine des ordres militaires dans la péninsule ibérique', *Collectanea Ordinis Cisterciensium Reformatorum*, xx (1958), and xxi (1959).

*Colección de documentos inéditos del Archivo general de la Corona de Aragón*, ed. P. de Bofarull y Mascaró, etc. (Barcelona, 1847–1910).

*Colección de fueros y cartas pueblas de España* (Madrid, 1852).

CONDE, J. A., *Historia de la dominación de los árabes en España* (Madrid, 1820–1).

CONSTABLE, G., *Monastic Tithes from their Origins to the Twelfth Century* (Cambridge, 1964).

*Constituciones Baiulie Mirabeti*, ed. G. Sánchez (Madrid, 1915).

*Cortes de los antiguos reinos de Aragón y de Valencia y principado de Cataluña* (Madrid, 1896–1919).

COTS I GORCHS, J., 'Les "Consuetuds" d'Horta (avui Horta de Sant Joan) a la ratlla del Baix Aragó', *Estudis universitaris catalans*, xv (1930).

COTTON, BARTHOLOMEW, *Historia Anglicana*, ed. H. R. Luard (London, 1859).

COY Y COTONAT, A., *Sort y comarca Noguera-Pallaresa* (Barcelona, 1906).

DANVILA, M., 'Origen, naturaleza y extensión de los derechos de la Mesa Maestral de la Orden de Calatrava', *BRAH*, xii (1888).

DEFOURNEAUX, M., *Les Français en Espagne aux XIᵉ et XIIᵉ siècles* (Paris, 1949).

DELAVILLE LE ROULX, J., 'Les archives de l'Ordre de l'Hôpital dans la péninsule ibérique', *Nouvelles archives des missions scientifiques*, iv (1893).

—— 'Bulles pour l'ordre du Temple, tirées des archives de S. Gervasio de Cassolas', *Revue de l'orient latin*, xi (1905–8).

—— *Cartulaire général de l'Ordre des Hospitaliers de Saint-Jean de Jérusalem* (Paris, 1894–1906).

—— *Documents concernant les Templiers extraits des Archives de Malte* (Paris, 1882).

—— *Les Hospitaliers en Terre Sainte et à Chypre* (Paris, 1904).

—— 'Un nouveau manuscrit de la Règle du Temple', *Annuaire-bulletin de la Société de l'Histoire de France*, xxvi (1889).

—— 'L'Ordre de Montjoye', *Revue de l'orient latin*, i (1893).

DELISLE, L., *Mémoire sur les opérations financières des Templiers* (Mémoires de l'Institut National de France, Académie des Inscriptions et Belles-Lettres, xxxiii. 2, 1889).

DESCLOT, B., *Chronicle of the Reign of King Pedro III of Aragon*, ed. F. L.Critchlow (Princeton, 1928–34).

DESSUBRÉ, M., *Bibliographie des Templiers* (Paris, 1928).

DEVIC, C., and VAISSETE, J., *Histoire générale de Languedoc* (Toulouse, 1872–1905).

DIAGO, F., *Anales del reyno de Valencia* (Valencia, 1613).

DIGARD, G., *Philippe le Bel et le Saint-Siège* (Paris, 1936).

——, FAUCON, M., etc., *Les Registres de Boniface VIII* (Paris, 1884–1939).

DOUËT D'ARCQ, L. C., *Collection de sceaux* (Paris, 1863–8).

DUBY, G., *L'Économie rurale et la vie des campagnes dans l'Occident médiéval* (Paris, 1962).

DUFOURCQ, C. E., *L'Espagne catalane et le Maghrib aux XIIIe et XIVe siècles* (Paris, 1966).

—— 'Prix et niveaux de vie dans les pays catalans et maghribins à la fin du XIIIe et au début du XIVe siècles', *Le Moyen Âge*, lxxi (1965).

DUPUY, P., *Histoire de l'Ordre militaire des Templiers* (Brussels, 1751).

DURÁN GUDIOL, A., *Colección diplomática de la catedral de Huesca* (Zaragoza, 1965–9).

DURBEC, J. A., 'Les Templiers en Provence. Formation des commanderies et répartition géographique de leurs biens', *Provence historique*, ix (1959).

ERDMANN, C., *Die Entstehung des Kreuzzugsgedankens* (Stuttgart, 1935).

—— 'Der Kreuzzugsgedanke in Portugal', *Historische Zeitschrift*, cxli (1929).

*España sagrada*, ed. H. Flórez, M. Risco, etc. (Madrid, 1747–1918).

ESTEBAN ABAD, R., *Estudio histórico-político sobre la ciudad y comunidad de Daroca* (Teruel, 1959).

FÁBREGA I GRAU, A., 'La dècima per a la conquesta de Sardenya en els pontificats de Bonifaci VIII i Benet XI', *VI Congreso de historia de la Corona de Aragón* (Madrid, 1959).

FERRANDIS, M., 'Rendición del castillo de Chivert a los Templarios', *Homenaje a D. Francisco Codera* (Zaragoza, 1904).

FERREIRA, A., *Memorias e noticias historicas da celebre ordem militar dos Templarios* (Lisbon, 1735).

FINKE, H., *Acta Aragonensia* (Berlin, 1908–22).

—— 'Nachträge und Ergänzungen zu den *Acta Aragonensia* (I–III)', *Spanische Forschungen der Görresgesellschaft: Gesammelte Aufsätze zur Kulturgeschichte Spaniens*, iv (1933).

—— *Papsttum und Untergang des Templerordens* (Münster, 1907).

FONDEVILLA, F., 'La nobleza catalano-aragonesa capitaneada por Ferrán Sánchez de Castro en 1274', *Congreso de historia de la Corona de Aragón*, ii (Barcelona, 1913).

FONT RIUS, J. M., *Cartas de población y franquicia de Cataluña* (Madrid, Barcelona, 1969–   ).
—— 'La comarca de Tortosa a raíz de la reconquista cristiana (1148)', *Cuadernos de historia de España*, xix (1953).
—— 'Franquicias locales en la comarca del alto Bergadá', *Pirineos*, x (1954).
—— 'Franquicias urbanas medievales de la Cataluña Vieja', *BRABLB*, xxix (1961–2).
—— 'Orígenes del régimen municipal de Cataluña', *AHDE*, xvi (1945), and xvii (1946).
—— 'La reconquista de Lérida y su proyección en el orden jurídico', *Ilerda*, vii (1949).
FOREY, A. J., 'The Order of Mountjoy', *Speculum*, xlvi (1971).
*Fori Antiqui Valentiae*, ed. M. Dualde Serrano (Madrid, Valencia, 1967).
FUENTE, V. DE LA, *Historia de Calatayud* (Calatayud, 1880).
*Fueros y observancias del reyno de Aragón* (Zaragoza, 1667).

GALBRAITH, G. R., *The Constitution of the Dominican Order* (Manchester, 1925).
GARCÍA-GALLO, A., 'La sucesión del trono en la Corona de Aragón', *AHDE*, xxxvi (1966).
GARCÍA LARRAGUETA, S. A., 'Fueros y cartas pueblas navarro-aragonesas otorgadas por Templarios y Hospitalarios', *AHDE*, xxiv (1954).
—— *El gran priorado de Navarra de la Orden de San Juan de Jerusalén* (Pamplona, 1957).
—— 'La Orden de San Juan en la crisis del imperio hispánico del siglo XII', *Hispania*, xii (1952).
—— 'Relaciones comerciales entre Aragón y el Hospital de Acre', *VII Congreso de historia de la Corona de Aragón*, ii (Barcelona, 1962).
GAZULLA, F. D., 'La Orden del Santo Redentor', *BSCC*, ix (1928), and x (1929).
*Gesta Comitum Barcinonensium*, ed. L. Barrau Dihigo and J. Massó Torrents (Barcelona, 1925).
GIMÉNEZ SOLER, A., 'Caballeros españoles en Africa y africanos en España', *Revue hispanique*, xii (1905).
—— 'El poder judicial en la Corona de Aragón', *Memorias de la Real Academia de Buenas Letras de Barcelona*, viii (1901).
GIRONA Y LLAGUSTERA, D., 'Mullerament del Infant En Pere de Cathalunya ab Madona Constança de Sicília', *Congreso de historia de la Corona de Aragón*, i (Barcelona, 1909).
GONZÁLEZ HURTEBISE, E., 'Recull de documents inèdits del Rey en Jaume I', *Congreso de historia de la Corona de Aragón*, ii (Barcelona, 1913).
GRASSOTI, H., 'Homenaje de García Ramírez a Alfonso VII', *Príncipe de Viana*, xxv (1964).
GUAL CAMARENA, M., 'Estudio de la territorialidad de los Fueros de Valencia', *EEMCA*, iii (1947–8).
—— 'Mudéjares valencianos. Aportaciones para su estudio', *Saitabi*, vii (1949).
—— *Precedentes de la reconquista valenciana* (Valencia, 1952).
—— 'Reconquista de la zona castellonense', *BSCC*, xxv (1949).
—— *Vocabulario del comercio medieval* (Tarragona, 1968).

GUIRAUD, J., and CADIER, E., *Les Registres de Grégoire X et de Jean XXI* (Paris, 1892–1960).
—— *Les Registres d'Urbain IV* (Paris, 1892–1958).

HIGOUNET, C., 'Mouvements de populations dans le Midi de la France du XIᵉ au XVᵉ siècle', *Annales*, viii (1953).
HINOJOSA, E. DE, *El régimen señorial y la cuestión agraria en Cataluña* (Madrid, 1905).
*Historia Compostellana*, in *ES*, xx.
*Historia social y económica de España y América*, ed. J. Vicens Vives (Barcelona, 1957–9).
HUICI, A., *Colección de crónicas árabes de la reconquista* (Tetuán, 1952–4).
—— *Colección diplomática de Jaime I, el Conquistador* (Valencia, 1916–22).

IBANÈS, J., *La Doctrine de l'Église et les réalités économiques au XIIIᵉ siècle* (Paris, 1967).

JACOBS, J., *An Inquiry into the Sources of the Jews in Spain* (London, 1894).
JAVIERRE MUR, A. L., 'El archivo de San Juan de los Panetes de Zaragoza', *EEMCA*, iii (1947–8).
—— *Privilegios reales de la Orden de Montesa en la edad media* (Madrid, n.d.).
——, ARROYO, C. G. DEL, *Guía de la Sección de órdenes militares* (Madrid, n.d.).
*Jean XXII (1316–1334): Lettres communes*, ed. G. Mollat (Paris, 1904–59).
JOINVILLE, *Histoire de Saint Louis*, ed. N. de Wailly (Société de l'Histoire de France, 1868).
JORDAN, E., *Les Registres de Clément IV* (Paris, 1893–1945).

KEHR, P., 'El papado y los reinos de Navarra y Aragón hasta mediados del siglo XII', *EEMCA*, ii (1946).
—— *Papsturkunden in Spanien. I. Katalanien* (Abhandlungen der Gesellschaft der Wissenschaften zu Göttingen. Phil.-hist. Klasse, N.F., vol. xviii, 1926).
—— *Papsturkunden in Spanien. II. Navarra und Aragon* (Abhandlungen der Gesellschaft der Wissenschaften zu Göttingen. Phil.-hist. Klasse, N.F., vol. xxii, 1928).
KING, E. J., *The Knights Hospitallers in the Holy Land* (London, 1931).
KLÜPFEL, L., *Verwaltungsgeschichte des Königreichs Aragon zu Ende des 13. Jahrhunderts* (Berlin, 1915).

LACARRA, J. M., 'Alfonso II el Casto, rey de Aragón y conde de Barcelona', *VII Congreso de historia de la Corona de Aragón*, i (Barcelona, 1962).
—— 'Documentos para el estudio de la reconquista y repoblación del Valle del Ebro', *EEMCA*, ii (1946), iii (1947–48), v (1952).
—— 'Gastón de Bearn y Zaragoza', *Pirineos*, viii (1952).
—— 'Notas para la formación de las familias de fueros navarros', *AHDE*, x (1933).
—— 'La repoblación de Zaragoza por Alfonso I el Batallador', *Estudios de historia social de España*, i (1949).
—— *Semblanza de Alfonso I el Batallador* (Zaragoza, 1949).

LACARRA, J. M., 'Les villes-frontière dans l'Espagne des xIᵉ et xIIᵉ siècles', *Le Moyen Âge*, lxix (1963).

LAMBERT, E., *L'Architecture des Templiers* (Paris, 1955).

LAMBERTO and RAMÓN DE HUESCA, *Teatro histórico de las iglesias del reyno de Aragón* (Pamplona, 1780–1807).

LANGLOIS, E., *Les Registres de Nicolas IV* (Paris, 1886–93).

LECLERQ, J., 'Un document sur les débuts des Templiers', *Revue d'histoire ecclésiastique*, lii (1957).

LECOY DE LA MARCHE, A., *Relations politiques de la France avec le royaume de Majorque* (Paris, 1892).

LEDESMA RUBIO, M. L., *La encomienda de Zaragoza de la Orden de San Juan de Jerusalén en los siglos XII y XIII* (Zaragoza, 1967).

—— 'Notas sobre la actividad militar de los hospitalarios', *Príncipe de Viana*, xxv (1964).

LEES, B. A., *The Records of the Templars in England in the Twelfth Century* (British Academy Records of the Social and Economic History of England and Wales, vol. ix, 1935).

LÉONARD, E. G., *Introduction au cartulaire manuscrit du Temple du Marquis d'Albon* (Paris, 1930).

*Letters of Peter the Venerable*, ed. G. Constable (Cambridge, Mass., 1967).

*Liber Censuum*, ed. P. Fabre and L. Duchesne (Paris, 1889–1952).

*Liber Feudorum Maior*, ed. F. Miquel Rosell (Barcelona, 1945–7).

LLADÓ Y FERRAGUT, J., *Catálogo de la sección histórica del archivo municipal de Pollensa y de las curias de los Templarios y Hospitalarios de San Juan de Jerusalén* (Palma, 1944).

'*Llibre Blanch*' *de Santas Creus*, ed. F. Udina Martorell (Barcelona, 1947).

LOMAX, D. W., *La Orden de Santiago* (Madrid, 1965).

LÓPEZ POLO, A., 'Documentos para la historia de Teruel', *Teruel*, i (1949).

LOURIE, E., 'Free Moslems in the Balearics under Christian Rule in the Thirteenth Century', *Speculum*, xlv (1970).

LUNDGREEN, F., *Wilhelm von Tyrus und der Templerorden* (Historische Studien, vol. xcvii, 1911).

LUTTRELL, A. T., 'The Aragonese Crown and the Knights Hospitallers of Rhodes: 1291–1350', *English Historical Review*, lxxvi (1961).

MAGALLÓN, M., 'Los Templarios de la Corona de Aragón. Indice de su cartulario del siglo XIII', *BRAH*, xxxii (1898), and xxxiii (1898).

—— 'Templarios y Hospitalarios. Primer cartulario en el Archivo Histórico Nacional', *BRAH*, xxxiii (1898).

MAGNOU, E., 'Oblature, classe chevaleresque et servage dans les maisons méridionales du Temple au xIIᵉ siècle', *Annales du Midi*, lxxiii (1961).

MAHN, J. B., *L'Ordre cistercien et son gouvernement* (Paris, 1951).

MANSI, J. D., *Sacrorum conciliorum nova et amplissima collectio* (Venice, 1759–98).

MANSILLA, D., *La documentación pontificia de Honorio III (1216–1227)* (Rome, 1965).

—— *La documentación pontificia hasta Inocencio III* (Rome, 1955).

MAP, WALTER, *De nugis curialium*, ed. T. Wright (Camden Society, 1850).

MARCA, P. DE, *Marca Hispanica* (Paris, 1688).

MARÇAIS, G., 'Note sur les ribâts en Berbérie', *Mélanges René Basset*, ii (Publications de l'Institut des Hautes-Études Marocaines, vol. xi, 1925).

—— 'Ribat', *Encyclopedia of Islam*, iii (London, 1936).

MARÍA, R. DE, *El 'Repartiment' de Burriana y Villarreal* (Valencia, 1935).

—— 'Xivert y Oropesa', *BSCC*, xiv (1933).

MARTÍNEZ FERRANDO, J. E., 'Estado actual de los estudios sobre la repoblación en los territorios de la Corona de Aragón (siglos XII a XIV)', *VII Congreso de historia de la Corona de Aragón*, i (Barcelona, 1962).

MARTORELL Y TRABAL, F., 'Inventari dels bens de la cambra reyal en temps de Jaume II (1323)', *Anuari de l'Institut d'Estudis Catalans*, iv (1911–12).

MASIÁ DE ROS, A., *La Corona de Aragón y los estados del norte de Africa* (Barcelona, 1951).

MASSÓ TORRENTS, J., 'Inventari dels bens mobles del rey Martí d'Aragó', *Revue hispanique*, xii (1905).

—— *Repertori de l'antiga literatura catalana* (Barcelona, 1932).

MELVILLE, M., *La Vie des Templiers* (Paris, 1951).

MENÉNDEZ PIDAL, J., *Catálogo de sellos españoles de la edad media: Archivo Histórico Nacional: Sección de sigilografía* (Madrid, 1929).

MERCATI, A., 'Interrogatorio di Templari a Barcellona (1311)', *Spanische Forschungen der Görresgesellschaft: Gesammelte Aufsätze zur Kulturgeschichte Spaniens*, vi (1937).

MICHELET, J., *Procès des Templiers* (Paris, 1841–51).

MIGNE, J. P., *Patrologiae cursus completus. Series latina* (Paris, 1844–55).

MILÁ Y FONTANALS, M., *De los trovadores de España* (Barcelona, 1861).

MIQUEL ROSELL, F., *Regesta de letras pontificias del Archivo de la Corona de Aragón* (Madrid, 1948).

MIRALLES SBERT, J., *Catálogo del Archivo Capitular de Mallorca* (Palma, 1941–3).

MIRET Y SANS, J., 'La carta de franquicias otorgada por el Conde de Barcelona a los judíos de Tortosa', *Homenaje a D. Francisco Codera* (Zaragoza, 1904).

—— *Cartoral dels Templers de les comandes de Gardeny y Barbens* (Barcelona, 1899).

—— *Les Cases de Templers y Hospitalers en Catalunya* (Barcelona, 1910).

—— 'Lo castell de Montbrió', *Butlletí del Centre Excursionista de Catalunya*, ix (1899).

—— 'Enquesta sobre el trovador Vilarnau, amb algunes noves de Guillem de Bergadà, Ramon de Miraval i Guillem de Mur', *Revue hispanique*, xlvi (1919).

—— 'La esclavitud en Cataluña en los últimos tiempos de la edad media', *Revue hispanique*, xli (1917).

—— 'Inventaris de les cases del Temple de la Corona d'Aragó en 1289', *BRABLB*, vi (1911).

—— *Investigación histórica sobre el vizcondado de Castellbó* (Barcelona, 1900).

—— *Itinerari de Jaume I 'el Conqueridor'* (Barcelona, 1918).

—— 'Itinerario del rey Alfonso I de Cataluña, II en Aragón', *BRABLB*, ii (1903–4).

—— 'Itinerario del rey Pedro I de Cataluña, II en Aragón', *BRABLB*, iii (1905–6), and iv (1907–8).

—— 'Notes per la biografia del trovador Guerau de Cabrera', *Estudis universitaris catalans*, iv (1910).

—— *Los vescomtes de Bas en la illa de Sardenya* (Barcelona, 1901).

MIRET Y SANS, J., 'Los vescomtes de Cerdanya, Conflent y Bergadà', *Memorias de la Real Academia de Buenas Letras de Barcelona*, viii (1901).
MONCADA, J. L. DE, *Episcopologio de Vich* (Vich, 1891–1904).
MONFAR Y SORS, D., *Historia de los condes de Urgel*, in *CDI*, ix and x.
MONSALVATGE Y FOSSAS, F., *Los condes de Ampurias vindicados* (Noticias históricas, vol. xxv, Olot, 1917).
MUÑOZ Y ROMERO, T., *Colección de fueros municipales y cartas pueblas de los reinos de Castilla, León, Corona de Aragón y Navarra* (Madrid, 1847).

NEUMAN, A. A., *The Jews in Spain* (Philadelphia, 1944).
NOONAN, J. T., *The Scholastic Analysis of Usury* (Cambridge, Mass., 1957).
NOTH, A., *Heiliger Krieg und Heiliger Kampf in Islam und Christentum* (Bonn, 1965).
NÚÑEZ DE CEPEDA, M., *La beneficencia en Navarra a través de los siglos* (Pamplona, 1940).

O'CALLAGHAN, J. F., 'The Affiliation of the Order of Calatrava with the Order of Cîteaux', *Analecta Sacri Ordinis Cisterciensis*, xv (1959), and xvi (1960).
—— 'The Earliest "Difiniciones" of the Order of Calatrava, 1304–1383', *Traditio*, xvii (1961).
—— '*Hermandades* between the Military Orders of Calatrava and Santiago during the Castilian Reconquest, 1158–1252', *Speculum*, xliv (1969).
ODRIOZOLA Y GRIMAUD, C., *Ramón Berenguer IV, conde de Barcelona, caballero del Santo Sepulcro de Jerusalén. Memorias históricas referentes a la cesión en su favor de la Corona de Aragón, hecha por la Orden militar del Santo Sepulcro, la del Hospital y del Temple en el año 1140* (Barcelona, 1911).
OHLENDORF, E., 'Zur "cena in presentia" des Königs von Aragon', *Spanische Forschungen der Görresgesellschaft: Gesammelte Aufsätze zur Kulturgeschichte Spaniens*, xxi (1963).
OLIVER, B., *Historia del derecho en Cataluña, Mallorca y Valencia: Código de las costumbres de Tortosa* (Madrid, 1876–81).
OLIVER ASÍN, J., 'Origen árabe de "rebato", "arrobda" y sus homónimos', *Boletín de la Real Academia Española*, xv (1928).
OLIVEROS DE CASTRO, M. T., *Historia de Monzón* (Zaragoza, 1964).
OLMOS Y CANALDA, E., *Inventario de los pergaminos de la Catedral de Valencia* (Valencia, 1961).
ORDERICUS VITALIS, *Historia Ecclesiastica*, ed. A. le Prevost (Société de l'Histoire de France, 1833–55).
ORLANDIS, J., ' "Traditio corporis et animae" (La "familiaritas" en las iglesias y monasterios españoles de la alta edad media)', *AHDE*, xxiv (1954).

PALLARÉS GIL, M., 'La frontera sarracena en tiempo de Berenguer IV', *Boletín de historia y geografía del Bajo-Aragón*, i (1907).
PALOMEQUE TORRES, A., 'Contribución al estudio del ejército en los estados de la reconquista', *AHDE*, xv (1944).
PARKER, T. W., *The Knights Templars in England* (Tucson, 1963).
PAULI, S., *Codice diplomatico del sacro militare ordine gerosolimitano* (Lucca, 1733–7).
PÉREZ DE URBEL, J., *Los monjes españoles en la edad media* (Madrid, 1930–4).

PERKINS, C., 'The Knights Templars in the British Isles', *English Historical Review*, xxv (1910).

PERLBACH, M., *Die Statuten des Deutschen Ordens* (Halle, 1890).

PIQUET, J., *Des banquiers au moyen âge: les Templiers* (Paris, 1939).

*Poésies complètes du troubadour Marcabru*, ed. J. M. L. Dejeanne (Toulouse, 1909).

PRESSUTTI, P., *Regesta Honorii Papae III* (Rome, 1888–95).

PRUTZ, H., *Entwicklung und Untergang des Tempelherrenordens* (Berlin, 1888).

—— 'Forschungen zur Geschichte des Tempelherrenordens: I. Die Templerregel', *Königsberger Studien*, i (1887).

—— *Die geistlichen Ritterorden* (Berlin, 1908).

—— *Malteser Urkunden und Regesten zur Geschichte der Tempelherren und der Johanniter* (Munich, 1883).

PUIG I CADAFALCH, J., *L'arquitectura romànica a Catalunya* (Barcelona, 1909–18).

PUIG Y PUIG, S., *Episcopologio de la Sede Barcinonense* (Barcelona, 1929).

QUADRADO, J. M., *Historia de la conquista de Mallorca* (Palma, 1850).

—— *Recuerdos y bellezas de España: Aragón* (Barcelona, 1844).

RAMOS Y LOSCERTALES, J. M., *El reino de Aragón bajo la dinastía pamplonesa* (Acta Salmanticensia, vol. xv, 1961).

—— 'Textos para el estudio del derecho aragonés en la edad media', *AHDE*, i (1924).

RASSOW, P., 'La cofradía de Belchite', *AHDE*, iii (1926).

*Reconquista española y la repoblación del país* (Zaragoza, 1951).

*Regestum Clementis papae V* (Rome, 1885–8).

*Règle du Temple*, ed. H. de Curzon (Société de l'Histoire de France, 1886).

RÉGNÉ, J., 'Catalogue des actes de Jaime I, Pedro III et Alfonso III, rois d'Aragon, concernant les Juifs (1213–1291)', *Revue des études juives*, lx–lxx (1911–20).

—— 'Catalogue d'actes pour servir à l'histoire des Juifs de la couronne d'Aragon sous le règne de Jaime II (1291–1327)', *Revue des études juives*, lxxiii–lxxviii (1921–4).

REY, E., 'L'Ordre du Temple en Syrie et à Chypre', *Revue de Champagne et de Brie*, xxiv (1888).

RILEY-SMITH, J., *The Knights of St. John in Jerusalem and Cyprus, c. 1050–1310* (London, 1967).

RIQUER, M. DE, 'El testamento del trovador Guilhem de Berguedán', *Mélanges de linguistique et de littérature romanes à la mémoire d'Istvan Frank* (Annales Universitatis Saraviensis, vol. vi, 1957).

—— 'El trovador Giraut del Luc y sus poesías contra Alfonso II de Aragón', *BRABLB*, xxiii (1950).

RIUS SERRA, J., *Rationes Decimarum Hispaniae (1279–1280)* (Barcelona, 1946–7).

ROCAFORT, C., *Geografia general de Catalunya: Provincia de Lleyda* (Barcelona, n.d.).

ROCA TRAVER, F., 'Un siglo de vida mudéjar en la Valencia medieval (1238–1338)', *EEMCA*, v (1952).

RODRÍGUEZ CAMPOMANES, P., *Dissertaciones históricas del Orden y Cavallería de los Templarios* (Madrid, 1747).

RÖHRICHT, R., *Regesta Regni Hierosolymitani* (New York edn., n.d.).

ROMANO, D., 'El reparto del subsidio de 1282 entre las aljamas catalanas', *Sefarad*, xiii (1953).

ROTGER Y CAPLLONCH, M., *Historia de Pollensa* (Palma de Mallorca, 1897–1906).

—— 'Los Templers a Mallorca', *Congreso de historia de la Corona de Aragón*, i (Barcelona, 1909).

RUBIÓ, J., ALÓS, R. D', and MARTORELL, F., 'Inventaris inèdits de l'Ordre del Temple a Catalunya', *Anuari de l'Institut d'Estudis Catalans*, i (1907).

RUBIÓ Y LLUCH, A., *Documents per l'història de la cultura catalana migeval* (Barcelona, 1908–21).

RUIZ JUSUÉ, T., 'Las cartas de hermandad en España', *AHDE*, xv (1944).

RUIZ MORENO, A., 'Los baños públicos en los fueros municipales españoles', *Cuadernos de historia de España*, iii (1945).


SAGARRA, F. DE, *Sigillografía catalana* (Barcelona, 1915–32).

SALA-VALDÉS, M. DE LA, *Estudios históricos y artísticos de Zaragoza* (Zaragoza, 1933).

SALAVERT Y ROCA, V., *Cerdeña y la expansión mediterránea de la Corona de Aragón* (Madrid, 1956).

—— 'El Tratado de Anagni y la expansión mediterránea de la Corona de Aragón', *EEMCA*, v (1952).

SANAHUJA, P., *Història de la ciutat de Balaguer* (Barcelona, 1965).

SÁNCHEZ GOZALBO, A., 'Notas para la historia del Maestrazgo de Montesa. Castillo de Cuevas de Avinromá', *BSCC*, xiv (1933).

—— 'Notas para la historia del Maestrazgo de Montesa. Castillo de Culla', *BSCC*, xxv (1949).

—— 'Notas para la historia del Maestrazgo de Montesa. El castillo de Polpís', *BSCC*, xiv (1933).

SANDYS, A., 'The Financial and Administrative Importance of the London Temple in the Thirteenth Century', *Essays in Mediaeval History presented to Thomas Frederick Tout*, ed. A. G. Little and F. M. Powicke (Manchester, 1925).

SANPERE Y MIQUEL, S., 'Minoría de Jaime I', *Congreso de historia de la Corona de Aragón*, ii (Barcelona, 1913).

SANTACHS Y COSTAS, J., *Memoria sobre el archivo prioral de Cataluña de la Orden de San Juan* (Barcelona, 1885).

SAYOUS, A. E., 'Les méthodes commerciales de Barcelone au XIIIᵉ siècle, d'après des documents inédits des archives de sa cathédrale', *Estudis universitaris catalans*, xvi (1931).

SCHNÜRER, G., *Die ursprüngliche Templerregel* (Freiburg, 1903).

SCHOTTMÜLLER, K., *Der Untergang des Templer-Ordens* (Berlin, 1887).

SCHRAMM, P. E., 'Ramon Berenguer IV', in *Els primers comtes-reis* (Barcelona, 1960).

SENDRA CENDRA, D., *Aranceles aduaneros de la Corona de Aragón (siglo XIII)* (Valencia, 1966).

SEVILLANO COLOM, F., 'Bosquejo histórico de Oropesa', *BSCC*, xxvii (1951).

SOBREQUÉS I VIDAL, S., *Els barons de Catalunya* (Barcelona, 1957).

—— *Els grans comtes de Barcelona* (Barcelona, 1961).

SOLDEVILA, F., 'Alguns aspects de la política econòmica de Pere el Gran', *VI Congreso de historia de la Corona de Aragón* (Barcelona, 1959).

—— 'A propòsit del servei del bovatge', *Anuario de estudios medievales*, i (1964).

—— *Història de Catalunya* (Barcelona, 1963).

—— *Pere el Gran* (Barcelona, 1950– ).

STREHLKE, E., *Tabulae Ordinis Theutonici* (Berlin, 1869).

TESSIER, G., 'Les débuts de l'Ordre du Saint-Sépulcre en Espagne', *BEC*, cxvi (1958).

TORRES FONTES, J., *La reconquista de Murcia en 1266 por Jaime I de Aragón* (Murcia, 1967).

TOURTOULON, C. DE, *Jacme I<sup>er</sup> le Conquérant* (Montpellier, 1863–7).

TRAGGIA, J., 'Ilustración del reynado de don Ramiro II de Aragón', *Memorias de la Real Academia de la Historia*, iii (1799).

*Tresor de pobres* (Biblioteca de la revista catalana, 1892).

TRUDON DES ORMES, A., 'Listes des maisons et de quelques dignitaires de l'Ordre du Temple en Syrie, en Chypre et en France', *Revue de l'orient latin*, v (1897), vi (1898), and vii (1900).

TYRE, WILLIAM OF, *Historia rerum in partibus transmarinis gestarum*, in *Recueil des historiens des croisades: historiens occidentaux*, i (Paris, 1844).

UBIETO ARTETA, A., 'La campana de Huesca', *Revista de filología española*, xxxv (1951).

—— 'La creación de la cofradía de Belchite', *EEMCA*, v (1952).

—— 'Las fronteras de Navarra', *Príncipe de Viana*, xiv (1953).

—— 'Navarra-Aragón y la idea imperial de Alfonso VII de Castilla', *EEMCA*, vi (1956).

—— *El real monasterio de Sigena (1188–1300)* (Valencia, 1966).

USÓN Y SESÉ, M., 'Aportaciones al estudio de la caída de los Templarios en Aragón', *Universidad*, iii (1926).

VAJAY, S. DE, 'Ramire II le Moine, roi d'Aragon, et Agnès de Poitou dans l'histoire et dans la légende', *Mélanges offerts à René Crozet*, ii (Poitiers, 1966).

VALDEAVELLANO, L. G. DE, *Historia de las instituciones españolas* (Madrid, 1968).

VALL, G. DE SA, 'Rendición del castillo de Xivert', *BSCC*, xxiv (1948).

VALLS TABERNER, F., 'Les costums de la batllia de Miravet', *Revista jurídica de Cataluña*, xxxii (1926).

VALOUS, G. DE, 'Quelques observations sur la toute primitive observance des Templiers et la *Regula pauperum commilitonum Christi*', *Mélanges St. Bernard* (Dijon, 1954).

VÁZQUEZ DE PARGA, L., LACARRA, J. M., and URÍA RÍU, J., *Las peregrinaciones a Santiago de Compostela* (Madrid, 1948–9).

VERLINDEN, C., *L'Esclavage dans l'Europe médiévale*, i (Bruges, 1955).

VIARD, P., *Histoire de la dîme ecclésiastique dans le royaume de France aux XII<sup>e</sup> et XIII<sup>e</sup> siècles* (Paris, 1912).

VICH Y SALOM, J., and MUNTANER Y BUJOSA, J., *Documenta regni Majoricarum* (Palma, 1945).

VILAR BONET, M., 'Actividades financieras de la Orden del Temple en la Corona de Aragón', *VII Congreso de historia de la Corona de Aragón*, ii (Barcelona, 1962).

VILLANUEVA, J., *Viage literario a las iglesias de España* (Madrid, 1803–52).

VILLARROYA, J., *Real Maestrazgo de Montesa* (Valencia, 1787).

VINCKE, J., *Documenta selecta mutuas civitatis Arago-Cathalaunicae et ecclesiae relationes illustrantia* (Barcelona, 1936).

—— 'Das Gastungsrecht der aragonischen Krone im hohen Mittelalter', *Spanische Forschungen der Görresgesellschaft: Gesammelte Aufsätze zur Kulturgeschichte Spaniens*, xix (1962).

—— *Staat und Kirche in Katalonien und Aragon während des Mittelalters* (Münster, 1931).

*Volumen Fororum et Actuum Curiae* (Valencia, 1548).

WOHLHAUPTER, E., *Studien zur Rechtsgeschichte der Gottes- und Landfrieden in Spanien* (Heidelberg, 1933).

WÜRZBURG, JOHN OF, *Descriptio Terrae Sanctae*, in Migne, *PL*, clv.

ZAPATER, M., *Cister militante* (Zaragoza, 1662).

ZURITA, J., *Anales de la Corona de Aragón* (Zaragoza, 1610–21).

—— *Indices rerum ab Aragoniae regibus gestarum ab initiis regni ad annum MCDX* (Zaragoza, 1578).

# INDEX

The following abbreviations are used in the Index:

comm.  commander, commanders  prov.  provincial
conf.  confrater, confratrissa  T  Templar
dep.  dependency, dependencies

Dates are given in brackets when it is known that references under a name apply to more than one person and also when it cannot be taken for granted that they do not.

Aymeric, Bertrand (T), 432.
Aymeric, William, lawyer, 119.
Ayreis, Peter of, canon of Vich and public notary, 375.
Aytona, rector of, 358.
Azemar, Pons of (T), 345.
Azir Abeyanet, Abdella, Moor, 395–6.
Aznar (T), 450.
Aznárez, Fortún, lord of Tarazona, 38, 371.
Azylach, William of (T), 425, 438; prov. master, 420.

Bach, William of (T), 410–11.
Baco, Raymond of (T), 426, 429, 431, 434, 443.
Badat, Geoffrey (T), 425, 428.
Badels, William of (T), 428.
Badía, John of, 417.
Bafarul, Berenguer, 48.
Baibinum, T. dep. of, 451.
Bais, William of (T), 107, 437.
Balaguer, 54, 134–5, 137, 155.
Balaguer, Bernard of, scribe, 391.
Balaguer, Matthew of (T), 447.
Balaug, Peter of (T), 370.
Balcarca, church of, 78.
Balcarca, John of (T), 425.
Baldwin II, king of Jerusalem, 1, 10, 12.
Ballellas, 379.
Ballobar, church of, 78; vicar of, 177.
Bañolas, 389.
Banyuls, Arnold of (T), 267, 278, 410–11, 431, 439, 453.
Barbará, 15–16, 22, 54, 59, 114, 196, 198.
— convent of, 89, 99, 120, 320, 367, 416, 453; chamberlain of, 416; comm. of, 99, 266, 311, 398, 422, 425–6; dep. of, 271, 295, 451; sub-comm. of, 268.
Barbará, Berenguer of (T), 449.
Barbará, Bernard of (T), 433, 440–1, 445.
Barbará, Peter of (T), 449.
Barbará, Raymond of (T), 406, 439.
Barbastro, 119, 371, 378.
Barbastro, P. of (T), 438.
Barbens, 39, 55–6, 175, 372.
— convent of, 55, 90, 101, 320, 417; comm. of, 101, 424–5.
Barbonne, 5.

Barcelona, 8, 50, 62, 87, 101, 111, 124, 126, 129, 197, 234, 316, 323–7, 345, 358, 389–90, 402, 404, 409–10, 416; bailiff of, 389, 404; bishop of, 32, 172, 334, 370, 386.
— convent and commandery of, 102, 223, 230–1, 233, 404, 416; chaplain of, 295, 390; comm. of, 109, 223, 232, 237, 265, 293, 345, 400, 402, 407, 439; previously T. dep., 9, 162, 172, 271, 390, 451.
— cortes at, 31–2, 72, 116, 122, 127–8, 131, 406–7.
— counts of, 6, 8–9, 13–18, 20–6, 29, 33, 35–7, 44, 54–5, 57, 63, 66–70, 76, 84, 87, 91–2, 115, 117–19, 123, 244, 249, 290.
— crown archive in, 9.
— diocese of, 41, 173.
— Montjuich in, 51, 369.
— Usages of, 45, 136, 142, 252.
Barcelona, Hugh of (T), prov. master, 420.
Bargota, 306.
Barillas, Peter of (T), 422, 438.
Barrallus, lord of Marseilles, 374.
Barrio, Gasco of (T), 422.
Bartholomew (T): (1190) 435; (1255–63) 270, 448; (1260) 449.
Barufel, Raymond (T), 424.
Bassil, Berenguer of, scribe, 402.
Bastida, Raymond of (T), 266, 425, 428–9, 434, 443.
Bataia, Raymond (T), 439.
Batea, 26, 208–9, 215–16, 252–3.
Baths, public, 194.
Batizo, Dominic of, 46.
Bātx, John of, royal notary, 374.
Baux, Bertrand of, 374.
Baux, Hugh of, 341, 374.
Beaujeu, William of (T), grand master, 310, 329.
Bec, William (T), 437.
Bedocio, Arnold of (T), 87, 103.
Belchite, 6, 22, 67, 371; confraternity of, 6, 13, 15, 17.
Belissén, Bernard (T), 271, 293, 296, 424.
Belloch, Raymond of (T), 399, 424, 427, 435, 442–4.
Belloque, 209, 214; T. dep. of, 451.
Bellpuig, Bernard of, public notary, 412.

R